MW01492048

Nudity &
Christianity

edited by
Jim C. Cunningham

Bloomington, IN   Milton Keynes, UK

authorHOUSE®

AuthorHouse™
1663 Liberty Drive, Suite 200
Bloomington, IN 47403
www.authorhouse.com
Phone: 1-800-839-8640

AuthorHouse™ UK Ltd.
500 Avebury Boulevard
Central Milton Keynes, MK9 2BE
www.authorhouse.co.uk
Phone: 08001974150

First published by AuthorHouse 12/26/06

ISBN: 978-1-4259-7508-1(sc)

Library of Congress Number: 2006911040

Printed in the United States of America
Bloomington, Indiana

This book is printed on acid-free paper.

Contact the Author

To stay informed of the author's present projects and plans, visit: www.JIMCCUNNINGHAM.COM. To contact me regarding corrections, comments or to schedule a "Theology of the Body Retreat" in your area, just go to the "Contact" link at the web site.

Acknowledgments

I wish to thank the many people who helped to make this book a reality by their prayers, writing, editorial and reference work or by donations which greatly helped to support me during the several years it took me to edit and write this book.

First of all, I must thank the many authors who have contributed their writing to my publications over the years. Their names are in the Table of Contents.

Secondly, I wish to thank both my oldest daughter, Kate, and my wife, Linda, who did all the grueling proof-reading and also made many helpful editorial suggestions.

Last but not least, I am most grateful to my many supporters over the years who have believed in my work enough to contribute to it financially. I cannot list them all by name here, but those who subsidized my work with donations from $500 to $10,000 are listed here in alphabetical order:

Ernest Imus, Tom & Marilyn Pine, Andy & Beth Snider & Family, Martin V. & Janet Striegel. May God bless you all!

Dedication

For my wife, Linda, without whose love, friendship, help and willingness to question conventional assumptions, I could never have discovered and experienced so much.

A faithful friend is a sturdy shelter. He who finds one, finds a treasure. —Sirach 6:14

Whether you eat or drink, dress or undress, do all to the greater glory of God

In Memoriam, Pope John Paul II (1920-2005)

In loving memory of the 264th[1] successor of St. Peter, who understood so well, and taught so fearlessly and effectively the unpopular truth of the supernatural love for which man was perfectly designed by God and for which God Himself is both our perfect example and unfailing support. His predecessor, the great fisher of men, St. Peter, aware of his impending demise, once assured all Christians of his continued help from heaven.[2] Confident that the prayers of such holy men are powerful indeed,[3] with filial piety let us pray to these four giant saints, Pope John Paul II, Sts. Peter and Paul, and the apostle of divine love, St. John, to intercede for us, the People of God, so that we will "attain to the unity of the faith and of the knowledge of the Son of God, to mature manhood, to the measure of the stature of the fullness of Christ,"[4] truly glorifying God in our bodies.[5] By our example, may those who have not yet fallen in love with the Word made flesh, our Tremendous Lover, do so through the light of truth flaming through the torches of our bodies, so that Jesus' prayer "that they may be one"[6] may at last be fulfilled. Thank you, John Paul II, for helping us to understand that our bodies are precious gifts for love alone, created to be fully given to the Lord,[7] as is sacramentally expressed and effected through the awesome sacrament of matrimony, which St. Paul termed "The Great Sacrament."[8] Amen!

---

[1] Counting St. Peter, the 265th bishop of Rome.
[2] In II Peter 1:13-15 he promises to help them to be mindful of his teaching after the putting off of his body and departure from this life.
[3] Cf. James 5:16.
[4] Ephesians 4:13.
[5] Cf. I Corinthians 6:20.
[6] John 17:11 & 22.
[7] Cf. I Corinthians 6:13.
[8] Ephesians 5:32.

Foreword

There are various ways to use this book. I suggest that the reader first familiarize himself with the contents beginning on p. ii, as this will provide a thorough overview. While perusing the contents, certain items will likely appear so intriguing that you will want to fast-forward to that particular article. Go ahead, skip around to whatever interests you. The book is well suited for that.

Others will want to attack this tome "cover-to-cover"— men after my own heart. They will not be disappointed.

It was not possible (or even, necessarily, desirable) to avoid repetition of certain themes such as how baptisms were performed in the early Church. Nevertheless, each treatment of recurring themes sheds a somewhat unique light on the topic. Besides, we learn by repetition. Certain topics have been so under-represented in conventional Christian experience that, as G.K. Chesterton wood say, a little repetition is necessary to straighten the bent twig.

I, and many authors are Roman Catholics and believe there is nothing in our articles that is contrary to orthodox Catholicism. Other authors come from various Christian denominations and a few (e.g. Kahlil Gibran) may be questionably Christian. Nevertheless, authors have been included because of the unique light they shed on the themes. The Holy Spirit blows where He will,[1] and all things are given us for our growth in sanctification. I do not pretend to vouch for any author's opinions but my own. In at least one place (e.g. p. 67) I found it necessary to state an explicit disclaimer. Thus the entire book should be regarded as a broad discussion from many perspectives on the woefully neglected topic of the integrity of the human body, along with the ramifications for our daily life. The purpose of the book is to get people thinking on topics which they may have heretofore been afraid to contemplate, lest the men in white suits arrive with a strait-jacket and carry us off! There is a very powerful dynamic in culture that demands conformity and it is difficult to shake free from these shackles and think

---

[1] Cf. John 3:8.

afresh, daring to ask supposedly unaskable questions like four-year olds, of whom our Lord said the kingdom of heaven consists.[1]

Most of the aspects of our lifestyle are unwilled; much of what we do is done because it was how we were reared or how "everybody else" does them. Very few people are courageous enough to question what "everybody else" deems obvious and "common sense," though, when asked, they can only bluster and mumble in response because they really have no clue why they do the things that they do and uphold so "religiously."

So I want to stir things up a bit—no, I want to stir things up a lot, and especially among theologians of both the professional and "armchair" varieties. I want them to contemplate and discuss the topics of this book seriously. I ask them to be open-minded, honest, logical and courageous. I encourage people to hold formal and informal discussions and debates on these topics. Truths often become clearer as we Christians openly and honestly thrash them out in discussion. But, as I urge in the introduction which follows, as truths emerge from their moldy shadows, *talking* about them is not enough. In order to grow in wisdom we must continually *apply* what we learn to our practical, daily lives. We cannot see through the fog to the higher rungs of the ladder until we scale the few rungs revealed to us.

One of the best features of this book is the painstakingly accurate indices. Many will want to read sections of this book found in either the Scriptural Index (pp. 509-531) or the Topical Index (pp. 532-545). For example, suppose you have often wondered about the passage in Genesis 9:18-27 about Noah's drunkenness and nakedness. Many Christians cite it as a proof text against nudity. But, is it really? By using the indices, you can hone in on that single topic in two ways. You can look up the various verses included in that passage on p. 517 of the Scriptural Index. You can also simply look up "Noah" on p. 540 of the Topical Index. Then you can read various interpretations by authors from various denominations which will serve to provide you with food for thought.

---

[1] Cf. Luke 18:16.

As you can quickly see by perusing the Scriptural Index beginning on p. 509, this book seriously tries to be grounded in the Word of God. Almost every contributor to this book believes that the Bible must be the lamp unto our feet and light for our path.[1] Most of us live and even breathe within the revealed Word of Life. We do not ignore it, stand aloof from it, and dream up our own dream world. Most of the Catholic authors also try to be grounded in the tradition and Magisterium of the Catholic Church. But we make a distinction between actual "tradition" and mere "presumed convention." Accordingly, nude baptism by immersion is quite traditional, though so unconventional as to seem heretical, if not lunacy. Speaking only for myself, I humbly submit all my writings to the scrutiny of the Magisterium of the Catholic Church, acknowledging it to be a great blessing from God to guide us sheep along the straight and narrow way.

Various Bible translations are used by various authors, and they usually designate which they are using. Speaking for myself, I almost always use the Revised Standard Version (RSV), Catholic Edition, published by Ignatius Press of San Francisco, unless otherwise noted. Some authors cite the King James Version (KJV), unless otherwise noted.

The names of the Biblical books and the actual canon used in this book is that used by the Catholic Church. Thus those using Protestant Bibles may need to sometimes refer to the deutero-canonical books which they refer to as "the Apocrypha."

Explanation of Biblical notation: When a certain bible verse or passage is noted, I first give the full name of the book, followed by the chapter number and a colon (:), after which is the verse number. Thus, "I Corinthians 13:13" refers to "the First Letter of St. Paul to the Corinthians, chapter 13, verse 13." Wherever a single "f" is found, it refers to the following verse as well. Thus, "John 3:1f" refers to "the Gospel of St. John, chapter 3, verses 1 & 2."

Likewise a double "ff" refers to at least the following *two* verses, and possibly more. Thus "Mark 10:17ff" refers to "the Gospel of St. Mark, chapter 10, verses 17 and following therefrom." It is sort of a "ballpark" way to refer

---

[1] Cf. Psalm 119:105.

to the passage about the young man and his encounter with Jesus. At other times, when accuracy seems more important, both the beginning and ending verses will be noted, separated by a dash (-). Thus, that same passage might be noted as "Mark 10:17-31."

When pages are referenced, a single "p." refers only to that one page number. A double "pp." refers to a plurality of pages such as "pp. 7-10" or "pp. 7f" to include p. 8, or "pp. 7ff" to include at least pages 8 & 9 and maybe a few more therefrom.

Notes on language: I am sorry (not really), but I am not sympathetic to those of a radical feminist mindset who are in the business of grinding axes so fervently that they are trying very hard to alter what has always been standard English usage. In Latin, many (most?) modern languages and English, "man" could mean either "male" or "all people as a group," depending on the context, which any third grader until recently had no difficulty in figuring out. Furthermore, the generic third person singular personal pronoun has always been "he," "him," etc., and nobody in their right mind ever used it to exclude females unless such was obvious from the context. The new trend is called "inclusive language," but it is anything but "inclusive," as it is ever insistent on specifying a person's gender, even when it is irrelevant.

For example, the long established, highly reputed Revised Standard Version translation of Genesis 1:26-28 has always read:

"Then God said, 'Let us make *man* in our image, after our likeness; and let *them* have dominion over the fish of the sea, and over the birds of the air...' So God created *man* in his own image, in the image of God he created *him*; *male and female* he created *them*. And God blessed *them*, and God said to *them*, 'Be fruitful and multiply...'"

In the above context, everyone who knew basic English never was confused about what "man" meant. In the above context, everyone has always understood it to be inclusive of both genders, as is obvious when, in the same sentence, after using the generic term, "man," the next phrase specifically defines it as including both "male and female." There was never a problem until some radical feminists came along and decided to pontificate to the earth that such standard usage somehow "demeaned" them. But as anyone knows who is at all familiar with English literature, no author ever had such an intention; the whole idea is a figment of the imagination. There is absolutely no way that Jesus had any intention whatsoever of excluding "the fairer sex" when He preached, "*He* who eats My flesh and drinks My blood has eternal life, and I will raise *him* up at the last day."[1] But these axe-grinders would require revisionist translators to perform all sorts of linguistic acrobatics to make language conform to their own personal problems. So how else should it be translated, as: "*She or he* who eats My flesh and drinks My blood has eternal life, and I will raise *her or him* up at the last day?" In my humble opinion, such semantical acrobatics is entirely unnecessary and even ridiculous and only serves to weaken the Word of God and the words of great "men" (yes, that includes males and females, as well as blondes, brunettes, red-heads and those with black hair and even baldies!). So I hope this suffices to explain why you will not find this book cheapening the English language, as is the current fad almost everywhere else.

Whenever I refer to "Adam and Eve," I have written "Adam & Eve," which to me connotes them as a unit, rather than two individuals. After all, they did become "one flesh." But I admit this one is just a quirk of mine and hope it will not bug you overmuch.

As for the use of italics for emphasis, you can assume that I am responsible whenever they occur. My excuse for using them so frequently is my frustration when hearing even educated people read in such a way that their inflection betrays their insufficient comprehension. I agree that, all things being equal, italics for emphasis should be rarely resorted to, but in my experience, listening to even church lectors, I have found that italics can be helpful. Oh, well...

—jcc

---

[1] John 6:54.

Introduction

by Jim C. Cunningham

Imagine a wedding "made in heaven." Imagine a couple doing it the Lord's way—no fornication, no unchastity, no cohabitation, no previous, broken marriage vows. Before the church altar, witnessed by their parish priest, they exchange marriage vows—not just to each other, but also, and most importantly, to the Lord. Their oaths are irrevocable, solemnly swearing to almighty God to be faithful to one another and to love one another, whether rich or poor, sick or healthy, etc.—forever.[1]

Friends and relatives celebrate with feasting and giving gifts to boost the newlyweds as they begin a new life, not as best friends, not just as a man and a woman, but as "one flesh"[2]—man *and* woman.

As they drive off on their honeymoon, tin cans clanging behind their car, decorated ostentatiously with flowers and a "Just Married" sign, leaving all the party-goers behind, they have truly "only just begun."[3] They have solemnly promised, but they have not yet consummated their promises. Though others give them all kinds of material gifts and spiritual bouquets, they have only one possible gift to give each other. It is an absolutely priceless gift because only Jesus Christ had what it took to pay for it; He paid for it with His Precious Blood, down to the last drop. St. Paul tells us what that gift is: *It is their bodies.*[4]

Till now they have glorified God in their bodies by their deep appreciation for these awesome gifts and by their premarital chastity. Now they are to glorify Him even more by this new sacrament of matrimony. Elevated to a higher chastity, they at last mutually gift each other with their bodies. The husband's body now belongs to the wife, and vice versa. "My beloved is mine and I am his."[5] "The wife does not rule over her own body, but the husband

---

[1] I.e. "Till death do us part."
[2] Genesis 2:24 & Matthew 19:5.
[3] The title of a popular wedding song by Paul Williams and Roger Nichols, recorded by "The Carpenters" in 1970.
[4] Cf. I Corinthians 6:15-20.
[5] Song of Songs 2:16 & 6:3.

does; likewise the husband does not rule over his own body, but the wife does."[1]

Pile up all the other wedding gifts—the material things, the cash, real estate, vacation trips and even the prayers. What these newlyweds give each other on their honeymoon infinitely exceeds them all. They unwrap their gifts as eagerly and excitedly as little children on Christmas morning. Till that moment the bride's body was hers, but now she transfers ownership to her groom. Likewise, till then, the groom's body was solely his custody, but now he turns it all over to his bride—forever! They enter into a higher chastity because each gives all, mutually. This is the opposite of unchastity, which is nothing but selfish grasping, even if mutual. In unchastity, there is mutual taking; in this higher chastity, there is mutual, total, self-giving.

Her man stands in awe at such a priceless gift, and mumbles something as seemingly silly as Solomon, "Behold, you are beautiful, my love; behold, you are beautiful; your eyes are doves."[2] "As a lily among brambles, so is my love among maidens."[3] "Behold, you are beautiful, my love, behold, you are beautiful! Your eyes are doves behind your veil. Your hair is like a flock of goats, moving down the slopes of Gilead. Your teeth are like a flock of shorn ewes that have come up from the washing, all of which bear twins, and not one among them is bereaved. Your lips are like a scarlet thread, and your mouth is lovely. Your cheeks are like halves of a pomegranate behind your veil. Your neck is like the tower of David... Your two breasts are like two fawns, twins of a gazelle, that feed among the lilies... You are all fair, my love; there is no flaw in you."[4] "You have ravished my heart, my sister, my bride, you have ravished my heart with a glance of your eyes, with one jewel of your necklace. How sweet is your love, my sister, my bride! how much better is your love than wine, and the fragrance of your oils than any spice! Your lips distil nectar, my bride; honey and milk are under your tongue; the scent of your

---

[1] I Corinthians 7:4.
[2] Song of Songs 1:15.
[3] Ibid. 2:2.
[4] Ibid. 4:1-7.

garments is like the scent of Lebanon. A garden locked is my sister, my bride, a garden locked, a fountain sealed.[1] Your shoots are an orchard of pomegranates with all choicest fruits, henna with nard, nard and saffron, calamus and cinnamon, with all trees of frankincense, myrrh and aloes, with all chief spices—a garden fountain, a well of living water, and flowing streams from Lebanon."[2] "You are beautiful as Tirzah, my love, comely as Jerusalem...[3] "My dove, my perfect one, is only one, the darling of her mother, flawless to her that bore her. The maidens saw her and called her happy; the queens and concubines also, and they praised her. Who is this that looks forth like the dawn, fair as the moon, bright as the sun, terrible as an army with banners?"[4] "How graceful are your feet in sandals, O queenly maiden! Your rounded thighs are like jewels, the work of a master hand. Your navel is a rounded bowl that never lacks mixed wine. Your belly is a heap of wheat, encircled with lilies. Your two breasts are like two fawns, twins of a gazelle. Your neck is like an ivory tower. Your eyes are pools in Heshbon, by the gate of Bath-rabbim. Your nose is like a tower of Lebanon, overlooking Damascus. Your head crowns you like Carmel, and your flowing locks are like purple; a king is held captive in the tresses. How fair and pleasant you are, O loved one, delectable maiden! You are stately as a palm tree, and your breasts are like its clusters. I say I will climb the palm tree and lay hold of its branches. Oh, may your breasts be like clusters of the vine, and the scent of your breath like apples, and your kisses like the best wine that goes down smoothly, gliding over lips and teeth."[5] "Arise, my love, my fair one, and come away; for lo, the winter is past, the rain is over and gone. The flowers appear on the earth, the time of singing has come, and the voice of the turtledove is heard in our land. The fig tree puts forth its figs, and the vines are in blossom; they give forth fragrance. Arise, my love, my fair one, and come away. O my dove, in the clefts of the rock, in the covert of

---

[1] These two images declare his awareness of and appreciation for her faithfully kept virginity.
[2] Song of Songs 4:9-15.
[3] Ibid. 6:4.
[4] Ibid. 6:9f.
[5] Ibid. 7:1-9.

the cliff, let me see your face, let me hear your voice, for your voice is sweet, and your face is comely."[1]

And the bride is likewise overflowing with esteem and appreciation for the whole of her new husband, body and soul. She reciprocates what might seem sweet nothings to outsiders, but for her it is highest poetry and the best expression of her love. It is not to be *compared* to the physical act of consummation; *it is intrinsically bound up with it*: "My beloved is to me a bag of myrrh, that lies between my breasts. My beloved is to me a cluster of henna blossoms in the vineyards of Engedi."[2] "I am a rose of Sharon, a lily of the valleys."[3] "As an apple tree among the trees of the wood, so is my beloved among young men. With great delight I sat in his shadow, and his fruit was sweet to my taste. He brought me to the banqueting house, and his banner over me was love. Sustain me with raisins, refresh me with apples; for I am sick with love. O that his left hand were under my head, and that his right hand embraced me!"[4] "The voice of my beloved! Behold, he comes, leaping upon the mountains, bounding over the hills. My beloved is like a gazelle, or a young stag."[5] "My beloved is mine and I am his, he pastures his flock among the lilies. Until the day breathes and the shadows flee, turn, my beloved, be like a gazelle, or a young stag upon rugged mountains."[6] "My beloved is all radiant and ruddy, distinguished among ten thousand. His head is the finest gold; his locks are wavy, black as a raven. His eyes are like doves beside springs of water, bathed in milk, fitly set. His cheeks are like beds of spices, yielding fragrance. His lips are lilies, distilling liquid myrrh. His arms are rounded gold, set with jewels. His body is ivory work, encrusted with sapphires. His legs are alabaster columns, set upon bases of gold. His appearance is like Lebanon, choice as the cedars. His speech is most sweet, and he is altogether desirable."[7]

---

[1] Song of Songs 2:10-15.
[2] Ibid. 1:13f.
[3] Ibid. 2:1.
[4] Ibid. 2:3-6.
[5] Ibid. 2:8f.
[6] Ibid. 2:16f.
[7] Song of Songs 5:10-16.

This effusion of mutual, rapturous esteem naturally leads to the actual union of the two in one flesh:[1] "I am my beloved's, and his desire is for me. Come, my beloved, let us go forth into the fields, and lodge in the villages; let us go out early to the vineyards, and see whether the vines have budded, whether the grape blossoms have opened and the pomegranates are in bloom. There I will give you my love."[2] "Awake, O north wind, and come, O south wind! Blow upon my garden, let its fragrance be wafted abroad. Let my beloved come to his garden, and eat its choicest fruits."[3]

There is no arm-twisting here. Their wills are already fused as one, as they expressed publicly not long before in front of the altar.

The groom is ripe and ready: "I come to my garden, my sister, my bride, I gather my myrrh with my spice, I eat my honeycomb with my honey, I drink my wine with my milk."[4]

And the wife again reaffirms her willingness as they melt into the one flesh embrace of love: "I am my beloved's and my beloved is mine; he pastures his flock among the lilies."[5]

Such total love must be exclusive in order to be total. We, the wedding party, can only say from afar: "Eat, O friends, and drink: drink deeply, O lovers!"[6] "Many waters cannot quench love, neither can floods drown it. If a man offered for love all the wealth of his house, it would be utterly scorned!"[7]

The real party has begun. The altar has become a nuptial bed. Exercising their lay priesthood in Christ, they complete the sacred rites. Not conforming themselves to this age of fornication, self gratification and indulgence, but transformed by the renewal of their minds, putting on "the mind of Christ,"[8] they now offer their bodies as a living sacrifice, holy and acceptable to God, their spiritual

---

[1] Cf. Genesis 2:24.
[2] Song of Songs 7:10-12.
[3] Ibid. 4:16.
[4] Ibid. 5:1.
[5] Ibid. 6:3.
[6] Ibid. 5:1.
[7] Ibid. 8:7.
[8] I Corinthians 2:16.

worship.[1] Realizing that even Solomon's poetic words are woefully inadequate, they no longer intercourse merely on the level of words, but their words become flesh.[2] Their entire selves are like two flames coming together as one brighter flame. Their physical expressions of love and tenderness stoke the fire of love ever higher. She welcomes him into herself as intimately as possible, gladly giving him access to her holy womb, open to him and open to yet more wedding gifts, these, from the Lord—new life created in the very image and likeness of God. The bride has literally become "the heart of the home."[3] She receives her man and will deliver their "olive shoots around their table."[4] As they cling to one another in orgasmic joy, just as Moses wrote,[5] they can finally say with Christ, "It is consummated."[6] "They are no longer two but one flesh. What therefore God has joined together, let not man put asunder."[7]

Is this erotic? I certainly hope so! And it is *sacred*, just like the other six sacraments.

But why is it that, despite so saying, there yet lingers within us a feeling that, married or not, sex is somehow "naughty"?

Perhaps part of the answer is that it is one of the many negative effects of original sin. But if this is true, it does not follow that this lingering feeling ought to be accepted as something right and good. On the contrary, it should be treated like all the other negative effects of original sin over which we strive to triumph. As this is true of sickness, ignorance, lack of sanctifying grace and death, so it should be no less true of our seemingly innate feeling that sex and the body are somehow bad.

So how is it that civilization has canonized, of all the ill effects of original sin, only one—sexual shame? Many spiritual writers have called it a virtue, but it should be

---

[1] Based on Romans 12:1f.
[2] Cf. John 1:14.
[3] Psalm 128:3.
[4] Ibid.
[5] Cf. Genesis 2:23f & Matthew 19:6.
[6] John 19:30.
[7] Mark 10:8f.

obvious that none of the effects of original sin can possibly be virtuous. As Jesus taught, "a bad tree bears bad fruit."[1]

But even if such shame were not consequent upon original sin, negative acculturation alone would amply suffice to screw everybody up. By the time that honeymoon happens, we have already acquired an extremely negative attitude toward that one priceless gift of our bodies, priceless because to redeem them—to buy them back for His Father—the Incarnate Word had to bleed to death dangling naked on a cross.[2]

Let's face it: How many of us can look at ourselves naked in a full length mirror and feel even *a little* like our bodies truly glorify God?

Glorify? Or is it more like horrify? Looking at ourselves naked after years and years of negative acculturation in the body department induces us to experience many things, but "glory" is not likely to be among them. For most all of us, that would take some *really* deep faith!

The negative feelings we experience are complex, but one element of them is physical shame, even with the bathroom door shut and locked.

Why? Perhaps part of the answer lies in a recent editorial [3] about a dad at Rye Beach, New Hampshire, who allowed his toddler to play *au naturel* and was accused to the town selectmen of "neglect."

We teach shame from infancy. Why shouldn't junior frolic in the sprinkler without his wet, clammy swimsuit? Why can't baby scamper around the house in the buff after his bath? Okay, well, yes, there are *practical* reasons, as this father of five is well aware, but those are not in the forefront of our motivations. What motivates us is the same shame that was drilled into *us* when *we* were toddlers, long before we even reached puberty.

And, speaking of which, just what is it about that first, long-awaited pubic hair, that *ipso facto* exponentially ups the ante in the shame game? Why might it be tolerated for junior to wade in his little backyard pool naked, but his big sister, because she is older, as though that were really a logical reason, cannot dare to remove her

---

[1] Matthew 7:17.
[2] Cf. I Corinthians 6:20.
[3] See Editorial, *Portsmouth Herald*, August 20, 2005.

unfilled bikini, and would rather die a torturous death than let anybody see what lies beneath her minimal fabric? Everybody knows what lies there anyway—just about the same as lies behind the bikini of anybody her age. So why the big mystery? Big brother is just a larger version of junior brother. He has longer legs, and we might suspect him to have longer everything else also. So whence comes all the hoopla?

Okay, so you're standing in front of that mirror looking at what your faith tells you is "the image and likeness of God."[1] Yeah. right! The all-beautiful, all-holy, all-good God! Boy, are we Christians gullible or what?

But everyone who has ever tried to read the Bible cover to cover got at least *that* far—the very first chapter. Maybe that's why few of us ever got much further...

Oops! The door wasn't locked after all, and someone walks right in while we are reflecting and contemplating the divine image! Almost all of us then feel sheer panic. We scream, we ridiculously try to hide our nakedness behind our hands, we tear the shower curtain right off the rod in our desperation to shield such a supposedly godly sight from the intruder—even if it's only junior, anxious for his own bath so he can get at least a few minutes of *après le bain* scamper freedom.

Our screams of holy terror succeed in ensuring that if junior's diapers had been dry, they are now drenched as he scampers off in terror and tears to mommy.

We make sure the door is really locked this time. As our pulse heads back in the normal direction, we have another look. Another element of that negative shame surfaces: *We think we are ugly.*

No, we don't much like whatever we see. Nothing is quite right. Too bony, too chubby, too gangly, too fat, too small breasted, too large breasted, too pointy breasted, too-downright funny-looking breasted. Either those centerfolds are a lie or we are a complete joke. What we need for Christmas is a massive air brush. The belly-button looks funny, our pubic hair isn't quite right, our penises look ridiculous, especially with all their whimsical, uncontrollable ups and downs. Hardly any of us are happy

---

[1] Genesis 1:26f.

with our buttocks, and on down to our knobby knees and funny looking piggy-toes.

But do any of us look in that mirror and feel, maybe, like "gratitude"? Like, "Thank You, Jesus, You did a great job here, and I am just overflowing with gratitude and like, "glorifying You with my body"?[1]

Not likely.

Some of us feel outright disgust. We don't even want to *peek* at what we look like in the altogether.

Others feel dirty, like they were caught reading *Hustler* magazine or something.

So imagine an entire rearing like this, all the way to that special honeymoon we have waited for for so long. After all that negative, anti-body acculturation, all of a sudden we are supposed to gift our beloved with this ugly, horrid, obscene, dirty, disgusting body? Why not just fill an empty box with garbage from the nearest dumpster and wrap that up for our newlywed spouse instead? We might as well!

No! Our whole self—especially our bodies—are supposed to be regarded as *priceless gifts*. We are not giving the love of our life *garbage*, but something *very beautiful, good, holy and precious*.

This is how it's supposed to be. This is how Pope John Paul II, even long before becoming pope, wrote, preached and taught it is supposed to be.

So if such is the goal, don't you think we have a very lot of homework to do? We cannot conform ourselves to this age and the negative way it regards the body. Every woman's magazine tells women they are ugly and inadequate. Imagine what the men's magazines say about women!

As Pope John Paul II also explained, the opposite of this puritanical shame is not lust. Lust is no more true sex than gluttony and drunkenness is Holy Communion.

A positive attitude toward the body and sexuality has nothing whatever to do with lust. The pornographers and porn addicts don't love the body; they despise it. There can be no love in lust. That is why the pope also said that

---

[1] I Corinthians 6:20.

it is wrong for a man to lust after his wife.[1] There is no lust in my description of the honeymoon at the beginning of this introduction. Sexual union is not *lust*; *it is love*. It effects permanent union and is the potential source of new life. Enjoying sex is no more lustful than enjoying a banquet is necessarily gluttonous. Sex is *supposed* to be enjoyable. If one doesn't like it, he needs a good Christian psychiatrist.

Unfortunately, almost all of us have been reared in a culture that either did not teach chastity at all or taught it "ass end to." Instead of teaching *what sex is* as God intended it, as I have tried to do above, most of us were taught *what sex is not*. It is not masturbation; that is nothing but self gratification and the abuse of a great gift. It is not fornication; that is nothing but mutual self gratification (if that). Sex is not adultery; the neighbor's wife is already taken. Sex is not performing homosexual acts; that is even worse than fornication because coitus[2] is the defining sexual act, and it is physically impossible to accomplish with the same sex. Need I mention that sex is not bestiality either? I might as well, as Moses saw fit to do so.[3]

But none of this negative teaching has revealed just *what sex is*. Why don't we define a thing by what it is, and then go from there? After all, if the U.S. bishops have publicly admitted that some 4,500 priests have molested minors in the past fifty years alone,[4] isn't maybe high time to try a new approach?

How many married couples celebrate their sacrament of matrimony in a manner anywhere near what I described above? The sad truth is that pious people truly believe sex is somehow dirty no matter who engages in it. Friends of mine know a holy couple who think they are chaste because they never had sex in broad daylight, and never when naked, and always in the dark and under the covers, and clothed. Sorry, but that is certainly *not* marital

---

[1] Cf. Pope John Paul II, Angelus audience of October 8, 1980. In *Theology of the Body* (Boston: Pauline Books, 1997), p. 157.
[2] I.e. Penile vaginal penetration and intra-vaginal seminal ejaculation.
[3] Cf. Leviticus 20:15f & Deuteronomy 27:21.
[4] According to the report of the John Jay College of Criminal Justice of the City University of New York, as authorized by the U.S. Bishops in 2004.

chastity. Perhaps one of their sons is among those 4,500 perverted priests.

But my book is not a sex book. (Perhaps I will yet write one of those.) No, my book is just a "*body* book," because that is *where we must begin*. Even if one's vocation is to consecrated celibacy,[1] he still needs to learn to appreciate his own and others' bodies and to work at acquiring the mind of Christ as regards bodies. It does not matter whether you are a cloistered nun or a matron with several grandchildren to brag about. We all have been gifted with a body, and so we must all learn to deal with it as Jesus did.

Do you suppose Jesus was ashamed to allow St. John the Baptist to unfasten His sandals, disrobe Him completely and give Him a symbolic bath in public, in the Jordan River?[2] Nude baptism was the norm for the first half of ecclesiastical history. How come that past culture did not freak out about the naked body as people do today?

I don't think people back then were any more chaste. Even without internet porn, people have always managed to find ways to lust after each other; it is one of their favorite capital sins. So what was so different back then such that no one had a heart attack learning in RCIA[3] class that when the big day finally came they need not dress up for the big event; in fact, they must not wear even a comb in their hair?

I have studied this question for most of my life, beginning in my university days when I majored in Patristics. When I found out about nude baptism while studying St. Hippolytus' *Apostolic Constitutions*, my socks were knocked off. I was practically shell-shocked. There was no way I could imagine such a thing at my home parish of St. Therese's in North Reading, Massachusetts!

---

[1] Consecrated celibacy is in an unique order of chastity. It is a special gift from God inspiring a person to dedicate his whole being not to a human spouse, but to God and His people. Priests of the Roman Rite are not divided in their loving commitment, but more closely imitate Jesus, Who gave His all for all.

[2] Cf. Mark 1:7-10.

[3] "The Rite of Christian Initiation for Adults." This is the standard program in the Catholic Roman Rite that prepares catechumens for baptism.

But why not? I sought much and I have discovered much. Jesus taught, "Freely ye have received; freely give."[1] And St. Peter taught, "The gift you have received, give as a gift."[2] And that is precisely what this book is. I am sharing with you the fruit of much meditation, study and experience, as well as those of many others of like-mind. In some places, the theology of the body launched by Pope John Paul II has practically become a fad, yet many are beginning to sense hollowness and even hypocrisy in it because their talk has become yet more drapery to hide behind. Oh, in their seminars they will sound so *avant-garde*, but just let junior walk in on them as they step out of the shower!

We can no more talk ourselves healthy in the realm of body-appreciation than we can in the realm of physical afflictions.

We must *act* on the word. If all we do is listen to it and talk about it, we are deceiving ourselves.[3] The body of man, together with his soul, created in the image and likeness of God, must be the starting point of any theology of the body. Nevertheless, hardly anyone wants to begin at the body. Despite all their sophisticated theological lectures, they still dread the body.

But the focus of Christian revelation is precisely *that body*. When God created man in His Own image and likeness, it was not without his body. The body of man was an essential part of the whole. In His omniscience, God knew His plan of redemption before time began. He knew that He would redeem the *whole* of man—*body* and soul—by inseparably joining to Himself that very human nature. "The Word *became* flesh."[4] In that human nature He freely experienced death, even death on a cross.[5] Despite popular belief, redemption does not consist in "dying and going to heaven." Any Christian with such an attitude is not one who reads his Bible very carefully. In I Corinthians 15:14-19 St. Paul emphasizes that without the dogma of the resurrection of the flesh, all the rest of

---

[1] Matthew 10:8.
[2] I Peter 4:10.
[3] Cf. James 1:22.
[4] John 1: 14.
[5] Cf. Philippians 2:8.

Christianity—even all the good deeds of all the saintly servants of the poor—is less than worthless. To hear many Christians talk about the faith, one would think that the incarnation, passion, death and resurrection of Christ were all mere superfluous, extrinsic extras. Even if none of that had ever happened—so goes their warped theology—God would still be "unconditional love" and would somehow save us anyway. Thus they would relegate all revelation to the category of optional, superfluous accretions, putting all their chips on the sole doctrine of God's infinite mercy.

But it does not follow that God's infinite mercy should allow us to save ourselves any way we please. The truth is that He could not have revealed that infinite mercy any better than He did, via the incarnation, passion, death and resurrection of the *body* of Christ. If His mercy were such that this paschal mystery was superfluous, then God would contradict Himself. His mercy does not have competing expressions, but is one as He is one. The modern heresy of universalist salvation, not through Jesus Christ, but through God's unconditional mercy somehow apart from Jesus Christ, may well prove to be the most insidious heresy of all time.

The theology of the body hits the nail of this error straight on the head by viewing God's infinite love through the sacrament of matrimony. Man is called to be one with God as a wife is one with her husband. In Christ, God offered His love to man as His spotless bride—spotless because He first washed her stained garments in His Blood, making them white.[1] There is one only heavenly Groom and one only human bride. We begin preparing for the nuptials at baptism, when all stain of sin is removed.[2] We, the People of God, unite as one bride—one Church—and when our heavenly groom comes again, the longed-for redemption of our bodies[3] will occur and the eternal nuptials will begin.[4] This spousal union is only possible because the Second Person of the Trinity has humbled Himself to take on a human body just like ours in all

---

[1] Cf. Revelation 7:14 & Ephesians 5:26f.
[2] Cf. I Peter 3:21 & Romans 6:6f.
[3] Cf. Romans 8:23.
[4] Cf. Revelation 19:7 & 21:2.

things but sin.[1] He graciously provided all that we need to see to the purification of our own body by means of the sacraments, His word, prayer, charity, etc. Thus on that great and awesome day the bride of Christ will be readied for her heavenly Groom and be able to be one with Him in a way symbolized now by every conjugal union.[2] Even now, as we await that day, we yet continue to grow in grace and in union with Him Whom our heart loves, especially when we receive Holy Communion, where we meet Him in the flesh and become one with Him like branches on the vine.[3] Each Communion is a pledge of the final resurrection of our bodies that we long for.[4]

This revealed plan for redemption is so wonderful, how could anybody relegate it all to a mere superfluous option, and instead, invent some other way for God to reveal His infinite mercy? What starving man does not rejoice at being admitted to the royal banquet, but instead demands that the King satisfy his hunger without the banquet? Yet this is exactly what many modern Christians (*et al.*) are doing when they invent their own definition of divine mercy, as though they could possibly best what God, in Christ, has already done.

The body is at the very heart of revelation. The body is the instrument through which God's mercy is blindingly revealed. Whatever negative forces there are which are opposed to our true good (e.g. Satan, the world, the fallen flesh, etc.), all aim for one bull's eye—*the body*. Throughout history, in one form or another, these forces have battled against the truth of the Gospel and have tried to derail the Church precisely in this realm of the body.

The source of many of the most insidious and destructive heresies that, throughout history, have constantly persisted in popping up here and there like weeds in a sidewalk crack, is a denial of one or another aspect of the truth of the body. Somehow, it has not been a hard sell to convince spiritual people that the body is evil or, at best, indifferent. But the revealed truth is that the body stands front and center in the Gospel. Yes, the present

---

[1] Cf. Hebrews 4:15.
[2] Cf. Ephesians 5:25-32.
[3] Cf. John 15:1-9.
[4] Cf. John 6:54 & I Corinthians 11:26.

condition of our flesh is that of a "fallen state," tending toward self-indulgence. But why make the flesh the only whipping boy when our souls are also in that same "fallen state"? Without the animation of our souls, the flesh is neither self-indulgent nor self-denying. There can be no sin of any kind were it not piloted by pride, which is specific to the *soul* rather than the *body*. Yet ever since original sin we have had a penchant for excuses, placing the blame where it does not belong. Eve blamed the devil.[1] Adam blamed Eve, and even God, Who, after all, was responsible for giving him the woman in the first place.[2] Throughout history sinners have continued the attempt to shift blame from where it really belongs to some concocted scapegoat or other. The flesh has always been conveniently a hand to absorb much, if not most, of the unjust blame. This has become so convenient that we have even made a pseudo-spirituality out of it, resulting in pious people despising their bodies, and instead of yearning in hope of the resurrection of the flesh, they have all but denied this central Gospel truth in their fervent desire to simply be rid of the burden of the body and go to heaven only in spirit. They might get such wild notions from Plato, but they do not get them from the Judeo-Christian Bible.

Shifting blame is not true repentance, and without true repentance there is no Christianity. Thankfully, the Church has always preached this and it has always been entrenched in our sacramental rites. The woman caught in adultery[3] made no excuses. She did not blame the weakness of her flesh, her dirigent poverty, or invoke some Freudian defense of her sin. Nor did she even try to spread the blame around by mutually accusing some of her male clients who, no doubt, had dragged her before Jesus in the first place. No, she simply stood there, guilty, ready to accept the blame. Precisely because of this personal truthfulness, the blame she justly expected turned into total mercy and forgiveness. Her sackcloth was removed and she was clothed with joy.[4]

---

[1] Cf. Genesis 3:13.
[2] Ibid. v. 12.
[3] Cf. John 8:3-11.
[4] Cf. Psalm 30:11.

Likewise, the publican in the rear of the temple[1] made no excuses for himself, but honestly admitted his unworthiness, and because of this, the Gospel tells us that he left the temple justified.

Nor did the prodigal son[2] rehearse any excuses when he returned to his father, but first resolved to accept the truth that he had sinned against both heaven and his father, happy if only he could assume even the status of a slave. He did not blame the devil. He did not blame his carnal impulses. He knew the truth that the pilot of both his body and soul was his will—a *spiritual* faculty—and that he alone was to blame. Because of this honesty he was received back by his father and accorded an even higher status than before, what with rings on his fingers and bells on his toes, feasting on the fatted calf!

This truth is at the heart of the sacraments, especially of baptism and reconciliation. The Church has always made forgiveness and mercy easily experiential. After all, this was the essence of St. Paul's Gospel: "Be reconciled to God!"[3] It was the very first word Jesus ever preached: "Repent!"[4]

But so long as we keep preferring to shift the blame elsewhere, we separate ourselves from the most wonderful experience in this life: union with our all-forgiving Father through true repentance. To be able to approach the sacrament of Christ's Body and Blood after experiencing such awesome and undeserved forgiveness, is as close as we can get in this life to the eternal nuptials of heaven.

But we foolishly deprive ourselves of this awesome experience when we dodge personal responsibility for our sins and instead, adopt some form of blaming the flesh. This only leads to an abiding negativity about our bodies and it does us no good. It is not holy. It is just another substitute for holiness.

At Mass, in the *Gloria*, we sing, "You Alone are the Holy One!" Jesus is our pattern of holiness.[5] He never regarded either His Own or anybody else's body in a

---

[1] Cf. Luke 18:9-14.
[2] Cf. Luke 15:11-32.
[3] II Corinthians 5:20.
[4] Mark 1:15.
[5] Cf. I John 2:6.

negative way. His Own flesh was so holy that He gave it to us with His Own hand[1] as our spiritual food[2] such that, by consuming it, we would have eternal life,[3] and by not consuming it, we had only death to look forward to.[4]

And why did Jesus heal all[5] who went out to Him unless He highly valued and cherished their bodies and not merely their souls? All of His miraculous cures were signs of the one, ultimate, final cure of all cures—the resurrection of the body on the last day.

Spiritualities tainted with negativity about the body have not borne the good fruit of helping us yearn in hope for that awesome day. Instead, they have tended to make us forget about it, content to have our bodies rot in some grave forever, so long as we can be with the Lord in our souls. But as St. Paul repeatedly emphasized,[6] this is not the Gospel of Christ.

Why persist in failed pseudo-spiritualities, tainted as they are by Gnosticism, Manicheanism, Jansenism and Puritanism? Why not be like the wise man Jesus referred to who knows how to bring forth from his storeroom things *new* and old?[7] The negative approach to the body in the past has not only led to a neglect of the central dogma of the resurrection, but has also been largely responsible for all kinds of psycho-sexual problems and perversions. Just imagine if those 4,500 priests whom the bishops admit have molested children had been reared in homes, schools, seminaries and a Catholic culture that took an approach to the body and sexuality that was 180° differ-ent? How often do you suppose they heard anything positive about the body and right sexuality? I would bet it would fit into a thimble. But not only did they hardly ever *hear* the truth of the body, but they probably never *experienced* it, neurotically bound up in all their silly taboos.

I myself confess that I am a product of that failed ap-proach. As someone once famously said, "There, but for

---

[1] Cf. Luke 22:19.
[2] Cf. John 6:55-58.
[3] Cf. Ibid. v. 54.
[4] Cf. Ibid. v. 53.
[5] Cf. Matthew 8:16.
[6] E.g. I Corinthians 15.
[7] Cf. Matthew 13:52.

the grace of God, go I!" I could easily have become one of those perverted priests. But when I began to question everything at the age of nineteen, not only did this search lead me to Jesus Christ and the Catholic faith, but it also led me to reconsider absolutely everything in my assumed culture, not least among them the body and sexuality. Thanks be to God that the same grace of truth that led me to Jesus Christ, also led me to that fullness of life that Jesus said He had come to impart to us.[1] And that grace sill leads on and on, its purpose being to totally transform us into Christ, in Whom Alone we can regain our original innocence so hurriedly lost by our first parents. Jesus was talking about "fullness," and thus the body cannot be excluded.

We need to *think* differently about the body and we need to *act* differently. We need to change the many, mindlessly accepted social structures and taboos that work against acquiring a truly Christ-like attitude toward the body. I am talking about everything from moms uninhibitedly breast-feeding their babies in public to changes in public architecture. At least fifty years ago locker rooms in schools and health clubs were built with one large shower room which everyone (at least of like gender) shared openly. By today these have been replaced by not only private, individual shower stalls, but also private, individual dressing rooms attached to the shower. We cannot change culture overnight, but we can at least take steps in the right direction. First, we need to do what it takes for ourselves, personally. Each one of us needs to re-acculturate himself, trying to wash out the inherited negativity and gradually acquire the mind of Christ toward the body.

Our second responsibility is to our own families, especially our children. We must try to rear them in a healthy way. I know from experience how difficult this is when their sibling society and the dominant culture is all working against us, but this is no less true when it comes to any other area of Gospel growth, such as our attitude toward money and prayer. We are the shepherds of our children, and we must do what it takes to lead them to

---

[1] Cf. John 10:10.

green pasture, even if the odds are against us and we cannot do it absolutely perfectly.

Finally, we need to do what we can to influence our community and the world around us. Yes, of course we should still combat pornography, but we should use a new approach. Pope John Paul II once said that the problem with pornography was not that it revealed too much, but that it revealed too little.[1] In the past, this attitude was far from evident in our deportment as we crusaded against pornography. The impression we gave was that pornography, indeed, revealed *too much*. By so operating, we effectively threw the proverbial baby out with the bathwater. The end result was an abiding contempt for the body itself. "Decency" necessarily meant keeping the body out of sight and out of mind.

But instead of denying the body altogether, we should have asserted it in its rightful place. By undressing Michelangelo's figures on the ceiling of the Sistine Chapel, Pope John Paul II did just this.

But what about the ceilings of our own sanctuaries in Hoboken, New Jersey and Wichita, Kansas? You know as well as I do that anyone who suggested decorating an American parish church with tasteful nudes would practically be excommunicated from the local parish. This is why we must begin to move in the opposite direction, opposing pornography with new tactics—tactics which do not *negate* the body but which *elevate* it to its rightful, God-given place.

If the U.S. bishops truly want to heal the disease that abetted (if not caused) the horrendous sins of those 4,500 priests, then they must work in the direction proposed by this book. They must strive, at every level, from family life and the administration of the sacraments to social life, to create a wholesome culture where the body and sexuality are accorded there rightful places. Pope John Paul II has already led the way. We have only to follow, not by merely *talking* about it in stuffy seminars, but by *living* it in everyday life.

I know how difficult this is, because I have been in the thick of the struggle for about thirty years now. Many who would like to begin to walk the talk don't know where to

---

[1] Because it distorts the truth of man by focusing only on the erotic.

start. I have a concrete proposal that could help thousands of people, whether they live in a monastic cloister or a coed college dormitory. I propose a new kind of religious retreat; a new movement to help correct past wrongs. Let's call it a "Theology of the Body Retreat," but not one where the participants merely sit around all day listening to erudite conferences and participating in discussions, but a retreat which actually offers participants the *opportunity to encounter the body firsthand, in a new, positive way*. Many variations on the theme are possible, but essential to all are the following:

1. Silence. "*With God*, all things are possible."[1] The first imperative is that we create an *atmosphere* of prayerful silence where we can truly be "*with God*." Silence is essential as any retreat master knows. We need enough silence to hear God's gentle voice booming in. This alone is not easy and takes lots of effort, discipline and the cooperation of everyone. Silence is too little appreciated in today's world. Sadly, this is true even at liturgical functions, despite the repeated insistence of the Church leadership.[2]

2. Time. One cannot turn gabbiness off and silence on like toggling a switch. At the very least, such a retreat should extend from Thursday evening through Sunday evening. We cannot hear God unless we "unhear" the world, and *this takes time*. Listening to God requires *waiting* on Him. He is not on call by demand. To try to approach the Lord in this way is already to abort any real possibility of a divine encounter. A day of recollection is simply not sufficient.

3. Prayer. In our acquired quietness we need to incline the ear of our heart to God by lots of prayer.

First comes liturgical prayer, both the Liturgy of the Eucharist and of the Hours because this is the very prayer of the Only-Begotten, incarnate Son to His heavenly Father as well as the loving exchange between Christ, the Groom, and us, the Church, His beloved bride.

Secondly comes meditating on the Word of God. Selected passages pertaining to the body should be offered. It

---

[1] Luke 1:37.

[2] E.g. cf. *The General Instruction on the Roman Missal*, 2003, NN. 43, 45 & Vatican II, *Sacrosanctum Concilium*, N. 30.

is tragic that so many people of all denominations neglect the Word of God in their supposed attempt to know and do His will. If the Word of God is going to dwell in us richly,[1] then we have to read it, reread it and read it again. We need to breathe the Scriptures, just as Mary taught Jesus to do, as did the Apostles, the Fathers of the Church and the great saints. As St. Jerome wrote, "Ignorance of the Scriptures is ignorance of Christ."[2] We cannot possibly know the mind of the Lord unless we are devoted to meditation on the Word of God.

Then come other forms of personal prayer, according to each one's own inclination and spirituality.

4. Inspiring, insightful conferences. The retreat master and his assistants need to know their stuff and know how to communicate it to others. To be credible, they should not only be talkers, but walkers with experience.

5. Recreation. Retreats are notoriously sedentary. Especially during a retreat about the body, physical activity is essential, even if it is just walks or helping to peel potatoes in the kitchen. Whatever the activity, according to each person's ability and inclination, it should be some exercise that makes us well aware of our bodiliness.

6. Journaling. Recording our questions, impressions, insights, etc. is a great help to learning. It is as though the Holy Spirit teaches us as we write. Perhaps this was how it was for some of the sacred authors of Scripture. As we try to express what we learn, we are led deeper into truth.

7. The last essential element of such a retreat has to be real occasions for experiencing the body within this prayerful, holy, chaste context. I realize that some people are prepared for a more intensive experience than others, and some will have all they can do to barely get their feet wet. For this reason, retreats can be designed for different levels so that no one is intimidated, yet each person has the opportunity to be challenged.

Even within an introductory "Theology of the Body Retreat," there can be various options available, according to each retreatant's readiness and inclination. For such an introductory retreat, the opportunity to experience the

---

[1] Cf. Colossians 3:16.
[2] St. Jerome, *Commentary on Isaiah*, Prologue.

body first hand might be delayed till the second half of the retreat, the first half focusing on right-mindedness.

The ideal setting for such a retreat is unquestionably a country place with lots of natural privacy. A city retreat is not a good idea. City culture has gone far to divorce us not only from nature at large, but even from our own nature. Jesus preferred to commune with His Father on the mountains,[1] and this is where we, too, can best strip away artificialities and be naked with God, even if only in spirit.

One suggestion for a beginning experience is to take a solitary nature walk, find a favorable spot for meditation and spend at least a half hour there. If comfortable, the meditation should be conducted nude, even removing the discarded clothing from sight. The object is to meditate with one's entire self—including his body. He should listen and imbibe the nature around him with his whole being, translating it all into a prayer crescendoing up to God.

This experience is really minimal, yet for many, it will prove overwhelmingly powerful. After getting dressed, all return for common prayer and a conference, followed by journaling time to allow the retreatants to contextualize their experiences. Then, later, during a group sharing, those who wish to share their experiences may do so. This communal sharing will prove to be one of the most effective elements of the retreat.

Another possibility for encountering the body during an introductory retreat would be to host a life drawing session. First, an art instructor would give everyone a very brief class, advising a few pointers for those who doubt their artistic abilities. Then prayer and the actual session during which everyone draws a nude model of either (or each) sex. This should last at least a half hour during which the model offers more than one pose. Spiritual music such as Gregorian Chant might play softly in the background. This session might well occur outdoors, weather permitting.

The life-drawing session is followed by common prayer, private time for journaling, a conference and group sharing.

---

[1] E.g. Matthew 14:23; 17:1; 28:16; Mark 6:46 & Luke 6:12.

Dinner and Eucharist could conclude such an introductory retreat, though for certain groups there could be a postlude option of a clothing-optional Finnish sauna experience.

The main object of the retreat is to bring the retreatants face to face with the body in a completely new, positive, non-erotic light. But this must be seen as only a beginning and not the fulfillment. Just because someone has made such a retreat he should not imagine that he is all of a sudden a pro, has walked the talk, "been there, done that." Retreatants need to be challenged to return home to continue integrating their new awareness into their daily lives in their own creative ways proper to each person's own particular situation and lifestyle.

Such retreats could greatly help to move the talk into the walk and really begin making a difference in the lives of individuals, couples, families and even wider cultural practices.

This book represents the fruit of over thirty years of hard thinking, prayer and study on the theme by myself and many others. As a plaque on the wall of our home reads, "May the peace of Christ *disturb* you!" May the articles in this book stir up stale, failed, complacent, conventional modes of regarding the body and challenge you to truly strive to put on the mind of Christ and do what it takes to be like Him in every way.

May our Lady, whose selfless consent occasioned the incarnation of the Only-begotten Son of God,[1] guide us all as we grow in union with her Son, the Spouse of the Church, His one bride, united with Him as one flesh now, in the sacrament of the altar, and forever in glory after He returns at the resurrection of the just on the last day. *Ave Maria!*

---

[1] Cf. Luke 1:38.

"Nakedness Is not Immodest"

by Pope John Paul II[1]

Sexual modesty cannot then in any simple way be identified with the use of clothing, nor shamelessness with the absence of clothing and total or partial nakedness. *There are circumstances in which nakedness is not immodest...* nakedness as such is not to be equated with physical shamelessness. *Immodesty is present only when nakedness plays a negative role with regard to the value of the person, when its aim is to arouse concupiscence, as a result of which the person is put in the position of an object of enjoyment. The human body is not in itself shameful,* nor for the same reasons are sensual reactions, and human sensuality in general. Shamelessness (just like shame and modesty) is a function of the *interior* of a person. There is a certain relativism in the definition of what is shameless. This relativism may be due to differences in the makeup of particular persons—a greater or lesser sensual excitability, a higher or lower level of moral culture—or to different world views. It may equally be due to differences in external conditions—in climate, for instance...and also in prevailing customs, social habits, etc. *Dress is always a social question,* a function of...social customs. In this matter there is no exact similarity in the behavior of particular people, even if they live in the same age and the same society. The principle of what is truly immodest is simple and obvious, but its application in specific cases depends upon the individual, the milieu, the society. *There are circumstances in which nakedness is not immodest.* If someone takes advantage of such an occasion to treat the person as an object of enjoyment (even if his action is purely internal) *it is only he who is guilty of shamelessness...* not the other.

---

[1] Karol Wojtyla, *Love and Responsibility*, trans. H.T. Willetts (New York: Farrar, Straus & Giroux, 1981), pp. 176-192. Wojtyla authored this book many years before being chosen to succeed St. Peter in Rome. Editor's note: All italics mine.

Let It Shine!

by Jim C. Cunningham

If you are like me, Judeo-Christian tradition is an integral part of how you view God, yourself and the world. We evaluate new ideas in the light of that value system. Some of us do this because we have profound faith that this system is divinely revealed, and therefore true. Others, having less or no faith, nevertheless feel uncomfortable with anything that appears to be drastically divergent from that tradition which has become our cultural home.

I suspect that most readers are shocked at this book since, at first glance, it appears to contradict assumed standards of what constitutes the virtue of modesty. I argue, however, that this assumption, like many others, does not come from revelation, but from the dominant culture around us—what Scripture often refers to as "the world."[1]

Although we would like to believe differently, we are far more deeply affected by the dominant culture around (and within) us than we are by strictly revealed truths. Our prideful tendency towards self-righteousness rejects this, but one example will suffice to show what I mean:

The Gospel clearly teaches that poverty is blessedness. Such was Jesus' very first beatitude, His opener for His famous "Sermon on the Mount."[2] In His "Sermon on the Plain" He taught, "But woe to you rich, for your consolation is now."[3] When a rich young man deigned to become His disciple, Jesus required of him that he first rid himself of all possessions, which he, sadly, was unwilling to do.[4] Teaching His apostles, Jesus clarified this event, saying, "It is easier for a camel to pass through the eye of a needle than for a rich man to enter the kingdom of

---

[1] E.g. cf. John 7:7; 14:17 & 27; 17:14; I John 2:15ff; I Corinthians 1:26ff & James 1:27 & 4:4.
[2] Cf. Matthew 5:3.
[3] Luke 6:24.
[4] Cf. Mark 10:17ff.

2

God."[1] In Luke 16:19ff Jesus tells the parable of the poor beggar, Lazarus. Though poor and "a loser" by the world's standards in this life, he nevertheless inherited eternal bliss in Abraham's bosom, whereas the rich man, at whose gate Lazarus vainly begged, inherited eternal torment. St. James also has many clear moral teachings on the necessity and blessedness of evangelical poverty.[2]

But how many Christians do you know who seek this beatitude? When I go to church, which I do every day, I never hear anyone—not even the priest—praying for blessed poverty. Instead, they pray for the same things everyone else would pray for such as health, wealth, prosperity and happiness in the here and now. Obviously, then, the vast majority of Christendom has not progressed very far in "putting on the mind of Christ."[3]

Rather than live what the Gospel explicitly teaches, they accommodate it to their pusillanimity and true irreligion. This fact stimulated Mark Twain to comment, "There was only one Christian, and He died." Although I do not share this pessimism, his hyperbole illustrates my point. In our self-righteousness, we constantly kid our-selves into imagining we are faithful disciples, but if we would be stark naked honest with ourselves, we would have to fall on our knees in the back of the church, beat our breasts, and humbly pray, "Lord, be merciful to me, a sinner."[4]

St. Paul, who taught that "the love of money is the root of all evil,"[5] clearly assessed this state of affairs. He knew what was required for the Good News to really take root in culture. Thus it was that in his letter to the Roman Church, which he considered preeminent,[6] he neverthe-less exhorted a radically new way of thinking, and this, in fact, specifically with regard to our bodies: "I appeal to you therefore, brethren, by the mercies of God, to present your bodies as a living sacrifice, holy and acceptable to God, which is your spiritual worship. Do not be conformed to this world but be transformed by the renewal of your

---

[1] Mark 10:25.
[2] Cf. James 1:9; 2:5ff & 5:1ff.
[3] Cf. Philippians 2:5, etc.
[4] Cf. Luke 18:9ff.
[5] I Timothy 6:10.
[6] Cf. Romans 1:8.

mind, that you may prove what is the will of God, what is good and acceptable and perfect."[1]

If the truth be told, we Christians are no more conformed to the mind of God in our attitudes toward our bodies than we are toward wealth and worldly success. This is as true of bishops as it is of sextons. We are hardly conformed to the Gospel at all. The sad fact is that we have defined "religion" to mean conforming the Gospel to the world. Rather than set our light aloft on a lamp-stand to enlighten the world, we have more or less vainly persisted in trying to keep a vestige of a flickering flame alive beneath a bushel-basket.[2] Indeed, such is ecclesiastical history. Jewish history before Christ was no different. "Hard-hearted and stiff-necked,"[3] the Chosen People constantly rebelled such that God often compared them to a wife gone a-whoring.[4]

Since this book concerns only body values, I must limit my analysis to this specific topic.

The Gospel has hardly (if at all) affected the body attitudes of Christians. Almost all Christians say that they want "to die and go to heaven" (of course, they are in no particular hurry to inherit such bliss). There is no place for their bodies in their spirituality. Their view of the body is far more in accord with Plato than the Gospel. For Plato, the body was a weight and hindrance, a prison of the soul. Almost every Christian (and Jew) I know share this view, despite what revelation states to the contrary.

St. Paul expressed the pith of the Gospel when he taught, "If Christ be not raised, vain is our preaching, vain is your faith."[5] He went on to say that Christ's resurrection is not something extrinsic and remote, but on the contrary, our own resurrection is intrinsically, intimately and necessarily linked with it.[6] St. Paul said that Christ's resurrection is so necessary and sure, that without it, our own bodies will not be raised from the dead. Christianity is not merely about being good, going to church and "having faith." St. Paul said that if we take the resurrec-

---

[1] Romans 12:1f.
[2] Cf. Matthew 5:14ff.
[3] Cf. Exodus 32:9; 33:3, etc.
[4] Cf. Hosea 1:2ff.
[5] I Corinthians 15:14.
[6] Cf. I Corinthians 15:12ff.

tion of our bodies out of the mix, no matter how great, miraculous and charitable we may be, not only is it all a grand waste of time and energy, but we would actually be *the most foolish and pitiable of men.*[1] Yet hordes of Christians give no thought to the resurrection, and self-righteously believe themselves to be rather important, useful, significant and even holy. But Paul says you can found and finance all the homeless shelters in the world, but if the resurrection is not central to your spirituality, you are more than wasting your time. I know some Christians who actually long for heaven, but I know starkly few who give a thought to what should be the focal point of their hearts' deepest yearning—the Last Day, when our bodies will be raised no matter how much they have rotted. Most Christians miss the boat entirely, drowned in a flood of secondary and tangential matters.

The Christians in St. Paul's day tended to have the same deficiency of faith: "... some of you say there is no resurrection of the dead."[2] Although few of us Christian readers might literally deny the resurrection verbally, yet most deny it in practice, as it has no place in their spirituality, focused solely as it is on "dying and going to heaven."

According to the Gospel, then, the goal of true religion is not to "die and go to heaven," one's soul finally liberated from its fleshly prison. The true goal, judging by what the Scriptures say, is to have our now corruptible bodies put on incorruption,[3] rejoined to our souls in an unbreakable unity more perfect even than Adam enjoyed before the fall. Until our bodies are redeemed, they "groan in pain."[4] At least this is what they are supposed to do if the Holy Spirit really animates them. But alas, the problem today, no less than in St. Paul's day, is that Christians are really more deeply imbued with the spirit of the world, rather than the Spirit of Christ. If we rejected the world's false definition of the body and "put on the mind of Christ," we would not find ourselves so indifferent or even oblivious to the Gospel's most central teaching—the resurrection of the

---

[1] Cf. I Corinthians 15:19.
[2] Cf. I Corinthians 15:12ff.
[3] Cf. I Corinthians 15:53.
[4] Romans 8:23.

flesh. Our conformity to the world pollutes the purity of our faith.

It is our world, and not the Gospel, that promotes the far-fetched notion that women's breasts are somehow so erotic and lust-provoking that it is a sin to expose them or to look at them. "Upright" Christians are so fully imbued with this error that they blush when they have to read such passages as Isaiah 66:11 from the lectern: "Oh, that you may suck fully of the milk of her comfort, that you may nurse with delight at her abundant breasts!"

Jews and Christians believe that the Holy Spirit inspired the Scriptures. God Himself gave us this beautiful image of lush, abundant breasts. He says He wants to console us like a baby is comforted by those breasts. How can we understand what the image means if it is supposedly sinful to experience the image? If God Himself compared His love for us in this way, then it would be entirely fitting and pious for Christians to have a photograph of a mother's luscious, soft and comforting breasts hanging on our living room walls or as bookmarks in our Bibles. But you know as well as I that your self-righteous 'brethren" would condemn you. Maybe they would not burn you to death as did their forefathers, the "upright, godly" people of 17th century New England, but they would at least despise you, look down on you and calumniate you.

The metaphors in Scripture, like all metaphors, are drawn from *familiar, daily life.* Because God wants us to understand His revelation, He does not choose metaphors beyond our experience, but rather *those we are intimately familiar with.* Thus it is presumed (by God at least) that everyone should be as familiar with the sight of breast-feeding that His metaphor will have the desired effect.

Not long after my conversion back to Christianity in 1973, I was attending Mass at a Trappist abbey. I heard a distracting, slurping sound, and looked next to me to determine the cause. There, in sheer stained-glass church light, was a bare, female breast, with a very contented baby sucking away on it like there would be no tomorrow.

I gasped. But by that time I had finally made up for my squandered youth and had read deeply from the Scriptures, and knew passages like Isaiah 66:11 (which, by the way, upon first reading, also made me gasp). A seminarian friend of mine from Rhode Island once told me that his class was taught to banish nursing moms from the nave to "cry rooms" and that they should never allow such a thing in church. I wonder where the hundreds of nursing moms went when crowds of several thousand[1] flocked to hear Jesus preach. When the indignant disciples tried to usher the cry-babies into the cry-room, Jesus intervened, admonishing, "Let the little children come to Me, and do not hinder them, for to such belongs the kingdom of heaven."[2]

I beg to differ with those Rhode Island seminary faculty, and I know I have the testimony of revelation on my side. Any mother's breast is, in truth, infinitely more precious and sacred than the most highly bejeweled chalice. All chalices will rot; the Gospel says so.[3] But the breasts of Christian mothers will, like the rest of their bodies, put on incorruptibility[4] and live forever. Let's face it: when it comes to our bodies, like most everything else, we Christians are really messed up. We are far, very far, from the mind of Christ. As St. Paul admonishes, we are spiritually mere infants, still needing to be given suck, and are not ready for the real meat of the Gospel.[5]

And how do you suppose a young man can be expected to "handle" the "shocking" sight of a breast feeding a baby if our supposedly godly, upright, holy leaders unscripturally condemn our seeing female breasts as we grow up?

A woman does not need the "excuse" of nursing to expose her breasts, because according to revelation, there is nothing whatsoever "dirty" about her breasts to begin with. If Christian leaders truly want to help their flocks put on Christ's mind, then they should leave a few copies of this book in their church vestibules. They should actively do what it takes to think and live in accord with the *Word* rather than the *world*.

It is the dominant culture of the world, and not Scripture, that fetishizes the female breast. It is that culture

---

[1] Cf. Matthew 14:21, etc.
[2] Matthew 19:14.
[3] Cf. Matthew 6:19f & James 5:3.
[4] Cf. I Corinthians 15:53.
[5] Cf. I Corinthians 3:1f & Hebrews 5:11ff.

that "entertains adult men" by paying women to perform erotic dances, baring their breasts as though they were objects of lustful passion.

All Christians should react by rejecting this perverted definition of the female breast. Instead, they allow dominant culture, rather than Scripture, to define it. The only difference between such "good" Christians and the world is in their *response* to that mutually acceptable mis-definition. The world responds with lust; "good" Christians, accepting the heretical definition of the breast as an evil object of lust, respond by denying it altogether, throwing the proverbial nursling out with the bath water. In doing so they do nothing to get to the root of, and solve the problem. By allowing the world to define their values, Christians are really following the world, and not the Gospel, even though they *respond* in a way opposite to the world's way. True purity must go deeper than *mere responses*. Purity needs to begin with *true definitions*, and for this we must look to the Word of God. "Your Word is a lamp unto my feet and a light for my path."[1]

To clarify: The world says "The female breast is erotic, let's lust to our heart's content." The common Christian reply is, "Yes, the breast *is* erotic (because the world says so), so I must shun all experience of it."

In reality, in light of revelation, this is absurd. The Gospel response ought to be, "No, you are wrong in defining the female breast as erotic, calling unclean what God has made clean.[2] I am certainly going to shun all lust, but not what is holy, which includes the *whole* human body, for I take my definitions from *God's Word* and not from *the world*."

The conventional Christian response to the world's lie that the female breast is "dirty" is to accept that flawed definition and reject the breast along with lewdness. This is merely the opposite side of the very same coin, and *the whole coin* belongs to the world, because the head of Caesar, the emperor of this world, is on it, identifying it as belonging to him.[3] The truly Christian, Gospel response ought to be to give *the whole coin* back to unChristian

---

[1] Psalm 119:105.
[2] Cf. Acts 10:15.
[3] Cf. Matthew 22:21.

8

Caesar, because it has nothing whatever to do with Truth—the mind of Christ. *Only God* should mint the coin of the Christian economy of salvation as it pertains to morality as well as dogmas of faith, since our treasury does not lie in this world.[1]

Jesus said He passionately longed "to set a fire on the earth."[2] Is not this radical, truly Gospel reaction the very stuff of that *fire*? Is not the *conventional* "Christian" response no more than a validation of what is erroneous?

What I have said above about the female breast can also be said about every other part of the human body. Maybe you still doubt me, so let me hit the nail on the head (no pun intended).

The female breast is, after all, just a *secondary* sexual characteristic like a man's beard. Perhaps you imagine that what I have said above cannot be applied to *primary* sexual characteristics (i.e. genitalia). This is not true, because the *entire* human body was created *in God's Own image,*[3] and not one part of it can be unholy or dirty. The notion that some part of it is indecent or obscene is entirely unscriptural. Those who believe this (and most Jews and Christians do, in practice if not in word) are judging by the erroneous standards of the world, which we are not supposed to blindly accept, but rather illuminate and correct.

Consider the male body. What would the world say is the most "obscene" part of it? This is not hard to figure out if you simply look at the world's peculiar customs of dress. What is the last thing a male stripper reveals? Yes, he euphemistically calls it the "full Monty." When a stripper on "ladies' night out" gets down to it, he wears only a jock strap or G-string, exposing his entire body with the sole exception of his genitals. According to the world's perversion, it is then, when he has stripped this far, that the ladies, conditioned by the world and not at all helped by pastors who should have gone to the root of the error rather than accept the world's absurd definitions—it is at that point that the ladies' hype reaches fever pitch, awaiting the ultimate revelation, when the stripper at long

---

[1] Cf. Matthew 6:19f.
[2] Luke 12:49.
[3] Cf. Genesis 1:26f.

last removes the little pouch covering his genitals, and makes the ultimate revelation.

And what specific part of his genitals, according to the world's definition, is the most erotic and "obscene"? It is that part normally naturally covered with foreskin—the head (or glans) of the penis.

This idea that the glans is "dirty" and "obscene" could not be further from revealed truth. This idea is nowhere to be found in the Old or New Testaments. Scripture fetishizes no body part at all. Fetishes are one of the alloyed metals used in minting Caesar's counterfeit coin. They have nothing whatever to do with healthy minds. Fetishes belong to perversion. To become true disciples of Christ we are supposed to give *the whole coin* back to Caesar. We must leave all that worldly darkness behind us. It is supposed to be washed away in baptism. It belongs to the "old man" that we are supposed to have stripped off at baptism, when we were clothed with the New Man—Christ.[1]

According to many patristic documents such as the Apostolic Constitutions of St. Hippolytus of Rome, in the early Church, candidates for baptism sacramentally symbolized this stripping off of the old man by not only emptying their pockets of all coins, but by literally stripping off *all their clothes*, jewelry and even hair pins. And this was done *in Church*, especially at the solemn liturgy of Easter Vigil Mass. The sexes were not segregated, but boys, girls, men and women all stood stark naked in church in front of the bishop, presbyters, deacons, and the entire congregation attending this most important Mass of the year, which almost no one missed. Nudity was not an option; according to St. Cyril of Jerusalem and Theodore of Mopsuestia, it was considered to be a *necessary* part of the ritual. My university degree is in Patristics, and I have never read or heard of any early Christian making a problem out of this church nudity. The idea that some part of the body was sinful or "dirty" was impossible for people of that time to imagine. (Yes, there were dualistic, Gnostic heresies, but these held that everything physical was evil, not just certain body parts.)

---

[1] Cf. Romans 6:6 & Colossians 3:9f.

After all, back then everyone went to the public baths, and since the essential symbol of the sacrament of baptism is precisely a *bath*, it made perfect sense to do it *naked, communally,* and *in a pool.*

But this is the tradition of the early Church. Let's go back thousands of years earlier, to the roots of Judaism in the Pentateuch (Torah).

Abraham is the father of all Judaism, and is the Christians' "father in faith."[1] God made a special covenant with Abraham, and instituted a physical, visible sign of that covenant:

"This is My covenant, which you shall keep, between Me and you and your descendants after you: Every male among you shall be circumcised. You shall be circumcised in the flesh of your foreskins, and it shall be a sign of the covenant between Me and you. He that is eight days old among you shall be circumcised; every male throughout your generations, whether born in your house, or bought with your money from any foreigner who is not of your offspring... So shall My covenant be in your flesh an everlasting covenant."[2]

The foreskin naturally covering the glans of the penis was cut off, thus unnaturally perpetually *exposing* the glans.

Now, don't you think that if God thought as the world thinks (which he absolutely does not),[3] that this would be the very last possibility for a *visible* sign of His covenant? In fact, you know as well as I that it would not be a possibility at all. Imagine attending a Christian convention to decide on something to symbolize belonging to the People of God. No one would mind if you suggested using "Honk twice if you love Jesus" bumper stickers, or wearing a necklace of a dove. No one would object if you suggested wearing a white shirt and tie, or always faithfully carrying your bible around. In fact, they would think you rather pious.

But imagine the poor, sad sack who gets up to the podium and with a straight face, suggests that all boys and men expose the heads of their penises permanently

---

[1] Cf. Romans 4:11f & 16-18.
[2] Genesis 17:10ff.
[3] Cf. Isaiah 55:8f & Luke 16:16.

through the surgical removal of their foreskins. Would there be enough tar and feathers "in all tar-nation" for such a "heretic" and pervert? (Self-)righteous indignation would fill the heads and hearts of all present. Children's ears would be quickly covered by their pious parents. Children would be whisked from the auditorium. There would be a great clamor and cry of protest. In short, it would be tantamount to the unforgivable sin against the Holy Spirit[1] and excommunication, at the very least, would not be long in coming.

This only goes to prove, like the breast-feeding example I began with, how far afield Christians are from the mind of God. They are as far from the revealed mind of God as one can imagine. They have faith alright, but it is faith *in the world*, and the world's whacko ideas, and not faith in the revealed mind of God. This was St. Paul's assessment of the most eminent of the churches, and why he exhorted them to not conform to the world, but rather, to be *completely transformed* in Christ,[2] until we can truly say with him, "It is no longer I, but *Christ in me.*"[3]

No, do not think that I am saying that every Jew was supposed to walk around with his genitals exposed. No sign is *always* seen. Even the "Honk twice" bumper stickers are sometimes garaged. But signs would not be signs if they were *always compulsively hidden* as our culture tells us to hide our "dirty" parts.

The idea that anyone in Scripture ever bathed in a bathing suit is absurd. Read your Bible backwards and forwards; it is not there. Bathsheba was not blamed for not wearing a bathing suit, or for not making sure no one could possibly see her while she bathed nude, but only King David was blamed for being so perverse as to abuse such an innocent event and turn it to bad effect, lusting in his heart, and soon committing adultery and even murder to cover it up.[4] Obviously, he was not then in a godly frame of mind. Bathsheba's naked body was not evil, nor

---

[1] Cf. Luke 12:10.
[2] Cf. Romans 12:2. And note that the context (v. 1) specifically refers to *our bodies.*
[3] Galatians 2:20.
[4] Cf. II Samuel 11:2ff.

was the sight of it; what was evil was King David's immoral abuse of such a holy creation.

Before central plumbing, bathing was public, as it still is in undeveloped parts of the world. It was perfectly common and natural to know what bodies looked like because daily life provided ample opportunities to encounter ordinary, non-erotic nudity. Not only were people seen bathing, and mothers breast-feeding, but laborers often worked nude. In the Vatican there is a mural by Rafael depicting Noah's three sons constructing the ark in the nude. The apostles, especially St. Peter, seem to have routinely fished in the nude.[1] When St. John relates this towards the end of his Gospel, the thing that is noteworthy and peculiar is not that St. Peter was fishing in the nude, but that when he realized that the risen Jesus was on the shore, he quickly got dressed and dove into the water with all his clothes on. In other words, his "bags were packed" and in his customary impulsiveness, he was ready to do or go wherever Jesus commanded. St. Mary Magdalen may have mistaken the Risen Christ for a gardener[2] because, having left His wraps behind in the tomb as the Gospel clearly states,[3] He was probably wearing what gardeners often wore—nothing, and having a perfect, glorified body, He must have had a very handsome body at that, as one might expect of a sun-bronzed gardener accustomed to manual labor. St. Peter also slept in the nude even in prison.[4] Isaiah 20:1ff tells us that the great Isaiah even preached for three years, stark naked, and this was not *his* cockamamie idea, *but God's.*

So if God Almighty commands nude *preaching*, how can preachers today condemn nude *swimming, gardening, sleeping, communal bathing,* etc.? The answer is simple: *only* if they have the mind of *this world* rather than the mind *of Christ.*

Such pastors might argue that times have changed, and we now find ourselves in a very different world than Isaiah's, and thus we must adapt accordingly. But where in Scripture does it say that holiness means adapting to

---

[1] Cf. John 21:7.
[2] Cf. John 20:15.
[3] Cf. John 20:5f.
[4] Cf. Acts 12:8.

the world? Isn't evangelism supposed to be preaching so as to conform the world to Christ, subjecting all things beneath His feet?[1] Have they not hitched their donkey behind their cart, "ass end to," as it were?

If they concede that indeed, nude should not, ideally, be considered lewd, but since the fact is that *it is*, chastity demands that we shun nudity as we would shun lewdness, then my reply is that it simply does not work. Whether you lust at a nude or shun a nude for the sake of purity, either way you only serve to foment the fetish, and this does nothing to conform the world to the Gospel. Heads or tails, it is *still Caesar's* coin, and *not God's*.

God has a very different view of the human body than the world does, and it is *His* view that His people should follow and adopt. The authentic, unadulterated, Christian Gospel is far more radical than the sight of a naked preacher like Isaiah. If we would gasp at the sight of our pastor preaching nude in our church sanctuary, we should gasp far more at the Good News he is supposed to be proclaiming, for before that Word, "all lies naked and exposed,"[2] for it is so keen that it divides "soul and spirit, bone and marrow."[3] The Good News is that that "Word became *flesh* and dwelt amongst us,"[4] suffering and dying to get back for us what we had lost, and then some. He proved victorious not merely by believing in God, His Father, not merely by doing good works so plenteous that all the books in the world could not contain them,[5] not by "dying and going to heaven," but by doing a thing entirely new and beyond the realm of the most fantastic fantasies: *He rose from the dead!*[6] Death no longer has any power over Him! What's more, He would have every one of us share in a like resurrection. He is not content to save *only* our *souls*; He wants the *whole* of us. He redeemed the *whole* of us, and there is no longer any cause for shame, but only rejoicing and boasting in the Lord.[7] Alleluia! "Honk twice" and let your light shine!

---

[1] Cf. I Corinthians 15:25.
[2] Hebrews 4:13.
[3] Ibid. v. 12.
[4] John 1:14.
[5] Cf. John 21:25.
[6] Cf. Matthew 28:6; Acts 10:40; I Corinthians 15:20; etc.
[7] Cf. I Corinthians 1:31.

On Modesty

by Kahlil Gibran[1]

And the weaver said: Speak to us of clothes.

And he answered:

Your clothes conceal much of your beauty, yet they hide not the unbeautiful. And though you seek in garments the freedom of privacy you may find in them a harness and a chain. Would that you could meet the sun and the wind with more of your skin and less of your raiment, for the breath of life is in the sunlight and the hand of life is in the wind.

Some of you say, It is the north wind who has woven the clothes we wear.

And I say, Ay, it was the north wind, but shame was his loom, and the softening of the sinews was his thread. And when his work was done he laughed in the forest. Forget not that modesty is for a shield against the eye of the unclean. And when the unclean shall be no more, what were modesty but a fetter and a fouling of the mind? And forget not that the earth delights to feel your bare feet and the winds long to play with your hair.

Nudity not Immodest

by Giovanni Agnesti, Archbishop of Lucca

"Nudity is not in itself an offense to modesty. It is not vulgar or sinful. The human body is God's creation and as such it is good work."

---

[1] Excerpted from: Gibran, Kahlil, *The Prophet* (New York: Alfred A. Knopf, 1976), p. 33.

Born again in Bethlehem

by Jim C. Cunningham

This is *not* an autobiographical account of my *spiritual* rebirth in 1973 when I returned home to the Catholic Church. That rebirth followed a grace-inspired enlightenment as to the existence of my soul, how filthy I had let it become, and how profound is our Father's mercy offered through His Only-Begotten Son, Jesus Christ. In the wake of that tender and awesome discovery, I made up for years of spiritual neglect by spending several hours a day in liturgical worship, personal prayer, meditation, study of the history of the Church, the lives of the saints, and the Holy Bible, which I am ashamed to admit I had not read through even once until I was about twenty years old. Somehow I could plow through the 900+ pages of Michener's *Hawaii* at age fourteen, but I don't think I even *thought* of taking on the Word of God. The Holy Spirit, the Re-Creator, was re-fashioning me, and obviously the first department to work on was the much neglected *soul*. Other areas of growth would all come in their due time, but first a solid *spiritual* foundation was needed.

Throughout all this soul-attention, I paid very little attention to my body, or "Brother Ass" as St. Francis of Assisi called it. After two decades of selfish self-indulgence and satisfying (or trying to) every physical craving I might have had, penance, self-denial and physical discipline was very much in order. All this resulted in my having a very low opinion of Brother Ass. At times this probably bordered on Jansenism, so far did I react from the self-indulgence of my dead years. There were a few subtle challenges proposed by the Holy Spirit that would nudge me to rethink this anti-body attitude, but I paid very little attention to them and just continued my program of 100% *soul*-development, regarding the body as a *nuisance* at best.

I'd like to share with you how the ignored nudges culminated in my getting my socks (and a lot more!) knocked off. It was actually a sort of born-again experience, but with respect *to the body*.

It happened in Bethlehem, in the Holy Land, in 1975, two years after my spiritual rebirth. I was the only American pilgrimaging to the Holy Land with a group of youth from the *Basilique du Sacre Coeur de Montmartre* in Paris. Unable to understand the French tour guides, I would go off on my own as often as possible. One day I was thus on a solo excursion to Bethlehem. After visiting the site where the miraculous, virginal birth occurred, over-hung by seemingly a zillion hanging oil lamps, I ventured off to another nearby Franciscan shrine known as the Milk Grotto. I had no idea what it was, or what I would find therein, but with open mind I entered and explored, always in a spirit of prayer.

I discovered that, according to tradition, it was the place where the Holy Family stopped on the flight into Egypt, in order for the Blessed Mother to breast-feed Baby Jesus. He surely picked the darnedest times, because it is not at all far from the stable, and they were supposedly in quite a hurry to skip town before Herod tried a form of birth control even Planned Parenthood hasn't yet dared to suggest!

"So they made a *whole shrine* out of this, huh?" I thought to myself, amazed at how little it took the Catholic Church to justify building another shrine. But I remained open.

As I entered, I did not really expect to find much more than a zillion more hanging oil lamps. I expected to just say a prayer and move on. But this shrine was decorated with many, many unique artworks, so I thought I might as well check them out.

Both to my astonishment and embarrassment, every single masterpiece seemed to have the same theme, and despite ten years of Catholic education by the Sisters of St. Joseph and the Augustinian friars, it was a theme they had somehow masterfully shielded from my experience.

As you might have guessed by now, the theme was Mary breast-feeding her Infant Jesus. In some paintings it was not all that obvious to this stupid, puritanical, bottle-fed American just what the little Baby was doing, but in others, Mary's breasts and even nipples were clearly depicted. I had never seen such a thing! In my brief twenty years of life just about the only place I had *ever* seen a depiction of *any* female breast was in my dead years, ogling pornography.

"But this can't be pornography!" I reasoned to myself. "If it were, it would not be a bona-fide, *Catholic* shrine!" I was quite confused, not to mention poor, neglected, Brother Ass, who had gotten nothing but grief from me during the previous two years.

Had they been anyone else's breasts I would have called them "dirty" and practiced the "custody of the eyes" which, with the help of God, I had gotten pretty good at. But during those two years I had read and reread the Gospels too often to be so heretical. The phrase from Luke 11:27 (which had also always embarrassed me when I read it) kept reverberating in my mind, "Blessed are the breasts that You sucked!" Nor did her blessedness stop there. She was and is entirely blessed. Blessed is the womb that bore You!"[1] And previously both St. Gabriel the Archangel and St. Elizabeth, referring to her entire immaculate being, exclaimed, "Blessed are you among women!"[2]

Still utterly consternated, Brother Ass had to wait while the bridle of right reason was fitted over his bucking head.

Other Gospel texts seemed to be suggestingly whispered by the re-fashioning, sanctifying Spirit: "You can know a tree from its fruit. A good tree bears good fruit."[3]

I ruminated, "The obviously good fruit here is the nourishing of the Incarnate Word—nourished, certainly, as God the Creator intended. Thus the 'tree' whence comes this holy nutrition must also be entirely holy." I prayed, "Yes, All-Blessed Mother, your breasts are, indeed, most blessed."

I began to understand more keenly than ever before that this is precisely why it is so evil to distort God's intention by exploiting the female breast by pornography and other perverted forms of "entertainment for adult men." The bridle began to fit better.

Suddenly I recalled an image I had seen about two weeks before while visiting a friend in Sperlonga, Italy on

---

[1] Luke 11:27.
[2] Ibid. 1:28 & 42.
[3] Matthew 7:16ff.

my way from Rome to visit another friend in Palermo. On the Sperlonga beach I remembered seeing a woman sunbathing without a top. Given my cultural upbringing, coupled with my anti-body zeal that I had thought was holy, I had been prone to judge such a woman in a most negative way. "Did I judge her wrongly, Lord?" I prayerfully questioned, more open than ever to the Sanctifier's reconstruction of my culturally ingrained way of looking at things.

I sang to myself the beautiful, Gregorian Sanctus I had sung with the French group at Mass hours earlier, "*Pleni sunt caeli et terra gloria Tua.*" Of course, this is the celestial hymn of the seraphim in Isaiah 6:3: "Heaven *and earth are filled* with Your glory!" My lips kept muttering, "And earth... and earth... are filled!" I prayed, "*All* the earth is truly filled with Your glory, Lord, not just spiritual things, but even material things. And certainly man whom You made in Your Own image and likeness is included— the *entire* man—mind, soul, spirit *and body*[1]—and *the entire body.* I'm sorry, Lord, for having failed to acknowledge this glory in the past. Teach me; Your servant is listening."[2]

Yet more Scriptural treasures surfaced from the wellsprings of my memory to confirm this new awareness: "What God has made clean, you are not to declare unclean."[3]

"God looked on *all* that He had made, and found it *very good.*"[4]

"Hmm, I certainly have not been regarding *everything* God made as good, let alone *very* good," I thought, slowly moving through the gallery to view more masterpieces of this awesome theme which best expresses the whole idea of the incarnation and Mary as no less than very Mother of God.

Hugh Heffner and Larry Flynt[5] do not have a monopoly on the human body; it *all* belongs to God, *and it is all holy.* With all my Catholic education, I couldn't remember

---

[1] Cf. I Thessalonians 5:23.
[2] Cf. I Samuel 3:10.
[3] Acts 10:15.
[4] Genesis 1:31.
[5] Pornography magnates of magazines such as *Playboy* and *Penthouse.*

ever being taught this. Was it really necessary that Brother Ass be so confused by these holy pictures? Obviously that was not the intent of that shrine, which was certainly no New York 42nd Street peep show!

I began to understand the pervasive influence of a very warped culture, and a culture, unfortunately, too often deferred to by Catholics. A truly wholesome cultural upbringing would have properly bridled Brother Ass such that he would have experienced no confusion while contemplating those sacred images. My own culture had failed in many, many respects.

Those well-meaning Sisters of St. Joseph should not have censored out holy cards depicting Mary's truly blessed breasts nursing Jesus. Culture should never distort historical truth. A perfect example of this is the lie of the silly loincloth on most crucifixes, despite the fact that Christ was clearly crucified nude, the soldiers having divided all His garments.[1] Must the Gospel be filtered through the lens of a corrupt culture? Shouldn't Christians do what it takes to bring culture into conformity with Christ, rather than distort the reality of Christ to warped cultures? We are supposed to be laboring to subject all things to His feet[2] and not to be doing the opposite, tailoring Gospel truth to the perverted tastes of the world.

Another classic example of this contamination is how, despite umpteen hundred years of tradition, the Feast of the Circumcision of Christ is no longer to be found in the Western liturgical calendar. Instead. it has been supplanted by a "World Day of Prayer for Peace." The whole idea of circumcision is embarrassing to our culture; lectors blush whenever they have to read about it from the pulpit. But just whom do we serve: our warped culture. or God, Who saw fit to institute circumcision as the *visible* sign of His covenant with Abraham?[3] Who should blush at *God's* ideas? "If you are ashamed of Me and My doctrine, I will be ashamed of you when I come in My Father's glory..."[4]

---

[1] Cf. Psalm 22:18; Matthew 27:35; Mark 15:24 & John 19:23ff.
[2] Cf. I Corinthians 15:25.
[3] Cf. Genesis 17:9ff.
[4] Mark 8:38.

Another mistake in our culture regards breast-feeding. Very many mothers squelch their better maternal instincts and choose to give their babies simulated breast milk through a plastic nipple. If culture supported nature as God intended, then most women would not hesitate to choose the natural way, and the very idea of blushing at it would be inconceivable, as it should be. But what do most "pious" Christians do? They pusillanimously defer to the warps instead of bravely contributing to the re-structuring of culture, bringing it into conformity with nature, right reason and the Gospel.

Indeed, Brother Ass was confused in Bethlehem largely because culture had so cunningly and successfully contrived to deprive him from ever witnessing the womanly art of breast-feeding. If you were to ask people from most distant times and places whether they could believe that it were possible for a man to grow to full adulthood without ever having witnessed such an ordinary act, they would think the very question was at best preposterous. It would be like asking people today if they can believe that a twenty year old young man has never seen an adult eat; they'd think you were completely bonkers! Well, that's just how skewed our culture is, and because of two decades of being stewed in this nonsense, Brother Ass was quite justified when he cried out in agony, "Gimme a break!"

Since the Holy Spirit had already been accustoming me to radical change ever since my return to Jesus, I was not afraid to ask radical questions and make even more radical changes. Thus I questioned my *entire* culture, from top to bottom.

Two years before I had been born again to re-address matters pertaining to the *soul*; now I was on the threshold of another rebirth, re-evaluating all my former attitudes as regards the *body*. As I meandered through that Bethlehem gallery, I thought, "As wrong as my culture is as regards *spiritual* things, so also is it wrong as regards *physical* things. I have been brought up—even by churchmen—to canonize what is 'normal'—the 'status quo'—as if it were divinely revealed."

I resolved, then and there, to do *whatever it took* to re-educate myself, exposing the warps and wounds inflicted on my psyche by my culture to the healing rays of the

Sanctifying and Re-Creating Spirit. I renounced my former culture; it was not Gospel-centered. It was Mammon-centered. It was all about self indulgence, and not at all about subjecting everything, body and soul, to the love of Christ.

I thought of the nudes in Michelangelo's Sistine Chapel and also of his glorious statue of unarmored David at the Uffizi, clothed only with complete divine trust (another image expertly hidden from us by the good sisters). It is aesthetically and theologically *essential* that there be no fig leaf hiding the sign of the covenant. For David (or any Jew) to have been ashamed of his circumcision would have been tantamount to blasphemy, as is shown by the Maccabean revolt, when many Jews were admonished for trying to hide their circumcision, some even resorting to reconstructive plastic surgery.[1] He was *Jew, pure Jew*, David, the Friend of God. He needed nothing but that divine friendship, symbolized by his circumcision, with which to go out against Goliath. In that beautiful statue is absolutely nothing negative or erotic. It is entirely holy, and it depicts something entirely holy and wonderful. So what if "the world" takes images of similar body parts and uses them for sordid purposes? What has that perversion got to do with us?[2] They are simply wrong. The dogs have usurped what is holy; swine have trampled pearls.[3]

Christians ought to counter perverse culture and assert the body's rightful, dignified place. Certainly Michelangelo did this; certainly the Franciscans at that Bethlehem shrine are doing that.

I had never been taught much about the *wholesome, positive* virtue of modesty. It effectively meant nothing more than scrupulously hiding our bodies, especially certain so-called "private parts." The result was unfortunately not the (supposedly) hoped-for chastity, but rather a conviction quite opposed to revealed truth—that our bodies are dirty, and even evil. "Naturally," this alone could only lead to a sort of neo-Jansenist view of the body, and ill-prepared me for a pilgrimage to the Milk Grotto, let

---

[1] Cf. I Maccabees 1:15.
[2] "What accord has Christ with Belial?" II Corinthians 6:15.
[3] Cf. Matthew 7:6.

alone a chaste view of others' bodies (like the lady in Sperlonga) and the right understanding of the sacredness of conjugal love. Rather than define modesty in purely *negative* terms, it should have been defined as the virtue by which the body's rightful place is asserted, and never used in a negative way. Thus the virtue of modesty would keep a woman from ever using her body to arouse (outside the covenant of marriage), but at the same time true modesty would induce her to assert her body's rightful place (e.g. nursing her babies). Thus the virtue is not merely *negative*, as though her body were nothing but a prospective lustful provocation, but *positive*, never hesitating to use her body as God (and the nature He designed) intended. Great harm is done, both psychologically and spiritually, if this *positive* aspect of the virtue is not asserted.

Christians should assert truth—all truth—and refuse to conform to the perversions of any culture. As St. Paul admonished, "Present your bodies as a living sacrifice, *holy and acceptable* to God, your spiritual worship. Do not be conformed to this world, but be transformed by the renewal of your mind, that you may judge what is the will of God, what is good, acceptable and perfect."[1]

This means growing into the full maturity of Christ,[2] striving to put on His mind and heart.[3] Wherever culture hinders this progression, it is every Christian's duty to adapt or destroy it. Surely Jesus regards the body as integrally holy. As we acclaim with the seraphim before the sacred canon of every Mass, "*All* the earth is filled with His glory!"[4] Evil people misuse money all the time, but is the mature, Christian response to refuse to use (or even look at) money? Why should the human body be any different? It devolves upon Christians simply to use the body as God intended and not to react to perversion by defining modesty in a way that in effect negates the body altogether. Indeed, the revealed truth is that the body is so awesome that God Himself assumed one, and made it the very condition of eternal life: "Unless you eat My Body, you

---

[1] Romans 12:1f.
[2] Cf. Ephesians 4:13.
[3] Cf. Philippians 2:5.
[4] Cf. Isaiah 6:3.

have no life in you."[1] And what is God's loving purpose in requiring such Holy Communion? "And I will raise him up on the last day."[2] The revealed truth is that our bodies are so positively precious that they are destined for resurrection and everlasting life. Culture must not stand in the way of these truths. My culture was not at all conducive to the correct assertion of the body's integral holiness. In effect, the body was regarded as a great obstacle rather than the means to holiness.

Bethlehem was a turning point in my renewal of mind as regards the body. It changed the way I view many things. For the last thirty years I have tried to implement what I learned at the Milk Grotto, by refusing to conform to a culture that withdraws the body from its natural, rightful place and abuses it by myriad forms of unchastity. This positive assertion has led to a liberating, wholesome purity quite unlike the unpeaceful, unnatural and downright neurotic version of chastity propounded by well-intentioned nuns, tainted by a kind of dualistic Gnosticism, many of whom have since abandoned the veil[3] altogether, or at least that stifling spirituality fraught with neuroses on every level. Church renewal is largely about re-evaluating culture in order to establish a sane, sensible cultural milieu for the life of grace. Let's not forget the vital Thomistic principle, "Grace builds on nature." Perhaps there is a dearth of vocations (and saints) today precisely because our age is itself an horrendous foundation for the life of grace. The sacraments are all in place. The constant infallible teachings are still there—more accessible than ever with modern technology. But the Good News can hardly be heard due to the cacophonies of contemporary culture. The liberating light of Christ is bushel-basketed by a culture inimical both to grace and nature. Radical,

---

[1] John 6:53.
[2] Ibid. v. 54.
[3] It is worthy of note that since 1983 when I began promoting Christian naturism world-wide, while many priests and religious brothers have "come out" as practicing naturists, I am still waiting for the first nun. My take on this interesting datum is that many nuns have whole-heartedly embraced worldliness since Vatican II, and that neo-Jansenism must have been even more deeply ingrained in them than in us pupils, such that they are still awaiting the realization of their bodies' integral goodness.

substantial changes are in order. Vatican II called for them, and laid down the guiding principles. It remains for us to truly implement *aggiornamento*[1] at long last. My "born again" experience at Bethlehem taught me one very important thing: authentic renewal must begin by asserting the integral goodness of all nature—especially the human body!

De Nuditate Habituque

by Jim C. Cunningham[2]

True Catholics are vitally interested in holiness—in striving to grow to the full maturity of Christ in mind, body and spirit.[3] All virtues, including chastity and modesty, are important to us.

By chastity we mean never deliberately seeking sexual pleasure outside of marriage. We believe that sex is very sacred, ordained by God to lovingly unite husband and wife, and raise up new life.

By modesty we mean never deporting ourselves so as to sexually arouse others (or ourselves). We regard charity as the most important virtue,[4] and it is not charitable to willfully lead anyone into sin.

Some Roman Catholics are nudists or naturists. Many others simply believe in certain occasions of social nudity (e.g. family nudity, skinny-dipping) without making an "ism" out of it. Certain demagogues sometimes accuse us of immodesty, insisting that "nude is lewd" except when nudity is absolutely necessary (e.g. medical exam). This essay is being written to defend social nudity against such demagogues who would like to equate the Gospel with

---

[1] Roughly translated, this Italian term favored by Pope John XXIII, means "updating."

[2] Latin, meaning "On Nudity and Dress." This article first appeared in *Clothed with the Sun*, 3.1, May, 1983, pp. 57-61. It was reprinted as the lead article in the premier issue of *Divine Reflections*, I,1, Fall, 1983, and is presented again here in very slightly edited form.

[3] Cf. Colossians 1:28; Ephesians 4:13; I Thessalonians 5:23.

[4] Cf. I Corinthians 12:31-13:4 & Colossians 3:14.

their own opinions (hang-ups?), and who do not represent the true tradition of the Roman Catholic Church.

Modesty is not just a matter of being clothed. Karol Wojtyla (who became Pope John Paul II) wrote, "Sexual modesty cannot then in any simple way be identified with the use of clothing, nor shamelessness with the absence of clothing and total or partial nakedness."[1] "There are circumstances in which nakedness is *not* immodest... Nakedness as such is not to be equated with physical shamelessness. Immodesty is present *only* when nakedness plays a *negative* role with regard to the value of the person, when its aim is to arouse concupiscence, as a result of which the person is put in the position of an object of enjoyment."[2] "The human body is *not* in itself shameful, nor for the same reasons are sensual reactions,[3] and human sensuality in general. Shamelessness (just like shame and modesty) is a function of the *interior* of a person."[4]

In his book, *Love and Responsibility*, Wojtyla says that a sense of shame is indeed necessary, but he does not define this as certain "hung-up" demagogues would like to define it. Wojtyla says that what we are ashamed of are *interior, disordered, lustful inclinations* (movements of concupiscence), and not of simply being seen nude. This latter is false modesty, an influence of such perverse systems as Jansenism and Puritanism—not of Catholicism.

According to St. Thomas Aquinas, an immodest act is one done with a lustful *intention*.[5] Therefore, at a nude beach, for instance, one who disrobes with the innocent intention of bathing or recreating is not to be accused of immodesty. Such a person should be ashamed only of lustful inclinations he might experience, but not of merely being seen nude. According to Aquinas' definition of modesty, such a person would not be immodest even if he were at a clothes-compulsory beach, so long as his intention was not to arouse. However, he might be guilty of

---

[1] Karol Wojtyla, *Love and Responsibility*, trans. H.T. Willetts (New York: Farrar, Straus & Giroux, 1981), p. 176.
[2] Ibid., p. 190.
[3] E.g. male penile erections.
[4] Wojtyla, p. 191.
[5] Cf. St. Thomas Aquinas, *Summa Theologica*, 2a 2ae, 151.4.

discourtesy and lack of charity. Pope John Paul II, who received his doctorate in theology from St. Thomas Aquinas University in Rome, follows the same train of thought.

The official teaching authority of the Church does not define what is immodest, because She teaches that it is *relative*: "There is a certain relativism in the definition of what is shameless. This relativism may be due to differences in the make-up of particular persons—a greater or lesser sensual excitability, a higher or lower level of moral culture—or to different 'world-views.' It may equally be due to differences in external conditions—in climate for instance... and also in prevailing customs, social habits, etc."[1] "Dress is *always* a *social* question, a function of... *social* customs."[2] "In this matter there is no exact similarity in the behavior of particular people, even if they live in the same age and the same society."[3] "The principle of what is truly immodest is simple and obvious, but its application in specific cases depends upon the individual, the milieu, the society."[4]

The Roman Catholic Church, then, is not opposed to social nudity unless 1) one's *intention* is lustful, or 2) such nudity is *not customary*.

Some History

The Roman Catholic Church has known nudity from its earliest days. Jesus was baptized and crucified nude.[5] For centuries it was the custom to baptize men, women and children together nude.[6] In his *Apostolic Constitutions*, St. Hippolytus of Rome (c. 200 A.D.) wrote that total nudity was required. Women were directed to remove even their jewelry and the combs from their hair.

We have details of how St. Cyril of Jerusalem (c. 350 A.D.) baptized. After those about to be baptized had taken

---

[1] Wojtyla, p. 186.
[2] Ibid., p. 190.
[3] Ibid., p. 189.
[4] Ibid., p. 190.
[5] Cf. John 19:23ff.
[6] In 1970, Pope Paul VI ordered a return to the early Church rite of baptism by complete immersion as the norm, with the more conventional rite of baptism by sprinkling or pouring on the head only for use in exceptional cases such as emergencies.

27

off all their clothes, St. Cyril would address them: "You are now stripped and naked, in this also imitating Christ despoiled of His garments on His Cross, He Who by His nakedness despoiled the principalities and powers, and fearlessly triumphed over them on the Cross."[1] They then remained standing naked for quite some time while they prayed and received more instruction from St. Cyril. Then their entire bodies (St. Cyril says, "from the top of your head to your feet")[2] were smeared with holy oil. After being baptized one by one in the baptismal pool by immersion, they emerged and were clothed in white albs. At a subsequent instruction St. Cyril would congratulate the newly baptized thus: "How wonderful! You were naked before the eyes of all without feeling any shame. This is because you truly carry within you the image of the first Adam, who was naked in paradise without feeling any shame."[3]

Nudity was not only a baptismal *option*. Theodore of Mopsuestia (c. 400 A.D.) seems to say that it was *necessary*: "Adam was naked at the beginning and he was not ashamed of it. This is why your clothing must be taken off, since it is the convincing proof of this sentence which lowers mankind to need clothing."[4]

For some ancient monks and nuns like St. Mary of Egypt and St. Onuphrius,[5] nudity was an ascetical discipline. One monastic chronicler relates an amusing story of a monk who thought he was somewhat advanced in the spiritual life, traveling from one Egyptian monastery to another. Along the way he encountered three naked monks who greatly impressed him by their total detachment and "other-worldliness." When he arrived at his destination, the porter queried whether he was a "monk." Humbled by his encounter with the three nude monks, he replied, "I? No, *but I have seen monks!*"

In the rubrics of many religious orders candidates for the monkhood were required to strip in church before receiving the habit. St. Benedict prescribed: "At once,

---

[1] Jean Cardinal Danielou, S.J., *The Bible and the Liturgy* (Notre Dame, Indiana: Univ. Notre Dame, 1956), p. 38.
[2] Ibid., p. 38.
[3] Ibid., p. 40.
[4] Ibid., p. 39.
[5] There is an outdoor chapel in the Vatican Garden in honor of this saint which depicts him wearing only his body hair.

therefore, in the oratory, let him be divested of his own clothes which he is wearing and dressed in the clothes of the monastery."[1]

Religious art of all times contains lots of nudity. The Vatican Museum is filled with it. In the Catholic shrine of the Milk Grotto in Bethlehem there are very many pictures of Our Lady's "blessed breasts"[2] nursing Jesus. The Church encourages nude art, but condemns pornography, which distorts the reality of man by portraying erotic values as primary. "Pornography is a marked tendency to accentuate the sexual element when reproducing the human body or human love in a work of art, with the object of inducing the reader or viewer to believe that sexual values are the only real values of the person..."[3] On May 6, 1981, Pope John Paul II condemned "pornovision" which views the human body only for sensual pleasure. He was not objecting to the nude, as he explained later: "Our preceding reflections were not meant to place in doubt the right to this theme [of nudity]... In the course of the ages, beginning with antiquity—and above all in the great era of classical Greek art—there have been works of art in which the theme is the human body in its nudity, the contemplation of which allows us to concentrate, in a certain sense, on *the whole truth of man*, on the *dignity* and *beauty*—including that which is *above* the sensual—of its masculinity and femininity."[4] Elsewhere the pope has said that the problem with pornography is not that it reveals *too much, but too little.*

Though the Church has certainly known nudity, unfortunately it has also had its share of prudery, being influenced by the particular spirit of the age. Things got so bad at one point that we read in an old Dominican rule for nuns that it was immodest for them to look at their own hands![5] Michelangelo's nudes in the Sistine Chapel of the Vatican were dressed and then undressed once again, according to the particular sensibilities of whomever happened to be pope.

---

[1] *The Holy Rule of St. Benedict*, Chapter 58.
[2] Luke 11:27.
[3] Wojtyla, p. 192.
[4] Pope John Paul II, quoted in *Clothed with the Sun*, 1.3, p. 81f.
[5] Also proscribed in the *Ancrene Riwle*.

Some Suggestions

Today's Church is experiencing its own cultural influences. One strong influence is our repudiation of former prudery and Puritanism. More and more, people are refusing to accept the old cultural value that the body and its functions are ugly and disgusting. Nudism, naturism, skinny-dipping, the wide popularity of nude beaches, family nudity, and nudity in non-erotic, family magazines and cinema, etc., are other strong influences.

How should the Church deal with these modern trends? She should assimilate whatever helps us to be whole and holy in mind, body and spirit.[1] She should reject whatever elements there may be in these influences that are lustful, pornographic, truly immodest and which overemphasize our sensuality, hedonistically making pleasure out to be a good in itself. Because of the very many good elements in these modern trends, today there is an opportunity to acquire, socially, a better handle on chastity, modesty and proper attitudes towards the body, than ever before.

I suggest working towards making modest nudity *truly customary* in our society. Since what evokes the sense of shame is relative, variable and learned,[2] we have the power to have a real say in shaping our culture. We can work to re-educate our society, teaching it to be ashamed of nudity *only* when it expresses a lustful intention. Rather than compulsively covering up as though the human body were shameful, I suggest wearing clothes only for practical and charitable reasons such as warmth, protection, comfort, cleanliness, and social courtesy.

At the same time I propose that we strive to educate ourselves and others in greater chastity, opposing pornography and every sexual aberration that is contrary to the Gospel.

In our re-acculturating we should beware of giving scandal. We should not flaunt our nudity. However, we are not responsible for the lusting of gawkers who go out of their way to look. Wojtyla says, "There are circumstances

---

[1] Cf. I Thessalonians 5:23.
[2] Cf. *New Catholic Encyclopedia*, Vol. 13, p. 164.

in which nakedness is not immodest. If someone takes advantage of such an occasion to treat the person as an object of enjoyment (even if his action is purely internal) *it is only he* who is guilty of shamelessness... not the other."[1]

Though we must not flaunt our nudity, we cannot expect any cultural change if we remain "in the closet," afraid to admit our preference for nudity. It is possible but improbable that our reputations would be harmed if people discovered our preference. But even though we may have to suffer a little persecution, it will be well compensated by the many good fruits of social nudity, among which are:

1. Greater experiential appreciation for the beauty and dignity of the body.
2. A greater feeling of unity with others, as external fences of clothing are done away with.
3. A greater appreciation for the distinctive complementarity of our masculinity and femininity, as we become convinced of how good it is to be a man or a woman.
4. Many people suffer from feelings of not being accepted. Social nudity is marvelous therapy for this psychological malady.
5. Curiosity about the naked body, which is often the source or occasion of lust, will be removed; much food for fantasy being sloughed off.
6. Our children will grow up with healthy attitudes towards their bodies.
7. Concupiscence will be diminished. When the sight of the genitals is reserved only for sex, then the mere sight is arousing, but when the genitals are seen on many occasions, the mere sight of them loses its propensity to occasion lust.
8. Nudity is healthy because it exposes the whole body to the air and sun, and gives people an added incentive to be fit.
9. Nudity is more recreative, more joyful, and thus our recreation is more effective. Who truly prefers a bathing suit to a birthday suit?
10. The false, puritanical shame ingrained in us by our upbringing is overcome.

---

[1] Wojtyla, p. 190.

11. By being accustomed to nudity we can react maturely to social situations of nudity that used to embarrass us, such as locker rooms, gang showers, hospitals, and modest nudity in cinema and art.
12. Married love is increased. Because marriage is a union of two in one flesh, the more that flesh is loved and appreciated, the stronger the marital bond.
13. We will not hypocritically admire the nude only in art, but in reality as well.

God made nothing more beautiful and dignified than the human body, which He especially designed in His Own image and likeness.[1] God's Own Supreme Beauty is reflected in the human body as well as the soul.[2] Whatever is beautiful in all creation, finds its perfection and fulfillment in the human nude. To love chastely and admire the naked body is to contemplate God. "Blessed are the pure in heart, for they shall see God."[3]

"I give You thanks that I am fearfully, wonderfully made; wonderful are Your works!"[4]

Look Mom, No Clothes!

by Linda S. Cunningham

Dear Mom & Dad,

It was hard to send you the pictures of the birth and especially the other pictures of Jim and me that I thought were cute. The pictures of the birth were justifiable, after all, because how can one show a birth without showing some nudity? Impossible! Then why is it okay to show my body *during* a birth and not *after* the birth? It's the *same* body. The body didn't change. The attitude changed. "But," one might say, "the body was yuck during the birth

---

[1] Cf. Genesis 1:26ff.
[2] Cf. Pope John Paul II, *Original Unity of Man and Woman* (Boston: Pauline Books, 1981), p. 75. Also cf. *Catechism of the Catholic Church* (San Francisco: Ignatius Press, 1994), N. 364 (see below, p. 194 for complete text from catechism).
[3] Matthew 5:8.
[4] Psalm 139:14.

too, but the birth made it tolerable!" But I say, "Is the body yuck *at all?*" God is not an old man up in the sky. He is the Lord of all the universe. He created all things. "And behold, He saw that it was very good."[1] And mankind is the crown of all creation. We were created in His image and likeness.[2] "And behold, it was very good."[3]

If I am liked by others, do they like *all* of me, or just my head and hands? Why is it always such a shock to see someone's bum or genitalia? We *all* have them! What did you expect to see? We are all walking around with these bodies and at the same time we are denying that we have them.

Jesus has a body. Can we dare say parts of His body are ugly, or are bad and lustful and sinful? We cannot! Neither are ours! No part of our bodies are bad or sinful in themselves. Only our thoughts or actions can be sinful. Pope John Paul says, "There are circumstances in which nakedness is not immodest... Immodesty is present *only* when nakedness plays a *negative* role with regard to the value of the person, when its aim is to arouse concupiscence, as a result of which the person is put in the position of an object of enjoyment."[4]

Seeing nudity in innocent situations like a birth, doing dishes, in the bathtub, is not bad. It is at least indifferent, and in my opinion, can be good and even necessary to have a healthy, wholesome attitude about our bodies.

Nowhere and never has the Church condemned nudity, and it never will. But it does condemn pornography and lewdness. The Pope says, "Pornography is a marked tendency to accentuate the sexual element when reproducing the human body or human love in a work of art, with the object of inducing the reader or viewer to believe that sexual values are the only real values of the person..."[5] Nude is not lewd. It depends on what your aim is.

The world (or at least most of it) is in a sorry state today. Society is both puritanical and pornographic. Both are bad; both do untold harm. And one feeds upon the

---

[1] Genesis 1:31.
[2] Cf. Ibid. 1:26f.
[3] Ibid. 1:31.
[4] Wojtyla, p. 190.
[5] Ibid., p. 192.

other. Everyone is affected by it. Why is it that it is quite acceptable for a man to buy porn at the local drug store, but if he was caught skinny-dipping with his whole family in a secluded place he would be condemned? Why is it when I babysat at Holy Innocents' Academy and changed the baby's diaper, a little boy would come over and point and laugh at her vulva? Why is it, at Jim's Catholic high school during a play, a boy had to take his nice jacket off to pick up a chicken, and all the kids in the audience cried out, "Take it off! More! More! Woo! Woo!"

Why is it that people who seem to be holy and God-fearing hate their bodies and hate the sexual part of their marriages even though Jesus made it a sacrament and said it is holy and good? And these same good Christian people let their daughters buy *Glamour* magazine and let them wear tight, alluring pants. But she turns her back in front of her own mother to change her shirt, and refuses to wash anyone's back in the tub. When one thinks about it, one realizes it is crazy and bad. I am stuck in it, you are stuck in it, Pam, Diane, Mark, John and everyone is stuck in it.

I've been wanting to bring this subject up with you for a long time. I hope you want to pursue this topic further. I hope we can even open this correspondence up to Pam and Diane. I think we can all benefit by it. I want to be healthy and wholesome—in the true sense. "Seek truth and follow after it."[1] It is hard for me to go against society, but after all, "the road to damnation is wide and many there are who follow it."[2]

Love,
Linda

---

[1] Psalm 34:14.
[2] Matthew 7:13.

Don't Be a Ham— Respect Nudity!

by Joan Turner

Noah had drunk new wine, the strength of which he did not realize until he felt the effects.[1] Therefore, he did not sin in drinking or accidentally finding himself drunk. Yet he was drunk, lying flat on his back in this tent and fully exposed, unaware, and looking pretty foolish to those who were accustomed to the dignified, God-fearing Noah. Only weeks before, he had the courage to listen to the voice of God and obey it, building the ark and allowing himself to be subject to the unceasing derision of his neighbors (until it started to rain).[2] Now he was totally naked, sprawled on his bed, and sleeping heavily from the new wine while his own son and grandson did him the very same injustice—laughed derisively at a situation over which he had no control, rather than help him out. Shem and Japheth proved the sensible and worthy compassion-ates. They covered Noah's nakedness to stop the ridicule of their good and holy father.

How do we know Ham and Canaan laughed and poked fun at Noah? It is implied first in Ham's telling of his father's nakedness to his brethren and their reaction to the news, and second in the heavy curse Noah laid on Canaan, Ham's son—a curse that must have been equal to the offense.

How do we know it was not nakedness itself that Ham laughed at or Shem covered? Noah and his family were very likely used to each other's nakedness. It seems next to impossible to be on an ark for any length of time with other people and limited space and never see each other's naked bodies. Nakedness itself would not have tempted Ham to laugh disrespectfully, but rather the situation as a whole is what prompted it—Noah, naked, drunk, helpless, unaware—a man to be understanding towards, and then left alone to sleep off his mistake. Ham and Canaan chose

---

[1] Cf. Genesis 9:20-27.
[2] Cf. Genesis 6:11ff.

rather to laugh at their father's situation. Shem and Japheth, appalled probably more at Ham's disrespect than Noah's helplessness, covered the object being ridiculed— Noah's naked body—without looking, as if to dramatically disapprove of Ham's laughter. Was it sinful to look at Noah's nakedness? No, but it was sinful to look and laugh.

Is there a lesson in this for us? The utmost respect should be shown the human body because it is the only created object made in God's image and likeness.[1] It is certainly not a thing to be laughed at or made fun of, but to be cared for and respected.

Correspondence with Bishop John A. Marshall

In the autumn of 1983 the Cunninghams and Joan Turner[2] moved from Newport, Vermont to a small town east of St. Albans where we planned to found "Mt. Carmel Academy" (MCA), an alternative private school characterized by solid Christian faith and dogma, individualized curricula and the naturist lifestyle. Though MCA was barely in the embryonic stage, no sooner had we moved to our new location near Maple Glen Nudist Park than we received a letter (see below) from the local Catholic pastor, Fr. Karl Schmidt.[3] Evidently, he wanted to disassociate himself from us from the outset, and essentially took it upon himself to excommunicate us from his little parish. He told us not to approach Communion until he received further direction from his superiors. This was problematic for all of us, as we had been going to daily Mass and Communion for many years, and his was the only nearby parish in our rural area. Plus, the three of us shared one very clunky gas guzzler and our work schedules took us in different directions.

We knew the pastor rather well, having once briefly been his tenants, and knew that appealing to him was

---

[1] Cf. Genesis 1:26f.
[2] Not her real name.
[3] Not his real name.

vain. Since Fr. Schmidt himself wanted direction from his superior, I resolved to appeal directly to the local ordinary—Bishop John A. Marshall. We also welcomed the opportunity to be completely candid with our spiritual leader, hiding nothing from him, and sincerely welcoming his direction.

There follows the brief, slightly edited correspondence between the three parties. Bishop Marshall's comments are especially interesting because he was reputed to be a very faithful, orthodox bishop to whom Pope John Paul II entrusted the unenviable task of investigating all United States seminaries and reporting back to him. John Paul II knew that some undesirable elements had crept into many U.S. seminaries and wanted an accurate report before taking corrective measures.

September 16, 1983
Mr. James Cunningham
Mt. Carmel Academy
Sheldon Springs, Vermont

Dear Sir:

It has been brought up to my attention both the name (quite Catholic) and the nature (quite pagan) of your Academy.

Until further notification from my Religious Superiors about the authenticity of your Academy as part of the Diocesan enterprise, and quite sure that His Excellency does not approve of an educational Center that upholds nudist philosophies and values in the territory of his Diocese, I will not be in the position to offer my personal or Parish endorsement of the said Academy.

Likewise it is my understanding that you have used my name as a supporter of nudism while you were trying to convince Mr. George McDonough[1] to be part of your "group". Please, be informed that if you have a hospital next to your dwelling it does not necessarily imply that you are sick. The fact that the Maple Glen Nudist Camp is part of the geographical area of this Parish does not imply

---

[1] Not his real name.

the Roman Catholic Community is supportive of it or participate in it.

Likewise I will follow the guidelines of my superiors concerning Sacraments. Consequently until clearance comes on your behalf and the members of the Academy as to reception of the Sacraments I will appreciate that you refrain from attempting the reception of the Sacraments in this Parish.

Sincerely in Xp. and the Theotokos,
(Rev.) Karl Schmidt

October 14, 1983
Most Rev. John A. Marshall
Bishop of Burlington, Vermont

Your Excellency:

I recently received a letter (copy enclosed) from Rev. Karl Schmidt that greatly disturbed me and my family.

It is my understanding that priests should refuse to distribute Holy Communion only to non-Catholics (with few exceptions) and to Catholics who they know, without a doubt, are in the state of mortal sin.

Rev. Schmidt asked us even to "refrain from attempting" the reception of the sacraments in his parish because we embrace a nudist lifestyle and enjoy recreating at Maple Glen Nudist Park here in Sheldon Springs.

Now, it seems to me that for Rev. Schmidt to declare us in mortal sin means that to be naked amongst others is objectively and intrinsically evil. As I understand it, there is no objective sin in being clothed or unclothed; the virtue or vice of how we dress is dependent on our motives, which we are sure are pure and holy. *The human body is not in itself shameful...* Shamelessness is a function of the *interior* of a person."[1] "Immodesty is present *only* when nakedness plays a *negative* role with regard to the value of the person, when its aim is to arouse concupiscence, as a result of which the person is put in the position of an object for enjoyment."[2]

---

[1] Wojtyla, p. 191.
[2] Ibid., p. 190.

These matters are most especially confusing because over the past few years Rev. Schmidt has, in fact, helped us form our ideas regarding nudism, though he may have been unaware of his influence. In various conversations he revealed to us:

1. That he condoned nude psychotherapy.
2. That some girls once found him skinny-dipping in his beautiful brook on his land.
3. That he permits a very large group of altar boys, priests and counselors who camp on his property each summer, to skinny-dip in his brook.
4. That while visiting his brother in Scandinavia he attended a co-ed, nude sauna, and he emphatically said it was perfectly moral.

I know that Rev. Schmidt has some personal grudges against me, as he has against everybody who has ever had him for their landlord. Now that we are in the jurisdiction of his parish, I feel like he is wreaking his vengeance on me by thus insulting, humiliating and bullying me.

Dear bishop, if I am convinced that the motives for my nudism are not sinful in any way, do I not have the "right" (albeit we are all unworthy, miserable sinners anyway) to go to Holy Communion in absolutely any Roman Catholic Church in the entire world, including my own town?

Perhaps you are not familiar with nudist philosophies, so I would like to share what I think is an accurate definition. I am also enclosing a copy of the official introductory brochure of the American Sunbathing Association,[1] which is the oldest and largest nudist organization in the United States and Canada. Though the brochure avoids religious questions, I cannot find anything in it that should be objectionable to a Catholic.

Before I attempt my own definition of nudism, I want to make it clear that we do not accept any and every nudist philosophy. People become nudists for a variety of reasons, many of which we do not share. But then, people also go to church for a variety of reasons, many of which we do not share. A few warped nudists do not make

---

[1] Now renamed "The American Association for Nude Recreation," headquartered at 1703 N Main St., Suite E, Kissimmee, FL 34744.

nudism wrong, any more than a few hypocritical Roman Catholics do not make church-going wrong. I will attempt a definition that almost any nudist would accept.

Nudism teaches that the naked human body is good, and not something to be ashamed of. Very many nudists (including us) go even further, saying that the naked human body is most beautiful as God's special handiwork (even though it is not yet in its most perfect form), and that it is sacred, made in His very Own image.[1] Nudists, then, wear clothes for *practical* reasons, and not just because convention demands dress, or because they are ashamed of any part of their bodies. Nudists may or may not be Christian. They may or may not believe in Original Sin and all its evil effects, including shame of nudity. Most Christian nudists believe that shame of nudity is one of the evil effects of Original Sin and, like all sin and all evil effects of sin (e.g. death, suffering, ignorance, loss of sanctifying grace, etc.), were never part of God's plan for man. Jesus said a good tree produces good fruit and a bad tree produces bad fruit.[2] Shame of nudity is a bad fruit of the bad tree—Original Sin. Is not sanctification the process of conquering in oneself (with God's help) sin, and its evil effects?

We don't relish our ignorance, but beg for light.

We don't glory in death, but in the sure hope of resurrection, triumphing over death.

We don't wallow in our sad state of lack of sanctifying grace, but seek to be full of grace.

We are not masochists, but seek to identify our burdens with the Redeemer's Cross, thus making them light and sweet.[3]

Similarly, it seems to us, and to most Christian nudists, that we should not relish the evil effect of Original Sin called "shame of nudity," but should strive to regard our bodies as the holy, beautiful and dignified creations which they are, members (no less) of Christ[4] and veritable temples of the Holy Spirit,[5] outdoing even Solomon's

---

[1] Cf. Genesis 1:26f.
[2] Matthew 7:17.
[3] Cf. Matthew 11:30.
[4] Cf. I Corinthians 6:15.
[5] Cf. Ibid. 6:19.

temple in splendor and beauty. If Jesus said that even Solomon in all his finery could not compare to the beauty of naked grass,[1] how much more dignified and beautiful must Solomon have been without his finery since he was worth more than a whole flock of sparrows?[2]

St. Cyril of Jerusalem was quite clear about the evil effect of "shame of nudity" being overcome by the symbolic nudity of the ancient baptismal rite. He told the newly baptized: "How wonderful! You were naked before the eyes of all without feeling any shame. This is because you truly carry within you the image of the first Adam, who was naked in paradise without feeling any shame."[3] The old man had been doffed, and they had now been donned with Christ.

Almost all nudists do not flaunt their nudity; that is why nudist camps exist like Maple Glen. They do not want to offend anyone, nor do they want their nudity to be misunderstood or abused by perverted, worldly people who see nudity as a *signum venereorum*.[4]

"Dress is *always* a social question, a function of... social customs."[5] In nudist society, nude is not lewd, and therefore total nudity is not a *signum venereorum*, and is *not* immodest. This explains why we have encountered no sexual suggestiveness at the several nudist parks we have visited. Their traditional motto, "A healthy mind in a healthy body," seems to ring true in effect. Women, newly initiated into nudism, universally attest to how much more comfortable they feel at a nudist park than at a conventional, "clothed" beach. The looks, the ogles and the whistles just are not to be found at a nudist park. I know at least a couple of very religious women who regarded their bodies as ugly and dirty despite their prayerfulness, holiness, right theology and daily Communion. Only by experiencing nudism were they able to effectively acquire a godly perspective on the body, regarding it as His greatest material creation.

---

[1] Cf. Matthew 6:29.
[2] Cf. Luke 12:24.
[3] Danielou, p. 39.
[4] Latin moral theological term meaning "sexually suggestive sign."
[5] Wojtyla, p. 190.

I am not aware of any official, Magisterial statement condemning nudism, and I have researched the topic more or less avidly for eight years now. Everything I learn, both through study and personal experience, confirms my nudist beliefs.

I would also like to respond to some inaccuracies in the enclosed copy of Rev. Karl Schmidt's letter to me:

1. I do not call the Academy that I am trying to found, "Roman Catholic." I understand clearly from *Apostolicam Actuositatem*[1] of Vatican II, that that adjective can only officially be given to foundations sanctioned by the Ordinary. I understand Mt. Carmel Academy to be a *private* school. However, *we* are Catholics. We believe teachers, like Christ, must give what they *are*. How could I table my Catholicism and presume to lecture on history? Or art? How can I teach multiplication and stifle dogma and morality? I cannot. I have to give what I *am*.

Though private, MCA's doors are open to you. We are ashamed of no aspect of our philosophy, methods or nudist lifestyle. (By the way, "nudism" is only one aspect of MCA; unfortunately it gets all the attention from shallow sensationalists.)

2. I do *not* seek Rev. Schmidt's personal or parochial endorsement of MCA. I do, however, want access to the sacraments he administers.

3. Rev. Schmidt has indeed helped us form our nudist philosophy as mentioned above.

4. I never tried to convince Mr. George McDonough[2] to be part of my "group," as he himself would attest. If someone finds our lifestyle and fellowship to be to their spiritual advantage, they are welcome to live with us, remaining completely independent. I assume no spiritual authority over anyone, even my wife and children. Some have asked me to be their spiritual director, but I consistently refuse.

If you have any other questions regarding my personal philosophy or my educational enterprise, etc., I will be happy to openly, honestly and candidly answer all of them.

---

[1] Vatican II, *The Decree on the Apostolate of the Laity.*
[2] Not his real name.

Perhaps you clearly see that I am in error, and can cast some light on the matter that somehow I haven't seen. I know that everybody's spiritual vision has "blind spots," which is why "the wise man has many counselors."[1] If the Church truly teaches that social nudity is intrinsically evil, then I will follow the guidance of the Church, the gate of salvation, for as the wise man says, "There is a way that seems right to a man, but the end thereof leads to ruin."[2] May God guide my steps in the way of peace.[3] I sincerely want only what is good and what truly glorifies Him.

Respectfully yours in Christ,
Jim C. Cunningham

October 28, 1983

Dear Mr. Cunningham:
Thank you for your very thorough explanation of your defense of the practice of nudism. You seem to be honestly convinced of its value and its moral integrity. That being the case, it would not be my intention in this letter to try to persuade you to think otherwise.

Indeed, I find no evidence in the September 16, 1983 letter of Reverend Karl Schmidt, which would indicate that he is trying to argue that point, even if both he and I might disagree with you. I see no mention whatsoever in his letter of excommunication, nor does he accuse you of being a public sinner.

The problem that Father Schmidt confronts is one of scandal. In judging scandal in the area, Father Schmidt must take into account the mentality of his people. He has discussed the matter with other pastors in the area and it is their conviction that the people understand nudism as an immoral or a potentially immoral (occasion of sin) activity. Perhaps this mentality may change in the future, or perhaps in Montreal or in some more sophisticated area, nudism would be understood differently. However, Father Schmidt must deal with the moral understanding

---

[1] Proverbs 11:14 & cf. 24:6.
[2] Proverbs 14:12.
[3] Luke 1:79.

of his people here and now. Although nudism might not be objectively immoral, if the people understand it that way, Father Schmidt would be granting carte blanche to the people to disregard all moral standards, if he were seen by the people to tolerate what they consider to be clearly immoral.

Accordingly, I think that you are following the proper course of action in receiving the sacraments in a place where your convictions on nudism are unknown. In this way, you are not giving scandal, whereas you would be doing so in the Sheldon area in the judgment of Father Schmidt and his fellow priests. Not being on the scene myself, I am unable to judge the circumstances; however, I must accept the judgment of my brother priests until they are proven wrong.

Since you seem to be fairly well acquainted with theology, I trust that you will give a sympathetic understanding to the distinctions that I have made.

With every best wish, I remain,

Sincerely yours in Christ,
(Most Reverend) John A. Marshall
Bishop of Burlington

December 15, 1983[1]
Most Rev. John A. Marshall
Bishop of Burlington, Vermont

Your Excellency:

In your letter you said Fr. Schmidt's concern was one of scandal, but isn't it curious that he never mentions the word in his entire letter to me of September 16, 1983?

Let me assure you that we do *not* want to scandalize anyone by giving bad example by our sinfulness, or even by any innocent action which might *appear* to be sinful. We love our brothers and sisters in Christ and want only what is for their temporal and spiritual good.

Fr. Schmidt says that we will commit indirect (or direct—after all, he did call us "pagan"!) active scandal[1] if we

---

[1] Editor's note: This is the original letter except for certain passages omitted either on account of their irrelevance to the topic or their overly personal nature.

44

received Communion in his church. Yes, if we believed his judgment—that his parishioners would take that for a *carte blanche* for all sorts of immorality, then he would be correct. But though they may mostly be "just farmers," we have a higher opinion of their level of "sophistication."

Maple Glen Nudist Park has been here for some eighteen years now. The concept is not new to the community. Their sign is right by the local Elementary School, which the supposedly scandalized have not been angry enough to have vandalized. Many have had direct involvement with Maple Glen, and I have heard them speak well of the nudists there.

People around here do not blush at the mention of Maple Glen—it is part of their community. When I applied for my waitering job in St. Albans, the application asked for the organizations (non-religious) that I belong to. I wrote down that I was a nudist. The hiree did not read that and recoil in some scandalous fright, but she matter-of-factly asked me whether I attended Maple Glen. When I said that I often went there with my family, her response was to tell me that she also used to attend a couple of years back—no scandal that I am aware of, not even in the simplest sense of just being shocked.

Last May we spent two days at a nude beach known as "The Ledges" on the Harriman Reservoir in Wilmington, Vermont. When we got home to Newport, Vermont, our "unsophisticated" neighbors (truck driver and a factory worker) asked us where we had gone for the weekend. Linda (my wife) told her exactly where we had gone. The result was far from scandal of any sort! Those neighbors—a family of five—ended up accompanying us to Maple Glen on a weekend. They loved it very much and are now avowed nudists. Fay declared the day after: "I never felt good about myself before!" Scandal? What is Fr. Schmidt talking about?

And again, as for community acceptance of nudism as an alternative lifestyle, did you know that the local motel offers a discount to nudists?

---

[1] Theological note: There are two different kinds of scandal: 1) "direct," by which we do evil *intending* to cause others to sin, and 2) "indirect," by which we do something that is *not* intrinsically evil, yet nevertheless has the *unfortunate* effect of causing others to sin.

What does Fr. Schmidt think—that his people have so little regard for his integrity that they will easily believe he is giving them *carte blanche* for orgy-mongering by giving us Communion? I can't believe it! It is utterly preposterous!

I myself have never met anyone like what Fr. Schmidt supposes his parishioners to be!

A friend of mine owns Paradise Mountain Nudist Camp near Oneonta, New York. What was the public attitude when she just opened up last Spring? Why, the Chamber of Commerce invited her to have a booth at their trade show, and the Rotary unanimously voted her into their club. Dear Bishop, Fr. Schmidt is wrong. What must I do to prove it?

But to make sure his people do not think he is condoning immorality by giving us Communion, why can't he just tell them he isn't, and why?

Or maybe Fr. Schmidt has taught his people that nudism is pagan and immoral. Maybe he has tried to instill that value into them. Maybe the truth is that the people *of themselves* do not consider nudism to be immoral, but rather that Fr. Schmidt *wants* them to consider it so (sort of like the missionaries of Polynesia teaching that being topfree is immodest—instilling a value which is not natively there?)

Even were it true that indirect active scandal would be given, such is perfectly moral because the four conditions of the principle of double effect apply:

1. It is not intrinsically evil for nudists to receive Communion (or to simply disrobe). Though Fr. Schmidt called it "pagan," nowhere in your letter did you tell us we were sinning and should not go to Communion. You did not even try to influence us away from nudism.
2. The evil effect of someone *perhaps* being truly scandalized would not be *intended*, but merely *tolerated*.
3. The good effects in no way come from the evil effect, but both result simultaneously from a common act.
4. The good effects far outweigh the evil effect.

The evil effect is not a finding in fact, but merely a subjective supposition that "unsophisticated" parishioners *might* be induced to sin.

Here are the factual, provable good effects:

1. A Roman Catholic family (and its clients) entitled to live the life of the Church is not kicked out of parish life as though they were great sinners and scum of the earth.
2. The Church is shown as truly catholic and transcultural, welcoming all men of good will.
3. An innocent Roman Catholic family (and its clients) entitled by baptism to receive Holy Communion, striving hard daily to live the life of Christ to the full by chanting the Divine Office in common, meditation, constant study of the faith and community life is not forced to attend Church where they must drive twenty extra miles, and where such a great distance makes daily Communion highly impractical, whereas they have been accustomed to daily Mass for some ten years now.
4. The good Cunningham name is not thereby slandered where everybody knows they are "excommunicated" from the local parish. In fact, our very forced absence appears to the community to be an admission of our guilt. Therefore, for the Cunninghams to be told they may not go to their local church is for that authority to be ensuring the slander of the Cunningham name. If, however, the Cunninghams attend that church, there is no slander.
5. Mt. Carmel Academy's good name will not be slandered. Dear Bishop, Mt. Carmel Academy is *our livelihood!* Fr. Schmidt's stance greatly hinders business—my putting bread on the table for my family.
6. The local parishioners are taught that Jesus, and His Mystical Body, the Church, loves everybody, no matter how exotic their lifestyle may seem.
7. The local parishioners will learn something about true modesty—that it is not a matter of minimum dress, but of deporting ourselves so as not to arouse others.
8. My children will not grow up confused, getting the wrong message from our local ostracism.

9. We can continue to attend Mass daily, as has been our revered custom for several years.
10. Fr. Schmidt will now have an excuse to offer daily Mass, which is not his custom. He used to say that no one wanted it or could attend. Now he'll have at least 3 adults begging for it daily.
11. Last, and by no means least (maybe first!):

Our work is with a lot of nudists. We speak to them of the love of God—of His profound love for them. The Church is *supposed* to be a sign and sacrament of that great love. Thousands (millions?) of nudists in the USA and overseas are aware of our excommunication from the local parish. What kind of message of God's universal, all-embracing love is that giving to them? Who is scandalizing whom? How does the Church reach out to those of a nudist persuasion? Many of them are very spiritual. I have certainly held far more edifying conversations at nudist parks than I have at any coffee hour following a Sunday Mass! My point is that nudists are a worthy group ready to listen to the Catholic message. What message are they getting by my ostracism?

Many nudists are not Roman Catholic or even Christian because *they* have been scandalized by the local church (not the Magisterium)—bigoted demagogues calling them "pagan" for a cultural practice that they are deeply persuaded is good—at least for them. Good missiology requires that the Word be preached in its purity, free of cultural accretions. Yet this is not done locally, though the missionary orders may be doing it in far away places in the Amazon jungle. The modern world is so pluralistic that cultural anthropologists say there are as many cultural varieties within a given section of America as there are in the entire world.

Jesus was with the outcasts. Where is Jesus to be seen today among the nudists—cast out not because they are sinners, but because they are different, like a racial minority? But no, to many (and sometimes I must agree) the local church seems more interested in maintaining the *status quo*, striving at all costs (even justice, sometimes) to see that the feathers of the Pharisees (whose names are engraved in the vestibule for paying their parish dues) are not ruffled. That is not how Christ's Church should be.

The eleven good effects I enumerated are all *factual* and not merely *possibilities*. The one evil effect is not even *certain*! It is clear that the good effects far outweigh the bad, meaning that it would be perfectly moral for us to receive Communion at our parish even if, regrettably indeed, someone might be *truly* scandalized thereby.

It won't be long before I am recognized by everyone in the whole region as a nudist. I advertise locally. *Boston Magazine* did a write up on MCA. A reporter from *USA Today* flew up from Washington, D.C. to interview me. I don't hide my nudism. I write it down on job applications! So what do I do when I am known in St. Albans and Enosburg Falls as well as I am here? Am I supposed to go to Mass in Canada? Where will it end? When will the good effect (1 of 11) of my not having to drive so many extra miles, outweigh the evil effect of someone *possibly* being scandalized? Can you give me a mileage figure? To me, it seems like a *reductio ad absurdum*.[1]

Perhaps no one actually sat down and thought about the good effects. Perhaps I have cast new light on the matter of whether the local people are indeed scandalized by nudists receiving Communion. Not only have we probably talked about it with more local people than Fr. Schmidt, but also it is a fact that people are not as up front with priests as they are with skinny-dipping religion teachers [like me]. Sometimes (usually?) they react the way they think the priest expects them to react. Very few people are themselves with priests...

Be that as it may, we are totally up front with you. We have nothing to hide, and are certainly non-conventional enough not to pretend we are what we think you want us to be. I couldn't live with such mental complications!

Oh, how we hope for a happy Christmas gift from you!

Joyeux Noel!
Jim C. Cunningham

---

[1] Latin philosophical term meaning "reduction to the absurd." In logical argument, you can prove the truth of a thesis by showing how its opposite would lead to absurdity.

December 20, 1983

Dear Mr. Cunningham:
It is not my intention to debate the presentation that you have made concerning the moral goodness of nudism. I appreciate your sincerity and your desire to receive the Eucharist daily. I must disagree with you, however, on some points:

1. Regardless of your theoretical arguments, there still remains the very real possibility of scandal on the part of the local people in a small community where everyone knows everyone else and it does not take much to create "*admiratio.*" Reverend Karl Schmidt must remain the judge of that.
2. You are not being forbidden to receive the Eucharist, even daily, if you wish. There are two other parishes within five miles of Sheldon Springs and several others in the general area.
3. Although other pastors have agreed with Father Schmidt that it could very well be scandalous to receive the Eucharist at St. Anthony's in Sheldon Springs, that might not be the case in their own parishes. If you should refrain from flaunting your commitment to nudism and quietly participate in the Eucharist at one of these other parishes, it could very well be that no problem will arise. Much depends upon your own style of behavior.

With sympathy for your plight, with the counsel that it is best not to advertise publicly your commitment to nudism in the rural area in which you live, and with every prayerful best wish, I remain,

Sincerely yours in Christ,
(Most Reverend) John A. Marshall
Bishop of Burlington

Catholicism and Nudism

by Fr. David Alton, Ph.D.

Can a Catholic be a nudist? The easiest answer to that question is the fact that thousands of Catholics in Europe and the United States *are* practicing nudists. I, who write these lines, am a Catholic priest in good standing. I know of a number of other priests who are members of [nudist] camps throughout the country. Hence the fact that large numbers of Catholics *are* nudists is ample proof that they *can be.*

Yet though there are many Catholics already enjoying the great benefits of nudism, still their numbers are not in proportion to their numbers in the world. What is holding them back?

It seems the reason is that many Catholics who are attracted hold back because they feel that nudism is condemned by the Church or that they would have to mention it in confession.

Is nudism condemned by the Church? No, the Church simply has not taken any official cognizance of the movement. Certainly the Pope has not condemned it, nor do I know of any individual Bishop who has condemned it. What is more, most authorities on moral theology do not even explicitly consider the subject of nudism. One of the few who does is the English Jesuit, Fr. Henry Davis, and he takes a rather stern view. He says: "Sun baths and air baths taken by members of both sexes together and without costumes are fertile sources of grievous sins, and there is no justification for them. Gymnastic exercises of nude males and females together are unnecessary and an offense against modesty."

At the outset it must be realized that this is *one* theologian's *opinion,* and so the entire authority of his opinion rests on the value of his arguments. He has two objections to nudism: 1) It is a source of impure thoughts and desires. 2) Sunbathing in the complete nude is unnecessary.

Neither of those objections is valid. The good Father just is not sufficiently informed about modern nudism. Let's look at his objections:

As to the first, no one could deny that if nudism were "a fertile source of grievous sins," it would indeed be morally unjustifiable. But the experience of all nudists *unanimously* affirms that nudism is *not* sexually stimulating!

At first glance this seems incomprehensible. The uninitiated think that if a *partially* clothed person is often an occasion of sin, then one *completely* nude would be even more so. That too seems to be Fr. Davis' impression. But such an opinion overlooks one important fact of human psychology: anticipation is usually greater than realization. Partial revelation focuses attention on what is concealed and thereby gives undue emphasis to one small aspect of the personality, whereas the completely revealed person can be viewed as just what he is: a person composed of soul and body (of which the sexual parts are one small portion). Then too, the nude sunbather is seen in the most unsuggestive circumstances—out-of-doors and exercising. Nudists, therefore, view one another with the same sort of casualness and objectivity with which one looks at nude statues and paintings. The Vatican museum is filled with objects of art in the nude, and even Fr. Davis recognizes the perfect legitimacy of viewing such works of art.

What is more, far from being a "fertile source of grievous sins," nudism actually is an *antidote* to the unwholesome attitude towards the body and all its functions, and in many ways it *reinforces* moral standards.

This is brought out in an excellent article by a Catholic teenager who had been in a convent preparatory school for three years before returning to the world and joining Sunny Rest Nudist Camp. She wrote: "My moral standards have been upheld and strengthened by regular visits to Sunny Rest... When I left the convent and began going to Sunny Rest Lodge, it was no transition from saint to sinner. If any influence is exerted at all, it is that which *reinforces* moral standards."[1]

---

[1] Dorothea Sullivan, "A Teenager Talks on Nudism," *Sun & Health*, Vol. 16, No. 3, p. 10.

Fr. Davis' second objection to nudism is that it is unnecessary. He thinks one could gain the same benefits if he did his sunbathing in some abbreviated costume. But that is not true. First of all, the abbreviated costume is actually *more suggestive* than nudity, for the very "protective" costume calls attention to what is hidden. The 1953 ASA Queen[1] refused to pose for press photographers in a bathing suit or in shorts. She said, "If you're looking for sex or cheesecake, you better go to the beach where bikini bathing suits and uplift bras are the rage, because you won't find that sort of thing at a nudist convention."[2]

But even more, nude sunbathing makes positive contributions that more than justify its existence. It gives a complete freedom and relaxation that cannot be gained by any other way. It promotes in adults, and especially in children, a wholesome and sane attitude towards the body and all its functions. It provides the motive and the means for maintaining better bodily and mental health. It contributes mightily towards the development of the fundamental Christian virtues, develops lasting friendships, and mightily promotes family unity.

So much for the Catholic's first reason for hesitancy and joining the nudist movement: the unfounded fear that nudism would violate the Church's moral principles. Implicitly we have answered the second difficulty, i.e. the fear that one would have to mention nudist membership in confession, coupled with the greater fear that he would be denied absolution unless he promised to give up membership. The answer is simple: in confession one tells his sins; and since nudism is not a sin nor does it lead to sin, there just is no call to mention it in confession. If, by way of extreme thoughts or desires, then not only would

---

[1] At its yearly conventions, the American Sunbathing Association used to hold beauty pageants as was also customary in clothed society of the time. There were some major differences, however: 1)Whereas contestants in clothed society were always restricted to only young females, nudist society had separate contests for all age groups and both genders. 2) "Sexiness" was not the criterion of judgment, but rather overall health and fitness. 3) Since all contestants wore only their tans, there was no suggestive titillating by barely concealing certain body parts. Though beauty pageants have not been in vogue anywhere in the past few decades, the former ASA variety provided chaste opportunities to admire God's greatest material handiwork—the human body.

[2] "ASA Queen Rips Bikinis," *Modern Sunbathing*, July 1954, p. 25.

he have to mention it in confession, but he should drop out of the nudist movement. But for the normal person such a reaction will not take place, and there would be no cause to mention that one had gone to a nudist camp, any more than there would be to tell the priest that you have gone to a golf course.

In conclusion we can say that nudism fits well into the context of Catholic doctrine. Catholicism teaches that the body is not sinful or shameful, but good and noble since made by the All-Holy God. The Church teaches that Original Sin did *not completely* vitiate or corrupt human nature, but *merely wounded* it. One of those wounds is concupiscence, the inordinate inclination to bodily pleasures. While pornography and burlesque and many fashions do indeed arouse concupiscence, nudism does not supply the stimulus that touches off the inclination.

Furthermore, nudism aids the practice of religion in many ways. It helps us observe the Fifth Commandment,[1] by promoting better physical and mental health. It helps us to observe the Sixth Commandment[2] by acting as an antidote to unhealthy curiosity about, and concentration on, sex. It strengthens our faith by bringing us closer to the beauties of nature that are a constant illustration of the proof of God's existence. It fosters humility by helping us to acknowledge our dependence on God and the essential equality of all men. It promotes charity by helping to break down selfish individualism and building up unselfishness and cooperation.

Can a Catholic be a nudist? He certainly *can*, and he will be a better man and a better Catholic for it!

---

[1] I.e. "Thou shalt not kill." The Church teaches that this commandment obliges us to take proper care of our own and others' bodies.
[2] I.e. "Thou shalt not commit adultery." The Church teaches us that this commandment obliges us to be chaste in thought, word and deed. Genital sexuality is for marriage, and conjugal chastity requires that sexuality conform to natural law.

Naked Truth

by Jim C. Cunningham

From babe to boy, from boy to man,
In clothes enwrapped, 'cept head and hand.

Baby born bare, image of God;
Boy dressed up—oh, what a fraud!

Beauty hid by mendacious cloth,
Destined to be but food for moth.

Truth has no end, and skin so true
Shall shine forth light in haloed hue.

Clothes aren't the man, yet cloaked so long,
We feel that we to garb belong.

Let us be free from custom's spell,
Stripping to skin that cannot sell.

Naked and pure, God's reflection.
Divine design, His confection.

Be not ashamed as 'ere you would,
God Himself says: "It's very good!"

Don't contradict God's opinion,
Clinging to clothes, confined, pinioned.

Don't act as if you're disgusting,
Good for nothing but man's lusting.

If they abuse what God made pure,
That's their problem; not what you wore.

We must teach the body's holy
By being nude chastely solely.

When only porn presents the nude,
It's 'nother lie—that nude is lewd.

Let's get naked and show the truth,
Men and Women, aged and youth.

So burn your bra, bathing suit too.
Be what you are, to self be true.

Body gently stroked by water,
Happy to be ocean's daughter.

Roll in the sand from whence thou art,
Thrilled to be of nature a part.

Wind delights in your undressing,
Balmy breezes all caressing.

Clothed with the sun oh may you be,
Warmed by those beams embracingly.

Naked walk through woods, streams
    and fields,
That do not know fences or shields.

If someone should see, say "Good day!"
Don't hide or blush, or run away.

Share your gladness by being kind,
Calmly pleasant and he won't mind.

Perhaps he'll see convention's curse,
Choose to be as he was at first.

Let us set the Prisoners free,
Showing them our Chaste nudity.

We have a gift So great to give.
Nude, help others Nat'rally live.

Tolerant Pluralism

by Paul Redkovich II

The message St. Paul wishes to give in Romans 14 is that the love and service of God may take many forms. That the manifestation of our dedication takes different forms is in each individual's perception of how he can best gain salvation. Some people follow traditional paths. Others choose a religious, monastic life, a few seek solitude to avoid temptation and serve God. We Christian naturists feel that living without clothing in appropriate situations is a return to innocence, a freedom to glorify God free from the badges and trappings of a so-called "civilized world."

Yet we must not be quick to condemn those who disagree with us. In their eyes, the perception of nudity as sinful or an occasion of sin is real, albeit in our eyes a misguided judgment. Thus, we must be tolerant and understanding, explaining our reasons, yet not condemning if in sincerity they still disagree. On our part, to not offend, our service to God in our natural state must be practiced with discretion.

In our own way each of us is trying to become closer to God. With God's help and love, in our innocence and in our pure, nude and natural state, along with our clothed brethren, may we all attain salvation.

Occasions of Sin

by Fred J. Gerty, Jr.

Romans 14 seems to cut both ways—just as we should seek and expect—tolerance from others in our beliefs and practices, so should we tolerate and respect others with opposite beliefs. In practice this means we respect others by not forcing them to witness our beliefs. So we modify our naturist lifestyle, even at home, when friends and neighbors are about. Though comfortable in our beliefs, indeed, wishing to advocate and even preach them to others, we find we have abstained from anything else that offers your brother an occasion for stumbling or scandal.[1] The true cusp is approached when we ask how we should modify our own beliefs and practices when others are not directly involved, or likely to observe, yet would be scandalized if they were. There, we should put thoughts of others aside, and be true to ourselves.

RE: the occasion of sin:

We ought to find a good approach for dealing with the seemingly major objection of some religious people to nudity—that it is an "occasion of sin." Yet the occasion of sin seems only to apply to purity instead of *all* the virtues. Are not banks with all that money, or stores will all those goods, an occasion of sin to steal or shoplift?

Should we avoid the occasion of sin of gluttony and refrain from sitting down with the family for dinner?

Occasions of sin can be anywhere. Yet we avoid it with our state of mind, and banish it from our thoughts, whether at the free[2] beach, or shopping, or banking, or eating, or any of the too numerous to mention temptations of the real world. When clothes-compulsory religious people so readily accuse us of providing "near occasions of sin," let's label that phrase for what it really is—just a simplistic and unthoughtful reaction to a new, expanding, and joyful activity—naturism.

William Shakespeare: *Hamlet*

What a piece of work is a man! How noble in reason! How infinite in faculties! In form and moving how express and admirable! In action, how like an angel! In apprehension, how like a god! The beauty of the world! The paragon of animals!

—Act II, Scene 2, Line 319

---

[1] Cf. Romans 14:21.
[2] I.e. clothing-optional.

Establishing Nude Customs

by Jim C. Cunningham

In the fourth part of the Altogether Christians[1] creed we profess:

That social nudity is truly chaste and modest if: 1) its *purpose* is not to arouse lust, and 2) it is *customary*, not disregarding the *legitimate* sensibilities of others.

Let's face it—social nudity is not very customary in our culture. Without offending "the legitimate sensibilities of others," we must work to make social nudity more and more customary. Otherwise, there can be no cultural progress in this area. Since Altogether Christians nudism is not admixed with hedonistic, but rather Christian, values, we Altogether Christians ought to be right in the forefront here, tastefully and tactfully presenting the positive cultural value of social nudity to a non-nudist culture.

We must do this by witnessing to them in word and work. We cannot communicate anything to them unless they hear what we have to say about nudism and see us live it. Therefore, we must let them know about our lifestyle. Since they already regard us as respectable Christians, they are apt to react differently when they hear the nudist idea from *us*, than when they hear it from *others*. For example, the Woodstock rock festival was ill-suited to preach the sacredness and dignity of nudity because a very large element of our society looked down on the "hippies" who flocked there. How different when a Christian family they respect invite them to swim in their pool, and automatically swim nude!

Closet nudists communicate nothing. Even when their nudism is occasionally discovered, the message that they give is that they ought to be ashamed of themselves for being nudists as if it were a sin!

We must speak. One gentle way of letting them know of your belief is to leave nudist periodicals in areas of your

---

[1] Altogether Christians International Nudist Club was founded by Jim C. Cunningham in 1983. To our knowledge, it was the first organized Christian naturist club.

homes where guests will see them. Or how about hanging your nudist photos on the same wall with your family pictures?

But word is not enough. Though "faith comes through hearing"[1] (according to St. Paul), yet for most people (identifying with doubting St. Thomas), "seeing is believing." As you know, a tasteful nudist photo says more than 1,000 eloquent words about the virtues of nudism. If that is true, then actually seeing real, live, family social nudism must be worth 1,000 of those wonderful photographs.

I remember having long discussions on nudism with some neighbors. I gave them lots of nudist publications to read. That all had effect, but 1,000 times more effective was their first few minutes at Maple Glen Nudist Park in Sheldon Springs, Vermont. Everything I had said, and they had read, suddenly became a reality that couldn't be contradicted.

Therefore, we must let our non-nudist culture see and experience our modest nudity. No, on second thought, "let" is too passive; rather, we must *show* it to them. But we must do it in such a way as not to offend their legitimate sensibilities (not all sensibilities are legitimate). If we merely attend nudist parks and well known nude beaches, we will not be very effectively witnessing to a non-nudist culture that does not frequent such places. If we are going to have any *real* effect on them, then we must *show* the wholesomeness and goodness of our nudism in other places and on other occasions. Where? How?

First of all, naturally, there is your home which is your castle. You alone have every right to establish customs of domestic nudity there. No one can legitimately say they are offended by your domestic nakedness. In fact, you have a greater right to be nude at home than at a nudist park or famous nude beach. Your home is your little Rome, and you decide what the Romans shall wear therein.

Oddly, however, it seems easier for non-nudists to see us nude on a nude beach than at home. That's probably because there's little chance that anybody knows us at a nude beach whereas those dropping in on us at home are likely to be people we know. But it is with these very

[1] Romans 10:17.

people we know that we can have the most effect! Since we already have their respect, no one can show them the integrity of nudism better than we! By failing to do so we pass up a grand opportunity to further the cause.

What kind of domestic nudity am I talking about? Any kind you decide, because it is *your* home. Although you might not answer the door nude, you might at least do nothing to prevent being seen nude at home. Go about nude freely in the daytime without pulling any shades. Anyone who happens to come to the door will see that you are nude therein. Without crossing your arms across your crotch and dashing for a hidden cranny, calmly and pleasantly ask the caller to wait a minute, put something on, and then answer the door. Your calm, pleasant and unabashed deportment will teach more than 1,000 photographs.

Once friends and neighbors are aware of your domestic nudist customs, and act as if they at least respect it *for you*, ask them if they'd mind if you didn't have to bother getting dressed the next time they drop in. They will probably (ironically) tell you to make yourself at home, and then you and your whole family will have lots of excellent opportunities to show them the dignity and wholesomeness of nakedness. It wouldn't be long before they would choose nudism for themselves, because your example of the purity and goodness of modest nudity simply can't be contradicted. It is breathtakingly, incontrovertibly *right*.

And your yard is yours, too. Don't hesitate to establish nude customs there. Although you might not mow the lawn nude, every yard is suitable for *some* degree of nudity that will not offend anyone's legitimate sensibilities.

Again, the principle is that we *want* to show non-nudists our modest nudity so as to make nudism more socially acceptable. Therefore, we do not want to act in such a way that we will *never* be seen nude in our yard, but rather, we *want* to be seen nude there in a way that won't offend anyone's *legitimate* sensibilities.

If you live in the country regard your yard as a nudist park and be freely nude there whether you are mowing the lawn or playing horseshoes. Sure, occasionally you will be seen nude, like you *want* to be, and no one's *legitimate* sensibilities can be offended.

If you live in a less private location, there are still lots of possible customs of nudity you can establish in your yard. Whenever you have to go outside for half a minute (e.g. to get something off the line) don't bother to put anything on. If someone does surprise you, act as calm and pleasant as you would if they had come to the door and seen you nude inside.

Almost every yard (even in Detroit, where I used to live) is suitable for nude sunbathing, by simply erecting at least a gesture of a screen (even if only a chaise lounge on its side) to show that you do not intend to offend anybody. You don't have to ensure that you are not visible from *any* vantage point, but simply from the places people often go (e.g. driveways, doorways, etc.).

If you have a pool, that is an excellent occasion to establish customary nudity. Many yards are private enough to allow daylight skinny-dipping. Even if a couple of neighbors have a view of your pool, swimming with clothes on is simply too ridiculous for compromise, and you may well swim nude even if you know they are watching. However, if this seems too radical for you, just about every pool allows for daytime nude use at least under water. You can wear your suit to (or into) the pool and take it off to swim. At night, darkness itself is a sufficient gesture of a privacy screen. There are few pools that are unsuitable for complete skinny-dipping at night (as long as the spotlight isn't turned on). If you invite guests to use your pool, do nothing differently than if you were alone or just with your family. Do not apologize for your birthday suit. It is *your* pool, and nude swimming is *your* custom. If you have a cottage on a lake, the same principles apply. Don't forget that we *want* non-nudists to see us nude without offending their legitimate sensibilities. When no one voices offense, assume that they don't mind.

When you are someone else's guest, you must conform to *their* domestic customs. However, if they invite you to use their pool it would not be offensive to simply inquire if it would be acceptable if you didn't wear a suit. They will probably tell you to make yourself at home, and if they do not then and there follow your lead and skinny-dip with you, you will have at least shown them a fine example of the purity and integrity of social nakedness.

If you are a nursing mother, no matter where you are (e.g. church, bus, court) you can very legitimately show the beauty of (at least) partial nakedness at its best. Don't nurse in such a way that no one knows you're doing it. This is a golden opportunity to teach others that the breast is not the property of *Playboy*, but a most beautiful and sacred creation of God. Make no attempt whatsoever to hide your breast—even when your baby is off the nipple for awhile taking a little breather. Never apologize for nursing in front of anyone, and never ask anyone's "permission." You have *God's* permission!

When you are out in God's country—out in the mountains, woods, fields, lakes and streams, and nobody is around at the time, go freely nude without giving the matter so much as a thought. Should a couple of people pass by, or stop to swim, do nothing differently unless they complain. Remember, we *want* them to see our modest nudity in order to influence them in a positive way. In such places the only time we have to wear clothes is when there are enough people there to have already established a custom of clothes-compulsiveness. In that case we have no right to impose our own custom, but must defer to their legitimate sensibilities.

A good way to establish a custom of social nudity at a place where suits are the custom, is to be there nude first in the morning as others show up. You must do this regularly and with as large a group of like-minded people as you can muster. Before others arrive don't congregate at some remote end of the beach. Take the whole beach. Run, play Frisbee and ball tag. Then, as a lot of clothes-compulsives arrive, move over a bit and charitably give them a section. In this way, we are deferring to their sensibilities to a reasonable extent. It will seem more like *we* are giving *them* the right to be clothed, rather than *they* are begrudgingly tolerating *our* birthday suits.

There are a lot of people on clothes-compulsive beaches who would love to skinny-dip. Your example is the best invitation for them to be rid of their shackles. If we all do what I am here suggesting, it will not be long before nudity is customary on every beach.

If, for some reason, you decide to attend a clothed beach, though you can't go nude, you can make certain inroads that will *gradually* lay the foundation for nudism. For example: 1) Once in the water you can anchor your suit under a rock or hang it on a raft and freely swim nude. 2) At least while lying on your belly, you ladies can sunbathe topfree. 3) You can change in and out of your bathing suit without scrupulously hiding. 4) You can freely skinny-dip at night.

Some people think it would be best to reside in a private nudist park where they could be nude whenever they pleased. But whom are they influencing there? How are they spreading the good news of naked freedom?

Rather, the truth is that all of you who read this now are *already* in ideal situations for social nudity. If you take full advantage of it, our cultural change will be marvelously effective. Try it!

Hiding the Evidence

by Jim C. Cunningham

It is interesting to note that after Adam & Eve sinned, they made only *loincloths* for themselves.[1] It seems that they were ashamed only of their loins—not the rest of the bodies. This should at least signify to even the most conservative fundamentalist, that at least bare-chestedness for both sexes is perfectly upright and in accord with Sacred Writ.

If we are to draw our moral interpretation of Genesis 3:7 directly from the literal Word, then we must conclude the absurd—that husband and wife are supposed to be ashamed of each other's nakedness, because Adam & Eve were husband and wife.[2] Obviously, then, we cannot draw our moral interpretation directly from the *literal* story. But then, what does this passage mean?

As everyone knows, there are two accounts of creation. The first is found, roughly, in Genesis 1, and the

---

[1] Cf. Genesis 3:7.
[2] Cf. Ibid. 2:23f.

second in the following chapter. In each account Adam & Eve are given only one commandment. In the first account God commands them to "be fruitful and multiply"[1] (i.e. to continue His creative act). In the second, he forbids them to eat of the tree of the knowledge of good and evil.[2] This command is the same as the one found in the first account, only it is expressed *metaphorically*.

Adam's & Eve's sin must have been some form of sexual abuse—they participated in some form of infertile sex (bestiality?) which gravely displeased God. They abused their sexuality, became piercingly aware of their guilt, and tried to cover up the evidence (i.e. their genitalia) like a murderer who casts his pistol into the Hudson River.

In inheriting that Original Sin, we also inherit all of its evil effects, one of which is this "natural" (according to fallen human nature only) urge to cover up our genitalia. Clothes-compulsiveness is not, then, merely a *cultural* curiosity. It is an *universally inherited* hang-up which gives evidence of the existence of Original Sin.

But through baptism, Original Sin is totally removed. Thereafter, its ill effects are unfounded. Why should we thereafter give in to an urge to cover up, especially when the original crime we are supposedly thereby inclined to hide, has been fully remitted? Does Jesus expect us to go on carrying the guilt and shame of a sin He has forgiven? Is it gratitude for His Infinite Mercy for us to go on acting like He has *not* forgiven us? Of course not! Nudism/naturism ought to be better suited to Christians than to any other group of people.

In Genesis 3:21 God gives Adam & Eve leather tunics before He banishes them from Eden. Some opponents of nudism are fond of citing this as proof that God wants us dressed, but the text proves nothing of the sort. Would they have us believe that God *never* wanted them to *temporarily* doff their leather duds in order to launder them, or to bathe, or to adjust to the hotter seasons, or to relax a bit from the burdens of this "valley of tears" by recreating nude? (Remember that He wanted us to rest so badly, that He devoted one of ten commandments[3] to it!)

---

[1] Genesis 1:28.
[2] Ibid. 2:17.
[3] Cf. Deuteronomy 5:12ff.

65

So you see, this passage lends no support to the anti-nudists. Rather, I see in it God's great, condescending mercy. Out of *justice* He is banishing Adam & Eve from Eden into a harsh, inclement clime. It seems more likely that He made them leather garments out of *compassion*, knowing that they would need them for protection and warmth. Mere fig leaves certainly sufficed to cloak the shame of nakedness, but it would not count for much, practically, out in the "valley of tears." Even the very mention that the tunics were made out of *leather* indicates that their purpose was warmth and protection, and not merely a covering for shame.

Nakedness: God's Plan

by Wayne C. Olson

And the man and his wife were both naked, and were not ashamed. —Genesis 2:25

Then the eyes of both were opened, and they knew that they were naked; and they sewed fig leaves together and made themselves aprons. —Genesis 3:7

But the Lord God called to the man, and said to him, "Where are you?" And he said, "I heard the sound of Thee in the garden, and I was afraid, because I was naked; and I hid myself." He said, "Who told you that you were naked? Have you eaten of the tree of which I commanded you not to eat?" —Genesis 3:9-11

And the Lord God made for Adam and his wife garments of skins, and clothed them. —Genesis 3:21

The first of the above passages refers to them before the fall, when people were sinless, perfect, as they had been created. In this state they were naked and had no feeling of shame about it. Nakedness is mentioned by the writer because, at the time of writing, the fall had already taken place and nakedness had become a social "problem." That he took the trouble to comment on their freedom from shame about their nakedness only serves to emphasize how truly desirable nudity and shamelessness are! His pointing this out demonstrates how very clearly it was the intention of the Creator that people be nude and not be troubled about it. In their original state, without sin, nudity is the desirable state. Is there a better endorsement for nudity than this?

The second passage refers to a time after the fall. It deals with the attempts made by the man and the woman to deal with their nakedness and shame. They made loincloths ("aprons"). Notice, this was before their encounter with the Lord God. Loincloth-making was *their human response* to their discovery that they were nude. It is not clear in the story *why* they chose to cover their genitals. The relationship between the sin they committed—eating the forbidden fruit—and their sex organs is not established. It was not until after they had sinned that their eyes were opened to their nakedness. The Original Sin then had nothing at all to do with nakedness or sex, but rather with disobedience over the eating of the forbidden fruit. The element of "shame" over nakedness was a result of the disobedience, not its cause. So from our earlier history, the abandonment of nudity, our intended state, is one of the consequences of the presence of sin in our lives.

The third passage confirms the fact that the Original Sin had nothing to do with nakedness or sexual activity.[1] The man used his nakedness as an excuse for hiding from God. The Lord God had to search him out and when found, the man answers: "I was naked and I hid myself." He had been naked before and did *not* hide. This time he was wearing his apron and was *not* naked, *and he hid*! He knew that the wearing of a garment meant that as soon as the Lord God saw him, he would know something was wrong.

Now begins the interrogation. "Who told you that you were naked?" As every psychiatrist knows, the first reason given is never the real one. Using nakedness as a cover-up

---

[1] Editor's note: Though there already is a general disclaimer in the Foreword of this book, I wish to emphasize my specific disagreement with this particular author's assertion regarding the non-sexual nature of the original sin. For my own take, see pp. 220ff.

(no pun intended!) is clear proof that both the man and the Lord God knew it was irrelevant. The problem was sin, not nudity. So the Lord God ignored the statement and proceeded to question the man until he learned the deeper truths.

The fourth passage is almost comic. The man and woman are in their loincloths and God made for them tunics, garments of skin—animal skin, presumably. He seems to be saying to them, "If you're going to wear clothing, then, by God, wear clothing! Skimpy loincloths won't do! If you're ashamed of your bodies, then let's cover them up altogether." So He judges their provocative garb unfit for their state and Himself provides the fuller garments that will *really* cover their shame! There s nothing half-way about *this* God!

Looking at the four passages together then, let us conclude:

1. Nakedness is the *intended* state of mankind; it is desirable, it represents the Creator's purposes and it is both natural and preferred for man and woman to be naked.

2. There is no shame inherent in nudity *per se*; quite the opposite is implied. In our perfected, ideal nature, there is no reason to feel shame about our bodies at all. The shame is apparent when we put on clothing; *clothing* is the badge of sin, not *genitals*.

3. There is no validity in the loincloth syndrome. Merely covering the genitals won't do, for it doesn't speak to the problem. Loincloths, provocative clothing, accentuate the genitals, and only call further attention to the shame and the basic problem people have with sex. Hiding the body is symptomatic of the soul's need to hide from God. If you must wear clothing, wear that which will call least attention to the body parts that give most people the most problems.

Different Kinds of Naked

by Le Roy E. Pickard

There are few truths in the Bible that are more strongly attested than the fact that the Bible approves social nudity as a part of a *normal* lifestyle.

If we believe that when God provided one woman for one man, that He was establishing a principle for life (and He certainly was), and confirmed it in such passages as Matthew 19:4-6, then, when He brought Adam & Eve together nude, walked with them and communed with them in the nude, He was also establishing a principle for a *normal* lifestyle, and confirmed it in such portions of our Bible as Songs of Solomon, Ezekiel 16, and many other portions of scripture, even under the rigid Levitical legal system.

In Leviticus 8:1-9 we have the account of Moses bringing Aaron and his sons, "to the door of the tabernacle of the congregation" to witness the ceremony. Verse 6 says, "And Moses brought Aaron and his sons, and washed them with water." If it is questioned whether or not the whole body was to be washed consider the spiritual application to this in Hebrews 10:22 where "bodies" is specifically stated.

Genesis 2:25 says, "And they were both naked." The Hebrew word here for "naked" is "*ayrome*" and simply means "nude." In Genesis 3:7 we read, "And the eyes of them both were opened, and they knew that they were naked." The Hebrew word for "naked" here is a different word than in Genesis 2:25. Here the word is "*awram*," and is nearly always associated with destruction, helplessness, or ruin, as in Ezekiel 16:7 & 22, and in Deuteronomy 28:48. Adam said, "I was afraid, because I was naked." This could be paraphrased, "I was afraid because I was ruined, destroyed and helpless." Adam had sinned and was experiencing the judgment of God for it. God's question to him was, "Who told thee that thou wast naked?" As a matter of fact, Adam was *not* naked, for they had "sewed fig leaves and made themselves aprons."[1] Then, God's second question to Adam was, "Hast thou eaten of the tree, whereof I commanded thee that thou shouldest not eat?" The subject here was not "*physical* nakedness," but "ruin." This is proved further by the words of Job, in Job 31:33, where he says, "If I cover my transgression as Adam, by hiding *mine iniquity* in my bosom." It is obvious, then, that Adam & Eve were not trying to hide their *physical* nakedness with aprons of fig leaves, but their *guilt*, so when God provided coats of skins, He was not just covering their *physical* nakedness, but in fact, we have here the first promise of the Redeemer.[2] The shedding of blood, and the taking of life[3] looked forward to Calvary, providing for believers a cloak of righteousness.

Clothes Divide

by Joan Turner

No matter what kind of sin the Original Sin was, all sin is *divisive*. Undoubtedly the greatest division in history occurred in the Garden of Eden when man divided himself against all that was dear to him, and with which he once was so harmoniously united—his spouse, his land, and his God.

Adam & Eve lost God's supernatural life—that unifying force which made them so peaceful, so whole, and so one with God. Imagine the feeling of separation, of brokenness, that must have swept over them when they first realized their guilt, that hideous guilt. We all know the feeling of being torn away from those we love most because of sin and guilt.

And then Adam & Eve hid not only from their God, but also from each other. And what did they hide from each other but their genitalia, the very things that should

---

[1] Cf. Genesis 3:7.
[2] Editor's note: Actually, Genesis 3:15 is generally regarded to be the *first* promise of a Redeemer.
[3] Editor's note: The acquisition of skins implies killing and shedding the blood of animals.

have nobly served to unite them and bond them together such that the two would become one flesh?[1]

Adam & Eve covered their loins; we know that. Perhaps the simplest understanding of those loincloths is that they symbolize the hideous *division* of sin. These first clothes were a *fence*, as it were, signifying their separation from their Creator and from their fellow creatures.

But Jesus has achieved a more powerful unity for us than even Adam & Eve once enjoyed! "I pray that they may all be One as You, Father, are in Me, and I in You."[2] "But now in Christ Jesus you who once were far off have been brought near through the blood of Christ. It is He Who is our peace, and Who made the two of us one by breaking down the barrier of hostility that kept us apart. In His own flesh He abolished the law with its commands and precepts, to create in Himself one new man from us who had been two and to make peace, reconciling both of us to God in one body through His Cross."[3]

Given this fact, how inappropriate clothes are among Christians! How can we worship together singing, "We are *one* in the Spirit, we are *one* in the Lord," while we stand there wearing those ugly symbols of the *separation* of sin? If the first symbol of *division* was *clothes*, then the best symbol of *unity* is *nudity*.

The Body's Place
in Christian Spirituality

by Jim C. Cunningham

Spirituality is the God-man relationship and everything that concerns that relationship. How does the body figure in this scheme? Does spirituality concern only our soul, or does it concern all of what we are—soul *and* body?

---

[1] Cf. Genesis 2:24.
[2] John 17:20f.
[3] Ephesians 2:13ff.

71

It concerns our body just as much as our soul! This is an astonishing statement. Many upon hearing this would begin to accuse me of heresy. But no, spirituality concerns our bodies just as much as our souls.

Spirituality concerns our personal relationship with God. Our persons are comprised of both soul *and body*. Angelic personalities are spirit only. Jesus never shared an *angel's* nature. No, He shared a *human* nature—soul *and body*. He did not give His *soul* as the Bread of Life, but His *body*. He did not save us by becoming just a human soul. He saved us by His death, and you can't die if you have no body. Spirits don't die, bodies do. His Sacred Body was the actual instrument of our salvation. This is wonderful! This is precious!

The body was not originally designed to die, but to live. Death is a result of Original Sin. Jesus triumphed over Original Sin by His death, purchasing eternal life for us all.

The eternal life He won for us is not only for our *souls*. It is for *us*, and we are both soul *and body*. It is for the *whole* human person. And that's why the doctrine of the bodily resurrection is so vital to Christianity. Without it all the rest of Christian life is vain.[1]

Is the human body really all that wonderful? Why has the body been put down so much in the past? Because it has been affected by Original Sin and is no longer perfect? Because it now has a propensity to unreasonably overindulge in sensual pleasure?

But the *soul* was also affected by Original Sin. We lost sanctifying grace and lucid intelligence. Is the body more to blame for our sins than the spirit? The Bible tells us that "pride is the root of all evil."[2] But pride is not a *physical* sin, but a *spiritual* one!

Now don't get me wrong. In no way do I want to exalt the body over the soul. My whole point is that this body vs. soul competition is meaningless and even harmful. We are *both* body *and* soul. *Both* were made by God as His divine reflection. *Both* are destined for eternal life. *Both* are wonderful. The true *naturist* should concern himself with *both* because *both* comprise His *nature*.

---

[1] Cf. I Corinthians 15:14.
[2] Sirach 10:15 (Douay Rheims).

Body and soul are different by nature. They complement each other, and together they image the beautiful unity of the divine. They have different spheres of operation. Mind, one of the soul's faculties, invents the suspension bridge. Bodies sweat to incarnate that idea. My mind has an insight. To share it with you I need my body—my tongue and my hands. I need symbols, which are *physical* realities to communicate *spiritual* ideas and realities. This is the essential mystery of the seven Christian sacraments. They are physical things, words and actions that really communicate what they symbolize.

Therefore we can see how vital the body is in order to love. We communicate through the body. Were this article not physically published in this book, held in your hands, read by your body's eyes, then your spirit and mine could not be one with the truths I am here conveying.

So we come to another fantastic discovery—the body is *essential* to love! Two human souls cannot unite without the body. How wonderful and necessary it is!

This conclusion not only applies to our human relationships, but also to our relationship with God. In order to unite us to Himself, *God became flesh* and dwelt among us so we could *see* His glory, "the glory of an only Son coming from the Father, filled with enduring love."[1] God Himself assumed a human body, and by means of that body He made complete union between God and man possible. He communicated with us by means of that body. He purchased our salvation by means of that body. He even went so far as to give us His body as our food, insisting that if we failed to eat it, then we would be lifeless.[2] Isn't it interesting to note that St. John "the Mystic" is the evangelist so seemingly preoccupied with the *body* of Christ? Mysticisms and spiritualities which ignore, denigrate or deny the body's essential place are false. The spiritual and the physical are not opposed; like man and woman, they comprise an essential, *complementary unity*. Nothing could be more false than to attempt to separate what God has joined together.[3]

---

[1] John 1:14.
[2] Cf. John 6:53.
[3] Cf. Matthew 19:6.

So whence have come all the negative attitudes towards the human body? Do you see how irreligious they really are? How unspiritual? Such perverted attitudes are a great obstacle to true spirituality—our union with God and others.

But fellow Christians, we cannot just sit smiling complacently at these delightful contemplations. *We must act.* In fact, we Christians must act even more than other naturists because there is a greater exigency in all this for us. Whereas *secular* naturists see in naturism merely mundane benefits such as greater rest and relaxation, and a healthier mind in a healthier body, we Christians see it from a *spiritual* perspective. We see how it concerns our religion—our relationship with God and others—our spirituality—our growth in holiness. For this reason we Christians ought to be way out in the forefront of the naturist movement. But where have we been?

What can we do to help restore the body's proper place in spirituality? There are many things we can do, but none of them seems to be as demonstrative or effective as unabashed naturism. Naturism, in one gesture, says it all. Standing naked in front of others says:

"I am both soul *and body*, and I fully accept and cherish that fact. I do not ridicule my body or wish it were not there. I am not ashamed of this precious gift. See, I am naked and unashamed.[1] Nothing about my God-given body is indecent, obscene, ugly or disgusting. It is all beautiful and wondrous. This is God's image! Why should I be embarrassed by this? I'm not ashamed of God! He's not disgusting! Sin occasioned the shameful hiding of this body, but my nudity itself proclaims the truth of the Gospel—that the Lamb of God has indeed taken away the sin of the world,[2] restoring everything in Himself,[3] seeking out and bringing back what was lost!"[4]

As we all know, one of the biggest problems is the unfruitful and perverted association of nude with lewd. To help rectify this, nothing is better than unhypocritically living the truth of the body's goodness and sacredness by

---

[1] Genesis 2:25.
[2] Cf. John 1:29.
[3] Cf. Ephesians 1:10.
[4] Cf. Luke 15:4-7 & 19:10.

dressing only for valid reasons and never out of shame of what God sees as "very good."[1] By unabashedly letting others see our bodies we prove the veracity of what would otherwise be just lip-service. We Christians are too often (and sadly, rightly) criticized for not practicing what we preach. Our tepidity annuls the power of the Gospel. Nothing convinces like *genuineness*. Jesus was genuine, to the last drop of His Precious Blood. If we follow Him as faithful disciples by our uncompromising living of the truth, we realize what He meant when He called us to be lights in the world[2] and salt that has not lost its flavor.[3]

We must correct the lie that "nude is lewd" by showing that "nude is good." If we allow people to only see nudity in lewd contexts, our neglect serves only to reinforce the lie. The corrective is simple—to show nudity in non-lewd contexts. Take off your clothes and teach by example. If we are seen doing everything nude but having sex, then that false association of nude with lewd has to disappear. Our simple, innocent nakedness itself speaks louder than words.

But our nakedness isn't worth much if it's in the solitude of our homes, nudist parks and well-established nude beaches. Naturists are too often like ghetto dwellers. We huddle together in our own little private groups. That's not going to do much for others. In fact, by thus isolating ourselves we make ourselves some sort of minority problem, and even appear to be some sort of "cult"! We give non-nudists the opportunity of pointing the finger at us and stereotyping us. We become "the *other* guys"—the "nudies." By living what we believe in everyday life we preach to far more than the choir only. It is more difficult for people to point to us as "other" when we are right in their midst. They see us as part of their "*us*" rather than just "*them*." A ghettoized nudism sets itself up for isolation, whereas a mainstreamed nudism that does not exile itself is harder to isolate. We are like cream in coffee. Once mixed, how can it be separated? Our very proximity with others tells them that what we believe and unabashedly

---

[1] Genesis 1:31.
[2] Cf. Matthew 5:14.
[3] Cf. Ibid. v. 13.

practice is not anything esoteric or eccentric, but is meant to be as common as, well, *having a body*!

Because of fear and tepidity, Christians who believe in naturist principles have allowed the secular element of the movement to lead while they sheepishly follow. This makes no sense whatsoever, as it is we who have been blessed with such abundant revelation. Let's get out of the trunk and assume the driver's seat in the naturist movement!

Pope Entertained by Topless Dancers

by Jim C. Cunningham

When Pope John Paul II visited Mount Hagen in Papua, New Guinea early in his pontificate, the press reported that he was fervently greeted by 180,000 native Melanesians, including bare breasted dancers and spear-carrying warriors wearing necklaces of pig tusks and dog's teeth, with their faces and bodies smeared black, red and white with ashes and pig grease. This is quite different than the way he is greeted in Krakow or Rome!

But did he ever try to impose Polish or Italian customs on these people in the name of "the missionary work of the Church"? Of course not. He was not scandalized by the sight of this customary nakedness. Surely he knows the difference between these topfree dancers and the lustful, belittling burlesque one could find in Roman night clubs.

When the Christian faith comes to a faraway place it does necessitate some cultural changes. For example, the Yanamamo Indians in Brazil practice infanticide. In order to truly share Jesus Christ with them, we would definitely have to advise against this particular cultural practice! But with clothing, no changes are necessary.

In the same press report, a fifty-four year old tribesman was quoted: "I didn't like to give up four of my five wives to become a Catholic." The faith of Christ required a change in his marital arrangement, but never in his or his wife's mode of dress.

This reminds me of another story I read in a book on chastity and modesty by a Marist priest, Fr. Aubin. It seems that Roman Catholic bishops in neighboring dioceses in Oceania had a dispute over modesty. One bishop admonished the other for permitting women to attend Mass bare-breasted. The other bishop defended this practice, stating that such partial nakedness was the ordinary custom for women in his diocese, and they meant nothing sexually suggestive by it. He then went on to rebuke the other bishop for allowing his women to drape themselves immodestly to allure. Truly, as Pope John Paul II wrote when he was still a Cardinal: "Sexual modesty cannot then in any simple way be identified with the use of clothing, nor shamelessness (i.e. immodesty) with the absence of clothing and total or partial nakedness."[1]

A Priest Discovers
the Christian Value of Nudism

by Fr. Jonathan Mueller

It is early in the morning. I am sitting nude by the pond at Mt. Carmel Academy. At this time of my life I am at peace with the world around me. It has been a very relaxing day and a half, and I'm sorry it will end tomorrow. It is also a peace that places me in harmony with my own body. I am thinking back to several years ago when I was first introduced to the nudist lifestyle.

I was in Germany at the time. On the advice of several friends, I had gone to see a doctor. While waiting to see him, I was wondering if this was another waste of time. For over twenty-five years I had a serious problem with acne on my back. I had seen many doctors and nothing had worked. My back had gotten worse over the years instead of better, and I had just about given up. As far as I was concerned, this was the final straw.

---
[1] Wojtyla, p. 176.

77

The receptionist called my name, and I went in to see the doctor. At the time I had no way of knowing that his prescribed treatment was to change my life.

After the doctor finished with the examination, he told me what I already knew—I had a very serious problem with acne and something had to be done right away before it got even worse. He then looked at me and said that something *could* be done for my back but I might be uncomfortable with the treatment. I had heard this before, so I said that I was in favor of *anything*, so long as it cured my acne.

He went to his medicine cabinet and took out a large jar of cream. The cream gave off an unpleasant odor, and I was thinking that I would have to walk around with the smell. He told me he wanted me to spread the cream over my back two or three times a week, and then lay in the sun for a couple of hours completely nude.

I looked at him for a few minutes and asked him to repeat the statement. He repeated it, and I knew I had not misunderstood him.

I found myself objecting that it would be impossible because there was no place I could lay outside nude. He looked at me for a few moments and said, "Go to a nudist camp; there is one in your area." I still objected, and when asked why, I decided to play my ace-in-the-hole. "Doc, I can't go to a nudist camp because *I'm a priest.*"

He laid his glasses down and said, "Father, there is nothing sinful about being nude or going to a nudist camp. *You* are the one making it sinful in the actions of your mind. You have tried other medicines that have not worked on your acne, so what do you have to lose? If you do not wish to follow my advice and treatment, then please see another doctor."

I left his office in a state of confusion, and I told a few friends about the treatment the doctor recommended. I even said to them, "Could you see *me* nude at a nudist camp?" My three friends said to me, "Why not? We all belong to a nudist camp. There is nothing wrong with it. It is only the imagination of you Americans. You don't even know what happens at a nudist park, so how can you judge it?" We continued to discuss the matter, and it was decided that I would go with them the following week.

When the day came, I remember hoping it would rain, but no such thing happened. My friends picked me up and after an hour's drive we arrived at the camp. After paying ten marks we were admitted to the camp.

The first thing I did was wrap a towel around my waist and place the smelly cream on my back. I then made a bee-line for the sun-field. I had already decided I was going to lie on my blanket on my stomach for the next few hours. This I tried to do, only to discover how silly it was. Plus, I discovered that no one in the camp cared about this silly American lying on his stomach. They were all enjoying themselves, so it did not matter what I did. Hence after an hour I began to relax and enjoy myself. This discovery changed my life and the way I understood myself.

I began to see the wholesomeness and goodness in my body. I also began to understand that nudism was not contrary to Christianity. We, as individuals, in our minds, have made it contrary and then invoked Christian principles to justify our position. Nudism is a liberating experience that enables our Christian faith to grow since we come to realize its wholeness to our world around us. The biggest barrier we have to cross is our fear, and once we have faced it, then we realize how liberated we are.

The Lustful Dead

by Joan Turner

You have heard that it was said, "You shall not commit adultery." But I say to you that every one who looks at a woman lustfully has already committed adultery with her in his heart. —Matthew 5:27f

Jesus came to fulfill the Old Law, not to abolish it. In this passage He does just that. He takes an old Jewish law, "Thou shalt not commit adultery"[1] and completes it:

---

[1] Deuteronomy 5:18.

"Thou shalt not even entertain thoughts of adultery, i.e. lusting in the heart."

Lusting in the heart is a spiritual adultery. It doesn't happen exteriorly but interiorly in the imagination. It is much like spiritual murder—although you do no physical harm to your enemy, you hate him with bitterness, wishing that evil would befall him. You have, in a way, murdered him in your heart.[1] About lusting interiorly, Jesus says, "Everyone who looks at a woman lustfully has already committed adultery with her in his heart."[2]

Those who lust, lust after the body, not the spirit, but nowhere does Jesus make reference to the body as the culprit or the cause of lust. Lust resides in the heart (which means the will) of man, not in his body or any one part of his body. Likewise, purity resides in the heart.

With that in mind, one could posit this theory: A man with a pure heart could be unmoved by a striptease burlesque show. He would probably avoid such places for they would afford him no entertainment. But if by chance he wound up at one, he may by the grace of God and an act of the will, remain pure, not entertaining any lustful thoughts in his heart. The steady dose of erotic behavior would find no audience in the man with a pure heart.

The same theory also says this: A man with a lustful heart can turn even the most innocent social nudist gathering into his own burlesque show if he chooses. His *heart* tells him that the naked human body is an object for sexual enjoyment. That is a lie. If we were tempted before to think Jesus was a bit harsh to impose such a strict interpretation on adultery, now we can see the reason behind it. Lusting after each other gives birth and nourishment to an ugly lie about humanity: we are sex objects—toys. This attitude destroys all sense of charity and compassion, the very things Jesus proclaims.

The playboy mentality that Christ condemns in this text takes one aspect of the human nature and makes it the entire essence of man and woman. It disregards the whole for the part. Certainly we are sexual beings but our sexuality must be taken as part of an entire human nature. We are sexual, healthy, loving, thinking, laughing

---

[1] Cf. I John 3:15: "Anyone who hates his brother is a murderer."
[2] Matthew 5:28.

creatures and a hundred other things besides. A burlesque act purposefully depicts us as one-dimensional—
erotic—twisting and warping the true perspective we
should have. Pornography, in all its forms, does the same.
Pornography is evil because it is intentionally false. It tells
a lie to gratify the lustful heart. In effect it destroys the
beauty of human nature.

Those who lust are spiritually dead. They cut themselves off from a loving mankind. They alienate themselves
from the saving power of Jesus. They know only fleeting
pleasures. They know no real joy. Jesus condemns this
state knowing with Divine wisdom how strongly we tend
towards it and how destructive the end results are. In
condemning the sin, Jesus saves the sinner. He opens for
us the channel to real joy, real happiness—not fleeting
earthly pleasure, but deep friendship with Him here and
eternal life hereafter.

Praise God
in your Sunday Best

by Jim C. Cunningham

[Tune: "Ye Sons and Daughters" (*O Filii et Filiae*)]

Refrain:
Alleluia! Alleluia! Alleluia!

1. Adam & Eve were created by God,
'Specially hand-crafted from the sod.
Oh, let us sing in thanks and laud. Alleluia!

2. God judged His work and gave men first prize.
They looked most like Him in all Paradise.
Why can't all know this and realize? Alleluia!

3. Then Satan tempted Adam and Eve.
They went and blew it, would you believe?
He gathered fig leaves for her to weave. Alleluia!

4. Man's first invention resulted from shame.
Sin made them fear their mortal frame.
But God still loved them just the same. Alleluia!

5. When time was ripe God sent His Son.
To take a body and human become.
He died for us and Heaven won. Alleluia!

6. Devil defeated, sin destroyed,
Free now from guilt and of shame devoid,
Life now worth living to be enjoyed. Alleluia!

7. No need for raiment now freed from the curse,
Though phys'c'lly faulty, clothes still look worse,
One day we'll shine as we did at the first. Alleluia!

8. Christ will perfect these bodies of ours,
Raising them up by His heav'nly powers,
Shining forth beauty better than flowers. Alleluia!

9. Christians, let's praise Him in our Sunday best,
Naked He made us, so let's get undressed,
And spend this day in holy rest! Alleluia!

Baring the Bible

by Harold Whitington

In the beginning God created the heavens and the earth,[1] He formed man of the dust of the ground, breathed into his nostrils and man became a living soul.[2] He placed him and his companion in a garden[3] of fertility with an abundance of nuts and fruit for food, shade that would protect them from the hot rays of the sun and a skin with pores that would contract to protect them from the cool of

---

[1] Cf. Genesis 1:1.
[2] Cf. Ibid. 2:7.
[3] Cf. Ibid. v. 8.

the night. They were in total harmony with God and nature.

After some time had elapsed, Eve's attention was attracted to the one thing that God had forbidden them to eat, warning them he would take away the tree of life and they would eventually die.[1] The tree was good for food and pleasant to the eyes, a tree desired to make one wise.[2]

Why not? They were very much alive and death seemed so remote. She ate the fruit and the eyes of her understanding were opened.[3] She knew of the evil thoughts that could be associated with the body. They knew of the pleasure of sin and corruption. Full of fear, they tried to hide and cover themselves.[4] Man has been full of shame and fear ever since, forcing everyone (even God's people) to cover themselves.

To the godly, the body is the holy temple of the Spirit.[5] There is no more reason to cover one part than another. Paul writes to Titus, "Unto the pure all things are pure but unto the defiled and unbelieving is nothing pure but even their mind is defiled."[6]

When everything was taken from Job, he immediately stripped the clothing from his body.[7] When Saul joined the prophets he stripped off his clothes and "lay naked also all the day and all that night."[8] In celebration of victory, David met Michal when he returned to his household. He uncovered himself and danced before the handmaids of his servants.[9]

Clothing should be used for protection against the cold. "They cause the naked to lodge without clothing that they have no covering in the cold. They take a pledge of the poor and cause him to go naked without clothing."[10]

Exodus 22:26 says, "If thou take thy neighbor's raiment to pledge, thou shalt deliver it unto him when the

---

[1] Cf. Genesis 2:16f.
[2] Cf. Ibid. 3:6.
[3] Cf. Ibid. v. 7.
[4] Cf. Ibid. v. 7f.
[5] Cf. I Corinthians 6:19.
[6] Titus 1:15.
[7] Cf. Job 1:20.
[8] I Samuel 19:24.
[9] Cf. II Samuel 6:20.
[10] Job 24:7.

sun goeth down for that is his covering only, it is raiment for his skin: Wherein shall he sleep?"

Ruth came home after gleaning wheat, dusty and dirty. Naomi told her to wash and don her raiment or veil and go to where Boaz slept in the field. She crawled under his skirt and when morning came, Boaz asked for her veil and she held it while he filled it with wheat.[1] Rebecca, after days of dusty travel, asked for her veil to adorn herself when she came within sight of her betrothed, Isaac.[2] Men and women alike worked in the field without clothing. "I am black, but comely, because the sun hath looked upon me. They made me keeper of the vineyard."[3] Matthew writes, "In the time of trouble when you are in the field do not return for your clothing but flee as you are."[4] Peter worked on his boat and fished in the nude.[5]

Clothing was always used as adornment. Peter writes, "Ye wives, your adorning let it not be the adorning of wearing gold or of putting on of clothing, but let it be the hidden man of the heart."[6]

The Garden of Eden seems to be a picture of Paradise, of heaven. No sin or evil thoughts. When we are resurrected, will our clothing be resurrected also?

Elijah was caught up in a whirlwind but he left his mantle behind. Elishah saw it and cried, "'My father!' ... and he took hold of his own clothes and rent them to pieces. He took up also the mantle of Elijah that fell from him."[7] There will be no clothing in heaven. Peter writes, "We look for a new heaven and a new earth wherein dwelleth righteousness."[8]

The story of this world is the story of the Bible. It began with *Adam & Eve* in the Garden. There was no feeling of guilt; they were innocent, holy and pure. How long they were in the garden, it doesn't say—a few days, a week or perhaps months. And all that time they were completely nude with no thoughts of clothes. Before they ate of the

---

[1] Cf. Ruth 3:3-14.
[2] Cf. Genesis 24:25.
[3] Song of Songs 1:6.
[4] Matthew 24:18.
[5] Cf. John 21:7.
[6] I Peter 3:3.
[7] Cf. II Kings 2:11-13.
[8] II Peter 3:13.

fruit there was no evil. They were innocent, just as a two-year-old child is innocent, and will go out in the yard or the street to play in the nude. But the parents teach them evil, and if they don't, society soon will. When Adam & Eve ate the fruit they became as a god to know good and evil.[1] The fruit gave them no material knowledge nor did it increase their cerebral capacity in the slightest. It gave them the knowledge of evil. They were attracted by the thrill of physical exploration. They chose the evil in preference to their former way of life. Man has been doing so ever since.

After 1,656 years had elapsed God saw that the wickedness of man was great in the earth and that every imagination of the thoughts of his heart was only evil continually, and the Lord said, "I will destroy man from the face of the earth for it repenteth me that I have made them."[2] But Noah found grace in the eyes of the Lord. He and his family survived by floating in the ark on the waters during the deluge.[3]

452 years later Jacob was born. He had twelve sons who became the twelve tribes of Israel. To them was given the responsibility of proclaiming the eternal Father of heaven who had created the world and all life. When the Jews failed to recognize Jesus Christ as their king, and crucified Him, they were driven from their homeland and dispersed throughout the world.

We are fast approaching the same conditions that existed at the time of the flood. The law of God is flouted. The prisons are so crowded there is no place to confine those convicted. All life is the building of a nest, a lair or a home for the raising of the young. The birds care for the fledgling until he flies away and is able to take care of himself. The animals watch over the young, protect them from harm, teach them the wiles needed to procure food and never desert them before they are grown. Not so man. We have child abuse, desertion by the parents, adultery and sexual promiscuity. The mating act is blown all out of proportion and we have pornographic magazines that dwell on nothing else. They contain pictures that are

---

[1] Cf. Genesis 3:22.
[2] Ibid. 6:7.
[3] Cf. Ibid. 6:8ff.

posed to suggest intercourse, or lewd pictures of nude women with a scrap of cloth covering only the breasts and the genitals which serve only to excite the evil passions of the heart. Seldom do we see woman portrayed in all the holiness and purity of Eve as she was presented to Adam.

Christ is expected to return shortly to set up the Kingdom of God that was refused Him the first time. It will be a time of resurrection including the Old Testament saints: "The bones came together, sinew and flesh upon them, skin covered them but there was no breath in them... I prophesied and the breath came to them and they lived. ... These bones are the whole house of Israel."[1] No mention of clothing. "And my servant David shall be their prince forever."[2] The saints of today will be caught up in the air to meet the Lord,[3] but without their clothing, as wind. Christ will rule and reign for a thousand years.[4] There will be no evil or evil thoughts. Clothing will be worn only for adornment. The whole world will be a paradise of holiness and righteousness. Paul writes to Titus, "We should deny ungodliness and worldly lusts and should live righteously and godly in this present world."[5] But he warns us, "All that will live godly in Christ Jesus shall suffer persecution."[6]

Do you believe in God? Do you believe the first verse of the bible? If so, by right of creation you belong to God. Paul writes, "God was in Christ, reconciling the world unto Himself, not imputing their trespasses unto them."[7] And John declares of Jesus: "Behold the Lamb of God, Which taketh away the sin of the world,[8]" or the sin of Adam & Eve. Paul writes of the latter days, "They shall turn away their ears from the truth and evil men and seducers shall wax worse and worse, deceiving and being deceived."[9]

Grace be with you all.

---

[1] Ezekiel 37:7-11.
[2] Ibid. v.25.
[3] Cf. I Thessalonians 4:17.
[4] Cf. Revelation 20:6.
[5] Titus 2:12.
[6] II Timothy 3:12.
[7] II Corinthians 5:19.
[8] John 1:29.
[9] II Timothy 3:13 & 4:4.

Nudity In Church

by a Roman Catholic Priest[1]

From the first days the Gospel was preached until well into the fourteenth century, the Christian Community carried out the baptismal ceremony by completely immersing the candidate's body in water. During the following two centuries only the lower part of the body was immersed, the priest pouring water over the head. Later on, when the numbers of adults for baptism steadily decreased, the Church began the practice of wetting the head only.

When the Apostles lived on earth, methods of baptism differed widely according to situation and necessity. Sometimes water was sprinkled on a group symbolically (this was probably the method adopted when the 3,000 were baptized on Whitsunday in Jerusalem),[2] and sometimes [just] the head was wetted.

But the Church preferred the method used by St. John the Baptist when baptizing Jesus, later propagated by the Apostles themselves—complete or semi-immersion of the body in a bath or running water.

When the Church decreed that pouring water on the head was to be the accepted practice from the sixteenth century onwards, this was not done from feelings of prudery; it was a precautionary measure for safeguarding the health of small children (dangers from impure water, cold water or water which had been infected by the frightful contagious diseases of the time). In various countries christenings were still carried out in rivers, or children were dipped in the baptismal font in accordance with the Milan Rite (Lombardy, Tessin).

During the baptismal ceremony, persons were put vertically into the river or christened in special bathhouses which were frequently erected near basilicas and cathedrals. These buildings were circular, octagonal or square in shape and enclosed a deep pool into which steps led

---

[1] The author has authorized this translation by Gottfried Bonderer, "al Roseto ob Lugano." First published in *Helios* in the 1950s (?) and made available as a separate tract.
[2] See Acts 2:41.

which were sometimes built in the direction of the cardinal points [of the compass]. Some of these baptisteries are very famous (e.g. Rome, Florence, Pisa, Rheims). The catechumens dipped in completely. At first there was only one immersion but later it was customary to have three. Three is not only a sacred number. The Apostle Paul had developed baptismal doctrine as the symbol of our Lord's three days in the tomb and in honor of the Holy Trinity.

The catechumens sometimes immersed only to the hips while the priest poured water over the head. The baptism of our Lord by John the Baptist is frequently represented in this way. Good examples are seen in the Aryan and Christian baptisteries at Ravenna where the delightful mosaics clearly show the sacred sex of the Redeemer through the transparent waters.

This custom was more widespread between the seventh and eleventh centuries when the simplest baptismal fonts became ever more frequent additions to the baptisteries. Children were immersed up to the hair, adults to their breasts. If certain bas-reliefs are to be taken as a guide, Chlodwig and his 3,000 warriors embraced Christianity in this fashion at Rheims.

It is stressing the obvious to point out that these baptisms demanded complete nudity. Archaeological remains leave no doubt whatever. Nor did the Church oppose it— quite the contrary!

It is certain that the gesture of pouring water over the body (if this is impossible, over the head) to the accompanying words, "I baptize thee in the name of the Father and the Son and of the Holy Ghost" confers grace infallibly through the will of Christ. That is the essence of the sacrament according to the basic doctrine of the Catholic Church. Yet the Church likes to surround sacred rites with symbolism taken directly from the Gospels (i.e. miracles performed by our Lord or parables spoken by Him) or from Paul's epistles. The Church holds one great day reserved for the masses thirsting for Christ—Easter. But first the future Christians must be carefully given religious instruction, strict examinations and they must make confessions of faith.

The solemn dedication itself is enveloped with a panoply of ceremony. There is the blessing by fire, blessing by water, questionings, prayers and exorcisms leading up to the ceremony of stripping naked, which has a purely mystical significance. The Catechumens are nude not only when entering the water, but also during a whole series of noble gestures intended to bring home the majesty of the body. Our bodies are married to the soul, to Christ and all that is godly, to humanity, sacredness, the priesthood and the Kingdom of Jesus Christ.

What does our Lord say: "Whoever keeps my word... my Father and I will be with him and abide in him."[1] On many occasions St. Paul tells us that Christians are the temple of the Holy Ghost.[2] St. Peter describes them as "verily partaking in the nature of God,"[3] "not from mortal but immortal seed."[4] Through His body the Christian becomes a temple. The Church therefore separates the profanity from the body [by] exorcisms, cleaning the ears and the nose, in this way repeating the gestures of Jesus Christ. Salt is given out to him that is the "salt of the earth"[5] a burning candle to him who is to be the "light of the world."[6]

Before entering into these honors the sinful man must be cleansed, and heathen beliefs and practices which have aged him through wickedness must be put aside. He must once again become a child of the Kingdom. Our Lord spoke about this to Nicodemus.[7] The act of exposure on entering the water is a symbol of abandoning the former life. As the Apostle Paul tells us, "To put off the old Adam in order to become a new man."[8] It amounts to casting out the marks of heathen practice and being reborn in a new garment. Who does not feel that this naked exposure is as difficult as death—"The death of sin"?[9] Well, after all, our Lord Jesus Christ did die only to rise from the tomb triumphantly in three days. From one symbolism to another, the Christian identifies himself with Christ's

---

[1] Cf. John 14:23.
[2] E.g. I Corinthians 3:16 & 6:19.
[3] II Peter 1:4.
[4] I Peter 1:23.
[5] Matthew 5:13.
[6] Ibid. v. 14.
[7] John 3:1ff.
[8] Cf. Romans 6:6.
[9] I Corinthians 15:26 & 54ff.

descent into the tomb by his own descent into the water. And he makes that descent three times in memory of the one day and two nights our Lord spent in the tomb.

Let us now have a look at how the Church prepares these Catechumens for the entry of God into their temple, for this pouring of sacred life into them. This is the perspective from which one must consider the Act of Baptism when carried out completely naked by the Church. No trace of false modesty here, despite the fact that there is a mixed congregation! The sacred mystery of our Lord's incarnation returns that original purity to our bodies in which they existed before the fall of Adam. Our bodies clothe themselves in the purity of the new Adam, Our Lord Jesus Christ, the First-born of all creatures.[1] It was to His image and likeness we were created.[2] The Word was made Flesh through His Conception in Mary's womb and our souls were renewed to the promise of Eternal Life through Him Who is Eternal Life Himself.[3] This Mysticism had cleansed the first Christians of prurient desire which would have drawn a condemnation like the following: "He who looks at Woman as to desire her, he hath already committed adultery with her in his heart."[4]

We have an interesting extant account of the Easter ceremonies at Jerusalem written by a high-born Galician about the year 400 A.D. This man, Etherie by name, describes what he saw during the night from Easter Saturday to Sunday. The candidates for baptism go into the baptistery and remove their clothing. Consecrated oil is then rubbed into their bodies "from the tip of their heads to their toes." Each then descends into the sacred bath and dips completely three times in the name of the Father, Son and Holy Ghost. This rite symbolizes the three days Christ spent in the tomb and His resurrection. The newly baptized, called "Neophytes," are clothed in white, symbolizing their fresh purity of the soul. They wear their baptismal tunic during the whole of Easter Week.

This report confirms Cyril of Jerusalem's *catecheses*: "The Chosen are entirely stripped of their clothing but care

---

[1] Cf. Colossians 1:15.
[2] Cf. Genesis 1:26f.
[3] Cf. John 11:25 & 14:6.
[4] Matthew 5:28.

is taken to prevent awkward situations from arising. Men are taken care of by a member of the clergy while women are tended by women (Canon 114 of Hippolytus), or else they are looked after by deaconesses."[1] This seems to be confirmed by the existence of a side oratory at the baptistery of St. John Lateran in Rome called "*ad S. Joannem ad vestem.*" Apparently, they undressed there. But a second symmetrical oratory was doubtless for the men, the other for the women.

The *apostolic Constitutions* [of St. Hippolytus of Rome] are more precise: "The deaconess is a woman who proves very useful especially when women are being baptized. The deacon himself anoints the forehead with oil and the deaconess rubs the remainder of the body very thoroughly, as men are forbidden to rub the women's bodies."[2] On seeing a group of naked people awaiting baptism, who either followed one another in single file into the baptistery (children, men and women, in that order) or else stood nude together at the side of a river, St. Cyril of Jerusalem called out, "Oh! Miracles! You were naked before the eyes of all and were not ashamed. Verily you carried within yourselves the picture of Adam who was naked and unashamed in paradise!"

St. Cyril cannot understand why "anyone should blush at seeing someone naked at baptism, when it signifies the renewal of Adam & Eve's innocence."

Complete nudity was not the rule everywhere however. St. John Chrysostom (d. 407 A.D.) reports that sometimes people kept a tunic on. But the Church, looking beyond the symbolism of the innocence of Adam & Eve, perceives in the chosen the naked figure of Jesus Himself on the cross, He Who did not vilify but sanctified our flesh. Naked and exposed like the dead and buried Jesus, the Christian enters the water (the grave). As a new man he steps out again, purified, cleansed, full of the promise of Christ's resurrection—a living member of his Christ!

---

[1] *Dictionnaire de Theologie Catholique* (French edition), p. 214. Editor's note: The patristic office of "deaconness" is not to be confused with that of "deacons," who not only assisted at baptisms but performed other clerical and liturgical functions as well.
[2] *Apostolic Constitutions*, III, 15-16.

What was the significance of this anointing with oil for which the recipients had to strip naked? The Church consecrated God's living dwellings as she does in the case of every other house of God. (Formerly pagan temples had to be washed and purified before being put in service for the Lord.) Oil specially blessed was used for this consecration. All the bishops blessed this holy oil for baptisms on Holy Thursday. One should not confuse the anointing prior to immersion, with the anointing afterwards. The former was carried out with "holy oil."

When the catechumens had been unclothed, the bishop or a priest poured this oil on the upper part of the breast and the back. Then the deacons or deaconesses (as the case might be) spread the oil in the form of crosses on the limbs. It is easy to perceive in this the dual symbolism of the Temple to exclude every profane usage and the warrior who can slip out of the clutches of his enemy (Satan) by covering his body with oil.[1]

The children led the procession, men and women following, in that order. They proceeded to the water and entered it naked, one by one their bodies glistening with oil. The male and female sponsors[2] held them by the hand while the bishop, priests and deacons dipped their hands into the water at the same time pronouncing the sacred words which turned these beings of flesh into children of God.

But another anointing awaited them when they left the water. This time it signified that the recipients should become perfect Christians by partaking in the priesthood[3] and the kingdom of Jesus Christ.

---

[1] Editor's note: Since ancient soldiery contained much hand-to-hand combat, before battle all soldiers would liberally oil their bodies. Like modern body-builders, this also helped to accentuate their muscularity, which had (hopefully) an intimidating effect on their enemies. Ancient competitive wrestlers also did this.

[2] Editor's note: i.e. godparents.

[3] Editor's note: The Catholic Church teaches that all baptized Christians have a share in the priesthood of Christ (cf. I Peter 2:5 & 9; Revelation 1:6 & 5:10), although from the many called to this general priesthood of the laity, few are chosen to Holy Orders, which confers a more intense sharing of Christ's sacerdotal powers such as to forgive sins in His Name (cf. John 20:22) and offer the Eucharistic sacrifice of the altar (cf. Luke 22:19). Also see *The Catechism of the Catholic Church*, N. 1546-1547 & 1591.

Who gave these anointings? Generally it was the bishop. It was his obligation in the case of men and women who wished to dedicate their purity to God. In this case oil was not used, but a special holy chrism which was a mixture of ointment and olive oil, also consecrated by a bishop on Holy Thursday. This fragrant substance gives the ceremony its title of "chrismation." The person was anointed on the forehead first so that "he might never be ashamed of the cross," then on the ears "so that he may hear the sacred mysteries," then in the nostrils "so that he may perceive the sacred fragrance, then on the breast "as the armor plate of honesty which repels the blows of wickedness." Is not this the way bishops, priests and kings were consecrated in both the Old and the New Testaments?

Does not the Christian in whom Jesus Christ lives on among men[1] and who "exudes the divine fragrance of Jesus Christ,"[2] supernaturally conceived from divine seed,[3] bear the same name as his divine Master, that is to say—"anointed"?

Surely it must astonish everyone who sees what honor the Church accords the naked bodies of her children? The Church has also arranged for the body to be incensed at solemn Masses and burials. She wants to see therein a vision of Adam's innocence created to God's image. She wants to see the innocent and pure limbs of Jesus born naked, baptized naked, dying naked on the cross and wrapped naked in His white shroud before entering the tomb, before He rose from the dead and drew us all into His glorious resurrection.[4]

How many Christians forget this fact and become accomplices of those who see in the body only shame, as if grace did not exist?

May I quote some texts which will bring applause from all the naturist community?

"The body is not for fornication, but for the Lord, and the Lord for the body... know ye not that your bodies are the limbs of Christ? Am I to take the limbs of Christ for

---

[1] Cf. Galatians 2:9f.
[2] II Corinthians 2:14f.
[3] Cf. I John 3:1-9.
[4] Cf. John 12:32.

fornication? ... Or know ye not that the body is a temple of the Holy Ghost, Who is in you, Whom you have from God, and not yourselves? You have been purchased dearly. Praise ye therefore, God in your bodies!"[1]

"For all God's creatures are good and nothing is bad that is received with thankfulness; for it will be sanctified by God's words and prayer."[2]

"To the pure in heart all things are pure; to the impure and the heathen nothing is pure."[3]

"You are all Children of Light and Children of Day; we are neither from the night nor the darkness. Let us not sleep therefore like the others but let us awake and be sober."[4]

"But He, the Lord of Peace, will sanctify you; and your mind, soul and body must be preserved unsullied for the future of our Lord Jesus Christ."[5]

Is not all that in the sense of our Lord's words?

"Let your light shine before men that they may see your good works and honor your Father in heaven."[6]

"The eye is the light of the body. If the eye is simple, the body will be bright."[7]

"And when your body is as brightness having no part of darkness, then it is brightness indeed."[8]

Is it not a real joy for every Christian to be able to find again the grace of the wonderful balance of the Garden of Eden before Original Sin came into the world? There is no doubt that those who live in naturist camps find a marvelous support for the balance of their soul and body in healthy, natural surroundings. Is it not the pure of heart that will see God?[9] The Christians in naturist parks may easily find God's image in their naked brothers and sisters beneath the trees or in the water. They certainly believe in the fall of Adam and its consequences. They know how difficult it is to get rid of the "Old Adam" in them. They

---

[1] I Corinthians 6:13-20.
[2] I Timothy 6:4-5.
[3] Titus 1:15.
[4] I Thessalonians 5:5.
[5] Ibid. v. 23.
[6] Matthew 5:16.
[7] Ibid. 6:22.
[8] Luke 11:36.
[9] Cf. Matthew 5:8.

know what a painful struggle must ensue if one is to rise each day as a new man redeemed by Christ. But they believe in grace. Are not lies the consequence of the fall? Does not vice often masquerade as virtue (e.g. our Lord's diatribes against the Pharisees)? Is it not this very lie which strikes our contemporaries so blind as to allow indecent fashions and permit the semi-nakedness of film, play and magazine? Is it not this very lie which causes confusion in their minds about the naturalness, sweetness and innocence of complete nudity which signifies a steady, loyal, brotherly life of purity? This is a cause of astonishment to those who can perceive it and a cause of joy to those who can find their way to the Savior once again through His first book of nature and who can find support in the Bible as in holy traditions which are all too soon forgotten.

The Apostolic Tradition

by St. Hippolytus of Rome

Editor's note: Also known as The Apostolic Constitutions, this is probably the oldest (c. 215 A.D.) extant patristic document describing details of ancient ecclesiastical life and worship. I am indebted to Kevin P. Edgecomb for this translation from the Latin.[1] Reprinted here with permission. ©2000 Kevin P. Edgecomb.

We have set forth as was necessary that part of the discourse which relates to the spiritual gifts, all that God, right from the beginning, granted to people according to his will, bringing back to himself this image which had gone astray. Now, driven by love towards all the saints, we

---

[1] Translator's note: My translation here is based on the work of Bernard Botte ("La Tradition Apostolique" in *Sources Chretiennes*, 11 bis. Paris, Editions du Cerf, 1984) and of Gregory Dix (*The Treatise on the Apostolic Tradition of St. Hippolytus of Rome, Bishop and Martyr*. London: Alban Press, 1992). My version (which it certainly is) is intended as a simplified one for ease of reading, directed primarily towards the non-expert. The complete translation can be found at:
www.bombaxo.com/hippolytus.html.

have arrived at the essence of the tradition which is proper for the Churches. This is so that those who are well informed may keep the tradition which has lasted until now, according to the explanation we give of it, and so that others by taking note of it may be strengthened (against the fall or error which has recently occurred because of ignorance and ignorant people), with the Holy Spirit conferring perfect grace on those who have a correct faith, and so that they will know that those who are at the head of the Church must teach and guard all these things. [Editor's note: Ordinations of bishops, priests, etc. omitted.] When they are chosen who are to receive baptism, let their lives be examined, whether they have lived honorably while catechumens, whether they honored the widows, whether they visited the sick, and whether they have done every good work. If those who bring them forward bear witness for them that they have done so, then let them hear the Gospel. From the time at which they are set apart, place hands upon them daily so that they are exorcised. When the day approaches on which they are to be baptized, let the bishop exorcise each one of them, so that he will be certain whether each has been purified. If there are any who are not purified, they shall be set apart. They have not heard the Word in faith, for the foreign spirit remained with each of them. Let those who are to be baptized be instructed that they bathe and wash on the fifth day of the week. If a woman is in the manner of women, let her be set apart and receive baptism another day. Those who are to receive baptism shall fast on the Preparation of the Sabbath. On the Sabbath, those who are to receive baptism shall all gather together in one place chosen according to the will of the bishop. They shall be commanded to pray and kneel. Then, laying his hand on them, he will exorcise every foreign spirit, so that they flee from them and never return to them. When he has finished exorcising them, he shall breathe on their faces and seal their foreheads, ears and noses. Then he shall raise them up. They shall all keep vigil all night, reading and instructing them. Those who are to be baptized are not to bring any vessel, only that which each brings for the Eucharist. It is indeed proper that each bring the oblation in the same hour... At the hour in which the cock crows, they shall first pray over the water. When they come to the water, the water shall be pure and flowing, that is, the water of a spring or a flowing body of water. Then they shall take off all their clothes. The children shall be baptized first. All of the children who can answer for themselves, let them answer. If there are any children who cannot answer for themselves, let their parents answer for them, or someone else from their family. After this, the men will be baptized. Finally, the women, after they have unbound their hair, and removed their jewelry. No one shall take any foreign object with themselves down into the water. At the time determined for baptism, the bishop shall give thanks over some oil, which he puts in a vessel. It is called the Oil of Thanksgiving. He shall take some more oil and exorcise it. It is called the Oil of Exorcism. A deacon shall hold the Oil of Exorcism and stand on the left. Another deacon shall hold the Oil of Thanksgiving and stand on the right. When the elder takes hold of each of them who are to receive baptism, he shall tell each of them to renounce, saying, "I renounce you Satan, all your services, and all your works." After he has said this, he shall anoint each with the Oil of Exorcism, saying, "Let every evil spirit depart from you." Then, after these things, the bishop passes each of them on nude to the elder who stands at the water. They shall stand in the water naked. A deacon, likewise, will go down with them into the water. When each of them to be baptized has gone down into the water, the one baptizing shall lay hands on each of them, asking, "Do you believe in God the Father Almighty?" And the one being baptized shall answer, "I believe." He shall then baptize each of them once, laying his hand upon each of their heads. Then he shall ask, "Do you believe in Jesus Christ, the Son of God, who was born of the Holy Spirit and the Virgin Mary, who was crucified under Pontius Pilate, and died, and rose on the third day living from the dead, and ascended into heaven, and sat down at the right hand of the Father, the one coming to judge the living and the dead?" When each has answered, "I believe," he shall baptize a second time. Then he shall ask, "Do you believe in the Holy Spirit and the Holy Church and the resurrection of the flesh?" Then each being baptized shall answer, "I believe." And thus let him baptize the third time. Afterward, when they have come up out of the water, they shall be anointed by the elder with the Oil of Thanksgiving, saying, "I anoint you with holy oil in the name of Jesus Christ." Then, drying themselves, they shall dress and afterwards gather in the church. The bishop will then lay his hand upon them, invoking, saying, "Lord God, you who have made these worthy of the removal of sins through the bath of regeneration, make them worthy to be filled with your Holy Spirit, grant to them your grace, that they might serve you according to your will, for to you is the glory, Father and Son with the Holy Spirit, in the Holy Church, now and throughout the ages of the ages. Amen." After this he pours the oil into his hand, and laying his hand on each of their heads, says, "I anoint you with holy oil in God the Father Almighty, and Christ Jesus, and the Holy Spirit." Then, after sealing each of them on the forehead, he shall give them the kiss of peace and say, "The Lord be with you." And the one who has been baptized shall say, "And with your spirit." So shall he do to each one. From then on they will pray together with all the people. Prior to this they may not pray with the faithful until they have completed all. After they pray, let them give the kiss of peace. [Editor's note: Description of the Liturgy of the Eucharist and other prescriptions omitted.] I counsel that these things be observed by all with good understanding. For if all who hear the apostolic tradition follow and keep it, no heretic will be able to introduce error, nor will any other person at all. It is in this manner that the many heresies have grown, for those who were leaders did not wish to inform themselves of the opinion of the apostles, but did what they wanted according to their own pleasure, and not what was appropriate. If we have omitted anything, beloved ones, God will reveal it to those who are worthy, steering Holy Church to her mooring in the quiet haven.

Circumcision:
A Theological View

by Jim C. Cunningham

Why did our loving God ever choose, and adamantly insist upon, circumcision in the first place? Husband and wife seal their covenant through the beautiful act of sexual intercourse. But God had the Jews seal their covenant with Him by having their foreskins cut off, exposing the heads of their penises. Very peculiar—or at least so it seems to me.

Well, one thing we can glean from it all is that our God certainly isn't puritanical. He made the unmentionable the central focal point of His covenant with Abraham. A lot of lectors would blush just by reading what God said:

"On your part, you and your descendants after you must keep My covenant throughout the ages. This is My covenant with you and your descendants after you that you must keep: every male among you shall be circumcised. Circumcise the flesh of your foreskin, and that shall be the mark of the covenant between you and Me... Thus My covenant shall be in your flesh as an everlasting pact. If a male is uncircumcised, that is, if the flesh of his foreskin has not been cut away, such a one shall be cut off from his people; he has broken My covenant."[1]

Along with the institution of this covenant of circumcision, God promised Abraham[2] tremendous fertility.[3] Phallic worship and fertility rites were common among all the non-Jewish peoples among whom Abraham sojourned. Sexual acts were often an integral part of public worship, and the phallus was universally recognized as a symbol of love and fertility. Thus it was fitting that the sign of this covenant have something to do with that particular anatomical part. And it seems that God wanted to impress this covenant on them so much that it had to be perma-

[1] Genesis 17:1-14.
[2] This was also the occasion when God changed Abram's name to "Abraham" (Genesis 17:5).
[3] Cf. Genesis 17:2ff.

nently carved right into their flesh;[1] it would not suffice just to have them wear a necklace symbolizing this covenant. Our God *means business*!

Another interesting observation is that since a sign doesn't have much significance unless it is *seen*, obviously there must have been occasions built into Jewish culture when male genitalia were exposed before the eyes of others in the community. Examples include: bathing, Levitical investiture ceremonies, ritual washing, heavy, perspiring labor, the community latrine, etc. Later, Moses would promulgate laws for every little detail of daily life, but among all this legislation there is never a mandate forbidding mixed, public nudity. In fact, one law specifically required priests to wear breeches, which clearly implies that, unless Moses had stipulated otherwise, they might well have thought nothing of performing those specific liturgical functions bottomless, and that bottomlessness in everyday life must have been routine enough to require proscribing it for these particular priestly duties.[2]

In fact, the Jews took particular pride in their circumcision. It meant that they were God's Chosen People. They were not merely a race among races; they were the *Chosen Race—God's* Race. To the ancient Jewish mind there were only two kinds of people—the circumcised and the non-circumcised. They must have been *proud* to show forth the sign of their special covenant!

Further proof that Jewish genitalia were sometimes on public display is found in a curious mention in I Maccabees 1:15. When *Antiochus Epiphanes* became head of the vast Greek Empire he tried to ram Hellenic customs down everyone's throats, including the Jews. He even had a Greek gymnasium built in Jerusalem (Moses hadn't thought to ask God about the regulations for discus throwing!). Many Jews apostatized and accepted these Greek customs. They even became ashamed of their circumcision and tried to hide it, not because they were embarrassed to expose their phalluses in public, but because they were ashamed to be identified as Jews. Of

---

[1] Cf. Sirach 44:21.
[2] Cf. Exodus 28:42f.

course, the Greeks required nudity in the gym,[1] and so one couldn't hide in gym shorts or even a jock strap. So what did these turncoat Jews do? The Latin Vulgate Bible has: "they made foreskins for themselves." And in case you suspect that they simply glued on a make-believe, "plastic" prepuce, a reference in I Corinthians 7:18 makes it quite clear. Both the Vulgate and the Greek New Testament render St. Paul's words as follows: "If you were circumcised when you were called, do not try to stretch down (or draw down) the prepuce." This clearly refers to some type of ancient cosmetic surgery (as if the mutilation wasn't bad enough the first time around!). In the Maccabean account it is interesting to note that the Bible does not at all condemn their *nudity*, but their *being ashamed* of their circumcision.

So the sight of the circumcised heads of every phallus was commonplace enough in the ancient Jewish world that it was a most significant, visible sign of their covenant with God. Even hundreds of years later, in St. Paul's day, it was so customary to see men's genitals that he had St. Timothy circumcised[2] for political expediency. It is hard for us today to imagine that it would have been impossible to hide one's genitals so no one could know whether you were circumcised or not. Anachronistic as it is, compare St. Paul and St. Timothy to Billy Graham and his evangelist assistant. Do you think it would be problematic for Billy to keep his assistant's genitals private (well, maybe if he were Jimmy Baker...!)? In the contemporary context it seems ridiculous, but that is because, unfortunately, our culture has become so pervertedly and unnaturally clothes-compulsive.

As we all know, there is a great deal of anti-Semitism in Russia. Over there, circumcision really has significance. I have spent a few months in Russia and have visited plenty of steam baths there. None of the Russian men in the baths were circumcised. A Russian Jew would not dare to visit the baths. Some of my circumcised American friends (not all Jews—Americans don't need a religious excuse for it; we do it out of blind deference to convention)

---

[1] Editor's note: "Gymnasium" comes from the Greek word for "nude"—"gymnos."
[2] Cf. Acts 16:1-3.

sensed how they were contemptuously treated and it finally dawned on us that it was because they were circumcised and were thereby mistaken to be Jews. I am not circumcised because my Jewish pediatrician knew it was neither medically nor religiously necessary for me, but after puberty, the growth of my foreskin did not keep pace with the rest of my penis, resulting in such a short foreskin that all but the left corona[1] of my glans is always naturally exposed. It took me several weeks before I figured out why so many Russian men approached me in the baths, asking me if I were a Jew (I was about to develop a complex over it!) Those Russian baths gave me a real taste for what it must have been like for the ancient Jews in the time of Antiochus Epiphanes.

St. Paul makes an interesting mention of circumcision in I Corinthians 7:18f:

"Was anyone circumcised when he was called? Let him not stretch down the prepuce. Was anyone with prepuce when he was called? Let him not get circumcised. Circumcision is nothing, and having the prepuce intact is nothing. The only thing that matters is the observation of the mandates of God."[2]

On Nudity in Art

by Pope John Paul II[3]

In the course of the various eras, beginning from antiquity, and above all, in the great period of Greek classical art, there are works of art whose subject is the human body in its nakedness. The contemplation of this makes it possible to concentrate, in a way, on the whole truth of man, on the dignity and beauty, also the supra-sensual beauty of his masculinity and femininity. These works bear within them, almost hidden, an element of sublimation. This leads the viewer, through the body, to the whole

---

[1] The ridge at the back of the glans where it meets the shaft.
[2] Editor's note: Translation mine, from the Vulgate.
[3] Excerpt from his General Audience of May 6, 1981, reprinted in *Our Sunday Visitor*, August 21, 2005.

personal mystery of man. But there are also works of art and perhaps, more often, reproductions, which arouse objections in the sphere of man's personal sensitivity. This is not because of their object, since the human body in itself always has its inalienable dignity. But it is because of the *quality* or *way* of its reproduction, portrayal or artistic representation.

Jesus: After the Resurrection

by Harold Whitington

Jesus was crucified on a cross for the sins of the world. After receiving permission from Pilate,[1] Joseph and Nicodemus took the body and prepared it for burial with over 100 pounds of myrrh and aloes. Wrapping it in linen cloths they took it to a nearby garden wherein was a sepulchre that had never been used. There they placed the body of Jesus. After rolling a great stone to the door of the sepulchre, they departed.

Four women watched from afar in tears and grief. They were Mary Magdalene, Mary the wife of Cleopas, the mother of James and Joses, who was also a sister of Mary, the mother of Jesus, Joanna and Salome, the mother of James and John. These four followed Him throughout Judea and Galilee ministering to His needs, washing His robe and bathing His body, preparing His food and helping Him in any way possible.

Upon the first day of the week, very early in the morning, these four came to the sepulchre and found the stone rolled away. Entering swiftly they found it empty. The body of Jesus was gone. Suddenly two men stood by them in shining garments. Trembling and full of fear they bowed their heads to the ground. One of them spoke, "Why seek ye the living among the dead? He is not here but is risen."[2] Hastily they returned to the apostles and His followers, perplexed and baffled by the words of the man and the disappearance of the body. When told that the body was

---

[1] Cf. John 19:38ff; Luke 23:50ff; Mark 15:43ff & Matthew 27:57ff.
[2] Cf. Luke 24:5ff; Mark 16:6ff; Matthew28:6ff.

gone, John and Peter ran to the sepulchre[1] and, stooping down, they entered and saw the linen cloths laying there and the napkin that was about His head.

Peter and John returned to their homes, but Mary Magdalene, who loved Jesus very much, could not leave. She had been with Him constantly for two years, ministering to His every need, watching over Him like a mother. She stood at the entrance weeping and looked back into the sepulchre with longing. "Jesus, my Jesus, where are You?" Suddenly two angels appeared in white, sitting, one at the head and one at the feet of where Jesus had lain. "Woman, why weepest thou?" "Because they have taken away my Lord and I know not where they have laid Him." Turning slightly, she noticed a man with no clothing standing nearby. Supposing him to be the gardener,[2] she said, "Sir, if thou hast taken Him, please tell me where thou hast laid Him and I will take Him away."

"Mary," the man spoke. She opened her eyes in amazement. It was Jesus. She ran toward Him and was about to throw her arms around Him. "No, no, please, don't touch Me, not now, I must go unto My Father first. You go and tell Peter and John and the brethren that you saw Me and that I am alive." Turning, she ran back as fast as she could and told them she had talked with Jesus. They looked at her in astonishment. Jesus alive? They had seen Him hanging on the cross. How could that be possible? "I tell you, Jesus is alive. I talked with Him.'

Cleopas and his wife, Mary, were in a quandary.[3] They had been so sure that Jesus was the promised King, that the government would be upon His shoulders,[4] that He would rule on the throne of David even forever. How could this happen? It seemed all their hopes were smashed.

How could He possibly have let the Romans kill Him? And now the body had been stolen. Sadly they started the long walk home. "I wonder who he could be?" "Hard to tell. Shepherds usually have a long robe to keep warm. They sleep in the field with the sheep but this man is nude."

---

[1] Cf. John 20:3ff.
[2] Cf. John 20:15.
[3] Cf. Luke 24:11ff.
[4] Cf. Isaiah 9:6f.

The man soon joined them and walked along in silence, but Cleopas and his wife couldn't keep their minds off of Jesus. As they talked, the man broke in, "What are you talking about? And why are you so sad?"

"You must be a stranger in Jerusalem. Don't you know what has just happened?" He answered, "No, suppose you tell Me." "About Jesus of Nazareth. He was a prophet. Mighty in deed and word. He healed the sick, fed the hungry and raised the dead. He was crucified three days ago by the Romans. This morning Mary Magdalene and I went to the sepulchre and found it empty. A young man sat on the right side and told us that He had risen and we would see Him."

"Believe Him. The prophets tell of Christ and His sufferings. Isaiah says He was led as a lamb to the slaughter.[1] It was necessary for Christ to die to enter into His glory."[2] As they drew nigh the village, the Man kept on going but Cleopas stopped Him. "Please Sir, won't You stop by with us for a while? We will have supper and You can rest and if You like we would be glad for You to stay the night."

Whereupon Jesus went in with them and when they sat down to eat, He took a piece of bread and blessed it and their eyes were opened and they knew Him. Before either could speak, He vanished out of their sight.

Returning to Jerusalem, they found the apostles and told of what had happened. While they were yet speaking, the nude body of Jesus appeared in the midst of them.[3] All but Cleopas and Mary were terrified, supposing Him to be a ghost,[4] but Jesus only smiled. "A ghost doesn't have flesh like you see I have. You can see the hole in My side and the nail prints in My hands and feet. Have you got any meat?"

They gave Him broiled fish and honeycomb and He ate. Thomas moved closer, he had been standing at the rear with doubt on his face. His eyes were riveted on the wound in His side. Reaching Jesus, he groped with his

---

[1] Cf. Isaiah 53:7.
[2] Cf. Luke 24:26.
[3] Cf. John 20:19ff.
[4] Cf. Luke 24:36ff.

hand, touched the flesh and felt where the spear had torn the hole in His side.

"My Lord and my God," he stammered.[1]

Jesus circulated among His followers and the people for forty days,[2] teaching of Himself and God, His father.

There is no reason to assume that Jesus [after the resurrection] ever wore any clothing or covering whatsoever. He lost everything when He was crucified. At one time, He talked to a group of over five hundred people.[3] They accepted Him as He was. When Jesus was assembled with His loved ones in Jerusalem and as they looked on, He was taken up and a cloud received him out of their sight.[4] If He had been wearing anything, it would have been left behind as the mantle of Elijah fell from him when he was caught up in a whirlwind.[5]

The Bible & Nudism

by Rev. La Rue C. Watson[6]

Many sincere Christians are, or would like to be, nudists. Naturally and properly, they are concerned with the Biblical attitude toward the subject. This is expressed both positively and negatively in the Bible. What the Bible *does not* say about nudity speaks as loudly as what it *does* say. Nudity seemed to be simply accepted as a commonplace condition, with no thought of immorality, and nothing to argue about.

The term, "nudity," is used in this article as it expresses a condition of the body, whereas "nudism" implies a general movement or organization along this line, which of course did not exist in Bible times.

It is common knowledge that the Greek and Roman "games" or athletic contests, of New Testament times were

---

[1] Cf. John 20:26ff.

[2] Cf. Acts 1:3.

[3] Cf. I Corinthians 15:6.

[4] Cf. Acts 1:9.

[5] Cf. II Kings 2:1ff.

[6] Reprinted from *American Sunbather* magazine.

conducted nude, by both males and females, in order that athletic effort might not be hampered in the least degree by clothing. New Testament writers refer to these contests as illustrations of phases of the Christian life, but there is not a hint of criticism of the nudity of the events.

Examples are I Corinthians 9:24: "Know ye not that they that run in a race run all, but one receiveth the prize? Even so run; that ye may attain.", and Hebrews 12:1: "Therefore let us also, seeing we are compassed about with so great a cloud of witnesses, lay aside every weight (encumbrance) and the sin which doth so easily beset us, and let us run with patience the race that is set before us." In this latter quotation, "lay aside every weight" makes clear and direct reference to the removal of the clothes by the athletes, with only commendation of the act as a symbol of the Christian life.

Crucifixion was a common method of execution in New Testament times. Jesus' case was typical. As He hanged nude on the cross, according to Mark 15:24, they "...parted His garments among them, casting lots upon them, what each should take." John 19:23-24 says of the same event, "The soldiers therefore, when they had crucified Jesus, took His garments and made four parts, to every soldier a part; and also the coat: now the coat was without seam, woven from the top throughout. They said therefore one to another, Let us not rend it, but cast lots for it."

A mixed company of men and women were gathered near the cross, but there was no hint of immodesty or indecency on their part.

As Jesus' body was removed from the cross at the beginning of the Jewish Sabbath, it was hurriedly placed temporarily in a tomb without embalming. Luke 23:55 says: "And the women who had come with Him out of Galilee, followed after, and beheld the tomb, and how His body was laid. And they returned, and prepared spices and ointments. And on the Sabbath they rested according to the commandment." Luke 24:1 continues, "But on the first day of the week, at early dawn, they came unto the tomb, bringing spices which they had prepared." Essentially the same is stated in Mark 16:1. To carry out this plan, they would have to see and handle His nude body, yet there is not the least implication in the story of any immodesty or indecency—only loving devotion.

Garments were often shed in public for strenuous activity, such as the stoning of Stephen. Acts 7:18 says of this, "and they cast him out of the city, and stoned him: and the witnesses laid down their garments at the feet of a young man named Saul." There were no moral implications regarding the nudity. It was simply accepted as just a matter of practical convenience.

Garments were removed from the victims for the purpose of public beatings, as recorded in Acts 16:22: "And the multitudes rose up together against them: and the magistrates rent their garments off them, and commanded to beat them with rods." To lay the whip most effectively on the condemned person, it was of course necessary to remove his clothing. This was in the presence of a large crowd, but again, it was just a practical matter, with no moral reflections on the factor of nudity.

Nudity seems to have been common among poor people in New Testament times, as indicated by the following sample passages:

I Corinthians 4:11: "Even unto this present hour we both hunger and thirst, and are naked, and are buffeted, and have no certain dwelling place."

James 2:15: "If a brother or sister be naked and in lack of daily food..."

Romans 8:35: "Who shall separate us from the love of Christ? Shall tribulation, or anguish, or persecution, or famine, or nakedness, or peril, or sword?" The writer goes on to develop the idea that neither nakedness nor any of these other things can "separate us from the love of God."

Speaking of Jesus, Luke 8:27 says: "And when He was come forth upon the land, there met Him a certain man out of the city, who had demons; and for a long time he had worn no clothes, and abode not in any house, but in the tombs." True, the story says the man was insane, but his nudity was merely an incidental fact, causing neither embarrassment to anyone, nor criticism. Nudity of the poor in New Testament times was never the subject of criticism; it was simply stated as one of the common hardships of poverty.

The Old Testament also presents nudity as one of the common hardships of the poor, with no criticism on moral grounds. Job 24:7 says: "They lie all night naked without clothing, and have no covering in the cold." Job 24:10 continues: "So that they go about naked without clothing, and being hungry they carry the sheaves." Isaiah 58:7 admonishes, "When thou seest the naked, that thou cover him." This act of charity was for the comfort of the recipient, not because of "modesty." Deuteronomy 28:48 warns: "Therefore shalt thou serve thine enemies, that Jehovah shall send against thee, in hunger, and in thirst, and in nakedness, and in want of all things." Here again nakedness is considered as simply one of the commonplace factors in poverty.

II Chronicles 28:15 implies that nudity was very common in those days. It was a cause of discomfort in cold weather, but not a matter of shame. The writer says: "And the men that have been mentioned by name rose up, and took the captives, and with the spoil clothed all that were naked among them, and arrayed them, and shod them, and gave them to eat and to drink."

In New Testament times clothing seemed to be considered a mere matter of adornment, comfort, convenience or choice, to be freely discarded when it got in the way. For example, note this casual statement in Mark 10:50: "And he (the blind man), casting away his garment, sprang up, and came to Jesus." No criticism of his nudity was even implied.

At the Last Supper, according to the thirteenth chapter of John, Jesus "layeth aside His garments" to wash the disciples' feet as a symbol of humble service.

Peter was nude among his companions in the boat as they fished on the Sea of Galilee. John 21:7 records quite casually: "That disciple therefore whom Jesus loved saith unto Peter, 'It is the Lord.' So when Simon Peter heard that it was the Lord, he girt his coat about him, for he was naked, and cast himself into the sea."

When the Bible speaks of someone rending or removing his garment, the reader may think, "Oh, well, it was probably only an outer garment. He doubtless had other clothing underneath." However, that was often not the case. In the above quotation, it is said that Peter was "naked" until he put on his coat. In the following case, the young man definitely had nothing under his outer garment but his naked body. Mark 14:51-52 says: "And a certain young man followed with Him (Jesus), having a linen cloth cast about him, over his naked body: and they hold on him; and he left the linen cloth, and fled naked."

Baptism was a religious rite long before the Christian era. It had three principal forms: sprinkling, pouring and immersion. In any form, it was a symbol of spiritual cleansing and a dedication to a certain form of belief and life. It was quite natural that first John the Baptist and then Jesus' followers, with Jesus' sanction, should adopt the ritual. Immersion was commonly practiced in the nude as a matter of practical convenience, and there is no reason to believe that early Christian baptism departed from this custom. The cult of the "obscene" body came later.

Jesus took a rather positive attitude toward nudity in Matthew 6:25 & 28-29 when He said: "Therefore I say unto you, Be not anxious for your life, what ye shall eat, or what ye shall drink; nor yet for your body, what ye shall put on. Is not the life more than the food, and the body than the raiment? And why are ye anxious concerning raiment? Consider the lilies of the field, how they grow; they toil not, neither do they spin (make clothes): yet I say unto you, that even Solomon in all his glory was not arrayed like one of these." Here Jesus very clearly and definitely commends unclothed beauty in contrast to the gorgeous clothing of the king. The above quotation from Matthew is similar to the record in Luke 12:22-23 & 27.

As to the sacredness of the human body, Paul in I Corinthians 6:19, says: "Or know ye not that your body is a temple of the Holy Spirit which is in you, which ye have from God?" How do we dare to call the temple of the Holy Spirit "obscene" or "indecent"? And it is nothing less than sacrilege to call God's handiwork "filthy." Along this line, Paul writes in I Corinthians 12:22-23: "Nay, much rather, those members of the body which seem to be more feeble are necessary: and those parts of the body, which we think to be less honorable, upon these we bestow more abundant honor; and our comely parts have more abundant comeliness."

Paul, in Romans 14:14 made the very practical statement: "I know and am persuaded in the Lord Jesus, that nothing is unclean of itself: save that to him who accounteth anything to be unclean, to him it is unclean." This agrees with the nudist idea that "nothing is unclean" about the human body except what we think about it or what we do with it, and clothing does not prevent thinking or doing.

We are told in Acts 10:14, "But Peter said, 'Not so, Lord; for I have never eaten anything that is common and unclean.' And a voice came unto him again the second time, 'What God hath cleansed, make not thou common.'"

Genesis 2:25 says of Adam & Eve: "And they were both naked, the man and his wife, and were not ashamed." This ideal state continued, according to the record, until a guilty conscience about other matters caused them to try to hide behind aprons of fig leaves. Then in Genesis 3:9-11 it is recorded, "And Jehovah God called unto the man, and said unto him, 'Where art thou?' And he said, 'I heard Thy voice in the garden, and I was afraid, because I was naked: and I hid myself.' And He said, 'Who told thee that thou wast naked? Hast thou eaten of the tree, whereof I commanded thee that thou shouldst not eat?'" Here is a clear implication that nudity is clean and proper and innocent. The story even represents God as criticizing Adam & Eve for trying to hide their nudity.

Nudity seems to have been a common practice among the Hebrew prophets, as it is today among some of the oriental "Holy Men." This is indicated in I Samuel 19:24: "And he (Saul) also stripped off his clothes, and he also prophesied before Samuel, and lay down naked all that day and all that night. Wherefore they say, 'Is Saul also among the prophets?'"

Where it occurs at all, Bible criticism of nudity is practically always when it is associated with sexual immorality, and is used as a symbol of such immorality.

I have visited many nudist parks and have never seen any conduct that would be out of place at a Sunday school picnic. Average moral standards among nudists are far above the average of non-nudists. Juvenile delinquency is very rare among nudist children and youth. The same cannot be said of non-nudists.

At a nudist park one sees people going about very much as at any picnic park, except that they are without clothes. But what difference does that make? Everyone knows what everyone else looks like anyhow, and clothes never proved a serious barrier to evil thoughts or deeds. In fact, immorality and sex crimes are often stimulated, rather than prevented, by clothes.

At a nudist park, one sees people going about, playing volleyball, horseshoes, miniature golf, tether ball, table tennis, and other games, hiking, swimming, sun-lazing, reading, chatting, working jigsaw puzzles, preparing and eating picnic lunches and other normal and wholesome activities, with no evidence of curiosity about other people's bodies or self-consciousness about their own. This is difficult to understand by one who has not had an experience of nudism, but, usually seems perfectly natural to the newcomer within a few minutes after entering the nudist world.

The bodies of patients of both sexes are seen and handled by doctors and nurses of both sexes without any implication of immorality. Parents see and handle the bodies of their young children of both sexes without any hint of wrongdoing. Husbands and wives practice complete nudity before each other. Why cannot the area of nude practice be expanded to include everyone? In many parts of the world, mixed bathing is common practice.

Frankly nude pictures and statues by some of the world's great artists adorn the walls, ceilings and corridors of many of the world's greatest Christian cathedrals and the Roman Vatican. This is generally accepted without question. The artists of all lands and all ages have considered the human body not as obscene, but one of the most beautiful and graceful subjects of art. No art gallery is complete without a group of nudes.

I do not feel that I am leading a double life. My conscience is clear on the subject. I do not believe that, as I have seen it practiced, there is anything immoral, un-Christian or un-Biblical about nudism. On the other hand, it fosters a clean, wholesome attitude toward the human body and toward the subject of sex, and greatly reduces juvenile delinquency and sex crimes. It helps to create clean minds in healthy bodies, and encourages high standards of thought and conduct. What can be wrong with that?

Streakers & Prophets

by Jim C. Cunningham

In 1973, while at the University of Massachusetts (Amherst), I experienced a radical conversion back to Christianity and, months later, to Catholicism. One of my friends who witnessed this change in me was a very popular student (president of the Greek system), intelligent, morally upright and spiritual. He used to go on Catholic retreats often, and even helped to lead them.

Perhaps feeling a bit guilty, one day he confided in me that he had done a solo streak in Amherst on a dare suggested by one of his frat brothers (these were the days when hundreds of students would streak en masse). At the time I was not a nudist, and told him that I thought he had done wrong because he failed to take into consideration innocent bystanders who might have been offended by his nudity. In other words, I considered the situation solely from the point of view of social propriety.

Years later, as a nudist, I reconsidered my friend's situation, and concurred with my previous judgment for the same reasons.

Then I saw Franco Zefferelli's movie about St. Francis of Assisi, "Brother Sun, Sister Moon." In it Francis strips naked in the town square in front of everybody—his family, the ecclesiastics, the townsfolk.

This was certainly improper behavior, apparently certainly unbecoming of a saint! But I realized that Francis was a prophet—a teacher—and that his message was greater than propriety. Prophets often interrupt propriety in order to get attention and deliver a powerful message. Francis' prophetic message was that all things really come from God our Father, and not from human beings. Pietro Bernardone, Francis' earthly father, was behaving in such a way that would usurp honor and gratitude due to God alone. Francis' nudity had great shock value. Even had he not preached a great sermon on the innocent trust of the lilies of the field and the birds of the air, his mere act of public nudity would have said it all. So I concluded that Francis' public nudity was not wrong. In his scale of values, propriety was less than prophecy. He had "prophetic license."

Subsequently, I reexamined the case of modern streaking. Although the motives of the streakers seemed far less solemn than Francis', I realized that it was really a prophetic statement. Society is wrong in its emphasis on clothing. As Jesus said, "As for clothes, why be concerned?"[1] Society is dead wrong in regarding the body in a negative way. Streaking is a positive, prophetic statement that says clothes don't matter, we are beautiful, and we're sick of the stupid oppressiveness of so-called "propriety."

So now, upon further reconsideration, I do not think that my friend did wrong in dashing nude around Amherst, and if he wants to do it again, this time I'll join him!

The Nudification of Culture

by Jim C. Cunningham

We naturists are often told that good nude beach etiquette means not straying from areas designated (by whom?) as nude. Supposedly, the purpose is not to aggravate the textiles and thereby perhaps lose the little we have.

That is, indeed, one approach—that of those whose naturism is motivated by recreational reasons. They are not out primarily to change culture, but to enjoy themselves in the state of dress that they prefer—nude. There is nothing wrong with this. However, there is another very valid approach which contradicts this. Those of us who primarily seek cultural change are among those who disagree.

---

[1] Matthew 6:28.

Our culture says nudity is "obscene, dirty, immodest and lewd." In order to change that culture we must show that this is not true.

Nude beaches and nudist parks show little or nothing. They only "preach to the choir." Instead, we need to show dignified, clean, modest and chaste nudity in ordinary, everyday situations to the non-naturists around us.

This does not mean that we must look for trouble. Such courage and activism can be misplaced and actually prove counterproductive. For example, I'm not suggesting going to work nude today.

I believe the situation can be compared to the controversy over civil rights for blacks of not too long ago. In many ways some naturists are like some timid blacks who were quite content to sit at the back of the bus—after all, at least they got to ride it, and surely it was a lot better than slavery!

But meekly waiting for a scrap to be cast our way is not going to win the respect of those who would keep us in that subordinate position, and surely we are not going to change them. Rather, we must hold our heads high and live according to the truth of nudity's goodness.

I once read an article entitled "Progress at Bondi," by Andrew Wayland.[1] It featured three photos of a woman in a G-string monokini. My initial reaction was that it was immodest. I thought, "If you want to go nude, then go *nude*!"

But I began to ruminate on it further. Maybe she couldn't go nude, or maybe she liked Bondi Beach enough to compromise and at least go as nude as could be tolerated there, hoping for (and truly and effectively ushering in) the day when she would be able to rewind that G-string onto her Yo-yo.

The fact of the matter is that the G-string was then the barest she could reasonably get at Bondi, and since it is certainly preferable to be as bare as possible while swimming and sunning, she did it. Thinking thus anew, I came to understand that that clothed (albeit scantily) lady was the true naturist. In fact, she might be far more naturist then women who go totally nude, but only at established places. (And who do these timid women think

---

[1] *Australian Sun & Health*, No. 15, pp. 8f.

established them in the first place?) The G-string can be truly naturist.

Beaches don't get nude overnight. But it's the likes of that lady in the skimpy G-string who will eventually accustom the textile public to innocent nudity in non-sexual situations.

Some people say that nowadays it's okay to wear a bi-kini because it's now quite acceptable, but they would call the girl who was the first to do it a "slut," "exhibitionist," or some other pejorative label. Jesus said a good tree bears good fruit,[1] so if bikinis are good today, then the root of the style (i.e. some brave and perhaps very chaste girl starting it) must also be good. Once again this means that the only logical definition of immodesty must include the *intent* to arouse others. You cannot define immodesty by merely what one wears or where he wears it, but by what he intends by it. Jesus said it's what comes out of the heart of man that is evil—lust, etc.[2] So bare trend-setters cannot be immodest unless they mentally *intend* to be.

The same argument for the G-string goes for obvious bralessness, etc. The first girl to ungird her breasts was probably considered "loose" by many. Now, however, it is a common sight and no one thinks the more of it, thanks to those courageous pioneers.

So that woman at Bondi may not have intended to draw attention to her scantily clad "sexual parts," but may simply have wanted to go as nude as possible because it was most logical, relaxing, or whatever. This is the kind of real naturism this article is about. These are the real naturists who are effectively changing cultural attitudes towards the naked body while card-carrying naturists who are content with their ghettoes (i.e. private clubs and remote beaches) change little or nothing. In fact their very secrecy and "closetedness" can be quite counterproduc-tive. Paradoxically, by wearing clothes (e.g. G-strings), people like that lady at Bondi are stripping our culture of its clothes-compulsiveness.

Those of us who really want to change cultural atti-tudes towards nakedness should not always frequent

---

[1] Cf. Matthew 7:17.
[2] Cf. Matthew 15:18ff.

nudist parks and nude beaches. Why don't we sometimes go to clothed places, and if we can't be totally nude, then be as nude as will be tolerated there? In this way we can effectively teach those who are caught up in prevailing clothes-compulsiveness. This is how we can convert hundreds of beaches to the chaste, respectable option of nudity. Indeed, this is precisely how those beaches got converted to bikinis—by gradually getting nuder—not by fighting to have their own, legalized, "bikini ghetto."

A "Scandalized" Catholic

Editor's introduction: Before moving to Vermont in 1982, I had a very brief tenure as the headmaster of Holy Innocents Academy, a private elementary school in Dearborn Heights, Michigan, founded by very conservative, Catholic laymen. Some of the prospective founding families were so conservative that they broke away when the majority decided in favor of the new, post-Vatican II Mass (Novus Ordo) promulgated by Pope Paul VI. Most of the other families who followed through with the founding were, in effect, reluctantly pro-Vatican II. My own position was (and still is) one of grateful delight with the reforms of Vatican II, while I deeply lamented (and still do) the many outrageous abuses of that enlightened ecumenical council perpetrated by "progressives" who seemed bent on destroying the Church altogether. Because of my vision, as well as my personal piety, energy and abilities, I got the headmaster's job—the tenth of ten principals in ten years. My tenure there lasted only a few months, illegally terminated by a certain clique on the school board with whom I soon locked horns. After several months I won my breach of contract suit in Michigan court.

Nudism had nothing at all to do with my termination. Since we had two school teachers boarding with us, we were not even "domestic" nudists; we kept our pants on, as it were. Domestic nudism did not resume until long after my termination while still living in the Detroit area and attempting to found a new school with the many families who resigned over my termination and the resulting turmoil.[1]

After a year in Michigan we Cunninghams and Joan moved to Vermont where we continued to work in education and our naturism matured and developed. Before our first year in Vermont was up, we unanimously decided to try to found a new private school embracing almost everything we believed in, from Jesus and the pope to daily naturism. Naturally, this made big waves in the media, one of the high points being a half page with our nude photo in Newsweek, August 20, 1984. When our former supporters in Michigan saw the article, they were stunned. To them it was like hearing that the pope had become a Mason, or President Ronald Reagan a Communist. The anti-Cunningham faction flaunted the article as though to justify their former opposition to me, though nudism had nothing whatsoever to do with my termination. Nevertheless, my supporters could not justify our newfound naturism and were understandably embarrassed.

Two families wrote to us, trying to correct what they saw as their wayward brethren. We regarded this as true, loving concern, but when we painstakingly tried to explain how naturism and Catholicism were not antithetical, they thought we were no better than stubborn heretics and we never heard from any of them again.

Those families badly need to learn what Vatican II and Pope John Paul II have to say about the human body. Their junior high school age boys used to refuse to change openly in the boys' locker room and since showers were required by me and the gym teacher, they would actually wear their skivvies into the curtain-less showers! I never dared to try to force nudity, but I recognized that excessive body self-consciousness as an unholy thing. One family donated many *National Geographics* to the new Michigan school we tried to found, assuring me that they had already "appropriately" taken scissors and literally cut out

---

[1] For the story of how we returned to domestic nudism, this time with a slightly "social" dimension, incorporating our one remaining boarding school teacher, Joan, into that lifestyle, see: Jim C. Cunningham, *Vermont Unveiled* (Troy, Vermont: Naturist LIFE International, Inc., 1996), pp. 10ff.

all the "pornographic" pictures! So you can see the kind of people who comprised my clientele.

There follows one of the two letters we received, followed by Linda's unanswered reply. The author had an M.D. but had never yet begun practice as a physician. It seems ironic that her profession should so directly concern the human body while she has such a fear of it. She and her husband, a professor, were what I would call "fundamentalist Catholics." I remember dining with them at their home and being flabbergasted that they literally believed the eternal fires of hell existed deep down within the center of this planet, justifying their convictions on various revelations of the Blessed Virgin Mary and other saints and angels. As a brief aside, I would like to assure the reader that the true teaching of the Catholic Church as enunciated by Pope Benedict XIV[1] is that, not only are Catholics not obliged to believe in any post-Apostolic apparitions or private revelations, but that it is theologically impossible to put divine faith in them. Only human faith can be placed in them, and, while human faith can aid religion, it cannot effect salvation.

One final clarification: When the author of the following letter refers to "scandal," it is not in the moral theological sense, since it is obvious that our naturism in no way caused her or her friends to sin. She means it merely in the ordinary sense of "being shocked." The author, like many other Christians, seems to confuse these two types of scandal, thus implying some sort of virtue in being "shockless" and "making no waves." But lots of teachers and prophets effectively use the "shock" tool to get attention or even as part of their message. Thus Isaiah's three years as a nudist achieved both purposes. If he had not preached nude, few would have troubled to listen to what they would have regarded as just another boring preacher. Isaiah's nudity caused them to pay attention, just like the nudity of anti-war demonstrators today. Secondly, his nudity was also part of his message; they, too, would soon be despoiled and denuded by invading foreigners as a punishment for their infidelity. Similarly, the nudity of today's anti-war demonstrators is also part of their mes-

---

[1] See Benedict XIV (1675-1758), De Servorum Dei Beatificatione et de Beatorum Canonizatione & Vatican II, Dei Verbum, N. 4.

sage; true peace requires disarmament—not arms build-ups. Nudity shows human unity, whereas uniforms accentuate national divisions.

Unfortunately, when we ask opponents like the below author how they can believe nudity is necessarily always a vice of immodesty if God Himself commanded Isaiah to preach nude for three years, they have no answer, accuse us of trying to justify ourselves, and stop communicating with us. They think their unreasonable close-mindedness is virtuous and are as smugly content to never read Isaiah 20:1ff as they are content to believe that if they dig deep enough, they will go to hell before China!

J.M.J.
Dear Jim, Linda and Joan:
Evidently nudity is a very big thing in your life now since you have taken the time to write to us all about it. My heart is heavy with grief and sorrow, and fear for your souls to see the state in which you have fallen. When I first got your letter, I showed it only to Fr. David[1] because I didn't want to spread the news of your mortally sinful conduct. I also thought, and still hope, you may someday bitterly regret your present actions, and it would be better not to destroy your reputation here in Michigan. But Paul caught (accidentally) some of my conversation with Fr. David, so they found out and so did Ann and Margaret. Then everyone saw your picture in the magazine (News-week) because Holy Innocents Academy people were passing it around and making sure we knew about it, as if to say, "I told you so," and those of us who supported you can only respond that, to some degree, they have a right to feel justified. They have every right to say, "I told you so."

Ann has been going through an extremely difficult year with serious illnesses in her family. We held off telling her about you all because of her trials. She had so much faith in you people and you all have added to her trials by what you are now doing.

Jim, I thought you were working so hard to become holy. Now I know why the saints say (St. Paul, too?), "We

---

[1] Franciscan chaplain at the Academy, who resigned in protest to my termination.

work out our salvation in trembling."[1] If nothing else, you all have made me realize that none of us is safe from sin and temptation, and even the most devout person can have a great fall. I tremble even more for my own salvation now. And also the saints say it is far more serious for a devout person to give scandal than a lax person because so many more people are scandalized by the devout person's behavior.

Not only that. Do you all realize the scandal you have given by that magazine article (Newsweek)? A national magazine. The harm is incalculable! You will never, never, never be able to know how much damage you did until the next life and then it will be too late to repair it.

And to claim that you are 100% magisterial[2]—that was only adding insults to Christ's wounds. The Church always warns us about occasions of sin and tells us that even one incident can open the door to disaster. You proved that by accepting that first invitation to the nude beach in Vermont.[3] It was wrong to go there in the first place. And now your whole life has changed! All because you gave in to that first temptation.

And who made the decision to go? I suspect, though I could be wrong, that you were the first to want to go to that beach, Jim. And Linda and Joan accepted your decision without much question. Linda and Joan, did you blindly follow Jim? Are you still doing so now? Linda, we obey in all things but sin. A wife must never cooperate with her husband in sin, no matter what the cost. Think! Think for yourself; Joan, you, too!

Which of you three has consulted a holy, magisterial priest and asked his advice about nudity? Oh sure, you found a nudist priest. But we all know that one can find any priestly perversion one is looking for today. The open (and hidden) scandals are increasing. But have you dared to ask a good holy priest, devoted to Our Blessed Mother, if nudity is permissible? Have you asked Our Blessed Mother if this is what she wants? Have you asked her if it conforms to God's holy will? Or is it very wrong and offensive to Him? And lastly, have you all become lax in

---

[1] Cf. Philippians 2:12.
[2] I.e. faithful to the official Catholic teaching.
[3] "The Ledges" in Wilmington.

your praying the Rosary? It is hard for me to believe that your fervor for the Rosary has increased or even stayed the same since we last met. Our Blessed Mother would never have let you go so seriously astray if you had asked her advice first. St. Louis de Montfort himself says we will not fall into public heresy if we devoutly pray the Rosary. And Our Lady once gave a gentle slap to a saint because he did not consult her before yielding to a temptation. She told him, "If you had asked me first, you would not have given in to this temptation."

And now to Fr. David. I don't know if he's written to you or not, but I will tell you what he told me. First of all, you gave the impression that Fr. David took no issue with your conduct. Your logic was faulty here. You drew a conclusion which was not based on fact. You acted the same as a doctor who diagnoses a certain disease without ever considering all the possible diseases a patient could have, and before he has all the information on the patient's condition on which to base the diagnosis. I'm dwelling on this point to show you that your reasoning is not always correct, and you have based your present conduct on faulty premises also.

Fr. David didn't write to you about conduct because he didn't have time. This past year has been a tremendous strain for him—the poor man has had very little rest and it shows. He didn't take issue with you because he simply did not have the time—not because he approved of your behavior. BUT he did tell me that in no way does he approve of your present behavior. In fact, when we were discussing the magazine article, he said he felt betrayed, which echoes the feelings of us all. Fr. David said that, because of Original Sin, the nudity that you speak of could never be condoned. Read Genesis again. Adam & Eve knew they were naked as soon as they committed their sin—Original Sin.[1] Because of the lingering effects of Original Sin, we must clothe our bodies. Fr. David read your first letter to me and said that he thought you "protested" too much. That is, you were trying to justify your position, but deep down you knew you were wrong. Fr. David fears for your family, as we all do. Think of the distorted example you are giving to those darling children

---

[1] See Genesis 3:7.

of yours. I can see nothing but serious harm for them. Your daughter may know how to read, but knowledge is nothing if a child is not properly brought up in the faith.

Linda, Fr. David said he used to admire you for your modesty.[1] Needless to say, you have now crushed that admiration. You have gone from one extreme to another.

Also, Fr. David disagrees with much of your reasoning in your letter, Jim. He doesn't believe in nudity in the family either. And I ask you this: Why did Our Lady convey this message at Fatima—"Fashions will appear which will offend our Lord very much."?[2] If partial uncovering offends Our Lord, then total uncovering must be totally offensive.

Furthermore, you have not discovered anything new. Nudity is just another heresy. It has reared its ugly head before. Groups such as the Adamites[3] believed in nudity. There were other groups, too. And lots of Catholic morality books and my confession book talk about modesty, especially modesty in dress. And it is definitely a virtue. And immodesty is a sin—a serious sin if the proper conditions are met.[4]

---

[1] Editor's note: Linda has always worn skirts/dresses of at least mid-calf length and would breast-feed our babies wherever she happened to be, even while receiving Communion. She never wore bras. We believed modesty meant dressing appropriately for the occasion. It was while we knew Fr. David that we began to practice domestic nudity with our boarder, Joan. We all deemed nudity at home appropriate, as when sharing the one bathroom, posing for figure drawing or simply to keep cool on warmer days. Tasteful, nude photographs in birth books had challenged our conception of true modesty. We showed one of these, *Birth* by Caterine Millinaire (Hampton Roads, Virginia: Harmony, 1974), to Fr. David, asking his opinion. He leafed through the book, looking at full frontal nudes of pregnant moms, a naked family (including the father) playing on a bed, and even a photo of a shaved vulva, spread wide for birthing. He said he found no fault with any of them except one of a pregnant woman standing by her tipi, for which opinion he gave no explanation.

[2] Editor's note: We did not and do not believe in any fashions designed to titillate, but God's Own design of the human body is not among such indecent fashions.

[3] Editor's note: To my knowledge, the Adamite heresy was condemned not for group nudity, which the Church herself used to require at baptism, but for erroneous doctrines such as denying original sin.

[4] Theological note: In Catholic theology, for a sin to be "mortal" (i.e. "deadly"), four conditions must be met: 1) The sin must be serious (e.g. stealing a car as opposed to penny candy), 2) one needs to know it is serious, 3) one must have given it sufficient reflection, and 4) full consent

Sorry I don't have time to write more. My dear people, I hope this letter does not sound harsh. Time prevents me from rewriting it. I hope you will go to the Blessed Mother after you read this letter and ask her to show you the truth about nudity. I have given you the opinion of an excellent priest. I hope you will heed it. Examining our sinful state, I tremble for myself, too. Our immortal souls hang in the balance. May Our Blessed Mother guide you and obtain many blessings for you all, especially your new little daughter.

Love,
Carol L., M.D.
P.S. None of us wants to discuss or argue further about nudity; we know where we all stand. Further arguing would be a waste of time. You never spoke of Our Blessed Mother in your letters. Why not?

J.M.J.
Dear Carol,

Peace to you and yours during this Christmas season [1984].

Thank you for your letter and your concern for our good. I would have written a letter just like that about eight years ago if I had thought that my Catholic friends were going astray. But since then my present outlook on the subject of modesty and nudity has been forming into what it is today.

First of all, I want to assure you that my conscience is clear, my heart is pure and my intentions are directed to pleasing God. All three of us have prayed, meditated, done research, consulted and discussed the matter thoroughly before making any decision. (I might add that Fr. David and Ann contributed to our present conclusion through certain discussions we've had with them, though they might not be aware of it.) We were already practicing domestic nudity when we were in Detroit, and you know what our spirituality was like while we were there. It

---

of his will. Mortal sin deprives a sinner of all sanctifying grace, forfeits his heavenly inheritance and erases whatever merit he had previously attained. The only (ordinarily) way to be restored to grace is through the sacrament of confession (also called penance or reconciliation).

hasn't regressed any since then. We firmly believe that we are not in mortal sin (or even venial), nor is it a mere occasion of sin. The two spiritual men who convinced us of this are St. Thomas Aquinas and the pope (particularly in his book, *Love & Responsibility*).

I have chosen the nudity lifestyle to imitate Mary's purity in that I would teach myself, my children and others that the body is not a sexual object, nor is it doomed to be considered such, but is the temple of the Holy Spirit,[1] purified by Baptism through the merits of Christ's passion and death, and raised up to its former dignity (and beyond) through His resurrection. It is possible to return to the innocence of children and that is what we experience daily without exception.

Our Lady of Fatima said, "More people go to hell for sins of the flesh than for any other reason." The devil has a hold on people's minds through pornography and puritanical attitudes. Both are bad. Both are condemned by the Church; each one feeds upon the other. We are at war with Satan and, like the nude Christ on the Cross, nudism crushes the head of the serpent. If the nudist attitude is that the sexual parts are no more arousing than a nose or an elbow, then pornography cannot find a place in it. If the nudist attitude is that the body is holy and good, then puritanical attitudes can't exist in it.

Ah, but you don't believe me! I feel that I am speaking to a brick wall with no door to receive me. A number of times we have gotten condemnations from good Catholic friends. They've shouted, "Mortal Sin! Mortal Sin!" at us and don't want to have anything more to do with us. Do they really love us as they say? Well, at least I am learning that the way to win the hearts of separated brethren is not to reject, but to dialogue with them with open arms.

We have received a nice letter from the H's and have written back, but alas, no answer from them! We are very disappointed. Have they shared it with you? Would it be "arguing" or rather, "sincere dialoguing"? We would turn on a dime if proven to be wrong. But one will have to go back eight years or more and disprove everything we found to be true. That will not be an easy task! What soul will be so generous? Missionaries go to the farthest ends

---

[1] Cf. I Corinthians 3:16; 6:19 & II Corinthians 6:16.

of the earth to preach the "Good News." Like Christ, they let themselves be associated with the poorest of the poor and the dregs of the dregs—or do they? There is a class of people that Catholics (no matter how fervent with love of Christ or Mary) will not touch with a ten foot pole. Are these people worse than those with leprosy? They are worms—not men.[1] Yes—nudists.

That horrible word—"nudist." That was the one thing that was keeping me from becoming a nudist once I was convinced of its philosophy. I was too proud to be rejected by my upright fellow Catholics, family and friends. What a stigma! But I wasn't filled with peace until, after fervently praying to Mary, I decided to go the way of the cross and be associated with the "scummiest" people on earth. Mary is teaching me humility. "He has looked with favor on His servant in her lowliness."[2] But here I go again! Is it my pride that is trying to justify myself in your eyes? Maybe I should imitate St. Therese of Lisieux. When someone would misjudge her she wouldn't defend herself. She would only long for heaven and the King of Justice all the more.

Christmas Peace,
Linda S. Cunningham

Vatican II on the Body

From *Gaudium et Spes*

"Though made of body and soul, man is one. Through his bodily composition he gathers to himself the elements of the material world; thus they reach their crown through him, and through him raise their voice in free praise of the Creator.[3] For this reason man is not allowed to despise his bodily life; rather he is obliged to regard his body as good and honorable since God has created it and will raise it up on the last day.

---

[1] See Psalm 22:6.
[2] Luke 1:48.
[3] Cf. Daniel 3:57-90.

126

"Nevertheless, wounded by sin, man experiences rebellious stirrings in his body. But the very dignity of man postulates that man glorify God in his body[1] and forbid it to serve the evil inclinations of his heart."[2]

Spirituality vs. Sensuality? Our Senses Are for Union!

by Jim C. Cunningham

Probably in an over-zealous attempt to disprove the "nude is lewd" myth, an ongoing theme in nudist publications has been the distinction between sensuality and sexuality, as if sensuality were morally permissible, but not sexuality. The truth is that both are not only morally permissible, but are wonderful gifts designed by God to give Him glory. Both can be abused and we are all more or less guilty of abusing them in the past.

There is perhaps a worse guilt that we all share regarding these natural wonders. We are all guilty of not using them—of not taking full advantage of them as God would have us do.

Many abuse sexuality by seeing the sense pleasure of sex as an end in itself. They ignore the fact that sex has a very special and specific place in God's design—to unite man and woman in a total, mutual, self-surrender—a God-like, indissoluble union that proves its holiness by its fruitfulness. Jesus said, "By their fruits you shall know them."[3] If the fruit of sexual love is the wonder of a brand new, tender, human life, then how holy and wonderful must sex be! To call sex (or sexual body parts) "dirty" is demonic. Whereas Jesus' deepest passion is to gift us with abundant life,[4] the devil hates life. He hates new souls created in the image of the God he despises, and destined

---

[1] Cf. I Corinthians 6:13-20.
[2] *Vatican Council II Vol. 2: The Conciliar & Post Conciliar Documents*, ed. Austin P. Flannery, (Collegeville, Minnesota: Liturgical Press, 1983), "*Gaudium et Spes*," N. 14.
[3] Matthew 7:16.
[4] Cf. John 10:10.

to share eternal life with Him. Because he hates life, it stands to reason that he hates sex. It is one of his major campaigns to confuse us about sex, which is why we see today the proliferation of so much pornography, rape, incest, abortion, premarital sex, self-sex, homosexuality, and various drugs and devices designed to render the God-ordained sexual relationship fruitless. Not only does the devil encourage all these abuses of sexuality (and I doubt there isn't a one of us who isn't guilty of some of them), but even where sex is right, holy and divine, he still manages to mess things up. How many marriages fall apart not only because of selfish abuses of sexuality, but even because of the lack of good, deep, rich sexuality? If we think sex is "dirty," then how strong can the marriage bond be—a bond consummated by that very sexual union? How can we truly honor a union while we condemn the God-ordained means to achieve that union?

Some Christians think sex is "dirty" because it is pleasurable. In fact, they feel guilty whenever they experience any sensual pleasure. They refer to a tasty dish as a "temptation." Did God make taste buds to tease us? Did He make them so we would eat repulsive things and get sick? This is also why some Christians think nudism is sinful. Even if you manage to persuade them that nudism is not sexual, it is still sensual, and because of this they condemn it. "It feels so good to swim nude, it must be wrong." That's how they think. If they cannot gladly accept the ordinate pleasures of this life, can they really yearn for heavenly beatitude? Our love for our Redeemer is commensurate with our passion for heaven, for which He gave the last drop of His Precious Blood.[1]

Sexuality is probably the height of sensuality. The Second Vatican Council described it as a most eminent human love.[2] The intense pleasure of orgasm beats a stuffed mushroom, a foot massage, a nude swim, or even a good Scotch on the rocks (well, I'm not so sure about the Scotch...). Precisely because sex is so great and pleasurable, many guilt-ridden Christians have a special problem with it.

---

[1] Cf. John 19:34.
[2] Cf. *Gaudium et Spes*, N. 49. Ed. note: I highly recommend this entire chapter which so beautifully defines the goodness of genital sexuality.

God is the source of our senses and sensuality. God must be the object of everything we do in life. I am writing this article because I want to help bring you closer to God by sharing the insights I have received. We need to abuse sensuality less, and use it much more, and even better.

The purpose of the senses is a spiritual one—union. Spirituality is about becoming like God, Who is all-holy: "You shall be holy, for I am holy."[1] "You must be made perfect, as your heavenly Father is perfect."[2] The greatest commandment is to love God with all our heart, soul, mind and strength.[3] Moses gave us the most pure, basic and simple motive—because "The Lord, our God, is One."[4] Jesus' whole mission was to unite all things in Himself.[5] True spirituality and sensuality are not opposed; the purpose of all sensuality is to attain the end of true spirituality. Senses are spiritual if used for union.

Genital sexuality is the means of union between husband and wife. Sensuality is a means of union between all of us, between us and God, and even between an individual's own body and soul. God certainly desires union.[6] He therefore must want sensuality, which is an essential means of effecting that union.

Compare the following: 1) You wave to a friend. 2) You shake his hand. 3) You give him a "kiss of love."[7] All are sensual, but the loving kiss is obviously most lush. Which is most apt to unite us as brothers and sisters? Obviously the kiss; then God wants us to kiss each other. "Greet all the brethren with a holy kiss."[8]

Or consider for a moment a banquet. The community assembles and together we feast. And maybe we gladden our hearts[9] with a few drinks, loosen up, and dance. All sensual, but all very unitive for the human community as long as there is no selfish excess.

---

[1] Leviticus 11:45.
[2] Matthew 5:48.
[3] Cf. Luke 10:27 & Deuteronomy 6:5.
[4] Deuteronomy 6:4.
[5] Cf. Colossians 1:15-20 & Ephesians 1:10.
[6] Cf. John 17:11 & 21; I Corinthians 1:10; Philippians 1:27 & 2:2.
[7] I Peter 5:14.
[8] I Thessalonians 5:26 & cf. I Corinthians 16:20; II Corinthians 13:12 & Acts 20:37.
[9] Cf. Psalm 104:15.

Consider being massaged by four friends. It is certainly a pleasurable experience (if they know what they are doing!), and the touch unites so powerfully.

Consider the pleasure of listening to good music. We are caught up in the beauty, order and harmony and are brought closer to reality thereby.

Besides uniting the human community, sensuality also unites us to God. Whose heart is not moved to adoration by the sensual experience of a beautiful nature scene? By the sight of the first spring robin? By the ocean breeze caressing one's whole naked body?

Sensuality is also proof of the union of body and soul (i.e. our life in this world) within each individual. It is an essential means of restoring the original, personal integrity man enjoyed before the fall. Death (the separation of body and soul) is not God's design. "God did not make death, and He does not delight in the death of the living. For He created all things that they might exist, and the generative [i.e. sexual!] forces of the world are wholesome, and there is no destructive poison in them."[1] It was commission of sin, by heeding the temptation of Satan, that death entered into the human experience. "Through the devil's envy death entered the world."[2] As Jesus said, "God is a God of the living, not of the dead."[3]

The cadaver has no sensuality. He is dead. The proof of life—of soul united to body—is sensuality. Jesus demonstrated this after His resurrection. When the apostles and Thomas doubted the resurrection, Jesus made them watch Him eat,[4] and feel His sacred wounds.[5]

Sensuality is so important that there could be no life-saving sacraments without them. The bath of baptism is the graphic sensual experience of being immersed in water. Eucharist utilizes bread and wine. Ordination requires the laying on of hands. All sacraments are sensual and they effect our union with God. "Truly, truly, I say to you, unless you eat the flesh of the Son of man and drink His blood, you have no life in you; he who eats My

---

[1] Wisdom 1:13f.
[2] Ibid. 2:24.
[3] Matthew 22:32.
[4] Cf. Luke 24:41-43.
[5] Cf. John 20:27-28.

flesh and drinks My blood has eternal life, and I will raise him up at the last day."[1]

We are, essentially, sensual beings. To deny this is to deny our humanity—to tell God He should have made us all angels and not men. Our corporeality, which includes sensuality, is precisely one of the main ingredients that make us different from angels. Pure spirits neither touch nor taste; they neither see nor hear, nor do they smell. They are not housed in a material world. We are not angels. To gratefully accept from God the gift of our humanity means that we are sensual.

But not hedonistic. Hedonism seeks pleasure for its own sake. Rather than unite, hedonism creates walls of selfish separation. This is why Pope John Paul II taught that a man must not lust—not even after his own wife.[2] Right sexuality is not selfish lust; it is loving union.

Christian sensuality uses the senses to unite. We were not put here to be pampered, but to serve.[3] But serving means uniting with God, nature and each other. That means sensuality.

And sensuality is not always pleasurable, either. Pain is sensual too. Both fasting and feasting unite us to God and each other. St. Paul said he was adept at both.[4] Often in the Bible an universal fast will often be proclaimed.[5] Everyone feels united in a common cause. On Ash Wednesday and Good Friday the Church proclaims a fast. We can look at each other sensually, our stomachs growling, and experience the union of mutual self-denial.

Christ's crucifixion was far from pleasurable, yet it was definitely sensual. Our pain is sensual too. We are sensual beings, whether we experience pleasure or pain. We should never seek either for its own sake. One is hedonism; the other is masochism.

---

[1] John 6:53-54.
[2] Cf. Pope John Paul II, Angelus audience of October 8, 1980. The exact quotation reads: " "Adultery in the heart (cf. Matthew 5:28) is committed not only because man looks in this way at a woman who is not his wife, but precisely because he looks at a woman in this way. Even if he looked in this way at the woman who is his wife, he could likewise commit adultery in his heart." In *Theology of the Body* (Boston: Pauline Books, 1997), p. 157.
[3] Cf. John 13:14-15 & Matthew 20:25-28.
[4] Cf. Philippians 4:12.
[5] Cf. Jonah 3:5 & Judith 4:9.

Rather, as Christians, we mutually admit the fact of our humanity (and therefore our sensuality) and use our senses for God's greater glory. "Whatever you do, do all to the glory of God."[1] Our senses must bring us closer to God and each other, whether they experience pleasure or pain.

We need to rest. It is so important that God dedicated 1 of only 10 commandments to it.[2] It is not bad, therefore, to enjoy a full body massage. But after we are renewed in body it is just as sensual to get out there and sweat in His service, performing the works of mercy[3] and all the duties of our state of life.

In fact, if we also approach the pain of sensuality with a different attitude, we will love life more. Hard work unites us to those for whom we labor, no less than massage. We experience God no less through working by the sweat of the brow, than we do by sunbathing nude. God is everywhere. All of our sensuality is designed to unite us to Him if we only approach it with the right attitude. Let us love life and surrender ourselves to its experience, seeing both in pleasure and in pain a means of union with God and each other.

Christian Nudist Manifesto

by Jim C. Cunningham

Christians of the world, unite!

Let us cast off the cumbersome shackles of cultural accretions which do not accord with Christ, our Lord, and live in the glorious freedom of the sons of God![4] Let us proclaim the dignity of our whole person, soul and body, because God has created us in no less than His very Own image, and has held us in such high regard that He Himself assumed our human nature—soul and body—and further showed His supreme love for us by His passion, death and resurrection.

---

[1] I Corinthians 10:31.
[2] Cf. Deuteronomy 5:12-15.
[3] Cf. Matthew 5:3-12 & 25:35f.
[4] Cf. Romans 8:21 & Galatians 5:1.

Let us disdain the wiles of the devil and those of his pernicious persuasion, who would denigrate our dignity and becloud the truth of God's love and mercy revealed to us in the mysteries of the Creation, incarnation and Redemption. Spirit only, the devil has always been jealous[1] of our precious bodies, specially fashioned by God's Own hand.[2] He either tempts us to hedonism, glutting our bodies in carnalities, or to "angelism," repudiating everything fleshly as something sinful.

Christians of the world, unite!

Let us, in the child-like simplicity which our Lord commends as rightful for His Kingdom,[3] resist both aberrations, dwelling single-mindedly in the innocence in which He originally created us, and to which, "in the fullness of time,"[4] after falling from His amazing grace by heeding the deceptions of the Master of Deceit,[5] He restored us, paying the "great price"[6] of His Own naked Body, nailed to the Tree of Life. Let us proclaim the truth of our bodily dignity by refusing to satisfy the jealousy of the Evil One, hiding our bodies as though they were something shameful. God created us to glorify Him. He created us unclothed. Let us glorify Him, then, in our bodies,[7] seeing in our very nakedness His glory and our true nobility.

And let not the devil foil us in the purity of our purpose by pretending that our Christian nakedness can somehow be impure and conducive to the scandal of the weak. God simply cannot create impurity. "He gazed upon all that He had made, and behold, it was very good."[8] As Christ Jesus, our Lord, taught, nothing external is impure; the source of wickedness is the human heart,[9] bemused by Satan's lies. Man's mind is free to foul up any divine purpose. Just because man can be tempted to sins of gluttony, should we therefore cover the apples in the

---

[1] Cf. Wisdom 2:24.
[2] Cf. Genesis 2:7.
[3] Cf. Matthew 18:3.
[4] Galatians 4:4.
[5] Cf. John 8:44.
[6] I Corinthians 6:19.
[7] Cf. I Corinthians 6:20.
[8] Genesis 1:31.
[9] Cf. Matthew 15:11 & 18-20.

marketplace? Just because man can be tempted to jealousy, should we therefore fail to strive for perfection? Should money be banned because man might make Mammon his god?

Of course not! Equally absurd is the demonic deception that just because man can be tempted to lust, then chastity and charity require that we hide the objects of man's mental fouling and assiduously cover our glory and reflection of the all-holy Deity. Bathsheba was never rebuked for not bathing privately, but King David for befouling the limpid pool by the adulterous lusting of his heart.[1]

Christians of the world, unite!

Let us proclaim the truth that these bodies of ours are no less than temples of the Holy Spirit![2] But how can we do this, shrinking in shame-faced pusillanimity, ever apologizing for the God-ordained fact of our flesh? Let us, rather, be bold beacons of the Paraclete Who is tabernacled within us,[3] putting our light on a lamp-stand and not under a bushel basket![4] Let us resolve, Oh Christian brothers and sisters, to be done with all such nonsense and never again don a robe out of shame or a misguided modesty which, in effect, declares God's marvelous image impure. To glorify God in our bodies we must proclaim the holiness of His handiwork, not from the dank darkness of our closets, but from the sunbeamed brightness of our rooftops, for "Nothing is covered up that will not be revealed, or hidden that will not be known."[5]

Christians of the world, unite in a long overdue revolution of Christendom and of the world! "The day is far spent."[6] It is now the time to rise from sleep, doffing deeds of darkness, along with their suffocating, fig leaf symbols, and donning the liberating armor of light,[7] not only "baring" arms, but our whole bodies! The curtains of our temples must be torn from top to bottom,[8] and the ancient

---

[1] Cf. II Samuel 11 & Matthew 5:28.
[2] Cf. I Corinthians 3:16f; 6:19f & II Corinthians 6:16.
[3] Cf. I Corinthians 3:16.
[4] Cf. Matthew 5:15-16 & Luke 8:16.
[5] Luke 12:2 & cf. 8:17.
[6] Luke 24:29.
[7] Cf. Romans 13:11f.
[8] Cf. Mark 15:38.

portals thrown wide open, that the King of Glory may come in,[1] His champion cup running over[2] with abundant life,[3] "and the life is the light of men."[4]

No less than a revolution is needed because change in our personal lives and in the world requires drastic action, especially after centuries of entrenched cultural encumberment. "The Kingdom of Heaven is won with violence, and the violent take it by force."[5] Let us live naked as God created us whenever possible and gladly show this glory to those around us. Let us support worldwide movements of social nudism by not only frequently attending existing areas for nude recreation, but ever establishing new ones. And since charity begins at home, nothing is more important or effective as establishing God's intention of nakedness as the norm in and around our homes, greeting all guests in our God-given glory and child-like innocence.

Christians of the world, I call upon you to thus unite and help prune the Tree of Life of sterile shoots that steal the sap destined for the fruit. Thus freed from the fowler's snare,[6] let us fly in the freedom of the sons of God![7]

The Naked Fishermen: 7 Reflections

John 21:4-13 (KJV)

But when the morning was now come, Jesus stood on the shore: but the disciples knew not that it was Jesus. Then Jesus saith unto them, "Children, have ye any meat?" They answered Him, "No." And he said unto them, "Cast the net on the right side of the ship, and ye shall find." They cast therefore, and now they were not able to draw it for the multitude of fishes. Therefore that disciple whom

---

[1] Cf. Psalm 24:7.
[2] Cf. Psalm 23:5.
[3] Cf. John 10:10.
[4] John 1:4.
[5] Matthew 11:12 & cf. Luke 16:16.
[6] Cf. Psalm 124:7.
[7] Romans 8:21.

Jesus loved saith unto Peter, "It is the Lord." Now when Simon Peter heard that it was the Lord, he girt his fisher's coat unto him, (for he was naked,) and did cast himself into the sea. And the other disciples came in a little ship; (for they were not far from land, but as it were two hundred cubits,) dragging the net with fishes. As soon then as they were come to land, they saw a fire of coals there, and fish laid thereon, and bread. Jesus saith unto them, "Bring of the fish which ye have now caught." Simon Peter went up, and drew the net to land full of great fishes, and hundred and fifty and three: and for all there were so many, yet was not the net broken. Jesus saith unto them, "Come and dine." And none of the disciples durst ask Him, "Who art Thou?" knowing that it was the Lord. Jesus then cometh, and taketh bread, and giveth them, and fish likewise.

Editor's introduction: Some Christians use this passage to argue *against* nudism. They contend that when Peter was aware of the Lord's presence, he also became aware of his immodesty, and hastily and awkwardly rectified it. Here are some reflections from Christian naturists of various denominations. It is recommended that readers prayerfully read all of John 21 to appreciate the broader context.

I.

by Steve Devore

The first thing to notice is that Peter was not dressed when he was on the boat. In other words, he was wearing what everyone else was (probably nothing). This shows that there are times when being nude is appropriate. Peter's lack of dress was appropriate while he was fishing; it probably wouldn't have been appropriate back on shore (it probably wasn't a very private place). Peter is the only one mentioned dressing because he was the only one who jumped into the water; the others probably did dress while the boat was coming to shore.

He might also have dressed because the water was cold, or he didn't want to carry his tunic above his head while he swam to shore.

II.
by Paul M. Bowman

It is true that this passage doesn't say why Peter put on his cloak. The Greek word used here is "*ependutes*," and this is, as far as I can find, the only time it's used in the New Testament. It probably was a type of coat specifically designed for a fisherman's work or conditions, so any answer will be open to question. The common sense answer, however, is contained within the passage, and seems so obvious to me that I can't see how people could use this verse as a reason to put on clothes.

It doesn't seem likely that Peter would fish naked with the other disciples and then suddenly become "modest" at the appearance of Jesus. If he did suddenly become "modest," it would certainly have to do with the fact that this occurred after the resurrection. I think most people would try to "hide" or instinctively try to protect themselves if they saw somebody whom their minds told them was dead!

Much more likely, however, is that Peter wanted to swim to meet Jesus on shore. They were out in a boat about a hundred yards from shore. Have you ever tried to swim a hundred yards with your coat under your arm? It seems much more practical to throw it on so both arms are free to swim. I say, then, that Peter thought it would be easier to swim to shore with the coat on his back rather than under his arm, and that he must have wanted it with him when he got to shore in case the boat did not follow him.

III.
by Rev. Jeffrey Hitt

We must take into account the time period in which this action takes place and look at the event through the eyes of the writer, along with the beliefs and customs of the time. As we read the Bible, we see it through our own eyes, but also through the writer's own bias, purpose, and his own eye witness accounts. We all know that six different people witnessing an accident will give you six different versions as to what happened. We are looking at a verse of Scripture that has been filtered through two thousand years of culture. It had been translated and interpreted many times before it reached us.

The Bethany Parallel Commentary on the New Testament states in its Matthew Henry column, "Peter was the most zealous and warm-hearted disciple; for as soon as he heard it was the Lord the ship could not hold him, but into the sea he throws himself that he might come first to Christ. He (Peter) showed his respect to Christ by girding his fisher's coat about him, that he might appear before his Master in the best clothes he had, and he girt it to him that he might make the best of his way through the water to Christ."

We must keep in mind that in New Testament times people were accustomed to dressing and looking their best when they appeared before royalty they respected, and Peter certainly respected Jesus Christ as his Savior. Peter was dressing up to go before his Master, just as people dress up today to visit governmental officials. Peter was reacting to his social conscience and the norms of his time which dictated he look his best, put on his best to be in the presence of the Lord. There were no naturist movements in New Testament times operating in this location so there was no need for further discussion. Peter got dressed out of reverence to his Lord, not because he thought that covering his body was hiding his shame.

Scholars disagree as to how naked Peter was. Some say completely, while others say he was only bare-chested.

It is a biblical and historical fact that nudity was very present in this time period. Children often played nude. People were accustomed to more nudity in biblical times than we are today. Nakedness is recorded of the prophets and King Saul and King David. Putting animal skins on Adam & Eve did not end nudity in the Bible.

IV.
by Don Haroldsson

If it were not so tragic, it would be laughable the way some of the cultists try to push their point. Let me take their point for a moment and press on to further observations and obvious conclusions.

If we take the position that Peter grabbed his clothes, but the other disciples did not, then we have a moot question in verse 15 where Jesus says, "Lovest thou me more than these?" These what? The obvious answer is clothes, because in verse 18 Jesus says, "When thou wast young thou girdest (i.e. clothed) thyself... but... when thou shalt be old... another shall gird thee." If we want to make a big point about Peter's clothes (for apparently he was the only clothed one), then from that position we must conclude that Jesus was rebuking him for his concern about his clothes.

Now, let's take a practical and realistic position regarding that event. You will remember that until Peter's conversion, he was a very impetuous and sometimes vacillating man. When Christ approached their boat one night, Peter wanted to go and meet Him.[1] When he realized that the One on shore was Jesus, Peter wanted to go to Him. An admirable quality. It was only natural to take his immediate, portable possessions. The question, then, is why did he put them on? He did not want to leave them in the boat all day because of the danger of theft from that offshore boat, and because they would be easier to carry that way, rather than rolled up in his hand while he swam ashore. The sad part about the sanctimonious question regarding this transition on the part of Peter is that it continues to beg the question of clothes-ism vs. natural living. The real question—the real issue—in this passage which is lost (buried) under verbiage of the "morality by material" philosophy, is that the Lord's concern, according to the text, is the degree of commitment and service which He expects from His followers.

V.
by Linda S. Cunningham

The scene in this passage is very similar to the scenes in the beginning of each of the synoptic Gospels where Jesus calls Peter to follow Him for the first time.[2] Jesus is on the shore and Peter is fishing with others in a boat.

---

[1] Cf. Matthew 14:25-32.
[2] Cf. Matthew 4:18-20; Mark 1:16-18 & Luke 5:4-11.

The men have caught nothing all night long. It is morning, and Jesus tells them where to cast their nets. They obey and catch a multitude of fish.

In the beginning of His ministry, Jesus asks them to follow Him. In this scene, about three years later, after they have recognized Jesus, Peter is so ready to follow his Lord and Master that he doesn't even wait for the call. He throws on his only possessions—the clothes on his back— and abandons ship to get to his Lord all the faster. In this way Peter showed his love and devotion, and his readiness to serve.

After Jesus questions Peter three times, "Do you love Me more than these?",[1] and after three affirmative answers, Jesus tells Peter what his new job is, "Feed and tend My sheep." Then, like the first time, Peter hears those blessed words once again, "Follow Me."[2]

VI.
by Rev. Dr. William Caple

It seems fairly obvious that what Peter was doing was not hiding his nakedness, because it was customary to fish either naked or relatively naked. What Peter was doing was rushing to be with the Lord, and again the custom was to wear a covering on shore.

I think also it is common courtesy to be attired as others are. If I were sunbathing on my patio and neighbors stopped in to visit, I would naturally cover myself, not because I am ashamed, but unless I knew my neighbors would join me it would be the hospitable thing to do. Common sense tells me that putting on clothes when appropriate does not say I am ashamed of my body, but is simply common courtesy.

VII.
by Fr. Jim Byrnes

Although I am not a Scripture scholar, being a priest I have some resources on hand to help find the answers to difficult questions. One of the really superb resources at

---

[1] John 21:15.
[2] John 21:19.

my disposal is The *Jerome Biblical Commentary*. I will quote directly from the JBC:

"Jews were sensitive about performing greetings without being properly clad. Peter's precipitate action is typical of the man as he is portrayed in the Gospels."

This action viewed in light of the JBC explanation is understandable. Haven't many of us "thrown something on" to greet someone coming to our homes? That is what Peter was doing. He threw something on to greet the risen Lord.

Keep in mind that even one as scholarly in the Scriptures as he who wrote this commentary on the Gospel of John calls this a "precipitate action." In the dictionary the word "precipitate," when used this way, has several meanings, among which are: "in sudden haste or without due deliberation; over hasty; rash."

Peter and Jesus were close friends. Jesus knew and understood his friend's background, occupation and lifestyle. Therefore, I would agree that if Peter had thought for a moment, he would have "skipped the formalities" and run to his Friend. But he acted before he thought; that was Peter.

The Lord understood him and picked him to be the Rock of the Church.[1] I think I can understand him too. His action does not negate the wholesomeness or holiness of being naked. I don't think we can learn anything from this action except a true reverence for the Lord and respect for Him in our lives.

Temple of the Spirit

by John R. Kane

A few decades ago I left Australia to teach in the United States for six months. While there, I came across an article in a magazine for Catholic clergy written by a priest about a holiday in a nudist club. As I recall, the priest had had a nervous breakdown. His doctor advised a

---

[1] Cf. Matthew 16:18.

holiday as remote from his ordinary life as possible, specifically in a nudist club!

Till then I had not thought deeply about nudism. Sunbaking nude was simply a pleasant way to pass an hour or two, but it had never occurred to me to consider what connection there was between social nudity and psychological health and religion. That article changed the situation. I must admit that I was deeply shocked (not scandalized) to see that a priest would go to a nudist club, that he would be willing to go public about it, and that an official clergy magazine would publish it.

While reading the article (and later through personal experience) I realized how stripping off clothes before others is almost literally stripping off all our disguises. In so many ways we feel exposed. We use clothes to express our personality, but naked we have no help. We use clothes to disguise all the "flaws" in our bodies, but naked we cannot hide them. We use clothes as symbols of our jobs and of our social and economic status, but naked we are on our own. The priest author made quite a powerful statement by his experience that psychological health relies on our ability to accept ourselves the way we are. Social nudity forces us to be honest about ourselves or gives the opportunity to accept what we see or not. At least we look at our age, the physique we have inherited, the results of our past way of life. It quickly dawns on us that that is what others see and should see irrespective of whatever steps we have taken to hide from them. We have to respect ourselves and others the way we are, not some imaginary selves. We often say we respect a person, that it is not important to us that they are thick or thin, tall or short, brilliant mathematicians or simple folk; we like them for what they are. Yet we would not trust them to like us if we let them see us the way we really are. We want them to like the disguised version of ourselves that we create using a template from the latest fashion conventions. Living in a dream world where we pretend that we are really some ideal person with ideal personality and ideal body (and where everyone else is also expected to be perfect) is a sure recipe for trouble. At the very least, it is a grave hindrance to any solid growth. Trouble has already started if we shudder when we see a little glimpse of reality and refuse to accept it.

I had already felt the need to integrate my religious beliefs after all the pop-psychology of those times. However, it hadn't occurred to me that I was keeping the naturist side of me in one compartment and my religion in another until the shock of seeing that article.

Why was I shocked? Because priests and religion should have hated naked bodies! Before this I hadn't even considered whether I should feel guilty about sunbathing nude or not; those two compartments were kept rigidly separate inside me. The author stirred in me a need for reintegration.

Christ's message to us is incarnation. We are, each of us, God's image, not merely in having an immortal soul. Aristotle's immaterial form stuck to a body, but the divine image is in our whole person, soul and body. Christ was not a spirit taking on the appearance of sinful matter so that He could bring us a message. His message was principally Himself—a real man, a real person on this earth. The earth was good enough for Him. A poor, second-rate country and a common working family were good enough. He lived and loved and worked and suffered. As a man, He didn't travel widely; He didn't learn many languages; He didn't get many degrees at college. He was human. It is good to be human like Him! It is good to be me, a man like Him. It is good to be that annoying guy next door, a man like Him.

Bodies are not a necessary evil to be hidden and ignored. They are "temples of the Holy Spirit"[1] indeed, but we have to remember that this metaphor is just a metaphor and is intended to emphasize the importance of the body—not to emphasize the dualism which so often leads to a contempt of the body.

It does not follow from the incarnation that we must go naked, just because Christ showed that the body is good, just as it does not follow that we must wear clothes because Christ mostly wore clothes. But it does follow that we can go naked if it is a suitable option. We can go naked if it helps to remind us that Christ was fully human, if it is useful to assert that the body is not evil, if it helps us to

---

[1] Cf. I Corinthians 3:16-17; 6:19 & II Corinthians 6:16.

143

see God's image better in ourselves and in our neighbor. Above all, the incarnation should have made us free from pointless restrictions.

My initial surprise that a Church magazine would take seriously the possibility that a priest could mix with naked bodies, and shock that a priest was actually able to do this and remain a priest, made me rethink my ideas of nudity, sex and priestly celibacy. It began to dawn on me that I had really a very low opinion of everyone's morality. My presumption had been that for a person of one sex to see a naked member of the other sex instantly resulted in lust for their body. My mind really did have a Manichean set about it. Bodies meant copulatory sex, and there was no way that one person could relate chastely to another person if bodies were noticed. It was quite a humbling experience to realize what a large blind spot was exposed here, and to realize that there must be other similar blind spots in me that remain.

Ashamed—
of the Way God Made Me?

Author Unknown

Ashamed—of the way God made me?
Ashamed—of my beautiful form
When Jesus was my pattern,
And this is the way I was born?

Then I must be ashamed of Jesus
And ashamed of my God above,
For He formed me by His pattern
And molded me in His love.

Ashamed—of what God pronounced perfect?
Ashamed—of His work divine?
When I am formed in His image
And He is the Savior of mine?

God forbid that I should turn traitor,
To condemn the work of His hand.
He pronounced His work good and perfect
And I will obey His command.

It was sin that brought shame into the garden.
Let's trample it down in the dust.
Let's lift our faces up to heaven,
Living clean and pure without lust.

The temple of God is our body.
Let's keep it clean for Him.
Do not defile or pollute it,
But be ruled by His Spirit within.

Some Interpretations

by Larry Hamilton

Leviticus 18:6-20

In the KJV[1] and RSV[2] translations of Leviticus 18:6-20, it says we must not be "naked" with a list of female relatives. This leads some to believe that you should not even be naked within the family. Then it says we must not be naked with another man's wife,[3] which would mean the majority of all women. However, several modern translations[4] say that it is sexual intercourse (not mere nakedness) that is forbidden here. The scripture really is against incest and infidelity. I have looked this up in several modern translations and they agree that it is sexual intercourse that is proscribed. Apparently the KJV was

---

[1] E.g. The KJV for v. 6: None of you shall approach to any that is near of kin to him, to uncover their nakedness...

[2] E.g. The RSV for v. 6: None of you shall approach any one near of kin to him to uncover nakedness...

[3] Cf. v. 20.

[4] E.g. The NAB (1970) for v. 6: None of you shall approach a close relative to have sexual intercourse with her...

145

modified by what was the moral standard at the time of King James,[1] but Leviticus is supposed to be the standard at the time of Moses.

As a matter of interest, verse 22 is against homosexuality, and verse 23 is against bestiality. Thus the entire context concerns serious *sexual* immoralities.

Luke 8:27-35

This is another passage that leads some to believe the Bible is against nudity. It describes one of Jesus' many exorcisms. In this case the man had never worn clothes, plus he hung around cemeteries (of all places). It is an understatement to say that the man was not like today's nudist. Because nudity was a compulsion with that man, Jesus clothed him.

To take this passage and say the Bible is against nudism would be like taking the story of the "Rich Young Ruler"[2] and say that it is sinful to have money. In this case, Jesus saw that the ruler's love of money was preventing spiritual values. So Jesus advised that particular person to sell all he had and give to the poor. But Luke 8:27-35 is another case; Jesus advises what is desirable for one particular person to do.

I Timothy 2:9

Here Paul says that a woman must dress modestly. When I read the context of this verse I suspect that Paul means humble dress, while avoiding fancy, opulent, and showy clothes.

Romans 14:14

Here Paul speaks against divisions within the church of Rome. He says not to judge your brother, who practices differently. Certain people abstained from pork. This verse says, "Nothing is unclean in itself; but it is unclean for

---

[1] Editor's note: Actually, the KJV and RSV literally translate the Hebrew euphemism for coitus; these modern translations forego the euphemism for greater clarity, thus explaining the euphemism.
[2] Cf. Luke 18:18; Matthew 19:16 & Mark 10:17.

146

anyone who thinks it unclean." In our case, this verse would say that nudism is not unclean in itself, but some people think nudism is unclean.

On Offense & Discretion

by Gene Caywood

For a Christian, choosing to be nude anywhere other than in the privacy of one's own home or the fenced security of a nudist resort, carries the possibility of being seen by others who might not understand. They are likely to have the idea that Christians should not take their clothes off where they can be seen by others. If they are bold enough to confront you, they will probably accuse you of offending them. If they are Christians they may claim you not only caused them to stumble, but possibly caused their friends who are not Christians to reject Christ. They will say that through your lack of discretion, their friends face eternal damnation. These are serious charges, not to be taken lightly by those of us who believe we do have some responsibility for others' physical and spiritual well being.

After more than a dozen years trying to relate Biblical Christian principles to naturism, I believe this to be the most difficult issue to be faced by serious, concerned followers of Christ. What answer can and should be given to those who might charge us thus? What follows only begins to address the question of giving offense, and the discretion which we must exercise.

Perhaps the key New Testament passage dealing with giving offense is Romans 14:1-15. Several points should be made relating to it.

First, the phrase "to cause to stumble," is not simply "to offend." It is very serious because it leads to eternal damnation. It should be translated "to lead away from the faith, to lead someone into apostasy." It is clear that some things others might become upset about do not reach this level of consequence. In fact there are some things of which Scripture specifically says we are not to let others judge us by such as food and drink, days of worship, etc.

There are also other things which, while not specifically listed in Scripture, clearly are not of eternal consequence. For example, even though some people might object to killing animals, it is hard to imagine that my going elk hunting is actually going to lead them into apostasy.

Clearly there are indeed also things which will lead others away from the faith, such as false teaching and sins specifically stated in Scripture. The question believers must ask themselves is, "Into which category does nudity fall?" Since it is not specifically listed as a matter over which we are not to judge another, we have two choices. Being caught nude is either not something which will lead another away from faith in Christ, or it is.

If you decide the latter, you had better not get nude where others have even the slightest chance of viewing you in that state, for James 4:17 says, "Anyone then who knows the good he ought to do and does not do it, sins." You had better limit your nude adventures to very remote places and times when you are sure no one will see you.

On the other hand, if you decide that nudity is similar to elk hunting (i.e. while some might object, it really has nothing to do with destroying faith), then you have much more freedom as to when and where you get nude. In this case, you must conclude that if the objecting person does claim eternal "stumbling" due to your lack of clothing, they are merely using it as a false excuse for their refusal to believe. What Paul is saying in Romans 14 and 15 is that we are allowed to exercise freedom in all questionable and disputable matters unless it causes problems for you, your companions, or those who might see you.

Most of what I have read by Christian writers on the subject of nudity and scandal addresses whether it causes you a problem—will it lead you to the sin of lust? Much less has been written on whether it really causes others problems. My conclusion is that nudity is not of eternal consequence to another who sees me. I base that on several points, each of which could be the subject of a full article. I list a few here:

1. God created the human body, looked at it, and pronounced it "very good" in its nude state.

2. The Scripture never condemns nudity, although there are several occasions where it would have been very easy and appropriate for the writers to have done so had it been God's purpose.

3. No one has ever been able to logically explain to me how viewing a body without clothes translates in another's mind to a rejection of a spiritual message proclaiming one's need to trust in Christ's substitutionary death as payment for my sins in order to give me a right relationship with God.

There is nothing in Scripture which makes the situation as grave as some might make it out to be.

It is interesting to note in the Romans passage that it is the stronger Christian who has the freedom to do the disputed thing. It is the weaker person who objects. Maturity brings freedom. The mature person has the strength to question disputable things, and determine and follow a proper course of action which is pleasing to God. This is the essence of freedom in Christ. Do not, however, allow this fact to be a matter of pride (we all know what that did for Lucifer), but when dealing with this issue, recognize that the free person is likely the stronger. "But do not use your freedom to indulge the sinful nature; rather serve one another in love."

My final point about this passage is that in spite of all the caution about causing others to stumble, it cannot be taken to mean that we always yield to the wishes of the objecting person. To do so would reduce the church to the consciousness level of the weakest person. All growth and freedom is for the sake of others even if it causes them to be upset. Why? Because it confronts them with their legalism. It challenges them to consider new possibilities. It is, I believe, the way God leads His people to changed positions and attitudes. Had some Christians never questioned the issue of slavery, we might still hold slaves today and not consider it wrong. Until just over a century ago, people (including Christians) over much of the earth held slaves without questioning whether it was right. As with nudity, Scripture never says whether slavery is right or wrong, it simply states it as being a part of the life situation of the people whose stories are told to make a spiritual point. Until some people in the West started questioning slavery (often based on Biblical principles), most Christians either didn't think about it or twisted Scripture to justify it. Today we look back and say unequivocally that those opposed to slavery were right, yet the consequences within the church were disastrous and still remain with us. Brother fought against brother in the bloody Civil War and most major Protestant denominations split over the issue, many remaining separate to this day.

So it may be, on a lesser scale, with the issue of nudity. If some of us Christians are convinced that it is not wrong, if we are convinced it is what God intended for His creation originally, and thus also intends for His new creation, and if we are convinced we must somehow share these convictions with others, even at the risk of fellowship with some of them being broken, then someday we (or more likely our descendants) may look back and say we did the right thing, even though the results at the time may have been painful.

So what do we do? Do we all take our clothes off at church on National Nude Weekend? Of course not! We practice nudity with discretion. What does that mean? It means we do practice nudity. We don't totally hide at home or at nudist resorts. We do go to nude beaches. We do camp and hike nude in remote areas. We do not wait until we are so remote that there is no chance whatever of being seen. Instead, we use discretion.

First, based on the distance from parking areas, and the number of people likely to be on the trail, we make a decision whether or not to remove our clothes.

Second, we prepare ourselves for the encounter which will inevitably come. We rehearse in our minds the specific words we will say when confronted. If you don't I guarantee you will be too flustered to be able to think of the best thing to say. When it happens, we don't grab our clothes to quickly cover up as if we had been doing something wrong. Instead we greet them in a cheerful voice, acting in a friendly manner. After an initial greeting, if we are going to remain in their presence more than the few seconds necessary to pass by on the trail, we say something like,

"We prefer wherever possible to swim (hike, camp, etc.) without clothes. Does that offend you?" I suggest the above words be specifically memorized. I have worked them out over several years and believe they express in a short statement and question the essence of what needs to be communicated at the moment of encounter. The statement implies we do this regularly, we weren't just caught about to have sex or go to the bathroom (the only reasons many people take their clothes off). It avoids use of the word "nude" which paints a much starker picture than "without clothes." The question is very important as it throws the ball in their court. They must react directly to our nudity. They must specifically and verbally say whether they object, and are given the opportunity to do so with the feeling that we will listen, respect them and react to their feelings. Thus, if they object, we should either put on some clothes or move on to another place. Our best response, in terms of a desire to communicate with them, is to get dressed while continuing the conversation, seeking to learn what misconception about nudity causes them to be offended.

Third, remember the words of Jesus' short teaching in Matthew 7:6, "Do not give dogs what is sacred. Don't throw your pearls to pigs." Why? Because pigs don't understand and appreciate the value of pearls. They will just trample them under foot, losing them in the mud. The Jews to whom He was speaking would have immediately connected "dogs" with the Gentiles—anyone not a Jew. Applying this verse to nudity, we should not bother trying to give our message to people who simply are incapable of accepting it. Instead, we should choose carefully to whom we try to convey the message. We should look for persons who might be receptive, but approach them with caution and discretion, gradually revealing our feelings to them and only revealing more as we are sure of their acceptance. This policy will minimize negative feelings and disrupted relationships, while reaching out to those who may possibly be open to new thinking on the subject.

Dialog of Conscience: Nudism & Scandal

by Jim C. Cunningham

TINA: I have no doubt that nudity is not a sin in and of itself. Of course, it would be sinful if a person used it to purposely cause someone to lust. But I am still confused about another point.

JIM: What's that?

TINA: Well, I can envision a situation where someone's motives for being nude were perfectly pure, but despite good intentions someone could yet be scandalized and caused to sin on account of this nudity. In other words, we could cause scandal and not even be aware of it. Aren't we responsible for the consequences of our actions no matter what our motives may be?

JIM: Yes, we are always responsible for our actions and their consequences. A good motive is not sufficient in itself to make any act pure. There is an old saying, "The road to hell is paved with good intentions." I think first we should clarify what we mean by "scandal."

TINA: What I mean by it is doing or saying something which causes another person to sin.

JIM: I think that is an accurate definition. Many people use the word very loosely, equating "scandal" with "shock." In this loose, non-theological sense, they say that someone is "scandalized" when they are merely "shocked," when no one may be caused to sin, but merely to be shocked.

TINA: I can think of at least one good example of that type of scandal. Someone might find out that a certain priest who was regarded as being very holy was an alcoholic. This would no doubt cause shock, but nobody is going to go out and get drunk or become an alcoholic upon hearing this news.

JIM: That's a fine example. So we're talking about something quite different—performing an action with good intentions, which nevertheless results in someone sinning. Of course, some people would say that other people's sins are not their problem. But this is contrary to the virtue of charity which motivates us to be concerned for the welfare of everyone.

TINA: So is there any solution to my dilemma?

JIM: Yes. I think it would be very helpful to review an age-old moral principle called "the principle of double effect."

TINA: What's that?

JIM: Morality is not so simple as merely always doing good acts, and never performing evil acts even though they may produce a good result, because we may not do evil that good may come from it. Besides this, many acts we choose to do are by their very nature neither good nor evil; they are indifferent. In fact, most of the things we do probably fall into this category. Examples are such things as when we decide to go to bed, what color car we decide to buy, what clothes we choose to wear, etc. But even though we perform acts which are either good in themselves or indifferent, morality is also concerned about one other thing—do these good or neutral acts produce good, neutral or evil effects? Obviously, if a good or indifferent act produces only good or indifferent effects and our motive for performing the acts is also good, then we cannot possibly be doing evil. But life is much more complicated than this. Many (if not most) of our acts have two or more effects which may be both good and evil.

TINA: Can you give me an example?

JIM: Sure. Let's say you plan to host a Thanksgiving dinner to which all your relatives will be invited. You plan to make it truly a festive occasion. There will be the turkey with all the trimmings, all sorts of *hors d'oeuvres* and desserts and, of course, champagne. Your motives are perfectly pure. You want to occasion a family reunion at which everyone gives thanks to the Lord for the blessings received. It is a time for happiness, rejoicing and recreation.

Now here's the fly in the soup. Uncle Harry is weak-willed. He always over-imbibes at such family gatherings and gets drunk. An unreasonably scrupulous person might conclude that since this evil effect results from the good act of arranging a Thanksgiving family reunion, then the family reunion should be called off, Uncle Harry should not be invited, or champagne should not be served.

If every decision we made were based on such scrupulosity, we would find ourselves doing nothing except going neurotic. The truth is that this Thanksgiving dinner may certainly be held, champagne may certainly be served, and Uncle Harry certainly must be invited since he is indeed a member of the family.

TINA: How can this be morally justified?

JIM: This is precisely where the principle of double-effect comes in. In order for an act to be performed which results in both good and evil effects, four conditions must hold true.

TINA: What are they?

JIM: First of all, the actual act you are doing cannot be in itself intrinsically evil; it must be either good or indifferent. Hosting a family gathering, serving champagne and inviting all relatives are not evil acts in and of themselves. They are either good, or at least indifferent. So, this first condition checks out.

TINA: But you don't want Uncle Harry to commit a sin!

JIM: Exactly, and that's the second condition. The evil effects which result from our good or indifferent act cannot be desired, but merely tolerated. Getting Uncle Harry intoxicated is not our purpose. We do not want it to happen. We merely tolerate it for the sake of other good effects.

TINA: But isn't the slightest sin bad enough to outweigh all possible good effects?

JIM: Not at all. If so, we couldn't do much of anything except go crazy. And this brings us to our third condition: the good effects to be attained by our good or indifferent actions must be equal to or greater than the evil effects.

TINA: How can you always know?

JIM: I grant that this can sometimes be a sticky area, but most of the time we can arrive at a mature judgment if our consciences are formed by the examples of Christ and the saints and other people of good reputation. Sometimes it may be necessary to consult those we consider wiser and more prudent than ourselves.

In this case, the good effects clearly outweigh the bad. By hosting this dinner, family ties will be strengthened, occasion is made to give thanks to the Lord for His blessings, our bodies and spirits are rested, and our bodies are nourished. These are just some of the possible good effects. If the good effect of celebrating a wedding did not outweigh the possible evil effect of some people over-indulging in their consumption of alcohol, then Jesus Christ would certainly not have turned vast quantities of water into wine to serve to guests at the wedding at Cana who had already consumed all the other wine that had been reserved for the occasion.[1] The Blessed Mother, too, had no problem with this as it was she who told Jesus to supply this new wine. Good people from all faiths cele-brate various occasions with good food and alcoholic beverages, not with the motive of getting anyone intoxi-cated, but merely to celebrate and relax together. Refer-ring to such examples, we can quickly see that our planned Thanksgiving meal is certainly morally permissi-ble, despite Uncle Harry.

TINA: But didn't you say we couldn't do evil that good might come from it?

JIM: Yes, and that brings us to our fourth and final condition: the good effects may not be the result of the evil effects, but rather the direct result of the indifferent or good act of hosting a Thanksgiving celebration. You see, Uncle Harry did not become intoxicated because he was invited to the family reunion. He did not become intoxi-cated because he participated in the Thanksgiving celebra-tion. Nor did he become intoxicated because champagne was served with which to celebrate, which nobody in-tended to serve in order to intoxicate anyone. You see, the good did not in anyway come from the evil. The evil effect was a result of the indifferent or good act of inviting Harry to this family reunion.

So you see, all these four conditions hold true, and that means that the celebration can go on without us suffering any scruples of conscience whatever.

TINA: This is really neat! It certainly helps clarify a lot of murky situations! Now let me try to relate it to the nudity question.

JIM: Okay, go ahead.

TINA: Well, condition number one stated that the act could not be evil in and of itself, but must be either intrinsically good or indifferent. Being naked is at least

---

[1] Cf. John 2:1-11.

indifferent. If it were evil in and of itself then God could not have let us be born naked, and Jesus could not have let them strip Him of His clothes before they crucified Him.

JIM: So condition number one checks out perfectly.

TINA: Now, condition number two says that the evil effect cannot be desired but merely tolerated. Certainly I do not desire anyone to commit sin on account of my nudity.

JIM: Then condition number two also checks out.

TINA: According to the third condition, the evil effects cannot be greater than the good effects. I can think of lots of good effects:

First of all, there's my own psychological health. To be able to dress as if no part of my body were shameful does immeasurable good to my own psychological health. Then there's the good socio-psychological effect. By being naked with others, we are confirming and reaffirming this fact as we regard each other as whole persons and not merely as acceptable parts and shameful parts. Then there's the good effect of education. Sexual morbid curiosity is not only nipped in the bud but even totally preempted! Then there's the good effect of openness and honesty presenting ourselves, at least physically, as who we really are with no pretenses. In a way, all clothes are lies. They hide part of the whole, or pretend what is not. Then there's the good effect of social, chaste intimacy. Social nudity seems to occasion an inexpressible togetherness. Everyone feels like family. You want to share with everybody as though they were your brother or sister.

And of course there are lots of good physical effects. When I come home from work and remove my sweaty bra, I don't think it does me much physical good if it feels so good to have it off and all I can do is scratch my suffocated, itchy breasts. Sunbathing may not be the politically correct vogue these days, but I can certainly say that being in the sun makes me feel very healthy. The more of my body that is exposed to the sun the healthier I feel.

Then there are practical good effects. You could cut your laundry down in half. In the summer, you could go for long periods without even thinking of having to put anything on. Nudity is also fun and relaxing. There's an inexpressible joy in being naked with others. It must be somehow related to that openness and honesty I referred to before. Also, it's got something to do with trust. In our culture, we are taught to regard nudity as a very vulnerable state. To be comfortable in this vulnerability requires a great deal of mutual trust.

And I can think of some good spiritual effects as well. By being totally naked I am saying, "God made me; He don't make junk!" Since I believe that people are created in God's Own Image, I must conclude that this applies to the entire body. Since the whole of our bodies is godly, we cannot attach shame to any particular part. Nakedness disposes me to pray better. I feel as though the veil is lifted and I can commune with my God face to face.

JIM: I'm sure you could go on, but I think that's enough for now. Now against all these good effects, weigh the one evil effect of someone possibly lusting on account of your nakedness. Even if you knew it was not only a possibility but a fact, this abuse of our nudity does not come anywhere near outweighing all the good effects you mentioned. Of course, we do not want anyone to sin, and your sensitivity in this regard is praise worthy, but being scrupulous about it is not the best response. Rather, let us live our lives with the freedom of the sons of God and pray that God's grace may dispel the evil in people's hearts, in whatever form it is found.

TINA: This discussion has been like a huge burden being lifted off my back. Thank you for making it all so clear.

Dialog of Conscience: The Cannes Principle

by Jim C. Cunningham

TINA: I was thinking about how many moralists today object to new customs or fashions of dress that, in one way or another, expose more of the body. They say that all such fashions are immodest and that it is sinful to wear them. What is puzzling is that they themselves wear fashions their own grandmothers and even mothers would not have approved of. When I mention this fact to them, they get defensive, saying that their situation is different because what they wear has long been established as customary.

JIM: For example?

TINA: A clear example is two-piece bathing suits or bikinis. Since these swimsuit fashions are now very common, they think that they are within the bounds of modesty. But when their mothers were their age no one would have dared to wear anything but a one-piece swimsuit, and even that would have had a kind of mini-skirt attached. And when their grandmothers were their age, even their legs would have had to be covered down to the ankles.

JIM: So what is puzzling to you?

TINA: They say that it is good—that is, within the bounds of modesty—for them to wear two-piece swimsuits that expose 95% of their bodies. I agree. At least it's better and more sensible than wearing all the cloth our grandmothers wore. But these moralists would claim that whoever began the trend were sinful and immodest just because such greater skin exposure was not yet common.

JIM: So?

TINA: So in effect they are saying that a good thing (i.e. the present, more sensible custom) had an evil beginning. But this seems to contradict a moral principle that Jesus taught.

JIM: Which one?

TINA: That good trees produce good fruit, and bad trees produce bad fruit. He said you can know a tree by its fruit. Bad trees cannot produce good fruit.[1]

So if we apply Jesus' moral principle to this matter, if today's commonly accepted greater exposure is admitted to be good fruit, then the tree from which it came must also have been good. Thus, just because those pioneers who initiated the trend were exceeding the bounds of what was then considered acceptable cannot mean that they were immodest.

JIM: What about the motive factor?

TINA: Well, I don't think we can put that into the equation because no man can ever judge that. For all we know, the

---

[1] Cf. Matthew 7:17f.

motive of the first lady who bared her breasts on the beach at Cannes on the French Riviera might have been entirely pure; maybe she was deeply convinced of the goodness of her breasts and she could see no reason why men's chests were somehow mysteriously holier than hers. Her motive could have been fairness. Or it could have been simply comfort. It is not sinful to try to be comfortable; after all, that's probably at least one motive why everybody goes to the beach in the first place.

And just as the motives of that topfree pioneer at Cannes might have been entirely pure, the motive of the above mentioned moralists, for all anybody knows, could be quite impure. Just because bikinis are common does not mean that all who wear them are truly modest in their hearts.

So, because motives are not knowable except to God and the individual, I don't think they can be a consideration in this discussion.

JIM: I agree; you explained it well. But though you aptly invoked a moral principle of Jesus about good fruit having to come from good trees, some people will probably still not be satisfied. Somehow, intuitively, they will still feel immodest if they dare to go beyond the customary limits (murky as they always are). Can you add anything to support your argument further?

TINA: I think I would apply the "principle of double effect" we discussed in our last dialog.[1]

JIM: Why so?

TINA: Because I think their concern is, "What if, since this new, 'barer' trend is not yet customary, it is, for that reason more likely to cause the evil effect of arousing lust in someone?" I think it is this anxiety that explains the feeling of somehow being "naughty" if you go beyond the limits.

JIM: I think there is another factor that causes the anxiety as well.

TINA: What's that?

JIM: Proverbs 22:1 says, "A good name is to be chosen rather than great riches." We all have a right to our good reputation. People fear being misjudged by others. The woman who first removed her top at Cannes somehow had

---

[1] See above, pp. 153f.

to overcome this concern. Either she believed others would not look down on her if she bared her breasts, or even that they would admire her and look up to her for it.

TINA: Like, "Way to go, Baby!"

JIM: Yes. Don't you feel that way when you see someone bravely step out and do something sensible that exceeds established norms?

TINA: Yeah! I recently read about a lady in Ontario who removed her top at a crowded, municipal pool and refused to put it back on when the authorities ordered her to. She said it was a matter of simple justice. There was no indication whatsoever that her motive was to turn anybody on. She just saw an injustice and wanted to make a demonstration to raise peoples' consciousness. Just because we are accustomed to injustices does not mean we should accept them. Jesus came to set us free[1] and we should work for greater and greater justice in this world. So, yes, definitely, when I read about that lady I felt inspired by her, and I think most others also looked up to her as some sort of a heroine, rather than as some sleazy slut or something like that.

JIM: So then we have isolated at least two main factors why we might feel uneasy about pioneering "barer" trends ourselves—

TINA: Right—fear of being misjudged and looked down upon, and not wanting to cause anyone to sin. And this latter consideration is why I think it will be comforting to apply the "principle of double effect."

JIM: Okay. Does the first condition check out?

TINA: Definitely. The first condition is that the act itself— the "object"—cannot be intrinsically evil. It is not intrinsically evil to wear less, or even to be completely naked. Most of us get naked every day, at least to shower.

And the second condition clearly checks out; the possible evil effect is not at all desired, but merely tolerated. Again, this one involves motives, which we cannot know, but if those pioneers truly did not want to cause any sin, then this condition checks out.

JIM: And the third condition?

TINA: Thirdly, the good effects cannot be the direct result of the evil effect, but rather, either of the act (object) itself

---

[1] Cf. John 8:32 & Galatians 5:1.

which we have already determined to be good, or at least morally indifferent, or from one or more of the good effects. In other words, we cannot have a situation where we dupe ourselves into thinking that good can ever come from evil. That would be a grave delusion. Indeed, this is what Jesus said when he said a bad tree cannot produce good fruit.

JIM: Can you relate this third condition more specifically to our case in point?

TINA: Sure. Let's suppose the good effects of the act of removing her top at Cannes before it was the norm included such things as comfort, affirmation of greater body acceptance for herself and educating others, a sense of freedom, etc. For all we know, maybe she had a rash or something which she hoped the sun would help heal, so health could also be among the good effects. What would cause all such good effects is not anyone's lusting, but rather, the act of removing her top. In fact, the evil effect is not even definite; it is only a possibility.

JIM: Good. One more condition to go. Do you remember what it is?

TINA: Yes, this is the hardest one because it requires prudence and good judgment. The fourth condition says that the good effect must at least be equal to the evil effect. I think in this case the fourth condition clearly checks out, especially because the evil effect is not even definite, but only possible.

JIM: But suppose it was definite. Suppose some voyeur openly manifested his lust to her in some way.

TINA: I don't think she caused him to lust. He was already an unchaste person before she removed her top. Speaking for myself, I know I would not be very comfortable in that situation. If my motives included greater physical comfort, the presence of such a voyeur would definitely spoil it. But I can at least hypothetically conceive of a lady who is so thick-skinned as to be able to ignore such a person and still enjoy the good effects of being topfree. Maybe she is so resolved to do what it takes to establish a more just, wholesome and sensible custom that she is willing to tolerate such nerds.

I was once at a quarry where skinny-dipping was long established. When I arrived at a small beach at one end, there was already a lady sitting nude in the sun on the sand. At that moment some young, rowdy, beer-drinking men hiked by and shouted untoward comments like, "Hey! Nice tits!" I thought those guys were nothing but pollution. It was such a quiet, beautiful, picturesque place, and nothing seemed more natural there than that nude lady. It was all so pure that I felt like it would practically be a sin for her to have to wear a bikini or something. Besides, they probably would have behaved the same way anyway.

JIM: What did she do?

TINA: Nothing; she ignored them. She made no attempt to cover up. I felt that she was so right that I decided to show her support by going nude also. I was wearing a bikini with my cut-offs on, and I had intended to only remove my shorts, but I was moved with a sense of justice and wanted to show her support, not despite those voyeuristic guys, but because of them. So, as I introduced myself to her, I took everything off and joined her on the tiny beach. Though she was probably pretty thick-skinned already, she showed a sense of relief and gratitude at what I did. Though those guys continued their comments from across the quarry, I have to say that I definitely felt more comfortable nude than if I had only removed my shorts and kept my bikini on. I would have felt like I had failed to support my sister and also that I would have compounded the problem by testifying to a lie rather than the truth.

Whether those guys committed any sins besides rudeness I do not know. I certainly wouldn't put it past them. They did not come off as paragons of purity, that's for sure. But I still think I did the right thing. The good effects of my stripping off—especially the consolation it offered that lady—was far greater, in my judgment, than any evil effects that our nudity might have occasioned. Those guys were crass and rude. Our nudity did not cause that; they already were crass and rude. Our nudity just occasioned them to demonstrate it. The same is true if they committed sins of lust. They were already impure anyway. We would not have caused them to be impure. At most, we would only have occasioned their impurity to be expressed.

JIM: But aren't you concerned about their souls?

TINA: Sure, I am, but wearing bikinis won't help any—it would only make things worse. They would be fantasizing about our "nice tits" covered by a very few square inches of cloth. It would be like flashing a red veil in front of a raging bull; it would only cause them to get more excited. I do not see how anything could be better than showing the body just as God made it. When you see the reality, there's nothing left to provide further fantasy fodder.

I think the same thing applies to that pioneer lady at Cannes. If her exposure did have the evil effect of causing someone to lust, the good effects such as I enumerated above, definitely outweighed the possible evil effect.

And, you know, I think the philosophical proof of *reductio ad absurdum*[1] applies here too.

JIM: How's that?

TINA: Suppose you knew that some voyeur was lusting after you even if you were wearing what was well within the normal limits. Would someone be obliged to wear a tent on account of such a person? Of course, that is absurd, so then we cannot say that that pioneer lady had to defer to such a voyeur either. If you know Uncle Harry always gets drunk at weddings, you still have to invite him to such an important family celebration. Life must go on; you just have to put up with such things.

JIM: I think you have done an excellent job explaining the morality of those who pioneer "barer" trends. You have clearly shown how those moralists who define immodesty simply as whatever exceeds the present norms are wrong. People desperately need to have a better attitude toward the body and as long as their motives are not impure, those who push the limits by daring to be "barer" are doing a noble work. I dare say it is even a spiritual work of mercy.

TINA: How's that? Which one?

JIM: Instructing the ignorant. They are teaching the best way—by example. They show that the body is good.

TINA: I think that's what we did at that quarry. If I had not undressed, and if that lady had covered up, we would actually have been teaching the lie that the body is evil, indecent, impure, and all that trash.

---

[1] See note on p. 49.

Suppose you are at the doctor's and the nurse shows you into a room and tells you to get undressed and the doctor will be along shortly. Most patients probably just undress down to their underwear, but since there's nothing he isn't going to see before you get out of there, you might as well go all the way. So suppose you do, but as the door opens, instead of the doctor, in walks another patient by accident. There are only two ways to react: You either scramble and try to cover up "certain" parts, or you hide nothing and just help him find his way. The first option is what is truly scandalous because it teaches the lie that the body is not good and holy, but that we should consider it bad and shameful. That is the message we send by scrambling to cover "certain" parts. And what does it say about those "certain" parts but that they, especially, are what are evil and shameful? But, as you said, it really is the spiritual work of mercy of instructing the ignorant if you choose the latter option. Your calm demeanor might actually floor him and effectively teach a lesson in truth that he will never forget.

JIM: I think you are very right.

TINA: I think we would all do well to push the limits. Bikinis certainly make a lot more sense than what our grandmothers wore, and it is obvious that it is precisely the greater degree of exposure that is what makes them so much more sensible. If some is good, why shouldn't more be better? Why not go all the way? Does there exist some "bottom line"—some "line of demarcation"? If so, the history of what people consider modest certainly does not bear this out. Since there is no defined line beyond which we enter into some kind of zone of intrinsic immodesty, then we ought not to behave as though we believed in such a nebulous unreality. We ought to push the limits and keep pushing until society finally recognizes the fact that the entire body is good and acceptable just as God made it. There is no virtue whatever in compulsively veiling any part of the body. Doing so only reinforces a lie; it does not teach the truth.

JIM: So should we all just live naked all the time?

TINA: Well, if somebody did, he would not be immodest, though people might think he is off his rocker.

JIM: And would that be an effective way to teach the truth?

TINA: No, I don't think so. No, we cannot do it in a way that would be counter-productive; that would be bad pedagogy. There are lots of ways you can push the limits without being counter-productive. A good example is openly exposing your breast when nursing your baby in public, or openly changing in a locker room so your naked body is not hidden. We ought to take full advantage of situations where nudity makes incontrovertible sense such as saunas, gang showers, locker rooms, swimming, sunbathing, keeping cool at home, sleeping, etc. Changing clothes necessarily entails getting partially or totally naked. We would do well not to close doors to change, but to change openly, even while we're conversing with people. The only reason to wear a towel to and from the shower is to hide the body, which reinforces the lie. Nudity here makes perfect sense and no reasonable person would think we were off our rocker for not wrapping a towel around ourselves. If we would all take advantage of these kinds of situations, we would go a long way toward teaching the ignorant about the body's goodness. I think the important thing is that we don't just always hug the shoreline, but instead, as Jesus said, "Put out into the deep."[1] That is where we will catch fish. But, as Jesus also said, we must be sure to cast our nets to starboard,[2] making sure our motives are always right.

JIM: I'm all for it! Let's go fishing!

TINA: And let's fish in the nude like St. Peter![3]

---

[1] Luke 5:4.
[2] Cf. John 21:6.
[3] Cf. John 21:7.

Open Letter to Evangelicals[1]

by Paul M. Bowman

Dear Pastor & Parishioners:

After considering your views on nudity I am compelled to write. I can scarcely recall a more biased, deceptive, and unscriptural opinion passed off as "Christianity.'

My family and I are now nudists/naturists precisely *because* of our Scriptural studies, not *in spite* of it (as some of you would insist). The question came up about nine or ten years ago and, being dedicated Christians, we turned to the Bible to determine how we should choose. We found repeated "evidence" in the church that social nudity is a sin, but found a far different truth in the Bible. I should point out that our study scrutinized every Biblical reference to "naked," "nakedness," "unclothed," "stripped," "uncovered," etc. We studied each reference in some six or seven translations, versions or paraphrases of the Bible. Your objections to nudity are so devoid of Scriptural knowledge, much less understanding, that it can hardly be called Biblical Christianity. Your incessant linking of nudity with sexual sin, to the exclusion of all else, makes about as much sense as insisting that fire can only be connected to the destruction of property and life, and is therefore totally immoral. Indeed, it makes me wonder just how shallow your understanding of sexuality must also be.

Your "logic" that because God made garments of skins for Adam,[2] He was thereby condemning the state of nakedness, is about as sensible as concluding that because God made the clouds that blot out the sun, He was condemning sunshine. It is much more likely that Genesis 3:21 shows that God ordained clothes as well as the already ordained nakedness.[3] Furthermore, because of the fall, Adam was no longer in Eden and was thus subject to the varieties of weather and climate, and God

---

[1] This first appeared in *Clothed with the Sun* 7.3 and is reprinted here with the author's permission.
[2] Cf. Genesis 3:21.
[3] Cf. Genesis 2:25.

knew they would need clothes. God loved and cared for them even after they sinned.

The Jewish prophets were apparently commonly naked, so much so that when Saul stripped off his clothes and prophesied naked, the people figured he must be a prophet also.[1] It must be a strange God indeed to use a vessel in a condemned state to bring His message to His people.

If the state of public nakedness is prohibited by God, then the story of Isaiah[2] is even more strange. In that case, God directly commanded Isaiah to loose the sackcloth from his hips—and he went naked and barefoot for three years. It seems that your God cannot make up his mind; or maybe public nudity is acceptable for some people but not others. My God's laws are the same for everybody.

Ezekiel's allegory pictures being naked and bare as a natural and totally acceptable state: "Your breasts were formed and your (pubic) hair had grown."[3]

The Song of Solomon is well known for its repeated appreciation of the naked body. I cannot understand why your God would several times use a state of sinfulness (i.e. nakedness) to depict His people in a proper relationship with Him.

Sexual intercourse is Scripturally ordained to be private and covered.[4] I take "covered" to mean "not public."

Clothes and jewelry are a gift to enhance and increase one's beauty,[5] but never Scripturally required except for priests in the presence of the altar[6] and for women during menstruation.

It is interesting that Noah was both drunk and naked in public view, but Ham—not Noah—was the one who was cursed when he called attention to Noah's nakedness.[7] It seems that your God should have been pleased that Ham notified his brothers to cover Noah—and that Noah should have been the one punished. My God knows that both the

---

[1] Cf. I Samuel 19:24.
[2] Cf. Isaiah 20:2ff.
[3] Ezekiel 16:7.
[4] Cf. Ezekiel 16:8.
[5] Cf. Ezekiel 16:10-14.
[6] Cf. Exodus 28:42.
[7] Cf. Genesis 9:22-24.

clothed and the naked are natural states of being and that calling attention to, or making light of the body, is giving it a position not ordained by Him.

While on the subject of drunkenness and nudity, the Bible clearly states that it is wrong to get a person drunk to be able to view his nakedness.[1]

Frankly, I think you are on very dangerous ground with your negative view of social nudity. King David danced naked in the City of David to celebrate the return of the ark. When his wife, Michal, criticized his dancing publicly in the nude, she was soundly rebuffed and ended up childless until her death.[2] How can your God be pleased with a joyful dance before Himself by one in a condemned state of nakedness? And all the maidens saw him![3] And why did God make Michal barren (I assume you believe fertility is determined by God) when she was merely espousing your God's point of view regarding social or public nudity? Your attitude today seems to be strikingly similar to Michal's many centuries ago; I would tremble if I had your attitude before my God.

Although some try to say Peter had underwear on, the probability is that he fished in the nude.[4] At least every other person in the New Testament who had his outer garments removed was left naked.[5]

Every Biblical association of nakedness with shame is in reference to a sin already committed. This is because one cannot hide from God behind literal or figurative clothes. God will remove whatever one uses to cover his sins, to expose a person as that person really is, i.e. "naked." All man-made excuses (for sin) will be removed. But this does not refer to physical nakedness.[6]

Historically, the early Christians were baptized in the nude, a fact conveniently ignored by today's church.

One statement I heard recently left me outraged at the open, callused deception practiced by many evangelicals. The statement that Leviticus 18:6-19 is God's law regarding the state of being unclothed, is either utterly irrespon-

[1] Cf. Habakkuk 2:15.
[2] Cf. II Samuel 6:20-23.
[3] Cf. Ibid. v. 20.
[4] Cf. John 21:7.
[5] Cf. Mark 14:51f & Acts 19:16.
[6] E.g. cf. Ezekiel 23:29; Hosea 2:3 & Micah 1:8 & 11.

sible or an outright lie. Every translation other than the King James version recognizes this passage to refer not to nakedness, but to sexual intercourse. Evangelicals have a responsibility to make this clear, not to contort it into a condemnation of nudity even within the family.

This letter is not meant to imply that nakedness cannot be used for sinful purposes. The sin comes, not from the *fact* of being naked, but from *how* the state of nakedness is used. A dead body, although openly naked, cannot sin. "God saw all that He made, and behold, it was very good,"[1] including human bodies. Some people choose to desecrate it; others try to deny it; still others accept their bodies as God created them. The reason is simple. These people are able to distinguish between nudity and sexual activity. They know that the "real" person lives within the body and that person is much more interesting and stimulating than the person's body. This is how it should be because God created us as spiritual, intellectual, social as well as physical beings.[2] When one places so much emphasis (either positively or negatively) on the body he is really idolizing the body over the sacred person God created. There are those who idolize the mind, others who idolize social relationships, and many so-called evangelical "Christians" who idolize the spiritual.

Finally, one has to consider the question of lust. I believe the problem lies in a misunderstanding of the word. Lust is a desire so passionate or strong that it very nearly compels action, especially action that breaks one's accepted bounds of behavior. This is not to be confused with exhilaration or the feeling of enchantment, or exhilaration in nature. Most people never forget the feeling of joyful pleasure when they see Yosemite Valley for the first time, or the enchantment they experience while driving along much of the California coastline. Yet, who would come home from vacation saying they "lusted" over these natural beauties? In the same way, a man may, indeed probably will, get much the same sense of excitement when viewing the natural beauty of a well proportioned female body. Such a feeling of pleasure or exhilaration, however, does not constitute lust, unless he is moved to

---

[1] Genesis 1:31.
[2] Luke 2:52 would suggest this.

take an action designed to result in a sexual union contrary to his Scriptural bounds of behavior. Mere appreciation, or even excitement at the wonder of the human body, is not lust. Lust begins when one is willing to start thinking of ways to sexually attract the other person in a union contrary to Scriptural morality.

I am comfortable spiritually with my open nudity because I know I am right with God and that I have nothing to hide from Him. Indeed, through Christ, I am returned spiritually to the same state Adam enjoyed in Eden. Because my heart (intention, desires) is right and my life is right before God, I choose not to pursue any of the sexual sins the Bible actually does condemn.

Last: I trust that you will study the more than fifty Scriptural references to nudity for your decision on public nakedness, and not rely on contortions of other Scriptural references that really don't address this subject.

Respectfully in Christ,
Paul M. Bowman

Naked, I Follow Naked Jesus[1]

by Greg Cook

"I am fully convinced that nothing is unclean of itself. If someone considers something unclean then for him it is unclean."[2]

Many people try to teach us that our bodies, or certain parts of our bodies, are somehow "unclean." With such thinking, being seen, or seeing others naked means we are somehow depraved, or that it will lead to depravity. These teachers promise freedom from depravity through being clothed. They promise freedom, while they them-

---

[1] "*Nudus nudum Iesum sequi*" seems to have been first coined by St. Jerome (d. 420 A.D.) in his letter to Rusticus (Ep. 125), and was often quoted by many mystics and saints such as St. Bonaventure.
[2] Romans 14:14.

selves are slaves to depravity for "a man is a slave to whatever has mastered him."[1]

Nudity is not unclean of itself. Nudity becomes unclean through its misuse. An example is pornography, which is an *exploitation* of the nude body. When a person drives a car drunk, it is a misuse of their driving privilege. Drunk drivers have caused great injury to many people, and we therefore pass laws against driving drunk—a misuse of the car. But we do not outlaw cars or driving. However, anti-nudity laws that outlaw nudity altogether, which are really intended to stop perverts (and they *should* be stopped), make every nude person into a pervert and criminal. The laws should only be against those who misuse nudity by committing lewd acts and who are causing harm to others. Just being nude is not lewd or impure. "Do not call anything impure that God has made clean."[2] We have been made clean through the blood of Jesus Christ.[3] Only in understanding that truth in a clothing-optional environment will people know the full freedom and benefits of the correct use of their bodies.

Satan and man through sin have perverted the good things of God so much, that now when we see the truth, it appears not to make any sense. Being naked before God and man has become foolishness. "But God chose the foolish things of the world to shame the wise; God chose the weak things of the world to shame the strong. He chose the lowly things of this world and the despised things—and the things that are not—to nullify the things that are, so that no one may boast before Him."[4] When we are stripped of our clothing we have no reason to boast, for then all that we are is what God made us to be—His good and "wonderfully made"[5] creation. "God saw all that He had made, and it was very good."[6] "Woe to those who call evil good and good evil..."[7] Jesus Christ, Who was God before the foundation of the world, is clothed in nothing but a brilliant light, the splendor of His Own glory. "O Lord

---

[1] II Peter 2:19.
[2] Acts 10:15.
[3] Cf. Ephesians 1:7.
[4] I Corinthians 1:27-29.
[5] Psalm 139:14.
[6] Genesis 1:31.
[7] Isaiah 5:20.

my God, You are very great; You are clothed with splendor and majesty. He wraps Himself in light as with a garment..."[1]

"His splendor was like the sunrise; rays flashed from His hand, where His power was hidden."[2] He needs no external garment, which is meant to hide the truth. Jesus said, "I am the Truth."[3] When He came to earth as a man, He "stripped" Himself of His heavenly glory, and He gave up all that was His, which is everything. "For you know the grace of our Lord Jesus Christ, that though He was rich, yet for your sakes He became poor, so that you through His poverty might become rich."[4] When it was time for Him to depart, He prayed, "Father, glorify Me in Your presence with the glory I had before the world began."[5] Then He was beaten and mocked and hanged naked on a cross. "... there were many who were appalled at Him—His appearance was so disfigured beyond that of any man and His form marred beyond human likeness..."[6] "When the soldiers crucified Jesus, they took His clothes, dividing them into four shares, one for each of them, with the undergarment remaining. This garment was seamless, woven in one piece from top to bottom. 'Let's not tear it,' they said to one another. 'Let's decide by lot who will get it.'"[7] Though He was in full view of everyone, He did not hide, and He was not ashamed. "Jesus, ...Who for the joy set before Him endured the cross, scorning its shame, and sat down at the right hand of the throne of God."[8] Now, after His resurrection, we see "... high above on the throne was a figure like that of a man. I saw that from what appeared to be His waist up He looked like glowing metal, as if full of fire, and that from there down He looked like fire; and brilliant light surrounded Him. Like the appearance of a rainbow in the clouds on a rainy day, so was the

---

[1] Psalm 104:1f.
[2] Habakkuk 3:4.
[3] John 14:6.
[4] II Corinthians 8:9.
[5] John 17:5.
[6] Isaiah 52:14.
[7] John 19:23f.
[8] Hebrews 12:2.

radiance around Him. This was the appearance of the likeness of the glory of the Lord."[1]

And "The Son is the radiance of God's glory and the exact representation of His being, sustaining all things by His powerful Word."[2]

The only required clothing is Jesus Christ Himself. All else is vanity. Those who do not believe had better get dressed in Christ, or their shame will not be covered, even by their high moral standards and right living (their "fig leaf apron"[3]). For those who are clothed in Christ, there is no shame or reason to hide. Therefore you can be "naked and not ashamed."[4] "If anybody is preaching to you a gospel other than ... the Good News that Jesus is the Christ,[5] ... let Him be eternally condemned!"[6]

Other facts supporting naturism:

Prophets were known for prophesying in the nude. Saul, and all those who went before him, prophesied naked after the Holy Spirit of God came on them.[7] Isaiah was commanded by God to go naked before everyone for three years.[8] God Who hates sin doesn't command people to sin.[9]

David danced naked before all Israel as an "act of worship." Michal claimed he was acting as a "vulgar man would," but she was cursed by God for trying to rebuke him.[10]

In the New Testament, a follower of Jesus fled naked.[11] Peter, one of the twelve disciples and founder of the Catholic Church, used to fish naked.[12]

Originally, baptisms were done in the nude. Even mass baptisms with men, women and children together. It signified their being restored to man's original condition, having their shame removed.

---

[1] Ezekiel 1:26-28.
[2] Hebrews 1:3.
[3] Genesis 3:7.
[4] Genesis 2:25.
[5] Acts 5:42.
[6] Galatians 1:9.
[7] Cf. I Samuel 19:23f.
[8] Cf. Isaiah 20:2f.
[9] Cf. James 1:13.
[10] Cf. II Samuel 6:14ff.
[11] Cf. Mark 14:52.
[12] Cf. John 21:7.

Public bathing was a common practice at one time. Whole families were together at the public bath (including Christians). The word "gymnasium" means to train in the nude; it was a common practice at one time.

Today there are several Christian naturist organizations. We Christian naturists believe that because our bodies are God's creation, they are good and bring glory to Him. We believe that Christ, having died for our sin, has taken away our shame; therefore, we no longer need to "hide." One pastor presented a good argument saying, "Who said it was okay to be naked at the doctor's office, the gym, or any other so-called 'appropriate' place?" He meant that there is no Biblical precedent for such a belief.

It is only the *misuse* of nudity, and also of clothing, that is wrong. But being clothed in Jesus Christ is a requirement, for we will not be accepted by God any other way.

So, even now, God is looking for you, to fellowship with you. He is calling out, "Where are you?"[1] "What have you done?"[2] He knows, but you must not doubt God's love for you, as did Adam & Eve. You must come forward and expose your sin. Let Him remove the fig leaves, and clothe you with His sacrifice—the Lord Jesus Christ!

Jewish Men Had No "Privates"

by Jim C. Cunningham

Male genitalia were not at all "private parts" in Hebrew culture. Biology itself requires them to be *external* organs, often needing to droop low in the heat in order to keep the semen at the right temperature, cooler than internal body heat. It is contrary to nature herself for culture to concoct customs denying the fact of the visibility of the body and the externality of skin. To contrive to "privatize" what is by nature external is as inane as outlawing the bark on trees or the feathers on birds. Yet one of the oddities of human culture is that we cannot

---

[1] Genesis 3:9.
[2] Genesis 3:13.

174

only imagine such absurdities but even forcefully impose them on ourselves, even according them the sanction of law and "religion."

Thus many religious people have created a pseudo-virtue out of compulsively hiding what God created to be external and visible. Their definition of the virtue of sexual modesty is at least partly intrinsically physical, requiring a nebulous quantity of coverings of fabrics, leather, etc. What other virtue is like this one? Just imagine if the virtue of humility depended—at least partly—on wearing a certain kind of hat or skipping, instead of walking, whenever going about in public! Yet despite the fact that all true virtue is by nature spiritual and not physical, such "religious" people staunchly insist on precisely the externalization of this one virtue of sexual modesty.

Despite Jesus' much lambasting of the Pharisees for doing this very thing—making religion a matter of external observances,[1] it seems that the Pharisee dynamic never rests, but always tends to turn what is spiritual into what is material. Indeed, this lies at the very core of idolatry, the sin which the Torah proscribed more than any other.[2]

It is a traditional Christian principle—especially elucidated by St. Thomas Aquinas—that "grace builds on nature."[3] Not only the system of grace (i.e. growing in godliness), but also the various schemata of cultures, including social customs concerning dress and body attitudes, should also be congruent with nature. In many ways Mosaic culture evidenced this respect for nature. This article focuses on the fact that Jewish culture had a very natural, practical acceptance of the human body, especially male genitalia.

This wholesome attitude was not unique to Jews; most of their Gentile neighbors shared the same unabashed attitude toward male genitalia as is evident from ancient art and writings, some of which would seem to go overboard in their emphasis of male genitalia, even going so far as to make phallic worship central in their public, religious rituals. At least this shows they were not at all bashful about phalluses and testicles!

---

[1] Cf. Matthew 15:17-20 & 23:13ff.
[2] E.g. cf. Leviticus 19:4; 26:1 & 30; Deuteronomy 31:16-20 & 32:16ff.
[3] See note 3 on p. 259.

Fertility and a numerous progeny were highly respected, and the most obvious, natural, physical symbol of this were the male genitalia because they were by nature external, highly visible, and obviously essential to procreation.

Although phallic worship *per se* was not part of the Jewish religion, the phallus nevertheless held a high and honored place. Abraham and Sarah were apparently not blessed by God because even at the ripe old ages of 100 and 99, respectively,[1] they were still without any progeny. Nevertheless, God revealed to Abraham that despite his apparent infertility, He would nevertheless yet bless them with progeny as numerous "as the stars of heaven and as the sand which is on the seashore."[2] It was in direct reference to this promise of copious procreation that God initiated a new covenant with Abram, the sign of which was to be surgically engraved "in the flesh of your foreskins."[3] God's choice of the phallus was not at all a random choice. As mentioned above, the phallus was universally held in high esteem as the symbol of fertility *par excellence.* Quite in accordance with nature, God accepted this fact, and chose it to symbolize His covenant with Abram and his descendants. The phallus itself was not to symbolize this, for that would not have been at all special since even the neighboring Gentiles valued the phallus as a prime symbol of fertility. What was to be unique to this new covenant was that even the foreskin that naturally covered the head (i.e. glans) of the penis would be surgically removed. Thus the symbol of the covenant was not simply the phallus, which was common even to their Gentile neighbors, but specifically the *perpetually exposed*, most sensitive *head* of every male's penis.

This surgery not only symbolized God's promise of abundant offspring through Abraham, and the fact that Abraham's family enjoyed a special relationship with God, unlike their Gentile neighbors, but it also expressed the Jews' covenantal responsibility to be sensitive to God, not

---

[1] Cf. Genesis 17:17.
[2] Genesis 22:17.
[3] Genesis 17:11.

hardening their hearts and stiffening their necks,[1] but being open, attentive, docile and responsive. It is in this context that both Old and New Testaments often refer to the circumcision of the ears,[2] heart[3] and lips.[4] St. Paul even refers to "the circumcision of Christ" by which the *whole* body of flesh is put off[5] (i.e. cutting off carnal lusts from our lives). Just as penile circumcision exposes the highly sensitive glans by removing its natural covering, so God wanted His people to be highly sensitive and responsive to Him by keenly listening to His voice, lovingly heeding His Word, and proclaiming His Word just as He revealed it.

When Joshua circumcised hundreds of thousands of Jews just before entering the Promised Land, Joshua 5:9 says the "rolling away" of their foreskins symbolized also their rolling away the reproach of Egypt.

Circumcision also expressed another thing. Naturally, the only time the head of the penis is exposed is during an erection, when a man's stiffening, rising penis outgrows its natural sheath, ready for the procreative act of sexual intercourse, when the drawn sword will be specially sheathed in the vagina of his wife. As a matter of fact, this is precisely how classical culture regarded it, as is proven even from the fact that the Latin word, "*vagina,*" literally means "sheath" or "scabbard." In John 18:11, when Jesus tells St. Peter to replace his sword into its scabbard, the Latin Vulgate literally says "*in vaginam.*" Such talk makes people in contemporary cultures uncomfortable, sweat and cringe, but such facts of life in ancient times were not only not embarrassing, but as I said, were often emulated to a hyperbolic degree, making them the central focus of sacred worship.

King Saul was not abashed to demand a wedding present consisting of one hundred Philistine foreskins,[6] and

---

[1] Cf. Exodus 32:9; Psalm 95:8 & Acts 7:51.
[2] Cf. Acts 7:51.
[3] Cf. Leviticus 26:41; Deuteronomy 10:16 & 30:6; Jeremiah 4:4; 9:26; Ezekiel 44:7 & 9; Acts 7:51; Romans 2:28ff; Philippians 3:3.
[4] Cf. Exodus 6:12 & 30.
[5] Cf. Colossians 2:11.
[6] Cf. I Samuel 18:25 & II Samuel 3:14.

David did not hesitate to go and fetch him twice that amount.[1]

The very special sign of not just the phallus, but specifically the surgically exposed *head* of the phallus, took on the added significance that the new relationship between God and man as sealed in this new covenant, was to be like unto the intimate, one-flesh, sexual union of husband and wife. Indeed, this was specifically how God originally created man to image Him. "God created man in His Own image, in the image of God he created him; male and female he created them."[2] God was originally mirrored in the faithful, enduring, exclusive, procreative *union* of husband and wife. Somehow Original Sin distorted this, but in His great mercy, through salvation history, God established various covenants to prepare the way for the final covenant in the Blood of Jesus Christ. The Old Testament often refers to the covenantal relationship between God and His people as a marriage.[3] He even compares the unique desire of a groom for his bride on their wedding night to His passionate love for us.[4] No, God is not at all embarrassed either by sexual parts or sex itself. In fact, it is the best symbol in all creation for His love for us. In the New Testament, Jesus takes all this even one step further. He is the heavenly Bridegroom[5] and we, the Church, are His bride,[6] His Chosen People, circumcised not merely in the flesh of our foreskins,[7] but in our *hearts*.[8] On the cross, He revealed both covenants, the new not abolishing the old, but perfecting it.[9] There He hanged suspended between God and man, revealing both covenants, both literal circumcisions—one surgically exposing the head of His phallus, and the other exposing His Sacred Heart.[10] As the emission of semen during ejaculation produced Abraham's physical descendants, so

---

[1] Cf. I Samuel 18:27.
[2] Genesis 1:27.
[3] E.g. cf. Ezekiel 16:8; Isaiah 62:4f; Hosea 2:19f & 3:1.
[4] Cf. Isaiah 62:5.
[5] Cf. Matthew 9:15; 25:1-13; Mark 2:19f; Luke 5:34f; John 3:29.
[6] Cf. II Corinthians 11:2; Revelation 19:7ff; 21:2 & 9ff; 22:17.
[7] Cf. Genesis 17:11.
[8] Cf. Colossians 2:11; Romans 2:28f; Deuteronomy 10:16 & 30:6.
[9] Cf. Matthew 5:17.
[10] Cf. John 19:34.

the emission of Blood and water from the Sacred Heart gave birth to the Church, at one and the same time both the children of God via adoption[1] and the Bride of Christ, the New Eve, created from the side of the New Adam as He slept the sleep of death on the cross.[2]

This was how and why matrimony became "the great sacrament"[3] in the New and Everlasting Covenant. The work of redemption, of restoring man to the original image of the God Who is love[4] was consummated[5] by, and in, Christ. All the other covenants till then were as so much foreplay, whereas by His death the marital union between God and man was consummated in the very Person of Christ—two distinct natures united in One Person. Christian marriage epitomizes this reality, expresses it, and even *effects* it. This is the theological basis for the new and exciting "theology of the body" as preached so powerfully by Pope John Paul II.[6] If we do not first have a very high regard for the body, its sexual parts, and sex itself, then we cannot even begin to understand this theology. It comprises the very nucleus of the Good News. There is nothing whatever shameful about it. Indeed, it is meant to be preached from rooftops![7]

Old Covenant body attitudes prepared the way for this heavy-duty Gospel. The grace of both covenants built on nature, and this presumed a healthy, wholesome, natural respect for the body and especially its sexual functions.

In Old Testament times male genitalia were far from private. They were in fact so commonly visible and public that they made a sensible, practical and likely location on which to engrave the *sign* of the covenant. A mere glance

---

[1] Cf. Galatians 4:4f; Romans 8:14ff & 23.
[2] This is a frequent theme in the writings of many Fathers of the Church. Archbishop Fulton Sheen, consistent with this patristic tradition, referred to the cross as Christ's "nuptial bed" where the Church was conceived.
[3] Ephesians 5:32.
[4] Cf. I John 4:8 & 16.
[5] Cf. John 19:30.
[6] His two main works that explore and lay the foundation for this theology are: 1. *Love & Responsibility*, written while still Karol Cardinal Wojtyla, (New York: Farrar, Strauss & Giroux, 1981). 2. *The Theology of the Body*, a compilation of many Wednesday "Angelus" talks delivered early in his papacy. (Boston: Pauline Books, 1997.
[7] Cf. Matthew 10:26.

between a man's legs sufficed to identify him as either a Gentile or a member of God's Chosen People. No one had to look hard, searching for some obscure tattoo or scarification. Right smack in the center of the body as a man stands facing you, where leg lines and torso lines converge, hang his "jewels," and no one needs a microscope to see whether his foreskin covers the head of his penis or whether it has been surgically removed by circumcision, permanently leaving his glans exposed. In a culture that *respects* nature, rather than *contradicts* it, there is, objectively, no better place for the mark of the covenant. It is only the strange, unnatural body attitudes of unnatural cultures that would make this in any way problematic. Yet it is so problematic in most contemporary cultures that Christians blush to read God's Word prescribing circumcision. In contrast, not only did the people of the Old Testament times not blush to read about it publicly, but neither did they blush to show it or see it. As Christians today do not blush to be seen wearing a sculpture of a naked, horribly tortured man nailed to a cross, and think nothing of hanging it around their necks or dangling it from their ear lobes, so no Jew in Old Testament times was ashamed to publicly show the sign of the covenant engraved in the flesh of his foreskin. As Christians are proud of the love Christ has for us and of the death He so lovingly suffered for us, and are proud to display its symbol around our necks and atop our steeples, so also the Jews were just as proud of the sign of their covenant which likewise expressed God's special, exclusive, faithful and fruitful love for them.

The idea that the circumcised penises of Jews should be kept fastidiously hidden is nowhere to be found in either the Old or New Testaments.

Genesis 17:14 says, "Any uncircumcised male who is not circumcised in the flesh of his foreskin shall be 'cut off' from his people; he has broken My covenant."

If it were not quite ordinary for people to see the genitals of boys and men, then how would anybody know who to cut off? If a male's foreskin was not cut off, then he would be cut off from God's people. There is no notion whatever that a special, Levitical, penis inspection team would have to go around peeking into men's pants or sneaking peeks while they urinated. Everybody could plainly see who was circumcised and who was not. To avoid suspicion, circumcised males certainly did not hide the fact, which would only have served to arouse curiosity, just as it does today when men and boys compulsively hide their genitalia. The very fact of hiding naturally arouses curiosity about just what it is he is hiding. If we enter a museum room of statues, if only one is veiled, that will be the one we are all naturally most curious about and most want to see revealed. When the curator is not looking, we might even try to sneak a peek. But among naturists today, like the Jews of old, there is no more curiosity about what a male's genitals look like than there is about what their noses look like. There is no shame in not hiding them, no more shame at looking at them than there is at looking at men's noses, and no one has to look long to determine if a man is circumcised or to discover other basic details about what his genitals look like. But most contemporary cultures not only ignore the dynamic of the veiled statue, but they even go so far as to make a moral virtue out of it, "fabricating" sins where there is no sin, but merely ordinary, natural, God-made curiosity. Many—including many Christians—perversely and un-scripturally actually do believe and state that their genitalia are "obscene, indecent and dirty," but many others hypocritically *pretend* that they truly esteem their bodies and their sexual parts; they claim that's *why* they compulsively veil them!

Such hypocrisy should be plain for all to see. What lady highly prizes a diamond ring so much that she never wears it and keeps it hidden in a secret compartment in her jewelry box? What man buys a highly prized sports car and is so proud of it that he keeps it garaged? Although the truth often stings, the truth is that compulsive clothing lies, failing to declare the truth of the body, and those who profess that they *respect* the body, yet *compulsively hide* it, are, in truth, liars; they have been deceived through immersion in a culture that cares little or nothing about nature or God. But Old Testament people would have been incapable of comprehending such an unnatural, exotic, weird culture.

Leviticus 21:16-21 says, "...None of your descendants throughout their generations who has a blemish may approach to offer the bread of his God. For no one who has a blemish shall draw near, a man blind or lame, or one who has a mutilated face or a limb too long, or a man who has an injured foot or an injured hand, or a hunchback, or a dwarf, or a man with a defect in his sight or an itching disease or scabs *or crushed testicles*; no man of the descendants of Aaron the priest who has a blemish shall come near to offer the Lord's offerings by fire; since he has a blemish, he shall not come near to offer the bread of his God."

And Deuteronomy 23:1 says, "He whose testicles are crushed or whose male member is cut off shall not enter the assembly of the LORD."

It is obvious from the above contexts that crushed testicles and a cut off penis shaft were as plainly visible as the other defects listed such as having an injured hand or being a dwarf. The Law of Moses was extremely detailed about all the ins and outs of the law, yet nowhere does Moses prescribe a special, "Testicle & Penis Inspection Patrol," simply because genitalia were not compulsively hidden as they are in much of modern culture, and the only shameful thing was not that genitalia were commonly visible, but that they, or any other body part, was defective in some way. It was as naturally easy to see if a man's testicles were crushed or his penis cut off as it was to see if someone was a dwarf or not. It didn't take a rocket scientist or even a family physician.

But if one had defective genitals and might want to hide the fact of their defectiveness, he would not hide it because this would obviously draw even more attention and curiosity, just as the modern custom does of hiding genitalia even when nudity makes incontestable, practical sense such as while swimming and relaxing on the beach. When a person is nude at the beach, those who see him simply satisfy their natural curiosity about his body, from his hair color to the shape of his knees and legs. But when certain parts are always compulsively hidden, it only serves to draw extra attention to those hidden parts, as people naturally wonder what the big mystery is. At least in the Old Testament, a man might have a half-reasonable motive for at least keeping his skivvies on—his testicles might be crushed or his penis cut off. But he knew that hiding would only have made matters worse, drawing even more attention to his physical defect. His best "cover," then, was "no cover." Nothing can possibly be more modest than total nudity, because it eliminates every last stitch of any striptease effect, and because God Himself designed the body, and He Himself pronounced it, along with all creation, "*very good*"![1]

In Old Testament times, poor people often owned nothing but the clothes on their backs. It was often the only collateral they had to offer a creditor as a pledge. According to the context of Exodus 22:26f, it seems that such pledges consisted of every stitch of clothing a poor debtor owned. This made sense for a couple of reasons.

First, the value of his few rags was probably a lot less than his debt, so the best collateral he could muster would have been literally all that he owned, i.e. all his clothes.

Secondly, if the debtor had to literally go naked until he made good his debt, he would surely have had a better incentive to settle his account than if he merely offered some article of clothing he could have done without. Just imagine if debtors today had to turn over all their clothing to their creditors until they settled up; needless to say, it would be a very effective incentive for most people to think twice about going into debt, and an incentive to get out of debt as soon as possible! And just imagine if government officials who wantonly spend tax-payers' money so as to create vast national debts, all had to go nude until they balanced the budget! Good idea? Should someone suggest it at the next Democratic and Republican Party Caucuses?

In the context of the passage cited below, such day-time debtor nakedness seems to have been quite routine. The Mosaic law was given to temper what could have been the excessive harshness of creditors who would be so overly demanding that not only would they make the poor debtor go nude all day by taking all his clothes as a pledge, but they would even show no mercy on him when night fell and the debtor really needed clothes to protect him from the cold. Here is the text:

---

[1] Genesis 1:31.

"If ever you take your neighbor's garment in pledge, you shall restore it to him before the sun goes down; for that is his *only* covering, it is his mantle for his body; in what else shall he sleep? And if he cries to me, I will hear, for I am compassionate."[1]

Evidently, all this did not apply only to males, because Deuteronomy 24:17 exempts only poor widows from this custom—not other females.

The custom of offering all one's clothes in pledge was not unique to ancient Israel. Even in late medieval Muscovy, at least into the reign of Czar Peter the Great, taverns routinely accepted people's clothes as a pledge, keeping them until the debtor could settle his bill in cash. Since the poor had nothing but what they were wearing, it was not unusual to see poor people walking around Moscow naked until they were able to earn or beg enough cash to redeem their clothes from the inn-keeper.[2] Since such public, urban nakedness was a sign of the most destitute poverty, one of Russia's favorite saints (comparable to St. Francis of Assisi in the West), St. Basil of Moscow, lived naked in the city—even in winter!

It seems that in Mosaic times public bathing was a given, for when the Lord commanded Moses to ordain the first five priests of the Levitical priesthood, no privacy was specified, despite the fact that for the first part of the seven-day ritual Moses was required to give all of the ordinands a bath *outside*, at the door of the meeting tent. Aaron was bathed first, followed by his four sons. All stood naked until the baths were given and they were invested with the priestly vestments, one by one. Exodus 29:4 reads: "You shall bring Aaron and his sons to the door of the tent of meeting, and wash them with water."[3]

Nor was there any hurry as though some anachronistic form of "modesty" might have required it. The baths must have taken a fair amount of time, and certainly the priestly investiture was not rushed. Here is the text that describes the investiture part of the ritual. Remember that while Moses is investing Aaron with all these vestments,

---

[1] Exodus 22:26f.
[2] Cf. Robert K. Massie, *Peter the Great* (New York: Alfred A. Knopf, 1980), p. 4.
[3] Cf. Exodus 40:12.

the other four ordinands are standing in attendance, naked, in public view, awaiting their turn:

"And you shall take the garments, and put on Aaron the coat and the robe of the ephod, and the ephod, and the breastpiece, and gird him with the skillfully woven band of the ephod; and you shall set the turban on his head, and put the holy crown upon the turban. And you shall take the anointing oil, and pour it on his head and anoint him."[1]

Only after all this are Aaron's four sons clothed: "Then you shall bring his sons, and put coats on them, and you shall gird them with girdles and bind caps on them; and the priesthood shall be theirs by a perpetual statute. Thus you shall ordain Aaron and his sons."[2]

If such an historically important ritual was meant to be performed privately, since the text specifies every last detail of the ritual, surely God would have stipulated such privacy somewhere, but there is not the slightest hint of any need for privacy. It is presumed that, like all other priestly rituals performed *outside* the meeting tent, it was an important community event, no less than ordinations today.

Exodus 29:42-44 actually specified "the seating plan" for religious ceremonies. The text says that God "will meet with the people of Israel... at the door of the meeting tent." Verse 44 makes it clear that this included this ritual of consecrating priests.

There is nothing to indicate that this ritual nudity was anything "shocking." For a half million people traipsing through the desert for forty years, daily public nudity was not noteworthy, just as it is not noteworthy for many cultures today who live close to the elements of nature. Even for modern people enculturated in a clothes-compulsive culture, when they go camping for any length of time, gestures of "modesty" gradually deteriorate because they are highly impractical and make no sense. Soon they no longer even attempt to change clothes privately. Likewise, donning bathing suits to bathe in streams and ponds, or segregating the sexes for bathing

---

[1] Exodus 29:5-7.
[2] Exodus 29:8-9.

seems artificial, unnecessary, impractical, contrived and ridiculous.

The Mosaic Law prescribed many, many baths besides the one described above, especially for the purposes of physical and religious hygiene.[1] If a person had a skin disease such as leprosy or anything that looked like it, he had to show himself to the priests for their diagnosis.[2] There is no reason not to presume that this required men, women and children to get naked for the priestly inspection. Although this skin inspection might have been performed in private, such privacy is nowhere stipulated in the meticulously detailed Mosaic Law.

Likewise, if the priests did diagnose some sort of uncleanness, the universal treatment always included bathing and a thorough laundering. There is no indication that these baths were taken in private. Since it was nothing less than public health at stake, it is reasonable to assume that such bathing was visible, assuring the community that proper hygiene and treatment was being faithfully executed. Neither one's clothing nor one's body was one's own; basic public health required that they were of high community interest. Also, such things as when a lady was menstruating,[3] when a couple had intercourse,[4] and when a male had a nocturnal emission[5] were also public knowledge. Deuteronomy 23:12f deals with the public latrine. There is no mention of any idea of "bathroom privacy," but only of a designated place. With hundreds of thousands of people using it, any notion of privacy is beyond being ludicrous.

Later Christian baptism would not abolish the Mosaic practices of bathing incoming priests, but rather, fulfill them.[6] Again, public nudity was required. Stripping off all clothing was sacramental of stripping off the "Old Adam," along with all the sin that went with that.[7] It was like getting naked for the Levitical priests' inspection of

---

[1] E.g. cf. Leviticus 14:8f; 15:1-33; 16:4, 24, 26 & 28; 17:15; Deuteronomy 23:10f; etc.
[2] Cf. Leviticus 13:1ff; 14:2f & Matthew 8:4.
[3] E.g. cf. Leviticus 15:19ff.
[4] E.g. cf. Leviticus 15:18.
[5] E.g. cf. Leviticus 15:16ff.
[6] Cf. Matthew 5:17.
[7] Cf. Colossians 3:9f.

uncleanness, followed by the bath of immersion in the baptismal pool. Many Christian exegetes also think that it was allegorical of the sacrament of confession, when penitents must get spiritually naked, confessing their sins to those who share in the Melchizedech priesthood[1] of Christ through apostolic succession.[2] Surely it is much more embarrassing to expose the leprosy of one's soul (i.e. sin) than body.

Baptism was also seen as fulfilling the priestly consecration of the Old Testament. Baptism not only made a person a lay member of the New Israel, but also consecrated him as a member of a new, royal priesthood.[3]

Exodus 20:26 & 28:42f require that priests not approach the altar naked; they must wear priestly breeches. If it were not quite ordinary to see males and even priests going about naked, this proscription against nakedness at the altar would make no sense. Scripture nowhere prohibits nakedness in ordinary, secular, daily life; it *presumes* it. That is why the Mosaic Law needed to stipulate that priests had to wear their sacerdotal skivvies when entering the sanctuary.

This does not suggest any taint regarding sexuality or genitalia. Rather, three possible reasons for this law are: 1) To clearly off-set things that are holy by outward signs (e.g. vestments) differentiating them from the secular and ordinary. 2) Since their uncircumcised, Gentile neighbors were into fertility cults and phallic worship, this priestly dress code constituted a sharp separation. 3) It could be allegorical of the celibate priesthood exemplified and taught by Jesus[4] and St. Paul.[5]

At least among themselves, nudity was normal for Old Testament prophets.[6] This continued well into New Testament times, with many monks and nuns of the desert going nude for the sake of asceticism and total evangelical poverty and simplicity. Even many Christians today, including myself, find that nudity disposes us to better prayer. It aids us in disposing ourselves to a "face to

---

[1] Cf. Psalm 110:4 & Hebrews 5:10; 6:20ff & 7:11ff.
[2] Cf. John 20:22f.
[3] Cf. I Peter 2:5 & 9 & Revelation 1:6; 5:10 & 20:6.
[4] Cf. Matthew 19:12; Mark 10:28ff; Luke 5:11.
[5] Cf. I Corinthians 7:1, 7f, 26, 32ff, 38 & 40.
[6] Cf. I Samuel 19:24.

face" encounter with God, before Whom all lies bare and exposed.[1]

But the nudity of the Old Testament prophets was not always only "among the guys." God commanded Isaiah to preach to the public for three years without ever wearing even a loincloth or sandals.[2] Prophets did not usually preach in the nude, and that was specifically why the symbolism of Isaiah's nudity was effective. It was as conspicuous as a naked preacher would be today standing on a soap box on Boston Common. But there was one huge difference. In Old Testament times, there was no notion that "nude is lewd." No "modesty police" would have arrested him for "public indecency," and no onlooker would have considered Isaiah to have been some sort of sexual "perv."

The same was true well into the Middle Ages. St. Kevin of Glandolough went nude even while standing in ice cold lakes and streams as a form of asceticism.[3] What was especially "shocking" was not his nudity, but the fact that he was nude in such flesh-mortifying circumstances. In his *Confessions*, the Father of Irish Christianity, St. Patrick, also casually mentions his extreme circumstances often including nakedness,[4] as did St. Paul a few hundred years before him.[5] There are many anecdotes about St. Francis' public nudity, his motives always being poverty and humility. No one would have thought of accusing him of sexual immodesty, but only of becoming a "fool for Christ."[6] Thus nudity has always been known among both Jewish and Christian prophets.

There is no indication in New Testament times to indicate that the sight of males' genitals were any less ordinary than it was in Old Testament times. As in the Old Testament,[7] Jesus,[8] St. John the Baptist[9] and St. Paul[10]

---

[1] Cf. Hebrews 4:13.
[2] Cf. Isaiah 20:2f.
[3] Cf. Thomas Cahill, *How the Irish Saved Civilization* (New York: Double-day Anchor Books, 1996) p. 156.
[4] Cf. The Confessions of St. Patrick.
[5] Cf. I Corinthians 4:11 & II Corinthians 11:27.
[6] I Corinthians 4:10.
[7] Cf. Leviticus 12:3.
[8] Cf. Luke 2:21.
[9] Cf. Luke 1:59.
[10] Cf. Philippians 3:5.

were all circumcised on the eighth day, and the New Testament refers to it as unblushingly as does the Old Testament. In fact, often in the New Testament circumcision is mentioned,[1] especially by St. Paul,[2] and it is always mentioned in as matter-of-fact a way as we refer to baptism. The nudity of Christ crucified is nowhere treated in the New testament as something shameful; the torturing and execution of Jesus was what was shameful.

Christ's circumcision was as obvious and unshameful as He hanged on the cross as it was when He was baptized in the Jordan River, where huge crowds of Jews went to be baptized.[3]

Later in New Testament times St. Paul had St. Timothy circumcised because his father was a Greek[4] and by thus accepting Jewish culture, Timothy could better become "all things to all men."[5] But if St. Timothy had "kept it in his pants" as compulsively as most preachers do today, then who would have been the wiser? The penises of both Gentiles and Jews were so publicly visible that whether or not a new Christian was circumcised became one of the hottest issues in the Apostolic Church.[6] If genitalia had been considered "private," and "nobody's business," then it could hardly have been such an issue, because no one would have known such "intimate" details about others' bodies. But the fact was that everybody knew because no one dreamt of such an unnatural, highfalutin contrivance as to "privatize" any body parts. Nothing could have seemed more ridiculous and outlandish to people of those more sensible, natural cultures. To sum up, there is nothing whatever in the New testament to indicate that male genitalia were any less exposed than in Old Testament times.

Nor did the common sight of male genitalia stop with Apostolic times. There is abundant proof from ancient art and writings that nudity was an everyday experience for centuries after the Apostles.

---

[1] E.g. cf. John 7:22f; Acts 10:45; 11:2ff; 15:1ff; 16:3; 21:21.
[2] The references are practically too numerous to list. Cf. Romans 2:25ff; Galatians 5:6 & dozens of others.
[3] Cf. Matthew 3:5f.
[4] Cf. Acts 16:3.
[5] I Corinthians 9:22.
[6] Cf. Acts 15:1ff et al.

Athletes publicly practiced and competed in the nude, including contact sports such as wrestling. Even in Old Testament times it seems that if a man got into a fight with another man both were presumably nude because Deuteronomy 25:11f says that if a man's wife helps him by grabbing his opponent's genitals, her hand would be cut off as a punishment. Thus it was not necessary to inhibit one's fighting ability by wearing any protective gear to shield his most vulnerable parts; the strict law was sufficient protection.

For many centuries after Apostolic times public bathing was common, and remained so in some places right into modern times. Even today, in Finland, boys, girls, men and women of all ages share public saunas, which is culturally considered a necessity of life. There is no opportunity for the build-up of any morbid curiosity about what others' bodies look like. At least every week or so everybody gets naked together, and this communal nudity is regarded to be no less proper or modest than dressing up for Sunday dinner. The only truly "private parts" in such cultures are one's *internal* organs; what is *external* is obviously and naturally accepted as being meant to be seen.

Nudity was the most common dress of children of all ages, and always has been in many places right up to the present. One of Michelangelo's more famous works, the "Doni Tondo," depicts the Holy Family. In the near background are several frontally nude male adolescents, as though such were normal. Even here in the city of Newport, Vermont, one spring afternoon in 2003 toddlers from both next door and across the street were outside, in public, nude. My vocational rehabilitation counselor told me that she and her friends were often nude on their farms as they grew up near Burlington, Vermont. When I attended a New Hampshire summer boys' camp in the 60s, everyone was nude while swimming, diving, boating and playing sports on the beach. None of us even thought of wearing swimming trunks, and if someone had, he would have been as ridiculous and conspicuous as any Jew of olden times who might have compulsively hidden his genitalia. The same was true at the Lynn, Massachusetts, YMCA where all bathing suits were forbidden in the

190

pool area. Everybody knew what each other looked like. Everybody knew who was circumcised and who was not. Everybody knew how far along us boys were in puberty. Physical facts were physical facts. Since they were naturally external, they were just as naturally public knowledge. True, the genders were not mixed, but even the males-only experience gave males of my generation (b. 1953) some idea of how ordinary nudity can be and how ordinary it also must have been in Biblical times. If any of us had dared to assert that his genitals were "private," he would have been just as ridiculed as any Jew in Biblical times who dared to make an issue out of being seen nude in public.

Even in our day there are occasions where female sports reporters have equal access along with their male colleagues to locker rooms and showers after a game. Male athletes behave no differently in the locker room even when female reporters are freely walking around looking for players to interview. There is no such thing as "privacy." The very idea is a joke. Women are free in the locker room to go wherever the players are, even standing in the entrance to the gang shower while several players shower nude, interviewing one or another of them, or asking them to step out for a lengthier interview. Nothing that belongs to natural, external anatomy is "private" as far as these reporters go. The dynamic is such that if anyone were to feign false modesty and turn his back when a female reporter approached, or, when interviewed, went out of his way to cover his "privates," he would be laughed at. The dynamic is to be natural and act no different than if only male reporters were issued locker room passes. This is the very same dynamic as was active in same-gender school locker rooms. Even if a male did feel somewhat shy about being nude in front of everybody, it was definitely "uncool" to feign any degree of false modesty; he just had to "grin and bare it"! The same is also true even for girls and women in contemporary culture when they have to "reveal all" for a male doctor or other hospital personnel. Even a nun would not make an issue out of having to expose her genitalia for her gynecologist, physician or technician doing a Pap smear. Such occasions simply slice through all the phony pretenses, and everybody accepts it. The same was true in ancient times when such occasions were much more common and involved a wider public.

One perfect example was the administering of the sacrament of baptism, which was ordinarily done in the nude, all ages and both genders together. No one made an issue out of it. Just as no woman hesitates to expose even her genitalia for her male doctor, so no woman would have thought twice about having to strip naked in front of everybody, including fellow male catechumens, family members, any male Christian observing the ceremony,[1] the male deacons, priests and the bishop. It was just an accepted part of life, just as are gynecological exams today or YMCA swims before the 70s. Ancient cultures were only healthier insofar as they offered far more opportunities for public nakedness, and the opportunities were common enough to preclude the contemporary phenomena of morbid curiosity, the assumption that "nude is lewd," and much of the impetus behind the proliferation of pornography.

Recently I met an East German priest who was 16 when the Berlin Wall came down. He said that growing up as a Catholic youth in East Germany meant that he and the other youth of his parish often had occasion to see each other nude when they went swimming along rivers and especially at beaches on the Baltic Sea. Nudity was no more an issue for him and his Catholic peers of both sexes than it was for me at the summer boys' camp. His mother would insist that they not go to beaches that required swimwear. She herself would always swim nude, and he and his Catholic friends felt no shame about being seen nude by each other. It was simply a fixed part of their culture, and they accepted it as we boys accepted the gang shower idea in junior high school. It was what was done, and one just did it. The notion of "private parts" simply did not compute any more for us boys than it did for those East Germans—or the Jews of Biblical times.

Art in the ancient and post-Apostolic world also helped insure against "privatizing" the naked human body. Nude sculptures and other nude art were on public display. In contrast, by the late 19th century, Mark Twain

---

[1] And all did, as baptisms ordinarily occurred during the most solemn liturgy of the year—Easter Vigil, attended by most Christians.

says that this became such an issue that fig leaf-style loin coverings were usually affixed to statuary when he visited Italy.[1] Culture had moved away from nature and had begun to make an issue out of what had never before been an issue. Sculptures very commonly depicted the nude human form as it was recognized as the most perfect and beautiful in all creation. Although today it is not very public, almost all art programs above the high school level include at least some nude figure drawing, and nature is still sufficiently strong in enough people to induce them to want to pose before their peers. Again, while our contemporary culture makes such an issue out of nudity, this universal experience alone slices clean through all the lies and pretense. Though all the students are reared in an unnatural culture that falsely teaches that "nude is lewd," in no time flat this lie is exposed as soon as the model's body is exposed. The museum veil has (at least temporarily) been lifted, and the skies did not come a-tumbling down. Once a model has banished the "private parts" idea by making his body public, those who view it are unable to remember what was supposed to have been so "private" about it. Drawing buttocks and genitalia is like drawing noses and elbows, just as seeing such body parts was just as ordinary in olden times. Such an experience should not be reserved only for art students and only for one art class once in their lives. The body should be a common enough experience as to thoroughly rout out all the vestiges of the lies that were inculcated in our rearing. In ancient times, there were no such lies to rout out, and lots of public nude statuary imitating life itself as it really was lived, and it went a long way to keep culture sane.

In conclusion, the notion that male genitalia were "private parts" was entirely alien to ancient Jewish culture. Skin is an *external* organ by nature, and thus it is naturally meant to be *seen*; it is not "private." Such common sense was unquestioned not only in the Old Testament, but also in the New Testament, and even for many centuries after that. Even in some contemporary cultures some sunlight of natural, common sense shines through, despite inorganic cultures that try to stifle nature. Nature will not be mocked. She always reasserts

---

[1] Cf. Mark Twain, *A Tramp Abroad*, chapter 50.

193

herself, like a river's banks whose man-made dikes often vainly try to direct their flow. Like the wind which man is also unable to control, rivers will flow where they will.[1]

God knew what He was doing by preparing the world for "the fullness of time"[2]—for the Messiah through the Jewish culture. We would do well even in these late, post-Apostolic times, to do what we can to steer culture back in a direction that most accords with nature, for "grace builds on nature," and we cannot allow stifling cultures to bushel-basket our light, for that light is Christ Himself, and if nature will not be mocked, much less will her Author!

The Catechism of the Catholic Church

by Jim C. Cunningham

N. 364 The human body shares in the dignity of "the image of God": it is a human body precisely because it is animated by a spiritual soul, and it is the *whole* human person that is intended to become, in the body of Christ, a temple of the Spirit:

"Man, though made of body and soul, is a *unity*. Through his very bodily condition he sums up in himself the elements of the material world. Through him they are thus brought to their highest perfection and can raise their voice in praise freely given to the Creator. For this reason man may not despise his bodily life. Rather *he is obliged to regard his body as good and to hold it in honor* since God has created it and will raise it up on the last day."[3]

---

[1] Cf. John 3:8.
[2] Galatians 4:4.
[3] This opening excerpt is directly from: *Catechism of the Catholic Church* (San Francisco: Ignatius Press, 1994), p. 93. The quotation at the end is taken from Vatican II: "The Pastoral Constitution on the Church in the Modern World" (*Gaudium et Spes*), N. 14,1.

"Man may not despise his bodily life"—thus says the *Catechism of the Catholic Church,* issued under Pope John Paul II. But the sad fact is that men—including Catholics—*do* despise their bodies. Many actually brazenly confess that they despise their bodies, and they think that such an attitude is true piety and chastity. Others profess the truth on their lips, but their hearts are far from it, as is evidenced by their speech and conduct.

Let's begin with the first group. These people are actually dualists, believing that the material world (or at least the body) is evil, and the spiritual world is good. They identify anything physical with sin. All that pertains to the senses is sin. They experience real guilt whenever they allow themselves anything actually pleasurable, whether it is a piece of strawberry shortcake, a massage, or a marital orgasm. With respect to this last example, they believe that sex is the most evil thing going. If they allowed themselves to actually enjoy conjugal love like the lovers described in the Song of Songs, they would feel like they committed a mortal sin and even after going to confession and doing penance, they will still feel residual guilt over it. They regard sex as a "necessary evil." I know one woman who tried to breast-feed her first baby but quickly stopped, calling the experience "gross" and "bestial." Such people see the body as ugly, and if they see someone with a beautiful body, they immediately think it is somehow evil because it is sexually attractive. Besides body functions like marital sexual intercourse and breast-feeding, they see all body functions as "gross" and "disgusting," the processes of elimination not least among them. They contrive grand rituals out of the human acts of urinating and defecating, going to absurd lengths to insure the strictest privacy. When they have to discuss such horrors, they use all kinds of euphemisms, unable to call a spade a spade. It is not sufficient for them to merely shut the bathroom door, but they must also lock it. One hospital roommate I once had was so terrified to have to ask for the bed pan and actually admit that he, too, alas, also had to stoop to the humiliation of defecation, that he resisted for days, despite great discomfort which he expressed with irritation. Finally, though, he could stand it no longer, and decided that if he had to humble himself to ask for help, he would wait till his wife showed up and ask her. It was hilarious to hear them behind the curtain, in whispers and hushed-up silence, trying to pretend they were doing something else, but alas, the olfactory nerve does not need to be too keen to know the truth. It is amusing to watch such people exit a bathroom trying hard to keep their composure, wearing a face like they "didn't do nothin'" in there, but knowing that as soon as the next user enters, he will know the truth either by the lingering bad odor or the profuse amount of air freshener they sprayed to hide the fact.

Euphemisms abound. When they need to excuse themselves to defecate or urinate, they will say such absurdities such as "I have to go see a man about a horse," or "I need to go and powder my nose." Even saying "I have to go to the *bath*room" is euphemistic; at least I have yet to see any baths in restaurant toilets. Or they call it a "*rest* room" or a "*men's* or *women's* room." I remember flying from Moscow to Tashkent when I was sixteen. I had to urinate, but not knowing how to ask the stewardess in Russian to show me where to go, I foolishly translated the American English euphemism literally into Russian, my pocket dictionary dutifully in hand, "Excuse me, where is the room for men?" She looked at me like I had three heads. Perhaps she thought I was asking for some kind of compartment on the plane where I could indulge my passions with women of ill repute. Whatever she thought, she cocked her head, frowned, and asked me what I wanted. I repeated myself, which was of no help at all. Then I frantically looked up the Russian word for "rest," and, bladder about to burst, desperately asked her for the "room for resting." She must have thought I was crazy. At last, someone nearby came to my rescue and called the spade a spade:

"He wants the *toilet*!"

I could have died! And everybody could hear him say such a word!

The stewardess was not abashed however, and made matters worse by shouting, "Oh, the *toilet*!" And pointing as an umpire behind home plate signifies strike three, she demonstratively indicated the location of my long-awaited haven. I was to learn a lot in Russia, especially at Sochi on the Black Sea where the toilets were all of the stand-up and squat variety which I had never seen before, and there were no partitions whatsoever, but everyone just lined up and did their business like there was no tomorrow.

Of course, body-hating people despise menstruation. They cannot even properly prepare their daughters for their first menses. Everything is hush-hush, or worse. Some girls are doomed to figure it all out for themselves. For these people, menstruation is really a "curse." Like spraying deodorant in the "bathroom" to hide the evidence of having done such a nasty, disgusting thing as defecation, they go to great lengths to hide the evidence of having had to change their tampon or menstrual pad.

Which reminds me of another true anecdote like my Russian flight story:

I was shopping with my wife at the open-air market at Piazza Vittorio Emanuele II in Rome, Italy, when I saw a couple of ladies looking at the wares at a certain booth. Inspecting the goods, they held up what appeared to me to be linen dinner napkins. Since we needed some, we ambled over to check it out. Since I spoke more Italian than Linda (which is not saying much), I asked how much the napkins were. The two female customers backed away, giggling at me, staring in disbelief. There was a lot of blushing all around. Finally, the vendor made it clear to me that I did not want to buy them for dinner napkins because they were for women only. Together Linda and I finally figured out that they were "*feminine*" napkins, laughed along with them and went our way. Evidently, in the Old Country, some older women still use washable linens when they menstruate. One irony is that in America, we euphemistically call menstrual pads "feminine *napkins*," even though they do not look like "napkins" at all, while originally they actually did look like napkins, and the term was appropriate and not euphemistic at all.

Not only do body-haters fail in their theology by hating their bodies, but this also has serious heretical ramifications when applied to other doctrines.

For example, in the Apostles' Creed which most Christians accept, it says, "And I believe... in the resurrection of the body." Yet such body-haters are perfectly content to be done with their bodies forever—even in their glorified, risen state. They just want "to die and go to heaven," and do not look forward to the resurrection of the dead at all. They are happy to merely be *souls* enjoying the beatific vision forever. But this is, arguably, the most perverse of heresies since St. Paul says that without the resurrection of the flesh, all the rest of the Christian faith is vain.[1]

But most Christians belong to the second group who *profess* that they do not despise their bodies, but in reality betray their hypocrisy in both their speech and conduct.

Like the body-haters, they too employ all sorts of euphemisms for certain body functions and body parts such as genitalia. They might even breast-feed their babies, but only in the most clandestine of ways, behind closed doors, denigrating such a holy, maternal function to the level of the processes of elimination, even nursing in restaurant toilets and not complaining about it! They *profess* that breasts are holy, but conduct themselves as though they were dirty and obscene. They might wear bikinis, but what do bikinis hide but breasts and the areas most involved in conjugal love and the processes of elimination? Thus they show by their *deeds* that they rank breasts with anuses!

Such people also do not call spades spades, and are uncomfortable with bathroom activities. Though the Vatican decorates its ceilings and walls with nudes, they would never decorate their walls or gardens with such "obscene" images. If their toddlers remove their bathing suits to frolic in the lawn sprinkler, these parents behave as though they had committed some unforgivable sin. They impose shame and indecency where there naturally is none. Their toddlers are rebuked as though they had committed some heinous crime. The toddlers are justly confused, but are forced to conform and thus learn a false shame foisted upon them by a culture that in reality resents the fact that God created bodies.

Their attitude toward sex is similar—or worse. They do not see it as "*celebrating* their sacramental covenant of matrimony," but as "fulfilling their marriage *debt*." Even in sex-segregated locker rooms, they will not undress at their lockers, but line up at the toilet stalls to change.

---

[1] Cf. I Corinthians 15:14.

Does all this proclaim the truth of what the *Catechism* teaches? How can any normal person not get the sense that they truly *do* despise their bodies despite what they might *say* to the contrary? Doesn't a mother who unabashedly breast-feeds her baby openly proclaim the truth of the *Catechism* far better?

If someone accidentally walks in on Christians of this second group while they are showering, they lose all composure as though some awful crime has been committed. Doesn't the person who acts calmly and without shame profess the truth far better?

Doesn't naturism proclaim this truth of the *Catechism* better than any other attitude or lifestyle? If we do not despise our bodies and are not ashamed of them, why insist on wearing bathing suits at the beach? Swimming and bathing are two activities (among hundreds) that certainly justify nudity. If we love and appreciate our bodies truly, and are not ashamed of them, what could possibly motivate us to wear clothing that has no purpose whatever except hiding what is wrongly believed to be obscene, dirty and shameful? How can this proclaim the truth?

Even if one could find reasons for doing so, to acquire the truth of the *Catechism* we need to do some "therapy" to wash out the false and heretical attitude. Naturism is the antidote. No, Jesus, Mary and Joseph probably did not go to nudist parks, but neither did they *need* to, because they had no perversions to counter. They were whole, in mind, body, soul and spirit. Their natures were in perfect balance so that grace, which builds on nature, could do wondrous things through them. They valued their own, and each others' bodies. In Michelangelo's famous "Pietà," Mary is not holding on her lap a body Who was no longer her Son. She holds her Son, though only His body, His Soul having separated from it by death. In a very short three days that very body was to be reunited with His soul in an immortal, glorified state. Having put on an earthly body like ours, He surrendered to the Father's will, letting His earthly body be sown in death so that it could rise incorruptible with a glorified body such as we, too, will one day enjoy if we persevere in faith, grace and bearing our daily cross.[1]

As the *Catechism* says, who we are—body and soul—comprises our persons. We are obligated to cooperate with God's recreating Spirit in refashioning who we are according to the pattern of the New Man, Jesus Christ. This is the true holistic health plan. Jesus was not only interested in healing *souls* by forgiving sins, but He was also vitally interested in healing *bodies*, as all the Gospels amply record. Obviously, He saw the body as an essential part of who people are. Just as He loved the body, so also must we. And since we must love our neighbor as ourselves, we must begin by cultivating a healthy love and appreciation for our own bodies. Perhaps one of the reasons why there is so little charity in our world—why the love of many has grown cold[2]—is because modern man has so little love for his own body. Does this not lie at the root of the present universal culture of death? Modern man fights not for the right to *life*, but for the right to *kill*—the "right" to die. If man does not love life, how will he yearn for Christ, Who *is* life,[3] the Holy Spirit, the Giver of life,[4] and our heavenly Father, the Source of all life?[5]

Some people—even many Christian naturists—imagine there is some sort of dichotomy between naturist life and their Christian life. However, if both their naturism and Christianity are orthodox, there can be no such dialectical tension. Grace builds on nature. By esteeming nature we dispose ourselves for grace. By cultivating a high regard for the body, we dispose ourselves to look to Christ, Who Alone can heal both body and soul and reunite both by a re-creation more glorious than the first creation of the universe, uniting us to Himself in glory forever.

Lust is like gluttony. People who lust do not truly love their bodies; they hate them. Nothing develops both body and soul more than love, which St. Paul tells us to put on over all else.[6] "Love is not self-seeking."[1] "Whoever seeks to

---

[1] Cf. Romans 8:16f; Matthew 10:38 & Luke 9:23.
[2] Cf. Matthew 24:12.
[3] Cf. John 14:6.
[4] Cf. Psalm 104:31 & John 6:63.
[5] Cf. John 6:57.
[6] Cf. Colossians 3:14.

gain his life will lose it, but whoever loses his life will preserve it."[2] Lust does not *value* anyone's body; it only wants to *use* bodies for its own self-gratification. This is why St. Paul often insisted that no fornicator or adulterer would inherit the kingdom of God.[3] No matter what one's lips might profess, if his conduct, whether in heart[4] or deeds is lustful, he shows that he is not seeking Christ, but only himself, and as Christ and St. Paul warn, this necessarily only leads to ruin and perdition.

By helping us see ourselves and others as whole persons—body and soul, naturism helps us to value the body and not to despise it.

I know a man who attends daily Mass and Holy Communion, but who told me, "To tell you the truth, nakedness scares the hell out of me!" For this reason he has blotted out the whole body issue from his mind and his life, refusing to deal with it. But if we love our bodies as the *Catechism* says we must, can we also fear them? St. John says "there is no fear in love."[5] If we love something, we are necessarily drawn to it; we are not repulsed by it, let alone "scared to death" of it. Are they not things that we hate and dislike that we shut out of our minds, and not things that we love and appreciate? Naturism shows this true love and appreciation.

Therefore, in order to profess the truth of the *Catechism* with our *lips* and our *lives*, how about "cleaning up our act"? How about avoiding those euphemisms that do not honor the body or its functions, but instead, saying yes when we mean yes and no when we mean no, calling a spade a spade, wary that anything else is from the devil?[6] How about working at acquiring a love and appreciation of our bodies rather than a hatred, dislike and fear of them? How about deporting our bodies like we really believe they are the temples of the Holy Spirit we say we believe they are? How about never teaching the falsehood that our bodies are "dirty" by not wearing bathing suits as though they hid what was unholy? No, we do not have to live nude

---

[1] I Corinthians 13:5.
[2] Luke 17:33.
[3] Cf. Galatians 5:19f.
[4] Cf. Matthew 5:28.
[5] I John 4:18.
[6] Cf. Matthew 5:37.

twenty-four hours a day, but can we at least move in the direction of truth and health rather than brainlessly accept the false standards of the dominant culture?

This was just what a Christian friend of mine did when she took her two daughters (pre-teen and teen) to a college pool for a Christian home-schoolers' swim. Though all the other mothers and daughters in the women's locker room stood in line at the toilets to change into their swimsuits, these three "let their light shine" by changing at their lockers as the architect (and Architect!) intended. My friend was not parading down Main Street in the nude, yet she was really moving in the positive direction that would help both her and her daughters, and the other females in the locker room, overcome the foolish fear of the body. By their unabashed deportment they showed that their bodies were holy and not dirty, sacred and not profane. Their bodies were not things to be repulsed by or afraid of, but esteemed as integral parts of their persons, just as the *Catechism* says.

Maybe we cannot change the whole world, but we can do a lot to change ourselves and a few people around us. When my own sons were pre-teens, though the other males in the YMCA locker room showered with their suits on before and after using the pool, they removed theirs and bathed with common sense. As a result, grown men were made aware of their foolishness and fears and followed my sons' example.

But we cannot change even a few people around us unless we change ourselves first. Let's try to alter our lifestyle in ways that will better help us love and appreciate the precious gifts of our bodies!

As Little Children...

by Jim C. Cunningham

At that time the disciples came to Jesus, saying, "Who is the greatest in the kingdom of heaven?" And calling to Him a child, he put him in the midst of them, and said, "Truly, I say to you, unless you turn and become like children, you will never enter the kingdom of heaven. Whoever humbles himself like this child, he is the greatest in the kingdom of heaven. "Whoever receives one such child in My name receives Me; but whoever causes one of these little ones who believe in Me to sin, it would be better for him to have a great millstone fastened round his neck and to be drowned in the depth of the sea." Matthew 18:1-6

Just what is it that children have that we must also acquire if we are to be saved? Obviously, Jesus is not commanding us to be child-*ish*, but child-*like*. He is not telling us to suck our thumbs, pick our noses in public and smear our oatmeal in our hair. But just what *is* He saying?

There are several passages like this in the Gospels. Besides the one quoted above, others include: Matthew 19:3-15, Mark 10:2-16 and Luke 18:9-17. As good exegesis requires, let's look at the *contexts* in which these admonitions appear.

In the passage quoted above, the immediate context is when the disciples question Jesus about who is the greatest in the kingdom of heaven. To answer them, He specifically calls a child over to Him, demonstratively places the child in their midst, and says that whoever humbles himself like that child would be the greatest in His kingdom, and that if they do not change and become like children, they cannot enter that kingdom. Then He intensifies His teaching even more by identifying Himself with children, saying that when His disciples welcome *them*, they welcome *Him*. Finally, He says that children are so precious to Him that if anyone scandalize one, he would be better off if he had a millstone tied around his neck and he were thrown into the sea.

It is obvious that the specific quality of children that Jesus is emphasizing is their *humility*. They had no social standing, no property, no power, no authority, nothing at all to puff themselves up about. Children are simple and unpretentious. They are the image of the poor in spirit to whom the kingdom of heaven belongs.[1]

Matthew 19:3-15 begins with the Pharisees approaching Jesus to trick Him with their sophistry, behaving quite

---

[1] Cf. Matthew 5:3.

unchildlike. In fact, their manner and method are eerily reminiscent of the Serpent in Genesis 3:1ff where he asks Eve, "Did God say, 'You shall not eat of *any* tree of the garden'?"

Like father, like son. Jesus called the Pharisees the children of the "Father of Lies,"[1] and here they sound just like their father when they ask Him, "Is it lawful to divorce one's wife for *any* cause?" Just as the devil knew fully well what God had commanded Adam & Eve, so here, too, the Pharisees know fully well that it is not lawful to divorce "for *any* cause."[2]

If the parallel between the Pharisees and the Serpent in the Garden of Eden was subtle, in His reply, Jesus brings it out, front and center, by immediately quoting Genesis 2:24, referring to the very wondrous, original union between man and woman that Satan deigned to destroy, and which the devil's children here, following their father's example, also want to destroy, pressing for the right to sunder what God has joined "for *any* cause."

They continue their unchildlike sophistry: "Why then did Moses *command* one to give a certificate of divorce, and to put her away?"[3] They know perfectly well that Moses never "*commanded*" divorce, yet they keep trying to trick Jesus, Who sees right through their guile. He immediately corrects them, saying that Moses never "*commanded*" divorce, but merely "*allowed*"[4] it, and by giving the reason for this concession, He boldly rebukes them, saying it was on account of the "hardness of their hearts."[5]

It is immediately after this exchange with the Pharisees that "children were brought to Him that He might lay His hands on them and pray."[6] Though His disciples did nothing to stave off the conniving, hard-hearted Pharisees, now they try to keep the innocent children away. Jesus reprimands them, and by doing so He juxtaposes the children with the Pharisees: "Let the children come to Me,

---

[1] Cf. John 8:44.
[2] Matthew 19:3.
[3] Matthew 19:7.
[4] Matthew 19:8.
[5] Matthew 19:8.
[6] Matthew 19:13.

and do not hinder them; for to such belongs the kingdom of heaven."[1]

Thus, the *context* of this second passage from Matthew about children and heaven isolates, by contrast to the Pharisees, two further qualities of childlikeness which Jesus is commending as disposing us for heaven: 1) honest, candid guilelessness and 2) sensitive, docility of heart.

Another passage is found in Mark 10:2-16, and is very similar to the one we have just examined. However, the conclusion is phrased a little differently: "Truly, I say to you, whoever does not receive the kingdom of God like a child shall not enter it."[2] Here He isolates the *manner* by which His kingdom must be received. The context still juxtaposes children with the conniving, legalistic Pharisees, who are always trying to find legal loopholes by which they can manage to follow the letter of the law while contradicting its spirit. This is not the childlike attitude that His kingdom requires. "The letter *kills*; the Spirit *gives life*."[3] Children are not duplicitous, but simple and straightforward. They do not try to connive ways to *appear* to be doing what they in truth are *not* doing; they simply do what they do.

Luke 18:9-17 introduces yet another context for the teaching about children and heaven.

The passage begins by identifying the specific audience for whom it was intended—"some who trusted in themselves that they were righteous and despised others."[4] Right away we can see two attitudes that are not childlike: 1) Children do not trust in themselves because they honestly admit their complete inadequacy; the very notion of even *trying* to trust in themselves cannot occur to them. 2) Children do not despise others by judging them as worse than themselves; they frankly accept themselves and others as they are without any judgmental comparisons.

Then Jesus tells the famous parable about two men, a Pharisee and a tax-collector, praying in the temple. The

---

[1] Matthew 19:14.
[2] Mark 10:15.
[3] II Corinthians 3:6.
[4] Luke 18:9.

Pharisee presumes to position himself right up front and his prayer ("*with himself*!)[1] consists of nothing but bragging about his *outward* piety as compared to the lowly tax-collector. In contrast, the tax-collector is sincere, honest and humble, frankly admitting his lowliness. Rather than *pretend* to be holy, he *confesses* his sinfulness. Jesus summarizes the parable thus: "Everyone who exalts himself will be humbled, but he who humbles himself will be exalted."[2]

It is specifically here that St. Luke inserts the passage about children and heaven. In fact, to make it clear that Jesus was not referring to older children who might have already been tarnished by the adult world they are gradually assimilating, he says that they were "*infants*"[3] who were being brought to Jesus. And again, when the disciples attempt to keep them away, Jesus admonishes: "Let the children come to Me, and do not hinder them; for to such belongs the kingdom of God. Truly, I say to you, whoever does not receive the kingdom of God like a child shall not enter it."[4]

Now, what does all this have to do with nudity?

Although Jesus is not, of course, telling us we have to get naked like infants any more than He is saying we should walk around in diapers holding a rattle, underlying social nudity there is the same childlike attitude that is required for admission into His kingdom.

First of all, unless you have that most elusive, "perfect 10" body, being naked in the presence of others is very humbling. There is no possibility of Pharisaical cover-ups and pretenses. If your breasts sag or your spare tire hangs on your hips, there is no hiding it; everyone sees you just as you are. As the tax-collector in Luke 18 honestly admitted his faults, so the nude openly and frankly reveals his physical shortcomings to all who care to look. There is a clear, undeniable honesty about nudity which is like the honesty of little children.

Nakedness, like children, is so starkly simple and frank. There are literally no put-ons (pun intended). There

---

[1] Luke 18:11.
[2] Luke 18:14.
[3] Luke 18:15.
[4] Luke 18:16f.

is no pulling the wool over anybody's eyes because there is no wool at all! You cannot have anything "up your sleeve" when you have no sleeves!

Unlike the Pharisee in the passage from Luke 18:9ff, children do not "despise others"[1] by judging them as worse than themselves. Instead, they frankly accept themselves and others just as they are, and so it is with social nudity. When one's own physical shortcomings are all too starkly exposed, it is natural to cut others plenty of slack. One automatically realizes Jesus' famous teaching, "Judge not, that ye be not judged. For with what judgment ye judge, ye shall be judged."[2] Practicing this with respect to others' physical qualities is very useful for learning not to judge others' spiritual, invisible qualities and motives. There is a certain guilelessness about social nudity. It does not even try to judge the possible guile in others.

My family was once at a local Vermont beach. We had been nude all day among other beach-goers, most of whom were clothed. By early evening the beach was abandoned except for us. Along came two young men fully clothed in duds so filthy it looked like they had spent the day in the dump. As they approached, grinning through missing teeth, Linda became self-conscious, quite unlike naked toddlers who, like Adam & Eve before the fall, are oblivious to their nudity. But she decided to give the newcomers the benefit of the doubt, despite her discomfort.

Sure enough, they walked right up to us to initiate a conversation. Quite unlike little children, we suspected that their motive was simply to get a close-up look at Linda's body. They said they had heard the rumors about the nude beach and, as soon as they finished their work at the local dump (at least *that* suspicion was correct!), they had come to check it out. Clothed only by the setting sun, it was not difficult for us to confirm the rumors.

Suddenly all our suspicious, judgmental, unchildlike attitudes were dispelled. Though they certainly did not need our permission, they asked us if we minded if they went swimming. I think they just wanted some assurance and encouragement, for as they began peeling off their

---

[1] Luke 18:9.
[2] Matthew 7:1f.

filthy clothes, their exposed skin betrayed the truth that the last time they had ever been naked was probably while frolicking in the lawn sprinkler as little children. White as ghosts, and wearing only their well-defined tan lines (around their necks and wrists!), they waded into the water and literally frolicked like little children.

When they waded back onto the beach they resumed their conversation with us. This time we knew that their motive was not to ogle Linda, but quite the contrary, to prove their childlike innocence, facing us and not hiding their nudity. If lust had been their motive, they would have shown the evidence, but there was no tumescence. Just like us, they simply delighted in the childlike innocence and purity of nakedness.

If Linda had acted on her suspicions, she would have quickly gotten dressed, but this would not have been guileless and childlike.

Indeed, whenever we wear clothes because we judge guile in an onlooker, we are not being simple, honest, straightforward, candid and innocent as children. A figure drawing model does not, and indeed, cannot, know what is in the minds of the artists drawing him. It really is not his business to know, but simply to do his job well and hold his poses. That is much how naturists are. They do not, and indeed, cannot, know what is in the minds of their beholders. Such speculations are not simple and childlike, so we naturists do not concern ourselves with them. One of our reasons for nudity is greater relaxation, and it would be quite counter-productive if we were only to be nervous wrecks, always on the lookout for evil motives.

A major reason why many Christians do not practice naturism is because they are afraid that they will be looked down upon by others who do not understand them. But in the above passages Jesus praises lowliness, saying that those who humble themselves would be exalted.[1] Often the motive for wanting to be seen, not only dressed, but *well*-dressed, is precisely the same as the motive of the Pharisee praying in the temple "*with himself*": to be esteemed by others. This is not childlike. Little children cannot even conceive of such a motive. A few people in my life have scorned me on account of my naturist beliefs and

---

[1] Luke 18:14.

practices, but what of it? As St. Paul said, "If I were still pleasing men, I should not be a servant of Christ!"[1] Besides, far more people have responded favorably to our nudity than not, and our mere deportment taught them more truth than if we had handed them this book.

Many saints did humbling things specifically to be looked down upon by those who exalt themselves and despise others whom they think fail to measure up to their high standards of perfection. Some saints intentionally became street people and some humbled themselves to go begging. Sure, they might have gotten a job and earned a "respectable" living, but begging not only managed to attain enough for survival, but earned them the added blessing of being looked down upon. Remember that Jesus does regard such as "blessedness" as He taught in His beatitudes.[2] St. John of God actually behaved like a lunatic in order to be scorned and to identify himself with the mentally ill whom those who exalted themselves despised. It is very sad that most Christians are "scandalized" by such behaviors instead of being scandalized by the Pharisees among their own number.

Some saints also went naked. Among their motives were: 1) to be truly evangelically poor, 2) to do penance, bearing the heat of the sun and the cold of night, and 3) to be despised as their Master "was despised and rejected."[3]

Recently, I was sitting on my back deck nude, praying with Linda, when a mother from the local Christian academy dropped by unannounced. I could have quickly wrapped the towel I was sitting on around me, but in the sight of God, what good would that have done either me or her? So, like a child, I remained as I was, honest and straightforward, hiding nothing. I knew there was a possibility that she would scorn me, but I knew that even if that did happen, I would be the victor in Christ, as it would serve to give me an opportunity for humility. As it turned out, her reaction was simply an apology for having intruded, and she subsequently invited us to dinner with her family. So many Christians panic at the thought of being "caught with their pants down," but experience

---

[1] Galatians 1:10.
[2] Cf. Matthew 5:3ff, especially vv. 11f.
[3] Isaiah 53:3.

proves that there are almost never any negative consequences. Jesus did say to treat others as we would like to be treated by them.[1] If it was *we* who were visiting *them* unannounced, wouldn't we want them to be themselves in their own castle and not panic and cover up as though they were guilty of some heinous crime? Of course, we would want them to feel free to remain calmly nude, not having to "defend" themselves against us by erecting breastworks of fabrics.

Because children are aware of their ignorance, they are docile and open to instruction. In fact, they are so eager to learn that they can be downright annoying, as the parent of any insatiably inquisitive four-year old knows. This childlike quality is opposite the Pharisees hardheartedness. They neither wanted to hear nor obey.

Nudity, because it is the state of openness and vulnerability, is *sensitive*. Just as a child does not pretend to know what he does not know, so the nude does not pretend to be other than who he is. True, though this honesty and transparency is only on the physical, visible level, chances are that such a disposition will carry over into the spiritual level as well. Indeed, social nudity can help us more easily acquire spiritual honesty. The one can effect the other.

St. Luke says that Jesus was addressing those "who trusted in themselves."[2] Nudity has a lot to do with trust because it is so utterly vulnerable. When I did not hurriedly cover up when that Christian mom popped in, it was obvious that I was showing her unilateral trust. Had I raced to cover up, I would have accorded her no trust at all. Without even knowing her, I would have presumed the worst. Why not presume the best in others? Even if they do not "deserve" it, is it not true that they will live up to the reputation and standard that we pre-establish for them? If you praise a guy for being an honest and hard worker, is he more likely to thereafter try to live up to our opinion, or prove us wrong? By not covering up, we lavish the onlooker with great respect and trust. We do not demand that he first prove his worthiness. Rather, we *begin* by believing he is worthy; we give him nowhere to go

---

[1] Cf. Matthew 7:12 & Luke 6:31.
[2] Luke 18:9.

from that pedestal but downhill, and who wants to do that? Nudity shows profound trust, and this is childlike. A little child unilaterally trusts that his big, strong daddy will certainly catch him when he jumps off a wall. He does not go to bed worrying that daddy will not provide breakfast for him the next morning. He has complete trust, from moment to moment. Social nudity can be an excellent, therapeutic tool for regaining such childlike trust, and wouldn't that help brighten our seemingly ever darkening world? When we smile at strangers we begin by presuming the best—that they are likeable. Just imagine if we went around frowning and scowling at them, requiring them to first prove they are worthy of our smiles! But isn't that precisely what we do when we cover up in their presence? A relationship has to begin with either trust or suspicion. Doesn't the former lead to a brighter, more joyful world?

Children receive the kingdom of God with total trust and confidence. They do not begin to doubt that Jesus might fail them, or that maybe Jesus really is still dead. We proclaim to them the Gospel that Jesus lives, and they naturally exclaim, "Alleluia!", and not "Prove it, Buster!" Shouldn't this attitude permeate our whole life and conduct, from smiling at strangers to not running for cover when "caught with our pants down"?

People love being trusted. Perhaps nothing else makes them feel better about themselves. I have often observed this joy at swimming holes when I was nude. Far from being "offended," those around me seemed to be delighted. My nudity had more to do with *them* than with *me*. They enjoyed my natural state not only because, as created in God's image, the human body is indeed beautiful, but even more, because it made them feel trusted. Sometimes—perhaps more often than not—one or more of them would be so deeply affected by that joyful feeling of being trusted that they, too, would get undressed, feeling hypocritical not to reciprocate that trust and pass it on to others. And isn't this just how a smile works? It is contagious; we want to pass it on.

In every way, nudity is childlike. It is even *literally* childlike, as every little child delights to run around all "bare naked." But to imitate children for that reason would be to seriously miss Jesus' point; it would be like sucking our thumbs to be childlike. Instead, sincere, candid social nudity can be of great advantage to acquiring the many vital, childlike qualities Jesus does say we must have in order to be saved. Since our eternal salvation is of such grave consequence, can any of us afford to refrain from using such an useful tool?

Commentary: Revelation 3:15-18

by Jim C. Cunningham

I know your works: you are neither cold nor hot. Would that you were cold or hot! So, because you are lukewarm, and neither cold nor hot, I will spew you out of My mouth. For you say, "I am rich, I have prospered, and I need nothing;" not knowing that you are wretched, pitiable, poor, blind, and naked. Therefore I counsel you to buy from Me gold refined by fire, that you may be rich, and white garments to clothe you and to keep the shame of your nakedness from being seen, and salve to anoint your eyes, that you may see.

There is no doubt that after the banishment from the Garden of Eden, nakedness became a negative, impoverished condition in this inclement valley of tears. To be clothes-less was to be in want of the barest necessities, to be the poorest of the poor—a truly pitiful and socially embarrassing condition.

In the Old Testament, material wealth and prosperity were thought to be proof of the Lord's blessing.[1] Conversely, to be poor was to shamefully lack that blessing. Furthermore, such material blessing was considered a just reward for personal righteousness. Psalm 128:1f says, "Blessed is everyone who fears the LORD, who walks in His ways! You shall eat the fruit of the labor of your hands; you shall be happy, and it shall be well with you." Since prosperity was a sign of one's just reward for

---

[1] E.g. cf. Psalm 112:3.

212

personal righteousness, poverty logically implied the opposite, i.e. since God is all-just, the poor must somehow be guilty of unrighteousness.

The sufferings of Job made no sense at all. Though he was a just man, Job was reduced to abject poverty, literal nakedness, disease and friendlessness. Only in the mystery of the cross of Christ, Who *fulfilled* the Law and the prophets,[1] was such suffering at all intelligible. The New Testament shows that the glory and beatitude of eternal life is not comparable to the trials of this present, fleeting life[2] and that our heavenly reward will be greater in proportion to our trials in this life.[3] St. Paul teaches that in all kinds of suffering "we are more than conquerors."[4] How can this be? "Because of Him Who loved us."[5] Furthermore, the New Testament reveals more clearly how suffering is a positive and even necessary[6] thing, perfecting the Christian[7] unto the full maturity of Christ,[8] Who Himself had to suffer in order to attain perfection,[9] and that such discipline was real proof of our heavenly Father's true love for us, His sons, for only neglected bastards are left undisciplined.[10]

Thus, the Gospel transformed all suffering—including poverty and nakedness—from something negative to something very positive. Whereas suffering had been very shameful, it became the only thing St. Paul would glory in and boast about.[11]

Therefore, in the light of the Gospel, the only truly negative kind of nakedness is being bereft of good deeds and virtues. If we are naked when it comes to these spiritual garments, then we have cause for great and true shame on Judgment Day when we are numbered among the goats and not the sheep.[12]

---

[1] Cf. Matthew 5:17.
[2] Cf. Romans 8:18 & II Corinthians 4:17.
[3] Cf. II Corinthians 1:5; Galatians 6:7 & I Peter 4:13.
[4] Romans 8:37.
[5] Ibid.
[6] Cf. Romans 8:17.
[7] Cf. Romans 5:3ff; I Peter 4:1 & James 1:2-4.
[8] Cf. Ephesians 4:13 & Colossians 1:28.
[9] Cf. Hebrews 2:10; 5:8f & I Peter 2:20f.
[10] Cf. Hebrews 12:5ff.
[11] Cf. Galatians 6:14; II Corinthians 11:30; 12:5 & 9f.
[12] Cf. Matthew 25:41ff.

In Revelation 3:15f Jesus rebukes Christians for their spiritual lukewarmness, saying He will vomit such from His mouth. To be spiritually naked—bereft of spiritual fruits—is to choose to be rejected by Christ.

Revelation 3:17f says: "For you say, 'I am rich, I have prospered, and I need nothing;' not knowing that you are wretched, pitiable, poor, blind, and naked. Therefore I counsel you to buy from Me gold refined by fire, that you may be rich, and white garments to clothe you and to keep the shame of your nakedness from being seen, and salve to anoint your eyes, that you may see."

Obviously, "naked" does not refer to physical nakedness, because it is clear that these worldly, rich, complacent Christians are, in fact, quite well-dressed. What they lack, however is *spiritual* treasure—the raiment of virtue and good deeds. Hence, in Jesus' Own obvious usage one can be "naked" even though physically rich and well-dressed.

Furthermore, note that He uses "poor" and "blind" along with "naked." Yet we know that being physically poor or blind is not a moral or spiritual evil,[1] but being willfully ignorant about spiritual matters is truly evil. Jesus here no more condemns physical *nakedness* than He does physical *blindness*.

That Jesus is speaking in images, and not literally, is also obvious from v. 18 where He bids us buy gold, white robes and salve from Him. He no more wants us to literally buy real gold and salve from Him than He wants us to be fully or well-dressed in white robes. If fundamentalists are so near-sighted that they cannot see Jesus' obvious meaning here, then they are hypocrites if they don't wear *literal, "white robes."* Furthermore, they're going to have to buy them *from Him*—I wonder where they shop, "K(ingdom)-Mart"?

Revelation 16:15 says, "Lo, I am coming like a thief! Blessed is he who is awake, keeping his garments that he may not go naked and be seen exposed!"

Again, any fundamentalist who thinks this means we should not be physically naked, should not go to sleep either! The truth is, just as we should be spiritually sharp, keen and vigilant, so also should we be spiritually clothed

---

[1] Cf. Matthew 5:3; Luke 6:20 & John 9:3.

with virtues and good works, as St. Peter, who liked to fish in the nude,[1] clearly defined true modesty for early Christian women: "...when they see your reverent and chaste behavior. Let yours not be the outward adorning with braiding of hair, decoration of gold, and wearing of fine clothing, but let it be the hidden person of the heart with the imperishable jewel of a gentle and quiet spirit, which in God's sight is very precious."[2] Obviously, the clothing God is interested in is of an *interior* sort (and I don't mean underwear!).

St. Mary of Egypt and other Christian ascetics went nude in order to be truly poor. They used that physical poverty and nakedness to gain spiritual riches and the true "white robes" Jesus referred to in Revelation 3:18. They completely divested themselves of this world's goods in order to more ardently long for the "heavenly habitation to envelop them."[3]

Finally, in conclusion, I can do no better than quote Revelation 19:7f which precisely states what I have said above, viz. that the fabrics we are supposed to be clothed with are not made of *physical* fibers, but of *virtues*, and it is only the lack of virtue that is truly shameful:

"Let us rejoice and exult and give Him the glory, for the marriage of the Lamb has come, and His Bride has made herself ready; it was granted her to be clothed with fine linen, bright and pure—*for the fine linen is the righteous deeds of the saints.*"

---

[1] Cf. John 21:7.
[2] I Peter 3:2ff.
[3] II Corinthians 5:2.

The Bible & Nakedness

From Fig Leaf Forum[1]

The Bible never describes nakedness as being *inherently* shameful or *inherently* sinful:

1. Mankind was created "in the image of God,"[2] "naked and unashamed."[3]
2. After they sinned, Adam & Eve covered themselves out of *fear*, not *shame*.[4] God mercifully clothed them out of *physical* necessity, not *moral* necessity.[5]
3. Except where forbidden in formal worship by specific religious or cultural conventions,[6] there are no Biblical prohibitions of nakedness.
4. Wherever shame is associated with nakedness in the Bible, it is:
   A. shame due to sinful conduct found in conjunction with nakedness;[7]
   B. shame due to status as vanquished people;[8]
   C. figuratively, shame due to spiritual deficiency.[9]
5. The act of "clothing the naked" spoken about in both the Old and New Testaments refers to the provision of *physical* needs, not *moral* needs.[10]
6. Though physical clothing is regarded as a moral necessity in our worldly society, such is *not* taught by the Bible. By contrast, the Bible teaches the ineffectuality of external prohibitions based on "human commands

---

[1] Reprinted with permission from *Fig Leaf Forum*. Address: POB 1955, Stn Main, Winnipeg, MB R3C 3R2, Canada
http://www.figleafforum.com.
[2] Genesis 1:27.
[3] Genesis 2:25.
[4] Cf. Genesis 3:10.
[5] Cf. Genesis 3:17-19, 23f.
[6] E.g. Exodus 20:26; 28:42f; I Corinthians 11:5f & I Timothy 2:9f.
[7] E.g. Genesis 9:20-25; Jeremiah 13:26; Ezekiel 23:29f; Nahum 3:5f & Habakkuk 2:15f.
[8] E.g. Isaiah 20:4; 47:3 & Micah 1:11.
[9] E.g. Revelation 3:17f & 16:15.
[10] E.g. Isaiah 58:7; Ezekiel 18:7; 18:16; Job 31:19; Matthew 25:36-43 & James 2:15f.

and teachings" in controlling sinful desires.[1] It instructs the redeemed to "clothe yourselves with the Lord Jesus Christ."[2] Holy conduct results from the *internal* work of the Holy Spirit, not *external* rules.[3]

Christians who choose to be naked in the presence of others must do so appropriately:

1. Their motives must be pure.[4]
2. Their activities must be:
   A. honorable and glorifying to God;[5]
   B. loving and respectful of others;[6]
   C. legal.[7]

Commentary: Leviticus 18:6-23[8]

by Jim C. Cunningham

First, the text from the King James Version:

None of you shall approach to any that is near of kin to him, to uncover their nakedness: I am the LORD. The nakedness of thy father, or the nakedness of thy mother, shalt thou not uncover: she is thy mother; thou shalt not uncover her nakedness. The nakedness of thy father's wife shalt thou not uncover: it is thy father's nakedness. The nakedness of thy sister, the daughter of thy father, or daughter of thy mother, whether she be born at home, or born abroad, even their nakedness thou shalt not un-

---

[1] Cf. Colossians 2:20-23.
[2] Romans 13:14 & Galatians 3:26f.
[3] Cf. John 14:16f; Galatians 5:22-24 & Hebrews 8:10.
[4] Cf. I Chronicles 28:9; Proverbs 16:2; 21:2 & Hebrews 4:12f.
[5] Cf. I Corinthians 6:19f; 10:31 & I Thessalonians 4:3-7.
[6] Cf. Romans 14:12-15:1 & I Corinthians 8:9.
[7] Cf. Romans 13:1-7 & I Peter 2:11-16.
[8] This commentary also applies to a similar passage found in Leviticus 20:11-21. Also note 20:11 which provides a key to understanding just what Ham's offense in Genesis 9:22 was—incest, an abomination for which Ham's descendants, the Canaanites, were notorious.

cover. The nakedness of thy son's daughter, or of thy daughter's daughter, even their nakedness thou shalt not uncover: for theirs is thine own nakedness. The nakedness of thy father's wife's daughter, begotten of thy father, she is thy sister, thou shalt not uncover her nakedness. Thou shalt not uncover the nakedness of thy father's sister: she is thy father's near kinswoman. Thou shalt not uncover the nakedness of thy mother's sister: for she is thy mother's near kinswoman. Thou shalt not uncover the nakedness of thy father's brother, thou shalt not approach to his wife: she is thine aunt. Thou shalt not uncover the nakedness of thy daughter in law: she is thy son's wife; thou shalt not uncover her nakedness. Thou shalt not uncover the nakedness of thy brother's wife: it is thy brother's nakedness. Thou shalt not uncover the nakedness of a woman and her daughter, neither shalt thou take her son's daughter, or her daughter's daughter, to uncover her nakedness; for they are her near kinswomen: it is wickedness. Neither shalt thou take a wife to her sister, to vex her, to uncover her nakedness, beside the other in her life time. Also thou shalt not approach unto a woman to uncover her nakedness, as long as she is put apart for her uncleanness. Moreover thou shalt not lie carnally with thy neighbour's wife, to defile thyself with her. And thou shalt not let any of thy seed pass through the fire to Molech, neither shalt thou profane the name of thy God: I am the LORD. Thou shalt not lie with mankind, as with womankind: it is abomination. Neither shalt thou lie with any beast to defile thyself therewith: neither shall any woman stand before a beast to lie down thereto: it is confusion.

The ancient Hebrews often used euphemisms when referring to sexual matters, just like we do. For example, when we say "sleep with" we mean "have sex with." There is nothing at all immoral with simply *sleeping* with any-body. In fact, formerly in American culture, and today in many other cultures, beds are even shared with guests. Since beds and sleeping concern sex insofar as sex usually happens in bed at night, we use euphemisms like "go to bed with" and "sleep with" when we really mean "to have sex with." If Mom says to her son, "Now don't go to bed with anybody till you're married," no sane person understands anything else by this but not to fornicate, whether in bed or on the kitchen table!

So it is with the ancient Hebrew euphemism "to uncover the nakedness of." Since nakedness and sex usually go together, their euphemism for "to have sex with" was "to uncover the nakedness of." It has no more to do with nakedness than beds have to do with fornication.

This is abundantly clear from the context. Note that the proscriptions concern relatives—not women whose consanguinity is more remote. Knowing well our hardness of heart and how we'll look for loopholes where we can, the Lord clearly delimits our "conjugal territory."

The whole passage is about sex. After proscribing incest, the Lord goes on to proscribe adultery,[1] infanticide (and abortion!),[2] homosexuality[3] and bestiality.[4] Nudity and dress have nothing to do with it. If it were nudity that was the big sin, how could it make sense for the Lord to say it was okay to be nude with all the females in the whole world, except a handful of designated close relatives?

Finally, look at the gravity of the other sins that are proscribed in the same passage. Does any sane person actually think the Lord ranks seeing your mother in the nude along with offering up your babies in sacrifice to Molech or having sex with an orangutan?

Our all-loving and all-just God is not arbitrary, making up ridiculous laws and ranking such things as simple nakedness next to adultery and infanticide. On the contrary, our God is All-Just and desires our true welfare. Incest is manifestly not in our best interest as a biological society. The verses in question clearly proscribe *incest— not nakedness.*

If it sounds sensible to Christians that God would put nakedness on a par with infanticide, then I don't wonder why there are so many atheists out there that think such a hokey Gospel is absurd. Belief in a stupid God cannot glorify Him. On the contrary, our God is not only All-Just

---

[1] Cf. Leviticus 18:20.
[2] Cf. Leviticus 18:21.
[3] Cf. Leviticus 18:22.
[4] Cf. Leviticus 18:23.

and All-Loving, desiring only what is for our true welfare, but He is All-Wise.

When we read Scripture we must beware of being so nearsighted as to miss the whole picture. We need to step back so we can "see the wood for the trees." All objects look the same if we look too closely. Let's always make sure to see things *in context*—just as God revealed them.

The Original Sin & the Fig Leaf

by Jim C. Cunningham

In their attempt to justify their clothes-compulsiveness, many Christians hark back to Genesis 3:7 where Adam & Eve sew fig leaves together to hide their loins. They never ask *why* they might have done this, nor do they ask just what the big Original Sin actually *was*. Apparently, they simply assume that the sin was literally partaking of some unidentified fruit. Nor do they ask how the panic to fabricate fig leaf aprons can possibly have anything whatsoever to do with eating fruit. They just take what they read at face value ("the Bible tells them so"!), and that's that. This absurd fundamentalism would not be so bad, but they insist on imposing their "interpretation" (if it can be called that) on all the rest of us. If we do not imitate Adam & Eve after their fall, and fastidiously hide our "unmentionables," then we are nothing but a bunch of heretics, or worse.

Man is created in the image of God, and his mind wants to penetrate truth, as far as it can, *through understanding*. Our passion for understanding is not blasphemous; on the contrary, it glorifies God, Who gave us the gift of reason, without which we would not image Him any better than an orangutan. There is no sense at all in God, from *His* end, revealing His will through Scripture, unless He had given man, at *his* end, the gift of reason with which to receive that revelation. Reason is not opposed to faith; faith illumines reason and defines its limits.

220

When we read the Bible, we must always ask the probing questions: "Who, what, when, where, why and how?"

The assumption of many fundamentalists is that, since Adam & Eve made fig leaf aprons, God wants everyone until the Second Coming to stay clothed at all times. Actually, they all make exceptions, such as for the bath or the doctor's office, even though these exceptions cannot be found in Genesis 3, nor anywhere else in Scripture. In fact, many go beyond, insisting that we must stay clothed till the Second Coming, and even insist that all the saints in heaven will wear clothes for all eternity (sounds more like hell to me!).

This, therefore, is a commentary on Original Sin and its relationship to the fig leaf loincloths Adam & Eve so hastily manufactured as their first response to that sin. I implore your patience in "baring" with me, because this is about as deep as revelation gets. Indeed, its antithesis is the mystery of redemption, which more than undid what sin had done. "Where sin abounded, grace abounded all the more."[1]

Since what follows is very deep, and deserves an entire book (which I yet hope to write), I strongly recommend all readers to prayerfully reread the first three chapters of Genesis before continuing. I also recommend rereading this article a few times, and pausing for meditation when moved to do so. There is a lot here. My aim is to show that the fig leaf thing has nothing to do with simple nakedness. To demonstrate this, I must explore the *nature* of the Original Sin to which the fig leaves were a feverish response.

In theology, the "what" of a sin is called its "object." Thus, the heart of this commentary explores just what the "object" of the Original Sin was. This not only sheds floods of light on the fig leaf frenzy, but on literally all of revelation, including the very heart of the Gospel.

First of all, in my interpretation of Scripture I am not a strict literalist because often only an idiot (and they exist, let me assure you!) could take everything literally. *Properly* interpreted, Scripture does not contradict itself because God, the Holy Spirit, is the primary Author, and

---

[1] Romans 5:20.

He is Truth Itself.[1] However, on the purely literal level, Scripture is full of contradictions. Even objective matters like the number of those slain in battle sometimes conflict.[2] This is easily explained by such literary techniques as hyperbole. No one in their right mind accuses a person of lying when he says, "There were a million mosquitoes in our tent last night!" We understand exactly what he means to convey. Also, sometimes words are chosen that literally mean the exact opposite of the intended meaning. For example, children say, "That roller coaster ride was *wicked*!", meaning it was *very good* indeed. How some people can understand such nuances of language in everyday speech, but then tie the Holy Spirit's hands by refusing Him the like liberties, is beyond me. (Oops—now they'll accuse me of teaching that the Paraclete has literal hands!)

The big question is, "Just what *was* that Original Sin that introduced clothing, suffering, ignorance, death, etc. into human existence?"

On one level it is immaterial; no matter what it was, they were proud and usurped God's prerogative by knowingly disobeying Him. Well, that is all well and good, but it tells us zilch why that sin would prompt a scrambling to cover genitalia. Tell me, if you were caught stealing an apple from your neighbor's orchard, would your first impulse be to make sure your fly was zipped up, or to hide the apple or pretend you were picking it for the farmer, and maybe even sampling it a bit just to make sure it was of sufficient quality to harvest for so kind and noble a farmer as he? Since there is no direct connection between apples and genitals (or is there something Mama never told me?), then the logical deduction is that the apple picking thing is *figurative—not literal.*

---

[1] Cf. John 16:13 & 14:6.

[2] E.g. II Samuel 3:14 says that David slew *one* hundred Philistines, duly counting out their foreskins in front of King Saul, and I Samuel 18:25ff says it was *two* hundred. Since we are certain that the same battle was being referred to, then we are free to interpret the *two* hundred as not *literal*, but *hyperbolic*. This does *not* mean that it is not true. In fact, hyperbole can convey more truth than bland statistics, because it adds the emotional significance and also other significances such as David's great military prowess which was all the more likely to arouse the envy of jealous Saul.

Other weight for this conclusion is that we know God is all-just. Were I to heavy-handedly establish a cocka-mamie law for my children like, "Thou shalt not drink milk from a tea cup," and then attach to this inane "crime" an unbelievably harsh penalty, everyone but an idiot would rightly accuse me of being an unjust, unloving rogue. But lo and behold, how many "pious" Christians have just such a "faith" in their supposedly all-merciful, all-loving and all-just, heavenly Father? It would be funny were it not so sad. Such stupid "piety" is sheer blasphemy. Indeed, Jesus said, "If you then, who are evil, know how to give good gifts to your children, how much more will your Father Who is in heaven give good things to those who ask Him?"[1] How is it that if we would all severely castigate any *human* father who was so unfair and arbitrary as to impose absurd rules with even more absurd, dispropor-tionate punishments, we at the same time, deem it a "pious" sentiment to think thus of our heavenly Father?

Likewise, in Genesis 4:10-15, Cain, a cold-blooded murderer gets off better than his parents did for suppos-edly picking an apple! Will somebody gimme (and God!) a break?

It is not "rationalism" to believe that Divine Revelation is worthless unless God first made us in His image, gifted with reason, in order to interpret it. Therefore, let's be *reasonable* (i.e. godly) for a moment. "'Come now, let us reason together,' says the LORD!"[2]

"God is love."[3] Out of love He created the cosmos, proclaiming everything that He made "very good."[4] The obvious grande finale of all His creativity was man. Unlike other creatures, before undertaking the creation of man, there is a special pause and incisive preface. There is an intramural consultation among the three Divine Persons of the Blessed Trinity, all of Whom were at work in creation. To "speak" things into being requires a Trinity of Persons: a Speaker, the Word and Breath. Before beginning this finale, the Trinity proposed, "Let Us make man in Our image, after Our likeness; and let them have

---

[1] Matthew 7:11.
[2] Isaiah 1:18.
[3] I John 4:8.
[4] Genesis 1:31.

dominion over the fish of the sea, and over the birds of the air, and over the cattle, and over all the earth, and over every creeping thing that creeps upon the earth."[1] Where is this Trinitarian "image and likeness" thus far reflected? Thus far it is reflected only in the fact of man's assigned "dominion" (from the Latin, "Dominus," meaning "Lord").

As the narrative poem continues, more is revealed about how man images the Trinity: "So God created man in his own image, in the image of God he created him; male and female he created them."[2] Hmm..., the duality of sexes in man reflects the Trinity. This apparent anomaly is explained when we consider just what unites male and female—fecund love. Only with this last component is the Trinitarian image in man complete.

We learn more about our lofty nature in the next verse: "And God blessed them, and God said to them, 'Be fruitful and multiply, and fill the earth and subdue it; and have dominion over the fish of the sea and over the birds of the air and over every living thing that moves upon the earth.'"[3] The Blessed Trinity is not static or passive; God is Life Itself.[4] He is Ultimate, Creative Power. Designed in God's "image and likeness," man reflects this creative sharing of life by *pro-CREATION*. This is at once both an integral description of who man is, and at the same time a command, or better expressed, a mission.

Also, once again, man is commanded to be lord of the earth.[5] These commands to procreate and have dominion are sublime, a most noble vocation. There is no absurd arbitrariness here—no revelation that God created man so He could make up ridiculous laws and play with man as pawns on a chessboard. In Genesis 1:25, after God had created all but man, He declared it "good." But in 1:31, after creating and installing man as the crowning glory of creation, "God saw *everything* that he had made, and behold, it was *very* good."

In the second chapter of Genesis we have what seems to be an entirely different story of man's creation, but this

---

[1] Genesis 1:26.
[2] Genesis 1:27.
[3] Genesis 1:28.
[4] E.g. cf. John 14:6 & I John 1:1.
[5] This purpose for man is first revealed in Genesis 1:26, and then again in 1:28.

is not so. The fact is that there is simply far too much to reveal about the mystery of man for one account alone to suffice. This second account corroborates (not contradicts) and extrapolates the revelation of the first, something like an inset story within a story as we see in news magazines today, or a "detail" as we find in art books, offering a magnified view of some highlight.

In this magnification we learn more about the sexes and man's lordship. This second story is more dramatic—more graphic:

"Then the LORD God formed man of dust from the ground, and breathed into his nostrils the breath of life; and man became a living being."[1] The creation of man is here described as far more special than that of the other creatures. Although made partly of the same mud of the earth (whence our resemblance to other creatures), there is, even in the formation of man's body a special molding and shaping, in some mysterious way reflective of God the Trinity's Own "image and likeness."

But there's even more! The very soul—life principle—of man is of a God-like order, signified by man's being enlivened by the very breath (Spirit) of God.

Then God assigns man his duty to use his dominion over creation to make it bear fruit ("till it")[2] and to be its steward ("guard it")[3] and not a destructive, tyrannical master.

Immediately afterwards, God assigns sensual parameters for this God-like earthling—parameters that are conducive both unto fecundity and right lordship. As is probably universal in all languages, the euphemism used for this is "eating":

"You may freely eat of every tree of the garden; but of the tree of the knowledge of good and evil you shall not eat, for in the day that you eat of it you shall die."[4] It is obvious that the so-called apple tree[5] is allegorical from the very name of the tree itself. Is it a Cortland apple tree, or a McIntosh? No, it is "the tree of the knowledge of good

---

[1] Genesis 2:7.
[2] Genesis 2:15.
[3] Ibid.
[4] Genesis 2:16f.
[5] Note that the text here does not specify the exact type of tree. Perhaps the apple tree tradition came from Song of Songs 8:5?

and evil"! Search as I might all the indices of all tree seed catalogs, I can't find that one anywhere listed. Why? Because obviously, it is not an actual "tree" at all! Its very name should indicate to anybody that it is an *allegory* of something far more profound and mystical than biting an apple!

Looking at our own moral experience, how do we come to *intimately* know good and evil? The answer is aptly given in Psalm 51 where we see King David "*knowing* evil" through the profound realization and admission of his guilt of adultery and murder.[1] He surely "tasted forbidden fruit" by committing adultery with Bathsheba.[2] Just as in Genesis 2:17, the consequences included deaths as well as "knowing good and evil." His sin was linked to the murder of her husband, Uriah,[3] and the result was the death of the bastard fruit of that illicit union,[4] much to David's grievous regret. Indeed, did David not then "*know* evil"? Isn't it obvious that Genesis 2:17 means this sort of thing, and not the mere eating of apples?

Furthermore, not only did David "know evil," but by plunging into the depths of his immorality, he gained an intimate "knowledge" of goodness as well. He keenly sees its desirability and longs for such virtue with passion that no poet or playwright has ever described better than David in Psalm 51. It may be unfortunate, but it is true, that humans keenly learn the glory of rectitude by falling into its opposite. You can tell a child, till you're blue in the face, not to touch fire, but only by disobeying does he gain that truly *intimate* knowledge of how good your counsel was, and how wrong (evil) he was not to trust you. Thus our daily experience corroborates my allegorical interpretation of "eating the forbidden fruit" of the "tree of the knowledge of good and evil." Far from making light of divine revelation, as some particularly mindless fundamentalists would accuse me of, I am in truth paying it much greater heed.

---

[1] Cf. Psalm 51:1-3.
[2] Cf. II Samuel 11:2ff.
[3] Cf. II Samuel 11:6ff.
[4] Cf. II Samuel 12:14-18.

No sooner does God assign the parameters of man's sensuality (which, if he heeds, he will "live" and keep his God-like pristineness), than He suddenly proclaims something quite opposite to what He has been saying all along: "It is *not* good that the man should be alone; I will make him a helper fit for him."[1] Why is it "not good" for the man to be alone? When God says something is "not good," we had better take heed. Something "heavy duty" is going on. It was "not good" for the man to be alone because alone he could not fulfill his divinely assigned purpose. The kind of fruitfulness God wanted from man was not merely that of an orchard keeper. God did not want the man to "fill the earth" with apples or Swiss chard, but human offspring![2] In no way could man manifest his God-like creativity than by procreating offspring "in his own image and likeness"—like unto himself. The greatest "garden" for man to "till" and "guard" is woman, for only thus can he raise up new life like unto himself.

Probably all cultures euphemistically refer to woman as a "garden" in whom seed is sown. In the Song of Songs Solomon has the woman refer to her younger virgin sister as a "garden enclosed," whose breasts are yet small.[3] So one would think that the Genesis narrative would go right into the creation of woman, but not so—not so at all! Most interestingly, the narrative continues:

"So out of the ground the LORD God formed every beast of the field and every bird of the air, and brought them to the man to see what he would call them; and whatever the man called every living creature, that was its name. The man gave names to all cattle, and to the birds of the air, and to every beast of the field; *but for the man there was not found a helper fit for him.*"[4]

If literalist fundamentalists want to insist that Genesis is primarily interested in scientifically revealing our origins, they have an impossible task. I once called in to a Christian radio show that tried to do just this. I

---

[1] Genesis 2:18.
[2] Interestingly, the Latin word for this is literally, "*semen*," and the Greek word means literally "sperm."
[3] Cf. Song of Solomon 8:8ff.
[4] Genesis 2:19f.

pointed out some obvious contradictions if we are to mindlessly insist on literalism. I had the guy backed into a corner when all of a sudden he feigned piety, lamely asserting, "Well, I guess I just have to have childlike (i.e. childish!) faith; after all, Jesus said, 'Unless ye become like little children, ye cannot enter the kingdom of heaven.'"[1] I wonder whether he sucks his thumb, too... Such "piety" is probably more scandalous than pedophile clergy. Good people who rightly value their God-given gifts of reason and intellect, hear that nonsense and judge that Christianity isn't worth investigating; pagans make more sense. If we would only read things *in context* we would come much nearer to the truth of things, and truly edify unbelievers.

Even in elementary school we were taught that sentences express complete thoughts. A prepositional phrase is meaningless unless in the context of a sentence. Words in a sentence derive their significance from their relationship to each other. "In the barn" tells me nothing. "Zeke is milking the cow in the barn," tells me several things, all because of *context*. It tells me *who* is milking, *what* he's doing, *to what/whom* he is doing it and *where* he's doing it.

This is how Scripture must be read or else it is nothing but an inane jumble of words which can be "interpreted" any way convenient to one's prejudice. Using our God-given noggins, however, and studying the context, we learn a vast amount of holy wisdom, probing realms into which even angels long to probe.[2]

The narrative has the creation of animals immediately follow God's proclamation to create a "suitable partner" to dramatically illustrate that *none* of those creatures would qualify. They are in no sense "partner" or equal to the man, but *lower*. By naming them, man shows his God-like dominion and lordship over them. *None* of them are "suitable" to be man's "partner" in fulfilling his God-like mission of procreation, and without procreating, neither can he hope to fulfill the command to subdue the earth; he will need billions of helpers for that one!

---

[1] Matthew 18:3.
[2] Cf. I Peter 1:12.

The stage is now perfectly set for the grande finale of creation—woman. The following verses are packed with more meaning than all of Shakespeare's works put together:

"So the LORD God caused a deep sleep to fall upon the man, and while he slept took one of his ribs and closed up its place with flesh; and the rib which the LORD God had taken from the man he made into a woman and brought her to the man."[1]

Why the "sleep"? Perhaps so man would know that he himself is not responsible for the creation of woman. Her origins are both mystery and yet intimately bound up with his very self. Many commentators have remarked on the significance of "the rib," signifying woman's equality of partnership. According to the original plan, neither sex "wore the pants"—they were equal.

God "brings" the woman to the man. Fathers of brides still do this at every wedding. Just as with the other creatures, God "brings" her to the man, but unlike all the others, the narrative omits "to see what he would name her." Finding her "suitable" beyond his wildest dreams, the idea of naming her does not even enter his head. His mouth is agape, he is head over heels in love; he would be her servant sooner than her master. He beholds a glorious queen far more beautiful than the bejeweled queen in Psalm 45:9 & 13f. His rapture for the woman is comprehensive. *All* of him is attracted to *all* of her. As she is also created "in the image and likeness of God," his passionate devotion for her is no merely profane love. It is beyond *eros*. It is, in truth, the original priestly sacrifice—the act of love that fittingly glorifies God. Man is priest and woman is temple. Their sacrifice is their love in which God Himself is intimately involved.

Though even man alone—without woman—in some sense reflects the Trinity by the fact of the union[2] of his body[3] and soul,[4] and, as St. Augustine says, even man alone, reflects the Trinity in the three primary faculties of

---

[1] Genesis 2:21f.

[2] The *union* reflects the Holy Spirit, the Principle of *unity*.

[3] The body reflects the Second Person of the Trinity, the *Logos*, who would become "flesh and dwell among us" (John 1:14).

[4] Which reflects the Father, the First Person of the Trinity, Who is Spirit (cf. John 4:24).

his soul, viz. memory, reason and will, yet such solitariness being non-procreative, it is far short of the sublime, divine, Trinitarian imaging God intended. With the creation of woman what was "*not* good"[1] becomes "*very* good,"[2] or, were the man to have been asked for his opinion, "GRR-REAT!" The reflection of the Holy Trinity is now a perfect one, and not the sullied sort, "as in a glass darkly."[3] Here we have the trinity of man (First Person), woman (Second Person—second only in number, not in rank), and the very real entity of that comprehensive love that beckons them to a fecund union in which, indeed, they will "eat of the fruit of all of the trees of the garden,"[4] rapt in the God-designed ecstasy of married love.

Now, just like the Divine Trinity, this trinity will indeed be fruitful and creative. Man will sow his seed in this garden of delights without his brow sweating; indeed, this garden has no thorns, and his only care is to "guard" her as he was commanded. Here's how the narrative expresses all this:

"Then the man said, "This at last is bone of my bones and flesh of my flesh; she shall be called Woman, because she was taken out of Man."[5]

The "at last" confirms my *contextual* interpretation. It refers back to all those other creatures in verses 18-20 that didn't quite "cut the mustard" as far as "suitable partnership" was concerned. The NRA bumper sticker has it quite wrong when it says, "My wife—yes; my dog—maybe; my gun—NEVER!" The truth is that woman is not only man's best friend, but his perfect complement, without whom he is such a veritable basket case that even God looked on naked man standing there all alone and declared, "Nope! Won't do—*not* good, *yet*!"[6] The most important part of the "bone of my bones" declaration is not only that man does not simply immediately name her as he did the aardvark, but speaks words of flattery like no other lover has ever equaled. Furthermore, there is emphasis on the "*my*" of this creation. She is not just

---

[1] Genesis 2:18.
[2] Genesis 1:31.
[3] I Corinthians 13:12.
[4] Genesis 2:16.
[5] Genesis 2:23.
[6] Cf. Genesis 2:18 (my free paraphrase!).

another item made from similar mud to man's; in fact, her origin is not mud at all; she is "*of*" him! How reminiscent this is of the Nicene Creed's description of the Second Person of the Trinity: "God (the Son) *from* God (the Father), Light *from* Light, true God *from* true God." This also echoes the description of the Second Person found in Hebrews: "He is a pure reflection of the Father's being."[1] Man does not name woman in the same way he did the other creatures. Rather, still in the stupor of love, he simply describes her as having come *from* him. Had he looked in a mirror, the reflection he would have beheld would not have impressed him overmuch, but how different this living mirror he described as "woman"! Perhaps the greatest wonder and mystery for him was that such glory and beauty could have been made from the stuff *of him*! Every man confirms this primordial sentiment when he prefers the sight of woman to looking into a mirror. Woman is thus far more than an object; somehow, mysteriously, he is looking at his "better half"—his perfection. Someone might argue, as I once did with a Franciscan theologian, and claim that man did name woman here in Genesis 2:23, but in truth he does not assign her a name until after the fall, when part of her punishment is suffering him as her "master." Genesis 3:20 says, "The man called his wife's name Eve, because she was the mother of all the living." Only here, at last, is there a bona-fide "name." But back to Genesis 2:

"Therefore a man leaves his father and his mother and cleaves to his wife, and they become one flesh. And the man and his wife were both naked, and were not ashamed."[2]

Conjugal union is the continuation[3] of God's creative work. Now it is man's godly mission to proCREATE via that loving, fleshly union.[4] Puritanical perversions not-

---

[1] Hebrews 1:3.

[2] Genesis 2:24f.

[3] Cf. John 5:17: "My Father is working still, and I am working."

[4] There are many interesting similarities between the initial work of creation via the Father speaking the Word (e.g. cf. Genesis 1:3, 6, 9, 11, 14, 20, 24 & 26; Psalm 148:5; John 1:3; Colossians 1: 16 & Hebrews 1:2) and the restoration (re-creation) of all things in Christ (cf. Ephesians 1:10 & Colossians 1:20). Consonant with this paradigm, the mission of Adam & Eve to procreate is symbolic of the mission of the New Eve, the

withstanding, this right sensuality is what God intended. As long as they did not taste the fruit of the tree of the knowledge of good and evil, but directed their sexual energies to each other (union) and new life (procreation), they were not only not sinning, but as I said above, were offering God the most sublime sacrifice of praise possible[1]—then.[2]

Nothing about this right sexuality was obscene or unholy. That's why the text says, "They were naked and not ashamed." We know from other Scriptural passages[3] that "nakedness" is an ancient Hebrew euphemism for coitus. Thus if the author were more literal and less of a poet (which he surely was!), he might have said, "And they freely and openly indulged in sexual love, and were incapable of even conceiving how this could be shameful."

Church, who is the one-flesh, spousal union of the New Adam, the Word Incarnate and man, to go forth and multiply (cf. Genesis 1: 28) via preaching and baptizing (rebirthing—cf. John 3:5): "Go therefore and make disciples of all nations, baptizing them in the name of the Father, and of the Son, and of the Holy Spirit, teaching them to observe all that I have commanded you..." (Matthew 28:19f) Thus all things (cf. Romans 8:19-23) were to be recreated not only in the image and likeness of the Blessed Trinity, but via the *indwelling* of the Trinity (cf. John 17:21-26). Also, as in Genesis 1:28 & 2:15-17, there is the imposition of commands, to the faithful observance of which man is an active, responsible, contributing and "suitable partner" (Genesis 2:18 & 20) in this new relationship.

[1] As an integral part of renewing all things in Christ, St. Paul in Romans 12:1f tells us that our spiritual worship is to offer our redeemed bodies as a living sacrifice. All previous sacrifices, from the fall through Calvary, were of the "dead" variety. But since the Paschal Mystery did not stop with Calvary, but was fulfilled in the resurrection of Christ, Christ completed the restoration and became a "living sacrifice" as is expressed in Eucharistic Prayer I at Mass. Since we are members of His Body (cf. I Corinthians 12:12ff), we also share in this offering; we, too, are offered, through, with and in, Christ. Christ, the New Adam, infinitely transcended the living sacrifice Adam & Eve were supposed to offer through their fecund, conjugal union. Romans 12:2 goes on to tell us to put on the mind of Christ that we may "know" what is God's will—what is good, pleasing and perfect. Thus the sacrifice of the cross is the tree of knowledge through which we not only regain the image and likeness Adam lost, but become veritable sons of God, crying out, "Abba! Father!" (Romans 8:15)

[2] As mentioned in the above note, the sacrifice of Christ via His death and resurrection, infinitely transcends even the sublime sacrifice Adam & Eve were originally called to offer.

[3] E.g. Genesis 9:22; Leviticus 18:6ff; 20:11 & 17ff. Also see the commentary on this theme on pp. 217ff.

Indeed, this is just how it should be now within the covenant of matrimony. I would dare say even more so in that matrimony is an actual *sacrament*. It transcends the already sublime purposes of loving union and procreation by mysteriously effecting what it now signifies in Christ— the union of Him with His Bride, the Church (i.e. the communion of believers). When husband and wife unite in the act which the Second Vatican Council called "the most eminent human love,"[1] there is infinitely more happening than meets the eye (or any other body part!): man is being more fully united to God by the Church becoming more fully one with her spouse, Christ, the Word Who became flesh for us.[2] The whole Genesis creation story climaxes in the climax of the man and the woman—literarily and literally. Thus ends the second chapter of Genesis.

Enter Satan, very, very displeased at these goings on. He had no objection to the creation of octopuses and flatworms, pelicans and hippopotamuses, and hardly any at the creation of man—alone. Even God had declared *solitary* man "*not* good."[3] But no sooner does God create woman and the man get all excited, than Satan is green with envy. He himself had been banished from celestial delights for attempting to usurp divinity, and now he has to behold this new, life-giving creation made in that very Trinitarian likeness. He is not a little miffed. Since, as St. Peter tells us, he "prowls about like a roaring lion seeking whom he may devour,"[4] then we can be sure that he was in his best form back then in Eden. And just what did he envy, if not that very creative union of man and woman? He was jealous that they could enjoy all the fruits of the garden—all the uninhibited joys of that sacred, sexual union—but one: "but of the tree of the knowledge of good and evil you shall not eat."[5] Somehow, by hook or by crook, he would have to drag them down to his own dust-licking level.

There was only one way to accomplish this: get them to imitate him in his presumptuous attempt to become

---

[1] Cf. *Gaudium et Spes*, N. 49.
[2] Cf. John 1:14 & Ephesians 5:22-33.
[3] Genesis 2:18.
[4] I Peter 5:8.
[5] Genesis 2:18.

God by inducing them to disobey their mission which was two-fold: 1) procreate via conjugal union, and 2) exercise dominion over all the other lower creatures. There is only one act that would simultaneously so grossly accomplish *both* of these dastardly ends. It is so hideous that many pious Christians will prefer to put their hands over their ears and stamp their feet refusing to hear it, finding it much more "tasteful" to believe the literal story of eating a forbidden fruit. Hold onto your seats; the object of Original Sin had to be the sin of *bestiality*. After you recover, and stop convulsing in incredulous horror, read the proof:

1. Certainly, bestiality would be diametrically opposed to that glorious loving union the man expressed when God brought the woman to him.

2. Certainly bestiality is not going to result in the procreation of the one species specially created in God's image and likeness.

3. Certainly bestiality is nothing but looking to the lower creatures for "suitable partnership."[1]

4. The fact that the Tempter is described as disguised as a serpentine *beast* hints further at the nature of the sin.

5. The after effect of the fall is not hiding the doubly bitten "apple" or wiping their mouths of apple juice, but rather something obviously completely unrelated to literal eating; they immediately sewed fig leaves together to hide their genitals.[2] Tell me, when you were a child and got caught by Mom sneaking pie, was your first impulse to make sure your fly was pulled up, or to shove the pie back into the box and wipe your mouth? The answer is obvious. But suppose Mom caught you and Susie "playing doctor" behind the barn. Would your first impulse be to hide food and wipe your mouths, or pull up your pants? The fact that the man and the woman impulsively hid their genitals obviously means that they had willfully gone outside the parameters of sensuality that God had clearly established for them. They had eaten "forbidden fruit."

6. Where do you suppose God got the skins with which to better clothe them when He exiled them from

---

[1] Cf. Genesis 2:18 & 20.
[2] Cf. Genesis 3:7.

Eden?[1] Is it not likely that along with inventing G-strings, they also tried to hide the evidence by destroying the animals involved? Indeed, later Old Testament law was to require the death not only of the person who committed the abominable crime of bestiality, but the destruction of the beasts involved as well.[2]

Cain will later pretend he did not know where murdered Abel was.[3] Similarly, his parents wanted to hide their victims. But it didn't work. They tried to cover their shame, but God exposed it, not by withering their fig leaves, but far more dramatically, by making them wear their sin by clothing them with the skins of the beasts they had used. Their noses were rubbed in their guilt. Indeed, their wish came true; how well they "knew" evil (and thus, conversely, the good they had so foolishly forfeited)!

7. The nature of the woman's punishment also hints at a sexual sin: "I will greatly multiply your pain *in childbearing*; in pain you shall bring forth children, yet your desire shall be for your husband, and he shall rule over you."[4] Fulfilling the two-fold mission will no longer be pleasant or easy; the party's over—for awhile. Her relationship with the man is no longer that blessed equality; she forfeited that by seeking partnership with beasts over whom she was created to be co-ruler. Now, not only in the bearing, but even in the conceiving of offspring there will be difficulty. If God is all-just, and hence His punishments perfectly fit the crimes, then how can anyone not understand that the object of Original Sin had to be something sexual in nature?

8. "To know" was a Hebrew euphemism for the act of coitus. There is no personal knowledge more intimate and total than that acquired by sexual intimacy. Thus the Blessed Virgin Mary was legitimately bewildered when the Archangel St. Gabriel announced to her that she was to

---

[1] Cf. Genesis 3:21.
[2] Leviticus 20:15f says: "If a man lies with a beast, he shall be put to death; *and you shall kill the beast*. If a woman approaches any beast and lies with it, you shall kill the woman *and the beast*; they shall be put to death, their blood is upon them."
[3] Cf. Genesis 4:9.
[4] Genesis 3:16.

assist in crushing the head of the serpent[1] by offering her virginal body for the incarnation of the "New Adam,"[2] the divine Word made flesh,[3] "Who takes away the sins of the world,"[4] the spotless lamb through Whose obedience unto death on a cross[5] revealed the Tree of Life, the leaves of which are the medicine of the nations,[6] and Whose very flesh would be given for our Bread of Everlasting Life,[7] the which, if a man eat, he will not die.[8] Obviously all this is in direct relationship to the first three chapters of Genesis—even Mary's perplexed response, "How can this be since I do not *know* man?" Like the author of Genesis,[9] she uses "know" to mean the act of coitus, the only way of procreating known. But the archangel explains that the conceiving of the Messiah will be of quite another kind, reminiscent of the conceiving of the cosmos in Genesis 1:2 where the Creator Spirit, the "Giver of Life"[10] "hovered over the waters." The angel says: "The Holy Spirit will come upon you and the power of the Most High will overshadow you; therefore the Child to be born will be called holy, the Son of God."[11] And this New Eve, quite unlike the former, was generously obedient, willing to be God's humble "handmaid,"[12] rather than try to usurp His authority by trying to procreate the Christ her own way. At the moment of her faith-filled assent, "the Word became flesh and dwelt among us."[13] We know this because she immediately hastens to visit St. Elizabeth, who, "filled with the Holy

---

[1] Cf. Genesis 3:15 & Luke 1:29.
[2] Cf. Romans 5:14ff.
[3] Cf. John 1:14.
[4] John 1:29.
[5] Cf. Philippians 2:8.
[6] Cf. Revelation 22:2.
[7] Note also that Jesus defines that life in familiar, Genesis terminology: "And this is eternal life, that they know Thee the only true God, and Jesus Christ whom Thou hast sent." (John 17:3)
[8] Cf. John 6:50-53.
[9] Cf. Genesis 4:1: "Adam *knew* Eve his wife, and she conceived and bore Cain..." In Genesis 19:5, the euphemism, "know," refers also to homosexual acts: The men of Sodom "called to Lot, 'Where are the men who came to you tonight? Bring them out to us, that we may *know* them.'" Also see Genesis 4:17 & 25; 19:8; 24:16 *et al.*
[10] Cf. the Nicene Creed.
[11] Luke 1:35.
[12] Luke 1:38.
[13] John 1:14.

Spirit," hailed her, "the Mother of my Lord,"[1] (hence also the Judeo-Christian doctrine that life begins at conception, not birth). My main point here is that the use of the verb "know" in Genesis was an obvious hint to the Hebrew mind of matters sexual—not intellectual. This lends yet more weight to my thesis.

9. We first see the idea of burnt offerings as acts of worship with Cain and Abel.[2] How can such destruction of God's good creations possibly glorify Him unless by destroying those lower creatures (whether from herd, flock or field), they thus graphically demonstrated *dominion* over those creatures? The ultimate power of dominion is shown by exercising the right over the subjects' lives. Old Testament animal sacrifices were rituals demonstrating the desire to right the wrong of Original Sin. If Original Sin disobeyed God's command by wantonly abandoning their god-like power of dominion by instead, seeking "suitable partnership" with the beasts, then nothing could be a more appropriate, symbolic expression of seeking redemption from this particular sin than by exercising that rightful dominion via the *killing* of those animals. Even ancient Gentiles, long before Moses prescribed umpteen rituals for the slaughter and sacrifice of many animals, somehow instinctively knew that such animal sacrifices glorified God. Such sacrifices were identified with redemption—setting things right with God. But none of those sacrifices ever availed—not even all of them taken together. They were all merely *types* of the *One* Sacrifice for *all* sin that would work: our all-merciful God Himself assuming flesh and freely offering His life on the cross.[3] By trying to become God, death entered the world. By becoming Man and dying, Life is freely offered to all who will "take and eat."[4]

10. St. Paul alludes to a similar theme when he tells us to "be clothed with Christ."[5] In explaining the many symbols in the baptismal ritual, the Fathers of the Church went to great lengths to explain the significance of

---

[1] Luke 1:43.
[2] Cf. Genesis 4:3f.
[3] Cf. Hebrews 7:27.
[4] Matthew 26:26.
[5] Romans 13:14.

237

candidates for baptism stripping off the "old man of sin" and standing completely naked before all before being "clothed with the New Man, Christ," by being immersed in the baptismal pool thrice to remove the shame of Original Sin and to restore the Trinitarian image, and then exiting to be clothed in a white robe, symbolizing having become "clothed with Christ." No longer do we wear the skins of our shame in disgrace; the serpent's head is crushed, death has lost its insidious victory, and we are now clothed in the Light of Christ as in a robe,[1] "clothed with the sun/Son" like our Blessed Mother herself.[2] The symbolic, sacramental disrobing of baptism takes off the shame of sin. But baptism does not merely restore us to Eden. The symbolic nakedness represents that Edenic state, and as in Eden, is not shameful, but natural. But then comes the symbolic, sacramental bathing which effects a rebirthing as children of God. To symbolize this new, supernatural state which is infinitely more sublime than that which Adam & Eve enjoyed before the fall, they are symbolically invested with the white robe—not as though to cover the shame of nakedness, but rather, to proclaim our boast in the glory of Christ,[3] in Whom we have redemption[4] and become partakers in the divine nature[5] and children of God by adoption, crying out, "Abba! Father!"[6]

11. Another piece of evidence I offer is the covenant of circumcision with Abraham. Just think for a moment: isn't this a queer way for God to ordain to show His love and fidelity? This covenant of circumcision is part of salvation history, directly related to Original Sin and the New and Everlasting Covenant in Christ's Blood.[7] The whole "deal" with Abraham was all about fecundity and procreation, multiplying Abraham's seed like the sands of the sea and the stars of the sky. Isn't this reminiscent of God's original commandment[8] to Adam & Eve? And old

---

[1] Cf. Psalm 93:1.
[2] Cf. Revelation 12:1.
[3] Cf. I Corinthians 1:31; II Corinthians 10:17 & Galatians 6:14.
[4] Cf. Colossians 1:14.
[5] Cf. II Peter 1:4.
[6] Cf. Romans 8:15.
[7] Cf. Luke 22:20.
[8] Cf. Genesis 1:28.

Abe, like his ancestors, Adam & Eve, lost faith and tried to fulfill the promise his own way, making a "suitable partner" out of Sarah's (his wife's) Egyptian slave, Hagar. And, as with Eve, it was Sarah's bright idea to start with.[1] The result of this adulterous affair was Ishmael, and his descendants have been enemies of Jews throughout history. But all-merciful God put up with Abraham's weakness, and the next time he did it right and Sarah herself conceived Isaac, through whom the world was blessed since Christ (according to His human nature) was his descendant,[2] and through rebirth in Christ saints have been multiplied like "the stars of the sky and the sand on the shore of the sea."[3]

If not circumcised, when, naturally, is the glans (head) of the penis exposed? The obvious answer is when erect, ready for the act of sexual love. By ritually surgically removing the foreskin, the penis with glans exposed, even if not erect, is reminiscent of coitus, when it would naturally be exposed. The mere fact that God chose such an outlandish (by puritanical standards) symbol for His covenant hints that the Original Sin it was related to also somehow concerned sexuality. But with Abraham, rather than tolerating Adam's fig leaf attempt to hide his guilt, and rather than merely making him wear his sin to "know" his evil more intimately, God removes even the natural covering of the "crime weapon" giving man in need of redemption no way to hide. At the same time, however, God shows His mercy in this covenantal sign, for it prefigures his redemption, for the People of God are often likened to a bride by the prophets. A prime example is Isaiah 62:5: "as a bridegroom rejoices over the bride, so shall your God rejoice over you." Surely there is nothing puritanical here! God's love for His People is likened to the sexual love of honeymooners! So the covenant of circumcision, reminiscent of an erection, was instituted by God as an apt symbol of His passionate ("unto death on a cross"![4]) love for His People. The important thing to note here is that it is undeniably sexual in nature, hinting that

---

[1] Cf. Genesis 16:2ff.
[2] Cf. Matthew 1:2.
[3] Genesis 22:17.
[4] Philippians 2:8.

so, too, was the Original Sin, towards the eventual redemption of which it was instituted.

12. If the object of Original Sin was, indeed, sexual in nature, it helps to explain why the Old Testament, in passages like Leviticus 18:3ff, rank the abominable sexual sins of incest, adultery, homosexuality and bestiality right next to idolatry.

Indeed, if the object of Original Sin was bestiality, and Eve's motive was to "become like God,"[1] does this not shed light on why such sexual sins rank so close to idolatry? In that case, that sin was idolatrous. In fact, it was even worse than idolatrous because whereas the sin of idolatry involves worshiping some other god before the Lord,[2] Original Sin attempted to enthrone self in God's place, just as Satan himself had done.

Modern man often reads the lists of sexual sins in the Old Testament with near incredulity, because, from his perspective, they do not seem as grave as the Old Testament considered them. This is because for him, their motive would be simple carnal lust, whereas for Eve, the motive could not have been more perverse. Just read the awesome account of God's creating the universe in Genesis 1, and then juxtapose to this, little ole pip-squeak, naked Eve presuming, at the behest of a stupid snake, to usurp that uncreated Supreme Being—it is utterly preposterous!

For all the above reasons it seems that the object of Original Sin was bestiality, as this thesis explains so many otherwise quite enigmatic peculiarities in Scripture. Bestiality is a single, master key that unlocks many doors. It is the only sin that Adam & Eve could have committed that would, *at once*, break *both* of God's original commandments. By looking to beast as "suitable partners," rather than to each other, they obviously could not procreate, and by regarding the beasts as "suitable partners" rather than as their subjects, they obviously also forfeited their God-assigned role of dominion over them. Adam failed to "till"[3] the "garden"[1] specially created

---

[1] Genesis 3:5.
[2] The first commandment is "I am the Lord, thy God. Thou shalt not have strange gods before Me." (Exodus 20:2f & Deuteronomy 5:6f)
[3] Genesis 2:15.

for him, and he also failed to "guard"[2] it, since he did nothing to protect his wife from temptation.

The New Testament sacrament of matrimony is antidotal to this because it is the husband's role to devote himself to his wife's sanctification, imitating Christ, Who laid down His life to sanctify His Bride, the Church.[3]

I hope I have shown how deeply significant those little fig leaves were, and that to interpret them as simply covering shameful body areas is, at best, very superficial, and tells us nothing about Original Sin or redemption. Therefore, for a clothes-compulsive, Christian moralist to cite Genesis 3:7 & 21 in order to fabricate a sin out of nudity is absurd. The idea of purely physical shame (embarrassment at an area of exposed flesh) is not theological or Scriptural. The only truly shameful thing is sin. And even if we have sinned with our sexual members, rather than falsely deal with our guilt by covering up, we should expose it to the healing rays of God's rich mercy, imitating David in his perfect contrition,[4] blaming only ourselves for our sins, and not blaming God as though it's all His fault by creating our genitals in the first place. God is glorified by our assertion of the truth, and the Gospel truth is that our physical beings are without shame; they are good and beautiful, and even sacred—temples of His Spirit.[5]

Morality has nothing to do with having a body or seeing it, but only with *how* we use it. If we use it to murder or to steal or to commit unchaste acts in deed or in mind,[6] then we have true cause for shame, and need to turn to the Lord for forgiveness. And if we truly accept His forgiveness, we should glorify and witness to such a merciful God by deporting ourselves as though we have indeed been forgiven. Nothing accomplishes this so convincingly as chaste naturism.

---

[1] Genesis 2:15.
[2] Ibid.
[3] Cf. Ephesians 5:25-33.
[4] Cf. Psalm 51.
[5] Cf. I Corinthians 3:16 & 6:19.
[6] Cf. Matthew 5:28 where Jesus tells us it is possible to commit adultery in one's thoughts.

All Things to All Men

by Bishop Alejandro Labaca[1]

Introductory note: When Christian Missionaries coming from a culture in which clothing is obligatory find themselves working with a new culture where clothing is almost unknown, they are forced to reconsider their assumptions regarding modesty and dress. The following is an unofficial translation by a Capuchin missionary of parts of the published personal journal of a Spaniard, Bishop Alejandro Labaca, the Roman Catholic bishop of the Aguarico Amazon region of Ecuador. Here he relates what happened after he had been living for awhile among the Huaorani Indians:

I decided to save my pants and shirt for when I had to leave to go to some other culture. Sweating constantly, my underwear soon became an offense against the marvel of God's work which was my body, and an indecency for living among the Huaorani.

One day they let me go alone to wash in the river. I took advantage of the opportunity to rinse out my underwear in the water (there was no soap), and then spread them out in the sun to dry, along with my towel and socks. Meanwhile I sat in the shade and meditated on St. Paul: "Let us strip off the works of darkness and clothe ourselves in the armor of faith and walk in dignity as in broad daylight."[2]

My solitude didn't last long. Two families suddenly showed up, guided by Peigo. They took it as quite normal that I should be there like that. Peigo took the initiative and said to me, "You don't have a Gumi," (the cotton cord their men tie around the waist and penis). He quickly got one and tied it on me.

---

[1] Excerpted from the books: *Cronica Huaorani* by Bishop Alejandro Labaca, published by CICAME, Ecuador & *Arriesgaron sus vidas por el Evangelio*, ("They Risked Their Lives for the Gospel") by Rufino Maria Grandez, published by Editorial Franciscana Aransazu, Madrid, 1989.
[2] See Romans 13:12f.

"Now let's go home," he told me. I tried to pick up my underwear, but Peigo insisted that it wasn't dry yet and that we would come back later. So we all went into the hut. No one thought it strange; there was no problem.

Whenever new missionaries join the group, once again there arise the same worries that arose on our first contacts with the Amazon culture of nakedness. The worry, sometimes bordering on obsession, centers on the fact that the Huaorani strip their visitors naked. Although all of us agreed that nakedness was legal in their culture, this practice was one of the biggest difficulties for the entrance of missionary personnel, especially [religious] sisters. We very soon came to the conclusion that the missionaries should not wait until they are stripped, but rather anticipate it and do it ourselves in order to show our esteem and appreciation for the culture of the Huaorani people. It should be a sign of our love for the Huaorani and their concrete reality which clashes with our own customs.

It is true that the Huaorani ask for clothing. But before we clothe them with our garments we would do better to heighten their own consciousness of the value and beauty of their customs and of their family moral values which have not needed, up till now, any type of rags. It would be better to show them that if they have to put something on in order to deal with other peoples, it is not because their own customs are bad or dangerous.

Likewise we must avoid an abnormal and false duality, putting on clothes for fear of the missionary who is visiting, then going naked in normal daily life. I feared being rejected by the culture and customs of the Huaorani if I showed myself to be too unyielding. I therefore judged that I should conduct myself with complete naturalness, just as they do, accepting everything they do, except sin.

Let's look at a practical case: I had only one set of clothes, and the time came when I couldn't stand the sweat and the dirt. In these circumstances I understood that the missionary, if he is to walk the jungle with them, should walk as they do, and put on clothing only when it is needed against the chill of the night. Blessed are the Missionaries who have a deep enough tan to stand the tropical sun!

Postscript: For several years Bishop Labaca successfully contacted and shared the Gospel with a number of Amazon tribes, and was outspoken in defending their interests against developers and petroleum explorers invading their territories. On July 21, 1987 he and Sr. Ines Arango were speared to death by Indians of the Tagaeri tribe with whom they were trying to establish contact. The Indians were angry over previous incursions by petroleum developers. Bishop Labaca had previously left the following instructions: "If the worst should happen, should they kill me, I ask that you communicate to my family, to the religious, to the missionaries, the faithful and people in general my last wish, that on account of my death there be no retaliation of any class whatsoever, nor revenge, and that not a single drop of blood be shed. I will die content, for those Indians whom I love dearly."

Editor's comment: Bishop Labaca did not have to leave the Spain of the 80s to find a culture that regarded nudity as practical, decent and modest, just as was done in the Aguarico Amazon region of Ecuador. Topfree females were as normal on any Spanish beach as in any primitive culture, and at many beaches and vacation resorts total nudity was the established norm.[1] A local Spanish lady told me that at some seaside locations people do not even dress to walk to the beach from their homes. If his mission had been to evangelize the secularized, spiritually starved people of Spain, Bishop Labaca would have been equally justified in adopting their definition of what constitutes appropriate dress.

---

[1] Some listings of such beaches can be found in *The World Guide to Nude Beaches & Resorts* by Lee Baxandall, published by The Naturist Society, Oshkosh, Wisconsin. An even more extensive listing can be found in the *INF Guide* published by the International Naturist Federation, Belgium.

On Modesty

by C. S. Lewis[1]

The Christian rule of chastity must not be confused with the social rule of "modesty" (in one sense of that word); i.e. propriety, or decency. The social rule of propriety lays down how much of the human body should be displayed and what subjects can be referred to, and in what words, according to the customs of a given social circle. Thus, while the rule of chastity is the same for all Christians at all times, the rule of propriety changes. A girl in the Pacific islands wearing hardly any clothes and a Victorian lady completely covered in clothes might both be equally "modest," proper, or decent, according to the standards of their own societies; and both, for all we could tell by their dress, might be equally chaste (or equally unchaste). Some of the language which chaste women used in Shakespeare's time would have been used in the nineteenth century only by a woman completely abandoned. When people break the rule of propriety current in their own time and place, if they do so in order to excite lust in themselves or others, then they are offending against chastity. But if they break it through ignorance or carelessness they are guilty only of bad manners. When, as often happens, they break it defiantly in order to shock or embarrass others, they are not necessarily being *unchaste*, but they are being *uncharitable*; for it is uncharitable to take pleasure in making other people uncomfortable. I do not think that a very strict or fussy standard of propriety is any proof of chastity or any help to it, and I therefore regard the great relaxation and simplifying of the rule which has taken place in my own lifetime as a good thing. At its present stage, however, it has this inconvenience, that people of different ages and different types do not all acknowledge the same standard, and we hardly know where we are. While this confusion lasts I think that old, or old-fashioned, people should be very careful not to

---

[1] Excerpted from *More than Coping* by Elizabeth R. Skoglund, published by World Wide Publications, 1987.

assume that young or "emancipated" people are corrupt whenever they are (by the old standard) improper; and, in return, that young people should not call their elders prudes or puritans because they do not easily adopt the new standard.

Noah & the Gerasene

by Fr. Pat, OFM Cap.

I would like to offer some thoughts concerning two Bible passages which might be interpreted as condemning social nudity as such.

Genesis 9:18-27

Concerning Noah's nakedness and his sons' different reactions, let's remember that all human beings are alike, even if separated by many centuries.

Put yourself in Noah's place. Suppose (God forbid) you committed the offense of getting yourself so totally drunk that you even lost consciousness. Waking up next morning feeling miserable, you are frightened to realize that you can't even remember what you did in the last stages of your fling, but have the awful feeling that you probably made a complete and disgraceful fool of yourself.

One of your sons comes in. You ask him what happened last night. He says he found you sprawled on the floor drunkenly unconscious and naked, averted his gaze as much as possible from the disgraceful scene, covered you up and put you to bed to sleep it off. So you feel miserable and ashamed of yourself, and also grateful that your poor son took pity on you and helped you.

In comes your other son. He explains that he had earlier also found you unconscious and naked, left you that way and went off to tell others so that they could come and see. You would be ashamed of yourself, and also disappointed and perhaps enraged that this son did not help you in your hour of helpless misery.

Luke 8:26-39 & Mark 5:1-20

Concerning the naked Gerasene demoniac who got dressed after being freed by Jesus, put yourself in his place. Suppose that because of mental illness, or even demonic possession, you were running around naked in the city cemetery, yelling insanely, gnashing yourself to the point of bleeding, and fighting off all who tried to help you. If some kind soul managed to cure you by the power of prayer, or the wisdom of medicine and psychiatry, or a combination of both, what would you do first? Put on clothes, of course, realizing you were naked in public.

I have been with many naked people at naturist clubs and beaches and not felt the slightest compulsion to cover them up. If I found those same people naked in an inappropriate place because of drunkenness or insanity I would do everything possible to cover them up. There is no comparison between the natural and chaste nakedness of a decent naturist club or beach, and the sad, pitiful nakedness of a person who is drunk or insane.

Jesus told us we can judge a tree by its fruit.[1] If I find that my practice of naturism leads me to a more chaste, mature, accepting relationship to God, others, and myself, that's a good sign that it is good for me. If, however, I find that naturism leads me to sin, I have to drop it like a hot potato. The testimony of devout Christians who find naturism a help in the Christian life should be listened to.

I Timothy 2:9 tells women to dress modestly. Modesty depends on circumstances. A modest bathing suit is quite acceptable at a beach. It would be condemned as immodest if worn to church, or at the office. In the context of a naturist gathering, mutual, non-exploitative nakedness is more modest than a bathing suit. Taking off your bathing suit in the middle of a crowded non-nudist beach would be immodest.[2] Nakedness is not morally good or bad in itself. It can be very good or very bad depending on the intentions of the person and the actual circumstances.

---

[1] Cf. Matthew 7:17f.

[2] Editor's note: For an alternative opinion, see above, pp. 257ff, "The Cannes Principle."

Commentary: I Timothy 2:9f

by Gary Pence

"...women should adorn themselves modestly and sensibly in seemly apparel, not with braided hair or gold or pearls or costly attire but by good deeds, as befits women who profess religion."

First of all, it is important to notice that this passage speaks about women only, not about men. Verse 8, directed to men, makes no mention of any dress code. Hence, if verse 9 were intended as a prohibition of nudity, one would wonder why that prohibition seems to apply only to women.

This Bible passage does not support a general condemnation or prohibition of nudity. In fact, it might even be used to *support* nudity, or at least lack of concern about it.

The contrast in verse 9 itself is not between modest dress and immodest undress; it's between modest clothing and immodest clothing, and immodesty seems not to do with sexual provocativeness, but with extravagant self-indulgence. The specific objects of disapproval are hair styles, jewelry, and clothing that are showy and vain (hair braided, gold, pearls, expensive clothes). Moreover, in verse 10 Paul defines suitable, modest, and decent clothing as "good works," as if to say that modesty implies no concern with clothing at all, but with *behavior*—don't braid your hair or dress yourself in gold, pearls, or expensive clothes, but dress yourself in your good works.

Not only is this not a prohibition of nudity, it implies that a nude woman who does good works is more modest than a woman dressed extravagantly who does none.

To the Pure...

by Rev. Jeffrey Allen Mackey

Many Christians ascribe to a dualistic spirituality which sees the spirit as good, and the body as evil. The *pneuma*, or the soul, can be redeemed, but the *soma*, or the body, is part of the cursed creation, and is therefore irredeemable. This type of dualism does not exist in Scripture. Rather, you find explicit declarations concerning the sanctity of sex, coupled with the explicit declarations that sex and the body are good.

Wendell Berry aptly writes, "Nothing could be more absurd than to despise the body and yet yearn for its resurrection."

The great Solomon in his Song of Songs lauds the naked body. The expression, "drink wine,"[1] in the Song of Songs means "to make love." It is quite likely that the feminine declaration of "my very own vineyard"[2] refers to openness in talking about, and displaying one's sexual parts. There is no contradiction here between nakedness and spirituality. For Solomon, the human body was a universe in miniature—a picture, type, or symbol of the whole grown smaller.

Robert Henri writes, "There is nothing in all the world more beautiful or significant of the laws of the universe than the nude human body. In fact it is not only among the artists, but among all people, that a greater appreciation and respect for the human body should develop."

That this appreciation of the body should develop among those in the Christian tradition presents no conflict. The goal for the Christian is to grow in Christ-likeness. Christ is Redeemer, Savior and Example, *par excellence.* Our pilgrimage toward Christ-likeness must include both body and soul. Each part of the human being, created in the image of God, must participate in the journey of faith.

---

[1] Cf. Song of Songs 5:1 & 8:2.
[2] Song of Songs 8:12.

Paul writes, "to the pure, all things are pure."[1] He understood our spiritual journey in terms of our minds being recreated according to the pre-sinful mind of Adam in the Garden of Eden. Before sin enters the world, all things are pure, including nakedness.

Philosopher Scott Shafer aptly comments on Paul's reflections about purity in his thoughts: "I am beginning to understand finally the meaning of Paul's 'to the pure, all things are pure,' now that I have been a Christian for a few years. The purified mind sees no evil in God's creation—it is not defiled by the perverse thought patterns of the carnal man. If a perfectly pure Christian mind should encounter nudity, for instance, that mind will not be moved to lustful thoughts. This is certainly a desirable state of affairs."

The Apostle Paul blasts away at sexual sin and perversion in the church at Corinth, but there is no condemnation of nakedness. The church is called to uphold a different standard of conduct than what the vile temples and their prostitutes manifested. But there would be plenty of room for a wholesome nakedness which shunned the perversions of culture. It is a well documented historical verity that persons—mostly adults—were baptized naked in the early Church. This was most often done with both sexes together. History is also replete with evidence of ascetics of the Church being comfortable with their own and others' nudity as they grew in dedication to their Lord.

This comfort with nudity is reflected in Christian art from the earliest depictions of Christ at Mary's breast, through contemporary artists such as Eric Gill.

Within the Christian tradition, ascetics and aesthetics alike lauded the wonder and greatness of the body redeemed. To celebrate spiritual redemption is wonderful. To celebrate physical redemption will be wonderful.

What the Judeo-Christian traditionalist is called upon to do now, is to know a foretaste of that which will come. According to the Book of Revelation (19:14), overcomers will be gathered together in heaven and will be robed in white. White, in this context, is a symbol of purity. Could it be that being "robed in white" means that all the re-

---

[1] Titus 1:15.

deemed stand before God in purity, needing no other covering? It would appear that this would be a full circle back to the state of the creature in Eden and would be most thorough in completing God's plan.

YITZ

by Joel S. Heller

"The Lord had spoken to Isaiah, son of Amoz, saying, 'Go, untie the sackcloth from your loins and take your sandals off your feet,' which he had done, going naked and barefoot."[1]

As Isaiah was deeply engrossed in the Scriptures, the Man of God heard his wife in the kitchen, "Oy! We're out of dates."

"So? I can run out and pick some up," he offered.

"No, that's okay, Yitz," she replied quickly, "I can do it. You need to study your Torah."

"No problem. I need to get out. Sitting there so long makes me foggy. The errand will get the kinks out and give me some exercise." He argued until she agreed. Picking up his staff, the shopping bag and his money pouch, he set out for the marketplace.

Isaiah was well-known in town, and recognized by most as a prophet of the Lord. Wherever he went, people would usually stop and watch—especially lately. He had made some strange prophecies, but they always panned out. Still, folks usually blamed him for the hard times he predicted, never mind that he was only the messenger.

After haggling, he got a good deal on a sack of dates and stopped in at Menachem's. Menachem himself was behind the bar.

"Hey, Manny! How's business?"

"I can't complain," said the barman. "Well, I could, but I won't. What'll you have? The usual?"

"Sure."

---

[1] Cf. Isaiah 20:2.

Manny set a flagon of goat milk in front of his customer. "I gotta tell you, Yitz," he said, "people are starting to talk about you again. That 'virgin shall conceive'[1] thing finally cooled down, and now this 'sign' bit."

"Yeah, I know. It's a kick in the tush, all right," he agreed, sipping his drink, but I can't be concerned about people kvetching. You know Who I work for. I gotta do like He says."

"Far be it from me to second guess the Big Guy, but I've got a problem. My customers have started complaining about 'that schlemiel' when you leave the place. There's that sign on the door, 'No tunic, no sandals, no service.' I'm afraid I'm gonna have to ask you to start wearing something when you come in here."

"Sorry, Manny. I gotta do this as a sign. I mean, you don't make a sign, 'Behold, a man shall get up in the morning and commute to his office and put in a full day before going home.' A sign's gotta be something outrageous, to wake the people up."

"Yeah, yeah, like a virgin conceiving. Okay, Yitz, you can come in here naked. You're the customer," Manny conceded.

"Thanks. You're one in a million. Besides, mark my words, Manny: Since they're all pinning their hopes on the Egyptians and Nubians instead of the Lord, they're gonna be led off into slavery with their tushes hanging out."

"I gotta admit, you've never been wrong yet. But tell me, what does your wife think of this barefoot and naked thing?"

"Well," Yitz chuckled, "she wasn't too thrilled at first, but she's kinda gotten used to it by now. She says it's an improvement over the sackcloth and ashes I had on before. You know what she told me?"

"What?" asked Manny in anticipation.

"She said the other women at the flat rock on the river envy her 'cause she only has half as much laundry to do! I think that's hilarious."

Manny chuckled and continued probing, "Can I ask a personal question?"

"Shoot," Yitz answered, draining his flagon.

---

[1] Cf. Isaiah 7:14.

"Don't you, you know, catch cold? Or at least a sniffle or something?"

"Well, no. Oddly enough, I've never been healthier, knock on wood. I get out in the sun, and—Oy! The sun! It's getting late. I gotta get on home. Sadie's waiting for these dates."

Yitz paid for his drink and hustled home. He got there with just enough time to wash up before Sadie lit the candles for Shabbat.

The "Less Honorable" Parts

by Jim C. Cunningham

There are varieties of gifts, but it is the same God Who inspires them all in everyone for the common good. Just as all the members of the body are one body, so it is with Christ. By one Spirit we were all baptized into one body. The body does not consist of one member but of many. God arranged the organs in the body, each one of them, as he chose. If all were a single organ, where would the body be? The eye cannot say to the hand, "I have no need of you." The parts of the body which seem to be weaker are indispensable, and those parts of the body which we think less honorable we invest with greater honor, and our unpresentable parts are treated with greater modesty,[1] which our more presentable parts do not require. God has so composed the body, giving the greater honor to the inferior part, that there may be no discord in the body, but that the members may have the same care for one another. If one member suffers, all suffer together; if one member is honored, all rejoice together.

—I Corinthians 12:4-31 (abridged)

The above passage perplexes some Christians who advocate nudity, and which some anti-nudists erroneously cite to prove us wrong when we say that we ought to regard the penis as we do the elbow.

---

[1] The Latin Vulgate here has "*honestatem*," literally, "honesty." The KJV has "comeliness."

The Situation at Corinth: Babes in Christ

The Church at Corinth was full of factions[1] and child-ish boasting that was very divisive. These "babes in Christ"[2] would boast about who their pastor was, some having allegiance to Paul, others Apollos, and yet others Christ![3] They also looked down on "less honorable" church members because they were poor in material wealth[4] or in spiritual gifts.

Some Christians were so materially poor that they could not even afford to bring anything to eat to their potluck suppers (*agape*).[5] Evidently, rather than share their food, they all ate their own, right in front of the "have nots." Because the rich were not showing greater concern for the "less honorable," St. Paul told them all to forget the *agape* and eat privately, at home, gathering only for the Liturgy of the Holy Eucharist,[6] which was too important to be dispensed with. Mass has been celebrated this way— without the *agape* feast—ever since, in both East and West.

In I Corinthians 12:4ff, St. Paul had to address yet another cause for dissension's, divisions and jealous rivalries. These were the various spiritual charisms, gifts and ministries that the one Holy Spirit had infused into each church member differently. He explained that no one has all of the various gifts, but the Holy Spirit gives to each, not as a basis for jealous divisions, but exactly the opposite: to build up the one Mystical Body of Christ in love and full maturity. A bit later he will tell us that each member's true worth must be measured by the supreme gift that will never pass away—love.[7] It is not important what charisms we have, but only how completely we love

---

[1] Cf. I Corinthians 11:18f.

[2] I Corinthians 3:1.

[3] Cf. I Corinthians 1:12 & 3:3ff.

[4] In his epistle St. James also admonishes the faithful not to despise the poor, but rather, to esteem them more than the wealthy. See James 1:9f & 2:1-9.

[5] Cf. I Corinthians 11:20ff.

[6] Cf. I Corinthians 11:23-27.

[7] Cf. I Corinthians 12:31-13:13.

one another. All the other gifts will not last, but true charity is forever.[1]

Pauline Pedagogy

Imitating Christ,[2] the Teacher *par excellence*, St. Paul draws analogies from the everyday experience and culture of his disciples. This twelfth chapter of I Corinthians is a classic example of Pauline pedagogy, as he draws analogies from both objective, human anatomy and subjective, Corinthian cultural attitudes, extracting from each as much mileage as he can to teach the Gospel truth.

The Anatomy Analogies

St. Paul explains that the Church is the one Body of Christ. Christians comprise the various members of that one Body. The eye should not disdain the foot, but each part needs and should appreciate the others. The *variety* of parts, paradoxically, does not offend the principle of *unity*. A body that consists of nothing but the eye, is not a body at all.

Not only is it essential that there be a variety of different gifts, but were someone to compare one to another in a purely human way, he would find that objective anatomy itself teaches that the parts of the body that *seem* to be weaker are *all the more necessary*. God Himself so constructed the body as to give greater honor to a part that is without it, precisely so that there may be no division in the body, but that the parts may have the *same* concern for one another. Proof of this is found by simply observing how proximate are both the organs of *elimination* (i.e. "less honorable") and those of *generation*. That these latter are "more honorable" is shown by the fact that the most essential drive of any biological species (besides survival) is the procreation of its own kind. Jewish culture echoed this natural fact by considering barrenness to be the ultimate disgrace.[3]

---

[1] Cf. I Corinthians 13:13.
[2] Cf. I Corinthians 11:1.
[3] Cf. I Samuel 1:2 & 5ff; Luke 1:25.

Not only does objective anatomy bestow greater honor on the less honorable by locating the precious organs of reproduction (AKA "family *jewels*") there, but objectively, even those "less honorable" parts are, in fact, "*more* honorable" and necessary in and of themselves. My own life these past several years has proven this, for I have adjusted to a productive life just fine though my "more honorable" organs of sight have completely failed me. But who can live or function long without a functioning urinary tract? I never appreciated how truly great and wonderful it is just to urinate, until my kidneys failed as a consequence of juvenile diabetes. Suddenly urination got the attention and appreciation it truly objectively deserved. What I had formerly ranked as "less honorable" suddenly got promoted to the head of the class. You can live without the organs of vision, but you cannot live without the organs of elimination.

In this analogy we can clearly see how "not as man sees does God see,"[1] for in His eyes, what appears to be weaker and of less importance, is, in fact, the stronger and most important. He chooses the weak to shame the strong.[2] Therefore, Christians should "put on the mind of Christ"[3] and begin to show extra honor to those members of the mystical Body of Christ whom they formerly spurned and derided in their worldly and human way of thinking and judging.

Deacons in the early Church were responsible for almsgiving; they held the purse. When pagan rulers wanted to rob the Church, they would go after the deacons. Thus they went after the great St. Lawrence, who preferred being roasted alive on a gridiron, to denying his Lord, Jesus Christ. When he was asked to fork over the riches of the Church, St. Lawrence gestured at the starving and ill clad beggars saying, "Behold, the wealth of the Church!" Thus he proved that he truly had the mind of Christ.

Sts. Paul and James tell us to have this high regard for the poor. Speaking to Greek Corinthians who had already admired the nude human form for centuries, he

---

[1] I Samuel 16:7.
[2] Cf. I Corinthians 1:27.
[3] Romans 13:14.

said that just as they customarily exalt body parts which others consider lowly, so we should do also for the Body of Christ, esteeming the poor.

Those who compulsively hide their "private" parts, do not have the attitude of the Corinthians, Paul or Christ. They imagine those parts to be somehow unseemly and unpresentable. At the beach, they expose all that they consider to be seemly, and fastidiously cover what they deem unseemly. Christian naturists, however, show the truth of the dignity of every body part by exposing all without shame. By removing the final few square inches of fabric that veil what are wrongly called the "unmention-ables," they effectively elevate those parts to equal status with all other parts that are routinely exposed. For us, as for the Corinthians, Paul's analogy makes sense, and we clearly understand that, if we are going to be consistent, then we must also honor Christians considered "less honorable."

One might explore the objective analogy further and observe that the Creator has deigned to locate the "less honorable" parts smack dab in the middle of the body, giving them pride of place. Pubic hair appears to be an adornment, drawing attention to an area "the world hypocritically pretends does not exist.

Let's consider for a moment, the vagina. Judging by the plethora of pejorative euphemisms, most cultures probably regard this body part to be one of the "least honorable" of all. Nevertheless, God designed the vagina to be the very gate of love and life itself. Perhaps no part of a woman's body receives more concentrated attention than the vagina, not only in the act of conceiving new life, but especially at the wondrous event of birth. Having helped to deliver five of my own six[1] children, I know well what I am talking about!

The shapeliness and design of buttocks, breasts and genitals further shows this greater attention by the Creator, as any first year art student can attest after a week of figure drawing. That's why art schools must have their students draw from the totally nude model. Drawing

---

[1] Stephen Elijah/Anna Victoria Cunningham miscarried after about six weeks gestation. Though he died in the very earliest stages of his development, he is no less one of our children for that unfortunate fact.

a model with these areas hidden would be as inane as attempting to paint a facial portrait of a Bedouin lady with her scarf across all but her eyes, or painting a beautiful sunset after it has descended behind the trees. The folly of this is so plain that even Christian colleges that ordinarily legislate that students should cover these areas, thereby defining an external, Pharisaic "modesty," nevertheless, when it comes to teaching serious art, do not hesitate to provide plenty of nude models for their students to study and draw, day after day, challenged in ever new ways by this, the most beautiful form in the universe.[1] Though St. James condemns double-mindedness,[2] these Christians play both sides. They live the world's lie that the body has "less honorable" parts, but when it comes to real art, they live God's truth and treat all body parts the same, unabashedly presenting every body part to art students, having them draw genitalia just as they would draw ears and hands.

Eric Gill, the Irish Catholic thinker and artist, took it one step further. He observed that what we most admire in the botanical world are specifically its *sexual* members. Blossoms are nothing but the genitalia of plants. And what do all cultures do with them? We adorn our hair with them, pin them to our lapels, put them in the center of our dining room tables, beautify our yards with them, smell them and even bottle their juices and sell it as costly perfume. Yet when it comes to the human body the attitude of most cultures is just the opposite. Objectively, however, the genitalia are the very flowers of the human body. If we esteemed them as we did botanical blossoms, we would be much nearer the mind of Christ and of nature herself.

By their dress codes, cultures show their nonacceptance of objective, anatomical fact, yet no one can even dream up a single improvement on human anatomy. Just consider for a moment trying to relocate the generative organs, separating them far from the organs of elimi-

---

[1] The *Catechism of the Catholic Church*, N. 364, says: "Through his very *bodily* condition he [man] sums up in himself the elements of the material world. Through him they are thus brought to their highest perfection and can raise their voice in praise freely given to the Creator."
[2] Cf. James 1:7 & 4:8.

nation. Try as you might, you will not come up with a place one quarter inch different from the Creator's original pattern. It is so ingeniously designed that we just continue to marvel in wondrous awe at this divine reflection.

To teach his message that the members of the Church should work toward having "the *same* concern for one another" by bestowing *greater* honor on those deemed "less honorable," St. Paul clearly alludes to these objective, anatomical facts. Surely, he hopes such analogies will not be without effect with Greeks who prided themselves on their scientific knowledge.[1] Truly "becoming all things to all men,"[2] he speaks directly to where his readers are at, utilizing the Christian maxim that "grace builds on nature."[3] This is true with respect to ecclesiology, no less than any other dimension of Christian life. In his day, St. Paul worked from the healthy body attitudes of Corinthian culture to the more important ecclesiological teaching that every member of the Body of Christ is precious and important. In today's world, however, we might do well to work his image in reverse: Just as we must honor our poor brethren in Christ, so also we should honor those body parts which the world deems "less honorable." Rather than be ashamed of them, we should exalt them, if not placing them on a pedestal, then at least treating them the *same* as any other body part. Thus it is not only naturist, but truly Christian, to be no more ashamed of a penis than an elbow.

The Greek Cultural Analogies

Wanting to make his point incontrovertibly, the Apostle further speaks to where his readers are at by drawing an additional, related analogy from their subjective, cultural experience.

Corinthians, like all Greeks, were not only known for their emphasis on scientific knowledge, but also for their glorification of the human body. This is shown in every

---

[1] Cf. I Corinthians 1:22.

[2] I Corinthians 9:22.

[3] In his classic, *The Spiritual Life*, Adolphe Tanquerrey says, "Our spiritual life, while preserving and perfecting our natural life, is grafted on it." Trans. Herman Branderis. (Tournai, Belgium: Desclée & Co., 1930) p. 29.

aspect of their culture, from art and sports to customs of dress. To a world that denied the integral goodness and beauty of the whole human form, the Greeks boldly asserted the opposite.

They did not hesitate to depict the nude in art, but made this their hallmark.

In athletics, too, the Greeks boldly asserted the beauty and wonder of the naked human physique viewed from every angle and in a multiplicity of poses as athletes performed their various sports, from wrestling and racing to javelin throwing and high-jumping. There was no debate over whether to hide the loins. Even if certain sports clothing might have some practical, useful advantage, it could not do so at the expense of hiding the very body they were trying to exhibit in all its integral glory. The very idea of "private parts" was unknown to Greek culture. St. Paul never condemns Greek athletics, or even the fact that they were performed in the nude. He often drew analogies to their sports and physical training,[1] and even to the specific fact that the athlete did it in the nude. He matter-of-factly taught that just as athletes strip off every least encumbrance to better attain the crown of laurel that withers, so also ought Christians let nothing get in the way of our pursuit of the higher things in order to receive a crown of glory that will not wither.[2]

In I Corinthians 12:4-31, the Apostle specifically refers to Corinthian customs of dress. Analogies to art or athletics will not avail him here, because he is specifically trying to teach that, far from disdaining Christian brothers who appear "less honorable," we should afford them greater honor. Referring to nudity in art and athletics does him no good, as nudity emphasizes no one part over others. So St. Paul finds it perfectly expedient to refer to the Corinthian custom of adorning body areas deemed "less honorable," as they continued their cultural program of correcting what it regarded as the negative body attitude of the day. Unlike many modern cultures like ours today, however, the Greek motive for adorning those areas with drapery was not shame, but quite the contrary, to give them the greater honor they objectively deserved. St.

---

[1] I Corinthians 9:24-26; Philippians 3:12-14; II Timothy 2:5 & 4:7.
[2] Cf. I Corinthians 9:24ff & Hebrews 12:1.

Paul wisely teaches that just so ought Christians to treat the "lesser brethren."[1]

In modern societies where, as in ancient Corinthian culture, partial or total nudity is normal, the purpose of clothing is more to adorn what they highly value and respect than to hide what they are ashamed of and consider "dirty," "obscene," "disgusting" or "indecent." In much of Europe where it is customary for women to go topfree, as at beaches, pools and parks, when women do wear a top it is not for the same reason as for women in societies such as most of America where breasts are regarded as shameful and indecent. Two excellent illustrations of this point follow:

1. Back around 1970 one of the large format, American, pictorial, family magazines such as *Life* depicted a high-society European (Monaco?) fashion trend. It featured a photograph of a lady dressed in an elegant evening gown which covered only her left breast. Her right breast, evenly bronzed by sunbathing, hung handsomely like an ornamental adornment. Obviously, the attitude of her society was not one that deprecated the breast, but rather, considered it as good, beautiful, dignified and honorable. Since one breast was exposed, the reason for the drapery on the other was not shame. The fabric was not intended to *hide*, but to *adorn*.

2. Back in the 80s I saw a video clip on television of a French daytime TV exercise show. It was their version of our old "Jack Lalane Show." To encourage viewers to perform the aerobic routines in their living rooms, a large group of women were shown doing the exercises in unison. Naturally, they had attractive uniforms for the cameras. The costume was a skin-tight leotard outfit, but again, only one breast was covered, the other fully exposed. Both the exposed breast and the covering of the other breast were obviously seen as *adornment*; body shame was no factor in the costume design.

The above two examples show something of how the Greeks viewed the body and its drapery. When fabrics were used, they did not conceal the unsightly, but bestowed greater honor on parts considered "less honorable" by *adorning* them.

---

[1] Matthew 25:40ff.

It is impossible for any Christian to hold the view that in this passage from I Corinthians we learn that Greeks covered their loins out of shame, and, by implication at least, so should we. This would be diametrically opposed to the Apostle's obvious point. The "lesser brethren" are not at all truly shameful, any more than Greeks thought the phallus was shameful. On the contrary, they glorified it in an exaggerated way, going out of their way to clothe it with greater honor as it rightly deserves. Just so ought we to do with respect to Church members wrongly considered to be of lesser importance. The end result of this exaggeration will be the ideal situation: all members having exactly the *same* concern for one another.

Jewish Culture

Nor were these concepts revelations given only to the Gentiles. God had taught the same truth to His Chosen People in even more graphic ways.

Under Emperor Alexander the Great (c. 325 B.C.) Greek culture clashed violently with every other culture in the conquered world, including Judaic culture. In their vain attempt to Hellenize Israel, gymnasia were established in Jerusalem,[1] and Jews were forced to participate.[2] The very word "gymnasium" is derived from "*gymnos*," the Greek word for "naked," because to the Greek, it was self-evident that only total nudity was the proper uniform for physical exercise and athletics.

Like the super-Jew, St. Paul, Jews in the Old Testament did not object to the idea of nude physical exercise so as to deem it in itself, contrary to their religious conscience. However, like Christians, they never could quite see what the big deal was about throwing a discus, no matter what the athlete happened to be wearing. But devout Jews like Judas Maccabeus vehemently objected when Hellenization went so far as to intrude into the realm of religion. This fine line was crossed when many Jews broke covenant just to be like the Greeks not by merely wrestling publicly in the nude, but by being so ashamed of their Jewishness that they tried to hide the

---

[1] Cf. I Maccabees 1:14.
[2] Cf. II Maccabees 4:12.

marks of their circumcision.[1] Thus these turncoats reprehensibly had their values in wrong priority, deeming their phalluses "less honorable" because, being circumcised, it showed that they were God's chosen people. Their nudity is nowhere condemned, but their wearing "the Greek hat"[2] is vehemently condemned.[3] Under the New and everlasting Covenant, Jesus said that if we are ashamed of Him or His teaching, then He will be ashamed of us when He returns on Judgment Day.[4] It was no different under the Old Covenant. Jews had to hold fast to their faith even if it meant martyrdom.[5] They should have been proud to be known as God's Chosen People, marked in their flesh with the sign of the covenant.

Just as it was the purpose of the Corinthian custom of clothing those parts to show them greater honor against a world that wrongly considered them "less honorable," so also it was the Jewish custom to give greater honor to those same parts. Unlike the Greeks, the Jews did not do this by clothing them. Nor did they merely expose them like Greek athletes. After all, a nude body fails to confer greater honor on any one part. No, the Jews showed this special reverence by circumcision, surgically removing the natural covering of the glans of every phallus in Israel.[6] In a way, they were even *nuder* than Greeks. Indeed, God, in the Old Covenant, had bestowed greater honor on specifically those parts Adam & Eve wrongly deemed "less honorable."[7] Pointing to the New Covenant which would effectively redeem us from true shame which can only be a matter of what is inside man's heart,[8] (i.e. sin), the Old Covenant not only removed the fig leaf, but even the very foreskin! How graphic can God get? *God's* ways are surely not *our* ways,[9] and He showed this by the very peculiar sign He chose for His Covenant.

---

[1] Cf. I Maccabees 1:15 & I Corinthians 7:18.
[2] I.e. foreskin.
[3] Cf. II Maccabees 4:12.
[4] Cf. Luke 9:26.
[5] See II Maccabees 6 & 7 for examples of Jewish martyrs.
[6] Genesis 17:10ff describes the covenant of circumcision with Abraham.
[7] Cf. Genesis 3:7.
[8] Cf. Matthew 15:17-20.
[9] Cf. Isaiah 55:8.

In His ingenious design of the male body, the Creator could not have more closely associated the organs of elimination and generation, some parts (e.g. the urethra) being used for both. In this, Judaism surely bested Hellenic culture! Furthermore, not only in His creation design, but also in His covenantal sign, He showed His preference for what the world disdained. In many cultures the phallus is considered "less honorable" as evidenced by their jokes, euphemisms and insults. But the Judeo-Christian God, "Who chooses the weak to shame the strong,"[1] specifically honed right in on the head of the phallus to place the sign of His covenant. Thus did the Jews surround the "less honorable" part with greater honor even better than the Greeks.

On Growing Straight

"On Growing Straight" is the title of a chapter by G.K. Chesterton.[2] In it he points out the scientific fact that, all things being equal, all living nature tends to want to grow straight. This natural ordination is normally only interrupted by external conditions, against which the nature of a thing yet tries to straighten out. Chesterton observed that the only way to straighten out a bent twig is to bend it back just as much in the opposite direction. Both Greeks and Jews correctly assessed that the world's attitude about the body was not in accord with God's mind and plan. To attempt to straighten out the warp, they had to exert enough pressure in the opposite direction to end up straight at last. Likewise, Christians who come to realize that they have been reared with negative body attitudes need to do a little exaggerating in their lifestyle to straighten themselves out. Thus seeking opportunities to be nude both alone and with others is necessary to regain natural balance, even if such nudity seems somewhat eccentric.

---

[1] I Corinthians 1:27.

[2] Editor's note: This was related to me orally nearly thirty years ago, but I have not been able to document it. Are there any Chesterton aficionados out there who can help? The same idea was earlier expressed by John Henry Cardinal Newman in his *Apologia pro Vita sua*, Part IV.

Conclusion

St. Paul was "all things to all men,"[1] were he preaching to modern Christian naturists who had problems of factions like the Corinthian Church, he might say something like, "See how you bestow greater honor on nakedness by being nude so often—even when the situation might not always warrant it? Well, you do this to show greater honor on what the world considers shameful and 'less honorable,' right? In the same way I want you to show special appreciation for your Christian brethren who *appear* less gifted, and whom many wrongfully disdain. By showing this extra honor where it is needed, you will amend the divisive situation, eventually attaining the full unity which the mystical Body of Christ must enjoy. You know how you often say we should have the same regard for the penis as we do for the elbow? Thus do I want you to have the same concern for one another. If only you would be consistent and do in the Church what you do in your nudist culture, we would quickly arrive at the 'unity of the faith and the knowledge of the Son of God, to mature manhood, to the measure of the stature of the fullness of Christ.'[2] And don't forget that it is first and foremost that maturity that we must seek, for 'the kingdom of heaven is not a matter of eating or drinking,'[3] or of the putting on or off of robes that rot,[4] nor does even the circumcision of the flesh account for anything at all.[5] 'All that matters is that we are created anew,'[6] our minds being wholly directed to all that reflect the divine—'to all that is true, honorable, just, pure, lovely, gracious, excellent and worthy of praise,'[7] for 'then will the God of Peace be with you.'"[8]

---

[1] I Corinthians 9:22.
[2] Ephesians 4:13.
[3] Romans 14:17.
[4] Cf. Matthew 6:19f & James 5:2.
[5] Cf. I Corinthians 7:19; Romans 2:28; Galatians 5:2-6 & 6:15.
[6] Galatians 6:15.
[7] Philippians 4:8.
[8] Philippians 4:9.

Benedict XVI's Encyclical

by Jim C. Cunningham

On December 25, 2005, within the first year of his pontificate, Pope Benedict XVI issued his first encyclical entitled *"Deus Caritas Est."* It surprised many Vatican-watchers who expected the new pope to issue something more in accord with his reputation as "God's rotwiler," since he had been known for his strict adherence to, and enforcement of, 100% orthodox Catholicism. But the pope evidently wanted to establish the foundational context for all truth—that love which is, essentially, God. Following the trail blazed by his predecessor, John Paul II, he refers to one of the central themes of the theology of the body, viz. that God's relationship to man is like that of husband and wife, united as one flesh. Since God created man in His Own image and likeness, the truth that God is love has profound implications for man. Since man is comprised of a unity of both body and soul, love involves the whole of man; it is not merely a *spiritual* activity.

He writes, "Nowadays Christianity of the past is often criticized as having been opposed to the body; and it is quite true that tendencies of this sort have always existed. ... Christian faith, on the other hand, has always considered man a unity in duality, a reality in which spirit and matter compenetrate, and in which each is brought to a new nobility."[1]

Note his frank admission of the heretical tendencies of the past to denigrate the body. Christian naturism can be an excellent tool for righting past wrongs and according to the body its rightful nobility. It is important to note that the pope clearly states that the body is *noble*. Sadly, there are still many Christians who are influenced by those negative, heretical tendencies of the past and think that their negative body attitude is actually pious. In reality, however, only a body attitude that considers and behaves as though the body is noble is truly pious.

---

[1] Pope Benedict XVI, *"Deus Caritas Est,"* N. 5.

Nudism & Christianity: A Dialog

by Jim C. Cunningham

I.
At the Office

HELEN: Sofia, you've been acting kind of strange the last couple days. Is everything alright? You used to join me for coffee during break, but you seem to be avoiding me like the plague. Do I need a better deodorant or something?

SOFIA: Yeah, Helen, I'm very troubled. I've been wanting to say something, but just couldn't bring it up. I'm a complete wreck holding it in.

HELEN: Well, you got me all curious, that's for sure. Please sit down and let's talk. There's no one else around right now.

SOFIA: Well, I feel stupid, but I guess I'll just come right out and say it:

Ed and I were at the shore last week. We decided to take a walk along the beach and were shocked when we ran into people swimming, sunning themselves, and playing Frisbee with absolutely nothing on! That was bad enough, but we just thought they must all be pagans who don't know better, and we started praying for them. Helen, you and Larry were there with your kids, weren't you? We saw you—*all over*! We've been so upset we've hardly been able to sleep since. Helen—*in public*! *Stark naked*? How could you? And in the presence of little children! And all those men! You must have caused a thousand mortal sins of lust!

HELEN: Oops! So you found out? We've been quiet about being naturists for years, knowing something like this would happen and someone would misunderstand and get all upset. I'm sorry it had to happen to you.

Look, I truly know just how you feel. Larry and I used to feel exactly the same way till we tried it for ourselves. Believe you me, we gave it lots of prayer and study.

SOFIA: You telling me Monsignor Bouchard approves of you runnin' around in public flashin' your boobs? You guys are mad!

HELEN: Well, we sure did consult some good priests in confession. To tell you the truth, there were some who disapproved, but others saw nothing wrong with it, so long as our intentions were pure, and the situation was not lewd like at a strip joint.

SOFIA: If you look hard enough, you can always find some whacko priest to bless sin. Look at how many tell people it's okay to practice birth control, when the popes have clearly and repeatedly condemned it.

HELEN: But Fr. Tom McNamara? He's the holiest priest we know!

SOFIA: Fr. Tom said nude beaches are okay? I don't believe it.

HELEN: Sofia, honey, you've worked here at city hall with me for ten years. I've been your good and trusted friend. Larry and I would lay down our lives for you and Ed. We're the ones who brought you to Jesus in the first place, aren't we? Do you really think I'd lie to you, or that Larry and I would intentionally do anything evil? You know our spiritual maturity and have seen its many good fruits, haven't you? You're hurting my feelings.

SOFIA: I'm sorry, Helen, but that's how confused and upset I am.

HELEN: Look, break is about to end. How about if you and Ed come over tonight after we put the kids to bed and pray and talk about this some more. If you have some light to shed on the issue, then you'll have a chance to correct an erring sister and brother. If not, at least maybe we'll be able to assuage your fears.

SOFIA: I don't have anything planned, but I feel funny. You ain't going to be bare naked, are you?

HELEN: Of course not. We don't want to hurt anyone's feelings, least of all you guys. You're among our very best friends. At that beautiful naturist beach we were among people who understood; we weren't forcing our nudity on anybody.

SOFIA: How about all those gawkers walking up and down the beach ogling every naked babe in sight?

HELEN: Gawkers? You mean, like you and Ed?

SOFIA: What? Are you calling us voyeurs?

HELEN: Well, you had to have walked through about a half mile of naked flesh before you found us.

SOFIA: We were just curious, that's all—*innocently* curious.

HELEN: And Sofia, believe you me—we were just *innocently* naked, just as the good Lord created us.

SOFIA: It doesn't make any sense at all. Not an ounce of sense. You guys have flipped. Okay, we'll come over, but we ain't getting naked!

II.
At the Apartment

LARRY: Hi, Ed, hi Sofia, sister, come right on in! Sounds like you guys "caught us with our pants down" and we've got a lot of fast talking to do. But we're going to try not to be defensive, but just open and prayerful. We just want to share with you how we became convinced that social nudity is okay. I hope you, too, can be open as we pray and explore this thing together. If the Spirit convicts us of any sin, you can be sure of our repentance. We only want to serve the Lord.

ED: I want to believe you, Larry. I've always respected you and looked up to you—both of you. You don't know how this has disturbed us.

LARRY: Have a seat in the living room and let's pray.

In the Name of the Father, and of the Son, and of the Holy Spirit.

ALL: Amen. Praise You, Lord Jesus!

LARRY: Heavenly Father, we gather in Christ's Name. We ask You to send us Your Holy Spirit to guide us to all truth.[1] Show us what is right, and give us the strength to do Your will.

SOFIA: Pass the Bible. I want a Word from the Lord. His Word is the lamp unto our feet and the light unto our path.[2]

A reading from the psalms:

"I give You thanks, O Lord, that I am fearfully, wonderfully made. Wonderful are Your works!"[1]

---

[1] Cf. John 16:13.
[2] Psalm 119:105.

269

HELEN: Thank You, Jesus. We are Your little children; teach us. With Your crook and Your staff, keep us in the green pasture of Your grace[2] and guard us against the wolves.[3]

ALL: Amen!

LARRY: Well, praise the Lord! Where do we start? That was a great reading, Sofia. Did you choose that on purpose?

SOFIA: No, the Lord did.

HELEN: It was that kind of thing that got us asking questions years ago. The Lord made us, and our bodies *are* truly wonderful.

At break today, Sofia, you said something about my "flashing my boobs" in public. "Boobs" doesn't really sound like a good term for something the Bible calls "wonderful."

SOFIA: I know. I'm sorry. I didn't really mean it. I agree that we shouldn't talk about our bodies in a derogatory way like that.

LARRY: You know I've been a lector at St. Mary's for about a dozen years. Once, before Helen and I became naturists I had to read that reading from Isaiah that begins "Oh, that you may suck fully of the milk of her comfort, that you may nurse with delight at her abundant breasts!"[4] Well, I practically gagged to death. I hadn't prepared ahead of time, and I thought I was going to have a massive coronary. Helen says I turned red as a beet.

We discussed it afterwards. It became obvious that I should not be embarrassed by any image the Holy Spirit chose to use to teach us. I asked myself why I had gotten so embarrassed by the mere mention of breasts. We figured that our upbringing had to have a lot to do with it. Let's face it, where does our culture see and talk about breasts?

ED: *Playboy* and *Penthouse.*

LARRY: Exactly. But God did not give women breasts to lure men to lust, but to nurse babies. Why should we Christians let *Playboy* tell us how to regard breasts? Is

---

[1] Psalm 139:14.
[2] Cf. Psalm 23:1f.
[3] Cf. John 10:12.
[4] Isaiah 66:11.

Playboy our Master and Lord? Instead of thinking of breasts as an erotic symbol, we ought to see them for what they really are—symbols of tenderness, nurturing, motherhood.

HELEN: And the same can be said for all other body parts. God didn't make one of them to be an erotic symbol.

ED: But what about *sexual* parts?

HELEN: Like what—Breasts? Hands? My hands are feminine. Aren't hands, lips—the whole body—used in the sexual act? Some parts can even get more use than genitals. How come nobody calls us obscene and immodest for not wearing gloves in public and covering our lips? The body is a sexual thing. God made man male and female.[1] But you look at my lips, tongue, hands, etc. without getting all aroused, don't you? That's not because they're not sexual, but because you know that it is adultery for you to look at them that way.[2] Now why should the rest of my body be any different?

ED: Adultery? Look, I can get aroused without *intending* to lust! To tell you the truth, I did get aroused by all the skin at Sandy Hook.

LARRY: Wait a minute! We must have been a half mile deep down the nude section! If you thought it was wrong for us to be nude, it would follow that it would be equally wrong for you to look. But I know you are a good, chaste, Christian brother, and I trust you when you say you did not want to be aroused. That's just our point. We want to take back our bodies from a perverted culture that wants to turn everything into sex or some other sin. We don't want to play the world's game and let it make up the rules for children of the kingdom.[3] The prince of this world of darkness and sin has been cast out.[4] We are children of light and of the day.[5] In Christ our King "we are more than conquerors."[6] "To the pure, all things are pure."[7] Our bodies—every inch of them—are holy,[8] pure and simple.

---

[1] Cf. Genesis 1:27.
[2] Cf. Matthew 5:28.
[3] Cf. Romans 12:2.
[4] Cf. Revelation 12:9 & John 12:31.
[5] Cf. John 12:36; Luke 16:8; Ephesians 5:8; etc.
[6] Romans 8:37.
[7] Titus 1:15.
[8] Cf. I Corinthians 6:13-20.

We want to act accordingly, that's why we no longer wear bathing suits that are only designed to arouse anyway, but the All-Holy God Who custom designed our bodies in His image[1] did not do it so people would lust after them. That's why we prefer nudity when we have every reason to believe there's no one around to offend.

HELEN: Believe you me, if we knew you intended to stroll down the nude beach that day, we wouldn't have even been there.

ED: But would Jesus or the saints do something like this? It's hard for me to imagine.

LARRY: It's hard to imagine Jesus and the saints doing lots of things we do today, from eating fries and cola at fast food restaurants to bowling. Can you picture Jesus on our bowling team?

ED: No, but we could sure use Him, couldn't we?

HELEN: Cultures are vastly different. Sofia, you wear bathing suits, but you can't picture the Blessed Mother dressing like that. But don't you suppose she took sponge baths in the tiny, one-room Holy House of Nazareth? And on the way to Egypt, don't you suppose she bathed in the rivers just like Bathsheba bathed where she might be seen?[2] They had no indoor plumbing in those days, and houses were small. It was customary for everybody to bathe in public, and false modesty among large Jewish families in cramped quarters simply didn't exist.

ED: Wait a minute. Bathsheba was King David's accomplice in adultery. It all started with her bathing naked where anyone on the castle wall could see her. That's at least one Scripture that seems to support our position.

HELEN: Reread that one, Ed. Nowhere is her ordinary bathing condemned—only David's reprehensible abuse of that modest, ordinary situation by choosing to use her as an object for lust.

SOFIA: But why nudism? It sounds almost cult-like.

LARRY: We admit that it is somewhat of an exaggeration, but that's what it takes to straighten out what the *Playboy* cult has warped. G.K. Chesterton said that the only way to straighten out a bent twig is to bend it back just as far in

---

[1] Cf. Genesis 1:26f.
[2] Cf. II Samuel 11:2.

the opposite direction.[1] The penances we do as Christians are like that. Our natures are warped by Original Sin. They are prone to evil, and not to righteousness. Penance is an exaggeration, but an effective therapy, and by practicing it we grow unto perfection.[2] That's why so many saints seem to have gone overboard in their mortification of the flesh.

ED: Well, what about mortification, now that you mention it? What's so penitential about frolicking in the buff, playing Frisbee on the beach?

HELEN: Come on, Ed! Don't you sometimes frolic? We all need recreation! Even the great founders of the religious orders were sure to require daily community recreation. When we do it nude we not only relax better, but take back our bodies at the same time. You have to understand that naturism is not the center and summit of our lives. Nevertheless, we have discovered it to be a very helpful ingredient in the total picture. Some of the most penitential saints were nudists.

SOFIA: Don't be ridiculous! Name one.

HELEN: Well, I'm no walking encyclopedia of the saints, but off the top of my head I can think of several, like St. Mary of Egypt, and St. Onuphrius. In the Vatican Gardens there's even an outdoor chapel dedicated to him. There's an icon of him wearing only his body hair. St. Francis of Assisi stripped naked in the village square to demonstrate that God Alone was His Father.[3] Sometimes when he encountered people who were so poor that they were absolutely naked, he would literally give all he had to them—even the clothes off his back, walking away clothed only in spiritual joy. Nakedness was evidence of dirigent poverty; it had nothing to do with sex. The same was true almost two thousand years before him when St. Isaiah prophesied completely nude for three years. That was not some wild idea of his own—God told him to.[4] Also, many traditional paintings of St. Jerome show him out in the desert, beating his breast with a rock, completely naked. Then there's the first pope—

---

[1] Cf. G.K. Chesterton, "On Growing Straight." See editor's note on p. 264.
[2] Cf. I Corinthians 9:25.
[3] Cf. Thomas of Celano, *The Life of St. Francis.*
[4] Cf. Isaiah 20:2f.

Sofia: You're crazy! St. Peter?

HELEN: Of course. He and the other apostles, and probably Jesus too, used to fish naked all the time, even within sight of the shore. Just reread the end of John's Gospel.[1]

SOFIA: You're too much!

What about Adam & Eve? After they sinned they made clothes out of fig leaves.[2]

HELEN: Then if you want to imitate them, you should be topfree now.

SOFIA: What?

HELEN: Reread that passage in Genesis. Eve only covered her bottom!

SOFIA: Well, then, don't I at least have half a point?

LARRY: Not really. Why do you suppose they made those aprons?

ED: Because they sinned.

LARRY: For almost half the history of the Church, the custom was to be baptized by immersion, nude, in church, along with others of both sexes and all ages. I read this in the *Apostolic Constitutions* of St. Hippolytus. This symbolized the fact that baptism removes *all* sin.[3]

SOFIA: But God Himself made them leather tunics before He expelled them from the Garden of Eden.[4] He must want us to wear—

HELEN:—leather? Does that mean we can't wear fig leaves anymore, or polyester double-knits? Did you ever stop and think just *why* He made those garments?

SOFIA: For modesty, of course.

HELEN: Sofia, honey, they were husband and wife! Did you ever see Ed naked? Do you run to confession afterwards? Don't make illogical conclusions! Look at the *context* of Genesis 3. God is punishing Adam & Eve and their descendants. He is banishing them from an idyllic paradise to a harsh, inclement, valley of tears. By giving them leather clothing, He was giving them sort of a farewell present—something practical they would need. Fig leaves would probably do quite well if all we are trying

---

[1] Cf. John 21:7.

[2] Cf. Genesis 3:7.

[3] Cf. Jean Cardinal Danielou, S.J., *The Bible and the Liturgy* (Notre Dame, Indiana: Univ. Notre Dame, 1956), p. 38.

[4] Cf. Genesis 3:21.

to accomplish is hiding genitals. But they won't do much good where they were goin'. God packed them a practical travel suitcase because although He is fully just in punishing them, yet He is merciful even as He punishes. Praise the Lord!

ED: While we're in Genesis, what about the time when Noah is caught naked by Ham and old Noah condemns the literal hell out of him for it?[1]

LARRY: Again, guys, you need to reread it carefully. Ham made fun of his father. That was the big sin. Shem and Japheth, on the contrary, showed proper respect for their father who was not merely naked, but stone drunk, by covering his condition with a sheet. But to make it clear that it was not the mere fact that he was naked that they covered him, the artist—it was either Michelangelo or Rafael—painted both good, reverent sons walking backwards to cover Noah, just like Scripture says, but he has *them* totally naked too!

SOFIA: Well, so what? That's just one artist's interpretation.

ED: Yeah, it ain't like that artist was the holy pope!

LARRY: Well, the popes—including ours today—must have liked his interpretation because that mural is right in the Vatican apartments.

HELEN: Yeah, we saw it ourselves, along with tons of other nudity in the Vatican Museum. There's also a mural in there showing Noah supervising the construction of the ark, and although he happens to be clothed in that one, all the workers building the ark are stark naked. Must've been how carpenters worked in those days. That artist was either Rafael or Michelangelo too; I keep getting those two mixed up.

ED: Carpentry in the altogether? Ouch! Thank God they didn't have electric circular saws back then! There surely wouldn't have been many offspring coming from the survivors of *that* deluge!

[Sofia erupts in knee-slapping laughter.]

HELEN: I'm glad to see you guys are lightening up a little. Thank You, Jesus!

ED: Well, I must say it helps to talk. We were miserable, holding it all in.

---

[1] Cf. Genesis 9:20-29.

SOFIA: I think it would have been better if you had told us right away, and even have involved us in your many prayerful deliberations as your brother and sister in Christ.

HELEN: Well, we often wonder about being more open about all this, but we're so afraid that someone will take it all wrong. It's a touchy issue.

LARRY: You know, this might sound weird, but for me, being nude is practically a spiritual experience—not that it, in itself, constitutes a spiritual experience, but it's just another external thing that greatly helps dispose me to the grace of God. I feel such a sense of appreciation for myself, others, and all creation. People look more beautiful, God-like and dignified to me when they are naked. Jesus said, "What is of human esteem is an abomination in the sight of God."[1] Men glory in riches and fine clothing, but Jesus said that a wildflower was more beautiful in His Father's eyes than even King Solomon arrayed in all his royal splendor.[2] But in the same passage He said that human beings are far greater in His eyes than wildflowers. Nothing is more beautiful, therefore, than a naked person.

SOFIA: Well, at least that proves you've never seen *this* turtle out of her shell!

LARRY: [Laughing] But you do know it's true. If we don't see it that way, then we do not have *God's* perspective.

ED: I can see you haven't jumped into this rashly, but I have more questions.

LARRY: Shoot, kid.

ED: What about the sense of shame? In my study of Original Sin I learned that "shame of nudity" is one of the effects of Original Sin. None of the effects of Original Sin are immediately removed by baptism. Baptism removes all sin, but the effects remain. Aren't you guys pretending this isn't true?

LARRY: Not at all! You are absolutely right. But who ever said we are supposed to surrender to any of the effects of Original Sin? Let's look at some of the other effects:

We don't surrender to disease; we strive for healing. We don't surrender to aging; we strive for longevity. We don't give in to a darkened intellect; we pursue knowledge

---

[1] Luke 16:15.
[2] Cf. Luke 12:27.

276

and learning. We don't give in to the lack of sanctifying grace, but like the Blessed Virgin Mary, strive to be full of grace.[1] Finally, we do not surrender to death, but triumph over it through our hope in Christ.[2] Why should "shame of nudity" be the one, single effect we pretend to be impotent against? No! We can easily conquer it! Did any of the thousands of nudes at that beach appear to be embarrassed?

SOFIA: No, that's what was so unnerving! Most of them seemed to wear their birthday suits with more pride than others wear their Sunday best.

HELEN: That's because the only *truly* shameful thing is sin. If I claim that my body is a precious gift of God, would I glorify Him by being ashamed to let anyone see it, or by putting it on a pedestal?

ED: Isn't there some guidance from the pope on this? Hasn't Mother Church condemned this somewhere?

HELEN: She condemns immodesty, but does not presume to define that for every culture. For example, Larry and I once read a book on chastity and modesty. It told a true story about neighboring missionary bishops in Oceania. One allowed his flock to come to Mass in their native garb, which, for females, meant bare breasts. The other forced his flock to adopt the standards of the European culture he came from. The latter reprimanded the former, saying how obscene it was, but the former replied defending the nudity, and accusing the elaborate fancy European dress as the *true* obscenity. I Timothy 2:9f does not say that immodesty has anything at all to do with nakedness; it says immodesty is dressing up *to show off*. It says that true, "seemly apparel" consists of *good deeds*.

SOFIA: Are you serious? I want to look that one up. Pass me the Bible.

"...women should adorn themselves modestly and sensibly in seemly apparel, not with braided hair or gold or pearls or costly attire but by good deeds, as befits women who profess religion."

Well, I'll be—it does say that. But bare boobs right in *church*?

---

[1] Cf. Luke 1:28.
[2] Cf. I Corinthians 15:55ff.

HELEN: There you go again. Them ain't "boobs"! They're "breasts"! And God made 'em and He loves 'em infinitely more than any religious statue.

LARRY: Speaking of the pope's views, we did buy a book he wrote when he was still just a cardinal in Poland. Here, let me read from it; I marked the margins:

"Nakedness itself is not immodest... Immodesty is present only when nakedness plays a *negative* role with regard to the value of the person, when its aim is to arouse concupiscence, as a result of which the person is put in the position of an object for enjoyment."[1] He even deals with the issue of scandal and says if a person goes to a place like that nude beach, knowing what is there, and lusts, he alone is responsible for his sin—not those of us who are merely following the established cultural norms.

HELEN: Look, guys, we don't mean to try to convert you to naturism, we just want to explain why we do it so you can sleep tonight.

LARRY: But it would be a lot of fun to share the experience with our dear brothers and sisters...

SOFIA: Well, I must say I do feel a whole lot better. I still think you guys are crazy, though, and don't hold your breath waiting to gawk at my boo—

HELEN:—breasts!

SOFIA: Oops, yeah.

ED: Well we gotta get goin'. God knows I have a lot of sleep to catch up on. You've given us a lot to think about.

LARRY: Can I give you more?

ED: What do you mean?

LARRY: We have lots of back issues of an excellent magazine called *Naturist* LIFE *International.*[2]

SOFIA: You mean a nudie magazine?

LARRY: Well, I wouldn't call it that.

HELEN: Sofia, it's like our breasts ain't "boobs."

SOFIA: Yeah, I'm gettin' it. But do these magazines have dirty pictures in them?

HELEN: Of course not! The beautiful photos merely show what you read from Psalm 139 when we began our prayer

[1] Wojtyla, pp. 176, 186, 189ff.
[2] For information on in-print magazines and books, see www.naturistlife.com & www.naturistlifemag.com.

this evening. They depict our wonderful bodies just as God made them, in His very Own image and likeness.

LARRY: And there are lots of interesting and inspiring articles about all this stuff. Some are on the lighter side, such as people describing how they discovered social nudity, and others are deep enough to keep a philosopher happy. Can I give you a bunch to take home? We can say it's your "homework."

ED: Well, okay, pal, but make sure they're hidden deep in an opaque grocery bag or something. I wouldn't want anybody catching me with that stuff and getting the wrong idea.

HELEN: So now you know how we felt, and why we kept it a secret from you for so long.

SOFIA: Look, thanks a million, honey. You're a terrific friend. And you, too, Larry. We are so blessed to have friends like you. See you at break tomorrow, Helen.

LARRY: Good night, guys. God bless you both!

HELEN: And don't stay up all night reading those magazines; get your sleep!

Nudity: Humble & Modest

by Fr. James G. Dodge, OCSO

All of the Old Testament texts concerning the nudity of Saul, Isaiah and David have to do with humility, a sub-virtue of *temperance*, and the need for us humans to understand the importance of humility in our daily lives and in our relationships with our fellows.

Only when I am completely stripped of everything—clothing, decorations, honors, and significations which we use to try to show ourselves to be better than others—only then can I appreciate my negative worth, my essential inferiority, my complete and utter dependency, and grasp my own identity and realize who and what I am before God.

Thus true, sincere, humble nudism is a serious way to a real union with God. But it can only be that, if and when our nudity is undertaken in a realization of our essential nothingness.

In my ongoing considerations and study of the whole underlying idea and philosophy of nudism, I come continually upon the concepts of modesty and humility. As I mentioned above, both of these are part of the cardinal virtue[1] of temperance. I am well aware that many today do not like to become involved in this kind of analysis; scholastic speculations are definitely passé and rejected by many who wish to put all their study and emphasis on the Scriptures alone without any reasoning or speculation. But what if a person does not accept the Scriptures but perhaps can be persuaded, at least in certain fundamental areas? I do not see how we can deny the strength and efficacy of our reasoning faculties.

"Temperance is the virtue which regulates the sensitive appetite in the pleasures of touch, viz. in the pleasures of food and sex."[2] The virtue of temperance can be divided into two integral parts: the sense of shame and the love of propriety. Under the subjective parts we find modesty, chastity and sobriety. And there is the further division, in part, overlapping, the potential parts: meekness, clemency, continence, humility and again, modesty.

Perhaps this kind of analysis bothers some in our day, most likely because they cannot be troubled with the precise definition of terms and conditions. Admittedly, this can be carried to excess, yet like excess in everything else, the abuse does not diminish the value of the method.

Here, however, I am only concerned with two aspects of the virtue, both coming under the subdivision of potential parts: humility and modesty. Modesty is defined "...as the virtue that moderates all the internal and external movements and appearance of a person within the bounds and limits proper to his state in life, intellectual ability, and wealth."[3] There are four virtues included under modesty: humility, studiousness, modesty in external behavior, and modesty in adornment.

---

[1] Editor's note: According to Wisdom 8:7, the four cardinal, or "hinge," virtues are: prudence, justice, temperance and fortitude. All other moral virtues fall within the scope of one or another of these.
[2] Dominic M. Prummer, O.P., *Handbook of Moral Theology* (New York: P. F. Kennedy, 1957), pp. 222ff.
[3] Ibid.

Does all of this seem to be extreme nitpicking and excessive subdividing? But look about you and observe the people on the street, in the shop, office, in the theater, at play or work. Each one of us can very quickly see individuals who fit hand-in-glove into one or the other or several of these categories. We don't like to be pinned down so clearly, defined so exactly. Of course, this has nothing to do with our purpose or intentions until it all comes down to *what* we do and *why.*

Is not a great part of the fashion industry built precisely on stretching one or more of these to the limits? The *haute couture* of the designers goes all too frequently to such ridiculous extremes that one wonders why so many otherwise apparently intelligent people really bother with them. But then all of this is just one relatively small aspect of the whole concept of modesty.

Modesty in external behavior is the virtue inclining persons to observe reasonable decorum in externals which include: 1) bodily movements, 2) recreation and 3) dress and adornments.

Here we come to the concepts that directly have to do with the whole nudist philosophy. As to the question of adornment and dress, it would seem that here there is room for quite wide variation, depending on local culture, custom, and the particular conditions prevailing. We have clothing for every conceivable situation: work, sports, afternoon or evening, for different activities from swimming to skiing or scuba diving. Thus there are times and places for many variations according to climate and culture. At the same time we are all aware of the deliberately sexually provocative nature of many forms of clothing, jewelry, and other adornment which the cosmetic and fashion industries have exploited to the Nth degree.

But one may ask, "Is modesty in these things themselves, or in the intentions and attitudes of those using them?" Today with our more extensive knowledge of cultures, we are aware of the essential and often exemplary modesty of completely naked groups of people living in tropical regions, the Amazon, the various islands, the more remote parts of Africa, etc. Thus it is patently clear that this form of modesty is not dependent on how many yards, meters, or square centimeters of cloth, leather, or skins one is wearing on any particular part of the body. It is equally clear that here, as in all aspects of true modesty, the intentions and actions of the individual appear to be determinant.

The second aspect of the virtue of temperance that I wish to explore has to do with humility, which again, by definition, is "...the virtue which curbs a person's inordinate desire for personal excellence and inclines one to recognize one's true worth in its true light."[1] It has two purposes: 1) to restrain an inordinate desire for personal excellence, and 2) to subject the person to God by the recognition that all the good one possesses comes from the Creator. Whereas humility is a most necessary virtue, it is perhaps one of the most ignored, forgotten and neglected in our day and age. Quite obviously there is the very powerful spiritual component for this virtue in the example of the incarnation and the promises in the Gospels of the elevation of the lowly.[2]

The German term for humility, *De-mut*, is perhaps more expressive: the restraint of excessive courage, the control of pride.[3] It "...moderates the desire for one's personal aggrandizement by honor and the esteem of others. It is defined by St. Thomas Aquinas as a praiseworthy depreciation of oneself to the very lowest degree."[4] When fundamentalist individuals or groups, professing to be following the Scriptures, attack all nudists, they are completely overlooking this very important virtue and aspect of God's dealing with us. By no interpretation can one show that God has any objection to nudity *per se*. On the contrary, Saul himself goes to Ramah to find David, after sending three delegations unsuccessfully. And Saul "...too stripped off his clothes and he too fell into ecstasy in the presence of Samuel and falling down, lay there naked all day and night."[5] It appears to me that the "too" is frequently overlooked, for this makes it clear that not only Saul but all the others whom he had previously sent

---

[1] Prummer, Op. Cit., p. 238.
[2] Cf. Matthew 18:4.
[3] Cf. Karl Rahner, S. J. & Herbert Vorgrimler, *Kleines Theologisches Wörterbuch* (Freiburg: Herder, 1976), p. 79.
[4] Henry Davis, S. J., *Moral and Pastoral Theology* (New York: Sheed & Ward, 1949), p. 269.
[5] I Samuel 19:22-24.

were naked, and had been so for some time, not just a day and night.

Furthermore, we have the very explicit case of Isaiah at God's command going for three years completely naked, clearly not hidden alone in the wilderness.[1] Again there was David dancing naked before the Ark of God.[2] In all these cases the purpose was to demonstrate humility, *Demut*, and recognize the complete unworthiness of the individual in relation to God. For them nudity was a means, just as it is for us today, to show that no decoration or dress, no signs of human honors or dignities has any meaning before God.

It is precisely this virtue of humility that is today neglected, rejected and deemed beneath the dignity of the arrogant individuals who know all about God and His presumed offense in the presence of naked humanity. Where or what can we hide that is not open and fully revealed in the presence of God?[3] Where is God not present? In the manure pile, or the sweet smelling flower, in the genitals as in the nose, in every square inch of bare or covered skin as much as in the covering, in the sun and in the darkness, in the heart and mind of every individual, He is there. So how can God in any way be offended by that which He has brought into being?

Is this pantheism? Not at all, for I am not saying that these things in themselves *are* God in any conceivable way, but they would not even exist without His presence.

Therefore, the humility that should inform our being and actions is expressed in the modesty of our intentions. By being naked and open one to another, divesting ourselves of all the accouterments of pride and vanity, accepting each other without regard for the shape, size, color, perfection or imperfection of form which we individually may possess, we can more fully carry out our functions and duties as truly human beings. May we learn to shed the artificiality of all the external adornments insofar as climate and conditions permit, avoiding all abusive exploitation, and grow in our knowledge and respect for one another.

---

[1] Cf. Isaiah 20:2f.
[2] Cf. II Samuel 6:14-16.
[3] Cf. Psalm 139:1ff & Hebrews 4:12f.

A Rational Choice

by Drew Corrigan

One of the driving impulses in my life has been the desire to seek out and take the most rational choices. I guess you could describe me as both an idealist and also as someone who prefers to live by principles rather than whim. These facets of my makeup were crucial in my decision to become involved in social nudity.

The Body Censored

My parents are wonderful people and were very good to me and my siblings. However, like the majority of people, they were the product of their own culture. When it came to body acceptance ours was not a particularly open household. Sex was only rarely and rather awkwardly discussed, and pictures of the naked human body were not tolerated in general.

I say, "in general," because my father is a professional photographer and at least once during his career he was commissioned to do a series of photographs on breast-feeding to be used for the teaching of nurses. However, generally there was little permitted to be said about the human body and its functions.

In retrospect I feel that this lack of openness was not healthy for me as I matured. Like most teenage boys I developed an intense curiosity about the bodies of the opposite sex, mostly because I had no real idea of what they looked like. My friends and I would sometimes thumb through our mothers' women's magazines just to see women in their underwear. My father had quite a number of photographic books and magazines and some of these carried sections on nude photography. When I could, I would sneak peeks at those pictures, again out of curiosity. In late high school other boys and I would watch the girls during sports or when they walked upstairs, hoping to catch a glimpse of their underwear. Very occasionally some of the other boys would get hold of a girlie centerfold and we would all gloat over it.

I am not proud of this, but it was mostly due to the nature of my upbringing. If you tell a child not to touch something, that particular something will often take on an irresistible attraction which leads to the child touching it. Hiding away some aspect of the human body and how it functions will only serve to produce a powerful curiosity about that particular body part. This is especially true when coupled with the immense hormonal changes accompanying puberty.

Guilt & Shame

One of the more damaging aspects of this behavior was the guilt which accompanied it. During my late teens my father discovered a schoolbag hidden by some teens in the brush. It turned out to be full of *Playboy* and *Penthouse* magazines. Since the bag had been out in the elements for some time, they had become wet. My father placed them in our small garden shed to dry out before burning them. Of course, when opportunity presented itself I looked through these magazines before they were consigned to the fire. I felt intensely guilty afterwards as though I had seen something that shouldn't be seen. Accompanying this guilt were feelings of shame and being "dirty."

Similar feelings are often voiced by adults when they first see a naturist publication. For example, Claire Walsh describes her introduction to naturism, "Browsing through the magazine racks... I came across a copy of *Australian Sun & Health*. Hoping the news agent wouldn't recognize me behind my sunglasses, I bought it. Coming from a strict, "socially correct" family, I had always been taught that nudity was rude, even "dirty." I almost felt naughty, even at my age of 40+... Now nudity to me is not rude or pornographic, but the way we were created, and very much the way we become part of His landscape."[1]

It is ironic that what God created and declared to be "very good"[2] could be turned around and be regarded by so many as evil, dirty and a source of guilt and shame.

---

[1] *Australian Sun & Health* No. 51.
[2] Genesis 1:31.

One is reminded of Isaiah's cry, "Woe to those who call evil good and good evil."[1]

Into Puritanism

In my late teens, searching for "the truth," I joined a very conservative, fundamentalist church. I met Vanessa in this church and we eventually married. We spent the next twelve years in this church before we finally decided to leave it in 1994. This particular church had an extremely conservative stance on the human body. It had no end of rules specifying precisely what constituted "proper" dress codes.

Women were taught that at all times, even in the hottest weather, they needed to wear stockings and slips to church. Little girls, from the time they were old enough to stand, were to wear dresses with slips. They were also to conduct themselves "modestly," meaning that their underwear was never to be seen, even during play. Two-piece swimsuits for women were forbidden, and men were to wear swimming trunks, not briefs. At the summer youth camps girls were issued with swimsuits to avoid any "immodesty." They were also issued T-shirts with high necklines to make certain that nothing of their breasts or cleavage could be seen when bending over. Ministers and their wives would police church functions and swimming meets in particular to ensure that "decency" and modesty prevailed.

One couple we met in this church moved into Canberra from a country region. Their previous pastor was ultra-conservative and taught his congregation that when they went swimming they were not only to have dark, opaque swimsuits, but also that they ought to wear underwear beneath their swimsuits. I recall one time we went swimming at a public pool with this couple and remember the feelings of embarrassment and awkwardness I felt for them when their cotton underwear began to sag down outside of their swimsuits. I suppose they felt that they were doing God's will and that was all that mattered.

---

[1] Isaiah 5:20.

Speaking for God

The man who founded this church was born in the 19th century and had written a book on marriage and sex which was required reading during marriage counseling sessions. He said the fact that God created humanity naked and did not clothe them in the beginning, does not mean, under any circumstances, that God would approve public nudity—not at all! God clothed man. God intended man to keep clothed. God intended that we never expose the pubic region of our bodies except in the privacy of marriage.

No proof, Biblical or otherwise, was offered to support these statements. He later even questioned the validity of nudity between a husband and wife in the bedroom. Above all, no man should display his body before the new bride on their wedding night. Though we generally abided by the rules of this church, this was one rule we ignored on our wedding night.

Ministers frequently denounced all forms of nudity from the pulpit, usually linking it to the demise of Western society and the cause of hedonism around us. I am certain none of these ministers had ever visited a nude beach or read a naturist publication. Some men in this church even became very upset at seeing naked Barbie dolls which young girls brought with them to church functions and sometimes left lying around in an undressed or semi-dressed state.

The one exception to all these anti-nudity ministers was a lay preacher who recounted the time he was stationed in Germany. He told us about a church trip to the beach and his amazement when all the members changed into their swimsuits on the beach with little regard for who saw them. This was apparently the cultural norm.

On the other hand, there was the time that another lay preacher told us that when we prayed to God we ought always to wear our best church clothes. His reasoning was that God is a great King and ought to be approached in only the very finest of apparel. The fact that God created man and woman naked and unashamed obviously hadn't dawned on him.

Hypocrisy & Sin

For all its anti-nudity preaching, this church had its share of ministers, particularly higher up in the hierarchy, who were beset by sexual sins and a general preoccupation with sex. One particularly fiery American evangelist bemoaned the state of dress on Australian beaches, yet after services he would embrace the women, single or married, who came to greet him, and grope them in inappropriate ways.

Woe to Those Who Give Suck

One of the worst ways this paranoia about the body was expressed was the manner in which breast-feeding women were treated. All public breast-feeding was forbidden. Mothers were often required to retreat to unsanitary toilets, or drafty, unheated rooms, in order to feed their children. Even in their own homes mothers would excuse themselves and nurse in the bedroom if male guests were present.

I remember one deaconess telling us of how "upright" her mother was—she made sure that none of her other children ever saw her newest addition—and this was in a family of all girls! Later when we were arranging matters for the homebirth of our daughter we asked this deaconess and her husband if they had a large mirror we could borrow in order for Vanessa to easily view the baby's head emerging from her vagina and thus be encouraged. Both the husband and wife were appalled, saying something to the effect, "Why would you want to see *down there*?"

Nudity = Sex (or Does It?)

Given such a background, nudity was linked to sex in my mind. Going to the beach could be a real problem given the scantiness of many women's swimsuits. Vanessa and I often spoke with our church friends of how brazen many women and men had become with no regard for morals. Many church women became very sensitive about their own bodies, condemning other non-church women with lesser attire, and accusing them of intentionally

288

trying to arouse lust in men, even if their actions indicated nothing of the sort.

The first real chink in this view that "nudity = sex" came when Vanessa became pregnant and we began to explore possible birthing options. One of our church friends introduced us to the idea of homebirth. We attended information nights where videos of homebirths were shown and where large, explicit posters and photographic essays of women giving birth were on display. We borrowed various books on birth and eventually bought several ourselves. Most women who give birth at home choose to do it sans clothing. This is to give them maximum freedom to move about and adopt different positions, to let them receive massages and hot towel compresses on the lower back and abdomen, to control their bodily temperature more readily; and lastly, to avoid staining clothing from blood and other fluids.

Seeing photographs and videos of many different women naked in non-sexual settings, I began to realize that nudity doesn't always have to be sexual. Along with this investigation of homebirth we also began to research breast-feeding and I saw, for the first time, breasts fulfilling their primary function.

Several years later we learned that one woman who was previously active in the homebirth movement and who had previously quite unashamedly shared videos of the births of several of her children, had joined a conservative Christian movement which taught the "nudity = sex = sin" message. Recounting the story of the birth of her fifth child in the homebirth newsletter, she related how she had learned about Leviticus 18:6-18 and its supposed prohibitions against family nudity.[1] Despite having been present at her previous births, all her family members except her husband were excluded from helping with the birth. Her brother, a qualified and practicing midwife, was excluded, as well as a close female friend because "she was too much like a sister to me"! Her once intimate birthing at home was turned into an exclusionary event limited to the husband, doctor, midwife and emotionally detached helpers.

---

[1] See pp. 145f, 168f & 217ff for some commentaries on this often misunderstood passage.

Questioning the Party Line

Gradually, we began to think more critically about the messages we were hearing from this church and those learned from childhood. If nudity is always an invitation to sex, why is it that men, women and children in many other cultures ranging from the Australian Aborigines before European settlement, to the indigenous populations of Africa and elsewhere, could go about in varying degrees of nudity without complete social chaos? I even began to have a sneaking suspicion that it is our Western society's obsession with covering up the body which is at the root of excessive preoccupation with sex. Perhaps if we were all just more relaxed about the body and nudity, many of the problems we see around us would decline significantly.

Escape from Puritanism

As the years passed, we became progressively disenchanted with this church. Its autocratic ways, its greater emphasis on the ideas of men than on honest Biblical scholarship, its economical approach to the truth, left us frustrated and discouraged. We decided that enough was enough; we left it in 1994. We began to question more and more of what we had been taught on a whole range of issues, including social nudity.

Despite the general anti-body mindset pervading the church, we had nevertheless still been very open at home. We had made no efforts to hide ourselves from each other or our daughter. In her early years Amy frequently had showers with us while she was learning to wash herself. Even today, at seven years old, she sometimes shares the shower if we are in a hurry or are running low on hot water. Amy learned the proper names for the male and female genital organs. Whenever she asked, we explained in simple terms the process of conception and reproduction. Amy knows what birth is like as we had a friend photograph her birth in considerable detail. Even while in that church we both felt that the proper and natural way of educating children was to let them see their parents naked, to see breast-feeding first hand, and to witness the birth of their siblings.

Our thoughts on *social* nudity began to shift significantly from about August of 1994. We decided to rent Alby Mangel's *World Safari* video. This is a true life documentary made by a young Australian man and a friend, about their travels across Australia, the ocean and parts of Africa. In one part of the movie Alby and his friend had a yacht and picked up a group of young men and women for a leg of their journey. While at sea they needed to wash themselves. The film shows them all stripping off and having fun pouring water over each other, hosing each other down and then drying off in the sun. They were unashamedly nude in a natural and non-sexual social setting. I remember Vanessa commenting afterwards, "My thinking about nudity has changed a lot. If we were with friends we knew it wouldn't bother me to go nude in a situation like that." Incidentally *World Safari* is rated "G" and not even "PG"!

I began to look on the internet for information on parental and social nudity, and particularly its impact on developing children. In the process of looking for information I came across *Australian Sun & Health* magazine and the books they sell. Two books I found especially helpful were *Growing Up without Shame* by Dennis Craig Smith[1] and *As Nature Intended.*[2] The most intriguing aspect of the many personal accounts I read was how people described their going nude as helping them relax, as giving them a sense of freedom, and of providing a feeling of being at one with nature and God.

I did some research into the Biblical perspective on nudity and could find nothing specifically against it. Indeed, there were some *positive* examples of nudity and some interesting theological arguments could be drawn *in support* of social nudity.

Having dropped the old notion that "nudity = sex" and that "social nudity = sin," and being an idealist driven to take the most rational path, I decided I would have to experience social nudity for myself. Vanessa, while not being wildly enthusiastic, was not opposed, and agreed to

---

[1] Smith, Dennis Craig & Sparks, Bill (Topanga, California: Elysium Growth Press, 1986).

[2] Clapham, Adam & Constable, Robin (United Kingdom: W. Heineman, 1986).

let me take Amy down to Karobah Pool one weekend afternoon. Karobah Pool is our local clothing-optional swimming hole located on the Murmmbidgi which flows through the Australian Capital Territory and Canberra.

I must admit that the first time I stripped off I did feel a bit self-conscious, although those feelings passed fairly quickly.

Some men fear that going nude in a mixed setting will trigger an erection. These fears are largely unfounded. From my own experience I can state that going nude in a mixed setting is profoundly non-sexual. When you see numerous naked bodies, of all different shapes and sizes, swimming, walking around, lying about and talking, you begin to see others as *people*, each sharing the image of God, and not mere *sex objects*.

The main thing I remember from that first visit was swimming nude, and afterwards feeling the warm sun and gentle summer breezes against my skin. I have always been annoyed at the way pockets of air get so easily trapped in swimming trunks. It's like wearing a child's flotation bands around one's waist and thighs! To be able to swim without that encumbrance was simply wonderful. Amy quite enjoyed herself too. She took readily to going swimsuit free. I guess she has always been a naturist at heart. She often wears little or nothing at home; going nude in the river was nothing new.

I reported our experience to Vanessa. I said that I enjoyed it so much that I intended to visit the river regularly. On the third visit Vanessa decided to come along too. I didn't know if she was going to strip off but she did.

The summer of 1994/95 rolled on and during that time we got hold of more naturist literature and decided to join the Australian Naturist Federation Supporter Group. That was an interesting exercise. We needed to send photographs of ourselves (not necessarily nude) signed by a Justice of the Peace. The JP wanted to know why we needed the photographs. We told him and hoped he would forget who we were. Over the months following we became more comfortable with being willing to accept the naturist label but there are some people who we would prefer not to tell for various reasons.

Naturism is a natural progression in my life. Though clothes serve their purpose, we live in a society which is more preoccupied with how people *look* than with who people *are*. God told Samuel, "The Lord sees not as man sees; man looks on the outward appearance, but the Lord looks on the heart."[1]

If social nudity were far more widely practiced we would have a less pretentious society, a society less concerned with status and making a good impression. It would be a world where people could more readily accept others as they are, and treat each other with respect and honesty. We would be more directly reminded that all humans are made in the image of God[2] and have been crowned with dignity and honor by him, and as such are worthy of our genuine concern and compassion. If nothing else, there would be less sexual hang-ups and sex crimes.

Being nude is not sinful; it is the way God made us and he declared it to be "very good."[3] Don't be discouraged or beset by doubts. Be assured that it is no sin to be naked in the company of like-minded humans. Enjoy your body. Treat it carefully as the Temple of God's Spirit[4] and rejoice in what God has given!

Spiritual Blindness

by Michelangelo Buonarotti

What spirit is so empty and blind, that it cannot grasp the fact that the human foot is more noble than the shoe, and human skin more beautiful than the garment with which it is clothed?

---

[1] I Samuel 16:7.
[2] Cf. genesis 1:26f.
[3] Genesis 1:31.
[4] Cf. I Corinthians 3:16 & 6:19.

Jesus vs. Naturism

by Jim C. Cunningham

One of the most frequent comments I hear from Christians who have adopted the nude lifestyle is, "But I will always be a Christian *first*; a naturist *second*." Of course, this sounds pious, and most probably always is, but it can be understood either in a correct or incorrect sense.

The correct sense would be an extrapolation on Jesus' dictum in the Gospel of Luke: "If any man come to Me and hate not his father, and mother, and wife, and children, and brothers and sisters, yea and his own life also, he cannot be My disciple."[1]

At first hearing, Jesus might seem a bit extreme, but all He is really saying is that if anything, howsoever good and noble it may be in itself, opposes our life in grace, we must hate it, reject it and refuse to consort with it. This is probably one of the main allegorical meanings of the Old Testament command given by God to Joshua (et al.) to put certain Gentile cities in the Promised Land "to the ban."[2] That meant they had to destroy everything about the place, killing every creature. That's how Jericho was pulverized.[3]

In our Christian spiritualities we must have exactly the same attitude toward anything that hinders the purity of our union with our beautiful Savior.

But there is also an incorrect interpretation of that pious platitude, "Jesus *first*; naturism *second*."

For example, let's look again at the example Jesus gives in the above passage—love of parents. In the Gospel of Mark Jesus chewed out the Pharisees for shirking their responsibilities toward their parents, using their temple religious duties as an excuse.[4] They were not *really*

---

[1] Luke 14:26.

[2] E.g. cf. Joshua 6:17 & Deuteronomy 13:12-16.

[3] With the sole exception of the family of Rahab, the harlot (cf Joshua 6:17 & 23), one of Christ's ancestors according to His humanity (cf. Matthew 1:5).

[4] Cf. Mark 7:9ff.

choosing God over absolutely everything, including parents. On the contrary, what they were really doing here, as they did in everything else, was choosing *themselves* over both God *and* parents. The Pharisees were the worst imaginable idol worshipers; they worshiped themselves in the name of God. What they should have done is obeyed Moses (God's faithful prophet) and kept the fourth commandment to honor their parents.[1] In the New Testament epistles this commandment is emphasized, pointing out that it was the *first* commandment of the ten that had a promise attached to it: "Honor your father and your mother (this is the first commandment with a promise) that it may be well with you and that you may live long on the earth."[2]

You see, there really is no dichotomy between loving parents and loving God. We love our parents precisely *because* we love God, Who gave us the fourth commandment. If we hate our parents, we cannot truly be loving God.

Am I here contradicting what Jesus said above in the Gospel of Luke? Of course not! It is possible to have *disordered* and *inordinate* affections for people and things. All must be loved *in God*.

Yesterday was the feast day of Sts. Perpetua and Felicity (d. 203 A.D.). They so truly loved Jesus above all things, that they gladly preferred a torturous martyrdom in the arena, to any compromising. Felicity had just given birth in the prison, yet chose death with Christ over the strongest maternal feelings. Perpetua had both a nursing infant, and an elderly, pagan father who would go to visit her in her prison cell. He could not understand how in the world God could possibly be glorified by her wasting herself to agree to have her bowels ripped out by the horns of a mad cow. Wouldn't God be better served by her playing the game of the authorities and offering a little incense (or whatever) to some Roman god or other? "Let's be *reasonable*!" must have been his fervent plea. St. Perpetua, who wrote the account herself,[3] told us that the old man tried every possible argument. He pointed to his

---

[1] Cf. Deuteronomy 5:16.
[2] Ephesians 6:2f.
[3] See *The Passion of Sts. Perpetua and Felicity* by St. Perpetua.

gray beard. Out of love and respect for it, wouldn't she please back down? Then he lost it completely, and plucked his beard right out in front of her. Surely, her pure heart was moved at the sight. Tearfully, Perpetua remained steadfast to her Lord, Whom she had to love even more than parents because, while her parents merely assisted in procreating her, God Alone created not only her, but her parents and the whole universe as well. She soon won the martyr's crown, and hundreds of millions of people still celebrate her valor over one and a half millennia later.

The martyr's father wanted his daughter to *disorder* her affection. She did not fail to truly *honor him* by choosing to *die for Christ*.

Another example is money. Jesus said we cannot possibly love both it and God.[1] Yet, out of love for God, we can (and must) seek to honestly acquire money to fulfill our obligations. How can we obey His command to clothe the naked,[2] unless we first earn the bucks to buy the garments?

No, Jesus was obviously referring to a *disordered* affection for money, whereby one actually *lives* for it. Money does not make the world go round. If all stock exchanges crashed tomorrow, the globe's rotation would not slow down, nor would one less raindrop fall. The cosmos would not feel it. Only those would feel it who worshiped it.

Finally, let's take the nude lifestyle. I sense in some of the correspondents who write to me, a *gnawing doubt* as to the morality of nudity. I suspect that this is really the reason for their even making the statement, "Christian *first*; naturist *second*." In the menu of life, Christians cannot have God as their entree, and naturism, money and parents as side dishes. No! *God is the whole gala banquet*, and He *Alone* must be the "All in all"[3] of every morsel, from the first sip of soup to the very last lick of liqueur. We must not look upon ourselves as Christians *and* naturists, but rather naturists *because* we are Christians! God must be our reason for everything. If you are not a naturist because you love God, then you should not be a naturist—yet. Your affections and motivations are

---

[1] Cf. Matthew 6:24.
[2] Cf. Matthew 25:36.
[3] I Corinthians 15:28 & Colossians 3:11.

assuredly disordered. Our passion is *solely* for God. Along the way, as we grow more mature in Christ, our lifestyle changes. In our spiritual journey we are being taught by the Holy Spirit the ramifications of such revealed truths as:

1. "God looked upon *all* that He had made and found it *very good.*"[1]
2. "In the *divine image* He created them; male and female He created them."[2]
3. "What God has declared holy, let *no* man deem unclean."[3]
4. "Do you not know that your bodies are *temples* of the Holy Spirit?"[4]
5. "Is not the body *more* than clothes?"[5]

Sanctification is nothing other than presenting our bodies as a living sacrifice, holy and acceptable to God, which is our spiritual worship, not being conformed to this world but being transformed by the renewal of our minds, that we may prove what is the will of God, what is good and acceptable and perfect.[6] It is "putting on the mind of *Christ.*"[7] We believe that God has given us naturism as a *tool* to help "Christify" our minds and hearts. The goal is to think and feel about our own bodies and the bodies of others the very same way *He* felt about His Body and those of others. Did He use nudity as a sexual turn-on? Perish the thought! When He saw a naked woman—maybe His Blessed Mother—did He see something disgusting or arousing? Of course not!

Do you know what He thought? He thought exactly the same then as He did on the sixth day of creation when the first two bodies were created through Him, the eternal Word: He looks at that naked woman and declares that His handiwork is still "very good."[8] "My Father worketh until now; and I work."[9]

---

[1] Genesis 1:31.
[2] Genesis 1:27.
[3] Acts 10:15.
[4] I Corinthians 6:19.
[5] Matthew 6:25.
[6] Cf. Romans 12:1f.
[7] Philippians 2:5.
[8] Genesis 1:31.
[9] John 5:17.

You, reader, were created by the divine Word in your mother's womb[1] no less truly than Adam & Eve were created by Him. The same, beautiful, wonderful, creative God *still* creates beautiful, wonderful things, including your body.

Our goal should be to see nakedness through *Christ's* eyes. If the good tree bears good fruit,[2] and we are the fruit of the Good Creator, then how marvelous indeed we are!

So, my friends, let's not be Christians *and* naturists. Let's not be Christians *and* anything else at all. Let's be *solely* and *purely* Christian. If naturism helps effect this lofty goal for you, then welcome to the nude lifestyle!

"I give You thanks, O Lord, that I am fearfully, wonderfully made. Wonderful are Your works!"[3]

Before Hearts Were Hard: The Way We Were

by Rick Means

All Christians know the story of the Garden of Eden, and that Adam & Eve were nude before God. Few Christians, however, are able to see that God's original intention for the conduct of our hearts concerning nudity are relevant today. The idea that Christ's supreme sacrifice was powerful enough to allow us innocence and the conquering of lust in our hearts is too hard for most to envision. To many Christians, after man's fall, the pleasures of Eden were taken from us for all time, and the principles man lived by while in the Garden were all erased, including nudity.

In Mark 10:2-12, Pharisees test Jesus by asking "Is it lawful for a man to divorce his wife?"

Jesus explains that it was because their *hearts were hard* that Moses wrote the law allowing divorce.[1] Christ

---

[1] Cf. Psalm 139:13.
[2] Cf. Matthew 7:17.
[3] Psalm 139:14.

goes on to explain that in the beginning (in the Garden) God intended marriage to be a *permanent* arrangement. "Therefore what God has joined together, let man not separate."[2] The principle taught here is that there are gifts and benefits God has offered us that we are kept from enjoying due to the hardness of our hearts. Christ uses God's plan in the Garden to explain this.

Today's society sees nudity as a radical form of expression, a "way out there," "on the fringe" type of thing. The same hardness of heart that keeps today's society from questioning the acceptance of divorce as normal, also keeps it from questioning its clothes compulsion.

Jesus' use of God's *original* intention to explain things to the Pharisees shows us that the Garden *is* relevant in our determinations of right and wrong *today*. The fifth chapter of Romans[3] tells us that what was lost in sin through the one man (Adam), was gained—and more—through the one Man, Jesus Christ.[4] If Jesus uses the *original* intention of God in the Garden as instruction even *before* His Own sacrifice, how much more should we be standing on it *now*?

Reason should tell us that just as in the Garden, *so all the more now*, Christ's sacrifice truly is capable of defeating lust of the flesh in the face of nudity. In Christ we can be "more than conquerors"[5] of lust. Why are so many Christians so reluctant to believe this when they accept it as a given with respect to other vices such as envy and covetousness? It is currently accepted that Christ's gift can defeat envy in the face of neighbors with plenty, and defeat hatred in the face of a sadistic and cruel society. Is God not pleased when we resist coveting others, and maintain a modest lifestyle amidst those who squander their prosperity? Is God not pleased when we show love amidst those filled with apathy and even hatred? And isn't God pleased when we "clothe ourselves with humility before one another"[6] in the midst of a society caught up in the significance of manipulating

---

[1] Cf. Mark 10:5.
[2] Mark 10:9.
[3] Cf. Romans 5:12-21.
[4] Ibid., but see especially vv. 15-17 & 20.
[5] Romans 8:37.
[6] I Peter 5:5.

others with, and hiding behind, personal dress? Isn't it the "human traditions and basic principles of this world"[1] that teach us we should always be clothed? Paul tells us we should *flee* from them. Instead, we should receive the kingdom of God as a child.[2] We should put "off the sinful nature."[3] Isn't lust part of the sinful nature? We should defeat, once and for all, that sinful nature by accepting Christ's salvation and sanctification.

To those who remain unconvinced, addressing a few questions will clear things up:

1. Is God's original intention relevant *today*? Did Christ Himself use it to explain the unacceptability of divorce?
2. Does the fifth chapter of Romans teach us that what was lost to us through Adam was gained—*and more*—through Christ?
3. Does Christ have the power to circumcise our hearts[4] and allow us to put off the sinful nature?
4. Does this sinful nature include lust? Is Christ's gift strong enough to allow us to defeat hatred, anger, and envy? What about lust?
5. If the Pharisees who questioned Jesus were to have asked Him if nudity were okay, do you think He would answer that the hardening of our hearts keeps us from being able to be nude together as we were before God in the Garden?
6. Scantily clad bodies and quarter-second glimpses of nudity are seen on the street, at swimming pools, beaches and in the media. Would it be easier for a person to defeat lust in a social nude setting than in the face of such tantalizing glimpses?
7. Would a young person not be able to deal better with the lust caused by such pseudo-nudity if he were raised seeing nude bodies from youth?
8. Read Colossians 2:20-23. Are not compulsive clothing requirements in our society an example of what Paul teaches here? Aren't clothes often examples of false

---

[1] Colossians 2:8.
[2] Cf. Mark 10:15.
[3] Colossians 2:11.
[4] Cf. Romans 2:28f.

humility,[1] and can compulsive clothing *really* restrain sensual indulgence? Should we trust more in garments than in overflowing grace?[2]

9. Jesus tells us we must be as little children to accept His message. Doesn't the putting off of the sinful nature allow us to be as little children concerning greed, hatred, malice, and yes, *even lust*?

So let us run the race before us, putting off all that hinders.[3] Let us pray for one another, that we each may defeat the sinful nature and accept the circumcision of the *heart* that Christ offers, rather than depend on the circumcision of the *flesh* (the Mosaic laws and today's standards including clothes compulsion).

Nudity for a Christian is like a light. As Christians we diligently work to sweep sin from our hearts. Concerning lust, most Christians sweep in the dark. Nudity throws open the shutters, and sunlight suddenly makes plain all of the spots we have missed over the years, and the cobwebs overhead. The question is, shall we slam the shutters and go on sweeping in the dark, or shall we rejoice for the light and clean out those places we missed?

Man Created "Modesty"

by Mark Twain[4]

...they heard God walking among the bushes (which was an afternoon custom of His), and they were smitten with fright.[5] Why? Because they were naked. They had not known it before. They had not minded it before. Neither had God. In that memorable moment immodesty was born, and some people have valued it ever since, though it would certainly puzzle them to explain why. Adam & Eve entered the world naked and unashamed[6]—naked and

---

[1] Cf. Colossians 2:23.
[2] Cf. John 1:16.
[3] Cf. Hebrews 12:1.
[4] Excerpted from his *Letters from the Earth*, #3.
[5] Cf. Genesis 3:8 & 10.
[6] Cf. Genesis 2:25.

pure-minded. And no descendant of theirs has ever entered it otherwise. All have entered it naked, un-ashamed and clean in mind. They entered it modest. They had to acquire immodesty in the soiled mind; there was no other way to get it. A Christian mother's first duty is to soil her child's mind, and she does not neglect it. Her lad grows up to be a missionary and goes to the innocent savage and to the civilized Japanese and soils their minds. Whereupon they adopt immodesty. They conceal their bodies, they stop bathing naked together. The convention mis-called "modesty" has no standard, and cannot have one, because it is opposed to nature and reason and is therefore an artificiality and subject to anybody's whim—anybody's diseased caprice. And so in India the refined lady covers her face and breasts and leaves her legs naked from the hips down. While the refined European lady covers her legs and exposes her face and her breasts. In lands inhabited by the innocent savage, the refined European lady soon gets used to full-grown natives' stark nakedness, and ceases to be offended by it.

A highly cultivated French count and countess, unre-lated to each other, who were marooned in their night clothes by shipwreck upon an uninhabited island in the eighteenth century, were soon naked. Also, ashamed—for a week. After that their nakedness did not trouble them and they soon ceased to think about it.

You have never seen a person with clothes on? Oh well, you haven't lost anything.

Brain-Picking Catholic

by Bob Contreras & Jim C. Cunningham

BOB: Jim, as a practicing Catholic, do you mind if I pick your brain a bit? You seem to be knowledgeable in matters of faith and doctrine. Is there any Church document or encyclical that specifically addresses the philosophy of Christian naturism?

JCC: Not to my knowledge, nor to that of Fr. Benedict Ashley, O.P., a theologian who captained the team opposing me on the PBS TV debate, "Is nudity God's will?"[1]

The Church has, of course, addressed the issues of chastity and modesty. Before becoming Pope John Paul II, Karol Cardinal Wojtyla wrote *Love & Responsibility,*[2] in which he clearly states that nakedness itself is not immodest, and that customs of dress are relative to many changing factors from climate to personal sensitivity.[3]

As Pope, he was warmly welcomed and entertained in New Guinea by bare-breasted native female dancers, and it is he who was responsible for "undressing" many of the Michelangelo figures in the Sistine Chapel.

The clear Catholic teaching is that we may never do anything to cause sexual arousal outside marriage. If we allow dominant culture to define all nudity as intrinsically immodest, not only does it lead to absurdities like prohibiting same-sex gang showers and even nudity with one's doctor, but it has proven to serve only to abet morbid curiosity that is far more detrimental to chastity. Our approach to chastity is bound to be counter-productive unless we teach it in a positive, rather than a negative way. The negative method has led to the denigration of both the body and even sacramental sexuality within marriage, and it has even led to psychological neuroses and God only knows how many sins against chastity.

The positive approach asserts the sacredness of the body and rightful sexuality. Immodesty and lust are therefore seen as aberrations of the true, the beautiful and the good. Many theologians believe that Pope John Paul II is stressing this positive approach, as is evidenced by his *Theology of the Body.*[4]

BOB: I once read excerpts from a G.K. Chesterton essay, where he mentioned the "Adamite heresy," which apparently (correct me if I'm wrong) originated in Germany in the late nineteenth century. Mr. Chesterton thought it was comical, but identified it as a heresy nonetheless. He was referring to naturism. Mr. Chesterton was more concerned

---

[1] See article below, p. 311.
[2] See note on p. 1.
[3] Cf. Wojtyla, pp. 176-192.
[4] (Boston: Pauline Books, 1997).

about other philosophies coming out of Germany at the time (or a bit earlier), Marxism and nihilism (Nietzsche) which originated after the French Revolution, which came about because of the Protestant Reformation—whether directly or indirectly is debatable (no offense to my Protestant brothers and sisters).

JCC: As I understand it, the Adamites were a lot more than just nudists. Their teaching was more like that of Matthew Fox' *Original Blessing*[1] which denies Original Sin and thus the need of redemption. On the contrary, we do not deny Original Sin or its many unhappy consequences, including concupiscence, which is the lusting of the spirit against the flesh.[2] The problem of concupiscence is exacerbated by fear of the body. Naturism, as we define it, provides a positive, wholesome assessment of the body and actually leads to greater chastity rather than greater lewdness.

Just look at the main dynamic behind striptease. The bare-breasted Papua New Guinea dancers are not at all like Las Vegas strippers. The dance of the former is as chaste and wholesome as any Polish folk dance. Las Vegas strippers, on the other hand, thrive on precisely the culture that proscribes innocent social nudity. The intention of Las Vegas strippers is to arouse lust. They do this by teasing their male audience, gradually revealing what non-naturist culture defines as erotic parts of their bodies, but hardly ever do they expose all as frankly as any Christian naturist lady.

Modern culture is so pluralistic and confused, that even in one society such as France, you can witness both nudities. The night life at the Parisian "Moulin Rouge" feeds on morbid curiosity and purposefully leads to lust, but the bare-breasted women at Parisian municipal pools give no evidence of any intention to arouse, but are simply taking advantage of an accepted custom, similar to the Papua New Guinea women. If lecherous men merely want nakedness, they do not have to pay a lot of money to see it. But the simple, chaste nudity of the pool or beach scene fails to satisfy them. They specifically want the erotic, striptease acts.

---

[1] (Santa Fe: Bear & Co., 1996).
[2] Cf. Galatians 5:17.

I find it hard to believe that Chesterton opposed all nudity. As a renowned art critic, he had to have a high regard for the nude in art. Surely he believed that "religion is the mother of art," and therefore it is difficult for me to believe that he was anti-nude. I suspect there was more than just nudity that he opposed in the Adamite heresy.

BOB: Furthermore, if I were to ask the average parish priest (who is loyal to the Magisterium) if my family and I could participate in Christian naturism, I don't think he would recommend it.

JCC: Ask, you might be surprised. Even the priest who opposed me on PBS TV, once he heard me out, did not condemn it, and emphatically declared that our beautiful, heavily illustrated book, *Vermont Unveiled,*[1] was not pornography, but "beautiful." True, you will find all sorts of priests out there, few of whom have even heard of John Paul II's theology of the body.

BOB: As an amateur historian, I see no Christian tradition of naturism throughout the last twenty centuries.

JCC: There was no need for it. Do you suppose mothers had to nurse their babies in toilet stalls two hundred years ago? The modern world is mad, and needs many *new* remedies to rectify its madnesses. The wise man knows what these are.[2] The hardened conservative keeps insisting on pouring new wine into old wineskins. Jesus said this does not work; it only leads to disaster.[3]

BOB: When St. Peter and St. Paul entered Rome two thousand years ago, didn't they encounter pagan naturism on a great scale?

JCC: No, naturism did not exist because there was no reason for it. Culture offered plenty of opportunities to encounter nudity in non-erotic situations such as breast-feeding, public bathing, swimming (bathing suits are a modern invention), heavy manual labor in the fields or loading ships, art, etc. Slaves were displayed in public

---

[1] *Vermont Unveiled*, 2nd Edition, by Jim C. Cunningham, is still in print. Practically speaking, it is a 100-page photographic guidebook to dozens of Vermont swimming holes where nudity is the norm, or is considered an acceptable alternative. But it is also a powerful graphic and textual statement of the positive attitude toward the body. In-print copies may still be available from www.naturistlife.com.

[2] Cf. Matthew 13:52.

[3] Cf. Luke 5:37f.

squares nude so the buyer could inspect what he was buying. St. Peter used to fish in the nude.[1] It was not *nudity* that these great apostles opposed, but *sexual immorality*, just as we Christian naturists do.

BOB: Wasn't it [pagan Rome] gradually replaced with a Christian culture which was very modest?

JCC: You call mixed nudity in church "modest"? Well, that was the normal way to baptize men, women and children for many centuries. If the apostles or fathers of the Church considered mere nudity to be sexually provocative, then they certainly would not have authorized or condoned nude baptisms! Obviously, "modesty" to them had nothing to do with merely hiding certain body parts.

BOB: What about St. Paul's directive to dress modestly?

JCC: Again, you wrongly assume that "modesty" means body coverings, but that's not what the Apostle said. He defines it himself, quite clearly: "I desire that... women should adorn themselves modestly and sensibly in seemly apparel..." He is not discussing naturism vs. textilism, but rather, what kind of textile dress constitutes true modesty, as is clear from what he continues to say: "not with braided hair or gold or pearls or costly attire *but by good deeds* as befits women who profess religion." He then goes on to admonish that women learn "in silence, with all submissiveness." "I permit no woman to teach or to have authority over men; she is to keep silent."[2]

From the context it is obvious that there was a problem with women taking courses and workshops in women's assertiveness, funded by Welfare programs,[3] and were maybe even going so far not only to try to usurp God-designed, male roles in society, but maybe even to claim that their bodies were their own and that they were not answerable to anybody, even if they chose to kill their babies in their wombs. In these senses, "modesty" is not the antonym of nudity, but of ostentatious audacity. Indeed, his description of immodest dress—"braided hair or gold or pearls or costly attire—has nothing to do with simply exposing their divinely crafted bodies, but only with brazen ostentation. It is ironic that many "pious"

---

[1] Cf. John 21:7.
[2] I Timothy 2:8-12.
[3] Anachronisms intended.

Christian women who do dress up to show off and "look good," look down their noses at other women who dress simply and unpretentiously, sometimes exposing more or less skin not to show off, but because it is natural, practical and comfortable. The modesty St. Paul is talking about concerns humility, not body-hiding.

Modern day feminists have so hoodwinked the mass of women in our society that they are almost all, in St. Paul's terminology, "immodest," even though they may never expose anything more than head, hands and feet— all jewelried and painted, of course, while their clothes are more and more looking like those of what they regard as a "successful" and "powerful" man. Where is the truly modest woman today?

In fact, nudity can help women acquire this true, Gospel modesty. Many women are too proud to be nude because:
1. They hate their femininity and covet masculinity. Nude, the truth of their femininity is all too obvious.
2. When we are nude we are weak and vulnerable. This is not a virtue according to women who crave power.
3. Nudity cannot hide what women's vanity considers to be defects. Small or sagging breasts, "spare tires," stretch marks, surgical scars, cellulose and chunky buttocks and thighs, are just humbly, honestly and plainly revealed for what they are.

Thus it is clear that according to the Pauline definition of modesty, nudity is not only not antithetical to it, but could truly be helpful in acquiring it.

BOB: One might then ask, "Then why didn't he tell women to go nude?"

JCC: Maybe he did. He does say women should dress *sensibly*. What is sensible about the foolish dresses and stockings women used to swim in at the end of the Victorian era? What is more sensible for swimming than one's birthday suit? And St. Paul says it should be "seemly." Were not Adam & Eve "seemly" attired before the fall? Are not all of Michelangelo's nudes in the Sistine Chapel "seemly"? If they were "unseemly," how is it that they have been tolerated by centuries of popes? Finally, is it pious to say that our bodies which God created are "unseemly"? How would that be glorifying the Creator in His works?

For examples of what St. Paul would call "immodesty," just leaf through any women's magazine like *Vogue* & *Harper's Bazaar*, every photo and every ad depicts immodest women, even if they are covered from head to foot.

I once saw a cover of one such magazine that featured a photo of a woman from her ostentatious hat down to her naked, left areola, which was positioned at the trim edge of the right bottom corner. From that modest nipple up to her neck she was bare, but everything above that was heavily cosmeticized and topped off with a very flamboyant bonnet. According to St. Paul's definition of immodesty as defined in I Timothy 2:9f, what was immodest was *above* her neck. He never defined the female body itself to be immodest. Nipples were naturally made for children to suck, and he (along with other New Testament authors) often refers to this as simply a fact of life.[1] Certainly, if he treats the act of breast-feeding so naturally, he would have no problem with viewing that act or the body parts required for it.

Many (most?) of the faces in women's magazines are immodest as is clear from the intentions they express. But the naked nipple cannot express anything other than what God Himself intended; it's just "there." Pardon my French (after all, I do live on the Quebec border!), but those faces express either brazenness ("F— you!") or lust ("F— me!"). They almost never depict godliness, naturalness, purity or simplicity.

In fact, I can recall only once having seen an exception in *Vogue*. It was a large, color photo of a woman facing the viewer, holding a bag of groceries on each hip. She was smiling simply and heartily. She looked healthy. If she had makeup on, it was so subdued as to be unnoticeable. There were no clothes making her look like some athlete or promoting some athletic sportswear company. No offensive textile colors to contradict the body's natural color. There were no high heels distorting her legs and stance. There was no jewelry anywhere. There were no false pads filling in gaps or accentuating any body part. There was no padded bra or anything to make her bosom appear to be different than how God made it. She wore no slacks mimicking the design that "successful" males wear,

---

[1] E.g. cf. Luke 11:26; I Corinthians 3:1f; I Peter 2:3 & Hebrews 5:12ff.

nor even a business suit skirt hiding the primary sexual characteristic of her genitalia. Even her pubic hair was bushy and natural—not shaved and shaped to "fit" into some skimpy bikini. Indeed, she was *sensibly* nude, posing for an article on nutrition, which, after all, is about producing a healthy body. And her nudity was so "seemly" that it did not belong in such a women's magazine, but rather should have been a poster on the wall of every high school health class. What a wonderful, refreshing exception she was! The facial expressions on the other faces all seemed to express ungodly intentions, but that one said, "Hi, this is me as God made me and which I try to respect by a healthy diet and by not despising my body or being ashamed of any part of it. Let's all remember that health has to begin with a good body attitude. Won't you accept and appreciate the gift of your body, too, and eat right?"

I can't imagine St. Paul having a problem with that, unless he were to think her a bit too didactic, whereas he did not want women to teach.[1] But then, *Vogue is* a *women's* magazine, and the model was not necessarily presuming to instruct men, but only to edify her sisters.

In I Timothy 2:9f we also read that St. Paul was not preaching a modesty in terms of textiles, because he specifically states what constitute "sensible" and "seemly" apparel for Christian women: "good deeds." Unlike the whitewashed sepulchres of the Pharisees,[2] St. Paul is specifically stating that true religion has nothing to do with the wearing of outward garments or jewelry. In God's eyes, clothes do not make the woman (or man); virtue does. He does not exhort Christians to hide their breasts while nursing, or to bathe in private, but rather to "put on compassion, kindness, lowliness, meekness and patience."[3]

Indeed, St. Peter, the nude fisherman, also admonishes us to clothe ourselves with *humility*.[4] He says, "Let not yours be the *outward* adorning with braiding of hair, decoration of gold, and wearing of fine clothing, but let it be the *hidden* person of the heart with the imperishable

---

[1] Cf. I Corinthians 11:3 & 14:34f.
[2] Cf. Matthew 23:26.
[3] Colossians 3:12.
[4] Cf. I Peter 5:5.

jewel of a gentle and quiet spirit, which in God's sight is very precious."[1]

Elsewhere, St. Paul lambastes those who would seek to render true religion impotent by *externalizing* it into a matter of diet, vocal prayers, or the observance of feast days.[2] He says, "for the kingdom of God is not food and drink but righteousness and peace and joy in the Holy Spirit."[3] There is always a negative tendency in religion to define it in terms of *external* observances. Externals have value only insofar as they represent *internal* realities, or help us to acquire those *internal* realities. All virtue— including modesty—is a matter of the heart. Clearly, this is what St. Paul meant when he said that the circumcision of the flesh was of no religious value whatever, but only the circumcision of the heart.[4] Isaiah was modest as he preached nude for three years.[5] Christ was modest as He was baptized by St. John the Baptist in the Jordan. Early Christians were modest as they stripped naked in church for baptism in front of all who were gathered for the Easter Vigil Liturgy. Likewise, all nudes throughout history, from Adam & Eve before the fall to Finns who sauna together as they have done from time immemorial, are modest if their nudity is as God intended and not for any untoward motive. God does not judge as man does, by appearances, but *by the heart.*[6]

---

[1] I Peter 3:3f.
[2] Cf. Colossians 2:16 *et al.*
[3] Romans 14:17.
[4] Cf. Romans 2:28f & I Corinthians 7:19.
[5] Cf. Isaiah 20:2f.
[6] Cf. I Samuel 16:7.

Debates... Debates!

by Jim C. Cunningham

David showed up with his slingshot, but Goliath was nowhere to be found! That's how I felt in 1997 as all of the big shot leaders of the so-called "Radical Religious Right" refused to pick up the gauntlet and engage me in publicly debating the question, "Is nudity God's will?" All of them very seriously considered the invitation from PBS, but in the words of the Assistant Producer, "began backpedaling" when they discovered they would be opposing Jim C. Cunningham of Naturist LIFE International. Some were already familiar with NLI through either print or the internet, or back-pedaled after checking us out. The funniest case was a very erudite Catholic apologist, a priest often featured on Mother Angelica's Eternal Word Television Network. He was invited to the debate in person when he happened to be at the Manhattan TV studio. They gave him NLI's guidebook, *Vermont Unveiled*,[1] to peruse while making up his mind. "These pictures are beautiful!" he exclaimed, and he refused the challenge, recommending Fr. Benedict Ashley, an 82-year old Do-minican Theologian from St. Louis University, a bioethicist who published a huge tome, *Theologies of the Body*. Well, it seems that Fr. Ashley did not know better, and accepted the challenge to be the captain opposing me. The rest of the opposition consisted of Peter Thiel, an evangelical attorney and research fellow with the Independent Insti-tute near San Francisco, and Bawa Jain, a Hindu Jainist United Nations interfaith director.

PBS allowed me to have input on the other members of my team, and I immediately suggested Fr. Jim G. Dodge,[2] an 82-year old Trappist monk-priest and naturist for about seventy years (nothing like a little experience!).

---

[1] See note on p. 305.

[2] Editor's note: Enjoying excellent health till the end, Fr. Dodge died the following February 1, 1998. I assisted at his funeral at Our Lady of Mepkin Abbey in Moncks Corners, South Carolina, where, according to Trappist custom, he was buried without a coffin, wearing nothing but his monk's habit. *Requiescat in pace!*

Our team now consisting of yours truly, a staunch Catholic lay father of five children who have never known anything but naturism, and an articulate and widely experienced Catholic priest, we racked our brains trying to perfect the team with an articulate, Christian naturist woman who could speak for the "better half" of humanity. We had almost given up when Fr. Dodge found Claudia Kellersch, a Bavarian living in the U.S.A. Northwest. She was known on the internet to be very articulate in defense of naturism. When I asked her about her theological background, she said she had read the Bible in both Greek and Latin, so I figured she was just the perfect complement to our team.

We immediately began to do our homework, researching the opposition, readying our best "guns," and planning strategies to utilize the strictly fixed professional debate format to our best advantage. We also practiced at the fine Manhattan hotel where PBS graciously accommodated us.

The evening before the big debate I called the two members of the opposing team who were also staying at the hotel, Fr. Ashley and Peter Thiel. They cordially accepted my invitation to dinner at the hotel restaurant. I wanted to enter the debate not with fire and ire, but with understanding, mutual respect and congeniality. There were ten of us at dinner: my wife, Linda, myself, and our three youngest children (who obviously did not look ill-adjusted or abused!), Claudia, Fr. Dodge, Peter and Fr. Ashley. Being completely blind and disabled (which I do not think they knew), I was the last to arrive with one of my children guiding me. I made a point to shake their hands and personally introduce everyone, always trying to "break ice" and remove imagined fences.

The dinner conversation was most amusing to me as I could see Fr. Ashley and Peter go through a series of massive mental readjustments as they discovered that we did not each have three heads, and in some respects, were even more conservative than they. Instead of being turned off by the type of godly nudity that we expounded, they seemed to be very intrigued. Most ironic was the fact that the Dominican and our Trappist found out that they had "met" before in 1941 at Gethsemane Abbey in Kentucky. Fr. Ashley had been there on retreat with Thomas Merton, while Fr. Dodge was being received into the order as a novice.[1] Small world!

To top it all off, upon parting for the night I asked them if I could make a present to them of a copy of *Vermont Unveiled*. They seemed enthusiastically glad to receive it. By the elevator, I said to Fr. Ashley, "Your theology of the body actually fits into our philosophy very well. What you have done on the *theological* level, needs to be done on the *practical* level; there ought to be retreats for Catholics focusing on the spirituality of the body in order to help straighten out harmful warps."

"You mean a nudist retreat?" he exclaimed.

"Well, not necessarily, but at least geared to address this neglected dimension of spiritual growth," I explained.

His response to this was a prolonged, pensive, "Hmm...," as he entered the elevator. The following day, September 30, was the taping of the debate. Ironically, it was the feast of St. Jerome, who said, "*Nudus nudum Iesum sequi.*"[2]

Fr. Ashley came to me between cosmetic make-ups.

"Did you check out *Vermont Unveiled* last night?" I queried.

"Well, I didn't read the whole thing yet, but the photographs are beautiful; they are definitely *not* pornographic!"

Linda felt sorry for the opposition, because by the time the debate began, it seemed they truly regretted being there, now that they better understood the naturist ideal as we presented it.

During the debate their best "guns" were not very powerful. Fr. Ashley asserted that it was unrealistic to suppose we could return to the Garden of Eden. Several times he said he agreed with us about public nudity; he just insisted that it be somehow regulated. Peter's "gun" was that we shouldn't practice naturism if it would scandalize a weak brother in the Lord who might not understand it the way we do. Bawa Jain's argument was that if naturism occasioned turmoil and public strife, it

---

[1] In his spiritual autobiography, Thomas Merton describes how impressed he was by witnessing Fr. Dodge's investiture. One day he was seen in choir in lay clothing, and the next day he had been swallowed up in the ocean of white. Cf. Merton, Thomas, *The Seven Storey Mountain* (New York: Harcourt, Brace & Co., 1948), p. 325.
[2] "Naked, I follow naked Jesus." See note on p. 351.

should be avoided so as not to create negative "karma." And that's the best they could do!

I think our team argued well and convincingly. Fr. Dodge, especially, was very funny, getting the live audience to laugh a few times. No matter who "won" or "lost" the hour long debate, what's really important is that the issue was seriously and respectfully addressed in a public forum, and among Christians. This alone had to get many PBS TV viewers to thinking, and it will be obvious to all that the assumption that "nude is lewd" may well be not adequately thought through.

PBS' "Debates Debates" ("Is nudity God's will?") was aired the week of November 5, 1997 on as many as 170 subscriber stations. Videotaped copies are available at www.naturistlife.com.

From *Pilgrim's Progress*

by John Bunyan

Editor's note: This three centuries old, charming episode allegorizing baptism and confirmation is excerpted from one of the oldest English Christian classics, *Pilgrim's Progress* by John Bunyan (Grand Rapids: Baker Book House, 1988) 2nd Part, pp. 257f. It is ironic that next to the Bible, this was one of the Puritans' favorite books, yet it contains chaste group nudity, wholesome dancing and responsible consumption of alcoholic beverages!

In the morning they [Christiana, her four sons, and Mercy] rose with the sun, and prepared themselves for their departure; but the Interpreter would have them tarry a while, "For," said he, "you must orderly go from hence." Then said he to the damsel that at first opened unto them: "Take them and have them into the garden to the bath, and there wash them, and make them clean from the soil which they have gathered by travelling." Then Innocent, the damsel, took them, and had them into the garden, and brought them to the bath; so she told them that there they must wash and be clean, for so her master would have the women to do that called at his house as they were going on pilgrimage. They then went in and washed, yea, they and the boys and all; and they came out of that bath not only sweet and clean, but also much enlivened and strengthened in their joints. So when they came in they looked fairer a deal than when they went out to the washing.

When they were returned out of the garden from the bath, the Interpreter took them, and looked upon them, and said unto them, "Fair as the moon." Then he called for the seal, wherewith they used to be sealed that were washed in his bath. So the seal was brought, and he set his mark upon them, that they might be known in the places whither they were yet to go. Now the seal was the contents and sum of the passover which the children of Israel did eat when they came out from the land of Egypt; and the mark was set between their eyes. This seal greatly added to their beauty, for it was an ornament to their faces. It also added to their gravity, and made their countenances more like them of angels.

Then said the Interpreter again to the damsel that waited upon these women, "Go into the vestry and fetch out garments for these people." So she went and fetched out white raiment, and laid it down before him; so he commanded them to put it on. It was "fine linen, white and clean."

Nude Baptism in the Early Church

by Larry Amyett, Jr.

Baptism in Judaism

In the Talmud the ritual of baptism was used as part of the initiation of proselytes. Proselyte baptism was a form of self dedication. Whether it was for repentance of sin (as in Christian baptism) is subject to debate. A person who wished to become a Jew would totally immerse himself in the nude under the instructions of the priest and the witness of three other individuals.[1] Lightfoot, in *Horae Hebraicae Talmuducae*, wrote, "Every person baptized must dip his whole body, now stripped and made naked, at one dipping. And wheresoever in the Law washing of the body is mentioned, it means nothing else than the washing of the whole body."[2]

The Jewish proselyte baptism probably dated back to the time of Jesus. Though the Talmud is a third to fourth century creation, there are some indications that this ritual existed during the time of Jesus. According to the Mishnah, the Schools of Shammai and Hillel had a dispute as to whether a proselyte might be baptized on the day before Passover and then take the Passover offering in the evening. If this dates back to those schools, then it would have existed during the time of John the Baptist. It may have even dated back to the time of Shammai and Hillel themselves. If so, then this ritual would be older than the New Testament.

John the Baptist

John the Baptist was one of very few Biblical personalities who was documented outside of the Bible. Josephus wrote of John: "He was a good man, and exhorted the Jews to lead righteous lives, practice justice towards one another and piety towards God, and so to join in baptism. In his view this was a necessary preliminary if baptism was to be acceptable to God. They must not use it to gain pardon for whatever sins they committed, but as a consecration of the body, implying that the soul was thoroughly purified beforehand by right behavior."[3]

Was Jesus nude when He was baptized by John? While the Bible does not say *how* John baptized, it may be possible to extract this information from outside sources. The early paintings of Christ's baptism do show Jesus

---

[1] Wilburn, Ralph G., Ed., *Renewal of Church: the Panel of Scholars Reports*, I, 2., p. 269.
[2] "Baptism," *The International Standard Bible Encyclopedia*, I, 1., p. 415.
[3] Wilson, Ian, *Jesus: the Evidence* (San Francisco: Harper & Row), p. 84.

being baptized nude. A good example of this is the fifth century mosaic in Santa Maria in Cosmedin, Ravenna.[1]

Baptism in the Bible

Unfortunately, there is very little in the Bible concerning the details of the rite of baptism. In Mark 14:51f we read, "And a young man followed Him, with nothing but a linen cloth about his body; and they seized him, but he left the linen cloth and ran away naked." One may speculate that the young man was going to be baptized by Jesus and that is why he was wearing only a linen cloth.

Cyril of Jerusalem

One of the best records of ancient rites of baptism is made by Cyril of Jerusalem (315-386 A.D.). He was the nephew of the patriarch of Alexandria, Theophilus. Cyril was one of the great leaders of the early Church. His influence can still be felt in the structure of the modern Church calendar, and his lectures give us an invaluable look into the theology and rites of the early Church. Cyril is important for our topic here because he wrote twenty-three lectures which were given to baptism candidates. As the bishop of Jerusalem, he was the head of the most important baptistery of that time. The basilica of Golgotha was considered special because it was built at the site of the crucifixion of Jesus and therefore considered holy.

There is good evidence to support the argument that the Church of Jerusalem maintained traditions which had descended directly from the time of the New Testament Church. As a result, the rite of baptism of the Jerusalem Church would contain many legitimate elements. We also know that Cyril's description of baptism was not a heretical doctrine. According to William Telfer, "Part of this heritage was no doubt a tradition of doctrine, and in particular of norms of baptismal catechesis. For all the freshness with which Cyril handles his matter, in catechetical lecturing, we may judge that he is guided by Church tradition, when we note how impervious he is to

---

[1] Wilson, Op. Cit., p. 85.

contemporary theological disturbances."[1] Therefore, Cyril's description of the rite of baptism is extremely reliable.

Because Cyril's record is so detailed and of such value, we should allow Cyril to speak for himself. In his "First Address on the Mysteries," he wrote of baptism:

You have been admitted to the divine life-giving baptism, and are now capable of receiving the more sacred mysteries[2]... Let us now instruct you in detail, so that you may know the meaning of what happened on the evening of your baptism. First you entered into the vestibule of the baptistery, and as you stood facing west, you heard the command to stretch out your hand; and you renounced Satan, as if he were present.[3] Then, when you renounced Satan, utterly canceling every covenant with him, the ancient alliance with hell, there is opened to you paradise of God, which He planted towards the east, whence our first ancestor was expelled. To symbolize this, you turned from the west to the east, the region of light. And you were told to say, "I believe in the Father, and in the Son, and in the Holy Spirit, and in one baptism of repentance." All this took place in the outer chamber. But when, God willing, we have entered the Holy of Holies in the succeeding explanation of the mysteries, we shall then understand the symbolism of the rites performed there.[4]

In the "Second Address on the Mysteries," he wrote:

As soon as you entered, you took off your clothes; this was a symbol of stripping off the old man with his behavior. After undressing, you were naked, thus imitating the naked Christ on the cross... And you bore the likeness of the first-formed Adam, who was naked in the garden without feeling shame. Then, after stripping, you were anointed with exorcised oil, from the hairs on top of your head to your feet, and were thus connected with the good olive tree, Jesus Christ. You were cut off from the wild olive and grafted to the good one... The oil symbolized participation in the richness of Christ, a remedy to drive away all trace of

---

[1] "Cyril of Jerusalem, St.," *Encyclopedia Britannica Micropedia* (15th Ed.). I, 3. p. 61.

[2] Editor's note: I.e. the Holy Eucharist.

[3] Bettenson, Henry, ed., *The Later Christian Fathers: Selections from the Writings of the Fathers from St. Cyril of Jerusalem to St. Leo the Great* (London: Oxford Univ. Pr.) p. 42.

[4] Ibid.

the hostile power... After this you were led by the hand to the holy pool of divine baptism, as Christ was taken from the cross to the appointed sepulchre. And each of you was asked if he believed in the Name of the Father, and of the Son, and of the Holy Spirit. And you made that saving confession; you descended into the water and came up again three times, thus alluding symbolically to the three days of Christ... In the very same moment you died and were born; and that water of salvation became both your grave and your mother.[1]

In the "Third Address on the Mysteries," Cyril wrote:

You were made Christ's when you received the symbol of the Holy Spirit, and all that was done representationally for you are representations of Christ. After His baptism in the River Jordan, when He imparted some tincture of divinity to the waters, He came up from them; and the Holy Spirit came upon Him in substantial form, like resting on like. Similarly, when you came up from the holy streams, chrism was given to you, an emblem of the anointing of Christ. This is the Holy Spirit... Christ was not anointed by men with oil or material ointments; but when the Father appointed Him as Savior of the whole world He anointed Him with the spiritual Holy Spirit... Christ was anointed with the spiritual "oil of gladness"; the Holy Spirit Who is called the oil of gladness because He is the cause of spiritual gladness. And so you are anointed with ointment, being made partakers and fellows of Christ. Beware of supposing that this is merely ointment. For as the bread of Eucharist, after the invocation of the Holy Spirit, is no longer simply bread, but the Body of Christ; so also this holy ointment is no longer merely ointment; not what one might call ordinary ointment, after invocation; it is the gift of Christ, and by the presence of the Holy Spirit it conveys the power of His divinity. It is applied symbolically to the forehead and the other organs of sense; and while the body is anointed with the visible ointment, the soul is sanctified by the Holy and life-giving Spirit. And you were anointed first on the forehead, that you might be freed from shame... Next, your ears, so that you might have ears ready to hear the divine mysteries. Then on your nostrils, that you might say, "We are to God a sweet fragrance." Then on your

---

[1] Bettenson, Op. Cit., p. 43.

*breast, that you might "put on the breastplate of righteous-
ness and withstand the devices of the devil." When you
have been granted this chrism you are called "Christians,"
verifying the name by your new birth. Before you were
admitted to this grace you had no genuine right to the title,
but you were advancing along the way becoming Christians.*[1]

Hippolytus

In *The Apostolic Tradition*, Hippolytus of Rome (c. 170-
236 A.D.) wrote extensively on many topics, including
baptism. It is best if we use his own words:[2]

Of the Conferring of Holy Baptism:

1. *And at the hour when the cock crows they shall first of
   all pray over the water.*
2. *When they come to the water, let the water be pure and
   flowing.*
3. *And they shall put off their clothes.*
4. *And they shall baptize the little children first. And if they
   can answer for themselves let them answer. But if they
   cannot let their parents answer or someone from their
   family.*
5. *And next they shall baptize the grown men; and last the
   women, who shall all have loosed their hair and laid
   aside the gold ornaments which they were wearing. Let
   no one go down to the water having any alien object
   with them.*
6. *And at the time determined for baptizing the bishop shall
   give thanks over the oil and put it into a vessel and it is
   called the Oil of Thanksgiving.*
7. *And shall take also other oil and exorcise over it, and it is
   called the Oil of Exorcism.*
8. *And let a deacon carry the Oil of Exorcism and stand on
   the left of the presbyter who will do the anointing. And*

---

[1] Bettenson, Op. Cit., p. 44.
[2] Dix, Rev. Gregory, ed., *The Treatise on the Apostolic Tradition of St.
Hippolytus of Rome, Bishop and Martyr* (Ridgefield, Connecticut: More-
house Publ.) pp. 33-38.

another deacon shall take the Oil of Thanksgiving and stand on the right.

9. And when the presbyter takes hold of each one of those who are to be baptized, let him renounce saying: "I renounce thee, Satan, and all thy service and all thy works."

10. And when he has said this let him anoint him with the Oil of Exorcism saying: "Let all evil spirits depart far from thee."

10a. And also turning him to the east, let him say: "I consent to Thee, O Father and Son and Holy Spirit, before Whom all creation trembles and is moved. Grant me to do all Thy wills without blame."

11. Then after these things let him give over to the presbyter who stands at the water to baptize;

11a. And a presbyter takes his right hand and he turns his face to the east. Before he descends into the water, while he still turns his face to the east, standing above the water he says after receiving the Oil of Exorcism, thus: "I believe and bow me unto Thee and all Thy service, O Father, Son and Holy Spirit." And so he descends into the water.

11. And let them stand in the water naked. And let a deacon likewise go down into the water.

11b. And let him say to him and instruct him: "Dost thou believe in one God the Father Almighty and His only-begotten Son Jesus our Lord and our Savior, and His Holy Spirit, Giver of life to all creatures, the Trinity of one Substance, one God-head, one Lordship, one Kingdom, one Faith, one Baptism in the Holy Catholic Apostolic Church for life eternal (Amen)?" And he who is baptized shall say again thus: "Verily, I believe."

12. And when he who is to be baptized goes down to the water, let him who baptizes lay hands on him saying thus: "Dost thou believe in God the Father Almighty?"

13. And he who is being baptized shall say: "I believe."

14. Let him forthwith baptize him once, having his hand laid upon his head.

15. And after this let him say: "Dost thou believe in Christ Jesus, the Son of God, Who was born of Holy Spirit and the Virgin Mary, Who was crucified in the days of Pontius Pilate, and died, and was buried, and rose the third day living from the dead, and ascended into the heavens. And sat down at the right hand of the Father, and will come to judge the living and the dead?"

16. *And when he says: "I believe," let him baptize him the second time.*
17. *And again let him say: "Dost thou believe in the Holy Spirit, in the Holy Church, and in the resurrection of the flesh?"*
18. *And he who is baptized shall say: "I believe." And so let him baptize him the third time.*
19. *And afterwards when he comes up from the water he shall be anointed by the presbyter with the Oil of Thanksgiving saying: "I anoint thee with holy oil in the Name of Jesus Christ."*
20. *And so each one drying himself with a towel they shall now put on their clothes, and after let them be together in the assembly.*

Conclusion

Since nude baptism appears to be correct and divinely endorsed, it raises larger questions about how we practice baptism in the modern church, and about the possible need for reform. Should we immerse someone during baptism three times or once? Should the subject's entire body be anointed with oil while nude and being prepared to be baptized? And what should we make of the practice of exorcism? It may be that abandoning the practice of nude baptism was just one step in which we ultimately lost so much more.

Editor's acknowledgments: Many thanks to John Kundert, editor of *Fig Leaf Forum (FLF)*, and author Larry Amyett, Jr. for permission to reprint this article in slightly edited form in the "Divine Reflections" feature of *Naturist* LIFE *International* magazine, No. 19, whence it is again here reprinted. Larry's original article appeared in the Feb. '97 edition of FLF. He writes from a non-Catholic Christian tradition. For contact information for FLF, see note on p. 216.

Curiosity

by Jim C. Cunningham

"Guess what's in my pocket."

"You're not wearing any clothes, so how can I guess what's in your pocket?"

"Oh, yeah. Then guess what I'm holding behind my back."

Naturally, everyone's attention has been arrested, and you can almost smell the proverbial wood burning as questions arise in each person's mind:

"Hmm..., could it be money? A pretty rock? A sea shell? A cat's eye marble? A baby Zebra?"

We want to know. Why? *Just because.* Our attention has been drawn to an unknown and we feel somewhat restless, disquieted and even distracted and disturbed until the mystery is solved.

There is nothing whatsoever prurient about such curiosity. It is simply how God wired us, gifting us with reason which has an in-built propensity to discover and to know. This drive is so essential to human nature that if we fail to strive to pursue it, we are morally culpable, for we have contradicted our very essence.

Furthermore, as "grace builds on nature," curiosity is also at the root of our *spiritual* search. Jesus tells us to seek, and guarantees success.[1] Likewise, we are told to seek in several other places of Holy Scripture.[2] Our natural sense of wonder is like an automatic motor, always motivating us toward the deeper discovery and experience of God's love and truth. Half the gifts of the Holy Spirit concern acquiring understanding.[3] Proverbs 4:7 says the very *beginning* of wisdom is "*Get* wisdom!" Without the desire to discover there would be no spirituality at all; there would be no humanity—nothing in the material universe created in the image and likeness of God. St. Thomas Aquinas taught that knowledge precedes love; you cannot love what you do not know. Thus the

---

[1] Cf. Luke 11:9.

[2] E.g. Proverbs 2:1-5; 8:17; Colossians 3:1 & James 1:5.

[3] Viz. wisdom, understanding, knowledge and counsel (cf. Isaiah 11:2).

innate human propensity to know is essential to man's fulfillment—love.

Whether consciously or unconsciously, our minds constantly ask questions like "Who? What? When? Where? Why? How? What if?" Our minds cannot receive knowledge but through the gate of inquiry, whose hinges are curiosity.

Knowledge is satisfying; it brings peace. You wake in the middle of the night hearing a peculiar sound. Toss and turn as you might, unless you are dog-tired, chances are you will not be able to "sleep like a baby" till you have taken the trouble to discover the source of the noise. It is not so much the sound that troubles you, but the *ignorance* of its source. There are all sorts of nocturnal sounds in my house, but none will disturb me but that one that is unfamiliar.

Why are mystery movies and novels so popular? Because their very essence is built on what is most fundamental in us. We rarely read the same book twice. Victor Hugo's *Notre Dame de Paris* (AKA *The Hunchback of Notre Dame*) holds and increases our attention to the end because we want to know the solution to all his intertwining plots and sub-plots. A good author quickly grips the reader's curiosity, and gradually builds it up more and more such that the book "cannot be put down"; we are glued to it like a desperate wrestler who will not let go till he has pinned his opponent.

Without being aware of it, our minds are constantly asking questions and receiving answers. I never understood this so fully until I became totally blind. When I had vision, I walked through the house unaware of the plethora of questions and answers mere routine glances provoked and provided:

"Is the power light still on on the stereo? Does the floor need washing? Did Junior put his chess game away? Is sunshine coming through the windows, or is it still overcast outside? Are the dishes done? Is Zebedee the cat up on the counter again where he is not allowed? That wallpapering still hasn't been done. Should we move it higher on our agenda? Etc., etc., etc. A sighted person—even unwittingly—takes in more data in one minute than a blind person does in a whole day.

When a sighted person reads *The Grapes of Wrath* by John Steinbeck, he anticipates some sort of sudden ending when he sees there is only one more page to turn at the end of the book. But when I "read" it via audio-tapes, I only knew it would end sometime within the following ninety minutes, as I had just flipped the switch to the last track of the tape. But when it ended with the highly creative, artful bang with which it does end, I was stunned. Had I fallen asleep? Missed something? *That's it?* That is the ending? Linda can testify how I paced the house in a daze and a dither. No ending ever hit me like that one, and it was all the more powerful simply because, being blind, I did not expect it.

The point is that man is naturally curious, and wittingly or unwittingly, through our senses and pure cognition, we are constantly asking and answering questions. It's called *intelligence.*

Though we all ask thousands of questions every day, we consciously pursue only the ones that "bug" us the most.

The best kept secrets naturally "bug" us the most. What people look like is one of—if not *the*—best kept secrets in our puritanical culture. We encounter sometimes hundreds of people every day, and each veiled body presents a question to our minds whether we are aware of it or not: "What does he look like?" If faces were veiled in a nudist camp, we would constantly wonder about what were behind all the masks.

In our clothes-compulsive society, it is the other way around. Our questions about facial features are quickly answered, since the answers are not hidden. However, since the bodies *are always* hidden, our natural curiosity with respect to that 95% of a person's physicality is chronically unsatisfied.

We respond to this fact in any of three ways:
1. Voyeurism: We seek to find out, "by hook or by crook," even invading privacy by long stares.
2. Repression: We sublimate the curiosity, intentionally denying the satisfaction of discovery.
3. Chaste naturism: We immediately satisfy the curiosity, as there are no veils to hinder vision.

Voyeurism

Perhaps the most common response to physical curiosity is voyeurism. The more "hard-to-get" this information is, the more quickly this response can devolve into a very negative, morbid type of voyeurism. The intensity can become so great that ordinary norms of personal privacy are violated in order to discover the answer. Also, admixed with natural curiosity is a selfish prurience.

Little Johnny is not supposed to tiptoe down to the Christmas tree on an Advent night and sneakily remove enough tape from his wrapped presents to discover what they are. Walking past them wrapped every day naturally drives a child nuts.

A "peeping Tom" does the same thing and for the same reason, though there is also an erotic element. He will sneak to peek, even violating established, accepted norms of privacy, so feverishly intense has his curiosity been titillated, tantalized and teased.

Thus once, when I was a young teenager, after changing out of my wet bathing suit, I tied my towel around my waist, exited our lakeside dressing room, and walked to the clothesline to hang it up. My older sister and her accomplices saw a golden opportunity to satisfy their natural curiosities about the parts of me that were chronically veiled. A quick, little tug on the towel, and "*Voila!*"— all would be bare and exposed. Such a deed surely violated my privacy and was inconsiderate of my feelings. All things being equal, they really would not have wanted to offend me in such ways, but in our senselessly repressive culture, all things were *not* equal. The chronic veiling, combined with the nature of human intelligence, created a situation that was grossly unequal, such that slight offenses might be tolerated in order to equalize things—in order to acquire the desired knowledge.

Voyeurs are like terrorists. They are so frustrated by what they see as injustice that they justify offenses against propriety, privacy, or, in the case of terrorists, even one's right to life itself. Sure, we can search out and destroy those surviving terrorists who have not yet violated even their own lives in venting their frustrations, or we can do what it takes to remove what causes that frustration. A truly successful "war on terrorism" had better be primarily concerned with the latter objective, or else its crusade will never win. Because the crusade itself breeds more of what it would annihilate, by its very nature, it ensures that victory can never be within sight.

What causes the voyeur's frustration? Part—if not all—of the answer is simply the chronic veiling of bodies. Society provides no way for natural curiosity to be satisfied.

This is not true at a nude beach. Anyone curious about what bodies look like has only to go to the beach and look. There are no secrets. Whereas formerly every body was another curiosity, at the beach the curiosity is satisfied before it is even aroused, and all this is accomplished within the norms of propriety, without offending anyone's personal privacy.

Thus, any "war on voyeurism" is best fought by simply removing the fuel from the fire rather than further fanning the flames as though to attempt to blow it out. Veils (AKA clothes) are the fuel. Society can remove this fuel simply by seeing that normal social propriety includes enough occasions where there are no veils. Beaches and bathing facilities are two good examples.

Repression

Another possible response is to resign ourselves to the fact that such knowledge is just "*verboten,*" and as soon as the question arises in our minds, dispel it by telling ourselves it is simply not morally knowable. This was precisely how the vast majority of Christians in our culture were taught to deal with such curiosity. In fact, it was defined as true chastity of mind.

But can these constantly recurring questions be harmlessly sublimated? Are they really dispelled, or are they perhaps relegated to depths even more morbid than the voyeur's, destined to eventually rumble and erupt in a destructive volcanic explosion? If the voyeur is *neurotic*, is the sublimator possibly *psychotic*?

Might this possibly be a key to disorders such as pedophilia? The typical voyeur is not a *bona-fide* "sicko"; he is likely an ordinary guy who just wonders what he might see if that girl sunbathing on her belly with her top undone were to turn over. He probably is not going to rape little children or jump in front of them on their way home from school and "flash" them.

I am no psychologist, but I do have some common sense. According to this latter wisdom, "Every action has an equal and opposite reaction." Therefore, what has been sublimated has not been dispelled. Instead, it has been stored away somewhere and is a time bomb waiting to explode.

The voyeur at least has an occasional valve. That sunbather actually does sometimes turn over, or at least show briefly some of what he longs to see. My sister and neighborhood friends did see something when my towel was yanked off, despite my pitiful, compensatory attempts to mitigate the consequences by covering my crotch with my hands. Since the voyeur does sometimes get what he is hunting, it pays him to hunt. Our society has actually deemed him "normal," and this explains why no one blames him for paying for *Playboy* along with his pills at the local pharmacy. This is why Howard Stearn was allowed to be on the air during prime time. This is why fashion accepts voyeurism as a given, and designs new modes of "veils" accordingly. This is why movies considered practically "family fare" contain at least some sexual nudity. All such gimmicks provide a valve, and society defines this as "normal" and thus "healthy."

But there is no socially acceptable valve for the sublimator. He is destined for dementia. Worse than merely offending against proprieties like personal privacy, the sublimator might end up committing actual serious crimes such as various forms of sexual assault.

In 2004, with the authorization of the U.S. Catholic bishops, the John Jay College of Criminal Justice of the City University of New York released a report revealing that in the previous 53 years 4,450 clergymen had sexually abused minors. The vast majority of these men were reputed to be upright and even pious. Few fit the stereotype of the sexual predator. But obviously, they were very sick individuals. Was their problem possibly abetted, if not caused, by a culture that taught a negative, repressive mode of chastity? If they had been reared in a Christian naturism that saw both the body and sexuality in the *positive* way in which God originally intended, would we not have a healthier priesthood and healthier marriages?

It is no secret that Catholics born before the 60s were "famous" for their apparently exaggerated "modesty." There were even sodalities, leagues and "armies" dedicated to ensuring that elbows and knees were never exposed.

You non-Catholics, and you younger Catholics cannot fully understand our upbringing in the 60s and earlier. The well-meaning Sisters of St. Joseph already had us practically neurotic wrecks by third grade. I was not the only seven year old who confessed to Monsignor Mullarkey (no kiddin'—that *was* his name!) having already committed adultery countless times. It would be nearly another seven years before I found out what adultery really was! There were (are) many of my generation and older who, to this day, feel "naughty" simply going to the toilet. I know it was a milestone *for me* to realize that it was not sacrilegious to pray on the toilet! After all, a little constipation ought to induce even hardened sinners to cry out from the depths for mercy!

That was about when I self-diagnosed that something was not right and began to ask questions and demand intelligent answers.

But suppose I had become an Augustinian priest like the blackfriars who staffed my prep school. Suppose, in my zeal for "purity" I had avoided all valves, thinking I was *dispelling* temptation when I was actually merely putting it in a pressure cooker, sublimating that natural curiosity. Suppose I had not begun to ask reasonable questions about the body and its functions. By now (age 52) might that repressed volcano not have exploded in quite undesirable, unwholesome and criminal ways as we read in the newspapers daily about so many priests and bishops? Many defend these perverts for being sincere, pious churchmen. Of course! That is just what I would have been, taking my pastoral ministry most seriously. But that has nothing to do with that subliminal volcano brewing for eventual, violent eruption, its floods of molten lava destined to destroy innocent villages. As St. Augustine said, "There, but for the grace of God, go I." Were it not for certain valves in my childhood, the number quoted above in the John Jay College report might well have been 4,451.

So we have now waged the "war on pedophile priests" just like our "war on terrorism." Our short-sighted objective is to find these "bums," yank off their Roman collars and lock them up where fellow inmates might well murder them, according to that so-called code of honor among thieves.[1].

Yeah, so? That's like a teenager squeezing his pimples and painting them with "Clearasil." The objective ought to be to discover the *sources* of such perversion and *do what it takes* to eradicate them.

I am *not* saying that "gettin' nekkid" will solve all the world's problems, but I *am* saying that society needs to find *positive, wholesome* ways to fulfill natural physical curiosity, or else it will pay the price in terms of volcanic devastations. If we really care about the innocent children preyed upon by these pervs, then we must not only restrain the aggressors from doing more harm, but we must recreate a society where those youths can themselves grow in a truly healthy way: "A healthy mind in a healthy body!"[2]

When we allow Boy Scouts to line up at toilet stalls in men's locker rooms to change into their bathing suits, although we may not be guilty of actual, perverted aggression, we are nonetheless guilty of fomenting an unhealthy environment. Ironically and foolishly, we condemn the monsters created by the "chaste" leaders whom we praise. Those responsible for allowing boys to change in locker room toilet stalls rather than in front of their lockers, are perhaps as perverted as those whom they derogate as "sickos."

In my own diocese of Burlington, Vermont, a handful of priests were removed from active ministry on account of allegations of child sex abuse. According to a very trustworthy priest friend of mine, the "crime" of one of them was simply changing into his bathing suit in a male locker

---

[1] E.g. On August 23, 2003, one of the Boston Archdiocese's most notorious, serial child molesters, Fr. John J. Geoghan, was brutally strangled to death at Souza-Baranowski Correctional Center in Shirley, Massachusetts, by a fellow inmate, Joseph L. Druce.

[2] "*Mens sana in corpore sano*," an ancient Roman proverb, has long been appropriated as the motto of many nudist organizations.

room where parish boys could see him. Heavens, God forbid! Those who maligned him are at least as perverted as bona-fide child sex abusers. The "purity" of such self-righteous Catholics is false, and perhaps, in God's eyes, more wicked than the lusty sins of many a lecher.

Chaste Naturism

Non-sexual nudity must be normal in culture. Natural nudity should be *de rigueur* in locker rooms, preferably of both genders, but even one's own gender is better than none at all. The gang shower ought to be standard custom as it once was, rather than individual stalls or no showers at all, as is usually the norm nowadays. At least *some* nudity should be normal at every beach and pool. By fastidiously veiling certain body parts we are proclaiming the false message that people are *parts*, and worse, "acceptable" parts and "unacceptable" parts.

By rearing children to see people as parts, we do violence to the very unity that images the One God. We are not parts. We are wholes.

Most influential education occurs in the home. Nudity in the home ought to be a daily event from infancy. Bathrooms should be openly shared. No one should hide to change clothes. Toddlers should be allowed to scamper around in the altogether. Indeed, it is "home," after all, and thus all ages ought to think nothing of being nude for comfort's sake. Especially if such homes are also places of prayer, and true chastity is understood and practiced, it is hard to see how any perv could be bred in such a wholesome environment. Before children were aware of asking the question, "What does the body look like?", they would already have found their answers. Such answers should be as ready to hand as any other. To deny natural curiosity about the body is to begin the creation of an ungodly, artificial, false mystique. It is to impose a problem where there naturally is no problem, as all creation is "very good."[1]

Moralistic gainsayers will accuse *us* of morbidly drawing attention to the body, but the reverse is true. *We* draw

---

[1] Cf. Genesis 1:31.

attention to nothing; *they* draw morbid attention to what they make such an almighty fuss about hiding.

Man is not a jumble of parts, but an integral whole. He is a unified entity. God created us in His image, and perhaps His most essential attribute is that He is One.[1]

By rearing children to see people as *parts* ("clean" parts and "dirty" parts), we do violence to the very *unity* that images the *One* God. *We are not parts. We are wholes.* Only this third response (i.e. chaste naturism) recognizes this fact and builds on it as on a foundation. The other two options (i.e. voyeurism, repression) deny this fact and are thus based on untruth. Virtue and godliness must be based on truth. Only chaste naturism accords with truth since it presents the body for exactly what it is as God created it. Catholics should abandon their former, failed, negative approach to purity and strive to imbibe culture with chaste naturism.

The Naked Pilgrim

Autobiographical Fiction by Jim C. Cunningham

In the middle of apparently nowhere, the rickety, old, Jordanian bus screeched its rusty brakes as it slowed down and came to a complete stop. Père Michel, the priestly Parisian leader of this Holy Land pilgrimage was just closing his rabbit-eared, omnipresent *Jerusalem Bible* as he finished his conference on Jesus' temptations in the desert.

"Here we are! Okay, everybody, take a final drink of water and let's begin our two hour hike to the camp. Leave everything possible on the bus, but be sure to take your hat."

We filed out anxiously, not knowing what to expect. It was only mid-morning, but the sun was already very hot in this arid desert.

As soon as the last pilgrim got off the bus, the Arabic driver shouted, "*Au revoir, mes amis!*" The doors slammed

---

[1] Cf. Deuteronomy 6:4; Galatians 3:20; I Corinthians 8:4 & 8; James 2:19; et al.

shut, and the old bus drove off into hazy oblivion, leaving a trail of rising dust in his wake. In a couple of minutes we could no longer either hear his broken muffler or smell the burning oil from his leaky engine. The intense, impending quiet began to descend on the small group of pilgrims— twenty-two Frenchmen of college age, and me, the only American.

"The purpose of this prayer walk is to experience the same environment that Jesus experienced," instructed the young assistant chaplain from the *Basilique du Sacre Coeur de Montmartre* in Paris.

"What you see, feel and hear is exactly the same as it was for Jesus, nearly two thousand years ago. Think of Him alone here, in this very valley, fasting for forty days and forty nights. Experience the solitude. Let it really saturate you. I see Marie and Jacques have their Rosaries in hand. I suggest that you put them away. Instead, walk here alone with God. Let the austerity of the environment be your prayer form. There must be no talking or even whispering, no hand signals. Keep your eyes on the desert and not each other. Hike in single file, and not too close to one another. Any questions before we begin?"

I think many of us wished we had had some questions, but nervously, we said we were ready to go.

The "road" was most generously called such. It was barely a sandy track passing through a rather narrow desert valley. Stark, barren, forbidding cliffs rose up to the left and to the right. My eyes combed them, searching for whatever—something—anything—to look at! I saw what appeared to be holes in the rock face—maybe caves. Had Jesus slept in one of these? I thought of His baptism by John in the Jordan River, not too far to the west.

What a theophany that must have been! John had been baptizing Jews by hordes. Scripture says, "Then went out to him Jerusalem and all Judea and all the region about the Jordan."[1] He was quite the craze. I tried to imagine thousands of people at the river bank, removing their robes before going down with John into the flowing water. "Surely that would not go over too well today," I mused, unable to imagine even our little group of pilgrims naked together in the Jordan.

---

[1] Matthew 3:5.

"No, I must not think of such impure thoughts. Jesus, I say with You Who might have been tempted right in this very valley, 'Get thee hence behind me, Satan!'"[1]

The haunting silence of the desert seeped deeper and deeper under my skin.

I returned to my meditation a bit frustrated, not knowing how to continue it without having impure thoughts about all that nudity. I took a deep breath of the hot, dusty air and prayed thrice, "O Mary, conceived without sin, pray for me who have recourse to thee."

I looked ahead at the single file of pilgrims walking before me. The women wore long, cotton dresses; the men, lightweight pants. Henri had removed his shirt and placed it on his head, Arabian style, protecting his head and neck from the increasing heat of the sun. His partial nakedness prompted me to try to imagine our whole group naked together in the Jordan, being baptized by John. It was hardly thinkable. "What a foolish thought," I said to myself, "but why? Why was it not foolish two thousand years ago?"

Then I imagined Jesus coming up to John, asking for baptism.

"Lord, I should be baptized by You! I am not worthy of scraping the camel dung from Your sandals!"[2] Thus he had humbly objected.

"Give in for now," Jesus had replied, "if we are to fulfill all justice."[3]

With that admonition, the saintly John gave in, resuming his role as valet, beginning to undress the Master for the ceremonial bath. As he had just alluded, he began by unfastening His sandal straps.

Soon they were descending naked together into the Jordan River as they had done so many times before as boys, but back then it had been much further north, in Galilee. Often they had played together while Mary and Elizabeth had washed the laundry on the rocks in the swift current.

But this time it was infinitely more solemn than a boyhood skinny-dip. Now a throng of thousands watched

---

[1] Matthew 4:10.
[2] Cf. John 1:27.
[3] Matthew 3:15.

in hushed awe. There was something indescribably serious and sacred about these two holy men.

As the pilgrims noiselessly hiked on, I meditated further on the baptism of Christ.

After immersing Jesus, John headed back towards the bank. Suddenly a deep, booming voice was heard from the skies, "This is My beloved Son in Whom I am well pleased."[1]

And to make it clear that Jesus, not John, was the subject of this divine pronouncement of praise, a beautiful dove suddenly appeared, hovering directly over Jesus' head, as the special star had once hovered over His manger,[2] and that brilliant dove literally alighted right on His wet, naked Body.[3]

Then began Christ's temptation in the desert. He exited the Jordan on the east side, and walked away from the crowds into the desert. Maybe He even trod this very same desert track.

"But what about His robe and sandals?" I suddenly wondered. "Did He enter His forty-day sojourn in the desert absolutely naked? I remembered certain desert saint hermits who actually did live naked out here. St. Mary of Egypt would bear the heat of this sun without any protection, and at night, she would sleep in the severe cold with no blanket. She did all this as penance for her sins.

My light exercise, combined with the unrelenting heat of the sun gradually rising toward its zenith in the cloudless, azure sky, caused me to perspire so much that my shirt was now so wet and clammy with sweat that it was uncomfortably sticking to my body. I considered removing my shirt like Henri, but decided to imitate St. Mary of Egypt not in her nakedness, but in her penance. I put up with the rolling sweat and my parched throat. Another hour or so and we'd be in camp anyway.

"After all," I thought, "if Jesus was so tough and austere as to go without food and drink non-stop for forty days and forty nights, then it's not that hard to believe He was naked all that time too.

---

[1] Matthew 3:17.
[2] Cf. Matthew 2:9.
[3] Cf. Matthew 3:16.

"Too bad we are so hung-up about nudity nowadays," I mused. "These young French women should not necessarily be considered immodest if they had nothing on instead of those dresses." I tried for a moment to imagine Solange, who was walking directly in front of me, without her dress on. I began to feel sexual arousal, so I banished the impure thought, and thrice repeated the prayer to Immaculate Mary.

"But why must I feel this way? She is pure. Were she hiking this prayer walk naked, she would not have immodest motives like the whores who display their wares on Montmartre, or the lewd dancers at the *Moulin Rouge*. "We are pure. Our intentions are pure, aren't they, Jesus?" I asked, as I continued my meditative hike.

As we rounded a bend around a hill, I thought I was seeing a mirage. In the distance I thought I saw a real waterfall full of naked people.

As we drew closer, I saw that the waterfall was indeed real, and so were the people, but they were not totally naked; they were wearing shorts or something. My wondering whether these bare-chested bathers included women was short-lived. As I drew closer, I could see that every single one of them had substantial facial hair. These were Bedouin men encamped here at this oasis. They waved to us, and we, a bit confused, waved back.

Where were the women? As we entered the camp, the answer became clear. The women were working outside their black, goat-skin tents, watering the camels, airing out the bedding, beating their carpets, and cooking on open fires. They were totally covered in black robes, except for their eyeballs. They did wave, timidly, but continued about their domestic chores. Children scampered about gleefully ululating like children anywhere. Seeing us, some of the younger ones hid behind the substantial folds of their mothers' robes, sheepishly and impishly sneaking peeks at us exotic intruders.

"This is ridiculous," I thought. "If the Bedouin men can strip half-naked and cool off in the waterfall, why can't their women?" I was experiencing the clash of cultures.

"Indeed, if 'modesty' says it's okay for the Bedouin men to be almost naked (some wore only their boxer shorts), while these women are totally covered, then it's not such a big step for us Westerners who are half naked compared to the Bedouins, to simply redefine complete nakedness as 'modest,' just as it must have been defined two thousand years ago when John the Baptist baptized thousands of naked Jews."

We ascended a hill at the periphery of the camp, and saw our dusty, old, rickety bus. The grinning driver greeted us in his best French and opened the doors for us. Eagerly, we entered and got a tall drink, and ate some flat-bread and salty, brittle goat-cheese. Our "*grande silence*" had ended at the waterfall, and everybody was excitedly talking about taking a plunge into the waterfall pool not only to cool off, but also to wash off the dust that had become a fine layer of mud on our sweaty bodies. Some had already changed into their bathing suits and happily ran off with their towels.

"You know, Jacques," I began, chomping an open goat-cheese sandwich and gulping some Tang, "it ain't right for those Arabs to be frolicking in the falls like that, while their women slave away buried in black."

"*Oui*, Jim, cultures are so different. I am certain our girls are glad they are not Jordanians!"

No sooner had he said this, then the first group of pilgrim bathers returned to the bus, extremely upset.

"*Mon Dieu*! We almost got raped!" exclaimed Solange, who was so upset that she was crying. "Those men are animals!"

"They actually threw a rock at me!" shouted Marie, obviously most distraught, her towel pulled around her bare shoulders and over her chest as far as possible.

She continued, "I thought it was too bad for the Bedouin women, but I didn't think they would hold us French girls to the same miserable standard! Why, back home in Bordeaux, boys and girls on the beach wear just *le minimum*—in fact, sometimes even nothing at all—and no one is ever treated this way! They made us feel worse than dirt." She was visibly shaking all over.

Père Michel listened with concern. "I forgot to warn you ladies. You ran off in such a hurry. I am very sorry. I'm afraid we must nevertheless be polite. This is not

Bordeaux, eh? You all know the expression, "When in Rome—"

"—do as the Romans do!" everyone chimed in together in spontaneous unison, prompting a chuckle that began to relax us all a bit.

"That's right. Sometimes Romans do fun things; sometimes not so much fun. I'm afraid you ladies will just have to do extra penance. Maybe you can offer it up for those oppressed Bedouin women," the good priest suggested.

"Well, we'll have to, but it's not fair," grumbled Solange, sure to get the last word.

"If the girls can't go swimming, then I don't think *any* of us boys should go either," generously offered Henri, sympathetically.

"No, no," assured Marie, "you boys ought to be able to go and cool off. Rome is Rome."

"*Oui*, you boys go ahead, urged Pauline. "It's okay. We're big girls. After all, better for *half* of us to be clean and refreshed than none of us at all." Then, pointing behind the bus, she continued, "Look! While you are gone we will go above the falls over there and splash in the hot wadi as best we can. Go on, now. Find out what those men have to say about the experience."

Reluctantly, our fun greatly spoiled by this culture shock, we males of the group changed into our bathing suits and went down to the falls.

The Bedouin men were having an animated discussion in Arabic, no doubt about the French women. They acted a bit stand-offish at first, but once Henri and Jacques began showing off doing diving stunts from a ledge about twenty feet high, they started loosening up again. One badly executed flip resulted in a spectacular, and most humorous belly flop. Upon contact, Henri let out some French word I did not understand, but the Bedouins evidently did, because they practically keeled over laughing.

One Arab spoke decent English. I approached him, "Excuse me. My name is Jim, from Boston in America."

"Ah, Boston? I have a brother in Somerville! Hello, I am Hammudi."

I was taken aback, picturing this one family so culturally divided. From this remote, back water oasis to the back yard of Harvard University and M.I.T. My mind could not contain such drastic dichotomy.

"Our women were very upset, you know," I began. "They meant no harm; they just wanted to rinse off after a two hour hike through this stifling desert."

"Yes, yes, I know, but this is no beach on Cape Cod! What would *our* women think?" he began to reason with me.

"Well, I suppose they'd be a bit jealous. But why can't they bathe here, too?" I asked.

"Ah! But it is not for *us* to make things up—not for *us*. We have traditions that go back to the Great Prophet, Mohammed. There is no changing *that*!"

"But you Bedouins drive buses and do other modern things not authorized by the Koran don't you?" I argued.

"No, no, that's different. Our mullahs and lawyers know about those things. Buses and Scud missiles are okay; Naked women are not."

"Naked? But they weren't *naked*!" I continued to argue, barely controlling my Irish testiness.

"Hey, you smart American. You see our women?"

"Yes—" I replied, unsure where he was going with this.

"Well, let me tell you, *your* women were n-a-k-e-d!"

I got his point. What one considers to be "naked" is a relative thing indeed. I knew it was useless to continue my polemics, and if Rome wasn't built in one day, I was certainly not going to rebuild Mecca in one day.

"Nice weather we're having," I said disheartedly, changing the subject, and gradually walked to the edge of the pool and dried off in the more than 100° air. "Culture can be so silly—so ridiculous and unfair," I thought to myself. "Heck, why can't everybody in the whole world just go naked and there'd be no big deal anymore? But then, Rome surely wasn't built in one day..." I reminded myself.

I walked back up the hill behind the falls with the Frenchmen. When we arrived, Père Michel was setting up a portable altar outdoors, while the women were unloading their sleeping gear from the bus.

"Père Michel, Where will we sleep tonight?" Marie asked, still looking quite hot and unrefreshed, despite her humbly accepted "splash" in the wadi.

"*O, pardon moi, ma cher,*" he replied apologetically. "We're staying in that stone pavilion over there." He pointed to the very top of the hill overlooking the entire camp. It was only a stone's throw away, but with all the excitement earlier, we had not even noticed it. Marie walked over to it with her overnight gear.

"Hey, there are no windows? And where's the door?" she wondered out loud.

Henri had run on behind the building and came racing back.

"*Amis! Mes Amis!* It's wonderful! The door's in the back. No, there are no windows—just three-meter high walls, and no roof. But guess what?" he baited us. "The wadi flows right through the center into a large stone pool, and out the other side. If that water weren't so hot, we could've had a pool party—French style—forget this Moslem madness! But it won't work. The water is hot enough to boil tea."

"We know," replied Marie, "we could hardly even splash in it up there above the falls. How could you boys stand it down at the waterfall?"

"It was actually rather cool and fresh after it fell over the falls through the air," explained Jacques.

"Oh, well, let's lay out our sleeping bags anyway and get set up for dinner and the night," suggested Pauline.

After everyone had found their space around the rectangular pool of hot water we gathered outside for Mass.

The readings were perfectly apropos—about bearing wrongs patiently. "All things come to him who waits," was the theme of the homily. At the consecration Père Michel always seemed a transformed man. He sort of went into another world. Instead of just elevating the Body of Christ and getting on with Mass, he would often do what he called a "adoration Mass" during which he would take the just consecrated Host and display it in a holder atop the chalice of the Precious Blood. Everyone would then pause for about fifteen minutes in complete silence and just bask in the Eucharistic Lord's Real Presence.

During this adoration, it came to me with the utmost clarity: "This is the Body and Blood of Jesus Christ. This is His perfect humanity in all His fullness. This is the whole Christ, and nothing but Christ. Of course, He is naked here before our eyes. His clothes did not rise from the dead. The soldiers rolled dice for his clothes,[1] and Peter and John saw the entombing linens laying on the floor of the tomb.[2] Of course, there are no clothes in heaven. Jesus did not come to save cotton and polyester. This is Jesus' whole Body here—Head, arms, legs, torso—and yes, penis, too! All is worthy. All is dignified and sacred."

Three Scripture passages came at me like arrows: 1) The words addressed to St. Peter in the Acts of the Apostles: "What God has declared holy, let no man call unclean."[3] 2) At the Last Supper: "Take and eat, this is My Body, given up for you."[4] and 3) In John 6:53 "Unless you eat My Body and drink My Blood, you have no life in you."

I then scanned our little congregation of two dozen Christians in that overwhelmingly Moslem place. These friendly faces gazing in attentive awe all belonged to that Body enthroned above (and in) the chalice that they were all adoring. And not merely their faces, but also all those other parts the Moslems considered so unclean and indecent. Indeed, many Christians down through the years have not been much more enlightened than these Moslems either. But not only each one of us, but *all* of each of us are members of His Mystical Body. How holy He is, and how truly holy are we in Him. My adoration of the naked Christ under the appearance of bread was now extended to the naked Christ in His people—His Church—His Mystical Body in Pauline, Henri, Jacques, Solange, Marie, Père Michel, and all the others. As I had tried unsuccessfully to do on our silent prayer walk, I tried now to do again: I imagined everybody being here without clothes in adoration of the naked Christ. Soon *we*—not our clothes, jewelry, etc.—would leap into His infinity, and He, simultaneously, in Holy Communion, would plunge

---

[1] Cf. John 19:23f.
[2] Cf. John 20:5ff.
[3] Acts 10:15.
[4] Luke 22:19.

341

into our depths, becoming truly our food, our never-ending life. Now, however there was not the slightest temptation of sexual arousal. We were all simply and purely brothers and sisters in the Lord. Like me, the Seraphim were not just adoring Christ on the altar; they were also adoring Him *in us*. Our bodies, His true temple, were actually far more sacred than that golden Host-holder or that bejeweled chalice. Those vessels merely housed Christ; we—bodies and souls—were, through baptism, a real, though mystical part of that Precious Body.

I was awe-struck at all this. The fifteen minutes had passed so quickly that I felt jolted, and somewhat jilted, when Père Michel got up off his knees, brushed the dust from his linen alb, and resumed the Liturgy. I felt such pure, effulgent joy. How sweet it was when we came to the Lord's Prayer, and, hugging each other around the little portable altar, prayed as one person in Christ, "Our Father, Who art in Heaven..."

Supper followed, and everyone was much lighter and more relaxed than when we had first arrived. After dessert, Henri took out his guitar and began playing by the pool. Pauline joined on her flute. They played so beautifully. The sweet music resonated cleanly off the stone walls and ascended to the glimmering stars which were now appearing by the handful every minute. A nearly full moon suddenly appeared over one of the walls, the soft, lush moonbeams gently flooding the interior court. On a lark, Jacques reached down into the pool and felt the water with his hand.

"*Mon Dieu!* The water—it is fresh! It is really cool!" he exclaimed.

Everyone rushed over to feel the miracle.

"The cold night desert sand! But of course!' shouted Henri.

Then eyes looked up at each other all huddled around the pool, and the widest grins I have ever seen began to break out on everybody's face. The glee and joy was so intense, I thought those walls would make Jericho's walls child's play. Without asking any questions, every single one of us began undressing. Reacting to the traumatic experience we had had several hours earlier, there was no thought at all of silly bathing suits. Everybody undressed right there right down to our birthday suits, and slipped into the cool, refreshing pool, the slow, wadi current gently flowing through it. Marie stood alone at one end of the pool, the moon shining on her sacred, naked body. Grinning triumphantly, she stretched out her arms to the twinkling stars above and unabashedly looking Père Michel right in the eye, said, "Hey, Père Michel! What were you saying at Mass about those who wait?"

And we laughed and splashed all night long. Not a typical Moslem pool party. Not a typical pilgrim pool party either. Not even a typical French pool party. No, it was a very special, unforgettable grace from our Blessed Lord, Jesus Christ.

On the Creation of Man

by Dietrich Bonhoeffer[1]

Yahweh shapes man with His Own hands. This expresses two things:

First, the bodily nearness of the Creator to the creature—that it is really He Who makes me, man, with His Own hands. His concern, His thought for me, His design for me, His nearness to me.

And secondly, there is His authority, the absolute superiority in which He shapes and creates me, and in which I am His creature. The Fatherliness in which He creates me and in which I worship Him—that is God Himself, to Whom the whole Bible testifies.

The man whom God has created in His image, i.e. in freedom, is the man who was formed out of earth. Darwin and Fauerbach could not themselves speak more strongly.

---

[1] This excerpt from the great Lutheran theologian, who was hanged for participating in a plot to assassinate Adolph Hitler, appears as the first entry in a Bonhoeffer anthology entitled, *The Martyred Christian*, edited by Joan Windmill Brown, published by Collier. This selection is entitled, "Created in His Image," and was taken from pp. 46f of Bonhoeffer's own book, *Creation and Fall*, also published by Collier. All italics, Jim C. Cunningham. The theology here expressed makes for a very solid foundation for naturism. Perhaps this is why history has proven Germany to be such a fertile seed-ground for social nudity.

Man's origin is in a piece of earth. His bond with the earth belongs to his essential being. The earth is his mother; he comes out of her womb.

Of course, the ground from which man is taken is still not the cursed, but the blessed ground. It's God's earth out of which man is taken. From it he has his "body."

His body belongs to his essential being. Man's body is not his prison, his shell, his exterior, but man himself. Man does not "have" a body; he does not "have" a soul. Rather, he *is* body and soul. Man in the beginning is really his body. He is one. He is his body as Christ is completely His Body, as the Church is the Body of Christ. The man who renounces his body renounces his existence before God, the Creator. The essential point of human existence is its bond with mother earth—its being as body. Man has his existence as existence *on earth*. He does not come to the earthly world from above, driven and enslaved by a cruel fate. He comes out of the earth in which he slept and was dead. He is called out by the Word of God the Almighty, in himself a piece of earth, but earth called into human being by God. "Awake, thou that sleepest, and arise from the dead, and Christ shall shine upon thee."[1]

Michelangelo also meant this. Adam, resting on the newly created ground, is so closely and intimately bound up with the ground on which he lies, that he himself, in his still dreaming existence, is strange and marvelous to the highest degree. But just the same, he is a piece of earth. Surely it is in this full devotion to the blessed ground of creation's earth, that the complete glory of the first man becomes visible. And in this resting on the ground, this deep sleep of creation, man experiences life through bodily contact with the finger of God. The same hand that has made man, touches him tenderly, as from afar, and awakens him to life. God's hand does not hold man in its embrace any longer, but it sets him free, and its creative power becomes the demanding love of the Creator toward the creature. The hand of God portrayed by the picture in the Sistine Chapel reveals more wisdom about the creation than many a deep speculation.

---

[1] Ephesians 5:14.

"And God breathed into his nostrils the breath of life, and man became a living being."[1] Here, body and life enter into one another totally. God breathes His Spirit into the body of man, and this Spirit is life and makes man alive. God creates other life through His Word. Where man is concerned, He gives of His life, of His Spirit. Man as man does not live without God's Spirit. To live as "man" means to live as body in Spirit. Escape from the body is escape from being man, and escape from the Spirit as well. Body is the existence form of Spirit, as Spirit is the existence form of body.

All this can be said only of man, for only in man do we know of body and Spirit. The human body is distinguished from all non-human bodies by being the existence form of God's Spirit on earth, as it is wholly undifferentiated from all other life by being from this earth. The human body really only lives by God's Spirit; this is indeed its essential nature. God glorifies Himself in the body—in this specific form of the human body.

For this reason God enters into the body again, where the original, in its created being, has been destroyed. He enters it in Jesus Christ. He enters into it where it is broken—in the form of the sacrament of the Body, and of the Blood. The Body and the Blood of the Lord's Supper are the new realities of creation—of the promise for the fallen Adam. Adam is created as body, and therefore he is also redeemed as body, in Jesus Christ and in the sacrament. Man thus created is man as the image of God. He is the image of God, not in spite of, but just because of his bodiliness, for in his bodiliness he is related to the earth and to other bodies... In his bodiliness he finds his brother and the earth. As such a creature, man... is in the likeness of his Creator—God.

John Donne (1571-1631)

Full nakedness! All joys are due to thee,
as souls unbodied, bodies unclothed must be,
to taste whole joys.

---

[1] Genesis 2:7.

What Would People Think?

by Jim C. Cunningham

What would people think of a guy who stood up at a civic center planning commission meeting and suggested that when the new structure is completed, the ceiling and walls should be decorated with nudes?[1]

What would people think of men who, at a meeting of a new, prestigious, family club, suggested that the initiation ceremony for new member families should require the applicants to take off all their clothes—men, women and children all together—while all the other members watch, and not get dressed again until the ceremony was over?[2]

What would people think of a man who, when asked his opinion on what type of insignia should mark the members of a club, suggested that the heads of all male penises be exposed by the surgical removal of their foreskins?[3]

What would people think of a bishop who commanded a preacher to go stark naked for three entire years, openly preaching to the public from pulpits and street corners?[4]

What would people think of a man who goes fishing with his buddies, trolling in a large boat, but takes off all his clothes and fishes in the nude?[5]

What would people think of a group of priests who kept vigil together all night—in the nude?[6]

What would people think of a man who would not give his noble daughter in marriage unless the would-be groom acquired one hundred foreskins of the enemy to be carefully counted out in his presence?[7]

---

[1] That man was Michelangelo and the building is the Sistine Chapel.

[2] Those men were the Fathers of the Church, like Sts. Hippolytus of Rome and Cyril of Jerusalem. The initiation ceremony is, of course, baptism.

[3] Such was God's idea as revealed to Abraham in Genesis 17:10ff.

[4] Such God commanded Isaiah in Isaiah 20:2ff.

[5] That man is the rock upon whom Christ built His Church (cf. Matthew 16:18), St. Peter (cf. John 21:7).

[6] Such was the custom of gatherings of prophets in the Old Testament (cf. I Samuel 19:20-24).

[7] Such was the dowry King Saul required of David for his daughter, Michal (cf. I Samuel 18:25 & II Samuel 3:14).

What would people think of that would-be groom if his zeal was such that he doubled the curious dowry?[1]

What would people think of a king who danced in the city streets, exposing himself?[2]

What would people think of a bishop who promoted nude wrestling as the ideal Christian sport?[3]

What would people think of a man who, while receiving a solemn promise from someone, required him to put his hand in his pants and hold his genitals while he made his promise?[4]

What would people think of an employer who required job applicants to show him their genitals, proving that their penises were not cut off or their testicles crushed?[5]

What would people think of a bishop who required newly ordained priests to let him strip them naked and give them a bath in front of the congregation?[6]

What would people think of border guards who required immigrants not only to show them their valid passports, but to show them their penises as well, requiring those with intact foreskins to submit to circumcision before entering, and who made such a huge heap of foreskins that they named it Foreskin Hill?[7]

What would people think of monks and nuns who chose perpetual nudity for their religious habit?[8]

What would people think of an archbishop who insisted on witnessing a doctor's inspection of the vaginas of all prospective first ladies of a bachelor president?[9]

---

[1] Such David did (cf. I Samuel 18:26).

[2] Such did the king whose heart was like unto God's (cf. I Samuel 13:14), David (cf. II Samuel 6:14-23).

[3] That man was St. Clement of Alexandria.

[4] Such Abraham required of his servant (cf. Genesis 24:2f) and Jacob required of Joseph (cf. Genesis 47:29).

[5] Such God required (cf. Deuteronomy 23:1).

[6] Such God told Moses to do to Aaron and his sons (cf. Leviticus 8:1-6).

[7] Such God required of Joshua as the Jews entered the Promised Land (cf. Joshua 5:2-9). The place was called "Gibeath-haaraloth" (cf. Joshua 5:3), which in Hebrew means, "Foreskin Hill."

[8] Such was the case with many anchorites, including Sts. Mary of Egypt, Onuphrius and Basil of Moscow.

[9] Such was the requirement in czarist Russia when the metropolitan of Muscovy assisted in validating the physical virginity of several fair maidens chosen to qualify for the final choice of the unmarried czar. Cf. Robert K. Massie, *Peter the Great* (New York: Alfred A. Knopf, 1980), p. 20f.

What would people think of a man who, when asked to give a metaphor of the consolation of God's goodness and bounty, suggested that it was like sucking on great, big, beautiful, buxom breasts?[1]

What would people think of an employee who played a prank on his boss by sneaking up on his boss while he was defecating and cut a piece off the back of his pants?[2]

What would people think of an archbishop who, every Easter season, led a solemn procession to the river, threw his crucifix in, and had all the altar boys strip naked and race, swimming and diving for it, and once retrieved, have the altar boys remain naked as they returned to the cathedral, the cross held high?[3]

What would people think of a man who, as a prophetic demonstration, takes off all his clothes in front of a village church with his family, bishop and fellow villagers all looking on?[4]

What would people think of an author who included a scene of two daughters who got their father drunk and took turns having sex with him? Would any respectable person keep such a pornographic book where children could access it?[5]

The honest answer to all the above questions is that people would think such men to be sexual perverts, exhibitionists, lechers, pornographers or at best, lunatics. The moral of this little study:

My thoughts are not your thoughts, neither are your ways My ways, says the LORD. For as the heavens are higher than the earth, so are My ways higher than your ways and My thoughts than your thoughts.[6]

---

[1] Such is the metaphor inspired by the Holy Spirit in Isaiah 66:11.

[2] Such David did to King Saul (cf. I Samuel 24:3f).

[3] Such was a traditional Easter ritual in Kiev.

[4] Such St. Francis of Assisi did as he began his new life in Christ, returning all to his covetous, earthly father and professing to be the son of his Father in heaven.

[5] The Bible is full of such "pornography." This episode is found in Genesis 19:31-36.

[6] Isaiah 55:8f.

The foolishness of God is wiser than men.[1]

Do not be conformed to this world but be transformed by the renewal of your mind, that you may prove what is the will of God, what is good and acceptable and perfect.[2]

Naked on the Cross

by Michael A. Kowalewski

"Having stripped yourselves, you were naked, imitating Christ, Who hung naked on the Cross... O wondrous thing! You were naked in sight of all, and were not ashamed..."[3]

In the pristine woods of Nova Scotia lies a Carmelite monastery.[4] Inside the rustic chapel I was awestruck by the incarnational, earthy mysticism expressed in their sacred art. The monks perceive nature, exalted by grace, as a means to enter God's embrace. The crucifix, above their stone altar, reveals Christ's natural nakedness, silently echoing the innocence of Paradise. From the dead wood of the cross blossoms a beautiful flower, a hint of the Resurrection. Christ's hand reaches down from the cross, and invites all believers to share in the grace of his suffering. As St. Rose said, "The only ladder to heaven is the cross," and so Christ, the Bridegroom, reaches out to His beloved bride.

Though naked crucifixes are a rarity in the Church, artists over the centuries have carved these sacred images. Michelangelo carved one in his youth. It is known as the "Santo Spirito Crucifix" and is displayed in his house, "Casa Buonarotti," in Florence. Also Benvenuto Cellini's white marble crucifix, intended for the artist's own tomb,

---

[1] I Corinthians 1:25.
[2] Romans 12:2.
[3] From St. Cyril of Jerusalem's *Mystagogy on Baptism*.
[4] Editor's note: The name of this monastery is "Nova Nada." This relatively new Carmelite branch has three communities of both monks and nuns. Recently, however, this one in Nova Scotia was evacuated. The others are in Colorado and Ireland.

evokes the cry of Job, "Naked was I conceived, and naked shall I die."[1]

When I first saw the naked crucifix, I was ashamed, but the holiness with which it was presented elevated my heart from senseless shame to veneration. The great Carmelite mystic, St John of the Cross, taught a doctrine of spiritual nakedness. The soul hides behind the fig leaf of religiosity, images, and ideas. The soul must strip off these hindrances, for it is only in the naked nothingness that the soul can climb the mystical mountain of divine union. Nakedness, first experienced as fear and shame, ultimately transcends into an inner freedom at which point the soul is no longer aware of its abandonment in the all consuming presence of God. The naked crucifix is a profound icon of Carmelite mysticism.

The mystical experience is a freedom of unclothing ourselves from worldly attachments and ego. Even religiosity can become, for many believers, an attachment—an end in itself, rather than a means to the end. So long as this continues, the purpose of religiosity is not served. The purpose of religiosity is to prepare our souls for the mystical. The fear of nakedness of spirit can lead us to hide behind vain good works and acts of piety in order to feel holy and close to God, yet in reality we are hiding from God, we are afraid of the nakedness of the cross.

Adam & Eve hid behind the fig leaf because of a lack of trust. Christ, the New Adam, is fully naked on the cross. This nakedness is a sign of contradiction as is the crucifixion in its entirety. Meant to be a sign of degradation, it becomes a triumphant sign of victory over, and detachment from, the powers and principalities of this world.

Any assertion that Christ was not completely stripped on the cross is the result of a false modesty that refuses to accept the full reality of the Christian mystery of salvation. In his Gospel, John the Evangelist gives an account of the stripping of Christ.[2] The Romans showed little mercy, humiliating their victims to the extreme. However, Christ's nakedness is more than a *historical* fact; it is of *theological* significance. Christ's nakedness is *sacramental*. It visibly

---

[1] Job 1:21.
[2] Cf. John 19:23ff.

350

communicates the poverty of spirit and purity of heart required for picking up our cross and following Christ. A Father of the Church, St Jerome, often said, "*Nudus nudum Iesum Sequi.*"[1]

Nakedness in the early Church was related to Christ as the New Adam. On the cross, Adam's garments of mortality have been divested. Jesus allows Himself to be stripped, so that in His nakedness He might restore to us the innocence lost by Adam & Eve. "The man and his wife were both naked, yet they felt no shame."[2]

Cyril of Jerusalem, in his *Mystagogy on Baptism*, exclaimed to the neophytes, "Having stripped yourselves, you were naked, imitating Christ, Who hung naked on the Cross... O wondrous thing! You were naked in sight of all, and were not ashamed; for truly you bore the likeness of the first-formed Adam, who was naked in the garden and was not ashamed."[3] Only Jesus Christ in His nakedness can free us from the shame of our own.

There is a prevalent fear of the body. Many popes reigning after Michelangelo were scandalized by naked bodies in a sacred building of worship and they had the nudes in the Sistine Chapel covered. But today we have a pope who, in the restoration project of the Sistine Chapel, ordered the removal of many of these loincloths. Pope John Paul II, when he rededicated the chapel, said that he dedicated this shrine to the theology of the body because Michelangelo was given the grace, like Adam & Eve, to behold the naked body in its truth. Man must learn to see the true language of the body, that the body is a gift of love, not an object of lust.

The Christian mystery, man's call to divine union, is revealed in and through the human body and man and woman's call to become one flesh. Many pious individuals would be shocked if someone told them that the naked body reveals God's love, or that sexual intercourse is an icon of the Holy Trinity and images the love between Christ and His Church. Yet this is precisely what Pope John Paul II asserts in "The Theology of the Body." He

---

[1] "Naked, I follow the naked Jesus." Found in St. Jerome, "Epistle 58 *Ad Paulinum.*"

[2] Genesis 2:25.

[3] From St. Cyril of Jerusalem's *Mystagogy on Baptism*.

declares that this Christian mystery is a scandal, even (and sometimes *especially*) for those who claim to be Christians. If such truth causes scandal, should it be talked about? St Thomas Aquinas states that if people are scandalized by the truth, it is better to allow the birth of scandal, than to abandon truth. There is a justified fear towards the body and sex because they have been so tragically misused and defiled. However, this fear must never hinder the realization of God's true purpose for our embodiment.

We tend to anesthetize and sanitize the Christian mystery in order to make it "comfortable" and appease our "prim and proper" sensibilities. In some ways this is understandable, but in the process many of us have become so detached from our humanity that we find it terribly difficult to face what Christ's Body actually reveals about the meaning of life. We must be bold in spirit and relearn the true language of the body. Redemption calls Man to see the mystery of God's love revealed in the body, revealed in His call as male and female to marriage, and that the body and sex are icons of the incarnation and Christ's love for the Church. The naked crucifix unveils this truth in all its simplicity and purity.

Our Lord in his spiritual and physical nakedness defeated the lies of Satan. People, who stood at the foot of the cross on Golgotha, would have seen Christ's circumcised penis. They would have known that he was a Jew. Christ the Son of God was a man, a fertile man. He was a true Bridegroom giving His Blood, which in Greek is translated "semen." St Paul says, "...a man shall leave his father and mother, and cleave to his wife; and the two shall become one flesh. This is a great mystery—I mean in reference to Christ and the Church."[1]

In modern culture we have sanitized this mystery. However, Renaissance art understood this well, at times portraying Christ with a voluntary erection, in the full virility of His manhood, most specifically at the moment of His passion. If you are shocked at this, continue to read for it is in your discomfort that you have something to learn. Far from being pornographic, such art was a response to that ever present temptation to deny the

---

[1] Ephesians 5:31f.

goodness of the body, to deny that Christ really became man. As Mary Rousseau states in her article "Eucharist and Gender," art that portrayed the virility of Christ was making a religious statement to the effect that "Yes, He really did have what it takes to generate new life in human beings, and it was functional."[1]

Portrayals of Christ on the cross with a voluntary erection were not blasphemous as we might be tempted to think. The artist conveys in his artistic symbolism of an erect penis that Jesus, in the exact moment of the utter depth of His love, also reached the height of His desire to generate new spiritual life. And that moment of most intense desire was also the moment of His fullest potency to do just what He desired. He wanted to, was able to, and did offer new life to sinners, even those who were then most directly causing His abjection. The crucifixion was the Eucharistic moment, the sacrament of the Bridegroom and the Bride, according to Pope John Paul II.

Remember it is the body that reveals spiritual reality. Christ had to have a Body capable of nuptial union and fatherhood in order to bring about His mystical nuptial union with the Church and generate new life in the Spirit.

There are numerous Old Testament passages that seem to foreshadow the indispensability of the Messiah's functioning genitalia. The animal sacrifices were fulfilled in the perfect sacrifice of Christ, the Lamb of God.[2] Animals that were sacrificed had to be unblemished. Any animal which had its testicles bruised, crushed, torn or cut could not be offered as a sacrifice.[3] Under the law, even men who had dysfunctional genitals could not participate in certain religious rituals.[4] This article does not assert that Christ did in fact have a voluntary erection on the cross. I only mean to bring to attention the symbolism artists of the Renaissance used to convey the depth of Christ's love and desire to become one flesh with His Church. Furthermore, it needs to be pointed out that

[1] *Catholic Dossier*, Sept-Oct '96, p. 20. For the theory of Christ's erection on the cross, also see Steinberg, Leo, *The Sexuality of Christ in Renaissance Art and In Modern Oblivion*, 2nd ed. (Chicago: University of Chicago Press, 1996), pp. 82-100ff.
[2] Cf. Hebrews 7:27.
[3] Cf. Leviticus 22:21-24.
[4] Cf. Leviticus 21:17 & 20; Deuteronomy 23:1.

Christ's love on the cross is related to conjugal love, not in *sensuality*, but in *charity*.

As described above, Christ's complete denudation on the cross is *historical*. To put a loincloth on what God allowed to be stripped off is a sign of our own fears regarding spiritual nakedness. Some individuals lack the purity to see what Christ's naked Body reveals. We become afraid and hide the nakedness behind a fig leaf.[1]

The body reveals the full grandeur of God. We are all still incapable of experiencing God fully and directly. The grandeur of God is so awesome and intense that to see him face to face in our present state of weakness would destroy us. The Eucharist can be seen as a buffer, giving a taste of our Bridegroom instead of the full heavenly consummation. The body is so powerful that clothing, for some individuals, becomes a necessary buffer. The grandeur of Christ's naked Body, "in which the fullness of deity dwells,"[2] is too much to handle, even for some Christians.

Carmelite nun Wendy Becket, an authority on art, gives an excellent example of this in her comments on the Botticelli masterpiece, "The Birth of Venus." Sr. Wendy states that Venus comes into the world naked. The saddest part of the story is that she is not permitted to step naked onto the land. Our world is not strong enough to receive such beauty. When Venus steps into our world, we shall cover her up, like Christ on the cross.

T. S. Eliot wrote that humankind could not bear too much reality. Love in its nakedness, beauty unadorned, is too luminous for us. We are challenged at some mysterious deep level of our being and some individuals are not ready to face this challenge. Our fears prevent us from entering courageously into the deepest mystery that is caught up into the fire of Trinitarian Love, the incarnation.

The naked crucifix reveals to us Salvation history. God is not concerned about the scandal the body may cause if it is for the purpose of revealing truth. God chose the penis to be the sign of the Old Covenant, which He established with Abraham.[3] The promise was that Abra-

---

[1] Cf. Genesis 3:7 & 10.
[2] Colossians 2:9.
[3] Cf. Genesis 17:10ff.

ham would have offspring as numerous as the stars.[1] The persons who saw the circumcised penis most often were husbands and wives in their marital relations. It would have been a reminder of God's promise to make Abraham exceedingly fruitful. The uncovering of the male genital organ points to nuptial union, life-givingness, and fatherhood.

It should not be assumed that only spouses saw the circumcision. It was not a private sign reserved for married couples. Circumcision was a visible witness to all of the promise of God's covenant, just as the New Covenant circumcision of the heart is now. St. Paul, in the New Testament, had St. Timothy circumcised. He was not married. St. Timothy was circumcised by St. Paul because Jews could easily see whether or not he was circumcised, and since St. Paul was into becoming "all things to all men,"[2] he had his disciple circumcised in order for him to be more effective as a preacher to the Jews.[3] Thus it is clearly implied that the congregation of Jews would ordinarily have had ample opportunity to see whether or not St. Timothy was circumcised.

Also, in the Old Testament First Book of Maccabees Jews sported naked in the gymnasium in Jerusalem, and hid not their *nakedness*, but their *circumcision*, ashamed to be Jewish.[4] In the New Testament this has significance when Jesus says, "If any man be ashamed of Me and My doctrine in this age, so will the Son of Man be ashamed of him in the age to come."[5]

The circumcision of flesh foreshadowed the circumcision of the heart made visible by the pierce of a lance through the Heart of Christ.[6] When Renaissance painters of Christ on the cross often chose to show Blood streaming from His side wound to His circumcised penis, they were revealing the history of Christ's passion. We have the beginning of salvation in the Circumcision that is linked with the completion of Christ's Circumcision of Heart.

---

[1] Cf. Genesis 22:17.
[2] I Corinthians 9:22.
[3] Cf. Acts 16:1-3.
[4] Cf. 1 Maccabees 1:14f.
[5] Luke 9:26.
[6] Cf. John 19:34.

God chose the penis as the sign of the Old Covenant, not only as a promise of many children, but of the nuptial love He wished to have with Israel. This covenant in the penis symbolizes the nuptial union predestined between God and humanity in the New Covenant with Christ. Christ's relationship with humanity is a nuptial love. He is a Bridegroom Who yearns to become "one flesh" with humanity.

Jesus' love for humanity was a masculine love, as made visible by His masculine Body. Pope John Paul II said, "Christ, in instituting the Eucharist... thereby wished to express the relationship between man and woman, between what is *feminine* and what is *masculine*. It is a relationship willed by God both in the mystery of creation and in the mystery of Redemption."[1] In other words, if you do not properly appreciate human sexuality, the mystery of creation, you cannot properly appreciate the mystery of Christ's redemptive love for His Church and furthermore, for the Eucharist.

St. John of the Cross in his poem, "Romance 9" on creation, poetically expresses this nuptial love of Christ for His Bride. I paraphrase:

Before there was anything, there was God, the Father, Son and Holy Spirit. God the Father says to His son, "It is time for You to have a Bride, so let Us create one for You. And You will love this Bride and ravish her with the divine splendors, the energies, the glories, everything that is Mine We will give to the Bride. You, My Son, will become one flesh with her and give her all the fullness of divinity. So, My Son, shall We create her?"

And the Son said, "Yes."

But then God gazed and said, "Well, Son, You do know what is going to happen? The Bride is not going to want to be the Bride. She will go after false gods and not love You. Your Bride will be a whore, a harlot in heat like a stallion with those who are not God and forsake the One Who loves her. If You are going to have a Bride, You will have to chase after her. You are going to have to win her love and become a Creator Yourself. You will become not only a Man, but also a Slave, not only dead, but also dead on a cross. You're going to have to chase her into the pit of

---

[1] John Paul II, *Mulieris Dignitatem*, N. 26.

hell and when she sins, You are going to have to become sin for her. When she curses, You are going to have to take upon Yourself the curse. When she kills herself and dies, You are going to die for her. Then maybe You will win your Bride and bring her back to the house of the Father."

So in other words, if the Son is going to have a Bride, it will not only be *incarnation*, it will have to be *humiliation, crucifixion,* and *death.*

The Father then asks the Son, "Are You sure you want to do this?"

The Son replies, "Yes, We must."

Then God said, "Let there be light!"

And the world began.

St. John of the Cross in his *The Ascent of Mount Carmel,* instructs us how to unburden ourselves of all earthly things, avoid spiritual obstacles, and live in that complete nakedness and freedom of spirit necessary for divine union. This is the nakedness of the cross. Christ held nothing back. Naked, the fullness of truth has been *literally* unveiled.

It would be dualistic not to relate physical nakedness to spiritual nakedness. Many saints and monks lived and prayed physically naked, such as St. Basil the Wonder Worker,[1] St. Onuphrius, St. Mary of Egypt. Such physical nakedness was an outward sign of the poverty and purity, reminiscent of the Garden of Eden. St. Francis, stripping himself naked, piled his clothes and what money he had in front of his father, saying: "Hitherto I have called Pietro Bernardone father; henceforth I will say, 'Our Father, Who art in Heaven.'" This moment marked a complete break for Francis with his past and the beginning of his life of abandonment to divine providence. This was not a nakedness of *shame,* but a nakedness of *liberation.* Spiritual-physical nakedness is a nakedness of poverty and purity, of abandonment and innocence. Blessed are the poor, the naked, for theirs is the Kingdom.[2] Blessed are the pure for they will see God[3]—*in the body.*

The garments of shame have no place in the Lord's Vineyard. The only way to climb the mystical Mount

---

[1] AKA St. Basil (Vasili) of Moscow.
[2] Cf. Matthew 5:3.
[3] Cf. Matthew 5:8.

Carmel, as described by St John of the Cross, is to be unconsciously naked, clothed in the strength of God. To be naked without God, is to be naked and ashamed: "God asked, 'Who told you that you were naked?'"[1] To be clothed in God is to be naked and so detached that one is not even aware of his nakedness. Hans Urs Von Balthasar eloquently expresses it thus: "...Jesus focuses on those who inwardly are so impoverished and emptied out that they have divested themselves of their inmost core, their 'conscience,' in order to yield the place to the Word of God..." It is in the poverty of the cross that we become divested of all the powers and principalities of this world. We become incarnations of Christ, the *Logos*, "naked and not ashamed."[2]

As man ascends Mount Carmel, he grows and transforms into the likeness of his Creator. The deification of Man, his perfect union with God made possible by grace, will be realized completely in the future age after the resurrection of the body. However, beginning in this life, this union which divinizes us can be made more and more real. As this happens, spiritual and physical nakedness become more and more united. We must learn to see in Christ's naked Body the revelation of the mystery of God's love. We must learn to see in our own naked bodies the incarnation of God.

It is written in Sacred Scripture, "The soldiers, therefore, when they crucified Him, took His garments... That the Scripture may be fulfilled which says, 'They divided My garments among them; and for My clothing they cast lots.'"[3][4] It is important that in our crucifixes we do not anesthetize and sanitize this unfathomable mystery, in the name of a false and immature modesty. The simplicity of the cross should not be complicated by human neuroses.

---

[1] Genesis 3:11.
[2] Genesis 2:25.
[3] Psalm 22:18.
[4] John 19:23f.

Body No Big Deal?

by Jim C. Cunningham

Dear Jim,

The reason why I have not yet sought opportunities to experience social nudity is that I have a conflict about the issue of making the biological life too much of an issue. In my life I take care of who I am, physically, but I do not make my biological body a serious issue. My relationship with God has to do with *how I think*. My physical body has nothing to do with my growing spiritually.

I have read somewhere that nudist Christians state that being naked is being closer to God. How is that different from being closer to God and wearing clothes?

Before I commit myself to a nudist lifestyle, I want to make sure the other participants are really putting the right aspects of the Word of God in the way that God wants it to be.

God is the most important thing in my life. No matter what else, His Word is paramount. If you shed some light on this conflict that I am facing, I would appreciate it very much.

Yours in Christ,
Caleb Browning

Dear Caleb, Peace!

One huge, massive objection to your present, a-physical spirituality looms large in my mind:

In I Corinthians 15:14, St. Paul tells us that if the resurrection of the flesh is taken out of the Christian mix, not only is all the rest of our pietism a total zero, but less than zero. All Mother Teresa's good works, all Billy Graham's sermons, all the church-goings of all Christians, all the martyrdoms of all the martyrs, is less than zero.

Christianity *is not*—I repeat—Christianity *is not*—about "dying and going to heaven." The body is not a banana peel, as Hindus believe, to be cast off eventually so the real banana (i.e. the soul) can attain Nirvana. The body is neither the launching pad nor the rocket booster for the space shuttle (i.e. soul) to get it into orbit (heaven). The body *is* the space shuttle. Scripture says, "God did not make death."[1] It says, "Through the envy of the devil death entered the world."[2] "Diabolical" comes from the Greek, meaning "division." Tearing down, separating, destroying, all constitute the very essence of who Satan is.

But in stark contrast, "God is One,"[3] and He created man in His Own image and likeness[4]—hence, *one*. Even when Eve entered the scene, her addition did not violate that divine reflection of oneness, for "the two became one flesh."[5] Division was the result *of sin*. The first sin was division, separating man from God. Plus, that Original Sin resulted in many divisions. Man was pitted against woman: "your urge will be for him but he will be your master."[6] The shame of nakedness divided man from his own body.[7] Adam & Eve even used nature—the Garden— to divide (hide) themselves from God,[8] just as Karl Sagan-type scientists, in the tradition of T. H. Huxley and Charles Darwin still do, pitting science against revelation, falsely creating dichotomies where none exist.

But there were two even more terrible divisions:

1. The eternal loss of heaven. Thanks be to "God, Who is rich in mercy,"[9] He deigned to become, not just your over-rated *soul*, but your vastly under-rated *flesh*, and dwell amongst us,[10] and then give us not just His *soul*, but His *flesh* to eat, making it so vital that if any fail to eat It, he dies—forever.[11]

2. The other horrendous, unthinkable division that resulted from that awful first sin, was *death*—the rending asunder of body & soul. Jesus came to restore all things,[12] and this includes the imparting of life to man, living in

---

[1] Wisdom 1:13.
[2] Wisdom 2:24.
[3] Deuteronomy 6:4; Galatians 3:20; etc.
[4] Cf. Genesis 1:26.
[5] Genesis 2:24.
[6] Genesis 3:16.
[7] Cf. Genesis 3:7 & 10.
[8] Cf. Genesis 3:8.
[9] Ephesians 2:4.
[10] Cf. John 1:14.
[11] Cf. John 6:53.
[12] Cf. Ephesians 1:10.

"the shadow of death"[1] ever since the fall of Adam & Eve. "I came that they may have life, and have it abundantly."[2]

And just what is life? It is union—one—God—love. And that does *not* mean that the body can rot as long as the "liberated" soul flies up to heaven, but rather, that both soul and body are restored to their original *unity*, imaging God, Who is One & Who is Life. This union—eternal life—will never again experience division.

The price for this certainty was no less than the *death* of Jesus. Jesus paid for it *with His Body*! And you would regard the body so casually?

Caleb! You are in the grip of age-old "angelism,"[3] which puts all the chips on the soul as though that were all that mattered to God.[4]

No way! Reread, reread, and then reread it again seventy times seven times: I Corinthians 15.

Early on in the infant Church St. Paul had to nip the angelist heresy in the bud. It is easy to fall into it, because the flesh—"Brother Ass"[5]—is, well, a pain in that ass,[6] and because of Original Sin, rebels against the spirit and vice versa.[7] If unaided by right-minded will and unaided by grace (without which we cannot even *desire* the good,[8] the fallen flesh has an in-built tendency to get into trouble like a pig on the loose (e.g. overeat, fornicate, etc.). It needs to be reigned in and disciplined, as does also our soul, whence comes man's worst evil, the root of all evil—pride.[9] Angelists denigrate the body because, in its fallen state, it tends toward self-indulgence. But the state of our souls after the fall is far worse, as they tend toward pride, the root of all evils. So why don't angelists contemn their souls

---

[1] Luke 1:79.

[2] John 10:10.

[3] My term for the pseudo-mysticism that values only the soul, to the denigration of the body. In my opinion, most of Christendom has been polluted by this heresy.

[4] In his first encyclical, "*Deus Caritas Est*," (N. 5), Pope Benedict XVI taught: "Should he aspire to be pure spirit and to reject the flesh as pertaining to his animal nature alone, then spirit and body would both lose their dignity."

[5] St. Francis of Assisi's nickname for his body.

[6] Pardon my French; after all, I do live on the Quebec border.

[7] Cf. Romans 7:22f & Galatians 5:17.

[8] Cf. Philippians 2:13.

[9] Sirach 10:15 (Douay Rheims trans.).

even more than their bodies? The truth is that *both* are precious, and *both* belong in a state of eternal *union* in God, Who is One. Any true mysticism must begin here.

As for some of those so-called Christian naturists who say God is "closer" to them when they are naked, well, don't you already have enough fruitcake left over from Christmas? They are not even at Theology 101 yet, and the best we can do is cut them slack, saying they are only speaking *poetically*, and not *theologically* or *philosophically*. There's a lot of that "poetic license" out there that vaunts itself as "theology," when in reality, it is only pious poop.

If God created man in His image, and Scripture emphasizes the fact that He created him *naked*,[1] then *somehow*, nakedness images God. This is (at least partly) because "God is love"[2] and gives His whole Self as Gift, even becoming a Body in Jesus, and giving that Body to us as food. "Giving all" is what revelation is all about. Hebrews 1:1ff explains that in the Old Testament, this Self-revelation on God's part was sketchy and incomplete, but in the incarnate Christ it is all there. As Jesus told St. Philip, "He who sees Me sees the Father."[3]

Human nakedness is like God in that, at least on a physical level, the self is revealed. We do not withhold the sight/knowledge of who we are, at least physically. When a figure model is willing to pose nude for hours in front of her peers, she is keenly aware of this gift she is making of unilateral self-revelation. I think it would be a profitable spiritual exercise for Christians to have the opportunity to stand nude in front of their brethren, meditating the while on Who God is: Self-Outpouring, revelatory gift. The experience of being revealed to their peers will aid them in better understanding & appreciating just Who our totally generous God is. They should not only meditate on Hebrews 1 & John 1 (especially v. 14), but also Philippians 2:5ff on the "*kenosis*"[4] of Christ, Who "emptied Himself, taking the form of a slave."[5]

---

[1] Cf. Genesis 2:25.
[2] I John 4:8.
[3] John 14:9.
[4] The Greek word for "self-emptying" used in v. 7.
[5] Philippians 2:7.

Nudity was the "uniform" of slaves. In John 13:4ff when Jesus took off His clothes to perform the slave function of washing filthy, manure & mud-caked feet, He wore what slaves wore, which is why He began by disrobing. Later, He specifically explained the significance of what He had done, teaching by example that to be "master" in His kingdom is to become slave.

Many spiritual truths can be more fully internalized via the tool of nakedness, and Christians would do well to avail themselves of it, "making the most of every opportunity,"[1] that "in all things [including the naked body] God might be glorified."[2]

I highly recommend getting my 100-page photo-book, *Our Wonderful Bodies!*[3] "Read" the over two hundred photos of ordinary human bodies, "naked and unashamed."[4] When we gaze upon the human body with purity of heart, what we are seeing is God Himself.[5]

In His image,
Jim

Belloc No Angelist

by Hilaire Belloc[6]

What do men mean by the desire to be dissolved, and to enjoy the spirit free and without attachments? That many men have so desired there can be no doubt, and the best men, whose holiness one recognizes at once, tell us that the joys of the soul are incomparably higher than those of the living man. In India, moreover, there are great numbers of men who do the most fantastic things with the object of thus unprisoning the soul. And Milton talks of

---

[1] Galatians 6:10 & Colossians 4:5.
[2] I Peter 4:11.
[3] Available from www.naturistlife.com.
[4] Genesis 2:25.
[5] Cf. Matthew 5:8.
[6] Excerpt from: Hilaire Belloc, *Path to Rome* (New York: Longmans, Green & Co, 1902), pp. 117f.

the same thing with evident conviction. And the saints all praise it in chorus.

But what is it?

For my part, I cannot so much as understand the very meaning of the words. For every pleasure I know comes from an intimate *union* between my body and my very human mind, which last receives, confirms, revives, and can summon up again what my body has experienced. Of pleasures, however, in which my senses have had no part, *I know nothing...*

Woman to Woman

by Pat Brindamour & Linda S. Cunningham

Dear Linda,

My pastor told my husband, Bob, and I that we are probably harming our boys (Christian, age 11 & Paul, age 10) by bringing them up with an exposure to naturism. Now that your five children are mostly grown and on their own, what would your response be? In retrospect, is it a bad thing? Our pastor wants us to give it up.

Thanks,
Pat

Dear Pat,

In retrospect, I think growing up in a naturist environment was a very good thing for our children.

I regret that society at large does not support us in our efforts. My children, now young adults, experience some confusion and frustration now that they are immersed into the perverted, anti-body world. But even so, I prefer this frustration over the more negative results that they would be experiencing if they, lacking in naturist experiences, grew up like their peers who are now scandalizing them with their "nude is lewd" attitudes. I found it a compliment when one of my daughters complained, "Mom, you brought us up too innocent!"

Should I have done the opposite and brought her up perverted? Which way, then is the truly harmful way?

I think, in the long run, when my children have grown a little older yet, they will realize that naturism was a blessing in their life.

If you gave naturism up at this point in your lives as your pastor suggests, what kind of message would you be giving your boys about their bodies? Aren't they going to be terribly confused? What was taken for granted as so innocent would suddenly become taboo.

I would not do that to the psyches of *my* children. Instead, I would do what I have done with my children: simply to explain to them that not everybody understands the innocence of the naked body; that some people feel extremely uncomfortable with even the *thought* of themselves and others being nude.

We must be patient and gentle with these people (like your pastor) and try to shed a little light on their darkness.

You know, Pat, when I think back on my own childhood, I wish I had been brought up in a naturist family. It would have prevented a lot of trouble and pain in my own life.

Let me encourage you to persevere!

Affectionately,
Linda

Nakedness: next to Godliness

by Jim C. Cunningham

Usually, when we think of the human body being created in the "image and likeness"[1] of God, we think of the various *qualities* and *conditions* of the physical body itself as comprising this image. However, there are two much more fundamental ways that God is reflected in the man and woman He created: 1) the *fact* of their *existence*, and

---

[1] Genesis 1:27.

365

2) the *fact* of their *nakedness*. Although it is about this second way that this article is mainly concerned, first, a brief word about the most fundamental way of all:

The first principle of beauty is existence itself, because a thing must be, in order to be beautiful. Since God, Who is All-Beautiful, describes Himself as "I am Who am,"[1] i.e. Supreme Being itself, then all that shares in being also shares in that beauty by the mere *fact* of its *being*.

The second most fundamental principle of beauty is *visibility*, for how can we say a thing has beauty if it is invisible or hidden? Thus, just as the very fact of existence presumes essential beauty, so the very fact of visibility also presumes beauty; and we have not yet even gotten to the different *qualities* and *conditions* of being where most people begin (and end) when they think of what constitutes beauty.

These first two principles of beauty are so fundamental and essential that, taken together, they far outweigh whatever negative physical conditions or qualities a thing might have.

God is "epiphanical"[2]; it is of His very essence to make Himself known. God's way is not to hide, but rather to enlighten. "He enlightens every man who comes into the world."[3] In His light, we not only see things thus illumined, but "we see light itself."[4] There was no hiding in the original order of grace designed by God. "And they were naked, but unashamed."[5]

On the other hand, concealment itself reflects sin and Satan—not the God of light. It was sinful men who, because of the guilt of their sin, hid their genitals with fig leaves and hid their entire bodies in the bushes.[6] Adam claimed the reason for hiding was the fact of his original nakedness, but he lied like all criminals attempting to cover up their guilt. "I was afraid, because I was naked; and I hid myself."[7] The real motive for hiding was sin, and ever since, man has been playing the game of hiding from

---

[1] Exodus 3:14.
[2] "Epiphany" comes from the Greek, meaning "manifestation."
[3] John 1:9.
[4] Psalm 36:9.
[5] Genesis 2:25.
[6] Cf. Genesis 3:7-10.
[7] Genesis 3:10.

himself, his fellow man, nature and God Himself. As lies beget lies, so this hiding abets sin like a dark bar room where one can fool oneself that his intoxication will not be seen as though the very darkness made it easier to sin. This dynamic is also played out by people who wear sunglasses at night while standing in line at an XXX-rated theater. Indeed, our Lord Himself says that people love darkness specifically because they do not want their sinfulness to be exposed.[1]

Sin and hiding go hand in hand. The psalmist says, "All of man is lie."[2] St. Paul says, "All men have sinned."[3]

On the other hand, grace and revelation also go hand in hand. To know is to see. Eve sinned in order to know good and evil like God.[4] One of the consequences was hiding—trying to deprive others of knowledge lest one's guilt should be known. A lie is a hiding of the truth. That's why we have the expression "*naked* truth"—because truth is, of its essence, stark naked. Any attempt to dress it necessarily obscures it, and truth obscured is simply lie. This is why Scripture describes God, Who is Truth Itself, as "clothed in light."[5] The eyes of faith are necessary not so much to see an otherwise very obscure God, but quite the contrary, God is so evident, bright and glorious that were it not for faith we should perish from the intensity of the glory.

The process of love is one of successive revelation—getting to "know" each other. This is why the Hebrews used the verb "to know" to mean "to unite with in conjugal love."[6] A virgin is "known" when she freely surrenders all she is to her spouse to become one flesh with him and to share this life and love via procreation. "God is One."[7] Indeed, He is the very principle of Unity Itself.[8] His purpose in redeeming man is to elevate us from our adulterous condition of knowing and consorting with evil, to knowing and uniting with him via participation in grace.

---

[1] Cf. John 3:19.
[2] Psalm 116:11.
[3] Romans 3:23.
[4] Cf. Genesis 3:1ff.
[5] Psalm 104:2.
[6] Cf. Luke 1:34; Genesis 4:1; etc.
[7] Deuteronomy 6:4; Galatians 3:20; etc.
[8] Cf. Colossians 1:16.

As with all lovers, the very beginning of this work of bringing to loving union is getting to know each other. God is already All-Knowing by definition. "Before Him no creature is hidden, but all are open and laid bare to the eyes of Him with whom we have to do."[1] Thus this process of knowing is one-sided: He already sees us naked; it is for God to make Himself known, and for us to know and love Him Who is thus revealed. Thus nakedness is clearly the way of the Lord of light, and concealment is the domain of the Prince of darkness.

Hebrews 1:1ff teaches, "In many and various ways God spoke of old to our fathers by the prophets; but in these last days He has spoken to us by a son..." Thus the process of redemption, i.e. making man holy, was a process of *successive revelation*. From this fact alone we can see how intrinsically connected are holiness and revealing (i.e. nakedness). The entire Old Testament since Genesis 2 is the record of this ever-increasing process of revelation, climaxing in the New Testament, when the fullness of revelation, the Second Person of the Holy Trinity, stripped Himself of glory and "became flesh and dwelt among us,"[2] and "we have seen His glory, the glory of an Only Son coming from the Father, filled with enduring love."[3]

Not only is this divine nakedness essential to the process of redeeming us for the new, promised kingdom, but this age of the valley of tears with its ignorances and concealments will fully end one great and awesome day, and what will follow will be a new realm of being characterized by such light that even our risen bodies will be glorious beacons, shining like the stars. Of this new and everlasting era Jesus said, "There is nothing concealed that will not be made known."[4] And St. Paul puts it another way: "I will know even as I am known."[5]

No one wants to be ugly; we all desire to be like God and share in His perfection of Beauty. This alone is proof not only of the existence of God, Who is All-Beautiful, but

---

[1] Hebrews 4:13.
[2] John 1:14.
[3] Ibid.
[4] Matthew 10:26.
[5] I Corinthians 13:12.

also of the fact that it is natural for man to strive to know Who God is and to be like Him. Deep down we know we were created in His image and likeness, and constantly tend to pursue the regaining of that perfection.

The devil, always "prowling about like a roaring lion,"[1] is relentlessly trying to destroy our pursuit of this perfect image. He utilizes a plethora of ploys to obfuscate the process. These ploys range from trying to convince us we are not beautiful and never can attain beauty, to trying to convince us that there simply is no All-Beautiful God to seek to emulate. He is the Prince of this world, and though his doom has been sealed by the paschal victory of Christ, his time has not yet expired. His world has its own ungodly principles, and constantly seeks to hinder our first purpose, viz. to seek God.

One lie the world tries to brainwash us with is that we are so ugly already that unless we live for Mammon[2] and constantly buy this and that cosmetic, weight and dieting program, or newfangled fashion, we are doomed to ugliness and inadequacy. Of course, nothing we do ever works very well, and most attempts are laughably pitiful, yet we go on allowing ourselves to be deceived into thinking that a little more Mammon will yet help our hopelessness.

The world even dupes people into believing that they can actually attain beauty—*through concealment*! Once, when I had to wear a "monkey suit" for some function or other, my secretary, who was accustomed to seeing me in my divinely tailored "birthday suit," commented, "My, don't you look spiffy today!"

How would she know? All she could see were my head and hands; all else was not only hidden, but even falsified, as by the padded shoulders in the suit jacket that pretended a build other than the reality. She regarded me with the eyes of the world, so brainwashed was she through so many TV commercials, "glamour" magazines, and vain opinions of men. If she had had God's perspective, she might rather have walked into the press room while I worked in the altogether and, awed at true (though imperfect) beauty, have exclaimed, "My, don't you look spiffy today!" As explained above, even if my own particu-

---

[1] I Peter 5:8.
[2] Cf. Matthew 6:24.

lar physical qualities and conditions were not perfect, two facts of beauty outweighed all else: 1) the fact that I existed as a human being—a veritable mirror cf God by definition, and 2) the fact that I was naked, "epiphanical," revelatory, completely exposed, just like our All-Beautiful God of revelation. In truth there is absolutely nothing to shop for that can improve our appearance, because anything we might buy is not us, but merely something hung or gooped on us.

If all classical literature is correct, women have always been especially susceptible to vanity. Like Eve who so readily believed Satan's lie, they easily believe they are truly ugly. I see this even in veteran naturist women. As a result, many women cannot bring themselves to accept their own beauty, and openly and honestly present the same to others. That is why, largely, many wives do not accompany their husbands in the lifestyle of social nudity.

One would hope that at least *Christian* women would see through the world's deceptions and proceed in more godly than worldly ways, but vanity runs so deep that one look at Tammy Fay Baker tells you it makes no difference at all. In fact, the problem is worse with Christian women because they fall easy prey to yet another sneaky ploy of the prowling lion. They readily believe that nakedness is not intrinsically connected with godliness, but quite the contrary, is intrinsically connected with sin! So convinced are they of this lie that they preach it as Gospel, when, in fact, it is nowhere to be found in the Gospel. Is their vanity so deep that they strive for the ultimate cover-up— disguising vice as virtue? Is their real motive for being zealots for false modesty not their deep despair of ever being beautiful? Are they not using religion to accommodate their own ungodly, unscriptural mindset?

I have already explained, objectively and philosophically, why nakedness is godly, but let me add some subjective, experiential proofs:

Both my wife and one of our daughters were college art majors. Most every day at school they drew nude men and women, sometimes their fellow students. Every life drawing class was such obvious, experiential proof that the notion that nakedness necessarily implies lust is utterly false. In that class there were ordinary college boys, reared by moms who believed they are ugly and that exposure means sin. Those boys might never have seen a naked female except in an erotic pose in some porno-graphic magazine, which, like the above-mentioned duped Christian women, propagate the lie that nakedness is sinful.

Suddenly their very first life drawing class arrives. They are gathered in a classroom with their peers of both sexes. The model, let's say a female peer, stands only a few feet away awaiting the art instructor's direction to remove her robe. The boys may be legitimately confused because for the first time they will be exposed to nudity in an other than erotic context—something their "pious" mothers and churches have thus far fastidiously pre-vented them from experiencing. Before they have time to try to reorganize their confused minds, the signal is given, the robe is dropped, and there, standing right in front of their eyes is their peer—a girl they sit beside in math class, and maybe even sing with in chapel choir. Every square inch of her skin is exposed to them. This is likely the same girl who otherwise always wore a bra, not because she needed one, but because she was brought up with the lie that "modesty" means taking pains to conceal one's gender characteristics like breasts—even the little bumps her nipples might make through the fabric of her shirts. Her skirts had been long out of "modesty," trying to prevent these same boys from seeing her leg above the knee. Even in the presence of only girls in gym class she had dressed and undressed not openly in the aisle in front of her locker, but in the private shower stall booth. Only last week, while swimming in the college pool, she had wondered whether her swimsuit was cut too high at the hips and clung too revealingly to her buttocks.

But now she stands completely naked before the pro-longed gaze of the same people. To those from whom she had previously painstakingly hidden even the bumps of her nipples through the fabric of her opaque shirt, she now exposes every square inch of her God-designed body. How moot did her hemline concerns seem now that there was no dividing line between "modest" and "immodest" leg? Whereas before she did not even briefly bare what was beneath her gym shorts to fellow female students in

371

the locker room, now she openly exposes every detail of her body to the prolonged gaze of not only girls, but also any boy who happened to be in that class. How silly her swimsuit anxieties must seem now.

And what are the dynamics of this experience for those boys? They are even more confused in that the exposure of the model's body is so simple and ordinary—so "in the light." There is no sneaking of peeks, no hiding one's stash of porn, not even any fantasizing about what lay beneath those heretofore teasing textiles. The devil's game is up. Not only her skin, but his lie is exposed for the phantom that it really is. Without having much time to think about it, those ordinary boys begin to draw; they draw her entire figure, and it is entirely different from any previous experience of nudity they had ever had, because it was in the plain light of day and not in shadows and hiding. There is a certain delight they experience, but it is not the illicit pleasure of sin, but the wholesome pleasure of finally perceiving naked truth in its stark simplicity. Truth is beautiful by definition. Beauty is pleasing by definition.

With no special preparation for either model or students, everyone easily and readily is able to have the right mind about the model's nakedness. There is no voyeurism, no untoward comments or looks. Three minutes of this first life drawing class for both model and students dispel a lifetime of intensely taught lies—lies even taught from pious moms and pulpits.

What is the secret behind life drawing classes? Why is that girl model able to stand there in the nude when the day before she was looking in the mirror to see if her bra and shirt were opaque enough? The answer is as simple as nakedness itself: it works because it is done God's way, not in darkness, but in light—God's very first creation.[1]

The life drawing experience proves my point that if only we are as up front about nakedness as God originally intended, we will dispel the dark lies of pornography and also come to appreciate our own unique, very real beauty. Many women have attested that they never felt beautiful until they began to practice naturism. Indeed, how can they have felt beautiful while living lives of deception and

---

[1] Cf. Genesis 1:3.

concealment? The first thing necessary to discover one's own beauty is unveiling ourselves just as we are. One immediate effect is the deep realization of one's own beauty, simply because the very *fact* of being *visible* is itself beautiful and God-like. Now add to this powerful awareness the positive response of those who behold us as we are, and the experience is all the more rewarding and affirming.

The fact of our visibility not only is beautiful in itself to others, but it also, as of itself, helps us to discover and believe in our own innate beauty. People will go to such great expense and labor to improve their physical *qualities*, but meanwhile there is something everybody can do that costs nothing and is as simple as nakedness because it *is* nakedness—no longer hide in the darkness out of fear and shame, but in trust and faith in the image of the All-Beautiful God that we are, respond to His call to step out into His marvelous light[1] and accept our baptismal birthright—the freedom of the children of light.[2] Rather than hide beneath a suffocating bushel-basket, everybody can stand tall on a lamp-stand, so that all may see the good work which we truly are and glorify our Father Who is in heaven.[3]

Since we are all reflections of God by definition, then we are all His neon lighted billboards. How can anyone be an atheist surrounded by thousands of mirrors of God? What quality of evangelization is it if we proclaim shame even in the *fact* of our physical being? Who wants to believe in a God Who is so ugly and raunchy that all His witnesses are deeply mortified if anyone should happen to glimpse Him in them? But to proclaim God with our bodies we need not enroll in any charm school to learn how to prance with pride and stride with style; simple, unabashed body-acceptance is already more profound than a thousand eloquent homilies. Although we can improve our charm, we already are charming by definition. Eve was already like unto God before she listened to the lie that sin would give her what she already had. In the Gospel parable, all three servants received talents to begin

---

[1] Cf. I Peter 2:9.
[2] Cf. Romans 8:21; Luke 16:8; John 12:36 & I Thessalonians 5:5.
[3] Cf. Matthew 5:14-16.

with. Two improved theirs further and were rewarded with joy. One hid his out of fear, and was severely punished by his Master; he was cast "out into the outer darkness where men weep and gnash their teeth."[1]

Furthermore, this revelation of self cannot be *selective*, but *universal* in scope. Even the world believes in selective revelation of one's nakedness, pre-judging those deemed "worthy" of it. But is this the way of nature as God intended? Are sunsets more spectacular for the saintly? To really experience one's own beauty and even find God in it, the scope must be *universal, without restriction.* After all, Him Whom we image is God, Who "...makes His sun rise on the evil and on the good, and sends rain on the just and on the unjust."[2]

One of the world's and devil's greatest weapons is fear. Fear binds us and buries us more firmly and surely than St. Lazarus' sepulchral wrappings and tombstone.[3] But just as Jesus loudly called him forth from those restrictive wraps into the freedom of light and life, ordering him to be unwrapped down to his nakedness whilst a crowd watched in utter amazement, so also must we respond to His loud call to be completely open and honest, having nothing to hide because we are not ashamed of anything we are, think or do. Just as there was no selectivity in the crowd that watched Jesus raise St. Lazarus from the dead, so also we, to experience true freedom and beauty, cannot be selective in who sees our nakedness, even if onlookers include sinful men. The divine Healer did not hang out with the healthy and self-righteous, but with the sick and sinners.[4] Gluttony is not cured by starvation, but by right eating. Porn addiction is created, or at least strongly abetted, by compulsively depriving people of the wholesome experience of the body's beauty. Pornography is a lie, not because it reveals too much, as Pope John Paul II taught, but because it reveals too little.[5] To assert that the whole is one of its parts is a lie. A whole is *all* its parts, *rightly composed.*

---

[1] Cf. Matthew 25:14-30.
[2] Matthew 5:45.
[3] Cf. John 11:17ff.
[4] Cf. Luke 5:30-32.
[5] Because it distorts the truth of man by focusing only on the erotic.

As the devil tricks millions of Christians into believing that exposure means sin, when we know it means grace, so also he tricks us again, telling us that this universality is "imprudent," or even sinful because sinful onlookers could possibly lust after us.

The truth is that they are lusters mainly because the world has prevailed in forming them to regard all nudity as erotic. If they could only experience non-erotic nudity more, rather than seeing ourselves as near occasions of sin for them, we would be healers in the order of grace, bravely and compassionately doing what it really takes to help make them chaste. By covering up, we give in to their deceptive game and let evil control us. But by letting them see us just as God created us, we are completely in charge and *we control* the context. We even dictate what is to be their response, which I will now show:

One of the main points in Dale Carnegie's classic, *How to Win Friends and Influence People*, is that people invariably live up to the expectations we set for them. If we show trust in others, they automatically want to prove themselves trustworthy. There is a funny but true scene in the book, *The Cross and the Switchblade* by Rev. David Wilkerson where he is preaching to an auditorium full of gang members in New York City. He takes up a collection and specifically asks a real crook to be in charge of the money, carrying it backstage behind the curtain where there is an exit and he could easily simply walk out into the alley and make off with the dough. This the extemporaneous "usher" surely intends to do, until it begins to sink in that for the very first time in his life someone actually *really trusted him.* Soon this meant more than all the money in the world, and he shocked his gang peers as he brought the basket from backstage to where the preacher was on stage.

The dynamic is as simple as it is powerful: show people *in advance* your high estimation of them, and they will live up to it. But if the preacher had engineered the collection with fears and suspicions, he would surely have presented a near occasion of sin for the "ushers," who, true to these negative expectations, would have made off with the haul.

This dynamic is as true in the realm of modesty as it is in honesty.

In the above example of life drawing, the whole context presumes the best in the art students. Nothing is done or said that would send a message that the students are expected to abuse the situation via lust. The lights are on. The model poses as frankly nude as any fruit basket positioned for a still life class. Trust is generously afforded to all right from the outset, and the students live up to it.

But take a different situation such as a strip-bar. The whole context expects the stripper's nudity to be abused via lust. It is even expressed on the sign on the door. The atmosphere is dark and dingy. Everything in the stripper's routine sends the message that no one's gaze is expected to be chaste. Sure enough, all the customers live down to such low expectations.

Although nakedness itself is a return to God's original intention for man,[1] He also intended that man be *unaware* of it: "Who told you that you were *naked*?"[2] Thus what imaged God was not only the visible fact of man's self-revelation in his naked state, but also his lack of self-consciousness concerning same. This oblivion is part of our birthright of freedom as children of God. The more self-conscious we are about our bodies, the more restricted we are. It would hardly feel much like "freedom" if, while nude, we were constantly fretting about being seen. The truly free person is one who gives no more thought to such concerns than a sunset does. Just as every tree falling in a forest makes noise whether or not anyone hears it, so every sunset is beautiful whether or not anyone watches it. It is what it is, because it reflects its divine Artist, Who is Who is.[3] If we are convinced that our true beauty comes from God, and not from the approval of any man, then we, too, will experience the freedom of such natural detachment. I recall seeing an antique cartoon consisting of two frames. In the first, a missionary bishop with miter and crosier shakes his fist disapprovingly at a naked African lady shouting, "In the name of decency, put something on!" The second frame has her walking back

---

[1] Cf. Genesis 2:25.
[2] Genesis 3:11.
[3] Cf. Exodus 3:14.

out to him from her grass hut *with a hankie on her head!* She really had no clue what his "problem" was.

I can validate the moral of that cartoon. My wife and I raised our children as naturists from their birth. They never knew their nakedness. Of course, living in the woods helped create the environment that made this possible. Once, when the whole gang accompanied me to my print shop in town, as the day warmed up, off went their clothes, with no inhibitions, despite the fact that they were playing on a city sidewalk. It was very awkward for us to try to explain to them why they could not do that in town. We had to tell them that city folks are just really weird, and "When in Rome, we should do as the Romans do."

Around the same time a Canadian family visited us in our woods. They aspired to naturist values, but were quite permeated with the weird ways of the world such as bodies being "indecent." After coming home from Sunday Mass our children naturally removed what the world considers their "Sunday best" and wore what Genesis 2 reveals is their true "Sunday best"—their naked bodies. But when they went out to play and quickly detected odd vibes from the other two boys who insisted on at least wearing their skivvies, like the African in the cartoon, they were made to feel that something was somehow wrong with them. So they reacted by trying to cover their nakedness with their hands. What was really funny and very revealing was that none of them knew just what body part they were supposed to hide. The oldest had a general idea, but her sister covered her belly-button, her mouth hanging open like she had no clue what was going on. The younger siblings were even more oblivious, not knowing what to do, but sensing that something was not right.

I relate this story because some argue that after the fall, it is natural to be ashamed of nudity. But we proved that, on the contrary, it is natural to be oblivious of one's nakedness. Children who are reared to believe that the body parts hidden by a bikini are "indecent" and who are compulsively deprived of ever seeing what lies behind those few square inches of fabric, will, upon encountering a woman clothed only in light like Him Whom she images, stare fixedly at those very parts. They cannot see the woman as a whole—as a person, but they can only see those body parts. Thus are children literally brain-washed into objectifying women by their pious, well-intentioned, but very ignorant Christian parents and pastors. Our children were reared to see people as whole persons. This would have been impossible had we reared them to wear bathing suits and never be naked, and if they were, to scramble and hide at the sound of approaching footsteps.

Jesus said that His Kingdom belongs to little children.[1] They have not yet acquired the perverted baggage of adulthood. Sadly, "education" means the gradual acquisition of that baggage, rather than the development of the good talents entrusted to us by our Creator and Master.

People actually break out into a sweat at the mere thought of being caught naked, just as people fear tarantulas or scorpions. Fear can be warranted when there is just cause such as imminent danger of harm. But such is not the case when, after taking off their pajamas and about to put on their underwear, someone should suddenly open the door and walk into the bedroom. What? Does one think one's own mother or father is going to assault him? Unwarranted fears are useless; they inhibit our experience of living as children of light and of the day.

The example of my family's uninhibited nakedness proved that no fear was warranted. In fact, very often, by deporting ourselves as the children of light that we are, others who encountered us imitated us. You could easily tell by their sharp tan lines that the idea of wearing only light as the most modest garb possible was new to them. The truth was obvious because it was not hidden beneath a bushel-basket, but placed on a lamp-stand. Truth speaks for itself; it only needs to be uncovered. And the truth of our innate beauty and purity is so utterly delightful that despite decades of reverse enculturation, many people cannot remain beneath their own bushel-baskets. In contrast to our honesty they are suddenly ashamed not of their bodies, but of their bathing suits. Even if all they are wearing is a skimpy bikini, it suddenly feels like shackles and they can't wait to be free of them. In an instant they prove the truth of the basic message of naturism. They instantly graduate from feeling ashamed of

---

[1] Cf. Matthew 19:14.

their nakedness to being ashamed of their bathing suits—their "fig leaves." If body shame were truly natural, then such conversions could not be so quick and easy. What else should we expect when we finally do things as God intended?

When we do not panic when others see our nudity, it shows we trust them fully. Rather than look down at us in some negative way, they have got to feel buoyed up by our unilateral trust in them. They do not think, "Aren't you going to cover up out of embarrassment and shame?", but rather, "Are you really not going to regard me as some predatory lecher and just stand there calmly letting me see your nakedness? Just what do you think of me anyway?"

Thus trusted, they are going to automatically live up to it. Rather than give into the lie that such nudity is "imprudent," we prove how supremely prudent it really is, converting whoever sees us into a trustworthy person. Thus have we imaged God, Who "...makes His sun rise on the evil and on the good, and sends rain on the just and on the unjust."[1]

We have also displayed something godly by the simple fact of our open nakedness. We have reflected to them something of God's beauty because we are His handiwork. In a sense, we are even His Self-portrait.

Nakedness is also godly because it is evangelistic. It preaches truth as of itself. We are, literally, His living Bible. "You yourselves are our letter of recommendation, written on your hearts, to be known and read by all men; and you show that you are a letter from Christ delivered by us, written not with ink but with the Spirit of the living God, not on tablets of stone but on tablets of human hearts."[2]

Besides loudly proclaiming both God's existence and his beauty, uninhibited nakedness preaches that He is a God Who reveals. He wants to be known so He will be loved, and by this love, man, who fell from grace, will share in that Beautiful Godhead.

So it matters not what a person's particular physical *qualities* may be; *everyBODY is beautiful.*

---

[1] Matthew 5:45.
[2] II Corinthians 3:2f.

Many say that they will reveal their own special beauty—after they lose thirty pounds! The truth is that it is absurd to say that a naked lady—however fat—is more beautiful when she cannot be seen. Clothing can only add bulk, and besides, it hides the real, fundamental beauty of the *fact* of one's nakedness. One lady I knew said she did not go to nude beaches because she did not want to "trash the beach" with her chubby flesh. On the contrary, I saw her naked at her house and at ours, and I can attest that she was definitely more beautiful naked, and that I did not have to see her nude to know she was chubby.

Let's remember that when God created man and woman in His image and likeness, they were completely naked.[1] Nakedness was God's idea from the start. The clothing idea came out of sinfulness and man's interaction with Satan. Jesus clearly told us "You can judge a tree from its fruit. A good tree bears good fruit, and a bad tree bears bad fruit."[2] It is impossible for the clothes idea to be good, since it is clearly the result of the biggest sin ever committed, another result of which was banishment into this inclement valley of tears where we often now need clothes, not to *conceal* God's beautiful creation, but to give us the warmth and protection our inclement climate now demands.

If anyone thinks he is not beautiful, then he can easily improve his condition not by buying any textiles or cosmetics, etc., but simply by returning to the godly state of nakedness as God intended. We cannot recreate every condition of Eden, but one—simple nakedness—is as attainable as taking off our clothes. Our very nakedness, by revealing who we are (at least physically) will loudly reflect our All-Beautiful God Who so much wants us to know Him that He became flesh and even died naked on the cross for this purpose. Can God possibly get any more naked?

Can you?

---

[1] Cf. Genesis 2:25.
[2] Matthew 7:17.

Tolkien's Naked Fellowship

by Linda S. Cunningham

J. R. R. Tolkien's books are making a comeback these days because of movies like "The Lord of the Rings" that have recently been produced. My curiosity was piqued because I am very interested in children's books and the reviews I've read, particularly from Catholic and Christian sources, were very positive. The latest one said that they hoped the movie would encourage children to read Tolkien's books because they are so wholesome and full of things like self sacrifice, noble goals, exciting adventures, and the good triumphing over evil.

I have recently read and am now in the middle of the first book of Tolkien's trilogy, *The Fellowship of the Ring*. So far I have encountered three nude scenes which were very wholesome and practical. I find it very interesting and hopeful for the "nude is not necessarily lewd" cause, especially among the pious, because Christians are actually encouraging their children to read Tolkien's books that have these nude scenes in them. I do hope this will have a positive influence on children to obtain a more wholesome attitude towards naked human bodies, including their own.

Here's what I found in *The Hobbit*:

Bilbo Baggins was chosen by the great wizard Gandalf to accompany a band of dwarves on a dangerous mission to reclaim their own Lonely Mountain, and all their treasures which lay confiscated by Smaug, a fearsome dragon, in the halls inside the mountain. During their long journey, after escaping goblins within the Misty Mountains which they had to cross, and from wolves and a raging fire, they were quite grubby, to say the least. So there is a little skinny-dipping scene at this point in the story:

They took off their clothes and bathed in the river, which was shallow and clear and stony at the ford. When they had dried in the sun, which was now strong and warm, they were refreshed, if still sore and a little hungry.

In *The Fellowship of the Ring* there was another bathing scene, this time within a house. Merry had preceded Frodo to his new home by a few days, in order to prepare it for him and his two other companions. When they finally arrived, Merry opened a door at the end of a passage and a puff of steam came out.

*"A bath!" cried Pippin... "Which order shall we go in?"
said Frodo... "Trust me to arrange things better than that!"
said Merry. "We can't begin life at Crickhollow with a
quarrel over baths. In that room there are three tubs... Get
inside and be quick!" ...*

*Snatches of competing songs came from the bath room
mixed with the sound of splashing and wallowing...*

*Frodo came out drying his hair. "There's so much water
in the air that I'm coming into the kitchen to finish," he said.*

Later in the book, Frodo and his three friends were captured by the Barrow-Wights. Old Tom Bombadil came to the rescue and delivered them from the dark chamber which was as cold as death. Merry, Pippin and Sam found themselves wearing thin white rags instead of their own clothing. They were upset at having lost their own clothes:

*But Tom shook his head, saying: ... "Clothes are but
little loss... Be glad, my merry friends, and let the warm
sunlight heat now heart and limb! Cast off these cold rags!
Run naked on the grass, while Tom goes a-hunting!" ... The
hobbits ran about for a while on the grass, as he told them.
Then they lay basking in the sun with the delight of those
that have been wafted suddenly from bitter winter to a
friendly clime, or of people that, after being long ill and
bedridden, wake one day to find that they are unexpectedly
well and the day is again full of promise.*

*By the time that Tom returned they were feeling
strong...*

*Merry, Sam, and Pippin now clothed themselves in
spare garments from their packs; and they soon felt too hot,
for they were obliged to put on some of the thicker and
warmer things that they had brought against the oncoming
of winter.*

Many of the movie reviewers praised the producers for sticking so closely to the story as Tolkien wrote it, but I disagree. So far in my reading, I am finding whole chapters missing, including both of the nude scenes. Perhaps they think that the audience can't handle it, but I think the audience desperately needs such innocent and healthy scenes.

Commentary:
I Thessalonians 5:22

by Bill Asseln

Some non-nudist Christians quote I Thessalonians 5:22 from the King James Version which says, "Abstain from all *appearance* of evil." The New International Version translates this verse, "Avoid every *kind* of evil," and the New American Standard Version says, "abstain from every *form* of evil." The Greek word that is translated here as "appearance," "kind" or "form," is "*eidos*," meaning "a view." While this word is found in a number of places in the Bible, this passage is the *only* place that the KJV translates it as "appearance." When the word "appearance" is used elsewhere in the KJV, it comes from other Greek words.

"Every kind of evil" is a better translation of the verse.

Editor's note: Other translations: Douay Rheims: "appearance," New American Bible: "semblance," Revised Standard Version: "form," Jerusalem Bible: "form," Vulgate: "*specie*" (whence derives our word "species").

That St. Paul's sense cannot possibly be what these anti-nudists claim can be proven by *reductio ad absurdum*,[1] because absolutely anything can "appear" evil to somebody, from driving to church (lazy) to going to the bank (avaricious). Even Jesus Himself "appeared" to be a glutton and wine-bibber to some people.[2] St. Paul, who, in the same epistle, tells us to imitate Christ,[3] cannot be setting a higher standard for us than for Christ Himself!

---

[1] See note 1 on p. 49.
[2] Cf. Matthew 11:18f.
[3] Cf. I Thessalonians 1:6 & I John 2:6.

More on Nude Baptism

from Fig Leaf Forum[1]

Hippolytus, presbyter in Rome after A.D. 212, specified removal of clothing for baptism, and in the fourth century instructions for baptism throughout the Roman Empire stipulated naked baptism without any suggestion of innovation or change from earlier practices.

A sampling of these instructions will demonstrate the central importance of naked baptism to Christians.

In the Eastern empire, Cyril of Jerusalem or John, Cyril's successor, bishop of Jerusalem from A.D. 387 to 417 ... explained to the recently baptized what they had experienced.

He wrote: "Immediately, then, upon entering, you removed your tunics... Having stripped, you were naked... Marvelous! You were naked in the sight of all and were not ashamed! Truly you bore the image of the first-formed Adam, who was naked in the garden and 'was not ashamed.'"

The Syrian bishop, Theodore of Mopsuestia (before 428), wrote: "You draw therefore near to the holy baptism and before all you take off your garments. As in the beginning when Adam was naked and was in nothing ashamed of himself, but after having broken the commandment and become mortal, he found himself in need of an outer covering."

About a century later, the Greek author, Pseudo-Dionysius, gave a similar detailed account:

"The deacons divest him [the initiate] completely and the priests bring the holy oil for unction. The hierarch begins the process of unction with a threefold sign of the cross, leaving it to the priest to cover the body of the man completely with oil... Then the priests guide the man to the water [and the hierarch] immerses three times the initiate whose name is called out across the water by the

---

[1] This excerpt was gleaned from *Fig Leaf Forum*, No. 24, and is used here with permission. For contact information for FLF, see note on p. 216.
FLF is citing Margaret R. Miles, *Carnal Knowing: Female Nakedness and Religious Meaning in the Christian West* (Burns & Oates, c.1989) pp. 33f.

priests to the hierarch with each immersion. Each time the initiate is plunged into the water and emerges, the hierarch invokes the three persons of the divine blessedness."

Similarly, John the Deacon, writing in about AD 500, said:

"They are commanded to go in naked, even down to their feet, so that [they may show that] they have put off the earthly garments of mortality. The church has ordained these things for many years with watchful care, even though the old books may not reveal traces of them."

Narsai, founder of the Nestorian School in Nisibis in the middle of the fifth century, described the candidate for baptism:

"Naked he stands and stripped before the Judge that by his wretched plight he may win pity to cover him."

On Spiritual Nakedness

by St. Neilos the Ascetic[1]

Let us strip ourselves of everything, since our adversary stands before us stripped.

Do athletes compete with their clothes on? No, the rules require them to enter the stadium naked. Whether it is warm or cold, that is how they enter, leaving their clothes outside; and if anyone refuses to strip, he excludes himself from the contest.

Now we too claim to be athletes, and we are struggling against opponents far more skilful than any that are visible. Yet, instead of stripping ourselves, we try to engage in the contest while carrying countless burdens on our shoulders, thus giving our opponents many chances of getting a grip on us. How can someone encumbered

---

[1] *The Philokalia,* compiled by St. Nikodimos of the Holy Mountain & St. Makarios of Corinth, is a compendium of the wisdom of the desert fathers and other early Eastern monks, mystics and ascetics. Several volumes are available in English translation, translated from the Greek & edited by G. E. H. Palmer, Philip Sherrard & Kallistos Ware, and published by Faber & Faber, London. This excerpt is from pp. 243-245.

with material possessions contend against "spiritual wickedness,"[1] since he is vulnerable from every angle? How can someone weighed down with wealth wrestle with the demon of avarice? How can someone clothed in worldly preoccupations race against demons stripped of every care? Holy Scripture says, "The naked shall run swiftly in that day"[2]—the naked, not the one who is hindered in running by thoughts about money and material possessions.

A naked person is hard or even impossible to catch. If Joseph had been naked, the Egyptian woman would not have found anything to seize hold of, for the Scriptures say that "she caught him by his garment, saying 'Lie with me.'"[3]

Now "garments" are the physical things whereby sensual pleasure seizes hold of us and drags us about; for whoever is encumbered with such things will of necessity be dragged about by them against his will. When Joseph saw that, because of his body's need for clothes, he was being dragged into intimacy and union with sensual pleasure, he abandoned them and fled; he realized that, unless he was naked, the mistress of the house would seize him and hold him back by force. So when he left he was naked except for his virtue, like Adam in Paradise...

This is why the writer of Proverbs says to the intelligence, our trainer: "Take away his garment, for he has entered."[4] So long as someone does not compete but stays outside the arena, he will of course remain clothed, smothering beneath the garments of sensory things the manly strength required for the contest; but once he enters the contest, his garment is taken away, for he must compete naked.

Indeed, we must be not only naked but anointed with oil. Stripping prevents our opponent from getting a grasp on us, while oil enables us to slip away should he in fact seize hold of us. That is why a wrestler tries to cover his opponent's body with dust; this will counteract the slipperiness of the oil and make it easier for him to get a hold.

---

[1] Ephesians 6:12.
[2] Amos 2:16.
[3] Genesis 39:12.
[4] Proverbs 27:13.

Now what dust is in their case, worldly things are in the case of our own struggle; and what oil is in their case, detachment is in ours. In physical wrestling, someone anointed with oil easily breaks free from his opponent's grip, but if he is covered with dust he finds it hard to escape. Similarly, in our case it is difficult for the devil to seize hold of one who has no worldly attachments. But when a man is full of anxiety about material things the intellect, as though covered with dust, loses the agility which detachment confers upon it; and then it is hard for him to escape from the devil's grip.

Detachment is the mark of a perfect soul, whereas it is characteristic of an imperfect soul to be worn down with anxiety about material things. The perfect soul is called a "lily among thorns,"[1] meaning that it lives with detachment in the midst of those who are troubled by such anxiety. For in the Gospel the lily signifies the soul that is detached from worldly care: "They do not toil or spin, yet even Solomon in all his glory was not arrayed like one of them."[2] But of those who devote much anxious thought to bodily things, it is said: "All the life of the ungodly is spent in anxiety."[3] It is indeed ungodly to pass one's whole life worrying about bodily things and to give no thought to the blessings of the age to come—to spend all one's time on the body, though it does not need much attention, and not to devote even a passing moment to the soul, though the journey before it is so great that a whole lifetime is too short to bring it to perfection. Even if we do seem to allot a certain amount of time to it, we do this carelessly and lazily, for we are always being attracted by visible things.

Editor's note: Although St. Neilos the Ascetic is not promoting the nudist lifestyle nor anything that belongs to the temporal order, like St. Paul,[4] he draws his metaphors from nude athletics which were customary in the first millennium.

Nudity for athletes was entirely acceptable; it would have seemed absurd back then to suggest that athletes

---

[1] Song of Songs 2:2.
[2] Matthew 6:28f.
[3] Job 15:20.
[4] E.g. cf. I Corinthians 9:24ff; Philippians 3:13f & Hebrews 12:1ff.

wear clothing. Not only would it have clearly been seen as a great hindrance, but it was specifically to see the glory of the naked bodies of the athletes that spectators flocked to the stadium.

Sadly, in modern athletics and especially in the Olympics, we cannot glorify God in *all* His works, but must impose a very narrow, skewed attitude on what is naturally wholesome, requiring athletes to hide the fruit of their labors.

But kudos to *Life* magazine who, in an attempt to re-institute sanity, published a beautiful display of athletes at a summer Olympics[1] performing their particular events (e.g. high-diving, basketball) attired as the Olympians of old—nude.

Just as it is difficult for American Christians to project themselves *in space* to other lands who have different customs of dress from ours, so too, it is difficult for them to project themselves back (or forward!) *in time to* when no one—not even ascetical saints—could have conceived of requiring athletes to wear even the minimum of clothing. Our individual and cultural perspectives are so minuscule, yet we self-righteously impose them on the entire globe and on all of historical time. What ever happened to the virtue of "humility"?

For Your Eyes Only?

by Jim Thurman & Jim C. Cunningham

Dear Jim,

One thing my wife brought up that I didn't have an answer for, and it is kind of funny that she brought it up:

She is of the mindset that our bodies and viewing them is *only* for the context of marriage. No one else is allowed to see her body except her female doctor and myself. She even gave an example of both of us being on a nude beach and some man walking by and looking at her, what would I do? At that time I didn't have an answer for

---

[1] As I recall, it was in the mid-nineties.

her. I realized that we were on two totally different planes and didn't know how to handle it yet.

In God's love & peace,
Jim Thurman

Dear Jim,
RE: Nudity reserved only for spouse:
1. It's not doable, so how can one think it's what God wants? God does not demand the impossible or absurd.
2. If God wants nudity reserved only for married spouses, why did He command Isaiah to preach to all the Jews nude for three years?[1]
3. Why would St. Peter fish "with the guys" in the nude?[2] There is no indication that if he had been within sight of women he would have done otherwise.
4. Why would Moses have stripped, bathed & invested Aaron and his sons while all Israel watched?[3]
5. Why would the Church, for about 1,000 years, have baptized catechumens in the nude—boys, girls, men and women together—with the congregation looking on?
6. Why would some saints such as Onuphrius, Mary of Egypt, Basil of Moscow, Kevin of Glendalough and Jeselinus of Luxembourg (whom St. Bernard of Clairvaux highly praised) have practiced nudity as a form of evangelical poverty and asceticism?
7. Why would all (or almost) Catholic colleges with art departments pay men & women to stand nude in front of their students? Does your wife have anything that those models don't have?
8. Why would Catholic schools and summer youth camps have taken same-sex nudity as a given in gang showers, locker rooms, pools and water and beachfront sports? Even though all were of the same sex, surely some participants were homosexuals, but the Church still condoned and even required it.

---

[1] Cf. Isaiah 20:1ff.
[2] Cf. John 21:7.
[3] Cf. Leviticus 8:5ff.

9. Why would even Billy Graham Studios produce films (e.g. "The Hiding Place") with dozens of full frontal, female nudes?[1] Many of these actresses had spouses, but all camera men, stage crew and viewers of all ages can see their bodies as naked as their own husbands can see them.

10. Why should her female gynecologist be a permissible exception to the rule? Does she know her doctor's sexual orientation? If it's supposedly a sin to be seen nude by anyone but our spouses, shouldn't a truly holy lady prefer death to the supposed sin of baring one's "private parts" for the inspection of gynecologists? One thing that can be said for extreme Moslem groups such as the Afghanistan Taliban is that, unlike many Western Christians who share their negative view of the body, they do not make exceptions. The Taliban teaches it is better for a woman to die than to be treated by a male doctor. Unlike those extreme Moslems, many Christians settle for compromises, contradictions and inconsistencies.

11. How will your wife keep the sight of her body "for your eyes only" if she is hospitalized? Privacy in hospitals is a joke, epitomized by the silly "Johnny" they make you wear. It is designed so that, for all practical purposes, personnel can easily get at any part of your body, and the parts they are usually most interested in accessing are "down there." Whenever I am hospitalized, I call their bluff and they readily admit that the "johnny" is a joke and are happy to let me just go nude, which is really nifty as far as they are concerned, because no clothing gets in the way of anything. But even if a patient attempts to maintain some modicum of (false) modesty, even Houdini himself couldn't keep his body private. So again, reserving the sight of one's body for one's spouse alone is just not doable unless, like extreme Moslems, you'd rather die than be hospitalized where eyes of the opposite sex might see your body.

12. Why, after 2,000 years of opportunities, hasn't the Catholic Church, who has the obligation to be a good

---

[1] I saw the original movie in the early 70s. In the 80s I saw it again and lamentably, most of the nudity had been expunged.

shepherd & guard our souls, has never, ever, come out and condemned nudism or defined just how much body must be veiled in order not to be "immodest"?

13. Why would God have commanded the surgical exposure of the heads of all the phalluses in Israel to be the sign of His covenant with His Chosen People?[1] Is He a perv? A bad practical joker? Are we not blaspheming Him by ungodly, prudish behavior and beliefs inconsistent with His revealed attitude?

14. Why would the Vatican Museum be loaded with nude art, from the ceilings of chapels to the murals on papal bedroom walls?

15. Why would some bishops in Oceania missions have permitted women to go to Mass topfree? And why would a famous Spanish Capuchin missionary bishop, trying "to be all things to all men,"[2] wear nothing but a cord around his waist to hold up his penis, sheathed in a leaf?[3]

16. Why would the All-Holy Christ have allowed Himself to be forced to become a scandal, provoking everyone to lust by allowing Him to be stripped & crucified nude?[4] He could have been sacrificed for our sins just as well wearing "Speedos."

17. Why would there be so many pious priests, Catholics, other Christians & ministers, & other upright people who practice the lifestyle of social nudity?

18. Why should only married people be gifted with the opportunity to come to terms with the body? We all have them. We all deal daily with people of the opposite sex who have them. Shouldn't it be just plain part of being human that everyone should learn to regard bodies chastely?

19. Isn't it obvious that, by compulsively hiding the body we insure good business for Hugh Hefner, Larry Flynt, Howard Stearn, & other vultures of their stripe who take advantage of the ridiculous & totally unnecessary situation that people like your wife create, and scandalize millions of precious souls for whom Christ

---

[1] Cf. Genesis 17:10ff.
[2] I Corinthians 9:22.
[3] Cf. "All Things to All Men" on pp. 242ff.
[4] Cf. John 19:23ff.

suffered & died? Almost all of their business comes from people who are simply (& rightfully & naturally) curious. *Playboy* could not have sold on the streets of Alexandria in 250 A.D. Nudity was common in daily life. If you were to have attempted to sell *Playboy to* some Alexandrian, he would likely have looked at you like you had three heads & would have reported you to the looney police. Wasn't this Alexandrian culture far better suited to chastity than the repressive culture your wife defends and fearfully cowers behind?

20. Why would St. Clement of Alexandria have recommended nude wrestling as the ideal Christian sport?

22. Why would some Catholic retreat houses allow nude body massage of the opposite sex? I know a Jesuit priest who timidly stripped down to his skivvies for his massage therapy by a nun masseuse, who insisted that he not be silly and get naked. Since he is a naturist, he gladly obeyed. I also know a professional masseur who is a practicing Catholic and he massages many women who are nude, including one client who is a nun. The bodies of these clients are not only for the eyes of their spouses any more than the sight of their faces are.

23. Before her demise, the Swedish wife of this Catholic masseur, who was also a masseuse, had a job as a live model for medical students. Not one square inch of her body was reserved only for her husband's eyes, but was probably better known to the students than their own bodies, or, if some were married, than the bodies of their spouses.

The "for your eyes only" idea is probably usually an excuse and cop-out, hiding real shame and self-contempt. I would bet that in almost all such cases the spouse who espouses this excuse exposes her hypocrisy when she is ashamed even before her husband's eyes, and who, in their conjugal life, cannot give her whole self as a gift because she does not regard it as worth giving. This is a recipe for a miserable marriage.

But suppose there actually is a wife somewhere out there who believes in Barbara Streisand's "for your eyes only" way without shame and self-hate. In the best of scenarios, her way can only be said to be "poetic."

My wife is my pride and joy—my boast. I want to put her on a pedestal and dance around her with the exuberance of King David before the Ark of the Covenant,[1] blowing bugles! Why on earth would I want to jealously hide her away in my closet, reserved in all respects, "for my eyes only"? When people buy a new car or suit do they hide it away in their garage or closet or rather, parade it around town, hoping to draw attention to what they are proud of?

Where the "for your eyes only" way is off base is in its root which is the same old, "nude is lewd" bugaboo. Yes, sacramental sex is only for those vowed to each other, but what does that have to do with social nudity? Sex involves the whole body—perhaps head and hands as much as genitalia. Thus, the only true way to live the "for your eyes only" way is to do as the strictest of Moslems do, hiding every square inch of the bodies (including hands and faces) of those in their harems.

This last little "detail" ought to tip us off to what is really going on—possessive, jealous, covetous, selfish, self-satisfaction. The wives of the harem are private toys for one's own pleasure. But this has absolutely nothing to do with Christian, sacramental sexuality which is the antithesis of narcissistic selfishness and carnal self-gratification.

To sum up, the "for your eyes only" way is a very thinly veiled cover-up for reprehensible shame and self-contempt. The ladies who have modeled for our publications have not stolen anything from their husbands. The truth is that they have given their husbands *more* because they truly believe and live that their bodies are noble, beautiful and worth giving to their husbands. This deep self appreciation not only glorifies their husbands, but also glorifies God, Who gifts them with all they are: "By the grace of God I am what I am!"[2]

Peace always,
Jim C. Cunningham

---

[1] Cf. II Samuel 6:14ff & I Chronicles 15:27ff.
[2] I Corinthians 15:10.

Nude Wrestling

by St. Clement of Alexandria[1]

From Book III, Chapter X, *Paedagogus*:

The gymnasium is sufficient for boys, even if a bath is within reach. And even for men to prefer gymnastic exercises by far to the baths, is perchance not bad, since they are in some respects conducive to the health of young men, and produce exertion—emulation to aim at not only a healthy habit of body, but courageousness of soul. When this is done without dragging a man away from better employments, it is pleasant, and not unprofitable. ... But let not such athletic contests, as we have allowed, be undertaken for the sake of vainglory, but for the exuding of manly sweat. Nor are we to straggle with cunning and showiness,[2] but in a stand-up wrestling bout, by disentangling of neck, hands, and sides. For such a struggle with graceful strength is more becoming and manly, being undertaken for the sake of serviceable and profitable health.

Book II, Chapter XI:

Accordingly, deriding those who are clothed in luxurious garments, He says in the Gospel: "Lo, they who live in gorgeous apparel and luxury are in earthly palaces."[3] He says in perishable palaces, where are love of display, love of popularity, and flattery and deceit. But those that wait at the court of heaven around the King of all, are sanctified in the immortal vesture of the Spirit, that is, the flesh, and so put on incorruptibility. ... And Isaiah, another prophet, was naked and barefooted,[4] and often was clad in

---

[1] St. Clement of Alexandria is among the earliest Fathers of the Church. He died in 215 A.D.

[2] Thus St. Clement would *not* have approved of the ostentaticus antics of the WWF!

[3] Luke 7:25.

[4] Cf. Isaiah 20:2f.

sackcloth,[1] the garb of humility. And if you call Jeremiah, he had only "a linen girdle."[2] For as well-nurtured bodies, when stripped, show their vigor more manifestly, so also beauty of character shows its magnanimity, when not involved in ostentatious fooleries.

Book III, Chapter III:

Man may, though naked in body, address the Lord. But I approve the simplicity of the barbarians: loving an unencumbered life, the barbarians have abandoned luxury. Such the Lord calls us to be—naked of finery, naked of vanity, wrenched from our sins, bearing only the wood of life, aiming only at salvation.

Book III, Chapter X:

... and also rubbing one's self when anointed with oil. To render one who has rubbed you the same service in return, is an exercise of reciprocal justice; and to sleep beside a sick friend, help the infirm, and supply him who is in want, are proper exercises.

Book III, Chapter XI:

The Instructor permits us, then, to use simple clothing, and of a white color, as we said before. So that, accommodating ourselves not to variegated art, but to nature as it is produced, and pushing away whatever is deceptive and belies the truth, we may embrace the uniformity and simplicity of the truth. ... But it is monstrous for those who are made in "the image and likeness of God,"[3] to dishonor the archetype by assuming a foreign ornament, preferring the mischievous contrivance of man to the divine creation.

---

[1] Cf. Isaiah 20:2.
[2] Jeremiah 13:13.
[3] Genesis 1:26.

Topfree Penitence

by Jim C. Cunningham

Isaiah 32:11 says:

"Tremble, you women who are at ease, shudder, you complacent ones; strip, and make yourselves bare, and gird sackcloth upon your loins."

Here God is commanding the sinful women among His Chosen People to do penance, and clearly prescribes their penitential garb: They are to be naked, except for a girdle of sackcloth. How, then, can any Christian (or Jew) think it is "immodest" to go topfree when God Himself clearly commands it here? Like St. Paul in I Timothy 2:9f, the immodesty that God condemns is not the mere exposure of the body He created, but rather, fancy, ostentatious clothing, no matter how much skin it may cover. Many Christians who do not have the mind of Christ, but rather of their own, very narrow world, judge women who go braless or topfree as "immodest." Topfree women at the beach may not be *penitential*, and may not wear G-strings made out of *sackcloth*, but they are definitely not exposing anything that God objects to. When will all the "back to the Bible" Christians practice what they preach?

Commentary:
I Corinthians 10:25-31

by Jim C. Cunningham

Some anti-nudist Christians oppose social nudity on the grounds that it scandalizes our brothers in Christ whose consciences we should respect. They refer to the early Church controversy over whether a Christian may eat meat that had been sacrificed to idols which, in some Gentile areas was all the meat sold in the marketplace. They say that even if it is true that "nude is not lewd" (which they really do not believe), even so, since many of our brethren *do* believe that "nude is lewd," our nudity necessarily scandalizes them. Surely, Christian charity requires that we be sensitive to our neighbor, but where do we draw the line?

Many Christians believe it is immoral to imbibe any alcoholic beverage whatsoever. They even insist that Jesus drank grape juice at the Last Supper! Of course, most of us know they are mistaken—that wine is God's gift to "gladden the heart."[1] So just what does Christian charity dictate in such situations?

We must always watch our behavior and make judgments about what is appropriate in certain circumstances and in the presence of certain people. But situations will occur that challenge our judgment.

Suppose you are celebrating your wedding anniversary at a nice restaurant. You have ordered a bottle of Asti Spumante, when in comes a party of Seventh Day Adventists whom the hostess proceeds to seat at the very next table. Do you quickly cancel your order? Imbibe the champagne "in their faces"? Just do as you would normally do?

Or suppose you are at a clothing-optional beach with your family. You are all enjoying sun and surf clothed as God intended. You are stretched out on your back, gazing up at puffy white clouds that look like little naked cherubim, when you suddenly turn and see some Christian brethren strolling toward you whom you know think "nude is lewd." Do you jump up, unabashedly waving for them to join your picnic? Do you bury your heads in the sand like ostriches and hope they do not recognize the part of you that remains visible? Do you scramble for your clothes? Or do you do nothing at all differently, but simply act normally, praying that your chaste example will not scandalize them but edify them?

St. Paul offers clear guidance on how to handle such situations in this passage. Below I reproduce the literal text (Revised Standard Version), followed by my para-

---

[1] Psalm 104:15.

phrase, substituting being nude for eating meat sacrificed to idols. The text speaks for itself, and only those will make problems out of it who will make problems out of it.

Literal Text:

25Eat whatever is sold in the meat market without raising any question on the ground of conscience. 26For "the earth is the Lord's, and everything in it." 27If one of the unbelievers invites you to dinner and you are disposed to go, eat whatever is set before you without raising any question on the ground of conscience. 28(But if some one says to you, "This has been offered in sacrifice," then out of consideration for the man who informed you, and for conscience' sake— 29I mean his conscience, not yours—do not eat it.) For why should my liberty be determined by another man's scruples? 30If I partake with thankfulness, why am I denounced because of that for which I give thanks? 31So, whether you eat or drink, or whatever you do, do all to the glory of God.

Paraphrased Text:

25Go nude where such is the custom without raising any question on the ground of conscience. 26For "the earth is the Lord's, and everything in it—including our bodies." 27If a nudist unbeliever invites you to a nudist event and you are disposed to go, be nude like the others without raising any question on the ground of conscience. 28(But if some one says to you, "This event is lewd," then out of consideration for the man who informed you, and for conscience' sake— 29I mean his conscience, not yours—do not participate.) For why should my liberty be determined by another man's scruples? 30If I go nude with thankfulness for the wonderful bodies God has made, why am I denounced because of that for which I give thanks? 31So, whether you wear clothes or go nude, or whatever you do, do all to the glory of God.

Designed for Nakedness

by Leigh Orton

Human behavior is both diverse and complex. What is considered normal human behavior varies greatly in different countries and cultures. The wearing of clothing is a major part of our lifestyles around the world. The suggestion that we should not wear clothing would be controversial to say the least. Global attitudes to public nudity range from indifference to outright opposition. In our western society, the majority of people spends as much time as possible clothed, even when sleeping. Most would consider that, except for the purposes of intimacy, the normal thing to do is to shield their bodies from the eyes of others, sometimes even their own family members. But those who promote social nudity in our culture have challenged this mindset in favor of a changed attitude to both the body, physical nudity and the need for clothing.

So which should be considered normal human behavior—to be clothed or to be naked? As I have contemplated the whole notion of nude living I have had to wonder whether nakedness should not only be considered *normal* for us human beings, but could be a significant and vital part of our *design* and *purpose*. Of course, clothing is, at times, necessary and appropriate. But is it *always* necessary? If we consider our human make-up spiritually, physically and socially, and the evident intentions behind our creation, we find good reason to suggest that covering our bodies with clothing should not be the *norm* for daily living, but rather the *exception*. I suggest that nakedness should be *normal*.

Most of us would be familiar with the adage, "If God meant us to be naked, we would have been born that way." Although laced with a degree of sarcasm, this statement speaks to God's intention. God does nothing by mistake or without a definite purpose in mind. Although much of what God created has since suffered decay, it is safe to say that how He originally created our world and everything in it, is the way He wants it to be. "God saw all that He had made and it was very good."[1] No one will deny that every baby born into the world is, without exception, naked. With every new birth God affirms nakedness as part of our make-up and therefore part of the way we were designed.

According to Genesis 2:25, the very first human beings were created naked and unashamed. However, we're also told that they hid from God and from each other after they had disobeyed God. In Genesis 3:10 Adam says to God, "I heard You in the garden and I was afraid because I was naked, so I hid from the Lord God among the trees of the garden." Also in verse 7, "Then the eyes of both of them were opened, and they realized that they were naked, so they sewed fig leaves together and made coverings for themselves." This was not so much a covering of their bodies out of embarrassment at being seen naked, as it was an attempt to escape judgment and rejection because of their guilt and sin. That is why Adam hid from God. We find that God subsequently made coverings of skins for them,[2] primarily to demonstrate their need of a spiritual covering for sin, and also for physical protection from a now hostile environment. But it is clear that for Adam & Eve to wear clothing was not really God's idea. God had created them naked and unashamed and His desire for that remains unchanged.

We might expect that when someone gives an account of something he has just made, he would be eager to describe his creation in detail as to appearance, color, size, shape etc. But interestingly, God, in his Word, gives us *only one* descriptive detail concerning the appearance of the man and woman He has just brought into being: that they were naked and felt no shame.[3] As for the other details of their appearance, God says nothing. Why would God appear to single out this one aspect of man's appearance? We've already suggested that God designed us to be physically naked. But could it be that God views nakedness as *characteristic* of the way he wants us to relate to Him and to each other? God's supreme purpose in creating us was for Him to love us and enjoy a spiritually

---

[1] Genesis 1:31.
[2] Cf. Genesis 3: 21.
[3] Genesis 2:25.

intimate relationship with us. This is why He made us in His own image and likeness. He wanted someone like Himself whom he could love and relate to. He desired a relationship with His creation that was open, honest, truthful, and without fear or shame. He created us with nothing to hide. Could this be why the only description He gives us is, "The man and his wife were both naked and they felt no shame"?[1] Fear, guilt and shame destroy relationships. We are designed to relate to God and to one another without fear of judgment or rejection and to be able to have others know what we are like underneath, and still find friendship, acceptance and love. Many people are drawn to social nudity because of an inner yearning to experience this kind of relationship—a life without shame, rejection or guilt at both a social and spiritual level.

There are also features of our physical bodies that suggest that nakedness is part of our normal design and function. The human skin is designed to be exposed to sunlight. One vitally important function of the skin is to produce Vitamin D which is necessary for maintaining healthy, strong bones. It is even more necessary with increasing age. Vitamin D is synthesized in the skin when exposed to sunlight. Although sunlight is not the only source of vitamin D, it is obvious that the skin was not designed to be covered, but rather exposed to sunlight in order for us to remain fully healthy.

The human sex glands are the ova in the female, and the testes in the male. The ova are designed to function at normal body temperature and are found deep in the pelvis of the woman. However, the testes in the male, whose function is, in part, to produce sperm, are found outside the body. This is because normal levels of sperm production occur best at a temperature lower than normal body temperature. Should they become too warm, the testes will move further away from the body, as in a hot shower or bath, to maintain a cooler temperature. It seems totally out of harmony with the purposes and function of the human body to wrap the male genitals in clothing for prolonged periods of time. Yet most in our society are prone to do this, even in hot weather conditions.

---

[1] Genesis 2:25.

The skin is sure to be cleaner when not covered by clothing. Three conditions necessary for the growth of bacteria are warmth, moisture and darkness. All three of these exist on the skin under clothing. Bacterial growth that is unchecked may give rise to illness and disease. On the skin of the naked body the environment is one of coolness, dryness and light. Such an environment is far preferable to one that harbors and promotes the growth of bacteria. The skin is also instrumental in maintaining a normal body temperature through the evaporation of sweat. The sweat on the skin is most efficiently evaporated only when the skin is exposed to the light and air. Sweat that is covered by clothing is trapped, promoting bacterial growth. Exposure of all of the skin to light and air as often as practical will go a long way to maintaining clean, healthy skin, especially in areas like the groin where skin folds and creases tend to trap sweat and harbor bacteria. It is unwise at best, to unnecessarily cover the body with clothing when the skin has been designed to function uncovered and exposed to it's natural environment.

Doubtless there are many more reasons than are mentioned here, why being naked could be the normal, natural thing to do. To refuse to wear clothes at all, regardless of conditions, could rightly be called an act of lunacy. But so is the compulsion to wear clothes regardless of conditions. For many people social nudity seems to be nothing more than a way to relax—a kind of hedonistic hobby. But like much of our human experience, social nudity is more than skin deep, encompassing our whole being. A lifestyle of being naked when appropriate, clothed when necessary, and enjoying the real benefits of social nakedness, is indeed a healthier, more balanced way to live in harmony with our intended design and purpose.

Pope John Paul II, Address to Priests[1]

Praise God every day for the gift of your manhood! Praise God every day for the gift of your bodies! If you are uncomfortable with the gift of your body, then you are uncomfortable with the very gift that God has given you.

---

[1] March 10, 2000.

Nothing Shall I Want

by Jim C. Cunningham

It is a hot, August day. You are standing in a lush meadow by a country road. Your neighbor's hay wagon has just passed on his way to his barn a mile away at the foot of majestic mountains that jut up into the sky as though piercing the puffy white clouds that drift indolently by. They look like colossal reflections of your sheep, which quench their thirst at a meandering brook babbling through a field of wildflowers not far away. Not long before, you too had refreshed yourself in that brook, lying in it as the bubbly water caressed you all over, rinsing away the heat of the morning's labor. Bejeweled with droplets sparkling like diamonds still clinging to you as the balmy breeze wafts over your bare, bronzed skin giving you goose bumps, your self-awareness increases and you are reminded that "thou art from earth, and unto earth thou shalt return."[1] But your very keen consciousness of yourself in the context of that glorious panorama of created splendor, also reminds you that you are existentially related to Someone infinitely transcendent Who created it all and Who, every moment, holds every puniest particle in being.[2] You are a paradox, like those massive, imposing mountains, so weighted to earth, yet by their nature, tickling the white and azure heavens. The transient clouds tease their stateliness to stretch ever higher, challenging them to the very zenith of their stature. An eagle hovers high aloft, like you, belonging to both earth and heaven. It seems to represent your soaring spirit which has welled up from within you, overpowering all your senses. You are possessed with a feeling of complete integrity and wholeness, in communion with all, and the All in all. "Behold, it is very good."[3]

Not long ago, when your neighbor had rounded the bend behind you on the winding road playing tag with the elusive, intertwining brook, you had suddenly become

---

[1] Genesis 3:19.
[2] Cf. Colossians 1:16f & Acts 17:28.
[3] Genesis 1:31.

aware that you had left your overalls hanging on the sheep fence on the opposite bank. But the powerful, ever increasing sense of total contentment had detached you from all such concerns. They seemed more distant than anything within sight. They seemed so alien, or even unreal, like a phantom of the night that vanishes in the light. But you belong neither to darkness nor night, but are a child of the day and of light.[1] Your bare feet are rooted in the cool clover, while buzzing honey bees busily zigzag among the white and purple blossoms, obsessed only with gathering pollen for their honey making, as unconcerned with you and your vast inner world of consciousness as you are to those dirty overalls and the unreality they represent. Despite the plodding but determined pace of the oncoming wagon, feeling as you do, you could no more scramble for those overalls than those mountains could skip like yearling rams.[2]

You can hardly discern any details of the wagon, though you are now able to barely see the two horses and their bobbing heads as they tug at their weighty load in the late morning heat.

Like the whale that expelled Jonah onto the Ninevite beach,[3] your inner rush of serenity suddenly spews forth Psalm 23 into the tranquil harbor of your drumming heart. Though standing still, all is dancing within, like an unself-conscious ballerina whose agile body is the enfleshment of the story's music and message, or like the naked dancing of King David, too overcome with the thrill of the presence of the Ark to care about the social proprieties that squelched the love and gladness of his wife's hardened heart.[4]

You "lift holy hands"[5] as Paul taught Timothy, extending your arms in the sign of salvation, palms up as though both to offer and receive. You pray with soul and body, from the cool timothy that tickles your ankles to the increasing warmth of your still damp hair, the sun tirelessly reclaiming that moisture for those sheep-like cloud

---

[1] Cf. I Thessalonians 5:5.
[2] Cf. Psalm 114:4.
[3] Cf. Jonah 2:10.
[4] Cf. II Samuel 6:14ff.
[5] I Timothy 2:8.

puffs. Your prayer comes from more than your own wholeness; the entire panorama that is your divinely designed temple looks to you as head cantor, eager to echo the cadences of your celestial chant unto Him for Whom they are. You are their high priest, offering all to God, through, with and in yourself.

But your hymn is infinitely more powerful because it is not merely the composition of creation, however exquisite it all may be, but it has its source in His Spirit praying in you, recognizing that you do not know how to pray as you ought.[1] The wind that rushed at Pentecost[2] now blows where He wills,[3] and He wills to blow in you like bellows fanning the flames of love in your heart, like the inspiration that overwhelmed David as he sat with his lyre,[4] the very first to be gifted with this hymn which you now chant:

"The Lord is my Shepherd; there is nothing I shall want."[5]

Their thirst now thoroughly quenched, the sheep hear your familiar voice[6] and climb the embankment and amble towards you, safe and secure in your unobtrusive presence. Grasshoppers leap this way and that, and honey bees make room for the oncoming sheep without being too grudging; there is abundance for all. None want for anything. Contentment lies as thick as the sweet clover.

What you are to your sheep, the Lord is to you. As they graze contentedly, peaceful and secure in your presence, so you, too, are content, keenly aware of the gentle presence of your Good Shepherd. The sheep want for nothing. When they began to get thirsty, you led them to the living water of the meadow brook, and now you have led them to delicious, verdant pasture. Some graze, while others lazily slumber, resting on the cushiony softness. They appear to mirror their fluffy, vaporous images drifting above.

You, too, want for nothing other than what your Good Shepherd provides at the moment. Though you have

---

[1] Cf. Romans 8:26.
[2] Cf. Acts 2:2.
[3] Cf. John 3:8.
[4] Cf. I Samuel 16:23.
[5] Psalm 23:1.
[6] Cf. John 10:4.

worked off your hearty breakfast, you are confident that lunch will come in its time. Anxious neither for food nor raiment,[1] but only to bask in His abundant goodness,[2] you want for nothing.

You recall your Shepherd's words, "Is not the body more than clothes?"[3] and it has never seemed so true. The flaccid fabric of yonder overalls looks so pathetic and even vile. Anxious? For *that*? Nothing could be more beneath human dignity. Is that eagle anxious to cover its feathers? The sheep their wool? The field its flowers? No, all of King Solomon's royal vesture is not equal to the splendor of one lily of the field,[4] and as you are more precious to the Father than a whole flock of sparrows[5] or field of wild-flowers, you know well that nothing could possibly enhance your natural beauty and purity.

You remember St. Paul from your morning's meditation, "Having whatever *we need* to eat and wear, we are content."[6] The Good Shepherd meets all your needs and you are as content as your sheep. As they know that nothing can disturb their contentment as long as you are with them, so you know that nothing—not even the approaching hay wagon—can disturb your contentment. No one and nothing can negate the Gospel truth that your body is more than clothes and more splendid than all of King Solomon's wardrobe.

The breeze has almost entirely dried you by now. You feel the increasing warmth of the sun on your bronzed skin. Like the "woman clothed with the sun,"[7] you are a "great sign"[8]—a sign of God's perfect, paternal providence.

Now you can faintly hear the clap-clops of the approaching horses and the exuberant ululations of happy youngsters. You can see that morning haying has been a family affair, as several people seem to be either on the wagon or trotting along beside it.

---

[1] Cf. Matthew 6:25.
[2] Cf. Matthew 6:33 & Psalm 145:7.
[3] Matthew 6:25.
[4] Cf. Matthew 6:29.
[5] Cf. Matthew 10:31.
[6] I Timothy 6:8.
[7] Revelation 12:1.
[8] Ibid.

"The Lord has robed me with a mantle of justice, like a bride bedecked with her jewels."[1]

You are not only content and want for nothing, but you are keenly conscious of the exquisiteness of your natural raiment as any bride on wedding day. Far from wanting to scramble for cover, you delight in showing forth the intricate fancywork of your Tailor.

"There is nothing I shall want." Yes, that is precisely what you want so keenly—nothing—nakedness. You crave that nothingness because it glorifies its Creator. It proclaims, as if of itself, how truly good your Shepherd is. Your sheep, which belong only to earth, are oblivious to such considerations. They feel neither pride nor shame in their wool. But you are not solely from earth. Glory from above was breathed into you at conception.[2] Thus indifference is not natural for you. It is of your nature to be aware, to proclaim, to glorify. You are a reflective mirror, and you are proud of Him Whom you reflect.

Oh! How you do want only that nothingness, that total nakedness both of soul and body! Not to want anything is not the same as to want nothing. In the first case, man is loveless; he has no soul. In the latter case, he loves with all his soul, because his sole object of desire is nothingness. The man who has nothing has everything. He dwells in perpetual contentment. He knows his Shepherd is Good, in all times and in all circumstances. He who has Him for his Shepherd has everything, even if he has nothing, because His grace is sufficient for us,[3] and when there seems to be a lack, His grace always compensates for it.[4] The verdant pasture He provides requires the eyes of faith to be seen. Imagine the following choice: Either nearness to the Good Shepherd with what merely human eyes see as nothing, or, as Satan offered our Good Shepherd when he tempted Him, everything in the whole world[5]—except nearness to the Good Shepherd. It is, as we say, "a fool's choice." We know through faith that He Who gave us the Good Shepherd will give us all things

---

[1] Isaiah 61:10.
[2] Cf. Genesis 2:7; Psalm 104:30 & 139:13ff.
[3] Cf. II Corinthians 12:9.
[4] Cf. I Corinthians 10:13.
[5] Cf. Matthew 4:8.

besides.[1] If we seek first to be near Him, everything else will be given to us besides.[2]

Thus the onset of your neighbors cannot affect your contentment. They do not require you to suddenly want for anything more than what you already have at the present. Your faith and confidence in the Good Shepherd is stronger than anything that anyone can impose from the outside. This is the primary lesson that the example of all the martyrs teaches us.

The Lord, the Almighty God, Who made those cloud-piercing mountains, is your Shepherd! See how good He is, how thoroughly He satisfies your needs! See how nobly He clothes you! Isn't it tremendous?

Now you can begin to make out conversation and you see the children pointing.

The Spirit continues praying in you:

"In verdant pastures He gives me repose."[3]

Yes! Repose! You are anxious for nothing. You repose—utterly—in what you are, who you are, just as you are at this moment. Just as the sheep nearby repose on the fluffy meadow verdure, so you, too, feel that total repose. You recall how "re-pose" derives from the Latin, "to put back." Yes, all your desires have been put back inside of you. You want for nothing other than what you are just as you are, reposing fully in that reality. The approaching neighbors have not destroyed your repose. On the contrary, for some reason (the Spirit praying in you?), they only serve to confirm it, to deepen it, to prove it. They have not infected you so as to disturb the complete repose provided by your Good Shepherd. On the contrary, you delight in the opportunity to witness to the abundant goodness of your Shepherd, hoping to lead them, too, to His perfect providence.

Yours is verdant pasture. Your all-sufficient, natural livery is part of that verdure, as are the blue sky, the clear, babbling brook, the wide valley peppered with multi-colored wildflowers and ringed round by those majestic mountains. It is all so utterly verdant. You are ecstatic

---

[1] Cf. Romans 8:32.
[2] Cf. Matthew 6:33.
[3] Psalm 23:3.

with the realization of its complete adequacy. You want for nothing because your cup already runneth over.[1]

"By restful waters He leads me; He refreshes my soul."[2]

As the Spirit prays this in you, you think how literally true it is. You had just come out of those refreshing waters minutes before, and now you stand in the golden sunshine like a statue of the gods, and your awareness of this refreshes your soul. You feel so clean, so holy, so utterly crystalline, that shame is not only impossible, but not even conceivable. Any notion of shame would be like a defiling chink in the marble of that statue. Your awareness is solely of glory. Like a prism broadcasting the varied colors of light, shadows have no place—not even in thought. "We belong neither to darkness nor to night."[3]

"He guides me along the path of righteousness; He is true to His Name."[4]

Yes! Not the path of lies, of fears and cowerings, of discontent with our bodies as He made them, but along the way of holiness and rightness. How right it is for you to stand there ·so pleased with your Shepherd and His excellent care for you! You want to proclaim the Good News of this righteousness from those distant mountain tops.[5] You know that your whole being is like a trumpet blown by the Spirit, proclaiming jubilantly the King of kings.

"If I should walk in the valley of darkness, no evil would I fear; You are there with your rod and staff that give me courage."[6]

You think of the possible misconceptions and misjudgments your neighbors might have, seeing you standing there so apparently brazen and unabashed. The mind of the world and the worldly is so full of shadows, so negative, so preoccupied with death rather than life. The Good Shepherd has called you by name and led you out to green pasture.[7] He has led you out from the world's

---

[1] Psalm 23:5.
[2] Psalm 23:2f.
[3] I Thessalonians 5:5.
[4] Psalm 23:3.
[5] Cf. Matthew 10:27.
[6] Psalm 23:4.
[7] Cf. John 10:3.

perversions and senseless proprieties, away from the trampled, disgusting barnyard with its weeds besmirched with filth of every kind, and into purity and righteousness. You have followed His gentle biddings, allowing your mind to be transformed and renewed so you could judge aright what God's will really is, and thus present to Him your whole body as a living, acceptable and pleasing sacrifice to Him.[1] No, you cannot feign shame now, you cannot pretend to be of the world and its disordered, cacophonic ways of thinking. Even though you are yet in that valley of darkness where the worldly are your neighbors, you fear no evils such as they fear. You do not even fear the evil of their castigation, for your sole care is to be approved by God. Your Shepherd, too, was rejected by men,[2] but approved nonetheless and acceptable to God His Father.[3]

Nor do you fear the evil of straying, confident in His corrective rod and staff which always steer you aright. All this emboldens you, strengthens you and gives you courage.

Others, with no faith in the Good Shepherd's loving care, are not emboldened by His rod and staff. Instead, they produce the opposite effect in them. They cower in fear, hide under their wool, or disguise themselves in sheep's clothing, feigning allegiance to the Good Shepherd with their lip-service, but whose hearts are far from Him, hating discipline and ignoring His corrective Words.[4] Some fear His rod of correction so much that they refuse to follow along "the straight and narrow way"[5] for fear of straying. They are like the servant who, fearful of his Master, buried his talent rather than risk investing it.[6] He feared the rod, seeing in it punishment and retribution, instead of loving guidance.

Yes, as you stand there so conspicuous in your golden tan, so starkly contradicting the mind and ways of the world, you are aware of your continued journey along that narrow path of righteousness and purity. Like the good and faithful servants, investing what has been

---

[1] Cf. Romans 12:1f.
[2] Cf. Isaiah 53:3.
[3] Cf. I Peter 2:4.
[4] Cf. Psalm 50:6f.
[5] Matthew 7:14.
[6] Cf. Matthew 25:14-30.

entrusted to you,[1] you venture into unfamiliar lands, but you look not at the tempting distractions on the roadside, but your loving focus is on your Shepherd. Your comfort comes from Him, rather than simply the familiar wayside mirages, which appear to be voluptuous damsels, but when embraced, prove to be old hags. You see His staff, ever visible, ever leading onwards. It is your guiding star, your only navigation device. As long as you keep that ever in your sight, you stand firm;[2] you know where you are; you are with Him Who called you by name and led you out of the stinking sty and into verdant pastures.[3]

Others look at that staff and their hearts sink in dismay. They do not understand that true freedom is found only in following that staff. They mistakenly think it restricts their freedom; they feel like slaves, rather than sheep. This is because they have not known His voice.

But you have experienced the thrill of seeing Him approach as you strained and struggled, helplessly caught in brambles and briars. You know the experience of the joy of that loving Shepherd Himself picking His way through the sharp thorns, having left the other ninety-nine far away until He found you. No, His rod did not come down on your head as you looked up into His gentle face. Instead, He laid it aside and, with His bare hands getting scratched, gouged and bloodied all the while, He got your wool untangled at last.

It was because of that wool and the worldliness it represents, that you got all tangled up in the first place. You were shorn of the world at baptism, and clothed with light, but gradually you returned to both the rags and the shame they represent and all the darkness that goes with them, and ended up stuck in brambles, helpless. The more you turned and twisted to free yourself, the more entangled you got.

Instead of being deservedly kicked and beaten all the way back to the ninety-nine, He lifted you up and laid you right on His Own bare neck! As He triumphantly marched back, He whistled and sang happy songs. When He came to the ninety-nine He presented you like a prized trophy to

---

[1] Cf. Matthew 25:14-23.
[2] Cf. Psalm 16:8.
[3] Cf. John 10:3.

be placed on a pedestal, and not a convict to be shamed by being locked in the stocks.[1]

Yes, that was true freedom—the freedom of again being able to run in the way of His commands with His gift of freedom in your heart.[2] It felt like the rush of wind beneath the wings of that eagle soaring aloft. Every time you glance at that staff you relive that joyous thrill of true freedom.

But those others do not know His voice and have never been carried in His warm bosom,[3] hearing the throbbing of His meek and humble Heart.[4]

Of course, the Good Shepherd loves them, too, but they stubbornly resist His love, choosing briars instead of the right road, and the filthy barnyard and its few trampled, prickly weeds, rather than the living waters and the boundless, fluffy, delicious, fresh pasture to which His staff never fails to lead.

As you stand there in a reverie of such meditations, you are not even tempted to play the world's game again. How will they see the light enkindled in you if you snuff it out beneath the bushel-basket[5] of the warped attitude of the world? "Woe to those who call evil good and good evil."[6] They see the good work of the Creator and see evil rather than good. Yet the irony is that they love what they wrongly deem to be evil. "Nude is lewd," they believe, and overtly or covertly, they are enthralled by lewdness; it is the guiding principle of their lives. Those happy children frolicking around the hay wagon are the fruit of those very body parts their parents deem evil. How can it be so? There is no rational answer to any irrational question. No, not now, any more than at the beginning, when Eve, godlike, naked and free, listened to the serpent's irrational question, "Did God *really* tell you not to eat of *any* of the trees?"[7] Everything the world does and thinks is packed with that kind of guile and dishonesty. How glad you are to be free of it all. You have well learned your Shepherd's

---

[1] Cf. Luke 15:4-7.
[2] Cf. Psalm 119:32.
[3] Cf. Isaiah 40:11.
[4] Cf. Matthew 11:29.
[5] Cf. Matthew 5:15.
[6] Isaiah 5:20.
[7] Genesis 3:1.

counsel: "Watch and pray lest you enter into temptation."[1] Keeping your eyes fixed on that guiding staff, and staying in communion with the Sacred Heart of that Shepherd, temptation seems further away than those distant mountain peaks and as pathetic and ridiculous as your overalls drooping on the sheep fence.

"You have prepared a banquet for me in the sight of my foes. My head You have anointed with oil; my cup runneth over."[2]

Yes, "in the sight of your foes." There they are now, almost up to you, their facial features clearly discernible. They are consternated as their suspicions of your nakedness are confirmed as you loom into clear view. You know so keenly that your body is nothing less than the temple of the Holy Spirit,[3] and far more noble and wondrous than the temple of Solomon, which was one of the seven wonders of the world. Psalm 48:5 suddenly comes to mind:

"At once, they were astounded; dismayed, they fled in fear."

That was the reaction of the world to the grandeur of the ancient temple. How much more true of the temple of your body?

Your neighbors are shocked, astounded. They do not know what to make of what they see. Since what they see is so unlike them, they think you have gone mad, just as the world, and even Jesus' Own people, thought of Him long ago,[4] even trying to destroy Him by pushing Him off a cliff.[5] But as then He miraculously walked through their midst, untouched, so now, He Who dwells in you Who is greater than he who is in the world,[6] Who promised to be with you always,[7] Who is the same, yesterday, today and forever,[8] will therefore again miraculously cause His escape right through their midst. If they could inspire fear in you, then they would have you dancing to music they understand. But like your Good Shepherd, they may pipe

---

[1] Matthew 26:41.
[2] Psalm 23:5.
[3] Cf. I Corinthians 3:16 & 6:19.
[4] Cf. Mark 3:21.
[5] Cf. Luke 4:29.
[6] Cf. I John 4:4.
[7] Cf. Matthew 28:20.
[8] Cf. Hebrews 13:8.

you a tune, but you do not dance to it.[1] If you did dance to their music, then they could not only touch you, but destroy you. But you are oblivious to their cacophonies, hearing the beat of quite a different Drummer, and this creates that protective shield of grace[2] that the fiery darts of the enemy cannot pierce or even scorch.[3]

Rather than feel any intimidation, you feel just the opposite. You feel like you are at a sumptuous banquet in your honor, such a table fit for a king. And this, right in the sight of your foes. Of course, they aren't really your enemies. It is their ways and wiles that are your enemies.

The royal banquet prepared for you in their sight is yourself, standing there so fully contented—more so than by any banquet. You are more satiate than any feast could effect. All of King Solomon's royal raiment could not make you feel more dignified and regal than you are now. All the sumptuousness of the banquets of Bacchus could not make you feel more satisfied. You lack nothing. Nothing do you want. You already enjoy repose in verdant pasture.

You stand there looking straight at them, as stately as when Samuel anointed David king.[4] Your cup runneth over with the ecstasy of your happiness and contentment. You would have it no other way. You are glad they are there, looking on. Every cell of your body longs for them to see the good work that you are and to give glory to your Father.[5] Rather than they infecting you with their diseased minds, you stand as confident as the boy, David, stripped of all heavy, restrictive armor, ready to face the giant Philistine, Goliath of Gath.[6] You radiate glory like nuclear power burning away malignant melanomas. Like an army led by General Patton, your never stopping, aggressive boldness stuns them into imbalance, and never allows them to regain balance. They are on their heels, and can only find balance by falling down.

Accordingly, you have succeeded in making them sing in *your* key. They cannot understand what you are doing, standing there so openly nude, clearly within their sight.

---

[1] Matthew 11:17.
[2] Cf. Psalm 5:12.
[3] Cf. Ephesians 6:16.
[4] Cf. I Samuel 16:12f.
[5] Cf. Matthew 5:16.
[6] Cf. I Samuel 17:39f.

They have not even thought of trying to shield their children from what they regard as obscenity. They are entirely perplexed. Why didn't you run when you saw them approaching? Why don't you, even now, rush over to your sad looking, formless overalls baking in the sun? They look as pathetic as picked over lobster shells after a feast. You glance at them and recall the opening verses of the Bible, "In the beginning, ... the earth was a formless wasteland..."[1] But God put form to that chaos, and the greatest form was the body of man. You stand now as the exhibit of that glorious work of the Creator, whereas those overalls hang as testimony to the original formlessness, and later, of course, as testament to all that Adam & Eve did wrong by failing to understand and fully appreciate their God-likeness in their original nakedness, but hearkened to the "Father of Lies"[2] who deceitfully promised them what they already had if only they would disobey the "Father of lights."[3] The result was shame, fig leaves, and those pathetic overalls flopped on yonder fence.

No, you know you are god-like, a son of the Most High.[4] You know you are amply clothed in the Good Shepherd's goodness and want for absolutely nothing.

Utterly confused, your neighbors instinctively wave, as if dazed, their mouths agape. The children stare, studying you in innocent wonder. Before their parents think to attempt to restrain them, they race into the lush meadow, smiling and laughing, grasshoppers leaping before them.

"Hey, what you doin' all bare naked like that?" They frolic all around, tumbling, wrestling, pushing and pulling.

"Hey, let's go bare naked like our neighbor! Let's splash in the brook! Last one in's a rotten egg!" Clothes come flying off as they giggle and shout with glee, impervious to their parents' pathetic remonstrances, muted by their shock. Knowing it would be useless to even attempt to restrain their children at this point, they just maintain their plodding pace, cross the bridge over the brook,

---

[1] Genesis 1:1f.
[2] John 8:44.
[3] James 1:17.
[4] Cf. Psalm 82:6.

415

gazing upstream at their children, sparkling white in the sun, gaily splashing and shouting with innocent glee.

You grin. The happy shouts are better than the accompaniment of David's harp as you again raise your arms, palms up, but this time reaching for the sky, and finish your inspired psalm:

"Surely goodness and kindness shall follow me all the days of my life. In [my body, this temple of the Spirit,[1]] the Lord's Own house, will I dwell, forever and ever.."[2]

You absorb the precious, delicious moment, knowing that your Shepherd will lead you "from glory to glory,"[3] from the present glory which is so delicious to eternal glory such as no eye hath seen, nor ear heard,[4] and that the very body that is now not only thoroughly dry but now hot as well, will be changed, clothed with immortality.[5] Yes, even the world's greatest asset—death—will not snuff out the light shining in your body. Instead, your glorified body will then even more luminously glow with His glory. Yes, from glory to greater glory, God indwelling forever and ever. Your body is the Lord's Own house.[6]

As you walk back towards the brook to be refreshed again, the children dare you to approach, their hands in the pure water, poised to deluge you with their splashes. You laugh, loving the moment, glad that at least children understand.

"Father, I give You praise, for what you have hidden from the learned and clever, you have revealed to the merest children. Father, You have graciously willed it so."[7]

Suddenly racing into midstream, you return their splashes, laughing and shouting with those who belong to the same Kingdom. Amen!

---

[1] Cf. I Corinthians 3:16; 6:19 & II Corinthians 6:16.
[2] Psalm 23:6.
[3] II Corinthians 3:18.
[4] Cf. I Corinthians 2:9.
[5] I Corinthians 15:53.
[6] Cf. II Corinthians 6:16.
[7] Matthew 11:25f.

The Baptism of the Lord

From an Orthodox Liturgical Book

O compassionate Savior, putting on the nakedness of Adam as a garment of glory, Thou makest ready to stand naked in the flesh in the River Jordan. O marvelous wonder! How shall the water receive Thee, O Master and Lord, Who, as it is written, hast covered the roof of heaven with waters? O Jesus our Benefactor, we all sing the praises of Thine Epiphany.

He Who was enthroned before the ages with the Father and the Spirit, and Who has now in the last times been made flesh of a Virgin, in ways that He Alone understands, even Christ, comes to baptism, and through the divine washing He grants immortality unto all.

Wishing to bury our sins with water in the streams of Jordan, Christ our God comes forth in His compassionate mercy, and through baptism He forms us anew Who had grown corrupt.

Thou Who once hast clothed the shameful nakedness of our forefather Adam, art now of Thine Own will stripped bare; and Thou Who coverest the roof of heaven with waters, wrappest Thine Own Self in the streams of Jordan, O Christ Who Alone art full of mercy.

Be glad now and dance, O Jordan; leap for joy, O John, and let the whole inhabited earth rejoice exceedingly. Behold, Christ has appeared: He is stripped bare and baptized, wrapping human nature in a garment of incorruption.

Seeing Thee stripped naked, with fear Jordan said to Him Who had been born of a barren womb: "Suffer the Lord, Who cleanses the whole creation by fire and Spirit, to be baptized, O John. For behold, for this cause He has come to sanctify the elements of earth and water."

The Scandal of Neglect

by Jim C. Cunningham

Scandal is the serious sin of causing others to sin. Jesus said that those who cause a child to sin will be punished so terribly that "It would be better for him if a millstone were hung round his neck and he were cast into the sea."[1]

In the penance rite at the beginning of Mass we pray, "I confess... that I have sinned in my thoughts, and in my words, in what I have done, *and in what I have failed to do*." The first three categories of wrongdoing are "sins of *commission*"; the last category comprises our "sins of *omission*."

Sins of omission are too little acknowledged. Most of us do not intentionally push little old ladies down as they carry their grocery bags across the street, but perhaps most of us see her struggling, but for some reason or other, fail to offer a helping hand. We tend to wrongly define "goodness" as "not hurtin' nobody," rather than actively performing charitable deeds for others.

Perhaps the best definition of goodness is to be found in Matthew 25:31-46 where Jesus judges the nations solely on the basis of their performance of the works of mercy such as feeding the hungry, clothing the naked, visiting the sick, etc. Those who had done these things were compared to sheep at His right, separated from the goats, and called to enter into the Master's joy.[2] But others were judged to be goats, separated off to His left, and eternally punished.[3] One of the most interesting things to note about this passage is that the goats were not condemned for anything they *did*; apparently, they *did no evil*. They were condemned *for failing to do good*—sins of *omission*.

Jesus specifically referred to scandalizing *children* in the millstone passage cited above, because they are so vulnerable and dependent. Adults have experience, and

---

[1] Luke 17:2.
[2] Cf. Matthew 25:34.
[3] Cf. Matthew 25:41.

know how to be on the lookout for ravaging wolves, whether they come in their scraggly, scabby, wolf-skins, or disguised in sheep's clothing. But the young, like Little Red Riding Hood thinking the wolf was really Grandma, are wide open to be taken advantage of. We have a duty not to *abandon* them—to *leave them alone,* but to *guide and protect* them. It is not enough *not to harm* them; *we must help* them.

Just as there are *sins* of omission, so also there are *scandals* of omission—"*scandals of neglect.*" An example of a scandal of *commission* would be luring an innocent child to take and distribute drugs. Children lack prudence and caution, and by nature, look up to, and respect adults. Nothing could be more unnatural than to selfishly take advantage of a child's innocence and trustfulness as by luring him into sin. This explains the severity of Jesus' millstone metaphor.

There is one vast area of scandals of neglect that few people recognize, or are willing to recognize. It concerns body education and body appreciation. When a little child innocently asks his mother questions about the body, the "traditional" response is to be evasive or downright mendacious.

A toddler will logically and naturally remove his bathing suit as he frolics in the lawn sprinkler because he can see no good reason for wearing the wet, clammy, cold, and apparently completely useless thing. The "traditional" response is for the mother to admonish her child, and with punitive threats, insist that Junior keep his trunks on. If he asks the reason, nothing better is offered but, "Because I told you so; now do what I said, or you're going to get it!"

If a child is smart enough to ask a question, then he is naturally smart enough to comprehend the answer—if it accords with truth. Every question is but the flip side of the answer. This is why agnosticism is erroneous at its deepest root. It is like a purseful of coins with all heads and no tails. Of course, this is absurd, and so is agnosticism and her sisters, cynicism and skepticism.

There can be no more ripe, "teachable moment" than when a child himself composes a question. That fact alone means that he is 100% ripe and ready for an explanation, adapted to his intellectual level. When it comes to body matters, though, such questions are usually either hushed up as though he said something "naughty," or adults provide very inadequate, and even ridiculous "answers," leaving the child with a very unfulfilled feeling.

Now think what this must do to a developing child as he grows into and through puberty, never getting straight, adequate answers. He always has the sense that the whole body subject is somehow "naughty," and this is constantly reinforced, not only by what is said, but even more, by what is *not* said. According to the idea of sins of omission and scandals of neglect, we can harm a child not only by intentionally teaching him error, but also by either teaching them inadequately, so that they are not fulfilled, or by *not teaching them at all*.

Now let's see how they make worse, worst by "canonizing" their neglect and falsely labeling it "chastity," "purity," "modesty," etc. In other words, rather than admit their gross neglect in this area, they falsely call their sins of omission and scandals of neglect "virtue"! They are then doing just as Isaiah condemned: "Woe to those who call evil good and good evil."[1]

It is incredible how many child-rearing books teach that parents should never allow children to see natural nudity. The way some books deal with the topic, one would think that they were discussing some top secret, government "star wars" defense strategies. Even to make such a big deal out of it is unnatural and harmful. To ask whether children should be allowed to see nudity is really as absurd as asking why people walk on their feet instead of their hands. It should be a complete non-issue. To deal with it as if it were some dangerous, highly volatile thing is already to choose to cause harm rather than healing.

Consider a mother who takes a shower. She necessarily must make a choice whether to do it openly or clandestinely. She must decide whether to teach Junior that there is something mysteriously taboo about seeing her body, or else that there is nothing more mysteriously taboo about seeing her take a shower (or shower with her) than letting him watch her bake cookies (and let him help). If he asks questions about anatomy, they are absolutely no different

---

[1] Isaiah 5:20.

than his questions about baking procedures. If Mommy shuts the door and rebukes him if he walks in, she has made a decision that affects her child. If she leaves the door open and lets him see her naked with absolutely no fuss about it at all, then she has made a decision that affects her child. She is not in moral limbo. There is no middle ground. She either allows him to see her or she does not. She is bound by Christian charity to opt for what will most benefit and least harm her child.

My point is that it is precisely in situations like this that countless scandals of neglect are committed by parents who think of themselves as good, caring, nurturing and loving. Remember in Matthew 25:44 when those judged to be damned goats were honestly shocked to find themselves on the wrong side. They did not think they had done any evil either. But they had *not done* the truly good thing, and that is why they were condemned.

We have an obligation to teach the young about the body and right sexuality. Perhaps the main reason why modern society is so completely confused about sex is precisely because "good" Christian parents and churchmen failed to adequately teach in this area, preposterously calling their criminal neglect "religious virtue"!

So what do children do when those they naturally most trust, viz. parents and pastors, fail miserably to give them satisfactory answers to their very excellent questions, and who, by their fastidious avoidance of the issues, necessarily ingrain negative body attitudes in their youth?

The answer is a no-brainer: children look elsewhere. And just who are eager to fill in the vast void created by such compulsive neglect? Of course, it's those wolves, in and out of their disguise.

Various birth control organizations and public school "health" classes will "help" them; they will teach them that there is only one thing to consider when it comes to sexual "morality"—the willingness of those who engage in it. They will teach them how to commit sexual sins that Scripture strongly condemns, such as masturbation, fornication, adultery, homosexual acts, etc. The wolves will teach the untaught youth that there is nothing immoral about killing unborn babies; they merely strongly advise practicing "safe sex" so as not to get pregnant in the first place.

The eighth grader next door said she was learning sex education at public school. It included infant "care." Part of this required having to keep a baby doll with her every minute of the day and night, "feeding" it every couple of hours, night and day when it cried, changing its diapers regularly, etc. All this is nothing but those wolves in sheep's clothing insidiously wounding the vulnerable lambs, and almost all Christian parents are duped, thinking what a "cute" gimmick it is, and what a "good" education youth get nowadays. But the truth is that the child[1] learns less about baby care than about what a pain in the neck babies are, and if they are smart, they will be sure to use those condoms available for the asking from the school nurse, and learn about and use all the other kinds of "birth control" devices they learn about. And if they "make a mistake" and get pregnant with an unborn pain in the neck (AKA "baby"), then they should get an abortion as soon as possible to get rid of the unborn "nuisance."

In the meantime, while youth are taught lies, and anatomical details far beyond what they would have even thought to ask (proving their unreadiness), boys in the all male locker room at gym class fastidiously avoid undressing in front of each other. They are shown pornographic movies and how IUD's destroy embryonic human life in the uterus, but do not even see the buttocks (or even chests!) of their male peers. Calling good evil and evil good, no one dares to expose the true nature of the problem, lest they be seen as "perverts," whereas the truth is that the whole system is what is perverted, and especially those who defend it in the Name of Christ!

This entire situation is no accident. It was directly created by Christian parents and pastors who compulsively failed to do their jobs and by their many scandals of neglect, forced the tender youths entrusted to them to seek the answers, which they failed to give them, from very questionable sources, to say the least.

If "modest," "virtuous," Christian mothers and fathers failed to naturally provide body education by letting their children see them naked, by that scandal of neglect, they in effect, referred them to pornography and sex experi-

---

[1] Both boys and girls were forced to play the maternal role!

mentation for their body education. Once exposed to the lies of pornography, these "chaste" parents have waxed the slide for their sons to slip into all kinds of unchastity. And such fools are truly surprised when Junior, now a teenager, suddenly "comes out," announcing that he is "gay"! By their false "virtue" they themselves have transformed their pure, innocent children into sexual monsters. Then their sons are dying of AIDS in some nursing home, and such parents and pastors are still oblivious to their own guilt, just exactly like those astonished goats in Matthew 25:44. "Amen! As often as you failed to do it to the precious children I entrusted to you, you neglected to do it to Me."[1]

When will people finally understand that "grace builds on nature"? God's order of grace does not—indeed, cannot—contradict His order of nature. Rather, nature is the firm rock on which the wise man builds his house of grace.[2]

There is much truth to the humorous saying, "If God meant for us to go nude, we would have been born that way!" Nudity is natural at least some of the time, and in some places, most of the time. It makes no more sense to compulsively cover body parts because someone might look and lust, than it does to compulsively cover bakery showcases lest patrons look and indulge gluttonous thoughts. God's way is always truth, and never deceit. We use the expression, "the naked truth," because truth is, by definition, *naked.* A lie is the hiding of part or all of the truth, but love rejoices only in the truth.[3]

Many years ago, my friend, Joan, and I were philosophizing as we swam and sunned at an out of the way swimmin' hole on the Clyde River near Newport, Vermont. As with toddlers in the lawn sprinkler, there was no reason whatever for any clothing, so we were, of course, most appropriately attired as God originally intended.

Suddenly, we heard the voices of young people approaching. It seemed that they were turning back because seeing our nudity, they very mistakenly thought we must

---

[1] Cf. Matthew 25:45.
[2] Cf. Matthew 7:24f.
[3] Cf. I Corinthians 13:6.

be having sex and therefore would not appreciate any spectators. We were confronted with a moral choice:

We could stay as we were, say nothing, and let them make their erroneous deductions. This could only serve to reinforce whatever "nude is lewd" lies their parents and pastors had already managed to ingrain in them. Besides, we might have committed a scandal of commission, perhaps sending the message that fornication or adultery was okay.

Another option would have been to scramble for our clothes and make believe "we weren't doin' nuttin'!" But this would have been as bad as the first option.

The third option, which we chose, was to do what we could to repair any incipient scandal of commission that might have begun to sprout, and to remain nude for our own comfort as well as their body education, so miserably neglected for so many tender, developing years. Thus we managed to communicate with them before they had fully retreated, and convinced them that no sex was going on. We explained that we just preferred our birthday suits to bathing suits, and we asked if they had any objection if we carried on as we were. Since *they* felt like the intruders, and no doubt also because they couldn't believe their good fortune at being able to hang out with real, live, bare naked people, finally able to satisfy their long repressed curiosities in plain daylight, they were graciously obliging.

It was the right choice. By our chaste deportment we surely convinced them that sex had nothing to do with our nudity, nor should it. By carrying on as we were, those young teen boys and girls had a great opportunity to learn about simple anatomy. They did not have to resort to pornography or playing sexual games among themselves behind their parents' backs. We were simply natural, and they could satisfy their normal, healthy curiosity the natural way—simply by looking. This is, of course, just as it should have been all throughout their childhood. There should be no need whatever to resort to pornography and sinful and dangerous sex play. All they should ever have needed to do to find answers to most of their body questions was look—look at each other in the school locker room and gang shower, look at family members nude at home at least while bathing or changing clothes, look at swimmers at pools and beaches. Seeing people's bodies should have been as ordinary as seeing people—because bodies *are* people!

But Joan and I were an oasis in the desert created by their parents and pastors. At least for that one time they were able to somewhat quench their thirst, though I did meet them there on other occasions, and my nudity was always accepted by them as a given—just as it should be for everybody.

Needing to see bodies is like thirst. Just as we need to drink periodically, so we all need the frequent opportunity to see bodies. It is not at all like seeing a drawing on the overhead projector in health class. That artificial exceptionality exacerbates the thirst. They need real water—pure water, and that is the frequent and ordinary opportunity to see bodies in the plain light of day. We could not fully heal them by only that brief experience, but we were able to at least give them a drink which they appreciated.

I doubt any of those teens will forget Joan and me, and our example might well stir within them as the years go by. Maybe someday the truth of the body will fully dawn on them. Maybe it already has. Maybe they are now rearing their own children in a healthier way than they themselves were reared.

When people look at one another on a beach, they are, without being aware of it, asking themselves what each person looks like. Their mental questions are instantly answered when it comes to facial features and some other body details such as weight and height. But whether they are aware of it or not, everyone also wants to know what the rest of people's bodies look like. By being compulsively ("religiously"?) denied such simple, natural information, a very unnatural situation is created that God never intended. An unhealthy mind is created. The truly healing thing to do is to choose to be part of the solution rather than the problem. When it is doable, such as at that swimmin' hole on the Clyde River, the most healing thing to do is to imitate the wisdom of toddlers who know that wearing their clammy bathing suits is for the birds.

People—especially children—are starving to death for chaste body education. By failing to provide it we are not

425

neutral. There are only sheep and goats. there is nothing in between. We either help quench their thirst or let them die of thirst. Those who fail to give drink to the thirsty commit scandal, and thus share in the sins that their neglect has helped to cause. If children have to resort to pornography and sexual sin, we share in their guilt by our scandals of neglect.

I would rather skinny-dip in the sea than sink to its bottom wearing a millstone round my neck. How about you?

The Naked Baptism of Christ

by Michael A. Kowalewski

At Matins on the Forefeast of the Theophany, the sessional hymn exalts, "O compassionate Savior, putting on the nakedness of Adam as a garment of glory, Thou makest ready to stand naked in the flesh in the River Jordan. O marvelous wonder!"[1] For Christians, accepting the incarnation of Christ implies that the human body possesses a special religious meaning. Brother Cyril Guilbeault, S. C.[2] witnessed a baptism in a local parish church. In an interview I had with him, he recalled that during this baptism a priest submerged an infant naked into a baptismal pool. After the invocation of the Trinity, the priest lifted the child above his head and wrapped him in a white garment. An onlooker, unsettled by the unabashed nakedness, yelled out, "Sacrilege!"

Tragically, this onlooker seems to represent the attitude of modernity—the inability to see the sacredness of the body. Jesus Christ purified the waters of baptism naked as that infant. How would we react to a naked baptism? Would we look upon it with suspicion? *Pope*

---

[1] *The Festal Menanion* (Orthodox Liturgy), The Forefeast of the Theophany, Matins, trans. Mother Mary and Archimandrite Kallistos Ware (South Canaan, Pennsylvania: St. Tikhon's Seminary press, 1998), p. 303.
[2] Brother Cyril Guilbeault, S.C., teacher at Mount St. Charles Academy, Woonsocket, Rhode Island.

John Paul II declared, in his *Theology of the Body*, that understanding the sacredness of the body is important and indispensable in knowing what man is and who he should be.[1] Who we are, where we come from, our relationship to God, and our final destiny are somehow revealed in and through the human body as male and female.

We tend to anaesthetize and sanitize the Christian mystery. We do this in order to make this—at times shocking—mystery comfortable, and to appease our prim and proper sensibilities. What evidence is there that Christ was baptized completely naked? What sacramental meaning does it hold?

During the time of Christ people had an ease towards nakedness because they had a familiarity with the body that does not exist in the West today. Nakedness was a requirement for early Christian baptism. Nakedness was both practical and an expression of Roman culture. Jewish rites of purification and initiation, precursors to Christian baptism, point to another and far deeper understanding. Jewish rabbinical traditions ritualized nakedness, thereby transcending it's meaning from the profane to the sacred.

Complete stripping in the awe-inspiring baptismal rites of the early Church, and as alluded to by St. Paul throughout his epistles, follow the example of Christ's Own naked baptism in the Jordan by St. John the Baptist. With the incarnation of Christ, the body entered theology through the main door. Nakedness in the baptismal liturgies had a profound sacramental value for early Christians insofar as it spoke of the incarnation.

Sacred Scripture & Art

St. John the Baptist declared that he was not worthy to baptize Christ, stating that he, not Christ, should be baptized, "I need to be baptized by You, and do You come to me?"[2] When confronted by the priests and Levites, John said, "I baptize with water; but among you stands One

---

[1] Pope John Paul II, *Theology of the Body*, (Pauline Books & Media, 1997), General Audience Address August 18, 1982.
[2] Matthew 3:14.

Whom you do not know, even He Who comes after me, the thong of Whose sandal I am not worthy to untie."[1] St. John the Baptist was so humbled by Jesus that he felt unworthy not only to baptize Him, but to undress Him for His baptism.

Early Christian baptism was done by full immersion. This continues to be the present practice in the East. In the West, effusion has become the most common practice, though immersion is still considered both praiseworthy and preferable. *The General Introduction to Christian Initiation* in the Latin Rite instructs that full immersion is more suitable as a symbol of participation in the death and resurrection of Christ.[2] This affirms the superiority of the apostolic practice of immersion. Baptism, as St Paul states, is a burial: "Do you not know that all of us who have been baptized into Christ Jesus were baptized into His death? We were buried [immersed in water] therefore with Him by baptism into death, so that as Christ was raised from the dead by the glory of the Father, we too might walk in newness of life."[3]

Baptism by full immersion in a river or bath would naturally be accompanied by the action of taking off garments. St. Paul throughout his letters gives a variety of metaphorical allusions to the natural action of taking off and putting on clothing during the rite of baptism. In St Paul's Letter to the Colossians, he writes: "...you have put off the old nature with its practices and have put on the new nature."[4]

Sacred art of the patristic epoch of the Church unabashedly illustrates this complete stripping of the neophyte. A positive symbolic value of nakedness in Christian baptism may be gained from a study of early Christian iconography. Reductionists suggest that the presence of nakedness in early Christian iconography is either a decorative use of mythological conventions or an imitation of classical Greek painting. The fixedness and reserve of the naked iconographic figures invalidates this theory.

---

[1] John 1:26f.
[2] *The Rites of the Catholic Church as Revised by the Second Vatican Ecumenical Council*, "General Introduction to Christian Initiation," (New York: Pueblo Publishing Co., 1976), N. 22, p. 8.
[3] Romans 6:3f.
[4] Colossians 3:9f.

428

Nakedness in this primitive iconography, such as found in the catacombs, is expressing a profound theological language.

As one would expect in these icons, Adam & Eve in Paradise are naked. The only other Old Testament figures who are depicted naked are Jonah emerging from the mouth of the Great Fish, Daniel emerging from the Lion's Den, and the resurrected vision of Ezekiel. It is hardly necessary to emphasize that these Old Testament scenes containing naked figures are precisely those that were held to foreshadow the resurrection. On the basis of this iconographic evidence, nakedness is clearly a symbol of new life as promised in the resurrection, and when appearing in connection with the baptism, must be interpreted as signifying a rebirth into Paradise. The reductionists fail to understand the profound symbolic meaning of nakedness for Christians. Throughout the catacombs primitive icons of naked figures from both the Old and New Testament are depicted, to include Christ's naked baptism.

Christian art outside the catacombs presents an interesting picture of the time of the early Church. A 4th century Roman bas-relief and a 6th century Byzantine mosaic reveal a naked Christ being baptized. Close examination of these icons, moreover, reveals a preoccupation with Christ's genitals. Many icons conceal Christ's nakedness with a fish. There are iconographic canons that prevent the full depiction of Christ's nakedness. Some icons remove Christ's genitals completely. There existed a heresy that Christ was physically a eunuch. The most common way of depicting Christ's full nakedness in icons while concealing his genitals is with a forward leg. There are some icons that depict Christ's genitals. The genitals are very childlike, probably to express a prelapsarian innocence.

The loincloth is responsible for the commonly held fallacy in the West that Christ historically wore a garment of shame into the waters of the Jordan. During certain periods and in certain geographical locations, people had more of an unease towards the body and would often cover those parts which identified Christ's sexuality. Incidents concerning Michelangelo's Final Judgment testify to the immaturity of many clergy towards the body. The artist Daniele da Volterra was ordered by Pope St. Pius V to cover the loins of Michelangelo's naked figures, earning the sobriquet, "*Il Barachetlone*," "the trouser maker." In the statue-lined corridors of the Vatican Museum, male genitalia of all the Greek and Roman nudes had been chiseled off. Michelangelo, if he were still alive at that time, would have lashed out over such ludicrous immaturity. Michelangelo said, "What spirit is so empty and blind, that it cannot grasp that the human foot is more noble than the shoe, and the human skin more beautiful than the garment with which it is clothed?"

Michelangelo painted during the Renaissance, an era that was naturalistic in its expression, one that explored the beauty of human form. During this period, Christ, Whose divinity had been firmly established in the West was often depicted naked to emphasize His humanity.[1] But many Post-Renaissance Christians, from the later 16th century onward, were to see something shocking in all this, and so the "offensive" members were painted out wherever feasible. Such prudishness and obsession with the naked body was not kindred in spirit to the early Christians who viewed nakedness in terms of divine restoration, as we have seen. This examination of sacred scripture and sacred art clearly reveals that the loincloth in depicting Christ's baptism is not a historical fact but an expression of certain periods of cultural unease towards nakedness.

Jewish Rabbinical Traditions & Roman Antiquity

Pertinent to a background for Christ's baptismal nakedness is the occurrence of nakedness in sacred Jewish Rabbinical traditions and in secular Roman antiquity. The Ancient post-biblical texts that describe Jewish neophyte "baptism," consistently suggest that the neophyte was naked: "A man is present at the immersion of a man; and a woman at the immersion of a woman."[2] The Halakah

---

[1] Steinberg, Leo, *The Sexuality of Christ in Renaissance Art and In Modern Oblivion*, 2nd ed. (Chicago: University of Chicago Press, 1996), pp. 3-15.
[2] Smith, Jonathan Z., "Garments of Shame," *History of Religions*, Vol. 5, 1966, p. 219.

states that it was essential that the water reach every part of the neophyte's body: "...nothing must interpose between his flesh and the water."[1]

The Torah indirectly alludes to Aaron's nakedness in the ceremony of his washing and investiture.[2] This rite of initiation into the priesthood took place in about 1000 B.C. It provides an interesting example of how unclothing was ritualized, giving it a deep religious meaning beyond secular understanding. Whatever the Jewish understanding of ritual nakedness might have been we can assume that there was a deeper symbolic reason for it beyond what the ancient texts themselves state and that this custom was clearly carried over into Christian baptism as will be seen in the patristic baptismal mystagogies. It needs to be understood that Jews did not always view nakedness as a sight of horror. In I Samuel Saul lies naked in prayer. The nakedness was not the sign of horror. It was the sign of a prophet: "And he too stripped off his clothes and he too prophesied before Samuel and lay naked all the day and all that night. Hence it is said, 'Is Saul also among the prophets?'"[3]

Sacred Judaic influences were not the only impetus for the use of nakedness in Christian baptism. 4th century Roman culture was familiar with nakedness to a degree that does not exist in modern society. Birth and death occurred in the home, and bathing often took place in public baths because of the lack of private plumbing. Only the wealthiest had the convenience of having private baths with running water.[4]

Due to the practice of public baths, there did exist an ease towards nakedness that seems to have been transferred over to the baptismal ritual of the early Church. Indeed, secular customs in public bathing may have given Christians experience with nakedness that made them more open to naked baptism. Prudery would most definitely have been an obstacle to such a ritual.

Christians, to a degree, participated in the Roman culture in which they lived, so long as it was not contrary

---

[1] Smith, Op. Cit., p. 220.
[2] Leviticus 8:6f.
[3] I Samuel 19:24.
[4] Miles, Margaret, *Carnal Knowing* (London: Orbis, 1982), p. 26.

to their religious beliefs. Public bathing in and of itself, is a morally neutral act; however, it often became for many bathers a medium for sexual promiscuity. The Christian use of the public baths became a debated issue. If the public baths were frequently misused and problematic for the pagan Romans, drawing the attention of emperors to their regulations, they were more so for Christians.

In the mid-3rd century, the North African bishop, St. Cyprian, argued that consecrated virgins should avoid the public baths. These Christian women protested that such measures were unnecessary in preserving their purity.[1] St. Augustine of Hippo (354-430 A.D.) was somewhat more lenient than St. Cyprian; he prescribed baths for consecrated virgins once a month.[2]

Though ambiguous, the evidence seems to prohibit mixed bathing for Christians, or at least to approach it with vigilance. Nakedness in the secular context was viewed as potentially a dangerous incitement to lust, which was substantiated by the indecent behaviors that often took place in the baths.

Baptism developed a context for nakedness that removed the body from secular meanings and identified it as the site and symbol of sacredness, recovering a chaste language of the body. There was made a distinction between secular and sacred nakedness. Baptism protected the proper context for nakedness, not making it scandalous or subject to suspicion.

Secular nakedness in the baths, even when practiced by well-intentioned Christians, may have caused scandal through having the appearance of evil, due to the licentious reputation of the baths. St. Thomas, in his *Summa Theologica* states that something is said to be less than right through having an appearance of evil: "...if a man were to 'sit and eat meat in the idol's temple,'[3] though this is not sinful in itself, provided it be done with no evil intention, yet, since it has a certain appearance of evil, and a semblance of worshipping the idol, it might occasion

---

[1] St Cyprian, "On the Dress of Virgins II", *Ante–Nicene Fathers* (New York: Charles Scribner's Sons, 1903), vol. V, p. 430.
[2] St. Augustine of Hippo, Letter 211, Fathers of the Church Vol. 32, (New York: Fathers of the Church, Inc., 1956).
[3] I Corinthians 8:10.

another man's spiritual downfall. Hence the Apostle says, 'From all appearance of evil refrain yourselves.'[1]"[2]

This logic carries over into Christian use of the public baths. The Church, however, affirms and protects the sacredness of the body, thus nakedness in the context of baptism, for early Christians, does not fulfill the condition of "appearance of evil." Clearly, the Fathers viewed mixed bathing as part of the larger issue of sexual immorality and with nakedness in particular.

Both the sacred Jewish rabbinical traditions and the secular Roman customs of antiquity influenced early Christian baptism which finds its model in Christ's baptism in the Jordan. Keeping Christ's baptism in mind, let us examine the ancient baptismal mystagogies more closely.

The Fathers of the Church

Many of the Fathers of the Church eloquently expressed the need for stripping prior to the neophyte's entrance into the baptismal pool. It was a powerful and deeply moving symbol that conveyed the Gospel's message of rebirth. St. Hippolytus, presbyter in Rome after 212 A.D., gives the first written account specifying the removal of clothing for baptism,[3] and in the 4th century instructions for baptism throughout the Roman Empire stipulated nakedness. Several Fathers of the Church such as St. Cyril of Jerusalem, St. John Chrysostom and St. Gregory of Nyssa all specifically mention it in their baptismal instructions, and many other Fathers also allude to nakedness. Though St. Augustine left no detailed description of the actual ceremony for reasons of secrecy, it is speculated that he stipulated nakedness.[4]

Entering into the baptistery signifies admission into the Church, that is to say, the return to Paradise, which was lost by the sin of the first man: "You are outside of

---

[1] I Thessalonians 5:22.
[2] St. Thomas Aquinas, *Summa Theologica,* trans. English Dominican Province (Benziger Bros., 1947), Part II-II, Question 43, Art. 8.
[3] Burton, Scott, *The Apostolic Tradition of Hippolytus* (Cambridge: Archon Books, 1992), p. 46.
[4] Van Der Meer, F., *Augustine the Bishop*, (London: Sheed & Ward, 1961), p. 349.

Paradise, O neophyte," says St. Gregory of Nyssa to those who would put off their baptism. "You share the exile of Adam, our first father. Now the door is opening. Return whence you came forth."[1] It is the Paradise from which Adam was driven out and to which baptism restores us.

Theodore of Mopsuestia (350-428 A.D.) writes that the old garment symbolizes corruptible humanity: "Your garment, sign of mortality, must be taken off, and by baptism you must put on the robe of incorruptibility."[2] Theodore's mystagogy on baptism emphasizes mortality in association with the wearing of clothing. Theodore explains that clothing is a symbol of our dying nature. By breaking God's commandment Adam became mortal; and as a sign of this, God clothed him in dead animal skin.[3] It is a reproving mark of disobedience by which Adam was relegated to the necessity of wearing an artificial covering. Theodore relates the animal skin to the clothes of the neophyte.[4] The neophytes are instructed to remove their clothing before entering the baptism pool: "You draw therefore near to the holy baptism and before all you take off your garments. As, in the beginning, when Adam was naked and was in nothing ashamed of himself, but after having broken the commandment and become mortal, he found himself in need of outer covering."[5] Completely stripped, they stand upon their clothes in remembrance of Original Sin. Following the symbolic undressing, the neophytes are reminded of man's original nakedness, when he was free of shame and fear. They are brought forward to a baptismal pool where they are submerged three times in the Name of the Trinity.

St. John Chrysostom (347-407 A.D.), using Pauline imagery, gives a different emphasis toward the clothing/sin relationship. He perceives the shedding of clothes in relation to the neophyte shedding his evil deeds. Chrysostom states: "We put off the old clothing, which had been made filthy with the abundance of our sins, we put

---

[1] Jacques-Paul Migne, *Patrologiae Cursus Completus, Series Graeca,* Vol. 46, (Paris: Migne, 1857-1904), p. 417, sec. C.

[2] Ibid., XIV, 3.

[3] Cf. Genesis 3:21.

[4] Reily, Hugh M., *Christian Initiation* (Catholic University Press, 1974), p. 178.

[5] Smith, Jonathan Z., Op. cit., p. 227.

on new ones, which is free from every stain."[1] This of course is based on what St. Paul said to the Church of the Colossians: "...you have taken off the old self with its practices and put on the new self..."[2]

Clothing in Chrysostom's time, like ours today, was often vainly and scandalously used. Unnecessary luxury in the matters of dress and bodily adornment, expensive clothing and jewelry, is a sin against the Kingdom of God, where man appreciates others more than himself. The clothing and jewelry is to be stripped off during baptism, since it leads to the deeds of the old sinful self. Chrysostom urges his people to adorn themselves with virtues, rather than clothing and cosmetics.

St. Cyril of Jerusalem (350-387 A.D.) gives a Christological explanation for naked baptism. He associates the neophyte with Christ Himself, who was stripped of his clothing and crucified naked on the cross.[3] "You are now stripped and naked, in this also you imitate Christ despoiled of His garments on His Cross, He Who by His nakedness despoiled the principalities and powers, and fearlessly triumphed over them on the Cross.[4] Since the power of evil once reigned over your members, you should now no longer wear that old garment. I am not speaking now of your sensible nature, but of the corrupt old man with his deceitful desires."[5] To the worldly eye Christ's nakedness is seen as a humiliation, but through the eyes of faith this is not a defeat, but a triumph over evil. Underlying Cyril's image of Christ's triumph on the cross is Colossians 2:15. St. Paul states that this is a triumph over the "principalities and powers" of this world. The stripping away of Christ's clothes signifies the stripping away of these powers, and the nakedness, meant to be a humiliation, becomes thereby a sign of victory.

Through the mystagogies of Theodore, Chrysostom and Cyril we see the relationship between the scene of paradise in which Adam, vanquished by Satan, is clothed

---

[1] St. John Chrysostom, "Second Instruction," *Ancient Christian Writers* (London: The Newman Press, 1963), Vol. 31, p. 178.
[2] Colossians 3:9f.
[3] Cyril of Jerusalem, "Second Lecture on the Mysteries," *Fathers of the Church* (The Catholic University Press, 1970), Vol. 64, p. 161.
[4] Cf. Colossians 2:15.
[5] *Patrologia Graeca* (P.G.), XXXIII, 1077 B.

with corruptibility; that of Calvary in which Jesus, the New Adam, the conqueror of Satan, strips off His tunic of corruptibility; and finally, baptism, in which the person being baptized takes off, with his old garments, the corruptibility in which he shared as long as he was under the domination of Satan.

This baptismal nakedness signified not only a stripping off of immorality, but also a return to primitive innocence. St. Cyril stresses this aspect: "How wonderful! You were naked before the eyes of all without feeling any shame. This is because you truly carry within you the image of the first Adam, who was naked in Paradise without feeling any shame."[1] This is also the interpretation of Theodore: "Adam was naked at the beginning and he was not ashamed of it, this is why your clothing must be taken off, since it is the convincing proof of this sentence which lowers mankind to need clothing."[2] St. Gregory of Nyssa says: "Shame and fear followed the sin, so Adam & Eve did not dare any more to stand before God, but covered themselves with leaves and hid themselves in the woods."[3]

Therefore, we see the true symbolism of stripping off garments. It means the disappearance of the shame proper to sinful man before God, and the recovery of the sentiment, opposed to that of shame, of the filial trust, the *parrhesia*,[4] which was one of the blessings of man's state in Paradise. It is what Pope John Paul II was to call a rediscovery of the true language, or nuptial meaning, of the body. St. Gregory describes this return to the liberty of the children of God accomplished by baptism: 'You have driven us out of Paradise, and now You call us back; You

---

[1] *Patrologia Graeca, Op. Cit.,* XXXXIII, 1080 A.

[2] Ibid., XIV, 8.

[3] Ibid., XLVI, 374 D.

[4] *Parrhesia:* Greek term used thirty-one times in the New Testament. It means openness, publicness, candor. In II Corinthians 3:12 *parrhesia* is based on apostolic boldness or openness. In contrast to Moses' veiled face, Paul presents Christ unveiled and not ashamed. *Parrhesia* specifically towards God refers to one's confident relationship to Him. In the context of naked baptism, nakedness makes visible the invisible reality of confidence in relationship to God, a reality to be fully expressed in the *eschaton.* Cf. Horst Balz & Gerhard Schneider, eds., *Exegetical Dictionary of the New Testament* (Grand Rapids: Wm. B. Eerdmans, 1993), vol. 3, pp45-47.

have stripped us of those fig leaves, those mean garments, and You call Adam, he will no longer be ashamed, no, under the reproaches of his conscience, hide himself among the trees of Paradise. Having recovered his filial assurance,[1] he will come out into the full light of day."[2]

Christ's naked baptism as depicted in icons and practiced by the Fathers points to a profound sacramental significance of nakedness. Nakedness was not an option, it was necessary.

Theology of the Body and Conclusion

The use of nakedness in the Ancient Church during the baptismal rites had a sacramental value. The sacrament of baptism does what it symbolizes, but the full fruit in the soul of the neophyte is proportionate to his receptivity. Sacramental nakedness helped dispose the neophyte to the reception of the full effects of the sacramental and sanctifying graces of baptism. Pope John Paul II has underlined the sacramental value of the body in a series of weekly general audiences known as "The Theology of the Body." They were given over a five-year period at the outset of his papal ministry. The Holy Father confronts head-on today's false spiritualism. As contrary to conventional wisdom as it might seem, the Church does not need a more *spiritual* Christianity but precisely the opposite. Christians must develop a less *spiritual*, and more *incarnational*, and more sacramental vision in living their faith.[3] If the Holy Father is right, and the incarnation places the body and material creation at the center of our faith, then the sacramental value of nakedness, as practiced by the Ancient Church, deserves serious attention. "The whole world is a sacrament," writes Peter Kreeft, "a sacred thing, a gift."[4]

John Paul II affirms the sacramental value of the naked body: "The body and it alone is capable of making

---

[1] I.e. *"parrhesia."* See above note.
[2] P.G. XLVI, 600 A.
[3] Miller, Michael J., C.S.B., "Sacramentals in Catholic Theology," in Ball, Ann, *A Handbook of Catholic Sacramentals* (Our Sunday Visitor, 1991), p. 11.
[4] Kreeft, Peter, *Fundamentals of the Faith: Essays in Christian Apologetics* (San Francisco: 1988), p. 284.

visible the invisible mystery of God."[1] Sacramental nakedness means that it possesses a spiritual, religious meaning, which disposes the neophytes to receive divine life during baptism. Nakedness was an action that helped put the neophyte in touch with God's grace in Christ. Sacramental nakedness makes available, in the words of Vatican Council II on sacramentals, "a stream of divine grace which flows from the paschal mystery of the passion, death, and resurrection of Christ, the fountain from which all sacraments and sacramentals draw their power."[2] The neophytes should understand the baptismal ritual as both a rebirth, as in breaking the waters of the womb; and a burial into the water. St Ambrose mentions that the neophyte's descent into the Jordan (i.e. the font) recalls the naked entry into life and his naked departure from it, and reminds him to avoid superfluities.[3] St. Ambrose is referring to Job 1:21: "Naked I was born and naked shall I die."

Christ's nakedness reveals the very love of God; our bodies reveal Christ. St. Symeon the New Theologian wrote in the 11th century: "I did not blush before the members [naked body parts] of anyone, neither to see others naked, nor to show myself naked, for I possessed Christ completely, and I was completely Christ, and all of my own members and everybody else's members, all and each one were always like Christ in my eyes; I remained motionless, unhurt and impassive; I was all Christ Himself and as Christ I considered all the baptized, clothed with the whole Christ. While others, if they are naked and their flesh touches flesh, there they are in heart like a donkey or a horse..."[4]

In naked baptism the body is given specific attention because a Christian conversion is a conversion of the body as well as of the soul. Christ came to redeem all creation. In the sacrament of baptism, the body is seen in its

---

[1] Pope John Paul II, Op. Cit., General Audience Address, February 20, 1980.
[2] Vatican Council II, *Sacrosanctum Concilium*, 61.
[3] Migne, Jacques-Paul, *Patrologia Latina*, St. Ambrosii, Enarrutiones in XII Psalmos Davidicos, vs 32, Patrologia Latina Database (eletronic version 1st ed.), pld.chadwyck.co.uk/
[4] St. Symeon the New Theologian, *Hymns of Divine Love*, trans. George A. Maloney, S.J. (Denville, New Jersey: Dimension Books), Hymn 15.

original meaning, the way it was experienced in the Garden of Eden. This restored vision of the body is intimately experienced in nakedness. The body as a beatific vision has not been lost, though Original Sin has made man's heart blind to this truth. Through redemption, the Christian is called to rediscover the true language of the body. In the apocryphal Gospel of Thomas it is written: "His disciples said: 'When will You be revealed to us and when will we see You?' Jesus said: 'When you can take off your clothes and put them under your feet as little children and tread on them, then shall you see the Son of the Living One and you shall not fear...'"[1]

Some scholars suggest that this ancient writing influenced the baptismal mystagogies of the early Fathers disclosed above in which the clothing was removed and tread on before entering the baptismal waters naked.[2] Through baptism, the body becomes dignified as the temple of the Holy Spirit.[3] St. Augustine preached that before baptism the body was an instrument of iniquity and following baptism the body became an instrument of justice. The human person, through the redemption of the body, learns to rediscover its true language. The body is seen not in lust, but in holiness. Instead of nakedness being shameful, the body becomes the very medium through which the mystery of God's love is revealed.

The person in whom all the strength of the passions has been crucified and transfigured radiates the peace of paradise. Around him wild beasts are calm, and human beings also, who can sometimes be wild beasts. For such a person the beauty of the body no long arouses lust, but rather praise. The Father of the Church, St. John Climacus, says in *The Ladder of Divine Ascent*, "Someone, I was told, at the sight of a very beautiful [woman] felt impelled to glorify the Creator. The sight of it increased his love for God to the point of tears. Anyone who entertains such feelings in such circumstances is already risen... before the general resurrection."[4]

---

[1] *The Gospel of Thomas*, ed. Richard Valantasis (New York: Routledge, 1997), v. 37.
[2] Smith, Jonathan Z., Op. cit.
[3] Cf. I Corinthians 3:16.
[4] Colm Luibheid & Norman Russell, trans., St. John Climacus, *The Ladder of Divine Ascent*, 15th step, (New York: Paulist Press, 1982).

Let us not underestimate the power of the cross. We can, through God's grace, as demonstrated by Christ and early Christians, strip off the garments of shame and behold the naked body with holiness and honor. The onlooker who yelled out, "Sacrilege!" as the infant before Br. Cyril was baptized, failed to see the mystery of God's love revealed in the naked body. The approach that says that it is impossible to ever see nakedness as holy is the very approach that masks a kind of impurity. Those individuals who refuse to accept that there exists another attitude other than lust towards the body underestimate the power of redemption. They themselves are impure because they do not believe in the goodness of the heart, always holding it in a state of suspicion. Christ's naked baptism is full and rich with meaning. Sacred Scripture alludes to it, Icons depict it, the Liturgy explicitly emphasizes it, and the Fathers of the Church modeled it in their mystagogies.

The loincloth covering Christ's nakedness and the use of clothing today in baptism anaesthetizes and sanitizes the Christian Mystery. We do this in order to make this—at times shocking—mystery, comfortable and to appease our prim and proper sensibilities.

St. Ambrose of Milan: The Virtue of Nakedness

by Michael A. Kowalewski

In Scripture, the meaning of nakedness has more than a literal sense. The Fathers of the Church often used motifs that extend nakedness beyond its literal meaning. An example of this is found in the writings of St. Ambrose, bishop of Milan.

Ambrose's exegetical work *De Joseph* and his *Letter to Bishop Sabinus* (Letter 58) reveal Ambrose's moral and allegorical interpretation of Scripture in regards to nakedness and virtue. In *De Joseph*, nakedness ironically becomes a sign of modesty. In his *Letter to Sabinus*, the nakedness of Isaiah becomes a sign of unashamed love for Christ.

Nakedness for the Fathers was not merely an ascetical discipline; the nakedness of the saints was also a sign of restoration and of glory. Some of the Eastern Fathers saw nakedness in the light of the self contradictory image of the naked Christ crucified, a humiliation turned victory. Nakedness in the ascetic sense was a sign of radical abandonment, but in a different spiritual sense nakedness became a sign of a prelapsarian purity.

Ambrose follows earlier Fathers such as Cyril of Jerusalem in applying metaphors to baptismal nakedness. St Ambrose mentions that the neophyte's descent into the baptism font recalls the naked entry into life and his naked departure from it, and reminds him to avoid superfluities.[1] Ambrose is referring to the text found in the Book of Job, "Naked I was born and naked shall I die."[2]

The asceticism of early monks mortified, not so much the body *per se*, but carnal passions. Fasting, vigils and sexual abstinence were not attacks on the goodness of the body, but attacks on disordered appetites. By virtue of the incarnation, the body has a special place of honor. St. Athanasius states in his treatise, *On the incarnation*, that Christ in no way was defiled by being in a body. "Rather, He sanctified the body by being *in it*."[3] The body, by virtue of the incarnation, has been divinized.

The pagans of antiquity, such as the Hellenists, had a great appreciation for the body but they failed in purity. The Manicheans of Ambrose's time had a great admiration for purity, but rejected the goodness of the body. Many of the Fathers give a uniquely Christian vision of the body, one that is neither prudish nor licentious, but truly *incarnational*. It is a vision of naked ascetical purity, a redemptive understanding of nakedness. Ambrose, more

---

[1] Jacques-Paul Migne, *Patrologia Latina*, vol. 14, *Sancti Ambrosii, Enarrutiones in XII Psalmos Davidicas*, vs. 32. *Patrologia Latina* Database, electronic version of 1st Ed, pld.chadwyck.co.uk/
[2] Job 1:21 RSV: "And he said, "Naked I came from my mother's womb, and naked shall I return; the Lord gave, and the Lord has taken away; blessed be the name of the Lord."
[3] St. Athanasius, *On the incarnation* (New York: St. Vladimir's Seminary Press, 2003), p. 46.

than any other Latin Father, understood this vision of the body in his writings.

The West's vision of the body has been mostly influenced by St. Augustine's somewhat deprecating theology of the body. Ambrose who, unlike Augustine, was well educated in the Greek language, imported an Eastern theology of the body. His writings had a strong Eastern influence, yet he did not loose his own Latin roots, remaining typically Roman in thought and language.

In Scriptural exegesis, Ambrose was profoundly influenced by the allegorical method of interpretation as developed by Philo and Origen. In theology, Ambrose was predominately guided by the writings of Athanasius, Didymus the Blind, Cyril of Jerusalem, Basil, and Hippolytus. He composed exegetical works, moral/ascetical works, homilies, letters and hymns.

St. Ambrose's *De Joseph* is a commentary on Genesis 37:2-46:27. It represents a single sermon, probably preached in 387 A.D. *De Joseph* exhibits a marked predilection for moral teaching, found in most of his works. He praises Joseph as a mirror of chastity who prefigures Christ. He states in his opening paragraphs that through Joseph's character modesty shines forth.

Ambrose traces the whole story of Joseph's life, but the central, identifying theme is Joseph's courageous chastity which culminates with Joseph's temptation by Potiphar's wife. Scripture describes Joseph as a handsome man.[1] Ambrose states "He thought that he would be the more attractive, if he were proved more handsome, not by the *loss of his chastity* but by the *cultivation of modesty*."[2] If a woman lustfully gazes upon his handsome features, it is only she who is guilty of immodesty. Ambrose sees the beauty of Joseph as not one that seduces the eyes of others, but gains the approval of all men.

Potiphar's wife said to Joseph, "Lie with me."[3] Joseph was unmoved by her words. In her persistence she grabbed Joseph and he slipped away; "he did not value

---

[1] Cf. Genesis 39:6.
[2] St Ambrose, *De Joseph*, in *The Fathers of the Church*, vol. 65, (trans. Michael McHugh: Washington, DC: The Catholic University of America Press, 1972), p. 203.
[3] Genesis 39:7.

the clothing of his body higher than the chastity of his soul."[1] Ambrose goes on to say, "He stripped off his garment and cast off the sin. He left behind the clothing by which he was held, and fled away, stripped to be sure, but not naked, because he was covered better by the covering of modesty. Yes, *a man is not naked unless guilt has made him naked*."[2] Joseph was naked but not naked. He was not ashamed of his physical nakedness because he was clothed in virtue. Ambrose asserts that it is Potiphar's wife who was truly naked—*naked in virtue.*

Ambrose parallels this naked vice to the shame of Adam in the garden. It was only after Adam abandoned God's commandments through his transgression that he was naked. Adam knew he was naked because, according to Ambrose, he lost the marks of God's protection. Adam hid because he did not have the "garment of faith" which he put aside because of his transgression. Joseph who stripped himself of his clothing which he left in the hands of the adulteress, was not naked for he kept the "uncorrupted garments of virtue, but he stripped himself of the old man with his actions so that he might put on the new, who is being renewed in perfect knowledge according to the image of his Creator." Ambrose here is clearly giving allusion to the sacrament of baptism as defined by St. Paul's letter to the Colossians.[3]

Ambrose states, "Joseph left his clothing behind and laid bare the shamelessness of the adulteress."[4] It was Potiphar's wife who was the one who had really been stripped, although she was keeping the clothing of another. She, according to Ambrose, had lost all the coverings of chastity, whereas Joseph was sufficiently provided for and protected.

Ambrose's *Letter to Bishop Sabinus (#58)* can be dated rather confidently at 395 A.D. He wrote five letters to Sabinus, bishop of Piacenza.

This letter begins with Ambrose learning of a married couple who distributed all their wealth to the poor in the name of Christ. Leading citizens believed such action was

---

[1] *De Joseph* 5:25.
[2] Ibid.
[3] Cf. Colossians 3:9f.
[4] *De Joseph* 5:25.

443

ridiculous, but the virtuous couple were unashamed to appear devoted to their holy religion. Ambrose praises this unashamed love for Christ and quotes Matthew 10:32 against those citizens who criticized such unabashed witness to the Gospel life: "Whoever is ashamed of Me before men, of him will I be ashamed before My Father Who is in heaven." Ambrose goes on to compare the radical abandonment of the couple to Isaiah, who was not ashamed to go naked and barefoot through the crowds proclaiming heavenly prophecies.[1] Isaiah's nakedness, though unseemly when viewed in itself, became reverential under the aspect of holy religion, much like the couple's poverty. Isaiah was naked before the people "not in mockery but gloriously." Jews were breaking God's commandments. As a sign of their impending destitution, Isaiah walked naked and barefoot. He was not intent upon bodily but spiritual affairs. He paid no attention to whether he was naked or clothed. Ambrose compares Isaiah to Adam who was naked before his sin and that Isaiah, like Adam, did not know that he was naked, for he was clothed in virtue. It was only after Adam committed sin that he knew that he was naked and covered himself. Ambrose goes on to parallel Isaiah's nakedness to Noah; "Noah was naked,[2] but he was not ashamed, for he was filled with joy and spiritual gladness, while the one who mocked him for being naked remained exposed to the reproach of everlasting disgrace."[3]

He then compares Isaiah to Joseph's chaste nakedness: "Joseph, too, that he might not be shamefully stripped bare [of purity], left his cloak and fled naked. Which of them was dishonored here, she who held another's garments or he who threw off his own?"

In this letter he interprets scripture on three different levels of interpretation. On the literal level, Isaiah is naked, and God commands this as a sign of Israel's own nakedness. The moral sense of interpretation is that the events reported in Scripture ought to lead us to act justly.

---

[1] Cf. Isaiah 20:1-3.
[2] Cf. Genesis 9:21-23.
[3] St Ambrose, *Letter to Bishop Sabinus* (#58, in *The Fathers of the Church*, vol. 26, (trans. Michael McHugh: Washington, DC: The Catholic University of America Press, 1972), p. 147.

Ambrose sees in Isaiah's public nakedness a model of Christian virtue; we should never be ashamed of our Christian identity. In the allegorical sense, Ambrose acquires a more profound understanding of Isaiah's nakedness. He sees nakedness as spiritual and *only those who sin are truly naked.* Isaiah is not naked because he is clothed in virtue, whereas the people of Israel are naked because of their vice.

St. Ambrose is a Western Father with an Eastern theological flair, without compromising his Latin identity. His motifs on the nakedness of Joseph and Isaiah show an influence from earlier Fathers. These motifs are not original to Ambrose, but echo the spiritual sense of exegetical orthodoxy found in the baptismal mystagogies of Eastern Fathers. Nakedness is a sign of holiness for the Christian who confesses the incarnation.

Commentary on Job: The Naked Poor

by Jim C. Cunningham

The Book of Job includes several references to nakedness, and never in an erotic context. Rather, nakedness is most often seen as dirigent poverty. In our affluent society, this is difficult to relate to. Our definition of "poverty" hardly resembles Biblical poverty. The "poor" in 21st century America have access to all the free (or nearly free) clothing they want, and free food is available from many sources. My own family has benefited from such abundance. Whenever I have been hungry or naked it was always volitional.

But even today, in some parts of the world, there are people who are so poor that they are literally starving to death and some have traded their last, pitiful rag of body covering for a morsel of food.

This poverty of total nakedness is sometimes portrayed in cinema, such as the Christian movie, "The Hiding Place" and the graphic film, "Schindler's List." Both are about Nazi concentration camps, and both show the total poverty of prisoners upon admission to the camp. They are totally depersonalized and denuded. All their possessions are taken away, including their clothes and even their head and body hair. Both movies depict full frontal nudity without resorting to cute camera angles for the sake of "modesty" or "propriety." Since nothing was "proper" about such camps, to artificially impose propriety by the method of filming would be contradictory.

But my main point concerns modesty. Even "The Hiding Place," geared at mostly Christian audiences, clearly understood that there was nothing in the least erotic about the nudity it depicted. One scene showed many women inmates passing through a gang shower after having all their clothing taken away. Then the scene shifts to a huge room where dozens of naked women are shown, fearful and anxious. Suddenly deloused clothing is dumped into the room and they frantically scramble to snatch what clothing they can.[1]

"Schindler's List," not claiming to be Christian, depicts both erotic and non-erotic nudity. There are graphic sex scenes that are truly immodest as well as other scenes such as those in "The Hiding Place" that have no sexual connotation whatever. The full male and female frontal nudity is really vital to what the film is trying to convey.

Like Biblical poverty, such scenes have nothing at all to do with sex, other than the fact that bodies are, by God's design, either male or female.

Here are some verses (RSV) from Job that refer to this type of naked poverty:

7:5 *My flesh is clothed with worms and dirt; my skin hardens, then breaks out afresh.*

---

[1] I saw this film at a public cinema when it premiered in the early 70s. About ten years later I saw it again at a small, evangelical church and was disappointed to discover that almost all the non-erotic nudity had been cut. Apparently, some "pious," falsely modest, Christian viewers complained and the producers deferred to their ignorance. Much was lost by this editing, proving how essential the nude scenes were. The nudity was not thrown in to attract a larger audience; it was cut for that purpose. How can Christians like that be "lights of the world" (Matthew 5:14)? If our light is darkness, how deep will the darkness be (cf. Matthew 6:23)?

Job is describing his own poverty. He was literally reduced to wearing filth. Though a filthy nude could be used for erotic purposes, there is no hint of that here.

22:6 *For you have exacted pledges of your brothers for nothing, and stripped the naked of their clothing.*

It so often happened that the poor had nothing but their last piece of clothing to give as a pledge for some loan, that Moses wrote laws about it.[1] Moses did not outlaw the practice, but only stipulated that, while it was okay for such people to go nude in broad daylight, since that pledge was their only protection from the cold of the night, even if they had not managed to redeem their clothing by evening, basic charity (not chastity!) demanded it be returned to them for the night. Moses clearly sees that the purpose of clothing is warmth and protection—not some fabricated "modesty." The Book of Job is in full agreement.

24:7 *They lie all night naked, without clothing, and have no covering in the cold.*

Confirmation of my above comment. No receiver of pledges of clothing should keep it at nighttime when the poor really need it. By day it was not so much an issue as it was not needed for its main purpose—warmth.

24:10 *They go about naked, without clothing; hungry, they carry the sheaves;*

This is proof that poor field workers labored in the nude, explaining why St. Mary Magdalen at first assumed that the risen Christ, His wraps left behind in the tomb,[2] must have been "the gardener,"[3] for who else would have been hanging around in the garden stripped for work at the crack of dawn?

---

[1] Cf. Exodus 22:26 & Deuteronomy 24:12f.
[2] Cf. Luke 24:12 & John 20:5-8.
[3] Cf. John 20:15.

12:17 & 19 *He leads counselors away stripped, and judges he makes fools... He leads priests away stripped, and overthrows the mighty.*

This shows how God can turn the *status quo* on its hatted head. Evidently, as is too often the case today as well, counselors and priests were puffed up with their marks of distinction which mean nothing to God. If the sight of naked people were a true source of lustful temptation, then God, "Who tempts no one,"[1] could not be responsible for the stripping of anybody. For the same reason, the nakedness of Isaiah could not have been a source of temptation for anyone. A male stripper who briefly delivers a "strip-o-gram," stripping to his jock strap while singing some bawdy happy birthday tune to Suzy Q. is sexually immodest, but not Isaiah, who was completely nude for three years straight.[2]

31:19f *If I have seen any one perish for lack of clothing, or a poor man without covering; if his loins have not blessed me, and if he was not warmed with the fleece of my sheep;*

Job professes that he customarily practiced the corporal work of mercy of clothing the naked which Jesus ranked after welcoming strangers and before visiting the sick in Matthew 25:35f. Just as it is no sin to be a stranger or to be sick, so Jesus clearly saw no immorality in being naked. What was immoral was failing to offer welcome to strangers, clothing to the naked poor (not wealthy tourists on a nude beach in Jamaica!), and failing to visit the sick. Being naked is no more immoral than being hungry or thirsty. Just as we might volitionally do without food (fasting) as penance and mortification of the flesh, so one might give up clothing for penance as many early monks did. When Jesus emerged from the Jordan after His baptism, the context of Mark's Gospel[3] sounds

---

[1] James 1:13.
[2] Cf. Isaiah 20:1-3.
[3] Mark 1:10-13 (RSV): "And when He came up out of the water, *immediately* He saw the heavens opened and the Spirit descending upon Him like a dove; and a voice came from heaven, 'Thou art My beloved Son; with Thee I am well pleased.' The Spirit *immediately* drove him out into the wilderness. And He was in the wilderness forty days, tempted by

like He began His forty day period of going without food also going without clothing, as the text says, "The Spirit *immediately* drove Him out into the wilderness," as though He did not dally to dry off and get dressed first. It is likely that those early nudist monks saw it this way. They fasted from both food and clothing, and this asceticism helped fortify them against temptation as it did for Jesus. Going without clothes was no more an occasion of sin than their going without food.

I would argue that going nude can be a superior form of penance than fasting from food. Not only can nakedness be as uncomfortable as hunger pangs, but it can be much more humbling. One might brag about fasting and win the respect of the Christian community for heroic asceticism, but it is hardly likely that the Christian who goes without clothes for penance is going to be respected by the parish council who happens to pop in that day soliciting pledges for the Bishop's Fund!

Finally, there is the classic quotation from Job:

1:21 *And he said, "Naked I came from my mother's womb, and naked shall I return; the LORD gave, and the LORD has taken away; blessed be the name of the LORD."*

Job is stating the truth of just what constitute "us." When we stand naked before a full length mirror, we are looking at "us." What we see is what God will raise up on the Last Day. Clothes might make the man according to the ways of the world, but not according to the ways of the Lord. Yet Christians, like worldlings, behave as though clothes were an essential part of their anatomy, so much so, that they feel "naked" without them. But wouldn't it be nice to be at home in our own skin? Wouldn't it be nice to know that clothes are *not* "us," but merely tools we utilize for personal comfort, when necessary?

Job realized this the hard way. We can realize it in a much more pleasant way, simply by going nude when clothes make no sense, such as when swimming or taking a nature walk.

Satan; and He was with the wild beasts; and the angels ministered to Him."

In sum, nothing in the Book of Job, just as nothing in the rest of the Bible, attaches any immorality to simply being naked. As Job said, it is, after all, just who we really are.

And what does Job do in his divinely tailored, modest, leather raiment of his skin?

Praise the Name of the Lord!

Behold: It Is Very Good!"

by Jim C. Cunningham[1]

This article not only aims to show that the naturist message is in perfect accord with traditional principles of morality, but also to provide the reader with clear moral guidelines as he applies these truths to his own life.

Some Definitions

Chastity is thinking, saying and doing nothing for the purpose of willful sexual arousal outside marriage. Sexual modesty is conducting ourselves in accord with chastity. On the other hand, immodesty is doing something to sexually arouse another outside marriage.

No physical thing is of itself immodest. On the other hand anything at all can be immodest if it is used to try to arouse another person.

When Isaiah, in obedience to God, preached nude for three years,[2] he was not immodest because his body was not in itself immodest and his intention was not to turn anyone on to anything but God's prophetic message.

The male stripper, on the other hand, even though he keep his jock strap on, thus exposing less than Isaiah, is immodest not because of what he exposes, but because of his motive. His intention is to turn the ladies on. If this

---

[1] Title based on Genesis 1:31.
[2] Cf. Isaiah 20:2f.

could be accomplished by wearing a 55-gallon drum, then he would wear that.

Lack of Experience

Fr. Jim G. Dodge, OCSO, of happy memory, used to say that people opposed the belief and practice of body-acceptance out of simple lack of experience; they have nothing but the "nude is lewd" lie to judge by. Their experience of nudity has always been in a lewd context. This frustrated him, as it does me, because experience is the best teacher, and it is hard to argue with someone who simply cannot know what he is talking about because he has no experience. It's like a swimmer reluctant to jump into the lake.

"How's the water? Isn't it cold?", he asks, wondering why the others have not emitted yelps of discomfort.

"Not at all! It's great! Come on in!" assures everyone in the lake.

Only by jumping in for yourself can you acquire the conclusive conviction that this book is truth. Short of that, all I can do is testify to my own experience, eager to dispel your fears and doubts so you too can enjoy swimming.

Our Experience

My family spent two long summers living at a camp-ground/park in Frelighsburg, Quebec where no one wears clothes except for warmth or protection.

In every way the people there were exactly like their clothed Quebec counterparts but for one thing: they could not accept the lie that their physical bodies were somehow intrinsically shameful and obscene. They disproved the myth that "nude is lewd" not by passively wondering about it, but by actively finding out for themselves. I have yet to hear of one newcomer to such a place who, actively testing the theory that maybe the world is all wrong in asserting that "nude is lewd," left after one day's real experience without having forever disproved the myth for themselves. As all false fears vanish when squarely faced, so this myth evaporates about as fast as one can get undressed. Let me tell you what it was like:

451

At poolside (and most everywhere else), no one wears any clothing, since it serves no purpose other than to support the "nude is lewd" lie. There are all kinds of people of both genders and all ages, shapes and sizes. Rarely have I seen anyone approaching what the world calls a "perfect 10." Teenage boys and girls, in varying stages of pubertal development, hang out together unselfconsciously. Nowhere is there any sign of sexual arousal which males, at least, cannot easily hide.

Since all of those people regard the body simply as part of who we are, and not as some kind of "automatic" sexual stimulus, to be immodest at such a place, one would have to seek some other medium—perhaps a certain look, word, gesture, etc. But I have never seen it.

Many Have *Some* Experience

Although few of you may have had the opportunity to experience something like that Quebec place, most have had at least *some* experience of disproving the "nude is lewd" myth, at least in same-gender situations.

For example, if you are over thirty-five, you are probably old enough to have experienced junior high school gym gang showers. Prior to your first actual experience, you were probably anxious that you would get an erection in front of the other boys and feel mortified. But once in that situation for real, it just didn't happen. Though enculturated to regard even same-sex nudity as something erotic, when you squarely faced this phantom fear, it vanished like a mirage.

So believe me: mixed nudity is no different. Nudity is not erotic of itself, nor is the opposite sex erotic of itself. If it were, then all society would have to be sex-segregated, nude or not nude.

A Note on Erections

Erections come and go. They can be the result of lustful fantasies or erotic touch, but as all males know, many (if not most) of our erections are completely unwilled. They can be the result of simple physical stimuli such as a cool breeze on our bodies after coming out of the water. During puberty and young adulthood when certain hormones are doing their thing, males can find themselves often getting erections which have no apparent stimulus at all. Many males routinely wake up with an erection. Just as menstruation is simply part of being female, so varying degrees of tumescence throughout the day is simply part of being male. That's just how God created us, and it is all "very good."[1]

The wonderful body does its thing. The heart beats without our consciousness and the lungs automatically respirate according to how much oxygen the blood needs. All of our body parts naturally do what they were programmed to do by our Creator, and an erection is no more "wrong" than a runny nose or a yawn. The same is true of nocturnal emissions (wet dreams). While asleep, the body continues to do its thing, and being sexual beings with sexual parts, it will do its sexual thing regardless of our will and consciousness.

Morality concerns thoughts, words and deeds *that are willed*. The great Franciscan mystic and stigmatic, St. Padre Pio, used to say it is not at all sinful to *have* dirty thoughts, but only to *will* to have them. Unwilled thoughts and actions have nothing whatsoever to do with morality.

As with unwilled thoughts, so with nocturnal emissions and other experiences of unwilled arousal even when awake. If a girl is riding a horse or riding in a bumpy truck at a time of month when her hormones make her especially sexually sensitive, and she happens to be aroused, she has not sinned against chastity, even if she happens to experience orgasm. As long as her motive for traveling was not that, but rather to get to her destination, etc., her body is simply doing what her Creator programmed it to do. Like the boy who awakes during a nocturnal emission, she might, in her true desire to be chaste and pure, feel guilt and confusion, but the mature and objective attitude is to realize that her body was simply acting independently of her will, as many body functions do. Since it feels great and enjoyable, and being conditioned by a puritanical culture that not only equates nudity with lewdness, but also equates pleasure with sinfulness, the experience of unwilled orgasm can also cause confusion. Again, objec-

---

[1] Genesis 1:31.

453

tivity tells us that of course it is enjoyable—God made it that way. Pleasure itself is not sin, but only the *seeking* of illicit or inordinate pleasure. If she chose to ride in that truck specifically to get aroused, then she was not chaste. Sex belongs only within marriage. Sex is good, great and holy, but only in its place. Both natural law and God's law tell us that marriage is that place, since it is obvious from the mere observation of sexual physiology, that sex concerns procreation[1] and union of husband and wife.[2]

Near Occasions of Sin

If we want to *be* good, we must not only *do* good and *refrain* from evil, but we must be responsible enough to realize that we should also avoid the near occasions of sin. Thus if a drunkard knows his weakness, and knows that if he hangs out in bars he will end up over-imbibing, it is his moral responsibility to avoid bars, since for him, they occasion sin.

Although I have never heard of it, if a person found himself committing sins of lust by camping at the above-described Quebec campground, he would be morally obliged to avoid going there.

But suppose someone who has been so deeply conditioned by the "nude is lewd" culture does experience unwilled sexual arousal when encountering innocent nudity such as at that camp, in a gang shower, or even by reading this book. Is he therefore morally obligated to avoid these as near occasions of sin?

But unwilled sexual arousal is not sin, and thus things which occasion it cannot be near occasions of sin. Just because a boy ejaculates semen in his sleep or wakes up with a full erection does not mean that sleeping is a near occasion of sin and he is morally obliged never to go to bed. You see how absurd it is. The drunkard who hangs out in bars invariably finds himself sinning. Unwilled arousal or even orgasm is no more sinful than sneezing or yawning. Would we avoid near occasions of yawning or sneezing? Of course not, at least not for *moral* concerns.

---

[1] Genesis 1:28.
[2] Genesis 2:24.

One of the great Christian mystics (I think it was St. John of the Cross) encountered novices in the mystical life who were greatly troubled because when they felt closest to God in contemplative union and were saturated with awareness of His infinite love, they experienced sexual arousal. I myself have experienced this, and I am not at all ashamed of it. Often in spirituality the body hasn't got a clue about what's going on. "Love?" it asks. "Okay, I'll respond." And so it does the only thing it knows as a response to its awareness of love happening. Rather than get scrupulous and upset, since we are called to peace[1] and "God is a God of peace, and not of confusion,"[2] we should treat unwilled sexual arousal during meditation, or anytime for that matter, as we would treat a distracting thought trying to disturb our contemplative union with God. If we entertain the thought, then it has succeeded in taking us from higher things. If we fight the thought and get upset over it, then it may have been even more successful in spoiling our prayer. The attitude which all mystics teach is to remain calm and gently turn back to our focus. Like the schoolboy who is teased, if he shows disturbance then his teasers have accomplished their objective. But if he remains undisturbed, the teasers get bored and go away.

Just as we should not quit our spiritual life just because we sometimes experience unwilled sexual arousal during deep prayer, neither should we feel we should avoid any other ordinary activity during which sexual arousal might happen of itself.

At the high school in St. Johnsbury, Vermont, one of the art classes offered is (or at least was) life drawing. 16 year old boys today hardly have any experience of the bodies of their own sex, let alone those of girls. Since they have been deprived of this natural knowledge all their lives, and taught (at least by default) that "nude is lewd," they might experience sexual arousal as soon as they encounter their first nude model. After all, they probably never even see the bodies of their own gender in the gym locker room since everyone nowadays seems to wear their gym uniform beneath their school clothes. All of a sudden,

---

[1] Cf. I Peter 3:11.
[2] I Corinthians 14:33.

standing right in the classroom is a stark naked female who could well be just two years their senior. While "righteous," "pure" Christian pastors are telling their girl parishioners (some of whom also take that class) that they should regard their bodies as near occasions of sin and therefore should make sure that boys not even be able to detect their bra straps through the back of their blouses, there, standing before them are those very breasts— "obscene" creations of God with no bra to deny their reality, pretend that they do not bounce, and that their nipples do not sometimes become erect. How does it make any sense for all those girls to be so concerned about hiding the fact that they have breasts by compulsively strapping them and shielding them (and even hiding the straps!), when right in front of them in class stands one of their own gender not hiding anything at all? If boys can draw a nude female for an hour or two, one should hope they could handle the sight of a bra strap on the back of their fellow student preceding them out of the classroom! The contradictions people seem to be content with never cease to gall me.

But my point is that a boy, totally unprepared for the experience by his parents and pastors, might well experience sexual arousal. I am sure I would have at sixteen. Need he drop the class?

The answer is no, unless his motive for taking the class was to lust. If his motive was art, or even merely the knowledge he had been deprived of, even if he does experience arousal, he is not morally bound to drop the class anymore than he is bound to never sleep because he wakes up with an erection every morning.

Experiencing unwilled sexual arousal whether in sleep or art class is not sin; it is just the body doing its thing. Thus, it should not disturb us any more than a sneeze during a lecture, a distracting thought during prayer or a yawn during our pastor's Sunday sermon. Note that morality demands the avoidance of near occasions of sin. Sexual arousal is not sin, any more than a runny nose is. To be sin, there would have to be willful lust. If he is not seeking sexual pleasure, then there is absolutely no sin, and thus the class can in no way be regarded as even a near occasion of sin.

The drunkard above must avoid bars because experience has shown him that he always sins when he frequents them. The art class situation is entirely different.

What Lust Is *Not*

There may be some confusion over just what lust is. It is not the delight we experience when we encounter beauty. Why on earth should we avoid that? God is the ultimate Beauty. Should we therefore become atheists? We are made to seek the good, the true and the beautiful. Although it is my studied opinion that the human body is the most beautiful thing in the physical world, just about everyone would at least agree that it ranks high on the scale.

For many, this book will serve as a therapeutic tool to regain a healthy mind with regard to the body. This health is no less necessary than medical health. I myself have experienced the kind of healing which it is all about. This healing is, in my opinion, so necessary for us that even if some of us do occasionally slip into actual unchastity, and not merely unwilled sexual arousal, this book loses none of its validity or usefulness. It is necessary to work for a living for economic health. If, on payday, we find ourselves slipping into sins of greed or covetousness, we nevertheless still need to support ourselves. We must strive for holiness not by *inaction*, but by *action*—maintaining what we do and seeking holiness in it.

Clear-Cut Moral Guidelines

Here is a brief and crystal clear teaching on morality which you can easily apply to any moral problem. As with body education, it is sad and reprehensible that our parents and pastors (for the most part) failed to teach us such clear principles. Because of this neglect most everybody in society is something of a moral midget. They have no higher way of knowing right from wrong than gut feeling. We are not only gifted with awesome, handsome bodies, but far more, we are gifted with reason. As we delight in the beautiful, so we delight in the true. To help you delight in the good, here are some true moral principles that will bring great peace, for nothing is worse than confusion and ignorance.

The Soul of All Morality

First of all, morality concerns *willed* thoughts, words and actions. Morality has nothing whatever to do with *unwilled* things. If your car, through no fault or neglect of yours, goes out of control and causes property damage or personal injury, this has nothing to do with morality.

Secondly, our willed thoughts, words and actions (hereafter simply "acts"), like every arrow, have three essential components. The arrow consists of a head, a shaft and feathers, all of which must be right for the arrow to hit its mark. If the feathers are rightly aligned and the shaft is perfectly straight, but the head is unbalanced, we miss the mark. Two right components do not make the arrow's flight true; only all three can do this.

The same is true for each of the three components of every moral act. All three must be right to hit the mark.

Three Components of Moral Act

1. Act: Naturally, something has to be thought, said or done.
Example A: An *indifferent* act: Nude swimming. In itself, it is neither good nor evil. It is indifferent.
Example B: A *good* act: Feeding the hungry. This is just one of three components, and if the other two are not also right, then even though this of itself is good, we do wrong.
Example C: An *evil* act: Adultery. No matter how right the other two components may be, adultery can *never* be good.
2. Motive: Our motive must be good, or at least not evil. Contemporary popular morality errs because it disregards everything except motive in judging right from wrong. As long as someone *means* well, the popular error is to say he did right. This is as absurd as trying to shoot an arrowhead without a shaft or feathers.
Example A: The nude swimmer must not intend anything evil. If his motive is recreation, relaxation, socializing,

or simply going with the flow, "doing in Rome what Romans do," then this component is right. But if he intends evil, such as trying to cause lust, he misses the mark; he sins.

Example B: The person who feeds the hungry out of compassion and charity, or even for the sake of a job, working on the payroll of some charitable organization, does right. But if his motive is to show off how good and philanthropic he is, though the hungry man is helped, the one who feeds him does wrong.

Example C: The adulterer whose motive is lust does wrong. But the adulterer whose motive is compassion, consolation, or some highfalutin thing like that, he still does wrong because adultery itself is *never* right.

3. Circumstance:

Example A: Nude swimming is in itself indifferent, and my motives may all be on the up and up, but if I attempt to do it in a place where it is illegal and likely to spoil the recreation of others who do not yet share the good news of body-acceptance, I do wrong. But at a clothing-optional beach or my private pool, I do right.

Example B: Feeding the hungry is good in itself, and my motive may be charity, but if I do it when the sign on the hospital room door says "NPO: *Nihil per orem*" ("nothing by mouth"), because the hungry patient is preparing for an operation, I do wrong. In most circumstances, of course, I would be doing right by feeding the hungry.

Example C: There is no circumstance where adultery is justified, as is the case with every other intrinsically evil act.

So, that's all there is to it. If you are confused about some issue, just sit down and run through the above three simple components of every moral act. You might not like what you end up with, but true peace will be found in following your properly informed conscience.

Oops! Did I say morality was simple? Well, there is one further little glitch that needs treatment, but it, too, is easily resolved.

The Principle of Double Effect

Suppose you do something which is not evil of itself, like nude swimming or feeding the hungry. Suppose your motives are proper and so are the circumstances; all three components check out. Does this mean you are absolutely in the clear morally?

Not necessarily. There is still one more thing to consider.

Suppose our act has a bad effect. Can we do it anyway? The answer is yes, but only if the four conditions of "the principle of double effect" all check out. They are:

I. The act cannot be intrinsically evil. Well, we already dealt with this one above, so there should be no problem here.

II. The bad result (evil effect) of our act cannot be something we desired to happen, but rather, we merely tolerated it for the sake of the good effect(s) that result.

Example A: If it turns out that some lecher was lurking in the bushes and lusting, that cannot be something we *wanted* to happen, but something merely *tolerated* for the sake of the good effects of our nude swimming experience.

Example B: Just because school authorities know that every time they hold a dance *some* students misbehave, fornicating behind the school, getting drunk in their cars, getting into fights, etc., this does not mean they do wrong by authorizing another dance. The first condition above holds true, as there is nothing intrinsically evil about melodic body movement (i.e. dance). This second condition also checks out, because they in no way *desire* the misbehavior, but they only desire healthy recreation and fund-raising. They merely *tolerate* the evil effects.

III. Since it is contrary to simple logic to believe that good can possibly come from evil, the good effect(s) desired cannot be the direct result of the evil effect(s), but rather, both good and evil effects simultaneously result from the same otherwise good or indifferent act.

Example A: Thus the nude swimmer's recreation, relaxation, etc. come directly from his nude swimming, and not from the lecher's abuse. Both good and evil effects directly result from the nude swimming.

Example B: Likewise, the good effects of raising money and having fun does not result directly from the misbehavior of some students. Both result from the holding of the dance itself.

Example C: Suppose an otherwise good, educational movie such as "Schindler's List" includes a sex scene (which it does). Is it sinful to watch it? Watching the movie has both good and evil effects. It educates us about real history, (and we should know it well so as not to repeat it), and it entertains, raises money, etc. But since it does show some sex, it may well also have the evil effect of causing lust in the viewers. Since the good effects do not result from the few sex scenes, but from the rest of the film, then this third condition holds true. But a purely pornographic film like "Deep Throat," does not even make it to the "double effect" test; it fails the "three components" test because the act of fornication which comprises the *raison d'être* of the film is already an evil act to start with, regardless of motive, circumstance and whatever "good effects" one might trump up.

Example D: Suppose a girl decides to model for that St. Johnsbury figure drawing class for good motives such as earning income, contributing to art education, desiring to demonstrate appreciation and acceptance of the gift of her body, desiring to be completely honest about who she is, desiring to grow in self-esteem, desiring to teach others about the body's intrinsic goodness and purity, etc. And suppose all of these good effects happened as a result of her nude modeling. But suppose one student abused this trust by lust, and she knew it. She satisfies this third condition because none of the good effects are the result of the student's lust, but rather, all effects directly result from her nude modeling.

IV. The good effect must be at least equal to, or greater than the evil effect, or else the whole thing is not worth doing. Since morality means striving for good and avoiding evil, we cannot do something that checks out on all points above if the end result will only be greater evil.

461

Example A: Nude swimming checks out on this condition as well. If we allowed the perversions of the few to stymie everything we should be able to do, we could not do anything. As the pope wrote in his book, *Love & Responsibility*: "There are circumstances in which nakedness is not immodest. If someone takes advantage of such an occasion to treat the person as an object of enjoyment (even if his action is purely internal) it is *only he* who is guilty of shamelessness... not the other."[1] If a sexual pervert tells a nun her habit is erotically stimulating to him, she is not morally bound to get naked. You can see how absurd life would be!

Example B: If experience had shown that every school dance resulted in one, massive, drunken orgy and brawl, the authorities do wrong to sanction the dance since far more harm would result than good.

Example C: Since the sex scenes are incidental to "Schindler's List" as a whole, and since, as a whole, there is much to be effectively learned from the film, the good effects outweigh the bad. This may not be true for less mature audiences who might be negatively affected by those otherwise incidental scenes. Unlike more mature audiences, the less mature may be unable "to see the wood for the trees."

Example D: If a figure model knows that a student is abusing her nudity, because he has communicated this to her in some way, she has no moral obligation to get dressed, but can continue modeling even if he is present. The good effects of art and education and the others mentioned above far outweigh the abuse of that student. But if all the students told her that all they did during the whole session was lust after her, the good effect (if any) would not be worth it, since more harm would be done by her nudity.

So there it all is—no more glitches. You can apply the above to every situation like a stencil, and see if something is right or wrong.

---

[1] Karol Wojtyla, *Love and Responsibility*, trans. H.T. Willetts (New York: Farrar, Straus & Giroux, 1981), p. 192.

Beatific Vision

St. Paul tells us to think about "whatever is true, whatever is honorable, whatever is just, whatever is pure, whatever is lovely, whatever is gracious, ... excellent, ... [and] worthy of praise."[1] All of these adjectives apply to the human body, created in the very image of the All-Beautiful, All-Good, All-True God. We are like mirrors reflecting divinity. If heaven is seeing God,[2] and if we were created in His image,[3] then far from being sinful, seeing the human body is a veritable *act of worship*.

Indeed, the Gospel says so: "Blessed are the pure in heart, for they shall see God."[4] The impure, taking their miscue from the world, see sin, but the pure, accepting the body as God revealed it, see God Himself.

Though "now we see darkly, as in a mirror,"[5] it is my most profound desire that we all one day "see God as He is,"[6] "face to face,"[7] for eye has not seen, nor ear heard what God has prepared for us.[8] Redemption has not merely restored us to the original garden, *but infinitely more*. We are blessed with "confident assurance"[9] that "the straight and narrow way"[10] which right morality requires leads not only to life,[11] but to the beatific vision of Him Who is the essence of Life itself.[12] May He bless you all with greater and greater knowledge and experience of His beauty and goodness in all creation, especially in yourself![13]

---

[1] Philippians 4:8.
[2] Cf. Matthew 18:10 & Psalm 27:4; etc.
[3] Cf. Genesis 1:26f.
[4] Matthew 5:8.
[5] I Corinthians 13:12.
[6] I John 3:2.
[7] I Corinthians 13:12.
[8] Cf. I Corinthians 2:9.
[9] Hebrews 11:1.
[10] Matthew 7:14.
[11] Cf. ibid.
[12] Cf. I John 1:1ff; 5:11f & 20; John 1:4; 14:6; etc.
[13] Cf. Ephesians 1:17ff.

Theology of the Body

by Pope John Paul II[1]

"The body, and it alone, is capable of making visible what is invisible: the spiritual and the divine. It was created to transfer into the visible reality of the world the mystery hidden since time immemorial in God [God's love for man], and thus to be a sign of it."[2]

"Only the nakedness that makes woman an object for man, or vice versa, is a source of shame."[3]

"...Man is ashamed of his body because of lust. In fact, he is ashamed not so much of his *body* as precisely of *lust*."[4]

"Purity is the glory of the human body before God. It is God's glory in the human body, through which masculinity and femininity are manifested. From purity springs that extraordinary beauty which permeates every sphere of men's common life and makes it possible to express in it simplicity and depth, cordiality and the unrepeatable authenticity of personal trust."[5]

The Oldest Excuse

One Saturday the new pastor in town went out to visit his parishioners. All went well until he came to one house. It was obvious someone was home, but no one came to the door, even after he had knocked several times.

---

[1] One of the many resources for the theology of the body is www.theologyofthebody.net, offering books, DVDs & CDs, emphasizing both theoretical and practical aspects of this new theology.
[2] Pope John Paul II, *Theology of the Body* (Boston: Pauline Books, 1997), Feb. 20, 1980, p. 76.
[3] Ibid., p. 75.
[4] Ibid., May 28, 1980, pp. 115f.
[5] Ibid., March 18, 1981, p. 209.

Finally, he took out his card, wrote on the back, "Revelation 3:20" and stuck it in the door.

The next day, as he was counting the offering, he found his card in the collection plate. Below his message was the notation: "Genesis 3:10."

Revelation 3:20 reads: "Behold, I stand at the door and knock. If any man hear My voice, and opens the door, I will come into him, and dine with him, and he with Me."

Genesis 3:10 reads: "I heard Thy voice in the garden, and I was afraid because I was naked."

Naked Crucifixion

by Winston & Jim C. Cunningham

Dear Linda & Jim:

Jim, you once mentioned that Christ "died naked on the cross." I accept this as fact because you say it. I know you to be extremely knowledgeable about these things. But, I would appreciate knowing about the source of this information. As you know current art, for many years, has Christ clothed, albeit scantily.

I have a friend who questions your information, citing that all crucifixes have Christ with a brief garment on. If you would, I would appreciate knowing more so that I can attempt to convince her of your position.

Many thanks and prayers in advance. God love you.
Winston from New Jersey

Dear Win, Pax!

RE: Christ's crucifixion garments, why on earth would anyone suppose that the Romans executed Him differently than any other criminal guilty of capital punishment by crucifixion? If the Gospel makes a point of the soldiers dividing up His garments amongst themselves,[1] why on earth would anyone want to assert anything different?

---

[1] Cf. John 19:23ff.

465

Such people are likely creating God in their *own* image, replete with their own, immature hang-ups.

If God commanded St. Isaiah to preach stark naked for three years,[1] why should He exempt His Son from any of the rigors of His execution by which we are saved? The burden of proof is on your friend—not on me. She needs to come up with some credible excuse for Christ to have been crucified on Calvary wearing His boxer shorts.

Evidently, she is influenced—among other things—by religious art that Irish nuns (and the like) censored for her viewing. There is quite a lot of art that depicts Christ crucified nude. A good source is the book, *The Sexuality of Christ in Renaissance Art and In Modern Oblivion* by Leo Steinberg.[2] It contains lots of images the Irish nuns themselves never saw. If she relies on religious art for her faith, I suppose she thinks Mary is black, since she is depicted thus in Loreto, Italy. Or Mexican, since she is depicted thus in the Guadalupe image. Other art has her orientalized. And does she think of God the Father with the white beard on the cloud as in the *Baltimore Catechism*? Grunewald has Christ crucified not only nude, but green! Is He, therefore, green? When I was a Benedictine postulant at Portsmouth Abbey in Rhode Island, daily I served at Bishop Ansgar Nelson's (former bishop of Sweden) private Mass in the sacristy where the large crucifix above the altar depicts Christ nude. The estate of the late Trappist monk of Mepkin Abbey (South Carolina), Fr. Jim G. Dodge, bequeathed to me his Austrian, hand-carved, wooden crucifix which has Christ clearly nude.

If you ask me, I suppose many artists depict Him immodestly clad in something like what male strippers wear because they themselves have problems about the body in general, and their own bodies in particular. I wouldn't doubt that they suppose Jesus never defecated or lifted up His tunic to take a leak. The fact is that even the holy pope sometimes has to have a nurse stick a catheter up his penis and an enema up his rectum. Why should this surprise anyone or cause the least discomfort (except, that is, for the pope!)? If it does, then that is a problem that

---

[1] Cf. Isaiah 20:1-3.
[2] Steinberg, Leo, *The Sexuality of Christ in Renaissance Art and In Modern Oblivion*, 2nd ed. (Chicago: University of Chicago Press, 1996).

they need to address, rather than attempt to refashion reality according to *their* own warps.

I seriously wonder whether they can fully accept the reality of the mystery of the incarnation if the kind of sanitized, dis-gendered "Flesh" which they suppose the Word became looked more like a sexless Mickey Mouse than "a man like us in all things."[1] Just Whom do they really believe in? Why do they suppose Mary stuck Baby Jesus in those swaddling diapers so quickly?[2] She knew what all babies do, and she didn't want to deal with the "mustard" with all the company about to come to adore the thumb-sucking Lord of lords & King of kings! She also knew that no angels were going to do some mystical intravenous on Him, and that, to feed Him, she would have to let Him suck away at her "blessed breasts."[3] She had no illusions like all the pious poopers who would feign to be her children & even her spiritual "slaves." Mary knew which end was up, and still does.

If folks like your friend were to read the above, they would be in about as fervent a dither as if their parish priest were to display a crucifix depicting Christ crucified as the Gospels say, or if he were to baptize adults by immersion, nude, as in the old days. By the way, Pope Paul VI in 1970 ordered baptism by immersion to again become the norm for the whole Latin Rite, with baptism by sprinkling being the exception, as in cases of emergency. But then, your friend may not be such a big fan of Paul VI either, or of John Paul II, who stripped so many Sistine Chapel figures. I suppose she would have voted for some other, "more pious," use of Vatican funds. It would be real piety for your friend to lie in her yard at night nude, looking up at the stars that crown Our Lady, otherwise clothed only with the sun, as Revelation 12:1 says, and pray all 15 decades on a Rosary with a real crucifix showing Christ with both signs of the covenants, old and new, the circumcision of His flesh (Old) and of His Sacred Heart (New). Why should the image of a wounded, open Heart be any "more tasteful" than of a circumcised penis? Objectively, most people would rather see a naked, un-

---

[1] Hebrews 2:17.
[2] Cf. Luke 2:7.
[3] Luke 11:27.

bloody man than a cadaver with His chest rent asunder, but such is some religious pietism that they declare the gore "holy" and the nudity "obscene." Go figure. I can't!

Naked in naked Jesus,

Jim C. Cunningham

Commentary: James 1:13-16

by Jim C. Cunningham

Let no man, when he is tempted, say that he is tempted by God. For God is not a tempter of evils, and He tempteth no man. But every man is tempted by his own concupiscence, being drawn away and allured. Then when concupiscence hath conceived, it bringeth forth sin. But sin, when it is completed, begetteth death. Do not err, therefore, my dearest brethren. (KJV)

Whence Temptation? God cannot in any way be responsible for temptation any more than He can be responsible for anything evil. Evils, and everything pertaining to evil, are absolutely alien to God, Who is all-good, all-holy and Who desires with the fullness of His being that every man be holy as He is holy. "As He Who called you is holy, be holy yourselves in all your conduct; since it is written, 'You shall be holy, for I am holy.'"[1]

God is the Creator of all things without exception.[2] Therefore nothing in all creation is evil of itself. "For He created all things that they might exist, and the generative[3] forces of the world are wholesome, and there is no destructive poison in them; and the dominion of Hades is not on earth."[4] St. Paul affirms, "Everything created by God is good, and nothing is to be rejected if it is received

---

[1] I Peter 1:15f; & cf. Leviticus 11:45, 20:7 & I Thessalonians 4:3.

[2] Cf. Colossians 1:16f.

[3] Sexuality is not *reluctantly* included among the good creations, but is here *specifically emphasized*.

[4] Wisdom 1:14.

with thanksgiving..."[1] Furthermore, not only is every created thing—including the body—good, but God loves them: "Thou lovest all things that exist, and hast loathing for none of the things which Thou hast made, for Thou wouldst not have made anything if Thou hadst hated it."[2]

Because of free will, man can abuse anything, turning it to evil purpose, but none of those things he abuses is in any way evil. Thus, stones are not evil, though man may abuse them by using them to stone his brother. Gold is not evil, though man may abuse it by coveting it or stealing it. Food is not evil, though man may abuse it by gluttony. Wine is not evil, though man may abuse it by drunkenness. So also, the naked body is not evil, though man may abuse it by coveting it and committing fornication or adultery in thought or deed.

In all of the above examples, none of the physical things that man is able to abuse is in any way evil. God created them all, holds them in being and loves each and every thing. All creation is good as He is good, and all creation glorifies Him simply by being what He created it to be. When Isaiah related the story of his vocation, he saw the heavens opened and the Seraphim attesting to the holiness of all creation: "Holy, holy, holy is the LORD of hosts; *the whole earth is full of His glory!*"[3] We pray that this right-minded, celestial attitude be ours when we pray "Thy will be done on earth as it is in heaven."[4] If we are to be holy as He is holy, there is only one right attitude to have toward all created things, including the body: "To the pure, *all things are pure.*"[5] How has it happened that people have veered so far from what Scripture clearly enjoins, that they deem a person pure and holy if he considers the human body to be obscene, indecent, filthy, disgusting, dirty, immodest, impure, evil, etc.? We are supposed to see *God* in all created things, but this false piety thinks itself holy if it sees *filth* in God's greatest creation—the one He specially crafted *in His very Own image*! "For from the greatness and beauty of created

---

[1] I Timothy 4:3ff.
[2] Wisdom 11:24.
[3] Isaiah 6:3.
[4] Matthew 6:9-13.
[5] Titus 1:15.

things comes a corresponding perception of their Creator."[1]

Thus, stones do not cause temptations to kill people with them. There is nothing in the nature of stones which in any way allures and entices man to murder. No sane person, on seeing a stone, suddenly gets aroused with murderous feelings. If a man uses it to kill, the source of his temptation cannot come from either the all-good God nor anything He created and sustains in being. If a man kills by stoning, the stones are as innocent as God Himself and have nothing whatever to do with his sin.

The same reasoning applies to all of the other above examples. Food, gold or the naked body cannot have anything whatever to do with any man's decision to use them for evil. There is absolutely nothing in any of these things that allures and entices to sin because the all-pure God created them, and they are therefore pure. Perhaps if Eve had seen the all-pure God in all the trees of the Garden (especially the middle one) instead of the Evil One, Original Sin would never have been so much as a theory.

St. James clearly states where temptation originates— in man's own concupiscence. Concupiscence is a tendency within man to selfishly crave what is illicit, heedless of right order, and passionately desirous only of satisfying his own selfish craving. It is always irrational and disordered. Since the nature of a stone has no free will, it can only obey the natural laws that pertain to it. The same is true of all living things except man. Because he was created with free will reflecting God Himself, and because he has concupiscence as a result of Original Sin, man can depart from natural law and right order. This is called sin. As St. James says, sin ultimately generates *death*, whereas it is God's will that we persevere through temptations so He can reward us with the crown of *life*.[2] "For the wages of sin is *death*, but the free gift of God is *eternal life* in Christ Jesus our Lord."[3]

The origin of concupiscence in man was not God, since He cannot have anything to do with anything evil. This is why Original Sin is of such unique magnitude; no

---

[1] Wisdom 13:5; & cf. Romans 1:20.
[2] Cf. James 1:12.
[3] Romans 6:23.

pre-existing concupiscence within Adam & Eve was in any way responsible for Original Sin. The source of Original Sin was fully extraneous to themselves. In the story in Genesis 3 this is clearly signified by the tempting serpent. Adam & Eve had free will which made sin possible, but free will itself was in no way a source of temptation or anything evil. Rather, free will is man's highest, most God-like faculty, enabling him to freely align himself with God, not merely by necessity, but by love. Since all of us descendants of Adam & Eve do have concupiscence, it is impossible for us to relate to the special dynamic of Original Sin experientially. Jesus, however, did experience it when He was tempted in the desert[1] and later, in Gethsemane[2] the night before He died. None of those temptations came from any concupiscence within Him because He had none. It is unthinkable that the person of Christ, Who had both a divine and human nature, could in any way contain anything evil. He was all-holy at all times, from the first moment of conception. Like Adam & Eve originally, the source of His temptations were entirely extraneous to Himself, originating solely in the devil.

But St. James is not talking about these exceptional temptations of which we have no experience, but rather, about *us* and *our everyday experience*. We *do* have concupiscence, and according to St. James, the itch and urge to abrogate right order by sin originates there.

My main point in this article, though, is that no created thing can in any way have any responsibility for temptation or sin. The forbidden fruit which God planted smack dab in the middle of the Garden of Eden was not evil in any way and did not in any way allure or entice Adam & Eve. They were allured directly by Satan. Note that the serpent began his dastardly work[3] before Eve even noticed the good-looking tree and its delicious fruit. Her temptation came not from any concupiscence within herself, nor from the forbidden fruit itself, but directly from the serpent, just as Jesus' temptations in the desert came directly from the devil.

---

[1] Cf. Matthew 4:1ff; Mark 1:12ff & Luke 4:1ff.
[2] Cf. Matthew 26:36ff; Mark 14:32ff; Luke 22:39ff & John 18:1ff.
[3] Cf. Genesis 3:1. Not till v. 6 does Eve take note of the tree's desirability.

The stones used to murder St. Stephen[1] had nothing whatever to do with the sin of murder. The gold owned by Ananias had nothing whatever to do with his sin of deceit and covetousness.[2] The wine that Noah made[3] had nothing whatever to do with his overindulgence in it. In exactly the same way, and for exactly the same reasons, the naked body of Bathsheba[4] had nothing whatever to do with David's sin of lust, first in his thoughts, and then in his bed. Scripture itself clearly attests to this in Psalm 51 which thoroughly explains all the dynamics of that sin and David's contrition for it. Nowhere in that psalm is Bathsheba's nakedness blamed as the cause of his adultery. In fact, she is nowhere even mentioned, clearly proving that she had absolutely no responsibility for David's sin. Her public bath did not cause it, her beauty did not cause it, her nakedness did not cause it. She was innocent of his sin,[5] no less than the stones were innocent of St. Stephen's murder. Even if the stones had had free will, they would have had no culpability whatever, nor would they have had any responsibility to dig a hole in the ground and bury themselves lest St. Stephen's murderers should decide to throw them at him. His murderers could just have well have dug a hole and killed him by burying him alive. Neither the dirt, the hole nor the stones had anything whatever to do with the murder. There is absolutely no difference in the case of naked Bathsheba and King David. Psalm 51:5 explains how David was conceived in Original Sin, and thus also the innate concupiscence St. James says was the cause of David's sin.

This inspired wisdom of St. James flies in the face of the conventional notion of (false) modesty which erroneously puts the blame (at least in part) on a naked body extraneous to the sinner. But this notion is heresy because it logically leads to the conclusion that God, the Creator and Sustainer of the naked body is at least partly responsible for enticing a man to sin. Because of this fundamental, erroneous assumption, "virtue" imposes a

---

[1] Cf. Acts 7:58ff.

[2] Cf. Acts 5:1ff.

[3] Cf. genesis 9:20f.

[4] Cf. II Samuel 11:2ff.

[5] I am not exonerating Bathsheba from the guilt of her own sin of adultery, but of David's.

moral obligation on the woman to hide what is "evil" lest it lead a man to sin. This is why such bogus virtue can only be called "*false* modesty." Yet such people are esteemed as "pure"! What other false virtue is thus esteemed? False honesty? False humility? False charity?

St. James says this is erroneous. He says the only source of temptation is the sinner's own concupiscence. Just as no one imputes blame for the sins of gluttons on the baker or his displayed pastries, so also no one should impute any blame for the sins of a lecher on either the object of his lust or its Creator.

Therefore, the onus is on the sinner who has the moral obligation to control his own lusts and pull the reins in on them, keeping his appetites within the bounds of justice and right order. By persevering in doing this successfully, persevering in temptation, St. James says God will crown him with life;[1] it is a sure promise.

If conventional "wisdom" were correct, then not only would a woman be obliged to hide herself lest someone sin by lusting after her, but for the very same erroneous reasons, we would be morally obliged to hide all the stones on our property, require stores to hide their wine in windowless closets, pass laws forbidding anything gold to be visible, and require restaurants to keep all food covered at all times. Somehow, covers would have to be designed allowing diners to eat without seeing what they are eating.[2] This is absolutely no different than the invention of clothes which allows bodies to function (even have sex!) without having to be tempted by seeing such "indecent filth," despite the revealed fact that "...we are *His* workmanship."[3]

Nowhere in Scripture is any naked person ever blamed for anyone else's sin. Adam & Eve's nakedness had nothing to do with their sin, Bathsheba's nakedness had nothing to do with David's sin, Susanna's nakedness had nothing to do with the sin of her would-be rapists who already had lustful intentions long before they hid themselves in the bushes near where she bathed.[4] The all-holy

---

[1] Cf. James 1:12.
[2] Shh! Don't give the Taliban any more ideas!
[3] Ephesians 2:10.
[4] Cf. Daniel 13:1-63 (Catholic Bible).

God commanded Isaiah to preach nude in public for three years.[1] The very idea that there was anything whatever alluring about his nudity is entirely alien to the Scriptural text. Since God tempts no one,[2] Isaiah's nakedness could not possibly have been a source of temptation for anyone.[3] Jesus was stripped more than once during His passion[4] and died on the cross wearing only thorns, dirt and His Precious Blood. If mere nudity were a source of temptation, then the all-holy Jesus would not have allowed Himself to be disrobed by St. John the Baptist for His baptism[5] or by the soldiers before nailing Him naked to the cross.[6] Search the Bible from cover to cover, inside and out, and you will not find any hint of the erroneous notion that any naked body ever was responsible for anyone's sin. Rather, as St. James so lucidly says, the source of temptation is in a man's own concupiscence.

One might argue that while this is so, it still takes something outside himself to complete the temptation, as a match needs to be struck against a flint to ignite. There is no denying that people sin by abusing what is extraneous to them. What I deny is that there is any moral obligation for any of those extraneous things to hide themselves from all prospective sinners. If there were such an obligation, then every man would have to live in his own vacuum. When Jesus perfected the commandment against adultery by teaching that any man who even merely *looks* at a woman lustfully has already thereby committed adultery in his heart,[7] He clearly lays the

---

[1] Cf. Isaiah 20:1ff.
[2] Cf. James 1:13.
[3] Thus the nudity of contemporary protesters who use nudity both to attract attention and to convey a message (e.g. disarmament, pacifism), as well as the public nudity of streakers or runners in races such as San Francisco's annual May "Bare to Breakers Run" is without any moral culpability. If this were not so, then God would have been immoral to tell Isaiah to go publicly nude.
[4] For example, in John's Gospel alone, cf. 13:4 & 12; 19:1-2 & 23ff.
[5] Mark 1:7 implies that the minister of baptism was responsible for disrobing the candidate, and John humbly protested that he was not worthy of performing the meanest part of this preliminary rite—the removal of the candidate's filthy sandals.
[6] Cf. John 19:23f.
[7] Cf. Matthew 5:27f.

blame on the lustful man—not the woman or His heavenly Father Who created her.

But St. James also states the *positive* side to all this. Although God can in no way be held responsible for any temptation, nevertheless, when a man does endure temptations he is sanctified—made more like the all-holy God, and will surely be rewarded with the "crown of life."[1] Thus, even our attitude toward temptation should be *positive*, realizing how we can actually benefit from it. This does not at all mean that we tempt God by presumptuously *looking* for trouble, but on the contrary, as Jesus taught us in the Lord's Prayer, we strive not to be led into temptation and to be delivered from all evil.[2] If we have this right mind and are committed to holiness, we can trust God to always abundantly supply all the graces we need to withstand any trial that befalls us. Scripture says, "God is faithful, and he will not let you be tempted beyond your strength, but with the temptation will also provide the way of escape, that you may be able to endure it."[3]

Thus, paying money to watch a peep show, looking through a window of a booth at naked lesbians having an orgy, is clearly tempting God, Who will not honor such wanton presumption by giving His grace to be sinless. But a person who encounters nudity in ordinary life as David did when Bathsheba was bathing and as all the Jews did while listening to the preaching of naked Isaiah, can be assured of all the grace necessary not to give in to any concupiscence within him. Although it was rare even for Jews to encounter naked prophets, it was not at all rare for them to encounter nakedness in all sorts of ordinary, everyday situations like dressing, bathing, baptism, manual labor, swimming, etc. Indeed, in order for circumcision to be in any sense an effective sign of the covenant, male genitalia must have been a common, everyday sight. Yet in no way can either God Whose idea circumcision was, or the exposed genitalia be blamed for anyone's sin of lust. The only way a naked person could share in any culpability would be if his *motive* for exposing himself was impure. And indeed, this is just how St. Thomas Aquinas

---

[1] James 1:12.
[2] Cf. Matthew 6:13.
[3] I Corinthians 10:13.

defined immodesty;[1] to be immodest, one must *intend* to arouse lust in others. Thus every stripper is immodest because arousing her audience is what she gets paid for. But no nude woman sunbathing in her yard or at the beach is immodest unless her *motive* is impure.

Just as nudity is nowhere in the Bible blamed for sin, so also in the early Church which operated within the context of Roman civilization which contained lots of everyday nudity. Male and female slaves were displayed naked for sale in public marketplaces. Children lived and played nude. Bathing suits did not exist, and if someone had suggested such a curiosity, he would have been looked at as if he had three heads. Public baths were for everyone, male and female,[2] as were public toilets.[3] Laborers worked nude in the fields and loading ships. Mothers would not have even thought of breast-feeding so as not to let their breasts be seen. In contrast, excluding my wife, I can count on one hand the number of times I have seen bared breasts nursing children, but 1,500 years ago I would not have been able to be in the marketplace for an hour without witnessing such a normal activity several times.

Large families usually lived in one room. Not only did they undress in front of each other, but somehow parents managed to keep propagating too, despite others snoring nearby. Much, if not most, art was nude and no one would have thought there was anything in the least erotic about it. Public theater almost always included nudity as a matter of course.

Athletes competed publicly in the nude, not only for sports like foot-racing,[4] but also for contact sports like wrestling. No wrestler would have thought anything sexual as he rubbed his sweaty, oiled, naked body against that of

---

[1] Cf. "Modesty" in: New Catholic Encyclopedia, 1st Edition, 1967.
[2] Some cities had communal baths that were usually all male, but women were not strictly prohibited, especially when there was no all-female bath available. Often, however, baths were simply co-ed.
[3] The excavations at Pompeii, Italy, reveal a common toilet room with no partitions, not unlike the multi-hole outhouse of American schoolhouses before modern times, except that these were sex-segregated.
[4] Hebrews 12:1 makes a comparison between Christian ascetic spirituality and nude races, without even hinting at anything negative in the latter.

his opponent. Likewise, no spectator would have thought anything erotic while admiring the skill as well as the beauty of their well-formed bodies. Contrast that sane, body-accepting culture to that of America in 2004 when the brief sight of one female breast of the half-time performer, Janet Jackson at Superbowl XXXVIII caused a national uproar and the television broadcasting company was fined $450,000 for its lack of "moral" vigilance! The hypocrisy and sad irony was that the breast, as God's creation, was, in fact, beautiful, holy and innocent; the true indecency and immodesty lay in the lyrics of the music being played to "entertain" the TV audience of over 100,000,000 people. But while millions of "decent" Christians had conniption fits over the innocent creation *of the all-holy God*, hardly anyone complained about the truly indecent lyrical creation *of perverted men*.

Nudity in the patristic age was so ordinary that it was practically impossible not to encounter it daily. Living in such a pro-body culture, early Christians thought nothing about being baptized together in the nude with the congregation looking on. Many monks and nuns who lived lives of penance and prayer in the desert went naked for the sake of poverty and penance. The idea that there was something erotic about it would not have occurred to them.

But then one of the earliest heresies began to rear its head—Gnosticism. Fundamental Gnosticism believes in two equal forces of good and evil that war against each other. Gnostics say that physical, material things are identified with evil and spiritual things with good. Thus the human body was seen as evil. The cosmic war of good and evil, spirit and matter, also raged within man, between his soul and his body. The physical body became the scapegoat for sins that should have been attributed instead to man's own pride and concupiscence. Thus the senseless "cover-up" began, leading to the idea that it was immoral to let your body be seen "unnecessarily" or to see another person's body "unnecessarily." By the Victorian age, even the bare legs of pianos had to be covered!

When matters get that absurd it always leads to a pendulum swing in the opposite direction, and the twentieth century was an accelerated evolution of that reverse swing. At the beginning of the century both male and female beachwear covered nearly the entire (evil) body. But attitudes began to change, especially after World War I when millions of Americans became personally aware of cultures different from their own, and yet no less Christian. The American body began to be redeemed. Attitudes toward the male chest changed as daring men called the bluff. Swim suit tops came off and, contrary to presumed expectations carried over from Victorianism, all hell did not break loose, ladies did not go sex-crazy—at least not any more than formerly. Essentially nothing changed other than greater comfort for men and less clothing for merchants to sell. Simultaneously, women also tested the accepted mores, gradually exposing more and more of their arms and legs till all limbs were completely bared. As with male chests, all hell did not break loose. Sure, legs were pretty, because the body is beautiful, but beauty does not demand covering. On the contrary, by nature, it demands exposure to admiration and appreciation. We don't cover works of art; *we exhibit them.* All across Western Christian culture more and more of the body was redeemed, and with each new development came the same result—all hell did not break loose. About mid-century, some daring women did what some daring men had done a few decades earlier; they bared their chests in public. In many places this quickly became as ordinary as the sight of bared male chests. The false mystique about female breasts that had been created by compulsively hiding them was exposed for what it truly was—false. As with all the other body parts that finally saw the light of day in the 20th century, female breasts crawled out of their bunkers and discovered that no bombs were falling after all; all hell still did not break loose.

Some people jumped the gun without waiting for the rest of culture to catch up. They saw that increased exposure always netted the same result—acceptance, the redemption of more and more of the body as more and more was exposed. So they went all the way, taking it all off, and just as they had hypothesized, nothing happened except immediate acceptance among those of like mind. But the rest of society was not ready to evolve as quickly, even though it was clearly moving in the same direction.

So while the rest of society kept on at its own, slower pace, always discovering that more exposure led to more acceptance and new redefinitions of "modesty," nudists, eager to experience the total redemption of the body, formed their own clubs and organizations and private parks where they could practice their lifestyle without "offending" those of a slower pace.

Gradually society caught up with nudists. The social climate of the sixties made it easy to challenge any of "The Establishment's" mores. Thus nude beaches began to appear here and there all over Christendom. One no longer had to belong to a private club in order to experience the full redemption of the body. The whole body could emerge from the dark, dank bunker into the fresh light of day without any negative repercussions.

In tiny Vermont, for example, nude swimming, sunbathing and even hiking and water-skiing[1] had become so common by 1971 that law enforcement was perplexed. Chittenden County State's Attorney, Patrick J. Leahy (now U.S. senator), in a famous memorandum, advised that skinny-dippers be left alone unless they were in public areas such as crowded beaches and there were complaints.[2]

Society in the rest of New England was also simultaneously catching up with nudists. Many nude beaches popped up all along the New England Atlantic coast, such as at Moonstone Beach in South Kingstown, Rhode Island. This was an ordinary public beach. Anybody could pay their parking fee and enjoy it as at any other public beach. The only difference was that those who attended Moonstone were in the vanguard of the rest of society for they had finally caught up with the nudists. They had come to see the entire body as intrinsically good, modest and decent. Just as some daring men had bared their chests on beaches fifty years earlier and discovered that the sky did not come crashing down, so by the seventies some daring people decided to call the final bluff, removing the last, very few remaining square inches of their bathing

---

[1] Yes—I myself had the pleasure of experiencing this form of recreation!
[2] For the complete text of this memorandum, see Jim C. Cunningham, *Vermont Unveiled* (Troy, Vermont: Naturist LIFE International, Inc., 1996), p. 79. Also available online at: www.jumbojoke.com/000138.html.

costumes. The result was the same as had been the case with every other previous abbreviation of modest bathing attire. People felt completely liberated, no longer oppressed with the lie that their bodies, or at least some parts of them, were sinful, obscene, immodest, etc. If there was any filth, it was only in the mind of the beholder. Very sorry to say, most of such filthy-minded beholders were Christians! "To the pure all things are pure, but to the corrupt and unbelieving nothing is pure; their very minds and consciences are corrupted."[1]

What does this teaching of St. Paul say about those who should be out in the forefront, leading the world to the fullness of purity? The irony is that these same "guardians of morality" who are so blind to the planks in their own eyes, somehow manage to be "scandalized" by the imagined specks in the eyes[2] of those who honestly live the goodness of God's creation. Yet they, and their teenage daughters, think nothing of wearing bathing costumes that their just as blind "Christian" forebears would have deemed unfit for whores and lechers. Thus their own lifestyle attests to the truth that attitudes change with time, and as they finally accepted what society had already accepted for decades, so also their grandchildren would one day be unable to comprehend how their grandparents could ever have thought that wearing a tiny bathing suit (as opposed to wearing none) was somehow "virtuous."

Such people are parochial not only with respect to place, but to time as well. Just as all they need to do is go on vacation from their Kansas farm[3] to Europe or the Caribbean, where they would encounter long-established customs of topfree bathing suits and total mixed nudity, so also, all they have to do is look back in time only a few decades to see that more and more skin has always and consistently been accepted as modest. As with graphing algebraic equations, all they need to do is continue the curve to see that it has to lead to the full redemption of the body from its unjust, Victorian verdict of guilty.

---

[1] Titus 1:15.
[2] Cf. Matthew 7:3ff.
[3] Kansans, forgive me!

My own family visited Moonstone in the mid-eighties. Literally thousands of ordinary people of all ages, shapes and sizes who would never dream of joining a private nudist club, were recreating like people on any other public beach, except they were nude, experiencing the joy of purity. Thus this vanguard of society had finally caught up with the nudists.

Or had they surpassed it? After all, the nudist park gate is a kind of "clothing" too. This vanguard of society had no gates, no private membership cards. They saw their bodies as so pure that they were not ashamed, no matter who might see them, and they regarded their bodies as so pure that they could not understand how any sane person could possibly be "offended" by the sight of them. These people came to be called "naturists," though most of them do not want to be clothed with any "ism," either. They see themselves as ordinary people who simply have taken the final step. Their beach bags are packed with the usual inventory, minus only one item, and their preferred beaches need not go to the trouble and expense of building dressing rooms.

There is no reason to believe that the nuder and nuder trends of the last century are suddenly going to stop and go in the other direction. On the contrary, there is reason to believe that the rest of society—even the self-righteous moralists who presently condemn the final stage in the body's total redemption, will, before too long, return to the innocence of early Christian times when no one would have seen the point of joining a private club simply to be nude.

If we Christians are supposed to be "the light of the world"[1] and "the salt of the earth,"[2] why should we be last to accept what we eventually will accept anyway? Why don't we demonstrate leadership and thus guide the naturist movement according to Biblical, moral principles? The early Christians did not initiate nude customs in their culture; they simply accepted them as they found them, even incorporating them into their sacramental rites. They proscribed only what was aberrant, such as immorality in the public baths or in the theater. The social milieu in

---

[1] Matthew 5:14.
[2] Ibid. v. 13.

which contemporary Christians find themselves is not yet as accepting of the body as that of our patristic forebears. We have the power (and responsibility?) of shaping the world around us. The fact is that our culture is becoming ever nuder. This trend, like all social trends, needs the guidance of those who understand man's true purpose and destiny, yet we Christians seem always to be in the back seat, dragging our feet. By shirking our responsibility to lead, many social trends can end in shipwreck. What begins in the Spirit can end in the flesh unless we step up to the plate and show how power reaches perfection in weakness.[1]

Not only can we lead by stressing moral parameters, but we can use this new body-acceptance as a starting point of a new, vigorous evangelization. After all, the Gospel begins with the Word becoming a body like ours.[2] This is a hard sell in a culture where the body is seen as something evil. But where the body is seen as good, the message that its Creator Himself fully shared this good thing becomes much more credible. The Gospel says our true end is the resurrection of our bodies[3] and eternal bliss with God such as no ear has heard and no eye has seen.[4] This should seem to be not only an *attractive* message, but an *irresistible* one to those who truly value their bodies. No one wants to insure trash and filth, but rather, what is precious and valued. The Christian Gospel offers the best life insurance policy imaginable, and the price has already been advanced by Him Who gave His life on the cross.[5] If we neglect this excellent opportunity to not only guide, but also to evangelize, aren't we a lot like the pusillanimous sap who buried his talents, rather than like the enterprising man who invested his?[6]

I suggest that we Christians "be transformed by the renewal of our minds"[7] and, making the most of every opportunity,[8] assess what is good and positive in the

---

[1] Cf. II Corinthians 12:9.
[2] Cf. John 1:1ff.
[3] Cf. I Corinthians 15:12ff.
[4] Cf. ibid. 2:9.
[5] Cf. ibid. 6:20.
[6] Cf. Matthew 25:14-30.
[7] Romans 12:2.
[8] Cf. Colossians 4:5.

naturist movement and welcome it as fertile ground for the seed of the Word,[1] and as we give the Truth to those who truly appreciate their bodies, we ourselves will receive many blessings,[2] not least of which is a liberating acceptance of our own bodies, not seeing them as evil, filthy or obscene, but rather as good, holy, works of divine art. Rather than see them as sources of temptation, let's see them as conduits of grace and truth. The law came through Moses, but grace and truth come from the Word of God Who became a body![3]

Nudity conforms to naked truth and therefore sets us free[4] and glorifies the Creator by boldly asserting the holiness of His creation and thus cannot be the true cause of any man's sin. In fact, like all truth, it can only have a beneficial effect on others. It causes them to realize the truth of St. James' teaching that their own concupiscence causes sin, and not anything outside themselves. They realize they cannot point the finger at anyone but themselves, and this is good, as it leads to true contrition as David so eloquently expressed in Psalm 51. Nakedness allows the individual to realize that his own body is entirely holy, and this realization brings a profound sense of relief and liberation. Many women who literally felt like they were sinful simply by *having* a body and were heavy-burdened by this oppressive feeling, are now liberated entirely, free to sprint nude along the beach flying kites and leaping for joy, feeling light as a kite themselves, instead of that former, awful, heavy feeling that their bodies were nothing but sinful lures to lust. Our entire bodies are as innocent as stones, gold, food, and wine. The notion that there is the least need to hide them is seen for the lie it is. Our nudity becomes a true prayer as we "exhibit"[5] our bodies as "holy and pleasing to God."[6] All who see us are invited to share in that prayer, owning the truth of the goodness of all God's creation and praising

---

[1] Cf. Mark 4:8.
[2] Cf. Luke 6:38.
[3] Cf. John 1:14.
[4] Cf. John 8:32.
[5] Romans 12:1. The Vulgate has "ut exhibeatis" ("that you should exhibit"). The KJV & RSV have "present," which is a bit weaker as far as the idea of displaying is concerned.
[6] Cf. Ibid.

him in His works, and more specifically glorifying Him in our holy bodies.[1] Lame excuses for sin such as "The devil made me do it" or "She allured me" are sloughed away, leaving every man with the stark truth that his sin is just that—*his*. And the purity now more evident all around him encourages him to be pure also by controlling his inordinate lusts and thus meriting the crown of life.[2]

Blessed Are the Persecuted

by Jim C. Cunningham

Blessed are those who are persecuted for righteousness' sake, for theirs is the kingdom of heaven. Blessed are you when men revile you and persecute you and utter all kinds of evil against you falsely on My account. Rejoice and be glad, for your reward is great in heaven, for so men persecuted the prophets who were before you.
—Matthew 5:10-12

There are many reasons why people do not put into practice the truths of this book. Perhaps the greatest of these are either because they have an horrendous body self image that they refuse to change, or because they fear the persecution they expect to receive if they really apply these truths to their practical lives.

Some have a horrible body self image. When it comes to their physicality, their level of self-esteem is very low. In truth, they hate their bodies and can't wait to be rid of them. Most people like this will not read much of this book once they discover, upon cursory perusal, that its message does not tickle their ears.[3] Sadly, they view everything with this anti-body perspective. If they disagree with this book it is not because they have read it with objectivity and a sincere desire for the truth and a yearning for the Spirit to conform them to all truth. their minds are made up before they have been exposed to the dozens of excel-

---

[1] Cf. I Corinthians 6:20.
[2] Cf. James 1:12.
[3] Cf. II Timothy 4:3.

lent points of this book. They already know what they want to hear. Whatever "truth" they manage to embrace must conform to their own hatred of their bodies. They do not see their bodies as gifts from God, but rather as curses, or at best, great "crosses." They are opposed to all nudity not on account of any virtue, but simply because they want to hide from their own bodies, let alone the bodies of others, and they do not even want to see *themselves* in a full length mirror. Their attitude toward the bodies of others, while masked behind a false veneer of virtue, really has nothing whatsoever to do with chastity or modesty, but much more likely, envy and jealousy. Most of the enemies of this book fall into this mold.

There are many other people who are truly open to the challenges of this book and are honestly attracted to its positive ideas on the body, but are doomed to remain wannabes because they are frightened to death at the mere thought of actually starting to live the truths to which their minds have consented. This fear is the same brand of fear that keeps most Christians from ever experiencing what St. Paul meant when he referred to "the freedom of the sons of God."[1] They are shackled by the fear of what people would think if they were to discover their newfound body attitudes. they are afraid of even admitting these convictions in conversation, let alone being "caught with their pants down." They would not want to be caught dead at a nude beach—even clothed to their teeth. They would never even dare to be nude outside their locked bathrooms. Even if all their shades were pulled and all doors locked, they would be afraid to simply relax at home in the nude. It would be anything but relaxing, as they would be constantly anxious about some peeping Tom "catching" them, or the parson stopping by on his annual, spontaneous home visit. It is very true that removing your clothes, but not your fear, can only be counter-productive. If "safety" means hiding the truths you have learned from others, then nowhere is safe.

One priest who contributed to this book tried to be ever so careful to keep his naturism in the closet. He resided in a rectory with the pastor of the parish. While in the rectory, he "behaved himself." No one would ever have

---

[1] Romans 8:21.

485

suspected that he was a nudist. When he could, he sneaked away to one or other of the area nudist parks, not being definite about his whereabouts with the pastor. Little did he know that the pastor was also a closet naturist and used to sneak away to a nude beach in the neighboring state. It was only through me, with each other's mutual permission, that many years later they discovered the truth. They both had a good laugh at the following annual priests' reunion. When the resident priest was stationed thousands of miles away he thought he was "safe" in his birthday suit disguise at another nudist park when, to his profound shock, he turned around after buying a hot dog and drink, only to come face to face with the couple behind him in line—the couple he had been meeting with at the parish for marriage counseling!

I could tell many other anecdotes like that. The fact is that while some people do try to straddle the picket fence, it is never all that comfortable—especially for naturists! The best policy really is perfect candor. You don't have to advertise your naturism, but you should at least be prepared to admit and explain it. What St. Peter said about the faith in general can also be applied to our naturist convictions in particular: "Always be prepared to make a defense to anyone who calls you to account for the hope that is in you."[1]

Just what is it that so many people are afraid of? They are afraid of persecution. They value (covet?) their good reputation and do not want to risk losing it. They do not want to be misunderstood, misjudged, ridiculed, looked down upon or talked about behind their backs (or to their faces!). An all over tan just isn't worth it.

Chances are that such people are wannabes with respect to lots of things. Fear holds them back from ever really getting a life. Chances are that they also fear participating in a pro-life demonstration for the same reasons. They don't want others—even fellow Christians—to think they are kooks or fanatics, etc. Sure, they believe that life begins at conception, but they aren't about to risk their reputation over it. Similarly, after reading this book they might believe in the truth and benefits of naturism, but they are not about to risk getting persecuted over it.

---

[1] I Peter 3:15.

For me, I don't think I could have come to Christianity if I lived in such a strait-jacket. When I confessed Jesus I got plenty of persecution, and even more when I confessed Catholicism once the Holy Spirit had nuked all my stumbling blocks (e.g. Mary, pope, Eucharist, confession, purgatory, statuary, etc.). It would practically have been more respectable for me to have become a "Moonie" than to have returned to the Catholic Church. But as Jesus said, "It was not you who chose Me, but I chose you..."[1]

If God ordered Isaiah to preach nude for three years,[2] isn't it possible that He give the same command to your pastor—*or you*? Suppose you were given such a revelation. Would you readily accept? My suspicion is that if you are unwilling to apply the truths the Spirit has led you to in this book, then you would also disobey such a divine command, coming up with all kinds of classic excuses and rationalizations, such as not being sure it was from God; after all, even Satan can disguise himself as an angel of light,[3] etc., etc. If we do not respond to the Spirit in *little* things, how do we expect to conform to Him in *great* things?[4] When you know it is right to step out of your timidity and help a needy person, you must not resist the Spirit's lead. To be open to the Spirit means just that—to be open—to hold nothing back. If you are serious about sanctification, then you know what I mean. If the Spirit is moving you to get up and speak in front of people to share your inspiration, and you hold back, you know the awful, heavy feeling. That is definitely not what St. Paul meant by "the freedom of the sons of God."[5] The same is true when we know we should apologize for something, but our pride holds us back. The path to true freedom is clear. We only need to run (or at least crawl) along it! To fail to do so is to dig your own spiritual grave. "Since we live by the Spirit, let us follow the Spirit's lead!"[6]

But what does all this have to do with the body and nudity? St. Paul admonishes us to grow in all dimen-

---

[1] John 15:16.
[2] Cf. Isaiah 20:1-3.
[3] Cf. II Corinthians 11:14.
[4] Cf. Luke 16:10.
[5] Romans 8:21.
[6] Galatians 5:25.

sions—mind, soul, spirit and body.[1] This whole book is about how the body is an *essential*, even *central*, part of the mix. Yet how much have you grown in your body attitudes over the course of your life? If you are like most people, your body attitude has not developed much since your mother yelled at you for removing your bathing suit and frolicking nude in the lawn sprinkler. Honestly, few of us have moved on from there.

Christianity is imitating Christ.[2] Do we regard *our* bodies as He regarded *His*? Do we regard the bodies of others as He did? He was heedless even of the shame of the cross,[3] yet we Christians are ashamed even to display that victorious cross on the walls of our homes or sanctuaries of our churches unless we dress it like a doll, diapering Jesus as we would compel a naked toddler to put his bathing suit back on and stop being "naughty." The Word of God became flesh[4] and used that body to help others and to teach them truth. He laid that body down freely on the cross and took it up again.[5] He invites us to share in His Body by being incorporated into it by baptism[6] and by experiencing it more fully through Holy Communion[7] and the other sacraments. He was grateful for His body and the bodies of others and did not resent His father for those gifts. He did not hate His body. He did not abuse it physically or sexually. He truly honored it.

Let's be honest; we fall far short of imitating Christ in all this. So what are we going to do about it? As I see it, there is only one answer—to grow, grow and grow unto the full maturity of Christ Jesus.[8]

Unlike us, Jesus did not inherit all kinds of problems, hang-ups and cultural baggage to have to sort out and overcome. That is why we cannot imagine the Holy Family picnicking on holidays at Mt. Tabor Nudist Park. They did not need it. Yet neither did they know any shame when they presented themselves to St. John the Baptist for

---

[1] Cf. I Thessalonians 5:23.
[2] Cf. I John 2:6 & I Peter 2:21.
[3] Cf. Hebrews 12:2.
[4] Cf. John 1:14.
[5] Cf. John 10:18.
[6] Cf. I Corinthians 12:13.
[7] Cf. Ibid. 10:16 & John 6:53.
[8] Cf. Ephesians 4:13.

nude baptism by immersion in the Jordan. Everyone bathed nude. Wearing clothes to bathe would have been absurd to them. Everyone bathed in the Jordan or Sea of Galilee. As stated elsewhere in this book, they fished and gardened nude. Nudity was an everyday experience. Yes, nude *preaching* was odd, and refusing to *ever* don clothes was downright *insane*,[1] but appropriate nudity was nothing to write home about.

Our culture lacks almost all of those elements that would naturally allow us to grow up with a healthy mind as regards the body. Thus, if we Christians are serious about healing, then it behooves us to do what we can to institute such elements in our own culture. This will result in our own deep healing as well as of those who encounter us. It will also result in some persecution from some quarter or other somewhere along the line.

So? All who resolve to do what is right can expect to be persecuted.[2] Since when does a true disciple of Christ shun righteousness from fear of persecution? Jesus said if we are really following Him, then we can expect to be persecuted as He was.[3] Speaking for myself, I have a long way to go. There are no nails in my hands and feet yet, nor have they stripped me and dangled me from a cross. "There is no redemption without the shedding of blood."[4] "You have not yet resisted to the point of shedding blood."[5]

Blood? Did I say *blood?* Most of us haven't even re-sisted to the point of someone misjudging us! Jesus said they will hate you as they hated Me.[6] I am not there yet. Look how St. Paul was persecuted.[7] He was often reduced to such poverty and want that he had to perform his apostolic ministry in the nude, as did other apostles.[8]

Many Christian wannabe naturists who fail to live the ideals out of fear of persecution argue that it's one thing to suffer for the truth of the faith, and quite another to suffer for the cause of "gettin' nekkid!"

---

[1] Witness the Gerasene demoniac in Luke 8:27 & 35.
[2] Cf. II Timothy 3:12.
[3] Cf. John 15:20.
[4] Cf. Hebrews 9:22.
[5] Ibid. 12:4.
[6] Cf. John 15:18-20.
[7] Cf. II Corinthians 11:23-28.
[8] Cf. Ibid. v. 27.

But this is not as it seems. Jesus is the truth—the *whole* truth.[1] The Spirit guides us unto *all* truth.[2] We need to appreciate the gift of our bodies. It is the truly Christian way to go. Therefore, we must do what it takes to acquire that appreciation and share it with others. The truths we learn in secret must be proclaimed on rooftops.[3] By failing to do anything, we default to the likes of Larry Flynt to monopolize the body and teach our children false definitions of the body. We Christians must step up to the plate and take the bull by the horns (to mix metaphors a bit!). St. Paul says we own the whole world![4] Our Daddy made the universe! No one should be able to steal or damage His property if we proud children have anything to say about it!

Being persecuted for implementing the truths of this book is not different from being persecuted for the Gospel, as the body is central to it. The Gospel begins with the incarnation and ends with the final resurrection of the body. It is about the body from A to Z. To be persecuted on account of upholding the goodness and dignity of the body is to be persecuted for the Gospel.

St. Paul commands us "Glorify God in your body!"[5] Who actually does this? Does the average Christian even know what this means? Most merely interpret this in a *negative* way, by *not* fornicating, *not* masturbating, *not* committing adultery, *not* performing homosexual acts and *not* doing sundry other sexual perversions St. Paul says are "unmentionable."[6] But what do we do in a *positive* way to glorify God with our bodies? St. Paul's command was in the *positive*, not *negative* form. He tells us to *do* something, not to *not do* something. The sad truth is that most Christians ignore this command. They do nothing *positive* with their bodies because their whole attitude toward the body is *negative*. The irony is that if only they cultivated a *positive* body attitude they would also find it much easier to fulfill the *negative* commands not to lust because they would experience the goodness of their bodies and the

---

[1] Cf. John 14:6.
[2] Cf. Ibid. 16:13.
[3] Cf. Matthew 10:27.
[4] Cf. I Corinthians 3:21-23.
[5] I Corinthians 6:20.
[6] Ephesians 5:3.

bodies of others so deeply that they would instinctively not want to pollute them in such sinful ways. It is when people regard their bodies as trash that they trash them. When we experience their sacredness, goodness, beauty and dignity, then we take care to use them honorably.

Just compare this issue to the command to love.[1] Do we really fulfill the commandment to love by translating this *positive* command *negatively* and merely not hating anybody? Do you want to be *loved*, or merely *not hated*? I trust my point is clear. Just as we fulfill the command to love much more fully and truly by *actively, positively* loving and not merely by not hating, so we fulfill the command to be chaste and glorify God in our bodies much more fully and truly by *doing what it takes* to cultivate the *positive* body attitudes expressed in this book than merely by *not lusting*.

Ah! You and I understand this, but our potential persecutors do not. So is *that* it? You only want to be persecuted when you can win the applause of men? If someone in the street spits on you because you are carrying a Bible or wearing a crucifix, you like that variety of persecution because it wins you honor in Christian circles. But is there any merit in that? Isn't it more meritorious in God's eyes when our persecution is truly humbling—even among our own? Jesus came unto His Own, and His Own received Him not.[2] Shouldn't we follow in His footsteps?[3] It is far more meritorious to be persecuted in a way we cannot take pride in.

So suppose you are swimming nude in your backyard pool and the UPS man, finding no answer at the front door, comes around back and happens to see you in mid air, *au naturel*, executing a perfect 10 belly flop and after you surface for air, calls you over to sign for a parcel. Suppose he is the pastor's cousin, and rumors start spreading. People talk. People who flaunt their Christianity talk. This may lead to raised eyebrows at the next parochial school PTA meeting. Perhaps it gets worse than that. Maybe you are so misjudged that you soon find your 3rd grade Sunday School class has been assigned a

---

[1] Cf. John 15:12; Galatians 5:14; I John 3:23; etc.
[2] Cf. John 1:11.
[3] Cf. I Peter 2:21 & I John 2:6.

parent monitor—to keep an eye on you. Maybe you discover your services are no longer needed. Maybe your children get razzed at school by their "loving," "Christian" classmates. You are persecuted for being a "nudie"—at best, an eccentric, at worst, a sexual pervert. Suddenly the idea of being arrested for chaining yourself to abortion clinic operating tables never looked so good. Is this persecution holy? Is it Christ-like? Is it being persecuted as Matthew 5:10 says, "for *justice's* sake"? Is it being maligned falsely as Matthew 5:11 says, for *Christ's* sake?

Of course it is! "Justice" is "rightness." Are you not striving to be right in your attitude toward the body? Are you not trying to put on the mind of Christ? Are you not rejecting the world's erroneous definition of the body and asserting the Bible's definition? Are you not *doing* something about the unjust definition of the body rather than just *dreaming* about it or, like the hypocrites, agreeing to the truth *mentally* but not *in practice*?

Many fear the possible negative repercussions that can result from such persecution such as losing a ministry, a job and a good reputation. They suppose they can do more for Christ if they do what it takes to avoid such unfortunate results.

But isn't that the *world's*, and not *God's* perspective? Doesn't He choose those the world considers fools to shame the wise?[1] God's ways are not our ways.[2] The humbler we are, the more God can use us, even if we do not directly experience this. For example, "the prayer of a holy man is powerful indeed."[3] Which man is more truly holy and just in God's eyes—the humble man who seeks justice come what may, or the proud man who craves the applause of men and a good position for himself in the community and in the Church? Jesus never sought any honors from men.[4] He did everything in a way exactly opposite the world's ways. When King David thought he'd assess his military might in the world's way, by taking a census, he was severely punished.[5] Blessed is the man

---

[1] Cf. I Corinthians 1:27.
[2] Cf. Isaiah 55:8.
[3] James 5:16.
[4] Cf. John 5:34 & 41 & Matthew 22:16.
[5] Cf. II Samuel 24:1-25.

who fears only the Lord and is not beholden to the vain plaudits of men. "This is the man I approve: the lowly and humble man who trembles at My Word."[1] St. Paul insisted that all that mattered was that we were created anew.[2] But it is we who hinder this true spiritual growth by our cleaving to worldly ways and values. Who would have thought that the best way for Isaiah to preach for three years was naked? Who would have thought any good could come from Nazareth?[3] Michal, thinking like the world, despised her husband, David for his nude antics in public, where even the low class girls could see him,[4] yet few kings have rivaled David's renown and regal prowess. David was such an unlikely, unworldly choice to succeed King Saul that his father, Jesse, did not even bother to call him in from tending the sheep when Samuel "interviewed" Jesse's other sons for the job.[5] Joseph was sold as a slave, naked, his beautiful coat having been stripped from him by his brothers,[6] and in Egypt he became even lower yet—a slave in prison,[7] yet God raised him up to be second only to Pharaoh himself.[8]

Just like most all other Gospel values, we ignore Christ's teaching that the persecuted are blessed. We fear persecution as much as we fear poverty, yet Jesus declared both to be truly blessed. As long as we do not believe Him, so long is our light hidden under a bushel basket.[9] Perhaps courageously implementing the truths of this book will occasion a real conversion within us at long last. That the body should effect such a conversion is not at all far-fetched, because the body is what the Gospel is all about. God so loved the world[10] that He humbled Himself, taking our bodily form[11] and offered that wonderful body on the cross so that our bodies might be freed from Satan's grip and share in a resurrection like unto

[1] Isaiah 66:2.
[2] Cf. Galatians 6:15.
[3] Cf. John 1:46.
[4] Cf. II Samuel 6:14-23.
[5] Cf. I Samuel 16:11-13.
[6] Cf. Genesis 37:12-36.
[7] Cf. Ibid. 39:20.
[8] Cf. Genesis 41:40 & Psalm 105:17-22.
[9] Cf. Matthew 5:15.
[10] Cf. John 3:16.
[11] Cf. Philippians 2:6-8.

His.[1] To attain this end He gave us His body to eat, saying that if we obeyed Him in this, He would raise up our bodies on the Last Day[2] to live forever in the celestial mansions He ascended with His body to prepare for us.[3] So if the body is so essential to the whole Gospel message, then it should not surprise us that it might be the efficient cause of our long-delayed conversion from a stultified faith clothed beneath bushel baskets, to a bright, shining faith clothed only with joy: "Thou hast loosed my sackcloth and girded me with gladness!"[4]

St. Cyprian of Carthage (c. 200-258 A.D.)

Shivering, you want clothing, but he who puts on Christ is abundantly clothed and adorned.[5]

St. Paul and the Body

By Jim C. Cunningham

Sometimes, when we read the letters of St. Paul, we can be tempted to think he is anti-body, such as when he said he would rather be free from the body and home with the Lord,[6] and when he rhetorically asked who would deliver him from the body of death.[7]

However, just as Scripture sometimes tells us to despise the world,[8] elsewhere the same human author says that God so loved it that He sent His Only Son for its sake.[9]

In both of these instances there are no contradictions. The problem arises from different uses of like terms.

---

[1] Cf. Romans 6:5 & I Corinthians 15:49.
[2] Cf. John 6:54.
[3] Cf. Ibid. 14:2f.
[4] Psalm 30:11f.
[5] Epistle 76, tr. R.E. Wallace.
[6] Cf. II Corinthians 5:8.
[7] Cf. Romans 7:24.
[8] E.g. I John 2:15.
[9] Cf. John 3:16.

In the negative sense, "world" means the system whose whole dynamic is away from eternal truths and realities. In its positive sense, "world" means us sinners whom God wants to redeem so we can be happy with Him forever.

When Scripture uses "body" in a *negative* sense, it is merely referring to our self-gratifying, carnal impulses—not the body itself. In the negative sense, it might be translated as "carnality" or "sensuality." But when Scripture refers to the body in a *positive* sense, as when it says "the Word became flesh,"[1] it is not referring to anything negative whatsoever, but simply to the fact of human nature, to which the body is intrinsic.

When St. Paul refers to "the works of the flesh" as in Galatians 5:19-21, he does not mean to derogate the body itself. In fact, some of the vices he lists out do not pertain to the body *per se*, but to man's perverted *soul*, such as idolatry, sorcery, enmity, strife, jealousy, anger, dissension, party spirit and envy. Thus we do St. Paul an injustice if we interpret him to use expressions such as "works of the flesh" in such a way as to think he did not appreciate the body. But he clearly did appreciate the body so much that he told us that we must dedicate it to the Lord[2] and that it is so precious and noble that it is actually the temple of the Holy Spirit.[3] St. Paul was not schizophrenic; he simply used words in different senses, just as all languages do. Today's youth even use the adjective, "wicked" to mean exactly the opposite, even combining "wicked" and "good" to describe the same thing: E.g. "Oh, Dad, it was a wicked good concert!"

Fundamentalists tie themselves up in knots all the time. Just as St. Peter tells us to love our wives "*with understanding*,"[4] so also we must interpret the Word of God. Otherwise, as St. Peter also warns us of the letters of St. Paul: "There are some things in them hard to understand, which the ignorant and unstable twist to their own destruction, as they do the other Scriptures."[5]

---

[1] John 1:14.
[2] Cf. I Corinthians 6:13.
[3] Cf. Ibid. 3:16; 6:19 & II Corinthians 6:16.
[4] I Peter 3:7.
[5] II Peter 3:16.

Never read the Bible as though it contradicted itself, pitting one verse against another, because the Holy Spirit, its Primary Author, cannot possibly contradict Himself. When things *seem* to contradict, usually all we have to do is stand back and get some perspective. If you look at an impressionist painting close-up, it is quite ugly, but when it is viewed from the perspective intended by the artist, it is quite beautiful. Everything in life is like that. In fact, that is why Pope John Paul II said that the problem with pornography is that it reveals too little.[1] It is a close-up of only one value of the human body—the erotic, and thus it is a distortion. God, its Artist, never intended His human masterpiece to be viewed from that perspective. The right response is not to remove the painting from sight entirely, but simply to stand back and view it as its Artist intended. That is the whole point of this book. We should view the body as we view Scripture. Just because we encounter apparent problems is not cause to stop reading the Bible *altogether*, but only to read it *properly*, as St. Peter would have us do. St. Peter's 264th successor, John Paul II, would have us do the same with another divine revelation—the human body.

I Timothy 4:4f

For everything created by God is good, and nothing is to be rejected if it is received with thanksgiving; for then it is consecrated by the word of God and prayer.

---

[1] Because it distorts the truth of man by focusing only on the erotic.

Leap of Faith

by (Rev.) Charles A. Waugaman

Easter approaches,
booted and scarfed,
singing squills and hyacinth
over the doomed drifts,
laughing birdsong
into the taunts of wind and flurry.

Racing to catch up,
my trumpet-crowded heart
flings fanfares and flourishes
in all directions;
anthems acres with praise
as triumphant as lilies,
bright as choirs of golden jonquils.

Appearance confuses.
Only Truth reveals:
and I dance adoration
clothed solely in the brilliance
of forgiveness,
knowing the tomb is not empty
after all.

Left behind, discarded, worthless
are the soiled, stained
death wrappings of my sin
and I, following the risen Shepherd,
leap free.

George Weigel, *Witness to Hope*

The Holy Father's teaching in the theology of the body is at last going to exorcise the Manichean demon from Catholic moral theology.[1]

---

[1] (New York: HarperCollins, 1999), p. 342.

Bodies Wonderful!

by Jim C. Cunningham[1]

"*Wonderful* bodies? Whose bodies—mine?"

Yes, yours, and mine. I am not referring to some "perfect 10," idealized form, but what we all see when we step out of the shower and dare to look into the full-length mirror.

This book teaches the revealed truth that our bodies are precious gifts of God, good and holy and beautiful, created as they are in the image and likeness of our all-good, all-holy, all-beautiful Creator. Sadly, culture (including conventional Christian culture) tends to ignore, belittle or deny this fact. Whatever is pure is, by that very nature, vulnerable to pollution, and throughout history this has certainly been the case with respect to the human body. Deep down, we all tend to want to believe the truth of the body's goodness and beauty, but this conviction finds little opportunity to be explored, expressed, proclaimed and celebrated on account of various elements in culture which relentlessly threaten to contaminate it.

There is something beautiful in most of us which passionately wants to believe the message of this book. This is because we are made for higher things—for ideals—and we would like to think they could be true. Man finds his highest fulfillment in hope.

Our bodies are, after all, an integral and major part of who we are as persons. The body only too frequently reminds us of its reality. It needs constant respiration, frequent nutrition and exercise. Touch tells us of pleasure or pain. Our senses constantly act as sensors for our

---

[1] Editor's note: this article (here slightly edited) first appeared as "Welcome to You!" and was the lead article in my 100-page photo-book, *Our Wonderful Bodies!* (Troy, Vermont: Naturist LIFE Int'l, Inc., 2001). Whereas this present book is 100% textual, OWB! is nearly all photographic, depicting ordinary bodies just as God created them, of both genders and all ages, shapes and sizes, from Siberia to California. Since culture woefully neglects to provide many opportunities to encounter the naked body in non-erotic contexts, this book was an attempt to somewhat repair that scandal of neglect. To purchase OWB! go to www.naturistlife.com.

souls. The various emotions we experience in the course of an ordinary day all have keen repercussions in our bodies. We are, by definition, enfleshed beings, and not an hour passes which permits us to lose sight of this fact.

Since our bodies are such a vast and keenly experienced part of who we are, our attitude toward our bodies is therefore of vital importance. Most of us cannot do a lot to physically sculpt our bodies to be much different from what they now are, but we do have a lot of control over how we regard our bodies.

Because we are people of hope and idealists by nature, if we were to put this book down right now, get naked and stand before a full length mirror, almost all of us would immediately begin to make critical judgments not about what we *like* about what we see, but about what we *do not like*. Because we were made to seek perfection,[1] we tend to first notice what we believe to be deficiencies. This is because we are comparing our bodies to some undefined but nevertheless firmly believed ideal.

Whence comes this ideal? It comes from our innate desire for perfection, and this is good, because it constantly prods us in better and nobler directions, but it also comes from sheer ignorance. We really do not know what the ideal we have for our bodies is. This being so, obviously we are doomed to discontent because we do not even know what it is we strive for. We are like the frustrated and exasperated witness of a crime trying to describe to a criminology artist the features of the perpetrator of the crime. No matter what he draws, the witness never feels it is quite right.

Our mysterious, elusive ideal is undefined largely because we have been deprived of knowing what bodies are "supposed" to look like. If only we could see one another as we used to do in locker rooms, gang showers and YMCA pools, we would have the opportunity of acquiring a much more concrete idea of what we are "supposed" to look like.

Without chaste opportunities to see what others really look like, we have nothing left as a measuring stick but myths like the air-brushed centerfold of *Playboy*. But if you were to visit a venue such as a nudist park or nude beach, you would be surprised to discover that you look

---

[1] Cf. Matthew 5:48.

pretty much the same as everyone else. That's just how it's supposed to be. We are acceptable; we do fit in; we have nothing to be ashamed of.

Our bodies, like our faces, have features that seem more attractive than others, and some which seem less attractive. But if we live with this with respect to our faces, without going around like a fundamentalist Moslem, veiling even our eyeballs, then why should we apply a different standard to the rest of our physical being? If the truth be told, many of us would fare better in the comparison game if we played with our whole bodies rather than just our faces. The most artistic sculpture, lying by itself on the floor is much more beautiful and complete when erected on a stately plinth. Our bodies are those handsome pedestals displaying our heads. God did not create heads, but whole persons.

One of the reasons why we would actually prove to be more attractive if we not only bared our faces, but our bodies as well, is that we are not a part, but a whole. The detail of one small area of a painting is less than the beauty of the whole painting, in proportion. I don't know about you, but I would sooner admire the beauty of an entire 8-point buck in the wild, than just the taxidermized head mounted over a fireplace mantle. Logic tells us "The whole is greater than the part," yet we constantly contradict this in everyday life.

Another reason why it is more beautiful to show the whole rather than only the part is that the very willingness to be known as we are contextualizes our bodies among certain spiritual values which are themselves desirable and beautiful. These include openness, honesty, trust and self-acceptance. A nude accepts not only himself, but also those around him. These beautiful, spiritual values all contextualize a body which already enjoys its own, physical beauty, and taken all together, the result is very pleasing and delightful.

Years ago, when I entered my print shop somewhat "dressed up," my secretary exclaimed, "My, don't you look nice today!" The truth was that I looked no different than the day before, and her compliments were not directed to me, but to the clothes I happened to be wearing that day.

If "clothes make the man," then we are but an heap of rags.

Can you imagine being taken on a tour of a fine art museum to admire the beautiful paintings, but every work of art is veiled? Surely, it would not be the paintings we admire, but at best, the fabric of the veils. It is no less oxymoronic to assert that we are more attractive clothed than nude. If a physical thing is not seen, then it is not beautiful. *Anything* is more beautiful than *nothing*. We do not consist of only heads and hands. As you can see by looking at your own body in a full length mirror, there is far more to who you are than that!

The discontent many of us experience looking at ourselves in a full length mirror, criticizing what seems to fall short of our undefined ideal, can be compared to riding a bus. If a traveler did not know Cincinnati was his destination, he would not know enough to get off the stuffy bus there, but would be a perpetual traveler, never arriving. I don't know about you, but judging from buses I have traveled on, this is no fun.

The truth is that you can arrive whenever you want to. You can pull the cord that rings the bell to stop the bus, get off, and as the bus disappears on the distant horizon, take a deep breath, stretch your cramped limbs, look around yourself at the wide cosmos, leap into the air and click your heels.

We were not created for perpetual bus riding; we were created for joy, freedom, peace and love.[1] We were created to enjoy "the liberty of the sons of God,"[2] to leap into the air and click our heels. "For freedom Christ has set us free."[3] We all know it. Though it may be hard for us to acknowledge, it is something we all crave to do. Many will grin as they read this, eager to make it happen.

There is no external condition for which we must wait until this joy can happen. This liberation is not dependent upon any external thing. It is purely dependent upon your own acknowledgment and resolution. You do not have to *become* beautiful; you *are* beautiful. Nothing that money can buy can bring beauty. Beauty is something you must

---

[1] Cf. Galatians 5:22.
[2] Romans 8:21.
[3] Galatians 5:1.

decide. You can look at your body in that mirror and complain about this or that imagined imperfection and always ride the cramped, stuffy bus never satisfied, or you can redefine that nebulous, impossible ideal as something all so very concrete and attainable. You can redefine it as *what you see*. You can redefine it as *who you are*. You can decide to get off the bus. You can decide to accept the beauty you already are. You can be so happy that you can literally thrill at being who you are. How can such delight and gratitude in who you are fail to please Him Whose gift you are? What giver does not delight in his gift being appreciated?

Just think what this decision to pull that cord and ring that bell will do to your personal happiness and self-esteem. Whereas formerly happiness depended largely on external conditions, now you alone are the arbiter of your own happiness. Like the proverbial King Midas, the new, miraculous touch you will have acquired simply by fully accepting your physical self, will turn everything you touch into gold. Those around you will experience the gleam of your inner gold, and the outward beauty you already have, polished and buffed by your newfound acceptance, will be greatly enhanced. You will walk differently, hold your head higher, and there will be an intriguing sparkle in your eye. Self-help books for decades have tried to deal with the apparently endemic, societal problem of low self esteem. Who can imagine suffering from this debilitating malaise if, beholding his body in a full length mirror unveiled, and just as it is, reaches up to pull the bell cord?

Do not get me wrong. I am *not* saying that body-acceptance is nirvana or the height of spiritual perfection. But I *am* saying that to aim for those other spiritual perfection's without first reconciling yourself with your physical reality which we cannot escape, is like trying to run the 100-yard dash with your shoe-laces tied to each other. Your other aspirations, however noble in and of themselves, cannot help but appear pathetic.

I can tell you in all humility that I am beautiful. I say this despite total blindness due to thirty-six years of juvenile diabetes. I have not seen myself in well over a decade. Two and a half years of kidney dialysis and a kidney transplant left me far from any form Joe Weider would place in the centerfold of his *Muscle & Fitness* magazine. I have even lost my right leg below the knee. Yet I know I am beautiful. I accept my physical being with exuberance. Clothed only with the sun, I have often walked or lain outdoors in nature and experienced sheer exhilaration. I do not gawk at the exquisite beauty of nature as though I were a spectator or a mere patron in an art gallery, for I have reached up and pulled that cord and have realized the truth that I am *the very centerpiece* of the museum. Neither sunrises nor sunsets, neither valley views nor mountain vistas, neither Monarch butterfly wings nor the colorful spread of a peacock's tail, nothing in all creation has anything over me in the line of beauty. I pulled that cord and got off the bus, I reached up to the very stars, and the cosmos that met me bowed down before me. Sound a little conceited? True humility accepts truth. This truth is not something presumptuous or out of harmony with Christian revelation, which tells us that if God has given us His Only-Son, He surely cannot fail to give us all things besides.[1] Nowhere in all literature was man's dignity expressed better than in the eighth psalm:

When I see the heavens, the work of Your hands, the moon and the stars which You arranged, what is man that You should keep him in mind, mortal man that You care for him? Yet You have made him little less than a god; with glory and honor You crowned him, gave him power over the works of Your hand, put all things under his feet.[2]

Morality concerns more than willful thoughts, words and actions. It also concerns willful inaction, willful neglect, sins of omission, rather than of commission. Scandal is causing another's moral fall. It comes from the Latin, *scandalum*, which means a "stumbling block." But there are two ways to cause another's fall. We can place something in his path (scandals of commission), or we can fail to remove something which is bound to cause him to stumble (scandals of omission, or neglect). It has been my firm conviction for nearly thirty years now that our cul-

---

[1] Cf. Romans 8:32.
[2] Psalm 8:3-6.

ture, and those within it in positions of influence and responsibility, from parents and pastors to educators and legislators, have been guilty of very grave scandals of neglect in the area of body education and body acceptance. As Edmund Burke once said, "All that is necessary for the triumph of evil is that good men do nothing."[1] This is perfectly true when it comes to body attitudes. Because it is difficult, and makes us feel queasy, we tend to avoid and neglect the entire area. This has had disastrous effects on millions of people who had a right to have expected clear teaching and guidance. Let me give just two examples:

1. There once was a time (before the mid-70s) when at least males enjoyed the commonplace opportunity to encounter other male bodies in totally non-sexual situations such as locker rooms, gang showers and YMCA pools. In my youth, when I was a member of the Lynn, Massachusetts YMCA, it was forbidden for anyone to wear a bathing suit in the pool. All boys and men of all ages swam together in the nude, and no one would have thought to have made an issue out of it. Diving and swimming competitions were all done in the nude. The same was true at most summer camps for boys. All waterfront sports were done in the nude. If a newcomer boy was unaccustomed to this, he got used to it after ten minutes. We were all like Huck Finn and Tom Sawyer who spent their boyhood summers on the Mississippi nude.

Over the past few decades, we have neglected to maintain this healthy, traditional, cultural practice. We let it slip away for various reasons, but this neglect has proven unhealthy and harmful. School gang showers are all but unknown. High school football players today go straight home after practice or games, muddy, sweaty, snotty and sometimes bloody. Today, if a boy dared to use the gang shower after practice, his peers would make untoward remarks, or worse.

The debilitating effect is that boys have little or no opportunity to even encounter bodies of their own gender. It used to be that the bodies of only the opposite gender were shrouded in mystery, but today it is any body.

---

[1] Letter to the Sheriffs of Bristol, April 3, 1777.

Our bodies are such a hugely significant part of our identity. The entirely unnecessary physical ignorance which our culture (i.e. its leaders) has, by sheer neglect, allowed to prevail, is reprehensible and scandalous; it has contributed to the unhealthy attitudes of millions of people.

2. How could I have lived into adulthood without ever having witnessed an act that should be as commonplace as eating, because it is, in fact, eating? I am referring to the "womanly art of breast-feeding." Boys in our culture have little or no opportunity to learn by witnessing it, just what female breasts are primarily designed for. Mothers who do nurse their babies do so in such a clandestine way that it only serves to heighten curiosities which may already have attained unto the morbid degree. If babies should be veiled while dining, then why not adults? Why don't we all go out to eat with baggy hoods pulled over our faces, lest anyone should be aroused by witnessing the supposedly erotic activity of adult dining? It would be hilarious if it were not so sad, yet "good men do nothing." Day follows day, year follows year and decade follows decade, and still, "good men do nothing."

In 1976, at the age of twenty-two, I pilgrimaged to the Holy Land. At Bethlehem I visited the Franciscan shrine known as the Milk Grotto, where legend has it that Mary paused on the flight to Egypt to offer her "blessed breasts"[1] to Jesus. I don't think I had previously ever wondered how Jesus ate as a baby, and if I had been asked at the age of eight whether I thought the Mother of God had any breasts at all, let alone "blessed" ones as the Gospel describes them, I would have been mortified by the already so debilitating influence of Irish Catholic culture of that time. The very thought would have induced me to lose no time going to confession to repent of my grievous "adultery," lest I be hit by a car before receiving absolution and go straight to hell. Some of you readers might laugh, and you are right to laugh, but many Catholic readers at least fifty years old know how woefully true this was.

So imagine a young man formed by this warped culture, entering the Milk Grotto and seeing seemingly hundreds of classical art depicting nothing other than

---

[1] Luke 11:27.

505

what legend says the Mother of God did on that spot. Not only did many paintings show the Virgin's breasts, but some even clearly depicted what my Irish American Catholic culture had conditioned me to particularly regard as the most obscene and indecent part of those "blessed breasts"—her nipples (gasp!).

I was not a little confused. I looked around. Yes, those were real, Franciscan friars in their brown tunics and knotted, white, rope cords who served as curators of this sacred shrine. No, it was not some New York City 42nd Street porno dive. But having been taught—by neglect— that the female breast was intrinsically erotic, and having only encountered this part of God's creation in "dirty magazines," my psyche could only respond as that culture had conditioned it to respond, with unwilled sexual arousal.

"But this is the Ever-Virgin Mary! And this is a *Catholic* shrine!" Such were the confused exclamations of my thoughts.

Why had not the "good" Sisters of St. Joseph included images of Mary nursing Jesus among the many holy cards they gave us pupils for rewards? Why had I never seen my mother nursing my kid sister? Why had I never seen *any* mother nursing any baby? Why, seeking simple, innocent knowledge of the human body, did my "pious" adult world leave me nowhere to turn for such knowledge than *Playboy*?

I now finally know the answer: because "good men did nothing," allowing evil to triumph.

But having attained adulthood, if not true maturity, my continued formation was then in my own hands. I had two choices. Like my deficient mentors, I could do nothing, or I could reach up and pull that bell cord and get off the perpetually lost bus. With the encouragement of a well-known Trappist monk,[1] I pulled the cord.

Cultural warps can be unwarped. As the famous Catholic apologist, G.K. Chesterton once wrote, warped twigs can be straightened if bent back just as far in the opposite direction. That is precisely what I am trying to do—to repair the scandal of neglect—to straighten out the warp of a truly sick body attitude. More than ever in many

---

[1] Fr. M. Basil Pennington, OCSO (1931-2005).

decades, our contemporary culture harmfully represses healthy body attitudes. Oh, sure, there may be more nudity in movies and the media, but it is rare when it is not contributing to the lie that the human body is intrinsically erotic. Nudity in the cinema is almost always synonymous with sex—and this, by the way, is almost always fornication or adultery. Even in rare scenes where sex is not directly implicated, such as some of the nudity in "Schindler's List," it is usually negative and pejorative, rather than positive and celebrative.

My father ingrained many wise proverbs into me, not least among which was "It is better to light one candle than to curse the darkness." This book will not set the world afire. It is just a little candle in the darkness of ignorance and foolishness. It is a statement of truth. It is a way of sharing hard won fruits with others. It might inspire some of you to reach up and pull that bell cord. Others may have already pulled it, but are tempted to waiver in their seeming solitude.

No, you are not alone. Most of us crave what this book advocates. It is, after all, our original, blessed state: "And they were naked, and knew no shame."[1] "Redemption" means getting back what we lost. Through sin we lost innocence. Ancient baptismal rubrics required catechumens to take off all their clothes which symbolized sin, the world and that lost innocence. Sacraments are symbols which *effect* what they signify. The fact is that we have been redeemed. Through baptism we have died with Christ to sin. "We were buried therefore with Him by baptism into death, so that as Christ was raised from the dead by the glory of the Father, *we too might walk in newness of life.*"[2]

Your good, sacred body is your patrimony. God gave it to you and it was part of what constitutes His image in which we were created.[3] To be ashamed of it, then, is tantamount to being ashamed of God Himself. "Whoever is ashamed of Me ..., of him will the Son of man be ashamed

---

[1] Genesis 2:25.
[2] Romans 6:4, and read the complete context (verses 3-14).
[3] Cf. Genesis 1:25f.

when he comes in His glory and the glory of the Father and of the holy angels."[1]

In the most solemn liturgy of the year, Easter Vigil Mass, Christians gather in total darkness, symbolizing the sleep of Christ's death. But then one paschal candle is lighted, and from this every taper held by every person present is lighted, and the chain reaction illuminates the nave and sanctuary as though all the electric lights were on, symbolizing the resurrection of the Body of Christ, Who left His wraps behind in the tomb.[2]

This book is like my lone, lighted taper. I invite you to touch your wick to it and light your own taper. Rather than do nothing as "good" men have done, I invite you too "to light one candle." Nothing external to you will cause you to recognize your destination outside the bus window. Your destination will have been recognized only when you pull the cord and get off the stuffy, cramped bus. Do it! With giddiness, watch the bus drive off polluting the air. Soon it will be out of sight and its sickening fumes will have dispersed. As you needed no one's permission to get off the bus, so now you need no one's permission to celebrate your arrival. Go ahead, leap into the air, click your bare heels and let out your yodel cr yahoo!

---

[1] Luke 9:26.
[2] Cf. John 20:5ff.

Scriptural Index

Topical Index

Augustine of Hippo, St. 229, 432f, 439, 442
Australian Naturist Federation 292
Australian Sun & Health magazine 291
Baker, Tammy Fay 370
Balthasar, Fr. Hans Urs Von 358
baptism (also see "nude baptism") 10, 27 (Pope Paul VI restores immersion), 65, 87, 130, 274, 276, 443, 445, 467, 488
baptism, infant 320
baptism of Christ 27, 87f, 189, 316, 333ff, 417, 426, 427, 429, 440, 448, 474, 488f
Basil of Cappadocia, St. 442
Basil of Moscow, St. 184, 347, 357
Basilique du Sacre Coeur de Montmartre 17, 333
bathroom privacy 186, 195
baths, public (also see "saunas" & "showers") 13, 99, 101, 174, 184, 190, 314f, 431, 433
Bathsheba 12, 134, 226, 272, 472f, 475
beauty 501ff
beauty pageants 53
Becket, Sr. Wendy 354
Bedouins 336ff
Benedict of Nursia, St. (also see "*Rule of St. Benedict*") 28f
Benedict XIV, Pope 119
Benedict XVI, Pope 266, 361
Bernard of Clairvaux, St. 389
Berry, Wendell 249
bestiality xxx, 65, 234f, 240
Bethlehem (also see "Milk Grotto") 17, 24
The Bible and the Liturgy by Jean Cardinal Danielou, S.J. 28
birth (also see "homebirth") 32, 235
"The Birth of Venus" 354
body (also see "temple of the Holy Spirit") xxi, xxxii, xxxiv, 71 (in spirituality), 343ff, 351, 354, 359, 494ff, 498ff
body functions 195
body image 484
Bonaventure, St. 170
Bonhoeffer, Dietrich 343ff
Botticelli 354
Brazil (see "Yanamamo")
breast, female 5, 7, 506
breast-feeding xxxviii, 6, 21, 63, 284, 288f, 308, 348, 505
breast-feeding Jesus, Mary (also see "Milk Grotto") 17, 505f
Brother Ass 16, 18, 20f
"Brother Sun, Sister Moon," movie 113
Burke, Edmund 504
Burlington, Catholic Diocese of (see "Marshall, Bishop John A.")
burnt offerings 237

epiphany 366

erections, penile 26, 177, 292, 352f, 452ff, 456

Etherie 90

Eucharist xxxiv, xxxvi, xxxvii, xl, 23f, 130, 319, 345, 353f, 356, 488

euphemism 146, 196, 198, 219, 235, 257, 264, 495

Eve (also see "Adam & Eve") xxxv, 82, 274, 360, 367, 370, 373, 412, 470

evil, intrinsic 460

Ezekiel, Prophet 429

fall, the (also see "Original Sin") 130

fallen state (also see "concupiscence") xxxv

fashions, immodest 123

Fatima, Our Lady of 123, 125

fear 374, 378

Felicity, St. 295

The Fellowship of the Ring by J.R.R. Tolkien 381f

fetishes 7, 10, 14

Fig Leaf Forum 216f, 322

fig leaves 66, 69f, 81, 111, 174, 220ff, 234, 241, 263, 274, 350, 354, 366, 379, 400, 415

Finland, coed saunas in 190

fishing nude (see "Peter, St.")

Flynt, Larry 19, 391, 490

forbidden fruit 84, 471

foreskin (also see "circumcision") 11, 98, 100, 102, 176, 177, 263, 346f

fornication xxx

Fox, Matthew 304

Francis of Assisi, St. 16, 113, 188, 273, 348, 357, 361

Franciscans 22 (custodians of Milk Grotto)

free will 470f

freedom in Christ 149, 157, 501

friendship i

Frelighsburg, Quebec 451

fundamentalism 495

garden 227

Garden of Eden 84, 94, 250f, 274, 298ff, 313, 318, 351, 357, 360, 380, 384, 439, 471

gardening, nude 13

gawkers (also see "voyeurism") 268

genitalia 9 (male stripper), 65, 67f, 70, 258

Geoghan, Fr. John J. 330

Gerasene demoniac 246f

Gethsemane Abbey 312

Gibeath-haaraloth 347

Gibran, Kahlil 15

incest 219, 240
"inclusive" language xix
interpretation of Scripture 220f, 228, 494f
investiture (see "Levitical investiture" & "monastic investiture")
Isaac, patriarch 239
Isaiah, prophet, nude preaching of 13f, 173, 188, 251, 273, 279, 283, 346, 389, 394f, 441, 444f, 448, 450, 474f, 487, 493
Ishmael 239
Jackson, Janet 477
Jain, Bawa 311, 313
Jansenism xxxvii, 16, 24, 26
Japheth 275
Jeremiah, prophet 395
Jerome, St. xli, 170, 273, 313, 351
Jerusalem Church (also see "Cyril of Jerusalem, St.") 317
Jeselinus of Luxembourg 389
Jesus (see "Christ")
Jewish culture 175
Jewish rabbinical traditions 430
Job 69, 83, 213, 350, 445ff
John XXIII, Pope 25
John, Bishop of Jerusalem 384
John, the Deacon 385
John Bunyan (see "*Pilgrim's Progress*")
John Chrysostom, St. 91, 433f
John Climacus, St. 439
John Jay College of Criminal Justice 2004 Report on Clergy Sexual Abuse xxx, 328ff
John of the Cross, St. 350, 356f, 358
John Paul II, Pope (also see "*Love and Responsibility*") xv, xxix, xxxii, xxxix, 1, 26f, 29, 102, 125, 131, 179, 278, 303, 351, 353, 356, 374, 462, 464, 495
John the Baptist, St. xxxi, 87f, 316, 337, 427, 474, 488
Jonah, prophet 429
Joseph of Arimithea 103
Joseph, patriarch 386, 442-445, 493
Josephus 316
Joshua 177
Judas Maccabeus (also see "Maccabean revolt") 262
Karobah Pool, Australia 292
Kellersch, Claudia 312
Kevin of Glandolough, St. 188, 389
Kiev 348
know, (Hebrew euphemism) 235f
Koran 339
Kreeft, Peter 437
Kundert, John (also see "Fig Leaf Forum") 322

modesty 2, 15, 22f, 25f, 51, 76, 123, 146, 164, 175, 183, 245, 247f, 274, 279ff, 302, 306, 309, 336, 350, 358, 370f, 376, 420, 440, 442f, 446, 450, 485

Mohammed 339

monastic investiture 28f

monks, nude 187, 347, 448

Montmartre (also see "*Basilique du Sacre Coeur de Montmartre*") 336

Moonstone Beach, Rhode Island 479ff

moral act, three components of 458

morality 450-463, 503

mortification 273

Moses 389, 447, 483

motive (morality) 458

Moulin Rouge 336

Mt. Carmel Academy 36f, 42, 47, 118

Murmmbidgi River 292

Muscovy 184

Mystical Body 341

nakedness, spiritual xlii, 358, 385

Narsai of Nisibis 385

nature 349

naturism 58, 294

Naturist LIFE International magazine 278

naturist movement 483

naturists 481

Nazi concentration camps 446

Neilos the Ascetic, St. 385ff

Nelson, Bishop Ansgar 466

New Adam 350f

New Guinea (see "Papua")

Newman, John Henry Cardinal 264

Newport, Vermont 423

Nicodemus 103

Nietzsche, Friedrich 304

Noah 13 (Rafael paints sons building ark nude), 35, 85, 246, 275, 444, 472

nocturnal emissions 453f

Nova Nada 349

nude baptism xxxi, 10, 27 (of Christ), 27f (of catechumens), 87-90, 92, 95f, 110, 168, 173, 186, 192, 237, 250, 274, 306, 310, 315ff, 346, 384, 389, 441, 477, 507

nudism (also see "domestic nudity") 31f (benefits of), 40, 156 (good effects of), 279

nudist parks (see "American Sunbathing Association")

nudists 479, 481

84166645R10357

Made in the USA
Columbia, SC
15 December 2017